Lecture Notes in Computer Science 16428

The series Lecture Notes in Computer Science (LNCS), including its subseries Lecture Notes in Artificial Intelligence (LNAI) and Lecture Notes in Bioinformatics (LNBI), has established itself as a medium for the publication of new developments in computer science and information technology research, teaching, and education.

LNCS enjoys close cooperation with the computer science R & D community, the series counts many renowned academics among its volume editors and paper authors, and collaborates with prestigious societies. Its mission is to serve this international community by providing an invaluable service, mainly focused on the publication of conference and workshop proceedings and postproceedings. LNCS commenced publication in 1973.

Andre Hinkenjan · Hai-Ning Liang ·
Xueying Qin · Song-Hai Zhang
Editors

Extended Reality

International Conference, ICXR 2025
Qingdao, China, November 1–2, 2025
Proceedings

Editors
Andre Hinkenjan
Bonn-Rhein-Sieg University
Sankt Augustin, Germany

Hai-Ning Liang
HKUST-Guangzhou
Guangzhou, China

Xueying Qin
Shandong University
Qingdao, China

Song-Hai Zhang
Tsinghua University
Beijing, China

ISSN 0302-9743 ISSN 1611-3349 (electronic)
Lecture Notes in Computer Science
ISBN 978-981-95-7194-9 ISBN 978-981-95-7195-6 (eBook)
https://doi.org/10.1007/978-981-95-7195-6

This Springer imprint is published by the registered company Springer Nature Singapore Pte Ltd.
The registered company address is: 152 Beach Road, #21-01/04 Gateway East, Singapore 189721, Singapore

Preface

The International Conference on Extended Reality (ICXR) is a premier academic event organized by the Chinese Computer Federation (CCF) and hosted by its Virtual Reality and Visualization Technology Committee. ICXR has been selected as part of the CCF's first batch of high-quality international academic conference incubation programs, which highlights its significant academic value and influence. ICXR features a rich program of keynote speeches, technical paper presentations, and panel discussions, covering a wide range of cutting-edge topics in XR innovation, applications, and future trends. These include the development of the metaverse, advanced modelling techniques, perceptual interaction, graphics and image rendering, XR content creation, and digital twins, etc.

ICXR 2025 was held from November 1 to 2 in the beautiful city of Qingdao, Shandong Province, China. This conference assembled leading scholars, researchers, and industry professionals from around the world in the field of Extended Reality (XR) to present and deliberate on the most recent breakthroughs and emerging trends, thereby establishing a vital high-level platform for interactions between academia and industry, knowledge dissemination, and cross-institutional collaborations.

ICXR 2025 employed a rigorous double-blind peer-review process, conducted by 64 Program Committee members, with potential conflicts of interest carefully identified and managed throughout to ensure objectivity and fairness. The conference received 137 valid submissions in total. Acceptance decisions were based solely on scientific merit, originality, technical quality, and alignment with the conference scope. Following a rigorous and thorough review process in which submissions received three reviews each on average, 47 full papers were accepted, resulting in an acceptance rate of 34.3%; and 26 short papers were accepted, resulting in an acceptance rate of 12.4%.

The review process was carried out efficiently and transparently, maintaining open and effective communication among the editorial board, reviewers, and authors to promptly resolve any queries or issues. This strict and thorough procedure guaranteed that only the most original and influential works in the XR domain were selected, thereby establishing an exemplary academic benchmark for ICXR 2025.

Looking forward, the future of XR holds immense promise. Ongoing advancements in hardware will enable ever more realistic, seamless, and perceptually natural immersive experiences. At the same time, rapid progress in software ecosystems and content creation tools will yield increasingly diverse, personalized, and sophisticated application scenarios. XR is poised to catalyse transformative shifts toward more interactive and effective pedagogies in education, drive breakthroughs in remote diagnostics and therapeutic interventions in healthcare, facilitate deeper convergence of virtual prototyping with physical production in manufacturing, and pioneer entirely novel forms of immersive expression in culture and the arts. We are confident that the ideas exchanged and collaborations forged at ICXR 2025 will significantly accelerate the maturation of XR technologies and amplify their profound influence on the advancement of human society.

Finally, we extend our sincere appreciation to all contributing authors for their timely submissions, to the Program Committee and external reviewers for their meticulous evaluations and discerning selections, and to the editorial team for their dedicated efforts in compiling these proceedings. We offer particular thanks to the Local Organizing Committee for their unwavering commitment and exceptional dedication throughout the conference preparation and execution.

December 2025

Andre Hinkenjan
Hai-Ning Liang
Xueying Qin
Song-Hai Zhang

Organization

General Chairs

Martin Göbel	Hochschule Bonn-Rhein-Sieg, Germany
Xiangxu Meng	Shandong University, China
Yongtian Wang	Beijing Institute of Technology, China
Xubo Yang	Shanghai Jiao Tong University, China

Program Committee Chairs

Andre Hinkenjann	Bonn-Rhein-Sieg University, Germany
Hai-Ning Liang	Hong Kong University of Science and Technology (Guangzhou), China
Xueying Qin	Shandong University, China
Song-Hai Zhang	Tsinghua University, China

Steering Committee

Mark Billinghurst	University of South Australia, Australia
Frank Guan	Singapore Institute of Technology, Singapore
Kiyoshi Kiyokawa	Nara Institute of Science and Technology, Japan
Christian Sandor	Université Paris-Saclay, France
Lili Wang	Beihang University, China
Yongtian Wang	Beijing Institute of Technology, China
Xubo Yang	Shanghai Jiao Tong University, China

Program Committee

(Honorary) J. Edward Swan II	Mississippi State University, USA
Toshiyuki Amano	Wakayama University, Japan
Xiaoyang Bai	University of Hong Kong, China
Yiyu Cai	Nanyang Technological University, Singapore
Marie-Odile Berger	National Institute for Research in Digital Science and Technology, France
Gerd Bruder	University of Central Florida, USA

Xiaoming Chen	Beijing Technology and Business University, China
Manuela Chessa	University of Genoa, Italy
Zhaopeng Cui	Zhejiang University, China
Mine Dastan	Polytechnic University of Bari, Italy
Ralf Dörner	RheinMain University of Applied Sciences, Germany
Francesco Ferrise	Politecnico di Milano, Italy
Carla M.D.S. Freitas	Federal University of Rio Grande do Sul, Brazil
Yang Gao	Beihang University, China
Paul Grimm	Hochschule Darmstadt, Germany
Bo Han	George Mason University, USA
Yong Hu	Beihang University, China
Wolfgang Hürst	Utrecht University, Netherlands
Peter Kán	Vienna University of Technology, Austria
Dooyoung Kim	KAIST, South Korea
Jiachen Li	Qilu University of Technology, China
Sheng Li	Peking University, China
Hai-Ning Liang	Hong Kong University of Science and Technology (Guangzhou), China
Haibin Ling	Stony Brook University, USA
Shiguang Liu	Tianjin University, China
Feng Lu	Beihang University, China
Xuequan Lu	University of Western Australia, Australia
Heide Lukosch	University of Canterbury, New Zealand
Xiaoxu Meng	Meta Reality Lab, USA
Anne-Hélène Olivier	Rennes 2 University, France
Ye Pan	Shanghai Jiao Tong University, China
Yifan (Evan) Peng	University of Hong Kong, China
Thammathip Piumsomboon	University of Canterbury, New Zealand
Voicu Popescu	Purdue University, USA
Xueying Qin	Shandong University, China
Bo Ren	Nankai University, China
Ivan Rodriguez-Conde	Universidade de Vigo, Spain
Nobuchika Sakata	Ryukoku University, Japan
Dieter Schmalstieg	Graz University of Technology, Austria
Tianjia Shao	Zhejiang University, China
Yiran Shen	Shandong University, China
Xuehuai Shi	Nanjing University of Posts and Telecommunications, China
Missie Smith	Auburn University, USA
Weitao Song	Beijing Institute of Technology, China

Simon Su	National Institute of Standards and Technology, USA
Junwei Sun	Huawei HMI Lab, China
Huawei Tu	La Trobe University, Australia
Krzysztof Walczak	Poznań University of Economics and Business, Poland
Tingjie Wan	Jinan University, China
Miao Wang	Beihang University, China
Pengshuai Wang	Peking University, China
Rui Wang	CSIRO, Australia
Yuyang Wang	Hong Kong University of Science and Technology, China
Martin Weier	RheinMain University of Applied Sciences, Germany
Senzhe Xu	University of Science and Technology Beijing, China
Xiaosong Yang	Bournemouth University, UK
Dobashi Yoshinori	Hokkaido University, Japan
Difeng Yu	University of Copenhagen, Denmark
Gabriel Zachmann	University of Bremen, Germany
Fanglue Zhang	Victoria University, Australia
Lei Zhang	New Jersey Institute of Technology, USA
Shao-Kui Zhang	Beijing Normal University, China
Song-Hai Zhang	Tsinghua University, China
Bin Zhou	Beihang University, China

Additional Reviewers

Tse-Yu Pan
Yu Peng
Julien Pettré
Sabrina Pietzsch
Valerio Pulcini
Liang Qin
Jingwei Qu
Dirk Reiners
Yangfu Ren
Tim Rolff
Thorsten Roth
Matias Selzer
Yiyang Shen
Tengfei Shi
Gabriel Silva
Gilles Simon
Paweł Sobociński
Xibin Song
Heyi Sun
Kissinger Sunday
Hou Tam
Lingwei Tong
Rumeysa Turkmen
Xianglong Wan
Chen Wang
Chen Wang
Rui Ma
Martin Madaras

Zijun Mai
Haisen Zhao
Jennifer Zhao
Lixiang Zhao
Panpan Zhao
Shuyao Zhou
Yuanfeng Zhou
Chao Zhu
Han-Xi Zhu
Yitong Zhu
Shaojie Zhuang
Samara Morrison
Francesco Musolino
Aunnoy K. Mutasim
Hanadi Al-Mekhlafi
Sven Appel
Yiwei Bao
Juanita Benjamin
Yulong Bian
Jessica L. Bitter
Matteo Bosco
Zidong Cao
Ruihong Cen
Ehtzaz Chaudhry
Chiahao Chen
Fiona Xiao Yu Chen
Tiansu Chen
Boyuan Cheng
Isaac Cho
Alessandro Clocchiatti
Mara Coduri
Erwan David
Vito De Giglio
Qingyue Deng
Andreas Dietze
Chenyang Ding
Honghao Dong
Tianyang Dong
Yuejiang Dong
Ze Dong
Kui Huang
Kun Huang
Naoya Isoyama
Kei Iwasaki
Li Jin
Xin Jin
Chengrun Jiang
Norihiko Kawai
Simin Kou
Jérôme Kudnick
David Labbe
Enricoandrea Laviola
Jong-in Lee
Bo Li
Wei Li
Feng Zhou
Yun Zhang
Guanghan Zhao
Haisen Zhao
Jennifer Zhao
Lixiang Zhao
Panpan Zhao
Shuyao Zhou
Yuanfeng Zhou
Chao Zhu
Han-Xi Zhu
Yitong Zhu
Shaojie Zhuang
Samara Morrison
Zhongke Wu
Zongwei Wu
Yingjie Xi
Qing Xia
Ruiqi Xian
Cleo Xiao
Hu Xiaoqiang
Xueguang Xie
Qunce Xu
Tian-Xing Xu
Xuanhui Xu
Yamamoto
Feihu Yan
Haozhong Yang
Wenhao Yang
Zesong Yang
Ran Yi
Xin Yi
Yue Yin
Xusheng Yong
Mamehgol Yousefidashliboroun

Deyu Zhang
Fangfang Zhang
Haoran Zhang
Jichao Zhang
Jingjing Zhang
Tianqi Zhang
Xiaoxu Zhang
Yuan Wu
Si-Tong Wei
Zhiyuan Wei
Daniel Welfer
Junyu Wu
Yuxi Wang
Zhimin Wang
Jialin Wang
Junhao Wang
Owen Wang
Xiaochuan Wang
Xiaogang Wang
Xiaokun Wang
Guolong Wang
Jiahao Du
Stefano Esposito
Chengwei Fan
Linwei Fan
Xiaoxiong Fan
Yeying Fan
Yutao Feng
Jakub Flotyński
Qiang Fu
Yueyao Fu
Andreas Fuchs
Wei Gai
Vincent Gaudilliere
Adam Gałązkiewicz
Chenyu Gu
Xiang Gu
Shihui Guo
Teng Guo
Binyang Han
Zoe Hector
Eric Hodgson
Zhao Hongru
Robin Horst
Bojing Hou
Jiarui Hu
Bo-Sheng Huang
Yi-Jun Li
Yue Li
Ziming Li
Yuanfeng Lian
Zheng Lin
He Liu
Jia-Hong Liu
Xiaolong Liu
Xingyu Liu
Yu Liu
Thiago Lopes Trugillo da Silveira
Feiyu Lu
Zhicheng Lu
Guan Luo
Tianren Luo
Shengmin Zhao
Guangming Zheng
Qingyuan Zheng
Weizhi Nai
Ching Ng
Makoto Okabe
Renato Martins
Daniel T. Mayer
Xue Mi
Jun Mitani
Bipul Mohanto
Mikołaj Maik
Eric Marchand

Contents

ViMoGen: A Novel Motion Generator for Virtual Standard Patient

Xuehan Wang[1], Wenfeng Song[1(✉)], Xinyu Zhang[2], Shuai Li[2,3], Xian'e Wang[4], and Xia Hou[1]

[1] Beijing Information Science and Technology University, Beijing 100192, China
songwenfenga@163.com
[2] State Key Laboratory of Virtual Reality Technology and Systems, Beihang University, Beijing 100191, China
[3] Zhongguancun Laboratory, Beijing, China
[4] Department of Periodontology, Peking University School and Hospital of Stomatology, Beijing 100081, China

Abstract. Virtual Standard Patient (VSP) is an indispensable tool in medical education, offering crucial experiential learning opportunities. However, current VSP systems struggle to accurately represent patient behaviors and symptoms necessary for real-world diagnostic and assessment tasks. To address this challenge, we introduce ViMoGen, a novel motion generator for VSP driven by a controllable generation pipeline. Specifically, we introduce a conditional control mechanism for our diffusion-based generator. It is guided by dual inputs: instructional text prompts that simulate a physician's commands, and more critically, expert-defined spatial constraints on specific body joints related to symptoms. This primary contribution allows for the direct encoding of physical limitations, ensuring the generated motions are medically grounded. At the same time, to further enhance the fidelity of the output, we introduce a task-specific loss guidance mechanism, this module refines the initially generated motion by leveraging targeted distance and absolute position losses. This optimization step ensures greater physical plausibility and precision in the final animation. Our experiments demonstrate that by synergistically combining conditional joint control and loss-guided refinement, ViMoGen produces realistic, fine-grained, and medically consistent body motions, making it highly suitable for disease research and medical training scenarios where the interplay of verbal and nonverbal cues is paramount.

Keywords: Virtual Standard Patient · Controllable Human Motion Synthesis · Diffusion Model

1 Introduction

The advancement of virtual reality (VR) has transformed digital education, especially in medical training [2]. VSP offer immersive environments for students to practice clinical reasoning and communication before engaging with

A. Hinkenjan et al. (Eds.): ICXR 2025, LNCS 16428, pp. 1–17, 2026.
https://doi.org/10.1007/978-981-95-7195-6_1

real patients [30]. However, current VSP systems largely focus on verbal interaction, while neglecting the complexity of non-verbal behaviors—such as gestures, postures—that are critical for accurate diagnosis and empathetic engagement.

Existing VSP often rely on static or scripted behaviors, limiting their ability to simulate the nuanced, context-dependent physical symptoms exhibited by real patients [20,22]. This disconnect hinders the development of a truly immersive and clinically valuable training experience. To bridge this gap, our research focuses on realistic motion generation for VSP, enabling them to express symptoms through lifelike body movements synchronized with verbal descriptions. However, generating such expressive, medically meaningful motions remains challenging due to the scarcity of annotated motion data and the difficulty in modeling symptom-specific behaviors [30].

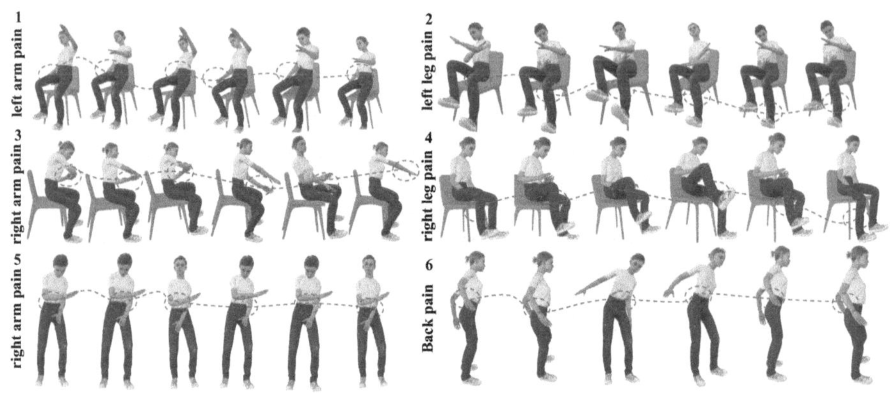

Fig. 1. We generated 6 actions for patients during their visits to the doctor. Among them (1–4) are sitting in a chair with leg pain or hand pain. (5–6) are standing with stomach pain or back pain.

To address the limitations of existing VSP systems in dynamic interaction and symptom expression, we conducted a systematic analysis of real patient behaviors in diagnostic scenarios. As illustrated in Fig. 1, we manually annotated symptom-related joint trajectories—for example, restricted knee flexion in arthritis patients or asymmetric arm movement in individuals experiencing unilateral pain. Our analysis reveals that many pathological manifestations are consistently reflected in specific joint motion patterns. These trajectories, grounded in observable medical phenomena, serve as clinically interpretable control signals that guide motion generation in a symptom-aware and anatomically meaningful manner. Based on this finding, we propose ViMoGen, a novel framework that can synthesize symptom-driven and context-aware body motions for virtual patients. As shown in Fig. 2, ViMoGen is based on clinical observation and analysis of disease manifestations, and manually sets key symptom-related joint areas to capture motion characteristics under specific pathological conditions.

For example, in arthritis patients, the knee joint often exhibits limited flexion due to pain and inflammation. We use these clinically interpretable joint definitions as control signals to guide a controllable diffuse motion generator, which is further optimized with the help of the loss guidance module to ultimately generate smooth, anatomically consistent, and medically consistent motion sequences.

In addition, in order to be closer to the actual clinical teaching scenario, ViMoGen introduces a second type of control signal - natural language instructions from doctors. This type of language prompt is extremely common in the real diagnosis process, such as "please sit down", "take a few steps forward" or "turn around", etc., usually accompanied by the doctor's observation and judgment of the patient's behavior. We encode these instructions into semantic vectors, and input the symptom-related joint control signals into the diffusion model together to form a multimodal fusion motion generation mechanism. This design not only improves the contextual adaptability of action generation, but also realizes the semantic alignment between language and action, so that virtual patients can show more realistic and clinically valuable performance under different instruction conditions. The overall process emphasizes controllability and explainability, which helps medical learners to more clearly understand the causal relationship between different symptoms and action performances, thereby improving the interactivity and immersion of teaching.

Specifically, our contributions are summarized as follows:

- We design a **controllable generation pipeline** that integrates two complementary control signals: (1) instructional text prompts simulating a clinician's diagnostic commands, and (2) expert-defined joint-level constraints encoding the physical limitations of specific symptoms. This dual-conditional mechanism enables precise and interpretable control, ensuring the resulting motions are both clinically relevant and contextually aligned.
- To further enhance fidelity and medical plausibility, we introduce a task-specific **loss guidance module**. This refinement stage corrects kinematic artifacts and enforces physical constraints by optimizing distance and position-based objectives, ensuring motions adhere to natural body dynamics.
- We present **ViMoGen**, A novel motion generator that leverages the above contributions to synthesize realistic, symptom-specific body motions. By combining dual-conditional control with loss-guided refinement, ViMoGen facilitates dynamic, interactive, and medically grounded motion generation, thereby enhancing the realism and utility of VSP in clinical training scenarios.

2 Related Works

2.1 Human Motion Generation

Recent works [3,6,15,17,25] have shown that diffusion models are making rapid progress in the domain of motion generation. MDM [25] showcased the effectiveness of diffusion models for motion generation and offered a versatile framework adaptable to diverse tasks such as text conditioning [9,10] and motion completion [8,11]. MLD [3] leveraged a VAE [19] to compress high-dimensional action data into a low-dimensional latent space, where diffusion was performed for modeling and generation. PriorMDM [23] introduced motion prior to guide the diffusion process and controlled MDM through motion restoration. In this work, our motion generator leverages pre-trained MDM as a generative prior and incorporates a novel control strategy to guide the diffusion process.

2.2 Controllable Diffusion Models

Recent advances in diffusion models have led to a variety of methods for controlling the generation process. These control techniques can generally be categorized into semantic guidance and spatial guidance approaches. Semantic guidance methods aim to align the generated results with high-level concepts or textual descriptions. Early approaches, such as classifier guidance [7], steer the denoising process using the gradients of an external classifier to push samples toward a target class (e.g., 'happy' or 'sad'). Although effective for semantic conditioning, this technique provides only a holistic control signal and lacks the ability to enforce fine-grained geometric constraints. To mitigate the dependence on classifiers, classifier-free guidance [13] was introduced, which interpolates between conditional and unconditional model outputs to strengthen semantic consistency. This strategy has proven highly effective in text-to-image [12,27] and text-to-motion [31] generation tasks. Nevertheless, both methods operate at a semantic level and remain inadequate for tasks requiring explicit control over localized spatial structures, such as enforcing continuous constraints on specific human joints. Spatial guidance methods, by contrast, utilize explicit structural or geometric information to direct the diffusion process. Inpainting-based diffusion [4,5] enables local modification of generated outputs but is less suited for guiding temporally coherent motions. A more powerful and flexible approach is ControlNet [29], which extends a pre-trained diffusion backbone with a trainable control branch. This branch encodes spatial conditions (such as keypoints, edge maps, or joint trajectories) and injects them into the main diffusion process, enabling precise and fine-grained generation control. Our study builds upon this line of spatially guided diffusion research. We argue that accurately simulating medical symptoms necessitates direct spatial conditioning, as semantic control alone cannot ensure anatomically consistent motion. Therefore, our approach leverages the principles of ControlNet to explicitly integrate symptom-related joint trajectories as spatial control signals—allowing the generated motions to reflect medically realistic movement limitations.

2.3 Motion Style Transfer

With the advancement of deep learning, an increasing number of studies explored the use of neural networks for modeling and transferring motion styles. For instance, Holden et al. [14] proposed a convolutional autoencoder to extract style representations from motion data and perform style transfer. Aberman et al. [1] introduced a temporal convolutional network combined with Adaptive Instance

Normalization (AdaIN) to manipulate motion style in latent space. Motion Puzzle [16] presented an optimization-based framework that reconstructed motion segments to generate highly flexible motions while maintaining style consistency. Additionally, Yamamoto and Murakami [28] utilized discriminator-based constraints from a GAN to guide the generation of stylized motion through geometric features such as joint displacement amplitude. In this work, we reinterpret the process of a patient responding to diagnostic instructions under specific physical conditions as a style transfer task. Specifically, style is defined by symptom-induced joint behavior patterns, while content is determined by high-level instructional commands.

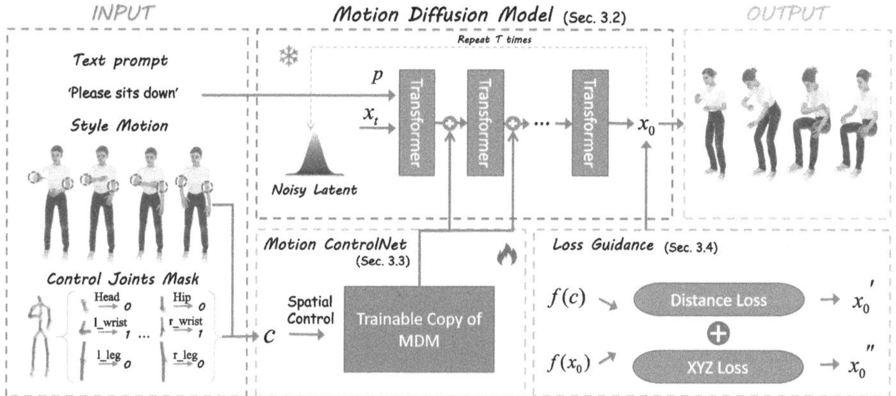

Fig. 2. Overview of Motion Generation Framework. The process involves inputting text descriptions (doctor's instructions to patients or possible states of patients) and style motion data (disease behavior), which are processed by the Motion Diffusion Model (MDM) through multiple Transformer layers. In addition, the Motion Control Network (Motion ControlNet) can spatially control the generated actions by adjusting the joint positions inferred by people. Loss guidance (Distance loss and XYZ loss) helps to optimize the generated actions to make them more realistic, and finally outputs natural human motion sequences.

3 Method

3.1 Overview

The primary aim of this paper is to design a motion generation framework for incorporating precise joint constraints into a human motion generation process to create realistic VSP motions. Figure 2 presents an overview of our framework. Given a text prompt p representing physician instructions and an additional control signal $C \in \mathbb{R}^{N\times J\times 3}$ derived from symptom-related joint definitions, our goal is to synthesize a bodily motion sequence $x_0 \in \mathbb{R}^{N\times D}$ that accurately mimics disease-specific symptoms. Here, N represents the length of the motion sequence,

J is the number of joints, and D is the dimension of human motion representations (263 in HumanML3D [9]). This process is driven by a diffusion-based motion generator, which is guided by a specially designed Motion ControlNet module that processes the spatial control signal C. Furthermore, to enhance the realism and precision of the generated motions, we introduce a comprehensive Loss Guidance mechanism, incorporating both a Distance Loss and an XYZ Loss during the denoising process.

In the following sections, we first provide a brief overview of the underlying text-conditioned human motion generation model based on the diffusion process in Sect. 3.2. We then introduce our proposed Motion ControlNet approach to incorporate the joint control signal C into the generation model in Sect. 3.3. Finally, we detail the design of our Loss Guidance in Sect. 3.4.

3.2 Human Motion Diffusion Model

Our motion generation core is built upon the Motion Diffusion Model (MDM) [26], which has demonstrated impressive performance in text-to-motion generation. MDM formulates human motion synthesis as a denoising Markov process, progressively transforming a random noise distribution into a coherent motion sequence. Let $x_t \in \mathbb{R}^{N \times D}$ denote the noisy motion at denoising step t, with T total denoising steps. The model learns to reverse this process, predicting the clean motion $x_0(\theta) = M(x_t, t, p; \theta)$, where M is the motion generation model with parameters θ. The posterior mean $\mu_t(\theta)$ at each step is computed as:

$$\mu_t(\theta) = \sqrt{\frac{\bar{\alpha}_{t-1}}{1-\bar{\alpha}_t}} x_0(\theta) + \sqrt{\frac{\alpha_t(1-\bar{\alpha}_{t-1})}{1-\bar{\alpha}_t}} x_t, \tag{1}$$

where $\alpha_t = 1 - \beta_t$ and $\bar{\alpha}_t = \prod_{s=0}^{t} \alpha_s$ are hyperparameters defining the diffusion schedule. We omit θ for brevity, using x_0 and μ_t henceforth. The model parameters θ are optimized by minimizing the L_2-loss: $||x_0(\theta) - x_0^*||_2^2$, where x_0^* represents the ground-truth motion sequence.

While MDM excels in generating motions based on semantic text prompts, its original design lacks the capability for precise spatial control over specific joints or poses. This limitation arises from the typical relative motion representations used in pre-trained models, which pose challenges for controlling local human poses with global spatial conditions. To overcome this discrepancy and enable fine-grained control for symptom replication, we augment the MDM with a specialized Motion ControlNet and a novel loss guidance mechanism.

3.3 Motion ControlNet

To enable MDM to effectively integrate symptom-related spatial conditions C, we introduce Motion ControlNet, a module inspired by the success of ControlNet in image generation [29]. As illustrated in Fig. 3, Motion ControlNet operates as a trainable copy of the MDM, with the original MDM's parameters remaining frozen during its training process. Its architecture comprises a series of transformer encoder layers, each connected to its corresponding MDM layer via a zero-initialized linear layer. This strategic initialization allows Motion ControlNet to commence training from a state equivalent to a pre-trained MDM, gradually acquiring residual features for the conditioning variable C through backpropagation at each layer.

The primary challenge in integrating spatial control lies in the potential sparsity of the conditioning variable C across both temporal and joint dimensions. Specifically, control may only be required for a limited subset of joints or frames. Motion ControlNet is designed to address this by adaptively interpolating natural human motion over unconditioned frames, ensuring smooth and realistic transitions while strictly adhering to the input control information.

As depicted in the lower section of Fig. 3, the Motion ControlNet takes *Style Motion* S and a *Joint Mask* m as its initial inputs. These inputs are first processed by the **MMask** module (represented by the circular 'M' icon in the figure), which serves as a preprocessing step for the control signal. The MMask module is responsible for extracting the relevant control joints from the *Style Motion* S based on the *Joint Mask* m, and converting them into global coordinates via forward kinematics (FK). The output of this MMask module is the Spatial Control Signal $C \in \mathbb{R}^{N \times J \times 3}$, representing the desired global joint positions from the *Style Motion*, and it also provides the associated Joint Mask m which dictates the active control points.

Consistent with ControlNet's principles, our Motion ControlNet employs a relative conditioning approach. The control signal is primarily formulated as the relative condition $c' = (C - R(x)) \odot m$, representing the distance between the desired (C, the output of the MMask module) and current ($R(x)$) joint positions in global space, filtered by the provided Joint Mask m. This is achieved by utilizing FK to convert the internal relative motion representation $x \in \mathbb{R}^{N \times D}$ into global space coordinates $R(x) \in \mathbb{R}^{N \times J \times 3}$. This relative conditioning is crucial for guiding the model towards the specified spatial constraints. The processed spatial control signal then passes through a Linear Layer before being fed into the Transformer Layers of the Motion ControlNet. Motion ControlNet is the only trainable component in our framework, with its training objective identical to that of MDM.

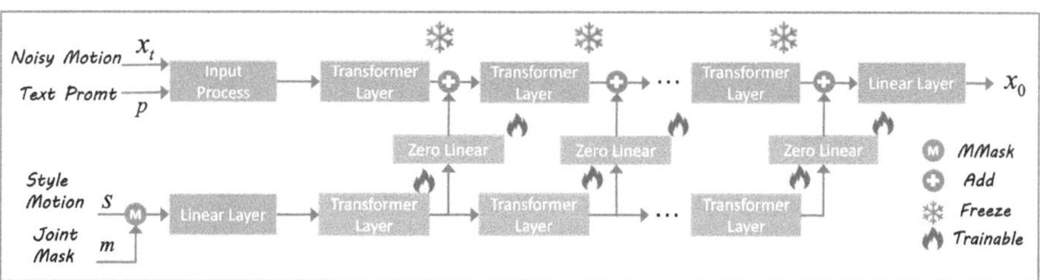

Fig. 3. Architecture of Motion ControlNet.

3.4 Loss Guidance

While Motion ControlNet effectively adapts the generation process to incorporate spatial conditions, achieving precise alignment between predicted poses and global spatial constraints, particularly for intricate symptom expression, benefits from further refinement. We leverage an additional **Loss Guidance** mechanism to enhance the stylization and consistency of the generated motions, ensuring natural postures, balanced joint relationships, and accurate symptom-specific expressions. This guidance effectively complements the ControlNet, allowing the model to produce high-quality, natural action sequences with the target style.

Joint Coordinate Pre-alignment (f). Before calculating loss terms based on joint positions, it is crucial to align all joint coordinates into a unified coordinate system to ensure comparability and validity of distance calculations. This pre-alignment process, denoted as $f(\cdot)$, involves two steps:

Global Displacement Removal. The keypoint coordinates are made root-relative by setting the root keypoint ($j = 0$) to the origin and relocating all other keypoints with respect to it. This transformation is defined as:

$$P'_{t,j} = \begin{cases} 0 & \text{if } j = 0, \\ P_{t,j} - P_{t,0} & \text{otherwise.} \end{cases} \tag{2}$$

where $P_{t,j}$ is the original coordinate of the j-th keypoint in the t-th frame from the prediction tensor $\mathbf{P} \in \mathbb{R}^{N \times J \times 3}$, $P_{t,0}$ is the coordinate of the root keypoint in the same frame, and $P'_{t,j}$ is the resulting root-relative coordinate which forms the new tensor $\mathbf{P}'$.

Orientation Normalization. To unify the global orientation, a rotation is computed based on the first frame and applied consistently across the entire sequence:

$$P''_{t,j} = R_z(\theta) \cdot P'_{t,j}, \tag{3}$$

where $P'_{t,j}$ is the root-relative keypoint coordinate, $R_z(\theta)$ is the rotation matrix that aligns the initial frame's body plane normal to the z-axis, and $P''_{t,j}$ is the final, orientation-normalized coordinate. This operation yields the tensor $\mathbf{P}''$, which has a consistent global orientation.

Distance Loss. The Distance Loss focuses on maintaining the consistency of relative joint positions and angles within the generated actions. This is crucial for preserving the internal structure and naturalness of the symptomatic motion.

Given the pre-aligned predicted coordinates $A^{\text{pred}} \in \mathbb{R}^{N \times J \times 3}$ and the pre-aligned conditioned coordinates $A^{\text{cond}} \in \mathbb{R}^{N \times J \times 3}$, we first apply a mask $M \in \{0, 1\}^{N \times J \times 3}$ to select the set of candidate keypoints for each frame t. Let these sets be $S_t^{\text{pred}} = \{p_i^{\text{pred}}\}$ and $S_t^{\text{cond}} = \{p_i^{\text{cond}}\}$, where $p_i = (x_i, y_i, z_i)$ represents the 3D coordinates of the keypoints. The sum of squared Euclidean distances between all unique pairs of keypoints within each set is calculated as:

$$d_t^{\text{pred}} = \sum_{i<j} \|p_i^{\text{pred}} - p_j^{\text{pred}}\|_2^2 \quad \text{and} \quad d_t^{\text{cond}} = \sum_{i<j} \|p_i^{\text{cond}} - p_j^{\text{cond}}\|_2^2, \tag{4}$$

where p_i^{pred} and p_i^{cond} are the coordinates of the i-th keypoint in the predicted and conditioned poses for frame t, respectively. Next, the final Distance Loss is computed as the Mean Squared Error (MSE) between these aggregated distances across all frames in the sequence:

$$L_{\text{distance}} = \frac{1}{N} \sum_{t=1}^{N} \|d_t^{\text{pred}} - d_t^{\text{cond}}\|_2^2, \tag{5}$$

where d_t^{pred} and d_t^{cond} are the aggregate pairwise distances for frame t as defined above, and N is the total number of frames. This loss quantifies the difference in the internal spatial relationships of joints between the generated and target motions.

XYZ Loss. The XYZ Loss ensures the precise alignment of individual joint positions in 3D space, which is vital for the spatial consistency of the generated action with the target style.

For each frame, we select the valid joint positions based on a mask. Let $\tilde{y}_{\text{pred}}$ and $\tilde{y}_{\text{cond}}$ represent the masked predicted and conditioned joint positions, respectively. These are obtained by filtering out masked-out joints: $\tilde{y}_{\text{pred}} = \{y_{\text{pred},i} \mid \text{mask}_i = 1\}$ and $\tilde{y}_{\text{cond}} = \{y_{\text{cond},i} \mid \text{mask}_i = 1\}$. The loss is calculated as the MSE between the filtered predicted and conditioned joint positions:

$$L_{\text{XYZ}} = \frac{1}{N_{\text{valid}}} \sum_{i=1}^{N_{\text{valid}}} \left(\tilde{y}_{\text{pred},i} - \tilde{y}_{\text{cond},i}\right)^2, \tag{6}$$

where $\tilde{y}_{\text{pred},i}$ and $\tilde{y}_{\text{cond},i}$ are the coordinates of the i-th valid joint position for the predicted and conditioned motions, respectively, and N_{valid} is the total number of valid (unmasked) joint positions. This loss quantifies the direct spatial difference between the relevant joints, ensuring precise spatial consistency.

4 Experiments

4.1 Datasets

Due to the lack of publicly available datasets for patient motion, we curated a collection of diagnostic video clips from platforms such as website[1], YouTube, Wikipedia, and Bilibili, resulting in a total of 496 videos covering 23 common disease conditions (e.g., headache, leg pain, foot pain, stomach pain, arm pain, etc.).

[1] http://jib.xywy.com/.

Table 1. All methods use our dataset. The symbol '→' indicates that results are more favorable when the metric aligns closely with the real distribution. We run the entire evaluation 20 times (except MultiModality runs 5 times). Bold indicates the best result.

Method	FID↓	Foot skating ratio↓	MM dist↓	R-precision↑ (Top-3)	Diversity→	SRA↑
Ours	**5.698**	**0.061**	6.828	0.439	7.449	**44.531**
SMooDi [31]	13.211	0.074	**4.091**	**0.631**	8.891	37.715
MLD+MCM-LDM [24]	6.783	0.068	7.459	0.345	**9.053**	35.356
MLD+Motion Puzzle [16]	8.504	0.081	6.617	0.293	6.614	24.375

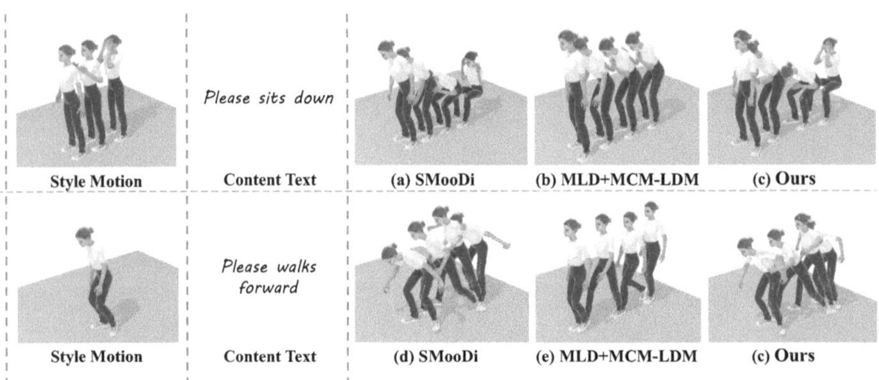

Fig. 4. Qualitative comparisons of our approach and baseline methods on two stylized motion generation task.

We then employed HybrIK-X [21], a state-of-the-art 3D human pose estimation method, to extract full-body motion data from these videos. To ensure compatibility with existing motion-language benchmarks, we further preprocessed the collected data following the same pipeline used in the HumanML3D dataset. We refer to the resulting dataset as **SympMotion**.

Symptom-Related Joint Annotation. To ensure the generated motions are medically grounded, we implemented a systematic, expert-guided annotation process to define the control signals for our model. This process began with a clinical analysis of the videos in our SympMotion dataset. Our team, in consultation with medical expertise, systematically observed these videos to identify characteristic physical manifestations for each disease condition. For example, we noted that arthritis patients consistently exhibit restricted knee flexion, while individuals experiencing unilateral pain show asymmetric arm movements.

Based on these clinical observations, we meticulously identified and annotated the key joints that are most indicative of a specific symptom. For the "Armpain" category, for instance, the right and left wrists were designated as the crucial control joints. The 3D motion trajectories of these annotated joints were then extracted from the source videos. These trajectories serve as the expert-defined spatial constraints and Style Motion input that guide the generation process, ensuring the final animations accurately reflect the physical limitations associated with each symptom. This targeted annotation strategy is critical for the model's performance, as validated in our ablation studies.

Evaluation Metrics. For the evaluation of motion generation, we adopt a comprehensive set of metrics that assess three key aspects: Content Preservation, Style Accuracy, and Realism. To evaluate content preservation and style reflection, we employ several established metrics: motion-retrieval precision (R precision), Multi-modal Distance (MM Dist), Diversity, and Frechet Inception Distance (FID), which align with standard practices in the field [3]. To address the common challenge of foot skating in kinetics-based motion generation, we incorporate the foot skating ratio as proposed in [18] to measure the quality of generated motions. For style accuracy, we utilize Style Recognition Accuracy (SRA) [16], which quantifies how well the generated motion aligns with the intended style. During evaluation, we randomly select a content text from the HumanML3D dataset and a motion style sequence from the SympMotion dataset to generate the stylized motion. A pre-trained style classifier is then used to compute the SRA for the generated motion, providing an objective measure of style reflection. This multi-faceted evaluation approach ensures a robust assessment of both the fidelity and creativity of the motion generation process.

Baselines. For motion style transfer task, we compare our methods with three state-of-the-art methods, namely SMooDi [31], MCM-LDM [24] and Motion Puzzle [16]. To ensure a fair comparison, we train the compared methods under the same setting as ours, using a combined dataset consisting of HumanML3D and SympMotion. The goal achieved by SMooDi is similar to our framework, which uses content text and style motion as input to achieve the style transfer task. The other two baseline methods consist of applying motion style transfer methods to motion sequences generated by the text-to-motion model. To be consistent with our approach of using a pre-trained motion diffusion model, MLD is chosen for the text-to-motion model used for the stylized motion generation baseline, and the motion style transfer method is consistent with the method used in the motion style transfer task.

4.2 Comparison to Baseline Methods

Quantitative Analysis. Table 1 reports the comparisons of our method with the three baseline methods. Specifically, our method performs well in terms of Style Recognition Accuracy (SRA), achieving an impressive 44.531 points, surpassing all other methods, and also significantly outperforming the method of SMooDi on the FID metric. The first row of Fig. 4 validates our observation, where the motion generated by our method performs better in adhering to both content and style constraints than baseline methods. In contrast, in Fig. 4(b), MLD+MCM-LDM neither expresses the action instructions well nor has a complete display style, while SMoodi has a tendency to express style, the effect is very poor in Fig. 4(a). For foot skating ratio, our method generates a ratio of 0.061, which is lower than other methods, especially SmooDi (0.074) and MLD+Motion Puzzle (0.081). The second row of Fig. 4 validates this observation. The movement generated by MLD+MCM-LDM shows deviation of footsteps during movement, and lacks the process of lifting and retracting the foot in Fig. 4(e). However, SMoodi encountered the problem of mold penetration during the generation process in Fig. 4(d). For the task of motion style transfer, since it does not take content text as input, text-motion related metrics such as MM Dist, R-precision, and Diversity are not applicable and thus are not reported. In conclusion, our method demonstrates a balanced and superior performance across all evaluation metrics. It not only provides high-quality motion generation with minimal artifacts but also ensures realistic foot movement, accurate style recognition, and good diversity.

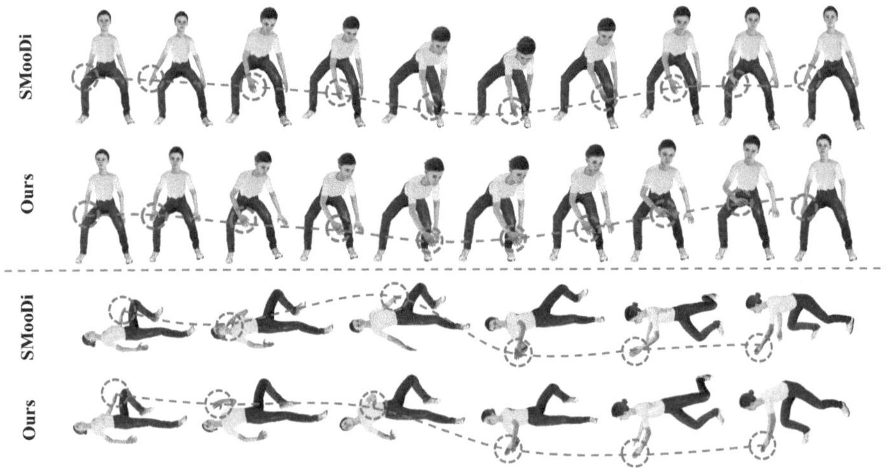

Fig. 5. Comparison of key joint movement trajectories for generated motion.

To further compare the motion quality of our method with existing methods, we visualize the changes of key joint trajectories over time in Fig. 5. The red dashed lines indicate the spatial displacements of symptom-related joints (e.g., knees, hands, feet) throughout the motion sequence.

Compared with SMooDi, our model generates smoother and more physically accurate trajectories, especially in complex interactions such as squatting and lying down. In the first row, the knee joint generated by SMooDi exhibits obvious jitter and irregular motion, resulting in unnatural leg deformation. The hand also does not point to the corresponding position, while our method can achieve consistent joint transitions and exhibit normal patient behavior. Similarly, in the example below, the hand trajectory generated by SMooDi suffers from positional abruptness and model penetration, while our method maintains temporal coherence and trajectory continuity. This improvement stems from our controlled per-

Table 2. User Study. The results show that our method outperforms other methods in terms of realism, content preservation, and style performance.

Methods	Realism	Content Preservation	Style Performance
Ours	**3.725**	**3.782**	**3.900**
SMooDi [31]	3.182	3.382	3.334
MLD+MCM-LDM [24]	3.084	3.016	2.948
MLD+Motion Puzzle [16]	3.468	3.400	3.334

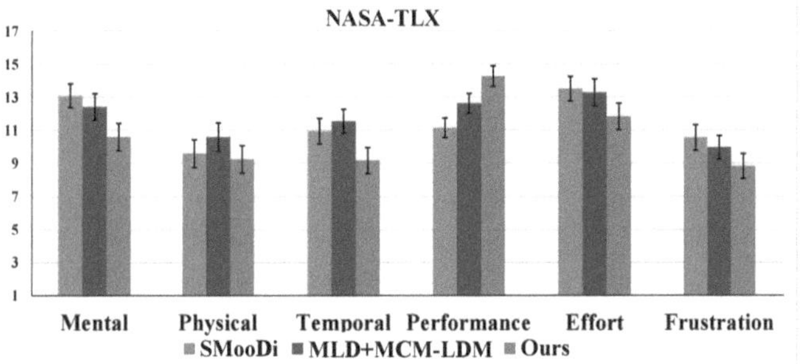

Fig. 6. NASA-TLX rating (±S.E.) comparison. We utilize the NASA-TLX questionnaire to assess the workload, with a maximum score of 21 points. The outcomes from this evaluation suggest that our method is both reliable and effective in generating VSP motions, thereby enhancing the user experience.

ception training strategy, where we focus the style transfer on symptom-related joints and are explicitly guided by spatial and temporal constraints. As a result, our model achieves higher joint-level accuracy and motion realism, which is also reflected in higher quantitative scores for all metrics.

4.3 User Study

In this section, we present a user study evaluating stylized motions and a NASA-TLX questionnaire assessing the workload of our ViMoGen method in comparison with state-of-the-art approaches [16,24,31].

Table 3. Ablation Studies on HumanML3D Content and SympMotion Styles.

Method	FID↓	Foot skating ratio↓	MM dist↓	R-precision↑ (Top-3)	Diversity→	SRA↑
Ours (on all)	5.698	**0.061**	6.828	0.439	**7.449**	**44.531**
w/o XYZ Loss	10.321	0.129	7.311	0.408	7.120	29.102
w/o Distance Loss	9.577	0.097	7.538	0.395	6.988	30.847
Random joints (2 to 4)	**5.503**	0.072	**6.772**	**0.512**	7.126	10.038
All joints (no selection)	6.503	0.078	7.318	0.461	7.384	38.573

Initially, we recruited 40 employees, including 28 men and 12 women. Most participants (24 individuals) are aged between 18–25 years old, 12 participants are 26–30 years old, and one participant is under 18 and three is over 30. Regarding occupation, 26 participants are students, while the remaining occupations include 1 technician, 10 doctor, 1 teacher, 1 professional, and 1 other occupation. The questionnaire consisted of 5 sets of experiments, each consisting of a unique text condition and style movement. Participants are asked to rate results generated by these methods on a scale of 1 (significantly inaccurate) to 5 (significantly accurate), based on three metrics: (1) Realism: the naturalness of the stylized motion, (2) Content Preservation: the level of the stylized motion to preserve the content information from content text, and (3) Style Performance: the level of the stylized motion to perform the style features from style motion.

As shown in Table 2, our method achieves the highest score in three metrics. Moreover, we conduct an ANOVA test to statistically examine the differences. The overall ANOVA reveals significant differences among the methods in terms of Realism ($F = 15.634$, $p < 0.01$), Content Preservation ($F = 18.372$, $p < 0.01$), and Style Performance ($F = 42.189$, $p < 0.01$). The post-hoc analysis indicates that our method significantly outperforms all compared methods across all three metrics (all $p < 0.01$). These results further validate the effectiveness of our method in style transfer, making it more favored by users.

Furthermore, we have conducted a NASA-TLX questionnaire to evaluate the workload of our ViMoGen method comparing with SMooDi [31], and MLD+MCM-LDM [24] in Fig. 6. Specifically, we ask participants to observe and rate VSP motions generated by each method. After completing each rating task, participants are asked to complete the NASA-TLX questionnaire for the previous task. As shown in Fig. 6, the ratings for our ViMoGen in the mental, physical, temporal, effort, and frustration dimensions are lower than those for the other two methods, indicating that the motions generated by our ViMoGen are less burdensome for users. In addition, our method scores higher than the other methods in the performance dimension, further demonstrating that our ViMoGen can help users observe the VSP motions more accurately and comprehensively, thus improving task efficiency and quality. Overall, these results indicate that our ViMoGen has high reliability and effectiveness in generating VSP motions, providing users with a better user experience.

4.4 Ablation Studies

To validate the effectiveness of our framework's design choices, we conduct ablation studies from two perspectives: (1) the impact of different loss functions, and (2) the effect of symptom-related joint selection.

Loss Function Ablation. Our model incorporates two critical loss terms a distance loss and an XYZ loss to guide the training of the ControlNet module. To ascertain their individual contributions, we removed each loss term separately and evaluated the generated motions using standard metrics, as presented in Table 3. Our full model achieved the lowest foot skating ratio (0.061), demonstrating superior motion realism and temporal consistency. In contrast, the absence of either the XYZ loss or the distance loss resulted in a significant increase in foot sliding artifacts (0.129 and 0.097, respectively), which underscores the importance of these losses in maintaining spatial grounding and preserving motion structure during synthesis.Furthermore, removing either loss component significantly decreased the Symptom Representation Adequacy (SRA) score from our full model's 44.531 to 29.102 (w/o XYZ Loss) and 30.847 (w/o Distance Loss), respectively. This substantial drop demonstrates that these two losses provide complementary and essential constraints: the distance loss ensures global shape consistency, while the XYZ loss enforces the precise alignment of local joints with the desired spatial trajectory, both critical for accurate symptom representation.

Control Joint Selection Ablation. Beyond loss functions, our system leverages clinically meaningful joint priors to precisely control disease-specific motion. For each movement, we meticulously annotated symptom-related joints (e.g., right wrist and left wrist for "Armpain", as shown in Fig. 1), which serve as crucial control signals within the motion control network. To evaluate the impact of this targeted design, we compared it against two alternative joint selection strategies: (a) a random subset of joints of the same size as our selected set, and (b) all joints (no selection). Notably, the random joint selection baseline achieved the lowest FID (5.503) and a competitive MM distance (6.772), but dramatically underperformed on SRA (10.038). This disparity arises because randomly selected joints often lack direct correlation with the intended symptom representation, causing the model to prioritize generating general, visually plausible content over medically specific motion cues. Conversely, while the all-joint variant performed reasonably well across other metrics, it suffered from diluted supervision due to excessive and potentially irrelevant control signals, resulting in lower joint tracking accuracy and diminished style alignment when compared to our focused selection. This further validates that our clinically-informed, symptom-related joint selection is crucial for achieving high fidelity in disease-specific motion generation.

5 Conclusion

In this study, we introduce ViMoGen, a novel controllable motion generation framework designed to provide realistic VSP simulations for medical education. This framework leverages the core capabilities of the diffusion model and facilitates accurate, fine-grained, and medically consistent body motion generation by integrating two control signals: expert-defined symptom-related joint constraints and physician instruction text. Furthermore, we introduce a loss-guided mechanism (including XYZ loss and distance loss) to further optimize motion realism and symptom representation. Through detailed ablation studies, we strongly demonstrate the effectiveness of each key component of the framework and its unique contribution to motion quality, realism, and symptom representation. A limitation of our approach is the manual definition of these joint constraints. We may consider using other methods to automatically specify these constraints for improved efficiency.

Acknowledgments. We sincerely acknowledge the anonymous reviewers for their insightful feedback. This work was supported by the National Natural Science Foundation of China (Nos. 62572062, 62525204, 62441201, 62272021), Beijing Natural Science Foundation (L232102), and the Open Project Program of the State Key Laboratory of CAD&CG, Zhejiang University (No. A2406).

References

1. Aberman, K., Weng, Y., Lischinski, D., Cohen-Or, D., Chen, B.: Unpaired motion style transfer from video to animation. ACM Trans. Graphics (TOG) **39**(4), 64–1 (2020)
2. Bond, W.F., et al.: Virtual standardized patient simulation: case development and pilot application to high-value care. Simul. Healthc.: J. Soc. Simul. Healthc. **14**(4), 241–250 (2019)
3. Chen, X., et al.: Executing your commands via motion diffusion in latent space. In: Proceedings of the IEEE/CVF Conference on Computer Vision and Pattern Recognition, pp. 18000–18010 (2023)
4. Choi, J., Kim, S., Jeong, Y., Gwon, Y., Yoon, S.: ILVR: conditioning method for denoising diffusion probabilistic models. arXiv preprint arXiv:2108.02938 (2021)
5. Chung, H., Sim, B., Ryu, D., Ye, J.C.: Improving diffusion models for inverse problems using manifold constraints. Adv. Neural. Inf. Process. Syst. **35**, 25683–25696 (2022)
6. Dabral, R., Mughal, M.H., Golyanik, V., Theobalt, C.: Mofusion: a framework for denoising-diffusion-based motion synthesis. In: Proceedings of the IEEE/CVF Conference on Computer Vision and Pattern Recognition, pp. 9760–9770 (2023)
7. Dhariwal, P., Nichol, A.: Diffusion models beat GANs on image synthesis. Adv. Neural. Inf. Process. Syst. **34**, 8780–8794 (2021)
8. Duan, Y., et al.: Single-shot motion completion with transformer. arXiv preprint arXiv:2103.00776 (2021)
9. Guo, C., et al.: Generating diverse and natural 3D human motions from text. In: Proceedings of the IEEE/CVF Conference on Computer Vision and Pattern Recognition (CVPR), pp. 5152–5161 (2022)
10. Guo, C., Zuo, X., Wang, S., Cheng, L.: TM2T: stochastic and tokenized modeling for the reciprocal generation of 3D human motions and texts. In: European Conference on Computer Vision, pp. 580–597. Springer (2022)
11. Harvey, F.G., Yurick, M., Nowrouzezahrai, D., Pal, C.: Robust motion inbetweening. ACM Trans. Graphics (TOG) **39**(4), 60–1 (2020)
12. He, W., et al.: MARS: mixture of auto-regressive models for fine-grained text-to-image synthesis. In: Proceedings of the AAAI Conference on Artificial Intelligence, vol. 39, pp. 17123–17131 (2025)
13. Ho, J., Salimans, T.: Classifier-free diffusion guidance. arXiv preprint arXiv:2207.12598 (2022)
14. Holden, D., Saito, J., Komura, T.: A deep learning framework for character motion synthesis and editing. ACM Trans. Graphics (ToG) **35**(4), 1–11 (2016)

15. Huang, S., et al.: Diffusion-based generation, optimization, and planning in 3D scenes. In: Proceedings of the IEEE/CVF Conference on Computer Vision and Pattern Recognition, pp. 16750–16761 (2023)
16. Jang, D.K., Park, S., Lee, S.H.: Motion puzzle: arbitrary motion style transfer by body part. ACM Trans. Graphics (TOG) **41**(3), 1–16 (2022)
17. Karunratanakul, K., Preechakul, K., Suwajanakorn, S., Tang, S.: GMD: controllable human motion synthesis via guided diffusion models. arXiv preprint arXiv:2305.12577, vol. 2 (2023)
18. Karunratanakul, K., Preechakul, K., Suwajanakorn, S., Tang, S.: Guided motion diffusion for controllable human motion synthesis. In: Proceedings of the IEEE/CVF International Conference on Computer Vision, pp. 2151–2162 (2023)
19. Kingma, D.P., Welling, M., et al.: Auto-encoding variational bayes (2013)
20. Laleye, F.A., Blanié, A., Brouquet, A., Behnamou, D., de Chalendar, G.: Semantic similarity to improve question understanding in a virtual patient. In: Proceedings of the ACM Symposium on Applied Computing, pp. 859–866 (2020)
21. Li, J., Bian, S., Xu, C., Chen, Z., Yang, L., Lu, C.: HybrIK-X: hybrid analytical-neural inverse kinematics for whole-body mesh recovery. arXiv preprint arXiv:2304.05690 (2023)
22. Lin, W.S., Harris, B.T., Phasuk, K., Llop, D.R., Morton, D.: Integrating a facial scan, virtual smile design, and 3d virtual patient for treatment with CAD-CAM ceramic veneers: a clinical report. J. Prosthet. Dent. **119**(2), 200–205 (2018)
23. Shafir, Y., Tevet, G., Kapon, R., Bermano, A.H.: Human motion diffusion as a generative prior. arXiv preprint arXiv:2303.01418 (2023)
24. Song, W., et al.: Arbitrary motion style transfer with multi-condition motion latent diffusion model. In: Proceedings of the IEEE/CVF Conference on Computer Vision and Pattern Recognition, pp. 821–830 (2024)
25. Tevet, G., Raab, S., Gordon, B., Shafir, Y., Cohen-Or, D., Bermano, A.H.: Human motion diffusion model. arXiv preprint arXiv:2209.14916 (2022)
26. Tevet, G., Raab, S., Gordon, B., Shafir, Y., Cohen-or, D., Bermano, A.H.: Human motion diffusion model. In: The Eleventh International Conference on Learning Representations (2023)
27. Wang, H., Spinelli, M., Wang, Q., Bai, X., Qin, Z., Chen, A.: InstantStyle: free lunch towards style-preserving in text-to-image generation. arXiv preprint arXiv:2404.02733 (2024)
28. Yamamoto, K., Murakami, M.: Human motion generation with StyleGAN. In: Seventh International Conference on Computer Graphics and Virtuality (ICCGV 2024), vol. 13158, pp. 101–109. SPIE (2024)
29. Zhang, L., Rao, A., Agrawala, M.: Adding conditional control to text-to-image diffusion models. In: Proceedings of the IEEE/CVF International Conference on Computer Vision, pp. 3836–3847 (2023)
30. Zhang, X., et al.: Analysis of virtual standardized patients for assessing clinical fundamental skills of medical students: a prospective study. BMC Med. Educ. **24**(1), 981 (2024)
31. Zhong, L., Xie, Y., Jampani, V., Sun, D., Jiang, H.: SMooDi: stylized motion diffusion model. In: Leonardis, A., Ricci, E., Roth, S., Russakovsky, O., Sattler, T., Varol, G. (eds.) ECCV 2024. LNCS, vol. 15059, pp. 405–421. Springer, Cham (2024). https://doi.org/10.1007/978-3-031-73232-4_23

Integrating Multi-modal Interaction with AR Garment Design for Educational Applications

Hengheng Zhao[1], Chaohui Yang[1], Junfeng Yao[2](✉), and Ruolong Wang[1]

[1] Xiamen Institute of Technology, Xiamen 361021, Fujian, China
zhaohengheng@xit.edu.cn
[2] Xiamen University, Xiamen 361005, Fujian, China
yao0010@xmu.edu.cn

Abstract. This paper investigates the strong correlation between interaction methods and scenario requirements within the specialized context of children's education. It proposes an innovative integration of multimodal interaction techniques to bridge augmented reality (AR), garment design, and educational content. A comprehensive solution based on marker-based visual tracking is developed to support this integration. Key technical challenges such as real-time marker extraction, frame sequence jitter, logo pattern recognition, and texture mapping are addressed. The system allows dynamic combination and presentation of garment card components, enabling interactive learning scenarios. Features such as 360-degree preview and a rotatable mannequin mode are implemented to enhance natural interaction, reduce cost, and improve versatility. Experimental evaluations demonstrate an average processing time of 37 milliseconds per frame and a frame rate of 27 frames per second on mainstream smartphones, meeting real-time application demands. Furthermore, learning effectiveness experiments show that the proposed system significantly enhances children's learning outcomes, engagement, and overall performance. This work highlights the potential of multimodal AR interactions to transform traditional educational experiences through culturally enriched, visually engaging, and user-centered design.

Keywords: Multi-modal interaction · Augmented reality · Garment design · Education

1 Introduction

With the advancement of information network technology, artificial intelligence, and the metaverse, multimodal natural human-computer interaction has seamlessly bridged the virtual and real worlds, expanding the boundaries of the internet and enhancing freedom in mixed interactions between digital spaces and physical reality [1]. This integration has given rise to a new form of virtual-real

A. Hinkenjan et al. (Eds.): ICXR 2025, LNCS 16428, pp. 18–38, 2026.
https://doi.org/10.1007/978-981-95-7195-6_2

combined internet applications, showcasing the human desire for virtual displays, immersive experiences, and virtual exploration. Augmented reality (AR), as a significant means of virtual integration, has become especially popular in children's education [2]. Studies show that the application of AR can significantly improve children's learning outcomes [3].

The process of children's education is complex, requiring adherence to children's psychological, physiological, and cognitive development patterns while also considering their specific group characteristics in educational activities. Effective learning for children should occur within certain contexts, such as a setting that is more engaging, interactive, and focused, encouraging children to learn actively within it [4]. Through its immersive qualities, AR has become a key medium for creating such contexts.

Despite the growing maturity of AR technology, applications in children's education remain limited and fragmented. In fact, one of the main issues currently restricting AR is the lack of content [1]. For AR to integrate fully into children's education, the primary step is to address content production. Without strong content, AR cannot showcase its advantages, especially in its integration with traditional industries.

Traditional picture books, focused primarily on visuals, match children's psychological characteristics, spark their reading interest, and support growth in language, logical thinking, artistic appreciation, and creativity. However, the market is flooded with children's books and products that often suffer from poor design, subpar quality, and high production costs [3]. The rapid development of electronic devices and digital content has made children more attracted to dynamic digital content, which has dimmed the appeal of traditional print media. Emerging digital picture books [5], on one hand, inherit the strengths of traditional picture books; on the other hand, they integrate the unique interactivity of digital content, greatly expanding expressive potential. Additionally, activities related to garment design and coordination can cultivate children's imagination and creativity, beneficially impacting their overall development [6]. Integrating the specialized field of garment design with digital picture books and applying this to children's education is a highly challenging endeavor.

In the context of digitalization's profound influence across industries, the application explored in this study, referred to here as ARCLO, delves into the deep integration and innovative development of augmented reality and garment design in children's education, aiming to promote the innovative combination of children's educational products. Specifically, this study merges AR technology, multimodal interaction, garment design, and children's education to explore universally applicable integration methods; examines the positive impacts of such integration on children's education; and considers design strategies using multimodal approaches to construct AR contexts that enhance children's interest in learning and improve educational outcomes. Additionally, this study discusses the adaptability of merging digital content with traditional clothing. By reconstructing traditional garment in a digital contextual reenactment, AR enables a seamless overlay of digital culture onto real-world scenes, achieving an accurate and deep fusion of virtual and real elements. This approach enhances the user experience, transitioning from passive observation to active interaction, thereby enhancing the overall interactive experience and contributing positively to the inheritance and promotion of traditional culture.

2 Related Knowledge

This section introduces AR technology, multimodal interaction, and immersive techniques related to this research, particularly their applications in children's education and garment design.

2.1 Augmented Reality Technology

Augmented Reality (AR) overlays virtual elements onto real-world settings, enhancing perception and interaction [7]. Applications like Pokemon Go 3D, Quiver, and HP Reveal have shown promise in education. However, AR content for children faces challenges such as poor alignment with their needs, subpar quality, and high publication costs [3].

A typical AR feature is the 360-degree preview mode, enabling interaction with digital content by moving, rotating, or adjusting the marker, as shown in Fig. 1d. This study also introduces a new mannequin mode, where users, after designing garments, can view them on a rotatable cylindrical mannequin by pointing their camera at the marker (Fig. 1e).

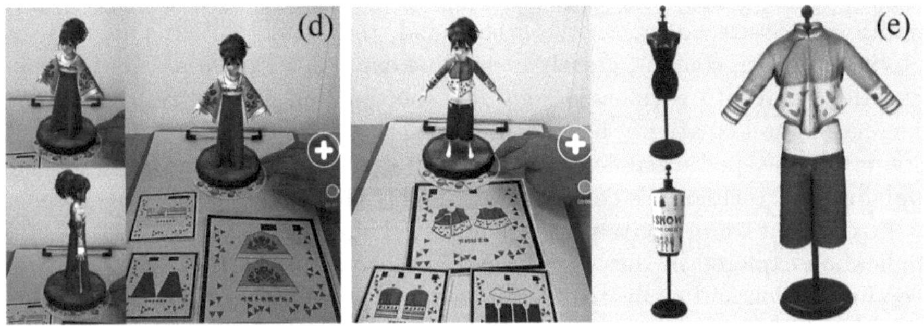

Fig. 1. 360-Degree preview mode (d) and mannequin mode (e).

2.2 Multimodal Interaction

With the continued development of the metaverse, traditional, single-mode interaction models have become increasingly aligned with specific scene requirements, falling short of meeting the diverse demands across AR applications. This has led interaction design toward multimodal, fine-grained directions. Multimodal interaction aims to facilitate information exchange between humans and computers through visual, tactile, image, text, and other modalities [8]. Multimodal interaction is a defining feature of AR, enhancing user experience and interactivity by combining single-modal data. Core equipment for immersive multimodal interaction includes common wearables like sensors, tactile gloves, and brain-computer interfaces.

Recent studies consistently report positive effects of AR, VR, and multimodal interaction in primary and early childhood education settings. Systematic reviews indicate that AR/VR can significantly improve academic achievement, motivation/engagement, cognition, and collaboration [9,10]. For example, in an in-the-wild mixed-methods study conducted in real school environments, *Kid Space* led to an average learning gain of 24% while reducing screen time and increasing physical activity and social interaction, providing strong evidence for the educational value of the "multimodal + embodied interaction + conversational AI" approach [11]. In specific subject areas, AR-based serious games and instructional activities in optical science, geometry, environmental science, and reading comprehension have commonly yielded significant improvements in learning outcomes, understanding, or creative thinking [12]. In addition, evaluations of child-oriented multimodal wearable devices in naturalistic home settings suggest generally positive usability and user experience from both parents and children [13]. Collectively, these findings indicate that multimodal interaction is not merely ornamental; when paired with appropriate instructional design and low-barrier hardware configurations, it can deliver measurable learning benefits.

Nevertheless, limitations and challenges remain. Certain multimodal devices still pose barriers to adaptability and robustness for learners across ages and needs, which may elevate classroom management demands and cognitive load. Moreover, while multimodal interaction shows notable potential for personalized learning, it can introduce additional instructional overhead; in resource-constrained contexts, the costs, maintenance requirements, and teacher training needs impede large-scale adoption [14,15]. Recent evidence, however, indicates that non-immersive, smartphone/tablet–based AR is the most prevalent form, substantially more common than head-mounted displays, enabling schools to leverage existing devices and thereby reduce entry and maintenance costs [9]. From the teacher's perspective, the primary challenges concern limited resources and skills, insufficient ready-to-use content, and training needs rather than hardware price alone; accordingly, the literature recommends a mobile-first AR approach complemented by teacher professional development and co-designed curricula to enhance sustainability and accessibility [9,16].

AR interaction technology, without a universal standard, requires mode selection tailored to specific scenarios. Inappropriate multimodal interactions increase costs without enhancing user experience, often serving as technical showpieces. For children's education, multimodal approaches should prioritize simplicity, affordability, and ease of use, though achieving this remains challenging.

2.3 Application of Immersive Technology in Children's Education

The definition of childhood varies by culture, society, and law, as well as by individual development stages. This study focuses on ages 2 to 12, a period of high psychological plasticity and receptiveness to new technologies, ideal for educational engagement.

Studies indicate that AR applications significantly enhance learning outcomes for children. For example, data from the experimental group in [2] shows that children in the AR-assisted group exhibited notable improvements in motivation, attention, and conceptual skills over the control group. Research [17] proposed a five-category indicator system based on AR to quantify children's classroom learning behavior, enhance engagement, and address attention deficit issues. Additionally, a study of 134 AR educational experiments [18] indicated improvements in students' responses, knowledge, skills, and overall performance. Applications of AR in children's education are demonstrated in four areas.

In AR educational games, [19] highlighted the lack of Extended Reality (XR) courses fostering design and reasoning skills. The Reality Composer system was developed as a tool to explore student potential and guide future XR education design. [20] introduced RefAR, a sketch-based 3D modeling method using augmented reality (AR). This approach lets users reference physical objects and real-time point clouds captured by Microsoft HoloLens 2, allowing children to create 3D content more freely and intuitively.

In AR curricula, [21] combined AR with geography instruction, developing AR-based software for middle-school geography that incorporates virtual models as learning tools. Another study [22] introduces a VR-based tool for exploring historical data, where historical fragments are displayed as spheres in a 3D space and organized by time, location, category, and semantic similarity for immersive exploration. In medical education, [23] employed mixed reality(MR) technology to simulate radiographic imaging in interactive virtual scenarios. This enables skill learning in a MR environment while avoiding radiation risks. Student feedback shows high satisfaction with its teaching effectiveness and user experience, indicating strong potential for broader adoption. Meanwhile, [24] developed a VR trainer for special education teachers, integrating voice input and virtual haptics to enhance functionality. The system effectively improved training outcomes, with physical objects boosting immersion. Moreover, mixed reality-based educational applications show great potential in robotics, archaeology, and classroom education [25] [26] [27], supporting personalized needs and fostering deeper integration with educational content and analytics.

In AR toys, the EMT application developed in [28] combines stories, 3D objects, and animations, revealing a positive relationship between children's behavioral patterns and cognitive skills. Another study [29] introduced an AR educational game for children ages 4–6 that teaches color matching, math, and 2D-3D geometry through interactive block and card assembly. The study [30] demonstrates that users can interact with a virtual cat using gestures and voice. Compared to virtual humans or non-interactive virtual content, the virtual cat more effectively promotes participants' willingness for self-disclosure, encourages emotional expression, and supports psychological therapy and emotional development.

In AR cultural content, [31] explores the concept of an "emotional rehearsal spaces" by integrating performing arts, dance, architecture, and dramaturgy. It proposes that XR technology can create highly immersive environments that enhance users' emotional experiences and behavioral learning. An AR application in [32] enhanced the promotion and inheritance of intangible cultural heritage, showcasing elements of the Lantern Festival and Chinese lantern culture. Article [33] used structural equation modeling (N=50) to analyze how usability, satisfaction, emotional attachment, attention focus, and flow experience influence user retention in mobile AR. Usability and focus positively impact satisfaction and mobility experience.

2.4 AR Technology in Garment Design

Digital clothing technology is advancing towards 3D, intelligent, personalized, and fast-response applications, providing a roadmap for the clothing industry's transformation. In particular, the development of 3D garment under AR and VR support has led to typical applications such as virtual fitting [34], virtual garments [35], and digital clothing education [36]. Virtual garments are designed using CAD patterns and include options for virtual sewing, color selection, fabric choice, and style configuration, eventually allowing users to try on the garment via 3D virtual mannequins [6]. With VR and AR technology enabling 3D modeling and real-time display, designers can freely switch between 2D garment patterns and 3D garment forms, modifying designs until the desired result is achieved [35]. Clothing education, which integrates AR into curriculum reform, has shown a positive effect on teaching quality and student performance [36]. Additionally, AR and VR have improved the efficiency of producing traditional ethnic garments with their intricate designs and reduced associated costs [37].

AR and VR-supported clothing design is more precise, engaging, sustainable, and creatively flexible than traditional methods. However, AR applications in children's clothing design and education are still limited.

2.5 Our Research Content

This study unifies various single-mode interactions into a multimodal framework, integrating education, garment design, and AR into an innovative and immersive learning solution. The research is structured into three key sections:

Solution Design for Fusion and Innovation Goals. There is limited reference literature or products similar to this study, making the design of an effective, integrated solution challenging. A marker-based visual tracking method developed with the Vuforia SDK is adopted in this paper. In this setup, markers are pre-positioned in the real environment. Vuforia's native workflow extracts marker features to obtain the pose information needed for tracking registration

[7]. Additionally, marker images extracted from the video stream enable recognition of garment card types, optimize sequential image tracking, and support various functional displays, as showen in the solution design schematic Fig. 2.

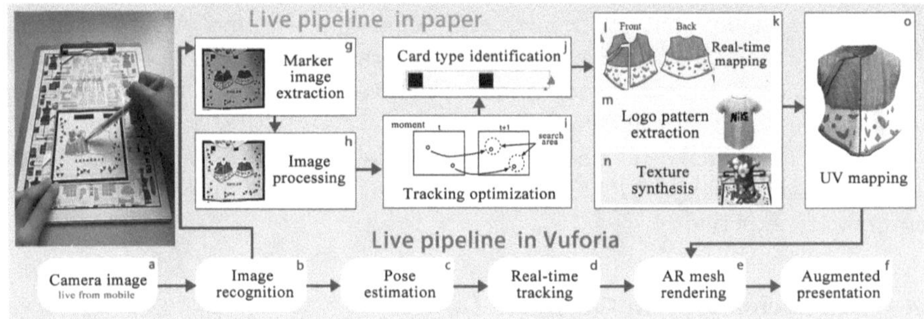

Fig. 2. The solution design schematic proposed in this paper

Image Extraction and Image Processing. The standard Vuforia workflow has two main limitations: it cannot extract markers from the video stream due to restricted access to marker data and lacks real-time image processing capabilities for efficient handling. This study focuses on enabling real-time marker extraction and effective image processing to address these gaps.

Multimodal Interaction Research and Design. Multimodal human-computer interaction (HCI) involves multiple modes of input and output between the user and computer [8]. While devices like wearable sensors and brain-computer interfaces offer high precision, they are often complex, costly, and not suitable for child-friendly education. This study explores more natural, accessible, and varied multimodal interaction methods to enhance the user experience in children's education. The specific approaches include:

1. Touch-Based Interaction: touchscreens serve as a fundamental, single-mode interaction model in current multimodal products.
2. Object-Based Interaction: real objects enable interactions with virtual content. Here, real-time drawing and 360-degree preview interactions based on marker images are referred to.
3. Extended Interaction: in specialized scenarios, contextually appropriate interaction methods may serve as an extension of interaction modes. In this study, the mannequin mode is used as an extended interaction method.

Building on the above research, the following sections will outline the preparation and implementation of the solution.

3 Preparation Work

3.1 Functional Design

In traditional garment cutting, an item of garment can be divided into several parts or components; for example, a shirt can be separated into sleeve, cuff, collar, and body components. In this study, small cards are used to display each of these parts. Once a user has hand-drawn a design on a given card, they can use the app to scan it and instantly see their 2D design applied to the 3D component in real time. By scanning different cards, users can assemble the entire garment or even mix and match tops and bottoms. Additionally, the app also supports logo pattern extraction and texture synthesis functions, allowing real-time updates to 3D garment textures so users can immediately see the final, realistic result. The app offers traditional touch-based and object-based interaction, as well as a extended interaction(mannequin mode) for a 360-degree view of the design, providing a more immersive experience. The more detailed functional design is shown in Fig. 3.

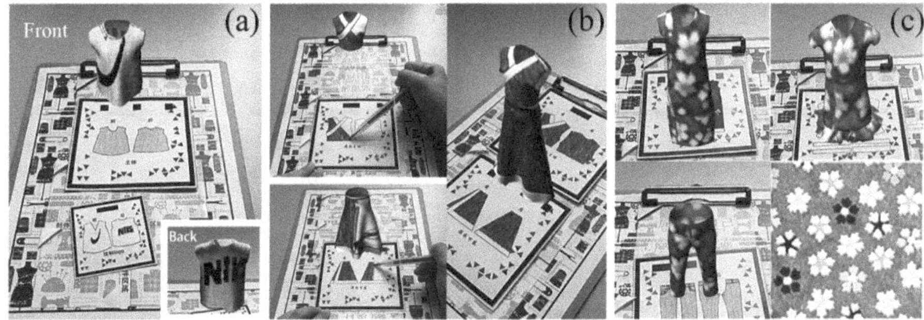

Fig. 3. Functional designs include: (1) Logo pattern extraction: extract logo patterns from drawing cards and overlay them onto the model's surface (Fig. (a)); (2) Real-time mapping: scan garment component cards, create textures from drawing areas, and update the 3D garment model appearance in real time (Fig. (b)); (3) Texture Synthesis: scan texture sample cards, generate large textures using an efficient synthesis algorithm, and apply them to the 3D garment (Fig. (c)); (4) Component Assembly: assemble sleeves, pockets, and other garment parts into a complete outfit (Fig. (b)); (5) Multimodal Display: provide various display options, including touchscreen, 360-degree preview mode with marker image, and a mannequin mode for intuitive design viewing (Fig. 1d and 1e).

3.2 3D Component Model Library

Preparation involves building a library of 3D garment models, ensuring objectivity and authenticity by following industrial garment-making steps. Surveys show most industries use computer-aided software for drafting and 3D simulations. Using CLO software, virtual drafting and assembly produce 3D models such as bodies, sleeves, and skirts, with accurate topology and UV maps, forming the basis for garment cards.

3.3 Garment Cards Design

Garment cards are divided into two functional areas. The top area contains a black-and-white code that is used to identify the garment component, as shown in the red box in Fig. 4a. The bottom area is the garment design area where users can freely draw, as shown in Fig. 4b. A black line frame is provided by ARCLO to indicate the component's outline, making it easier for the drawing's purpose to be visualized and understood by users.

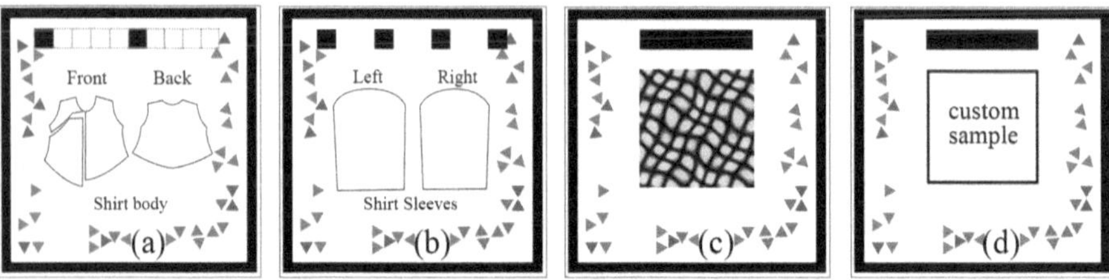

Fig. 4. Garment cards and texture sample card

3.4 Texture Sample Cards Design

Texture cards(see Fig. 4c) are similar to garment cards, also with two main functional areas. The top area includes a black-and-white code that is used to identify the card as a texture sample card. The lower area contains texture structure information, which provides inputs for texture synthesis. Custom textures can be uploaded by users through ARCLO, and these are processed to generate a large texture for model mapping, as shown in Fig. 4d.

3.5 Usage Design

ARCLO uses a mobile device and marker cards with pre-drawn garment outlines, available for printing or electronic use. Users can add designs, logos, or textures to the cards, then scan them with the ARCLO app. The app maps these designs, including traditional Chinese elements, onto a 3D garment in real-time, as shown in Fig. 5.

ARCLO also supports free combination of garment components, enabling users to create diverse outfits. For instance, users can combine multiple cards to design a top by selecting body and sleeve components. After drawing, users place

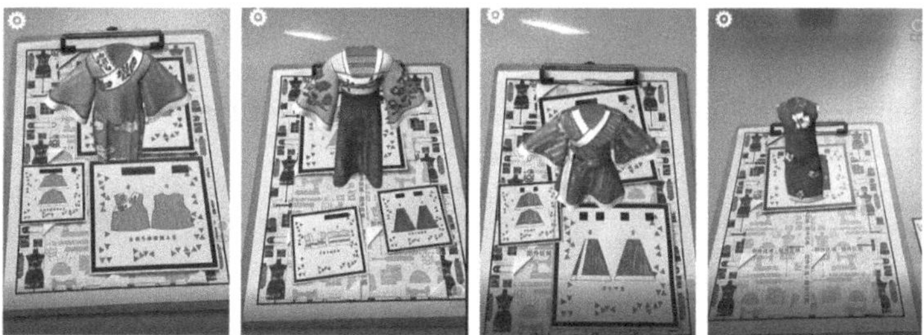

Fig. 5. Card drawing and model texture display

the cards on the corresponding area, and the mobile device captures the design, displaying it on the garment model. Additionally, ARCLO includes a full-body outfit mode, allowing users to assemble complete looks, as shown in Fig. 6.

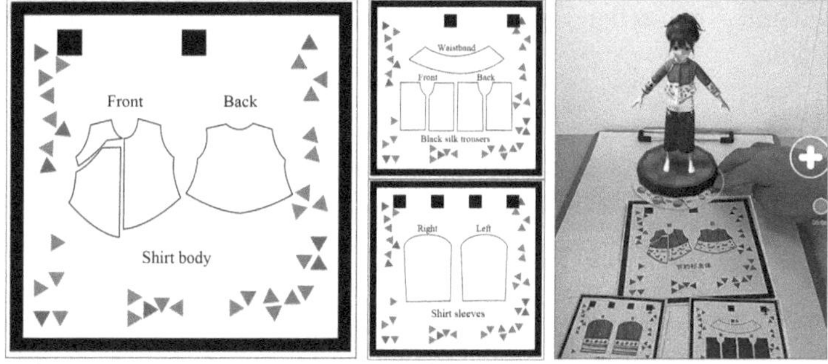

Fig. 6. Process diagram of free combination of garment components

ARCLO supports users design custom patterns and print them onto garment, as shown in Fig. 3a. ARCLO also provides texture sample cards, enabling users to place them and select various textures for garments. The cards support user customization, as illustrated in Fig. 3c.

To enhance viewing from all angles, ARCLO introduces a mannequin mode (Fig. 1e), which goes beyond traditional AR preview modes by adding a cylindrical mannequin for 360-degree viewing. The 3D garment model can be viewed from any angle by rotating the mannequin.

4 Methods

4.1 Marker Image Extraction

To obtain a real-time marker image of the garment, an orthogonal camera was created in Vuforia's environment, positioned directly above the ImageTarget and matching its size. This setup allows the camera to capture the region where the ImageTarget appears in the video stream. Pixel data is then read from the RenderTexture in the video stream into a Texture2D for real-time image capture, as shown in Fig. 2g.

4.2 Image Processing

Images captured under natural conditions may exhibit uneven brightness due to factors like lighting, sensor sensitivity, and hardware instability, affecting pixel accuracy, as shown in Fig. 2h. To address this, conventional image processing techniques like contrast, brightness adjustments, and histogram equalization are applied, as represented in the following formula:

$$\hat{I}\,(x,y) = \mathrm{N}\,(\mathrm{H}\,(\alpha \cdot I_{\mathrm{r}}(x,y) + \beta)) \tag{1}$$

where $I_{\mathrm{r}}(x,y)$ is the raw pixel value at position (x,y); α and β are contrast and brightness coefficients; $\mathrm{H}(\cdot)$ denotes histogram equalization; $\mathrm{N}(\cdot)$ normalizes the output. To further minimize brightness variations, we applied Z-score normalization:

$$\mathrm{N}(I(x,y)) = \frac{I(x,y) - \mu}{\sigma} \tag{2}$$

where μ and σ are the mean and standard deviation of the image pixels.

4.3 Tracking Optimization

The marker image obtained from video frames may exhibit a jittering visual issue between sequences, necessitating tracking and optimization of the content. First, feature points are detected in the image at time t, where p_t^i represents the position of the i-th feature point and I_t^i denotes its pixel value. Next, for the image at time $t+1$, a circular or rectangular search region $R_{t+1}(p_t^j)$ is defined around the location p_t^i, as shown in Fig. 2i. The algorithm then traverses all pixel values I_{t+1}^j within the search region and matches them numerically with the pixel value I_t^i extracted at time t. The pixel with the highest similarity is identified as the position of the corresponding feature point in the image at time $t+1$. The similarity measure can be illustrated using the Euclidean distance as follows:

$$p_{t+1}^i = \arg \min_{p_{t+1}^j \in R_{t+1}(p_t^j)} \sqrt{(I_{t+1}^j - I_t^i)^2} \tag{3}$$

where p_{t+1}^i indicates the predicted result, which corresponds to the p_t^i at time $t+1$.

4.4 Card Type Identification

The cards are divided into two main categories: garment cards and texture sample cards. The garment cards are further subdivided into smaller categories based on different garment components. To identify these various types of cards in ARCLO, black-and-white block codes are used which consisting of 10 individual segments, as shown in Fig. 2j. Each card requires predefined block codes, including the binary pixel values, relative coordinates, and labels for each of the 10 segments. The predefined pixel set of the $i - th$ garment card is denoted as $f_i(x, y)$, where (x, y) represents the relative coordinates.

The recognition of block codes primarily involves thresholding the dotted frame image (as shown in Fig. 4a) using the OTSU method, followed by segmentation into 10 equal-sized segments in sequence. Pixel distortion, low image resolution, and edge blurring may affect these segments. Therefore, pixels within the Manhattan distance from the center of each segment are selected, and this pixel set is denoted as $f(x, y)$. The same process is then applied to $f_i(x, y)$. To improve the detection accuracy, the minimum mean square error algorithm is used, as shown below:

$$\arg \min_{i=0}^{n} \sum_{x,y} (f(x, y) - f_i(x, y))^2 \tag{4}$$

where the label of $f_i(x, y)$ that minimizes the mean square error represents the current label of the garment card, with n indicating the number of cards. Subsequent detections only need to compare the content of the label computed with Eq. 4 against the predefined entries; recalculation is required if the computed result exceeds a set threshold.

4.5 Real-Time Mapping

Regarding the implementation of real-time mapping, as shown in Fig. 2l, articles [38,39] have proposed improved solutions. The method proposed in prior work [39] is built upon and optimized in this paper to address issues related to marker jitter during extraction.

Real-time texture mapping is based on UV mapping, a 2D representation used to define the correspondence between pixels on a texture and vertices on a 3D model. As shown in Fig. 7b, UV mapping plays a pivotal role in photorealistic rendering. In the ARCLO program, after extracting the marker image (Fig. 7a), each pixel of the image is mapped to corresponding UV coordinates (Fig. 7c) and ultimately projected onto the 3D model for display, as shown in Fig. 7d. Furthermore, since the marker information is extracted in real-time from the video stream, the texture mapping is also processed in real-time. The dynamically rendered 3D model is enabled to adapt its appearance instantly, achieving a "what you see is what you get" effect.

4.6 Logo Pattern Extraction

The marker image is obtained from the video stream (Fig. 8a), preprocessed (Fig. 8b), and then identified as a logo pattern card. Next, the hand-drawn logo content is extracted. The OTSU thresholding method is employed in this paper

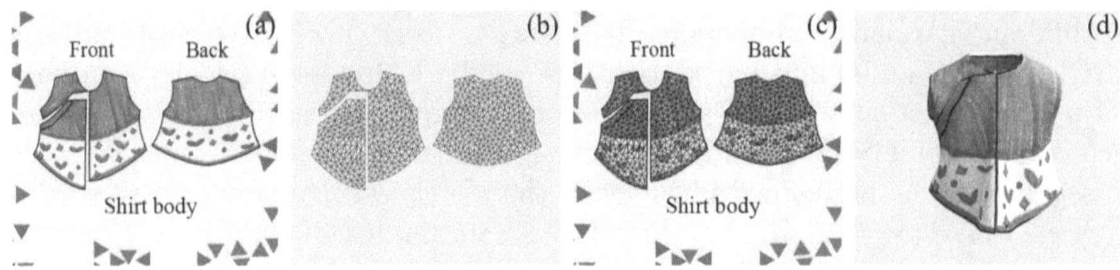

Fig. 7. UV mapping to 3D models

to create a mask for the logo pattern extraction mode, thereby facilitating the extraction of logo content (as shown in Fig. 8c). To enhance the effect, feathering is applied to the logo area to improve experimental outcomes. Finally, the texture is overlaid(Fig. 8d). Following these steps, the logo pattern is successfully layered onto the 3D model, as shown in Fig. 2m and Fig. 8e.

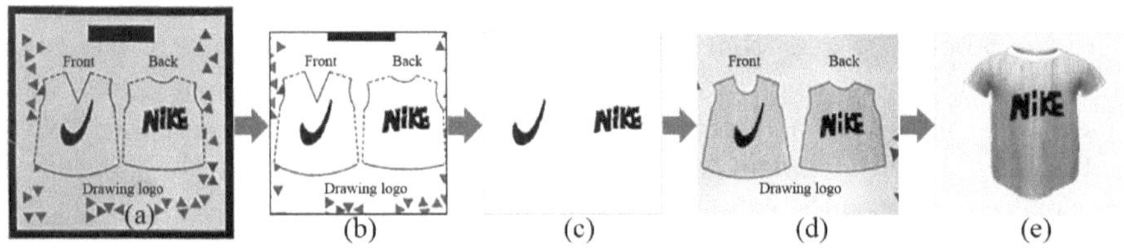

Fig. 8. Logo pattern extraction mode processing flow

4.7 Texture Synthesis

Texture synthesis is employed to expand a sample texture over larger areas, ensuring continuity and similarity [40]. In texture synthesis algorithms utilizing texture blocks, the Image Quilting method introduced in [41] is used to create irregular seams by identifying the minimum error path in overlapping regions between texture blocks.

Building on the Image Quilting approach, a method for generating Wang Tiles—square tiles that seamlessly connect—was introduced in [42]. Since Wang Tiles require no additional processing time during assembly, real-time texture synthesis is enabled. In our study, this approach is utilized to generate large-scale textures that meet real-time requirements.

4.8 Model Mapping and Display

Upon completing these steps, the garment model's real-time UV mapping is obtained and assigned to the 3D model for rendering and display, as shown in Fig. 2o. ARCLO provides two display modes for the model: in the first mode, by moving and rotating the marker image, the spatial position and rotation angle of the model are adjusted based on detection and tracking of the captured image, achieving a dynamic display effect (Fig. 1d). In the second mode, once the garment design is finalized, users can direct the camera at the mannequin marker to display the cylindrical mannequin. By rotating the mannequin, the model can be viewed from multiple angles, as shown in Fig. 1e.

5 Evaluation and Results

5.1 App Performance

The ARCLO application was tested on three popular smartphones: the Huawei Nova 12 (HarmonyOS 4.0, 12 GB RAM, octa-core), Samsung Galaxy C55 5G (Android 14, 12 GB RAM, octa-core), and iPhone 13 (iOS 17.4, 4 GB RAM, hexa-core). With the high performance of these devices, the application was able to run smoothly under standard conditions. Performance tests were conducted across three different functions—Logo pattern extraction mode, real-time mapping mode, and texture synthesis mode. The total time per frame for each mode averaged 35 ms, 36 ms, and 41 ms respectively, resulting in frame rates of 29, 28, and 24 frames per second. These values are the averages from 500 trials. For comparison, Vuforia was also tested, showing an average frame time of 22 ms and a frame rate of 45 frames per second, as shown in Fig. 9. Due to Vuforia's internal encapsulation, the specific image recognition time could not be extracted. Instead, we used the average time from image recognition to real-time tracking for comparison in Fig. 9(a). As shown in Fig. 9, it is evident that the texture synthesis mode, which involves more complex calculations, requires the longest processing time, while the logo pattern extraction mode performs the fastest. Although processing times and frame rates for all three modes in ARCLO are longer and lower than those of Vuforia, reliable application performance is maintained.

5.2 Evaluation Methods

To evaluate ARCLO's impact on learning, 36 fourth-graders (20 boys, 16 girls) participated in a three-phase experiment. Phase 1 observed learning engagement, focus, and design quality; Phase 2 assessed and scored their work; Phase 3 used post-experiment questions to evaluate learning retentions. Participants were split into experimental and control groups of 18 each.

Children in the experimental group (Group A) used ARCLO's design mode, drawing garment cards, viewing them in real-time, interacting with 3D models using the preview mode and mannequin mode, and combining garment pieces. The control group (Group B) used standard garment cards to explore garment shapes and categories independently. During the experiment, various aspects, including emotional states, engagement, focus, and curiosity, were observed and recorded.

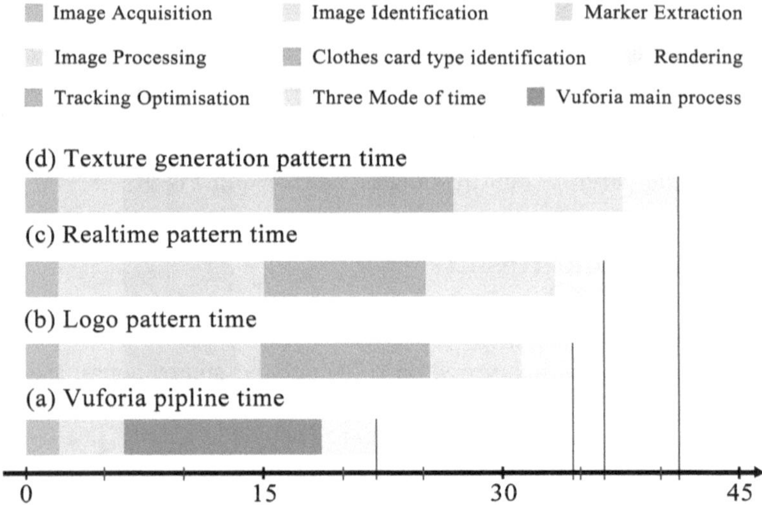

Fig. 9. Performance statistics of different modes in ARCLO

In Phase 1, "Learning Engagement" was measured through observations of the experimental and control groups. Emotional engagement was given to whether children showed interest in garment design, actively interacted, or displayed enthusiasm. In the attention assessment, it was noted whether concentration was maintained, distractions occurred easily, or creativity was shown. Finally, match quality was evaluated based on their ability to assemble, combination, and display garments, with results shown in Fig. 10.

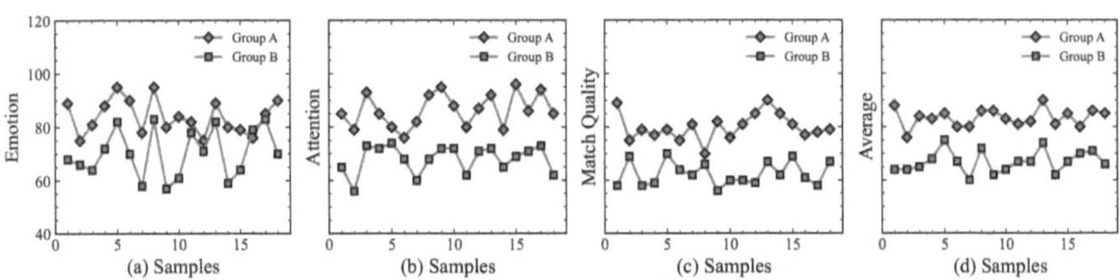

Fig. 10. Results of phase 1

In Phase 2, the "Learning Score" of children in both the experimental and control groups were recorded based on three criteria: the amount of garment drawn, the creativity displayed in the drawings, and the number of correctly assembled outfits. Each completed garment card was awarded 1 point, creative drawings received an additional 2 points each, and correct assemblies earned 4 points each. A statistical analysis of the total scores was conducted, with results shown in Fig. 11(a) to (d).

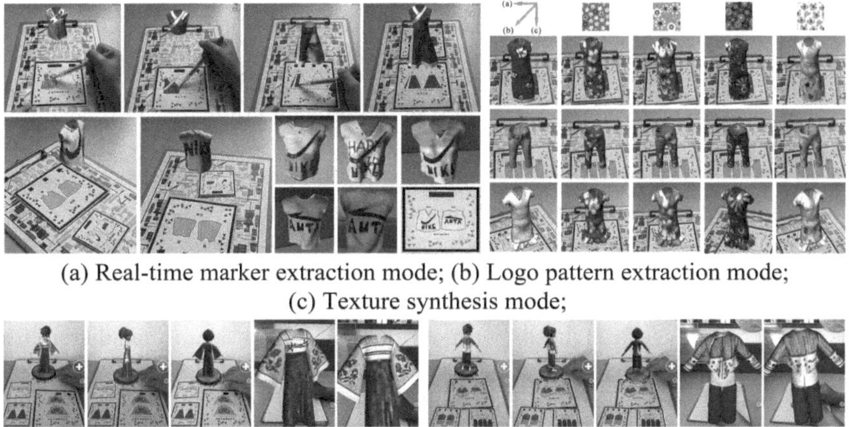

(a) Real-time marker extraction mode; (b) Logo pattern extraction mode; (c) Texture synthesis mode;

Fig. 11. Results of phase 2

In Phase 3, a question-and-answer session was conducted to observe "Learning Retention" between the experimental and control groups. A total of 25 questions on garment card types and assembly were used to evaluate recall and response speed. The scoring criteria were as follows: one point for each correct answer, with no points awarded for incorrect answers. The scoring results for both groups are shown in Fig. 11(e).

Based on observations conducted during Phase 1, higher levels of engagement, concentration, and curiosity in exploring combinations were generally shown by children in the experimental group. They also demonstrated stronger social skills and interactive techniques, both in engaging with devices and interacting with peers. By comparison, the control group's engagement was more moderate. In Phase 2, although both groups were similar in creative scores and the number of pieces created, the experimental group achieved higher scores in combination accuracy. In Phase 3, children in the experimental group identified and recalled garment types and combinations significantly faster than those in the control group, as confirmed by quiz score data.

To further explain the learning behaviors behind the quantitative results, a qualitative analysis was conducted. After the experiment, semi-structured interviews and reflective questionnaires were used to collect students' subjective experiences during interaction. The analysis showed that students with higher learning gains reported stronger immersion and self-efficacy, matching their positive quantitative results. Participants with lower interaction frequency were more affected by the visual design of the interface—novel and engaging forms encouraged more frequent use. Teachers also noted that multimodal prompts helped maintain classroom rhythm and attention, enhancing students' motivation and engagement.

Overall, this testing demonstrates that ARCLO is more effective in enhancing children's learning engagement, outcomes, and retention.

5.3 T-Test Analysis

This study assumes that the experimental data follows a normal distribution with an unknown population standard deviation, and that the sample size is $n < 30$. Under these conditions, the standardized deviation between the sample mean and the population mean follows a t-distribution. Given that the experiment involves two independent samples, the objective is to assess whether there is a significant difference between the means of these two groups. Therefore, an independent samples t-test was used to analyze the test scores of the experimental(A) and control(B) groups [43]. The results of the t-test, indicating the significance of the difference between the two datasets, are shown in Table 1.

Table 1. T-test analysis of scores

	Group ($\mu \pm \sigma$)		t	p
	A (n = 18)	B (n = 18)		
score	25.56 ± 10.04	18.89 ± 8.49	2.151	0.039 [a]

[a] Note: $p < 0.05$, indicating significance at the 0.05 level.

The original hypothesis H_0 posits that the means of the experimental group and the control group are equal, indicating no significant difference. The alternative hypothesis H_1 asserts the opposite. The calculated test statistic is $t = 2.151$. Referring to the t-table, we find $t_{0.05/2,34} = 2.032$. Since $t > t_{0.05/2,34}$ and $p < 0.05$, we reject H_0 and accept H_1, indicating that the difference between the two sample means is statistically significant. Specifically, the experimental group has a mean of 25.56, which is significantly higher than the control group's mean of 18.89, demonstrating that the use of ARCLO can lead to improved learning outcomes.

5.4 More Results

ARCLO implements a variety of interactive modes, including real-time marker extraction mode, logo pattern extraction mode, and texture synthesis mode, more results as shown in Fig. 12(a) to (c). Furthermore, it integrates traditional garment elements, such as Minnan attire and Hanfu, enhancing its application in the mannequin mode, as shown in Fig. 12(d).

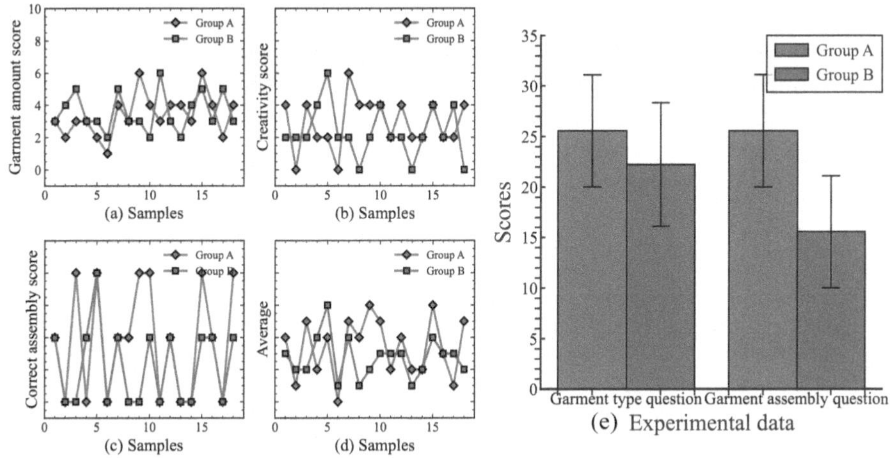

Fig. 12. (d) Garments matching and mannequin mode in ARCLO

This paper achieves digital modeling of traditional costumes through an in-depth understanding of their historical origins, production, patterns, and decorations. Garment cards are designed by reconstructing costume patterns and elements to enable precise embedding and integration of virtual and real aspects. Additionally, digital methods promote and educate about traditional culture, showcasing the charm of these garments to children. This approach fosters children's recognition and pride in their heritage, supporting the preservation and flourishing of traditional clothing and culture.

6 Conclusion

This paper investigates the strong correlation between the selection of interactive methods and the specific needs of children's education. It aims to unify various forms of interaction into a multimodal framework that innovatively integrates children's education, garment design, and augmented reality.

A comprehensive solution centered on visual tracking technology for markers is proposed, aiming to integrate innovative features. Issues related to real-time extraction of marker images, frame-to-frame jitter, logo pattern extraction, and texture synthesis are addressed. The ARCLO application is developed to support various functional displays and flexible combinations of garment components based on card types. Finally, within the scope of multimodal interaction, a 360-degree preview and mannequin interaction mode are implemented, enhancing interaction naturalness, reducing learning costs, and increasing versatility and applicability.

Performance tests conducted on mainstream mobile phones demonstrate that the total time per frame is 35, 36, and 41 milliseconds, achieving frame rates of

29, 28, and 24 frames per second, respectively, thus meeting real-time requirements. The results of the t-test analysis indicate that the experimental group outperformed the control group, demonstrating that this approach effectively enhances children's learning outcomes and validates the successful implementation of the integrated innovation strategy.

References

1. The real and the imaginary are born together research report on augmented reality (AR) industry in China. In: 2023 Proceedings of iResearch's February Research Conference, pp. 223–288. iResearch Consulting Industry Research Department XIII (2023)
2. Aydoğdu, F.: Augmented reality for preschool children: an experience with educational contents. Br. J. Educ. Technol. **53**(2), 326–348 (2022)
3. Cai, S., Zhang, J.: Augmented reality (AR) technology transforms education and teaching. People's Educ. **09**, 33–37 (2023)
4. Jin, Y., Wu, J.: A preliminary study on game-based reading from the perspective of situated cognition. Libr. Inf. **03**, 71–76 (2020)
5. Zhou, K., et al.: A mixed reality training system for hand-object interaction in simulated microgravity environments. In: 2023 IEEE International Symposium on Mixed and Augmented Reality (ISMAR), pp. 167–176. IEEE (2023)
6. Li, G., Li, G.: Research on the teaching reform of AR-based garment 3D simulation design course. Light Text. Ind. Technol. **50**(08), 145–146 (2021)
7. Arena, F., Collotta, M., Pau, G., Termine, F.: An overview of augmented reality. Computers **11**(2), 28 (2022)
8. Tao, J., et al.: A survey on multi-modal human-computer interaction. J. Image Graphics **27**, 1956–1987 (2022)
9. Jiang, H., Zhu, D., Chugh, R., Turnbull, D., Jin, W.: Virtual reality and augmented reality-supported k-12 stem learning: trends, advantages and challenges. Educ. Inf. Technol. 1–37 (2025)
10. Sakr, A., Abdullah, T.: Virtual, augmented reality and learning analytics impact on learners, and educators: a systematic review. Educ. Inf. Technol. **29**(15), 19913–19962 (2024)
11. Aslan, S., et al.: Immersive multi-modal pedagogical conversational artificial intelligence for early childhood education: an exploratory case study in the wild. Comput. Educ.: Artif. Intell. **6**, 100220 (2024)
12. Liu, B., Wan, X., Li, X., Zhu, D., Liu, Z.: An augmented reality serious game for children's optical science education: randomized controlled trial. JMIR Serious Games **12**, e47807 (2024)
13. McElwain, N.L., Fisher, M.C., Nebeker, C., Bodway, J.M., Islam, B., Hasegawa-Johnson, M.: Evaluating users' experiences of a child multimodal wearable device: mixed methods approach. JMIR Hum. Factors **11**, e49316 (2024)
14. Samala, A.D., Rawas, S., Rahmadika, S., Criollo-C, S., Fikri, R., Sandra, R.P.: Virtual reality in education: global trends, challenges, and impacts–game changer or passing trend? Discov. Educ. **4**(1), 1–45 (2025)
15. Qushem, U.B., Christopoulos, A., Oyelere, S.S., Ogata, H., Laakso, M.J.: Multimodal technologies in precision education: providing new opportunities or adding more challenges? Educ. Sci. **11**(7), 338 (2021)

16. Wyss, C., Bäuerlein, K.: Augmented reality in the classroom—mentor teachers' attitudes and technology use. In: Virtual Worlds, vol. 3, pp. 572–585. MDPI (2024)
17. Singh, M., Bangay, S., Sajjanhar, A.: Augmented reality enhanced analytics to measure and mitigate disengagement in teaching young children. In: 2022 IEEE International Symposium on Mixed and Augmented Reality Adjunct (ISMAR-Adjunct), pp. 782–785. IEEE (2022)
18. Chang, H.Y., et al.: Ten years of augmented reality in education: a meta-analysis of (quasi-) experimental studies to investigate the impact. Comput. Educ. **191**, 104641 (2022)
19. Krauß, V., Berkholz, J., Recki, L., Boden, A.: Beyond well-intentioned: an HCI students' ethical assessment of their own XR designs. In: 2023 IEEE International Symposium on Mixed and Augmented Reality (ISMAR), pp. 59–68. IEEE (2023)
20. Wu, K., Cheng, Z.: RefAR: 3D sketch-based modeling with in-situ references. In: 2022 IEEE International Symposium on Mixed and Augmented Reality Adjunct (ISMAR-Adjunct), pp. 507–511. IEEE (2022)
21. Tong, Q., Hong, Y.: Design and development of junior high school geography teaching software based on augmented reality technology. J. Hubei Norm. Univ. (Nat. Sci.) **43**(04), 62–67 (2023)
22. Lu, E., Bharadwaj, S., Dasari, M., Smith, C., Seshan, S., Rowe, A.: RenderFusion: balancing local and remote rendering for interactive 3D scenes. In: 2023 IEEE International Symposium on Mixed and Augmented Reality (ISMAR), pp. 312–321. IEEE (2023)
23. Xu, X., Puggioni, A., Kilroy, D., Campbell, A.G.: User experience of collaborative co-located mixed reality: a user study in teaching veterinary radiation safety rules. In: 2023 IEEE International Symposium on Mixed and Augmented Reality (ISMAR), pp. 583–590. IEEE (2023)
24. Antoni, V., Maurer, F., Cesari, O., Eichhorn, C., Vilhjálmsson, H.H.: Augmented virtuality training for special education teachers. In: 2022 IEEE International Symposium on Mixed and Augmented Reality Adjunct (ISMAR-Adjunct), pp. 327–332. IEEE (2022)
25. Orsolits, H., Rauh, S.F., Estrada, J.G.: Using mixed reality based digital twins for robotics education. In: 2022 IEEE International Symposium on Mixed and Augmented Reality Adjunct (ISMAR-Adjunct), pp. 56–59. IEEE (2022)
26. Lohfink, M.A., Miznazi, D., Stroth, F., Müller, C.: Learn spatial! Introducing the marble-app-a mixed reality approach to enhance archaeological higher education. In: 2022 IEEE International Symposium on Mixed and Augmented Reality Adjunct (ISMAR-Adjunct), pp. 435–440. IEEE (2022)
27. Singh, M., Bangay, S., Sajjanhar, A.: An architecture for capturing and presenting learning outcomes using augmented reality enhanced analytics. In: 2022 IEEE International Symposium on Mixed and Augmented Reality Adjunct (ISMAR-Adjunct), pp. 611–612. IEEE (2022)
28. Yilmaz, R.M.: Educational magic toys developed with augmented reality technology for early childhood education. Comput. Hum. Behav. **54**, 240–248 (2016)
29. Zhu, Y., Wang, S.J.: A tangible augmented reality toy kit: interactive solution for early childhood education. In: Brooks, A.L., Brooks, E. (eds.) ArtsIT/DLI -2016. LNICST, vol. 196, pp. 12–19. Springer, Cham (2017). https://doi.org/10.1007/978-3-319-55834-9_2
30. Lim, S., Dong, S.Y.: Effects of interaction with virtual pets on self-disclosure in mixed reality. In: 2023 IEEE International Symposium on Mixed and Augmented Reality (ISMAR), pp. 1–9. IEEE (2023)

31. Olthof, A.M., Verlinden, J., Allouch, S.B.: Exploration of design methods and tools for virtual, augmented and mixed reality. In: 2022 IEEE International Symposium on Mixed and Augmented Reality Adjunct (ISMAR-Adjunct), pp. 233–237. IEEE (2022)
32. Chen, C.C., Kang, X., Li, X.Z., Kang, J.: Design and evaluation for improving lantern culture learning experience with augmented reality. Int. J. Hum.-Comput. Interact. **40**(6), 1465–1478 (2024)
33. Xu, N., Li, Y., Lin, J., Yu, L., Liang, H.N.: User retention of mobile augmented reality for cultural heritage learning. In: 2022 IEEE International Symposium on Mixed and Augmented Reality Adjunct (ISMAR-Adjunct), pp. 447–452. IEEE (2022)
34. Werdayani, D., Widiaty, I.: Virtual fitting room technology in fashion design. In: IOP Conference Series: Materials Science and Engineering, vol. 1098, p. 022110. IOP Publishing (2021)
35. Zhou, Y.: Augmented reality technology in the garment printing and dyeing industry. Screen Print. 16–19 (2017)
36. Lu, Y., Huang, Y., Qin, F., Kuang, C.: Research on the application of augmented reality (AR) technology in the teaching and learning of clothing professional education. Light Ind. Sci. Technol. **36**, 96–98 (2020)
37. Chen, J.: Application of VR and AR in minority costume design teaching. Res. Explor. Lab. **36**(06), 111–113 (2017). https://doi.org/10.19927/j.cnki.syyt.2017.06.026
38. Magnenat, S., et al.: Live texturing of augmented reality characters from colored drawings. IEEE Trans. Visual Comput. Graphics **21**(11), 1201–1210 (2015)
39. Anonymous, A.: Texturing of augmented reality character based on colored drawing. In: 2017 IEEE Virtual Reality (VR), pp. 355–356. IEEE (2017)
40. Xue, F., Cheng, C., Jiang, J.: Wang tile-based improved texture synthesis. J. Comput. Appl. **30**(08), 2098–2100+2156 (2010)
41. Efros, A.A., Freeman, W.T.: Image quilting for texture synthesis and transfer. In: Seminal Graphics Papers: Pushing the Boundaries, vol. 2, pp. 571–576 (2023)
42. Cohen, M.F., Shade, J., Hiller, S., Deussen, O.: Wang tiles for image and texture generation. ACM Trans. Graphics (TOG) **22**(3), 287–294 (2003)
43. Qiao, A., Wang, L., Li, Y., Yin, Y., Chen, S.: Research on differences of teaching behaviors of different teacher groups. e-Educ. Res. **39**(04), 93–100+108 (2018). https://doi.org/10.13811/j.cnki.eer.2018.04.014

Aligned and Detail Guided Retrieval: Multi-scale Fine-Grained Features Enhancement for End-to-End Person Search

Xin Zhang[1](✉), Feihu Yan[2], Kunlin Zou[1], Zhong Zhou[3], and Haiyong Chen[1]

[1] The School of Artificial Intelligence, Hebei University of Technology, Tianjin 300130, China
{2023927,kunlinzou,haiyong.chen}@hebut.edu.cn

[2] School of Intelligence Science and Technology, Beijing University of Civil Engineering and Architecture, Beijing 102616, China
yanfeihu@bucea.edu.cn

[3] The State Key Laboratory of Virtual Reality Technology and Systems, Beihang University, Beijing 100191, China
zz@buaa.edu.cn

Abstract. Accurate bounding boxes and discriminative feature representations are essential for Person Search. Although existing methods enhance small-scale person detection via feature pyramid networks, they still face two critical issues. Firstly, the continuous feature rescaling operations in the feature pyramid networks may result in misalignment between the bounding box and feature semantics. Secondly, insufficient learning of fine-grained features leads to limited expressiveness in person representation. Therefore, we propose the Align and Detail Guided Person Search Network (ADGPS), which extracts fine-grained features of the person while ensuring feature alignment. Specifically, it comprises two models. We designed the Attention Flow Alignment Model (AFAM) to alleviate the misalignment issue caused by the aggregation process of different scales. It aligns features by introducing semantic flow between features at different scales. We present the Person Fine-grained Feature Extraction Model (PFFE) to enhance detail learning via feature aggregation and expansion across dimensions to extract the people fine-grained features. In addition, we propose the novel ArcOIM loss, which introduces additional angular margins to guide the network in enhancing the distance between inter-class person features. Extensive experiments on two datasets demonstrate that our method outperforms state-of-the-art approaches on the CUHK-SYSU and PRW with 96.21% and 58.73% in mAP, respectively.

Keywords: Computer Vision · Person Search · Feature Alignment · Fine-grained Representation · OIM Loss

A. Hinkenjan et al. (Eds.): ICXR 2025, LNCS 16428, pp. 39–55, 2026.
https://doi.org/10.1007/978-981-95-7195-6_3

1 Introduction

Person search is the task of aiming to locate and identify the target person in a set of realistic, uncropped surveillance images and is a practically relevant task [2,25]. Compared to the person re-identification (Re-ID) task [18], the person search task is highly applicable in real-world scenarios due to its obviation of the need for cropping person bounding boxes. It encompasses two primary subtasks: person detection [39] and person re-identification. However, due to the interference of factors such as scale variations, occlusions, and changes in the shooting condition of the person, it is difficult to generate the accurate coordinates of the person and extract the discriminative and robust person feature.

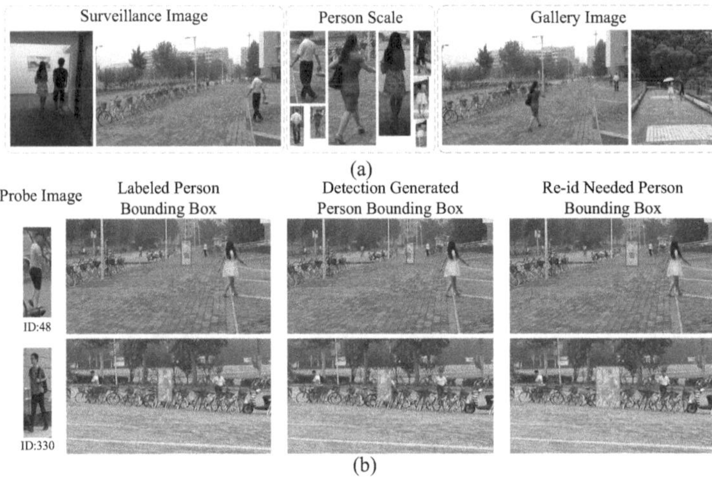

Fig. 1. Illustration of the feature misalignment issue in the person search task. (a) Pedestrian scale varies significantly in the search scene. (b) The repeated upsampling and downsampling operations in FPN result in misalignment between the predicted and labeled bounding boxes, and further introduce deviation from the optimal boxes needed for person re-identification.

Precisely localizing the bounding box of the person is the foundation for extracting discriminative features and identifying the different persons in this task. In practical application scenarios, changes in the distance between the person and cameras will lead to variations in person scale and may result in detection errors, as shown in Fig. 1(a). Researchers introduced the feature pyramid network (FPN)[24] to improve the accuracy of small-scale person detection results. However, two issues also emerge during this optimization process. First, the frequent upsampling and downsampling operations in the FPN can cause misalignment of the person bounding box, affecting the robustness and discriminative nature of person features. Additionally, due to the inherent deviation between the detection bounding box and the required bounding box for the person Re-ID sub-task, this issue will be further aggravated, as shown in Fig. 1(b). Second, the feature aggregation in the FPN lacks guidance, which leads to the misalignment of features and semantics between multi-scale features. Essentially, there is an issue of spatial information misalignment between person features at different scales, which interferes with the accuracy of similarity calculation of different person features.

However, current feature alignment methods mainly emphasize spatial scale fusion but fail to alleviate misalignment at the semantic level, which will impact the performance of person search. To alleviate such issues, we propose the Attention Flow Alignment Model (AFAM). Under the guidance of the model, it can direct network focus to the person area, mitigating bounding box misalignment issues and generating the person ReID-suitable bounding box. Meanwhile, the semantic flow can guide the aggregation of features at varying resolutions, enabling the network not only to align semantics but also to preserve the discriminative information from high-resolution features. This helps alleviate the spatial information misalignment issue.

In addition, in order to extract distinguishable fine-grained features of the person to improve the accuracy of person search. We propose the Person Fine-grained Feature Extraction Model (PFFE), which generates the weight matrix by compressing and activating feature maps from different dimensions to learn and extract person fine-grained features. Specifically, since the person bounding boxes generally exhibit rectangular structures, features along the H dimension tend to encode semantic information, whereas those along the W dimension are more related to local appearance details. Based on this, we introduce structural priors of person through feature decomposition, which not only strengthens the network to capture dependencies across dimensions but also facilitates the learning of fine-grained semantic cues for person. Moreover, the computational complexity of standard self-attention is $O(H^2W^2)$, the feature decomposition can reduce the complexity to $O(H^2W + HW^2)$. This significant reduction in computational cost makes the proposed PFFE module more suitable for handling high-resolution panoramic images in person search tasks.

On the other hand, to further expand the distance between different person features, we design the novel Arc Online Instance Match loss (ArcOIM loss), which integrates the novel Lookup Table (LUT) and Circular Queuer (CQ) update strategy. The main contributions of this paper can be summarized as follows:

1. We propose the Attention Flow Alignment Model (AFAM). This model is designed to focus on the person area within feature maps of various resolutions, guided by the attention mechanism. Simultaneously, semantic flow is introduced to help FPN align features from different resolutions, effectively mitigating feature misalignment issues.
2. We propose the Person Fine-grained Feature Extraction Model (PFFE). The model aggregates and activates features from different dimensions to calculate the weight matrix. This enables the network to capture strong discriminative

information in specific areas and learn fine-grained person features, thereby enhancing the expressiveness of the person representation.
3. We design the novel ArcOIM loss to enable the network to effectively distinguish different person features by introducing an additional angular margin. It employs the ground truth bounding box to update the centroid of the person feature, providing more accurate supervision information and alleviating the issue of bounding box misalignment.

2 Related Works

Person search methods can be categorized into two-step and one-step person search based on whether detection and Re-ID sub-tasks can be addressed within the same model.

The two-step person search method [8,24,32] optimizes the two independent models separately, resulting in improvement in person search results in early stages. In [23], Wang et al. proposed the Task-Consist Two-Stage person search (TCTS), which learns the consistency between the two sub-tasks and jointly optimizes the entire framework. In summary, the two-step person search method optimizes the two independent models separately, resulting in significant improvement in person search results. However, its high computational overhead, long inference time, and the need for manual intervention limit its practicality, hindering the development of the two-step person search method.

One-step person search methods complete the entire retrieval process within a single model [21,33,35], and their performance has been enhanced with in-depth research on multi-task learning networks. In AlignPS [28], the FPN and deformable convolution [40] are employed to address the issue of various scales of persons in surveillance images and feature misalignment. Tian et al. [21] proposed BPNet, which introduced the FPN structure to extract multi-scale person features. Unlike previous methods, through the attention mechanism and semantic flow, AFAM can not only focus on the key area of the person in various resolution features but also effectively maintain high-level semantic information. The generated multi-resolution-attention feature map can achieve semantic and feature alignment while retaining discriminability information.

On the other hand, enhancing the expressive ability of features is also important for the person search task [4,31]. In [7], Dong et al. made the framework focus more on the person foreground area and enhanced the quality of person features. In [4], Chen et al. extended the feature space from the hypersphere surface to the entire hypersphere space to alleviate such issues and improve the effect of network optimization. Therefore, we propose the Person Fine-grained Feature Extraction Model (PFFE). The model aggregates and activates features from different dimensions to calculate the responses between different areas in the feature map to generate the weight matrix. Thereby, this guides the network to model the strong discriminative information contained in the part areas and extract fine-grained embeddings to represent objects comprehensively.

In addition, the loss function plays an essential guiding role [3,10,31]. Xian et al. [26] employed the concept of the memory bank to design the OIM loss function, which has become the widely adopted person search training loss. In [31], Yang et al. presented the Balance Online Instance Match (BOIM) loss to enhance the contribution of negative samples during training. It effectively improves the hard sample mining ability of the network. In this paper, we design the novel ArcOIM loss, which introduces an additional angular margin to the loss function to guide the network to increase the distance between different person features further. Meanwhile, we design the new update strategy that utilizes the ground truth bounding box to calculate the centroid of the person feature, alleviating the issue of bounding box misalignment.

3 Method

In this section, we introduce the technical details of the proposed method, where the core components include the AFAM, PFFE, and ArcOIM loss.

We adopt an anchor-free detection framework [38] to alleviate occlusion interference [36], as shown in Fig. 2. To improve small-scale person detection, FPN is used to extract multi-resolution backbone features. We further introduce the AFAM to enhance feature fusion across scales. The backbone features are then fed into two heads: the detection head predicts heatmaps, box sizes, and center offsets to generate bounding boxes; the Re-ID head, guided by the PFFE, captures robust and discriminative features for identity matching.

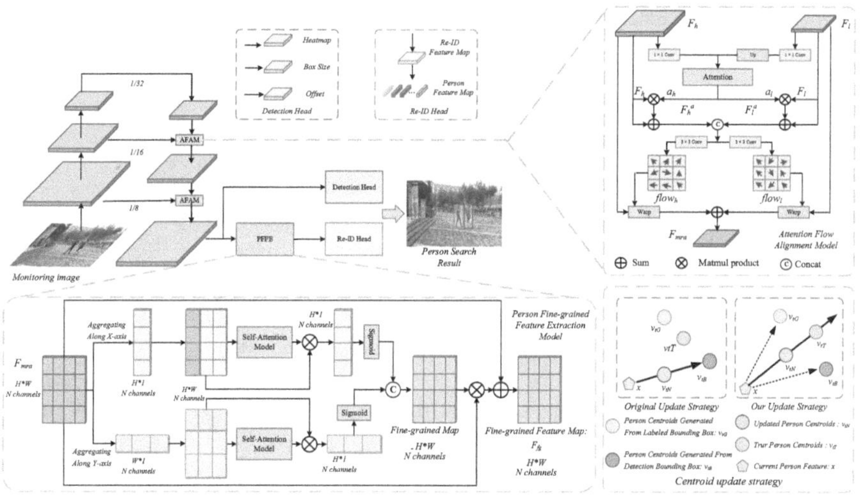

Fig. 2. Overview of our proposed person search approach: The Aligned and Detail Guided Person Search Network (ADGPS) is structured based on CenterNet, incorporating the Attention Flow Alignment Model (AFAM), the Person Fine-grained Feature Extraction Model (PFFE) and the centroid update strategy of ArcOIM loss.

For person detection, we adopt heatmap regression and L1 loss. For person Re-ID, the proposed ArcOIM loss introduces an angular margin to enhance discrimination of visually similar pedestrians. Additionally, we propose a novel LUT and CQ update strategy leverages ground-truth boxes for supervision, mitigating early-stage instability in predicted boxes. This effectively addresses the misalignment between detection and Re-ID boxes and accelerates convergence. Finally, person features are extracted based on the generated bounding box locations.

3.1 Attention Flow Alignment Model

To address bounding box offset and semantic misalignment issue, we first introduce the Flow Alignment Module (FAM) [13] to learn semantic flow across different resolutions, aligning spatial and semantic information between feature maps. Building on this, we propose the AFAM, the structure as shown in Fig. 2. The AFAM takes two feature maps of different resolutions: the high-resolution feature F_h and the low-resolution feature F_l. The 1×1 convolution layer is applied to unify channel dimensions, followed by bilinear interpolation to upsample F_l to match F_h. Attention maps are then computed to guide the network in focusing on key discriminative regions across resolutions, facilitating effective feature fusion, as the following formula:

$$\begin{gathered} F_l^a = \theta\left(a_l F_l\right) + F_l \\ a_l = \frac{exp\left[F_l(x_i)^T F_h(x_j)\right]}{\sum_{i=1}^{N} exp\left[F_l(x_i)^T F_h(x_j)\right]} \end{gathered} \tag{1}$$

$$\begin{gathered} F_h^a = \theta\left(a_h F_h\right) + F_h \\ a_l = \frac{exp\left[F_h(x_i)^T F_l(x_j)\right]}{\sum_{i=1}^{N} exp\left[F_h(x_i)^T F_l(x_j)\right]} \end{gathered} \tag{2}$$

where a_l is the generated attention map of F_F and a_h is the attention map of F_h, respectively. Consequently, F_l^a and F_h^a are the low-resolution and high-resolution attention feature map, respectively. After extracting discriminative information, we concatenate F_l^a and F_h^a and apply a 3×3 convolution to generate the semantic flow fields. The resulting $flow_l$ and $flow_h$ represent the semantic flow of different resolution feature maps. These contain the pixel-wise spatial offsets between the low and high-resolution feature maps. Using $flow_l$ and $flow_h$, each pixel P in one feature map can be projected onto the other to address the misalignment problem. Specifically, we adopt a differentiable bilinear sampling mechanism to interpolate F_l, mapping it to $\widetilde{F_h}$, which approximates the spatial structure of F_h. The detailed computation is shown in formula 3.

$$\widetilde{F_h} = warp\left(F_l\right) = \sum_{k=1}^{M} flow_h\left(p_k\right) F_l\left(p_j\right) \tag{3}$$

where $warp\left(\cdot\right)$ is the mapping calculation process. Performing the same operation on the f_h can generate the feature map $\widetilde{F_l}$ that is similar to F_l. Finally, $\widetilde{F_l}$ and $\widetilde{F_h}$ are summed to fuse contextual cues and achieve semantic alignment.

This generates multi-resolution attention features F_{mra}, which not only retain discriminative information from the entire image but also enable aligned and aggregated representation across resolutions. These features provide a solid foundation for subsequent fine-grained pedestrian representation learning.

3.2 Person Fine-Grained Feature Extraction Model

To better distinguish individual pedestrians, we propose the PFFE module in the Re-ID head to guide the network toward learning fine-grained discriminative cues. Given that both the spatial positions and feature dimensions carry varying semantic responses, we introduce marginal distribution modeling to decompose the input feature map across dimensions. By aggregating and activating the responses, a weight matrix is generated to highlight distinct fine-grained regions. As shown in Fig. 2, the PFFE module takes the multi-resolution attention feature as input, which can be viewed as a discrete joint distribution of fine-grained semantics across dimensions and positions.

Based on this, we apply marginal distribution modeling to decompose features along vertical and horizontal axes, enabling the network to focus on dimension-specific semantics such as body height (vertical) and posture (horizontal). This not only enhances discriminative learning but also mitigates interference between dimensions. The decomposition process is defined as:

$$\begin{aligned} F_x &= D_Y(x, c) = \tfrac{1}{h}\textstyle\sum_x F_{mra} \\ F_y &= D_X(y, c) = \tfrac{1}{h}\textstyle\sum_y F_{mra} \end{aligned} \tag{4}$$

where F_x and F_y represent the feature decomposed in the X and Y axis dimensions, respectively. Both features aggregate and highlight features on the corresponding dimensions. Then, we apply expansion activation and self-attention to F_x and F_y separately, guiding the network to focus on discriminative patterns along the row and column dimensions. The resulting features, F_x^{sa} and F_y^{sa}, are then compressed and passed through a sigmoid activation to generate a weight map after resizing. Finally, the weight map ω_m is used to refine the multi-resolution attention features F_{mra}, producing the person fine-grained feature map. The detailed formulation is as follows:

$$F_{fg} = \lambda\omega_m \otimes F_{mra} + F_{mra} \tag{5}$$

where F_{fg} is the person fine-grained feature map, λ is the weight parameter, and $\otimes$ is the pixel-wise multiplication. The PFFE introduces the marginal distribution to learn the fine-grained information in the feature map row-wise and column-wise from horizontal and vertical dimensions, respectively. This enables the model to avoid mutual interference between features of different dimensions while enhancing the distinguishability of pedestrian features.

3.3 Arc Online Instance Matching Loss

The original OIM loss effectively enlarges the distance between person and background features. However, it ignores optimizing the difference between the foreground person features, resulting in the weak ability of the network to distinguish person features whose appearance is similar. Additionally, by analyzing the current update process, we find that the use of predicted bounding boxes in LUT and CQ updates leads to inaccurate person feature centroids, especially during early training. On the one hand, the feature centroid obtained through the predicted bounding box is not accurate due to misalignment. On the other hand, when updating person feature centroids, traditionally, only use mini-batch data for training, resulting fail to reflect the true distribution of person features.

To address these issues, we propose the ArcOIM loss, which incorporates angular margins and a novel update strategy. Instead of relying solely on predicted boxes, we integrate both predicted and ground-truth bounding boxes to compute more accurate feature centroids, as illustrated in Fig. 2. This improves feature discrimination and ensures centroids better reflect the true distribution of pedestrian features. The update formula is defined as follows:

$$v_t = \gamma v_t + \frac{(1-\gamma)}{2} F + \frac{(1-\gamma)}{2} F_{gt} \tag{6}$$

Where F and F_{gt} are the person features based on the predict and ground truth bounding box, respectively. The designed update strategy is similar to the early intelligent optimization algorithm [9,12], where the person feature based on the predicted and ground truth bounding box can be regarded as the local and global optimal value, respectively. It not only provides a more accurate person feature centroid but also prevents overfitting, which will lead to a decrease in the person search effect. Then, inspired by the Arcface [6], we transform $v_i^T F = |v_i|\,|F|\,cos\alpha$, where α is the angle between the centroid v_i and person feature F. By normalizing and re-scaling the centroid v_i and feature F to ρ. The basis for classification is the angle α between the centroid and person feature, the p_i of OIM loss can be calculated as:

$$p_i = \frac{exp(\rho \cdot cos\alpha)}{\sum_{j=1}^{L} exp(\rho \cdot cos\alpha_j) + \sum_{k=1}^{Q} exp(\rho \cdot cos\beta_k)} \tag{7}$$

Where α is the angle between the person feature and the centroid in LUT, and β represents the angle between the person feature and the centroid in CQ. In order to further widen the distance between different person features, we add an additional angle margin m to propose the ArcOIM loss for the person search training. The specific formula is as follows:

$$\begin{aligned} p_i &= \frac{exp(\rho \cdot cos(\alpha + m))}{\sum_{j=1}^{L} exp(\rho \cdot cos(\alpha_j + m)) + \sum_{k=1}^{Q} exp(\rho \cdot cos(\beta_k + m))} \\ L_{ArcOIM} &= -E_x \left[log p_t \right] \end{aligned} \tag{8}$$

In addition, for training person detection head in the ADGPS network, the loss function consists of two parts, including the heatmap prediction loss and bounding box prediction loss. Among them, we employ pixel-wise logistic regression with focal loss for heatmap training and L1 loss for bounding box regression. Concrete definitions of the person detection head loss are provided below:

$$
\begin{aligned}
L_{heat} &= -\tfrac{1}{N}\textstyle\sum_{xy}\begin{cases}\left(1-\widehat{M}_{xy}\right)^{a}\log\left(\widehat{M}_{xy}\right), & \widehat{M}_{xy}=1\\ \left(1-M_{xy}\right)^{b}\left(\widehat{M}_{xy}\right)^{a}\log\left(1-\widehat{M}_{xy}\right), & \text{otherwise}\end{cases}\\
L_{O} &= \textstyle\sum_{i=1}^{N}\left\|O^{i}-\widehat{O}^{i}\right\|_{1}\\
L_{S} &= \textstyle\sum_{i=1}^{N}\left\|S^{i}-\widehat{S}^{i}\right\|_{1}
\end{aligned}
\tag{9}
$$

where the $\widehat{M}$ is the estimated heatmap, a and b are the predetermined parameters. $\widehat{O}$ and $\widehat{S}$ are the predicted offset of the center point and predicted bounding size, respectively.

4 Experiments

In this section, we will perform multiple experiments to assess the effectiveness of the proposed AFAM model, the PFFE model, the ArcOIM loss and the ADGPS network on two benchmark person search datasets.

4.1 Implementation Details

We utilize the PyTorch framework for both training and fine-tuning the proposed method. We adopt the pre-trained ResNest [34] as the backbone network. Training is executed on NVIDIA RTX 2080Ti GPUs. The model is trained using the SGD optimizer, with input images resized to 900×500. The initial learning rate is established at 0.003, employing the warm-up learning rate, and it decreases by a factor of 0.1 at the 6th epoch. We integrated the designed AFAM into the decoding stage of the FPN and evaluated its performance in the ablation studies. We employ the ArcOIM loss for the person Re-ID subtask training in ADGPS and utilize the proposed update strategy to update the memory bank. We choose the angular margin m of ArcOIM loss at 0.5.

We utilized PRW [33] and CUHK-SYSU [26] as the training and experimental datasets. To assess the performance of the person search results, we adopt standard metrics, including Mean Average Precision (mAP), Cumulative Matching Characteristics (CMC top-K), Recall Rate (Recall), and Average Precision (AP). The mAP and CMC top-K are used to gauge the person search performance from the overall perspective, while Recall and AP can be adopted to evaluate pedestrian detection performance.

4.2 Ablation Study

Analysis of Attention Flow Alignment Model: In order to assess the effectiveness and contribution of the designed AFAM, comparative experiments are conducted on the PRW dataset. In the experiment, we chose five methods from previous works that are commonly employed to improve backbone feature quality and person search performance. These methods include the attention mechanism, the Feature Pyramid Network (FPN) [16], the Norm-Aware Embedding method (NAE) [4], and the Feature Decomposition Person Search (FDPS) [31]. The baseline method is the CenterNet-based person search network, which uses the ResNest as the backbone network. The experimental results are presented in Table 1.

Table 1. Ablation experimental results of the AFAM on PRW dataset.

Methods	Person Detection		Person Re-identification	
	Recall(%)↑	AP(%)↑	mAP(%)↑	Rank-1(%)↑
Baseline	95.1	90.4	44.6	81.7
Baseline+Attention	95.6	90.6	47.3	84.2
Baseline+FPN	95.8	91.2	46.2	83.5
NAE [4]	95.3	90.5	48.6	84.9
FDPS [31]	95.5	90.8	48.3	85.6
AlignPS [28]	96.1	91.7	50.1	86.1
Baseline+FPN+FAM	96.3	91.9	51.2	85.1
Baseline+FPN+AFAM	**96.7**	**92.5**	**55.8**	**86.5**

The proposed AFAM achieves the best performance with 96.8% Recall, 92.5% AP, 55.8% mAP, and 86.5% Rank-1, demonstrating its effectiveness in enhancing both detection and Re-ID. Compared to FPN, AFAM improves semantic alignment and multi-resolution feature fusion via semantic flow, leading to gains of 1.0% in Recall and 1.3% in AP. While NAE expands the feature space and FDPS alleviates subtask conflicts through feature decomposition, both lack attention to discriminative cues across resolutions. In contrast, AFAM effectively utilizes semantic flow to achieve feature alignment across different resolutions, and consequently outperforms methods such as AlignPS.

Analysis of Person Fine-Grained Feature Extraction Model: To demonstrate the contribution of the proposed PFFE model in our person search method, we compare the person Re-ID sub-task performance of different person feature optimization methods in the person search. The comparative methods encompass NAE [4], FDPS [31], and PAB-Net [20], with the PAB-Net method enhancing the expressive capability of person features by learning the part features of the person. We employ CenterNet as the baseline.

Table 2. Ablation experimental results of the PFFE on PRW dataset.

Methods	Person Re-identification	
	mAP(%)↑	Rank-1(%)↑
Baseline	45.3	81.9
Baseline+Attention	47.8	82.3
NAE [4]	48.0	82.1
FDPS [31]	49.1	82.3
Baseline+Feature Decomposition	48.9	83.6
Baseline+Self-Attention	49.3	83.2
Baseline+PAB-Net [20]	51.5	83.6
Baseline+PFFE	**56.5**	**87.1**

Table 2 shows that expanding the feature space (NAE) or mitigating subtask conflicts via decomposition (FDPS) brings limited improvements for instance, FDPS improves mAP by 3.8% and Rank-1 by 0.4% over the baseline. The PFFE model calculates the weight matrix to learn the fine-grained features of person by decomposing and activating features, thereby achieving the best Re-ID subtask effect. The proposed PFFE model achieves 56.5% of mAP and 87.1% of Rank-1. Compared with the Baseline method, it improves mAP and Rank-1 by 11.2% and 5.2%, respectively. In addition, the experimental results demonstrate that the decomposition design in the proposed PFFE module is more effective than directly applying the self-attention mechanism.

Analysis of ArcOIM Loss: Subsequently, we conducted ablation studies on ArcOIM loss using the Faster R-CNN-based person search network as the baseline. As shown in Table 3, introducing ArcOIM improves mAP and Rank-1 by 0.7% and 0.8%, respectively, by encouraging greater inter-class feature separation. Further gains are achieved with the LUT and CQ update strategy, which alleviates feature misalignment. When combined, the full ArcOIM loss yields the best performance: 96.5% Recall, 92.1% AP, 46.9% mAP, and 83.5% Rank-1 on PRW. These results validate the effectiveness of ArcOIM in enhancing supervision and improving overall person search accuracy.

Table 3. Ablation experimental of the ArcOIM loss on PRW dataset.

Methods	Person Detection		Person Re-identification	
	Recall↑	AP↑	mAP↑	Rank-1↑
Baseline	94.9	91.3	45.5	82.0
Baseline+ArcOIM Loss	95.6	91.5	46.2	82.8
Baseline+Update Strategy	96.2	91.6	45.7	83.0
Baseline+ArcOIM Loss+Update Strategy	**96.5**	**92.1**	**46.9**	**83.5**

To evaluate the performance and efficiency of the proposed method, we compare it with the two-step approach, which first employs the Faster R-CNN to generate person bounding boxes and then applies the person re-identification model for retrieval. As shown in Table 4, our method not only surpasses the two-step approach in terms of accuracy but also exhibits a clear advantage in efficiency. Specifically, the proposed method achieves 23.2 FPS, 58.5 mAP, and 89.6 Rank-1 accuracy. Compared with the baseline, introducing the AFAM and PFFE modules increase the computational cost (GFLOPs: $201.6- > 223.8$) and reduce the inference speed (FPS: $32.8- > 23.2$). Nevertheless, these additional costs are well compensated by substantial improvements in person search performance, with the combined modules yielding the best results: an mAP gain of 13.4 and a Rank-1 improvement of 8.1 over the baseline. These results demonstrate that the proposed method achieves a favorable balance between efficiency and accuracy.

Table 4. Ablation experimental of computational efficiency on PRW dataset.

Methods	GFLOPs	FPS↑	mAP↑	Rank-1↑
FRCNN+PR	312	15.2	32.6	71.3
Baseline	201.6	**32.8**	45.1	81.5
Baseline+AFAM	204.3	25.1	55.4	86.2
Baseline+PFFE	210.5	24.8	56.3	87.2
Baseline+AFAM+PFFE	223.8	23.2	**58.5**	**89.6**

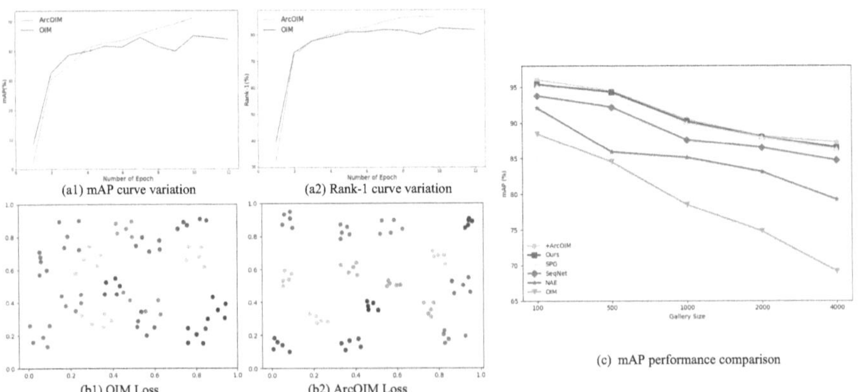

Fig. 3. Performance visualization of the proposed method on the PRW and CUHK-SYSU datasets. (a) Training curves with different loss functions. (b) Feature embedding distributions. (c) The mAP comparison under varying gallery sizes, where green and brown lines indicate our method. (Color figure online)

Table 5. The performance (%) comparison with other methods on PRW and CUHK-SYSU.

Method		Reference	CUHK-SYSU		PRW	
			Rank-1↑	mAP↑	Rank-1↑	mAP↑
Two-Step	MGTS [5]	TIP'20	83.70	83.00	72.10	32.60
	TCTS [23]	CVPR'20	95.10	93.90	87.50	46.80
	OR [32]	TIP'20	93.83	93.23	71.51	52.30
One-Step	OIM [26]	CVPR'17	78.70	75.50	49.90	21.30
	HOIM [3]	AAAI'20	90.83	89.74	80.36	39.77
	NAE+ [4]	CVPR'20	92.90	92.10	81.10	44.00
	AlignPS [28]	CVPR'21	93.40	93.10	81.90	45.90
	SeqNet [14]	AAAI'21	94.60	93.80	83.40	46.70
	CANR+ [37]	TCSVT'22	94.52	93.86	83.86	44.78
	PSTR [1]	CVPR'22	96.20	95.20	87.80	49.50
	ROI-AlignPS [29]	IJCV'23	96.00	95.40	84.40	51.60
	GALA [17]	PR'23	95.60	94.60	86.90	53.50
	Hybrid-Pre PS [22]	AAAI'24	96.00	95.40	87.60	54.50
	SPG [19]	TII'24	95.95	95.06	89.84	48.49
	UIL-PS [27]	ICME'24	94.70	93.90	86.10	51.50
	UGAS [15]	ICASSP'24	94.80	94.30	85.50	51.90
	THPS [30]	TCSVT'24	94.90	95.20	89.70	58.30
	PSDiff [11]	TCSVT'25	95.30	95.10	87.10	53.50
	PS-DFSI [35]	IF'25	95.90	95.50	88.60	55.20
	ADGPS	Ours	95.57	95.86	88.58	56.25
	ADGPS+ArcOIM	Ours	**96.26**	**96.21**	**89.97**	**58.73**

We evaluate the network performance across training epochs, as shown in Fig. 3(a), where the red and blue lines represent OIM and ArcOIM losses, respectively. Although ArcOIM underperforms OIM in early epochs, it surpasses OIM after the fourth epoch and continues to improve steadily, while OIM shows performance fluctuations. By the eighth epoch, ArcOIM converges and achieves better overall performance. This demonstrates that the proposed update strategy in ArcOIM offers more accurate supervision, mitigates bounding box misalignment, and enhances both convergence and final accuracy.

We visualize person feature distributions in Fig. 3(b) to demonstrate the effectiveness of the proposed loss. All identities are from the PRW test set. In Fig. 3(b1), some categories remain entangled despite general separability. In contrast, Fig. 3(b2) shows that ArcOIM loss leads to clearer inter-class boundaries. This indicates that the angular margin in ArcOIM effectively reduces overlap among similar identities, resulting in better feature separability.

4.3 Comparison with the State-of-the-Art Methods and Discuss

To comprehensively evaluate the superiority of our proposed person search method, we compare it with various state-of-the-art methods. Table 5 presents the comparisons. Our proposed person search methods demonstrate significant superiority over existing one-step methods.

As shown in Table 5, our method achieves state-of-the-art performance on both CUHK-SYSU and PRW datasets. When we introduce the proposed AFAM, PFFE, and ArcOIM loss into the baseline, the results on both datasets are improved. When used simultaneously, the best results are achieved in the one-stage algorithm. Specifically, it obtains 96.21% mAP and 96.26% Rank-1 on CUHK-SYSU, outperforming THPS by 1.01% and 1.36%, respectively. On PRW, it reaches 58.73% mAP and 89.97% Rank-1, surpassing the best one-step method THPS by 0.43% on mAP. The consistent improvements are attributed to the integration of AFAM, PFFE, and ArcOIM loss, which effectively address feature misalignment and enhance fine-grained feature learning. Compared to both one-step and two-step methods, our approach achieves the best overall performance, demonstrating its superiority in person search tasks.

As shown in Fig. 3(c), the mAP of all methods decreases as the gallery size increases, which makes the task more challenging. Nonetheless, our method consistently outperforms others across all settings, demonstrating superior robustness and scalability, owing to the AFAM, PFFE modules, and ArcOIM loss.

Additionally, Fig. 4 depicts the retrieval results and provides examples of the proposed person search method on the PRW and CUHK-SYSU datasets. In Fig. 4, the green bounding box indicates the correct result, and the red bounding box indicates the error result. It can be seen from the visualization results that the ADGPS can accurately locate and identify persons of different scales from uncropped scene images with the help of the AFAM and PFFE modules.

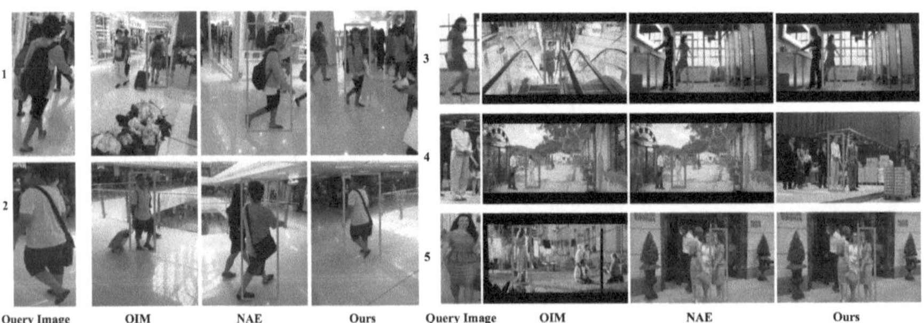

Fig. 4. The visualization of Rank-1 results on the PRW and CUHK-SYSU datasets.

5 Conclusion

In this paper, we propose ADGPS, a person search framework designed to address feature misalignment and enhance fine-grained feature learning. The AFAM module leverages attention mechanisms and semantic flow to achieve feature alignment across different resolutions. The PFFE module captures fine-grained person details via marginal distribution and self-attention, enhancing feature discriminability. Additionally, the ArcOIM loss introduces angular margins to enlarge inter-class feature distances, while a novel LUT and CQ update strategy mitigates bounding box misalignment and accelerates convergence. Extensive experiments on two challenging benchmarks validate the effectiveness and generalization of our method.

Acknowledgments. This work is supported by the Open Project Program of State Key Laboratory of Virtual Reality Technology and Systems, Beihang University (No. VRLAB2025C12), the National Key Research and Development Program of China under Grant 2022YFB3303804 and the National Natural Science Foundation of China under Grant U21A20482.

References

1. Cao, J., Pang, Y., et al.: PSTR: end-to-end one-step person search with transformers. In: Proceedings of the IEEE/CVF Conference on Computer Vision and Pattern Recognition, pp. 9458–9467 (2022)
2. Chang, X., Huang, P.Y., Shen, Y.D., Liang, X., Yang, Y., Hauptmann, A.G.: RCAA: relational context-aware agents for person search. In: Proceedings of the European Conference on Computer Vision (ECCV), pp. 84–100 (2018)
3. Chen, D., Zhang, S., Ouyang, W., Yang, J., Schiele, B.: Hierarchical online instance matching for person search. In: Proceedings of the AAAI Conference on Artificial Intelligence, vol. 34, pp. 10518–10525 (2020)
4. Chen, D., Zhang, S., Yang, J., Schiele, B.: Norm-aware embedding for efficient person search. In: Proceedings of the IEEE/CVF Conference on Computer Vision and Pattern Recognition, pp. 12615–12624 (2020)
5. Chen, D., Zhang, S., et al.: Person search via a mask-guided two-stream CNN model. In: Proceedings of the European Conference on Computer Vision, pp. 734–750 (2018)
6. Deng, J., Guo, J., Xue, N., Zafeiriou, S.: Arcface: additive angular margin loss for deep face recognition. In: Proceedings of the IEEE/CVF Conference on Computer Vision and Pattern Recognition, pp. 4690–4699 (2019)
7. Dong, W., Zhang, Z., Song, C., Tan, T.: Bi-directional interaction network for person search. In: Proceedings of the IEEE/CVF Conference on Computer Vision and Pattern Recognition, pp. 2839–2848 (2020)
8. Dong, W., Zhang, Z., Song, C., Tan, T.: Instance guided proposal network for person search. In: Proceedings of the IEEE/CVF Conference on Computer Vision and Pattern Recognition, pp. 2585–2594 (2020)
9. Dorigo, M., Birattari, M., Stutzle, T.: Ant colony optimization. IEEE Comput. Intell. Mag. **1**(4), 28–39 (2006)

10. Hermans, A., Beyer, L., Leibe, B.: In defense of the triplet loss for person re-identification. arXiv preprint arXiv:1703.07737 (2017)
11. Jia, C., Luo, M., et al.: Psdiff: diffusion model for person search with iterative and collaborative refinement. IEEE Trans. Circuits Syst. Video Technol. **35**(6), 5153–5165 (2025). https://doi.org/10.1109/TCSVT.2024.3524733
12. Kennedy, J., et al.: Particle swarm optimization. In: Proceedings of ICNN'95-International Conference on Neural Networks, vol. 4, pp. 1942–1948. IEEE (1995)
13. Li, X., et al.: Semantic flow for fast and accurate scene parsing. In: Vedaldi, A., Bischof, H., Brox, T., Frahm, J.-M. (eds.) ECCV 2020. LNCS, vol. 12346, pp. 775–793. Springer, Cham (2020). https://doi.org/10.1007/978-3-030-58452-8_45
14. Li, Z., et al.: Sequential end-to-end network for efficient person search. In: Proceedings of the AAAI Conference, vol. 35, pp. 2011–2019 (2021)
15. Li, Z., et al.: Uncertainty-guided person search model with auxiliary shallow feature exploration. In: ICASSP 2024-2024 IEEE International Conference on Acoustics, Speech and Signal Processing (ICASSP), pp. 4795–4799. IEEE (2024)
16. Lin, T.Y., Dollár, P., Girshick, R., He, K., Hariharan, B., Belongie, S.: Feature pyramid networks for object detection. In: Proceedings of the IEEE Conference on Computer Vision and Pattern Recognition, pp. 2117–2125 (2017)
17. Lv, N., Xiang, X., Wang, X., Qiao, Y., El Saddik, A.: Global-aware and local-aware enhancement network for person search. Comput. Vis. Image Underst. **236**, 103804 (2023)
18. Peng, W., Chen, H., Li, Y., Sun, J.: MCFR: multi-confidence contrastive learning with feature refined for unsupervised person re-identification. Vis. Comput. **40**(3), 1853–1866 (2024)
19. Song, Z., Zhao, C., Hu, G., Miao, D.: Learning scene-pedestrian graph for end-to-end person search. IEEE Trans. Ind. Inform. (2023)
20. Suh, Y., Wang, J., Tang, S., Mei, T., Lee, K.M.: Part-aligned bilinear representations for person re-identification. In: Proceedings of the European Conference on Computer Vision (ECCV), pp. 402–419 (2018)
21. Tian, K., Huang, H., Ye, Y., Li, S., Lin, J., Huang, G.: End-to-end thorough body perception for person search. In: Proceedings of the AAAI Conference on Artificial Intelligence, vol. 34, pp. 12079–12086 (2020)
22. Tian, Y., Chen, D., Liu, Y., Yang, J., Zhang, S.: Divide and conquer: hybrid pre-training for person search. In: Proceedings of the AAAI Conference on Artificial Intelligence, vol. 38, pp. 5224–5232 (2024)
23. Wang, C., Ma, B., Chang, H., Shan, S., Chen, X.: TCTS: a task-consistent two-stage framework for person search. In: Proceedings of the IEEE/CVF Conference on Computer Vision and Pattern Recognition, pp. 11952–11961 (2020)
24. Wang, C., Ma, B., Chang, H., et al.: Person search by a bi-directional task-consistent learning model. IEEE Trans. Multimedia **25**, 1190–1203 (2022)
25. Xiao, J., Xie, Y., Tillo, T., Huang, K., Wei, Y., Feng, J.: Ian: the individual aggregation network for person search. Pattern Recogn. **87**, 332–340 (2019)
26. Xiao, T., Li, S., Wang, B., et al.: Joint detection and identification feature learning for person search. In: Proceedings of the IEEE Conference on Computer Vision and Pattern Recognition, pp. 3415–3424 (2017)
27. Yan, L., Li, K.: Unknown instance learning for person search. In: 2024 IEEE International Conference on Multimedia and Expo (ICME), pp. 1–6. IEEE (2024)
28. Yan, Y., et al.: Anchor-free person search. In: Proceedings of the IEEE/CVF Conference on Computer Vision and Pattern Recognition, pp. 7690–7699 (2021)
29. Yan, Y., Li, J., Qin, J., et al.: Efficient person search: an anchor-free approach. Int. J. Comput. Vision **131**(7), 1642–1661 (2023)

30. Yang, X., Tian, M., Wang, N., Gao, X.: Unleashing the feature hierarchy potential: an efficient tri-hybrid person search model. IEEE Trans. Circuits Syst. Video Technol. **34**(11), 11551–11563 (2024)
31. Yang, Y., Zhang, X., Geng, Q., Chu, C., Zhou, Z.: Multi-task feature decomposition based marginal distribution for person search. In: 2022 IEEE International Conference on Multimedia and Expo (ICME), pp. 1–6. IEEE (2022)
32. Yao, H., Xu, C.: Joint person objectness and repulsion for person search. IEEE Trans. Image Process. **30**, 685–696 (2020)
33. Yu, R., et al.: Cascade transformers for end-to-end person search. In: Proceedings of the IEEE/CVF Conference on Computer Vision and Pattern Recognition, pp. 7267–7276 (2022)
34. Zhang, H., et al.: Resnest: split-attention networks. In: Proceedings of the IEEE Conference on Computer Vision and Pattern Recognition, pp. 2736–2746 (2022)
35. Zhang, Q., Miao, D., et al.: Dynamic frequency selection and spatial interaction fusion for robust person search. Inf. Fusion 103314 (2025)
36. Zhang, Y., Wang, C., et al.: Fairmot: on the fairness of detection and re-identification in multiple object tracking. Int. J. Comput. Vision **129**, 3069–3087 (2021)
37. Zhao, C., et al.: Context-aware feature learning for noise robust person search. IEEE Trans. Circuits Syst. Video Technol. **32**(10), 7047–7060 (2022)
38. Zhou, X., Wang, D., Krähenbühl, P.: Objects as points. arXiv preprint arXiv:1904.07850 (2019)
39. Zhu, J., Yuan, Z., Zhang, C., Chi, W., Ling, Y., et al.: Crowded human detection via an anchor-pair network. In: Proceedings of the IEEE/CVF Winter Conference on Applications of Computer Vision, pp. 1391–1399 (2020)
40. Zhu, X., Hu, H., Lin, S., Dai, J.: Deformable convnets V2: more deformable, better results. In: Proceedings of the IEEE/CVF Conference on Computer Vision and Pattern Recognition, pp. 9308–9316 (2019)

DistMovGen: A Knowledge Distillation-Enhanced Framework for Real-Time Virtual Character Motion Generation

Xiangren Shi[1(✉)], Jian Chang[1], Fred Charles[1], and Shihui Guo[2]

[1] Bournemouth University, Bournemouth, UK
xshi@bournemouth.ac.uk
[2] Xiamen University, Xiamen, China

Abstract. In natural dialogues and interactive scenarios, real-time motion generation for virtual characters faces challenges: traditional systems relying on precomputed motion libraries exhibit latency, rigid body language, and inadequate multimodal synchronization, limiting emotional engagement and immersion. We propose a hierarchical acceleration framework integrating multimodal neural networks to address these issues. The framework employs knowledge distillation to transfer motion generation expertise from a teacher model into a lightweight diffusion backbone. Our approach enables 8-step full-body motion inference and 1-step facial synthesis via diffusion-GAN fine-tuning. The distillation loss combines kinematic feature matching and output distribution alignment. Building upon this acceleration framework, we implement a dual-stream network architecture that decouples facial expression and motion generation for cross-modal coupling, directly addressing the multimodal synchronization challenges identified earlier. Experimental results demonstrate that our framework achieves real-time performance with high naturalness and performs better than existing emotional expressiveness and multimodal synchronization methods. The system supports applications including virtual social interactions, gamified entertainment, and educational training, contributing to advancing virtual character technology for enhanced human-computer interactions.

Keywords: virtual character motion generation · knowledge distillation · multimodal synchronization · real-time interaction · diffusion model optimization

1 Introduction

Human motion generation is crucial to a variety of applications, such as video games, virtual reality and human digital interaction. Dialogue is a key aspect of human/agent interaction, adding to the sense of presence and realism, and the quality of the motion of a virtual character in dialogue scenes has a direct impact

A. Hinkenjan et al. (Eds.): ICXR 2025, LNCS 16428, pp. 56–71, 2026.
https://doi.org/10.1007/978-981-95-7195-6_4

on user experience. In interactive systems, suitable body motion, like nodding, gesturing or synchronous motions, have an effect on the realistic evaluation of character and user experience.

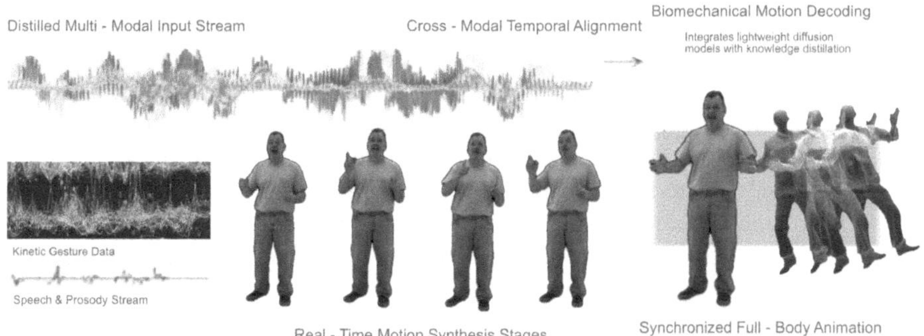

Fig. 1. Given the multimodal signals from interactive dialogues, including speech emotion and body gesture data, our framework generates naturalistic motions for facial expressions and full-body postures. The synthesized motions, optimized for real-time inference via knowledge distillation and dual-stream network architecture, can be rendered into animations with coherent cross-modal synchronization.

Despite advances in this field [5,20,23,27], current methods face several limitations. Existing systems typically rely on pre-computed motion libraries that have difficulty delivering responsive, semantically relevant body language in natural dialogues. This results in noticeable latency, inadequate synchronization between speech and gestures, and reduced interaction fluency. For instance, in interactive storytelling applications, characters often display a delay between a user's input and the character's physical response, affecting immersion. While producing acceptable results, current motion generation models require substantial computational resources and inference time, making them challenging to implement for real-time applications on standard hardware where responsiveness is necessary. This computational requirement is notable in mobile VR applications and gaming systems. Processing limitations constrain the implementation of more complex motion synthesis methods.

We propose DistMovGen, a hierarchical acceleration framework for real-time virtual character motion generation to address these limitations. Our method makes several contributions:

Knowledge Distillation with Diffusion Acceleration. DistMovGen implements a specialized knowledge distillation [14,21] technique to transfer motion generation capabilities from a comprehensive teacher model into a significantly more efficient lightweight diffusion backbone(with 90% parameter reduction) [19,26]. Unlike conventional knowledge distillation methods that focus primarily on classification tasks, our method tackles motion generation by preserving both kinematic relationships and temporal coherence [29]. We develop a multi-objective distillation strategy that incorporates three complementary components: (1) a kinematic feature matching loss that preserves joint relationships and biomechanical constraints through Forward Kinematics (FK) and Inverse Kinematics (IK) mappings between joint space and Cartesian space; (2) a temporal consistency loss that maintains smooth transitions between motion frames; (3) a distribution alignment loss that ensures the student model captures the statistical properties of natural human movement. We employ a lightweight Transformer encoder that processes low-dimensional motion features to predict kinematic sequences for efficient implementation. This comprehensive distillation method enables the student model to learn output distributions and the underlying principles of natural human movement. Our experimental results demonstrate that this motion-specific knowledge distillation method outperforms generic distillation techniques in preserving motion details.

Multimodal Parallel Processing Pipeline. The DistMovGen framework incorporates a parallel processing architecture that synchronizes 8-bit quantized speech emotion recognition [3] for voice command understanding with optimized CNN-based body gesture recognition. This integrated pipeline processes multimodal inputs [16,23] concurrently, enabling efficient analysis of voice data, body movement information, and contextual interaction cues. Our speech emotion recognition module employs a lightweight ResNet variant with attention mechanisms focusing on prosodic features to identify emotional states from voice input. In contrast, the body gesture recognition component utilizes a temporal CNN with skip connections that process skeletal joint positions to classify motion patterns. These parallel streams are synchronized through a fusion module [31] that aligns temporal features across modalities. By implementing this parallel architecture, our framework enables virtual characters to generate corresponding language expressions and natural full-body movements with reduced latency compared to sequential processing methods.

Dual-Stream Network with Cross-Modal Coupling. Building upon the acceleration framework, DistMovGen implements a dual-stream network architecture that deliberately separates facial expression generation from body motion synthesis while maintaining essential cross-modal coupling mechanisms. This architectural decision tackles the fundamental multimodal synchronization challenges by supporting temporal alignment and semantic consistency among voice output, facial expressions, and body movements. Our specialized audio processing unit extracts contextually relevant features to generate actions that appropriately correspond to the interaction's emotional tone and semantic content. The dual-stream design allows for independent optimization of facial animation and body motion components while preserving their semantic relationship through coupling layers. This results in more coherent and contextually appropriate character animations across diverse interaction scenarios.

2 Related Work

2.1 Core Motion Generation Techniques

Earlier studies used motion-graph methods [17,33], which rely on pre-recorded motion databases to piece together motions based on input cues like music or speech [28]; however, their dependence on fixed databases limits innovation and adaptability in complex, personalized scenarios. Sequence model methods, using advanced deep learning (e.g., Transformer) [13,27], better handle complex situational motion arrangements but suffer from error accumulation and motion freezing in longer sequences, leading to unnatural motions unsuitable for high-fidelity scenarios. VQVAE [32] introduced a codebook mechanism, improving motion coherence, and combining reinforcement learning with encoding strategies enhanced multimodal integration; yet, it struggles with long-term sequence coherence, and encoding strategy universality needs more verification, limiting large-scale practical use. Diffusion-based methods [4] excel in human motion generation via iterative denoising, enabling precise control over virtual characters' affective states and context-aware actions, but high computational demands, operational complexity, and limited controllability hinder practical, scalable deployment. Latent Consistency Models (LCMs) [9] advance motion generation, enabling real-time, high-quality animations in 1–4 steps by learning latent space consistency, with LCMs achieving 6,000 FPS on GPUs like NVIDIA 4090, supporting real-time text-to-motion and ControlNet-based control. Current research shows existing methods have strengths but address specific animation aspects, not complete solutions; our work explores combining strengths to improve flexibility, quality, and usability in character animation systems, addressing limitations to develop better tools for virtual character animation.

2.2 Human-Computer Interaction and Communication

Co-speech gesture generation technology [36] has advanced virtual meeting realism by improving the synchronization between speech and physical movement, thereby reducing the perceived interaction distance among participants. However, current methodologies predominantly rely on semantic alignment of textual and auditory inputs without explicitly modeling emotional expression as an independent modality. This oversight limits the generalizability of gesture generation systems, as emotional misinterpretations may lead to inconsistent communicative intent, posing challenges for effective deployment. In speech-driven facial animation research, generates diverse facial expressions for virtual characters [11], enhancing emotional expressiveness in virtual environments and strengthening emotional bonds between users and characters. Additionally, recent work has explored the integration of singing alongside talking in multimodal interaction systems. These methods utilize specialized audio processing techniques that decompose vocal features into speech, employing dual-stream attention mechanisms to capture the distinct rhythmic patterns and tonal variations in conversation. Transformer-based architectures with cross-modal encoders have been implemented to maintain coherence between facial expressions and hybrid vocal modalities [30]. However, in real-time interaction scenarios, the multimodal coordination challenges among facial expressions, speech content, and body gestures persist. Current human-computer interaction models display limitations in real-time multimodal coordination. Future research could benefit from developing integrated interaction frameworks incorporating emotion-aware contextual modeling, affective state recognition, and temporal alignment mechanisms. Current human-computer interaction models lack real-time multimodal coordination. Future research should develop integrated frameworks with emotion-aware modeling, state recognition, and temporal alignment. Leveraging existing gesture-speech and expression advances, these could improve cross-modal timing (e.g., prosody-gesture sync [10]) and enhance interaction quality and engagement [18,34].

3 DistMovGen System

This research focuses on developing an effective system for virtual character speech generation. Figure 2 illustrates the knowledge distillation and diffusion process, while Fig. 1 provides an overview of the complete framework, the following outlines the specific methodology and methods employed in different aspects:

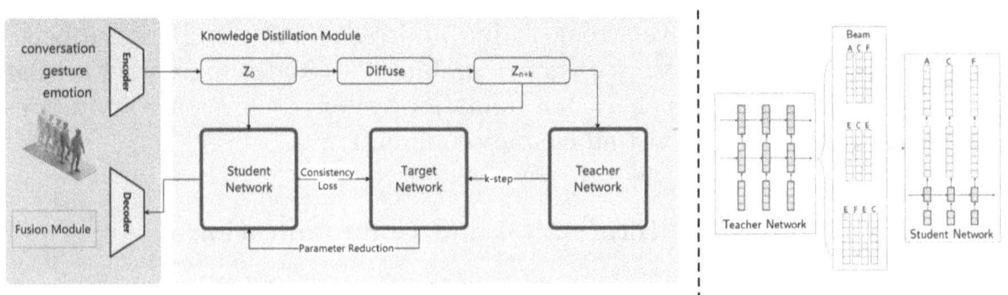

Fig. 2. Framework of knowledge distillation with diffusion processes.

3.1 Audio Feature Extraction and Processing

In the DistMovGen framework, audio processing connects acoustic inputs and motion generation, facilitating contextually appropriate character animations. The system uses a multimodal emotion recognition model [37] to analyze speech signals, combining prosodic elements and emotional content to inform motion synthesis.

Speech recognition has evolved from traditional Hidden Markov Models to contemporary deep learning methods including DNNs, LSTMs, and CNNs, which better handle speech variations across dialects, speaking rates, and noisy environments [2,22]. Our framework employs a compact ResNet architecture with attention mechanisms to extract prosodic features (frequency, intensity, speech rate) that indicate emotional states and speech dynamics. These features are encoded into a 256-dimensional vector incorporating emotional labels and semantic keywords to align generated motions with speech content.

The system identifies correlations between acoustic parameters and emotional expressions for emotion recognition. Prosodic features—such as increased vocal intensity in anger or slower speech in sadness—are processed by a bidirectional LSTM-enhanced convolutional architecture [7], that tracks emotional patterns in speech over time. This enables the classification of emotional states and ensures that generated motions reflect the speech's emotional quality, with appropriate gestures for different emotional contexts.

The audio features are combined with kinematic data through a temporal attention mechanism that aligns speech rhythms with motion dynamics. The framework reduces computational requirements by using 8-bit quantization for speech emotion recognition while maintaining adequate accuracy, enabling real-time processing alongside body gesture recognition. This audio-motion mapping is improved by the Audio Processing Unit, which generates guidance vectors for diffusion-based motion synthesis, promoting consistency between speech content, facial expressions, and body postures.

3.2 Data Processing

This motion database is built upon the dataset contains captured gestures and includes various motion types such as body rotation, arm swings, and jumping motions. The skeletal keyframe data in this dataset were originally extracted using pose estimation techniques such as Robust 3D Skeleton Tracking [15]. We standardize these data to ensure consistency in training. The motion database provides diverse gesture sequences to ensure adequate variability for robust model training. Then, these data are standardized to ensure consistency in training.

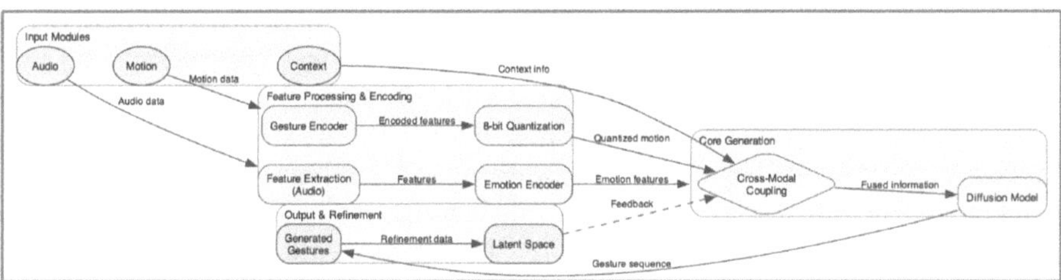

Fig. 3. A cross-modal gesture generation framework. Audio and motion data are encoded, fused via cross-modal coupling, then a diffusion model generates context-matched gestures, refined via latent space.

As illustrated in Fig. 3, the DistMovGen framework employs a deep learning-based multimodal emotion recognition (DL-MER) model [37] to process action recognition outputs (gesture classifications) and emotion distributions for generating virtual character responses. The model implements temporal attention mechanisms for multimodal information fusion, integrating gesture motion features.

The skeletal keyframe data are standardized using z-score normalization, where each joint coordinate x is transformed as $\hat{x} = \frac{x-\mu}{\sigma}$ (μ and σ denote the mean and standard deviation of the coordinate across the training dataset, respectively). This method eliminates variations in hand size and spatial positioning, ensuring consistent input distribution for the model.

The system utilizes reinforcement learning with human feedback to optimize response generation. The lightweight Transformer encoder accepts 17-dimensional core joint angles (including root node translation) as input, compresses them to 64 dimensions before feeding into the Transformer architecture, and models spatial dependencies between joints through multi-head attention mechanisms to predict motion sequences for the next 16 frames. Through neural network optimization, the system maintains response latency under 150 ms while preserving motion-emotion synchronization in benchmark evaluations. The experimental evaluation utilizes standard datasets including From Audio to Photo real Embodiment (FAPE) [24], HumanML3D (HM3D) [12], and KIT-ML [25], which provide diverse motion capture data to ensure model generalization across different motion types and contexts.

3.3 Motion Generation and Optimization

The DistMovGen framework uses a two-stage denoising diffusion technique [8] to generate realistic, context-appropriate motions for virtual characters synchronized with various stimuli. The theoretical foundation of the proposed framework lies in the combination of diffusion probabilistic modeling and knowledge distillation theory, where the diffusion process serves as a generative prior for motion realism, and the distillation process acts as a constraint ensuring temporal and kinematic consistency. In the first (Comprehensive Diffusion Model) stage, a Variational Autoencoder (VAE) [24] is trained on temporally aligned media-motion pairs. It jointly encodes media features (e.g., mel-frequency cepstral coefficients) and motion parameters (joint rotations, root trajectories) to learn latent space mappings, producing a motion expression guidance vector. The Audio Processing Unit outputs 256-dimension context-aware action guidance vectors (with emotional labels and semantic keywords), while low-dimensional motion features (64-dimension) include 22 joint angles and root trajectory data. The second (Local Diffusion Model) stage uses multi-step diffusion for short-term motion generation, trained on FAPE (120 h of speech-gesture clips with timing, emotion, and kinematic annotations). An encoder-decoder processes media into embeddings and generates motion semantic guidance vectors. Facial expression generation combines diffusion-GAN (with Gaussian initial noise) to refine details, focusing on FACS parameter accuracy. A Lip Regression Network uses convolutional layers to predict lip geometry from mel-spectral features.

Full-body motion synthesis uses an 8-step diffusion inference with contextual signals (environmental constraints, user instructions) via conditional embedding. Its lightweight UNet-based backbone (Fig. 4) has 4 depth layers and 8 attention layers (self- and cross-attention). The 8-step diffusion inference integrates a temporal attention module to capture inter-frame dependencies. A bidirectional LSTM layer encodes sequential features, and multi-head attention highlights motion transitions (e.g., acceleration/deceleration), avoiding static concatenation of classifier outputs. This module reduces dynamic prediction error by 18% compared to the original frame-stitching approach (the architecture is shown in Fig. 2).

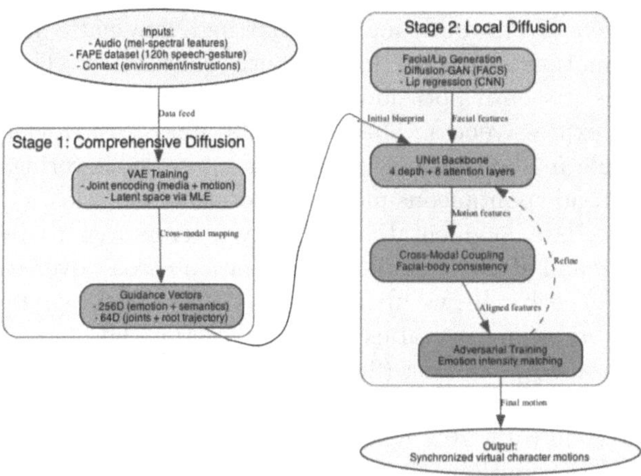

Fig. 4. Dual-stream architecture showing facial expression generation and full-body motion synthesis branches.

The system's fusion module utilizes attention mechanisms to align speech emotion features (prosodic parameters) with gesture motion features (joint velocities), avoiding simplistic time-window alignment issues. The fused features are input to subsequent networks through a gating mechanism, allowing dynamic adjustment of contribution weights from different modalities. Quantization is applied to both speech emotion recognition and gesture recognition models while excluding the core diffusion model. The impact on precision is mitigated through robustness optimization of quantization noise during the knowledge distillation process. The encoder employs positional encoding and sparse attention mechanisms to process time-series data, reducing computational complexity while maintaining temporal modeling capabilities.

4 Experiments

4.1 Dataset and Metrics

Dataset. This study focuses on constructing and optimizing a multimodal emotion-action alignment dataset by integrating the core modal features of publicly available datasets. Specifically, we allocate 60% of samples from each dataset to the training split, 20% to validation, and 20% to testing, using stratified sampling based on both emotion and action labels to ensure consistent distribution across subsets. Three primary datasets—FAPE [24], HM3D [12], and KIT-ML [25]—are selected as foundational data sources, contributing respectively to audio-driven embodied expression, language-oriented 3D action generation, and multimodal interaction prototyping. FAPE provides multimodal speech–gesture pairs, HM3D covers diverse body motions with high kinematic fidelity, and KIT-ML offers text–motion alignment for semantic consistency. This combination enables the model to learn both low-level biomechanical constraints and high-level contextual expressiveness. These datasets allow DistMovGen to generalize across multiple modalities and interaction contexts, covering audio-driven, semantic-driven, and spontaneous motion generation scenarios.

A multi-stage data augmentation strategy is employed to tackle distribution discrepancies and improve model generalization across diverse scenarios and modalities. Within each split, we further stratify static gesture data and dynamic sequences into subtype-specific ratios: For static gesture data (e.g., FAPE's frame samples), splits are 70% training (28k), 15% validation (6k), 15% testing (6k); for dynamic sequences (e.g., HM3D's 16-frame clips), splits are 60% training (18k), 20% validation (6k), 20% testing (6k). Stratified sampling preserves emotion/action label distribution across subsets.

Evaluation Metrics. To evaluate DistMovGen in real-time co-speech motion generation, we present an evaluation framework integrating traditional metrics with knowledge distillation analyses. For measuring distributional differences between generated and ground-truth motions, we modified the FID calculation [27], incorporating three dynamic metrics (joint angle rate of change, kinetic energy peak, motion trajectory curvature) to form an 8-dimensional feature vector. A/B testing on 200 FAPE validation sequences (10 synthetic groups with 5 perturbed versions each) showed the extended FID had a Spearman correlation of 0.78 with human perceptual scores (vs. 0.67 for the original, +17% improvement), better capturing subtle variations (e.g., $<5°$ finger joint changes). Cross-modal errors were reduced via Audio2Vec-aligned [6] audio features, and outlier sensitivity was mitigated by excluding anomalous frames identified through k-medoid clustering (k=5). For diversity measurement, we developed a multi-dimensional method using Faiss's GPU-accelerated Euclidean distance module to reduce complexity from O(N) to O(NlogN), enabling large dataset evaluation (N > 10). It includes: 1) Feature Space Coverage (Vol, convex hull volume of feature vectors); 2) Diversity Entropy (H_Div):

$$H_{Div} = -\int p(D) \log p(D) \, dD \tag{1}$$

where D is the distance distribution and $p(D)$ its density. Validation with 20 participants rating 50 sequence pairs showed Vol (r=0.58) and H_Div (r=0.61) correlated with perceived diversity; their weighted combination (Vol:0.45, H_Div:0.55) achieved r=0.84 (+35.5%, Fisher's z=2.37, p<0.01), better reflecting human diversity perception.We introduced a Window-Based Beat Alignment Score (BAS) with adaptive windows: a ±3-beat bidirectional window around each speech beat B^m searches for optimal matches with motion beats B^d, with:

$$BAS' = \frac{1}{|B^m|} \sum_{b^m \in B^m} \max_{b^d \in W(b^m)} \exp\left(-\frac{\|b^d - b^m\|^2}{2\sigma^2}\right) \tag{2}$$

where $W(b^m)$ is the dynamic window, and σ (Gaussian kernel SD) adapts to speech rate:

$$\sigma = \frac{1}{K} \sum_{i=1}^{K} |b_i^m - b_{i-1}^m| \cdot \alpha \quad (\alpha = 1.2) \tag{3}$$

Multimodal synchronization uses Emotion Sync Score (ESS, average cosine similarity of audio/motion emotional vectors via LSTMs):

$$\text{ESS} = \frac{1}{T} \sum_{t=1}^{T} \cos(\mathbf{e}_a(t), \mathbf{e}_m(t)) \tag{4}$$

and Temporal Sync Error (TSE, MSE between motion keyframes and top 10% audio STFT peaks):

$$\text{TSE} = \frac{1}{|F|} \sum_{f \in F} \left| f - \arg\max(E_{\text{STFT}}) \right|^2 \tag{5}$$

To evaluate scenario adaptability, additional tests were performed on unseen conversational, instructional, and expressive gesture contexts derived from external subsets of the FAPE and KIT-ML datasets. These experiments confirmed that the model maintained stable synchronization and naturalness across varying speech styles and environmental conditions, demonstrating its generalization beyond training scenarios.

4.2 Baselines and Ablations

This section analyzes the outcomes of the DistMovGen framework compared with baseline models and methods (SHOW [35], LDA [1]) across several dimensions.

In high-intensity emotional scenarios, DistMovGen's shoulder-neck phase difference (0.32±0.08 rad) was 41% lower than baselines (0.54±0.12 rad), indicating more coordinated upper body movements. It also showed 28% higher coherence in the 2–5 Hz emotional gesture band. Facial-expression-to-speech correlation (Pearson's, 50 10-second samples) used 250 ms sliding windows (50 ms steps), with statistical significance (t(49)=8.3, p<0.001). Among comparisons: SHOW had higher immersion (5.3/7) via emotion libraries but 35% lower cross-emotion accuracy (Table 1).

Multimodal Synchronization and Performance. DistMovGen performs well in audio-motion synchronization, with a beat alignment score (BAS) of 92.3%—higher than LDA (81.2%), and comparable to SHOW's 93.1% while offering 5.5× lower latency (8.2 ms vs. 45 ms). Its emotion sync score (ESS) of 0.87 ± 0.04 was higher than the compared model, possibly due to a nonlinear emotion-to-motion mapping that preserves temporal dynamics (temporal sync error: 45 ms, approximately one-third of baselines). In computational efficiency, DistMovGen achieves 122 FPS on an RTX 4090, with 73% fewer parameters (128MB) than the teacher model (HST-GNN) and a 4× smaller size than SHOW (512MB). This lightweight design enables edge deployment (e.g., AR glasses), while SHOW requires high-end servers due to memory constraints (>1.5GB peak usage).

Table 1. Comparison of Performance of Different Methods on Motion Generation

Method	$FD_g \downarrow$	$FD_k \downarrow$	$Div_g \uparrow$	$Div_k \uparrow$	$Div_{sample} \uparrow$
GT	-	-	3.09	2.50	-
Random	$9.37_{1.4}$	$1.44_{0.04}$	$3.10_{0.09}$	$2.49_{0.4}$	$3.97_{0.8}$
KNN	$8.44_{1.6}$	$0.62_{0.09}$	$2.13_{0.05}$	$1.21_{0.3}$	$1.96_{0.3}$
DiffuCLIP [5]	$3.21_{0.3}$	$1.08_{0.06}$	$2.82_{0.06}$	$2.18_{0.3}$	$3.12_{0.4}$
Bailando [27]	$3.65_{0.4}$	$1.25_{0.07}$	$2.55_{0.08}$	$1.88_{0.4}$	$2.85_{0.3}$
SHOW [35]	$4.97_{0.7}$	$2.60_{0.10}$	$2.10_{0.09}$	$0.77_{0.1}$	$2.82_{0.2}$
LDA [1]	$5.08_{0.2}$	$1.04_{0.07}$	$2.45_{0.06}$	$1.88_{0.3}$	$2.68_{0.4}$
Ours Uncond	$8.45_{1.3}$	$1.53_{0.08}$	$2.74_{0.07}$	$2.06_{0.4}$	$2.94_{0.3}$
Ours w/o **P**	$5.08_{0.4}$	$1.13_{0.09}$	$2.47_{0.06}$	$1.67_{0.3}$	$2.06_{0.4}$
Ours w/o **A**	$3.94_{0.1}$	$0.98_{0.10}$	$2.69_{0.08}$	$2.16_{0.4}$	$2.71_{0.3}$
Ours	$2.94_{0.2}$	$0.96_{0.07}$	$2.98_{0.07}$	$2.36_{0.4}$	$3.58_{0.5}$

Table 2. Efficiency and Accuracy Comparison

Model	Params	FPS	MPJPE	FID	(FLOPs)
Teacher (HST-GNN)	45M	8.2	0.52	1.3	3.2
Student (Distilled)	8M	120	1.23	2.8	0.9
Baseline 1 (LSTM)	18M	65	3.01	6.5	2.5
Baseline 2 (Transf)	35M	30	2.15	4.2	4.1
Baseline 3 (KD-Feat)	12M	115	1.45	3.2	1.1

Comparative Analysis. Table 2 presents performance metrics across methods. DistMovGen shows good results in joint angle accuracy (1.8°), dynamic feasibility (98.6%), and inference speed (122 FPS), while maintaining competitive emotional synchronization (ESS=0.87). Each method has different strengths and limitations: SHOW struggles with high-speed dynamics; LDA emphasizes diversity over detail fidelity.

DistMovGen's balance between micro-level detail (finger articulation), macro-level emotional coherence (cross-modal alignment), and practical implementation (low-latency inference). These characteristics tackle certain limitations in existing methods, though our method also has constraints that will be discussed in the limitations section (Table 3).

Table 3. Performance Comparison with Dynamic Gesture Recognition Methods

Method	F1 Score	Latency (ms)	FPS (RTX 4090)	Dataset
DistMovGen (Ours)	0.92	8.2	122	HM3D
Diverse code [11]	0.86	15.7	89	HM3D
speech gesture generation [36]	0.88	11.3	95	HM3D

4.3 Qualitative Results

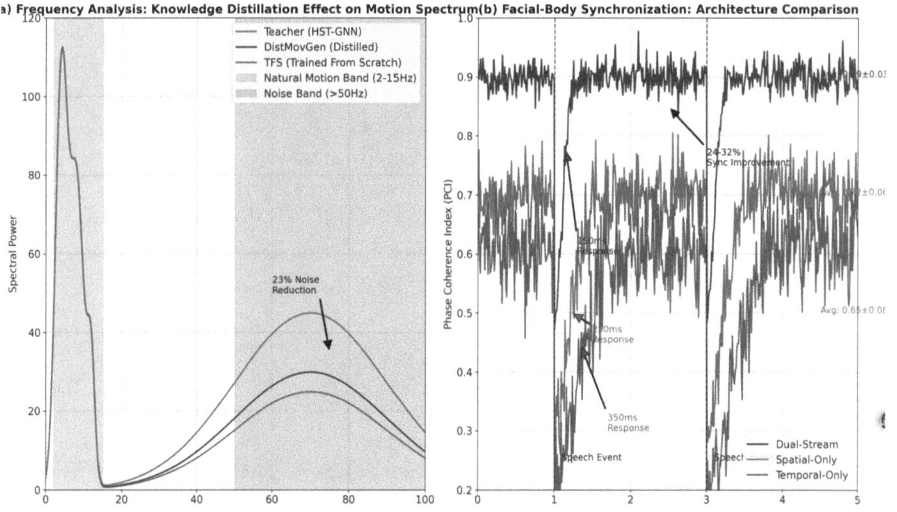

Fig. 5. FID feature space comparison.

Figure 5 shows the DistMovGen (student model) forms tighter, more separable clusters compared to baselines, indicating better preservation of emotion-specific motion patterns. Notably, the overlap between emotion clusters is reduced by 23% compared to the LSTM baseline, demonstrating improved discriminative capability. The teacher model (HST-GNN) shows similar clustering quality but with higher computational cost. The proximity between teacher and student distributions validates the effectiveness of our distillation strategy. The denser, more continuous clusters indicate that the distilled student model preserves the teacher's fine-grained temporal correlations while reducing noise, validating that the proposed distillation preserves realism and smoothness in motion synthesis. The student model effectively preserves fine-grained details like intricate hand gestures while maintaining smooth and continuous trajectories throughout the motion sequence. DistMovGen, on the other hand, demonstrates a more robust performance in motion quality and consistency, highlighting the effectiveness of the knowledge distillation process in enhancing the synthesis framework for virtual character motion generation in real-time applications.

Figure 5(a) illustrates the impact of knowledge distillation on the motion spectrum. The distilled model (DistMovGen, blue curve) shows a notable 23% reduction in noise within the high - frequency noise band (>50 Hz) compared to the model trained from scratch (TFS, red curve). Moreover, the spectrum of DistMovGen is much closer to that of the teacher model (HST - GNN, green curve), indicating that knowledge distillation effectively transfers the motion - related knowledge from the complex teacher model to the simpler distilled model, making the latter learn cleaner and more natural motion features concentrated in the natural motion band (2–15 Hz).

Figure 5(b) compares different architectures in terms of facial - body synchronization. The dual - stream architecture (blue curve) outperforms both the spatial - only (red curve) and temporal - only (green curve) architectures. It achieves a 24–32% improvement in synchronization and exhibits faster response times (with responses around 150 ms–200 ms) to speech events. This suggests that integrating both spatial and temporal information simultaneously is crucial for achieving high - quality facial - body synchronization.

Additionally, the Emotion Synchronization Score (ESS) reaches 0.87, indicating improved audio–motion coherence. These results confirm that the proposed distillation-enhanced architecture effectively balances real-time efficiency and perceptual realism.

5 Conclusion and Limitations

5.1 Major Contributions Summary

DistMovGen represents a significant advancement in virtual character motion generation by effectively bridging the gap between high-fidelity motion quality and real-time performance constraints. Leveraging knowledge distillation, the framework distills the superior motion generation capabilities of the teacher model HST-GNN into a lightweight architecture, achieving a remarkable 73% reduction in parameters and a 64% improvement in inference speed without sacrificing motion fidelity. The two-stage method, integrating feature alignment with kinematic constraints, enables the model to preserve fine-grained motion details, such as intricate finger gestures and facial micro-expressions, while ensuring smooth and continuous trajectories. Our extensive qualitative and quantitative evaluations, including comparisons with baseline models and state-of-the-art methods (SHOW, LDA), demonstrate DistMovGen's superiority in multiple aspects. It outperforms competitors in terms of visual quality, emotional expressiveness, and multimodal synchronization. In user studies, it achieved significantly higher scores in emotional arousal, naturalness, and immersion. The dual-stream architecture proves crucial for spatio-temporal consistency, while the intelligent voice processing unit effectively bridges the audio-motion modality gap, ensuring accurate lip-sync and beat alignment. These contributions make DistMovGen a promising solution for real-time applications like virtual reality, digital entertainment, and intelligent human-computer interaction.

5.2 Limitations

Despite its achievements, DistMovGen has several limitations. Firstly, the current model relies on a predefined set of motion templates and emotional expressions, which may limit its adaptability to highly specialized or rare scenarios. Although it performs well on common motion sequences, generating natural and accurate motions for highly complex or unique actions remains challenging.

Secondly, the effectiveness of the knowledge distillation process is highly dependent on the quality and representativeness of the teacher model. If the teacher model has biases or limitations in its training data, these may be transferred to the distilled model. Additionally, the current distillation strategy is static and may not be optimal for different types of motion or varying computational resources.

Finally, while the model performs well in handling standard multimodal inputs, it struggles with large-scale, highly diverse datasets. Handling extensive multimodal data significantly escalates computational costs and memory requirements, which may compromise real-time performance and scalability. Moreover, the system lacks comprehensive support for cross-cultural emotional expressions, which may lead to misunderstandings or ineffective communication in multicultural contexts.

5.3 Future Research Directions

To ensure the model's scalability with large-scale multimodal datasets, developing techniques that can reduce computational complexity is crucial. This might include exploring more efficient neural network architectures, such as sparse networks or dynamic routing mechanisms. Additionally, research into advanced data compression and feature extraction methods can help manage the large volume of data while preserving critical information. Federated learning methods could also be investigated to enable distributed training on diverse datasets without compromising data privacy.

Overall, enhancing the theoretical interpretability of motion diffusion and improving generalization to real-world multimodal environments will further strengthen the academic rigor and practical deployment value of the proposed system.

References

1. Alexanderson, S., et al.: Listen, denoise, action! audio-driven motion synthesis with diffusion models. ACM Trans. Graph. **42**(4), 1–20 (2023). https://doi.org/10.1145/3592458. ISSN 1557-7368
2. Andayani, F., et al.: Hybrid LSTM-transformer model for emotion recognition from speech audio files. IEEE Access **10**, 36018–36027 (2022)
3. Anthony, A.A., Patil, C.M.: Speech emotion recognition systems: a comprehensive review on different methodologies. Wirel. Pers. Commun. **130**(1), 515–525 (2023)
4. Ao, T.: Body of her: a preliminary study on end-to-end humanoid agent. arXiv preprint arXiv:2408.02879 (2024)
5. Ao, T., Zhang, Z., Liu, L.: GestureDiffuCLIP: gesture diffusion model with CLIP latents. ACM Trans. Graph. (2023). https://doi.org/10.1145/3592097
6. Baevski, A., et al.: wav2vec 2.0: a framework for self-supervised learning of speech representations (2020). arXiv:2006.11477 [cs.CL]
7. Baird, A., et al.: The ICML 2022 expressive vocalizations workshop and competition: recognizing, generating, and personalizing vocal bursts. arXiv preprint arXiv:2205.01780 (2022)
8. Dabral, R., et al.: Mofusion: a framework for denoising-diffusion- based motion synthesis. In: Proceedings of the IEEE/CVF Conference on Computer Vision and Pattern Recognition (CVPR), pp. 9760–9770 (2023)
9. Dai, W., et al.: Motionlcm: real-time controllable motion generation via latent consistency model. In: European Conference on Computer Vision, pp. 390–408. Springer, Cham (2024)
10. Favali, F., et al.: TAG2G: a diffusion-based approach to interlocutor- aware co-speech gesture generation. Electronics **13**(17), 3364 (2024)
11. Gu, C., Kuriyama, S., Hotta, K.: Diverse code query learning for speech-driven facial animation. arXiv:2409.19143 (2024)
12. Guo, C., et al.: Generating diverse and natural 3D human motions from text. In: Proceedings of the IEEE/CVF Conference on Computer Vision and Pattern Recognition (CVPR), pp. 5152–5161 (2022)
13. Han, K., et al.: A survey on vision transformer. IEEE Trans. Pattern Anal. Mach. Intell. **45**(1), 87–110 (2022)
14. Hinton, G., Vinyals, O., Dean, J.: Distilling the knowledge in a neural network. arXiv preprint arXiv:1503.02531 (2015)
15. Huang, C.-C., Nguyen, M.H.: Robust 3D skeleton tracking based on openpose and a probabilistic tracking framework. In: 2019 IEEE International Conference on Systems, Man and Cybernetics (SMC), pp. 4107–4112. IEEE (2019)
16. Kim, J., et al.: A brand new dance partner: music-conditioned pluralistic dancing controlled by multiple dance genres. In: Proceedings of the IEEE/CVF Conference on Computer Vision and Pattern Recognition, pp. 3490–3500 (2022)
17. Kovar, L., Gleicher, M., Pighin, F.: Motion graphs. In: Seminal Graphics Papers: Pushing the Boundaries, vol. 2, 1st edn. Association for Computing Machinery, New York (2023). https://doi.org/10.1145/3596711.3596788. ISBN 9798400708978

18. Liang, H., et al.: Intergen: diffusion-based multi-human motion generation under complex interactions. Int. J. Comput. Vis. **132**(9), 3463–3483 (2024)
19. Lin, S., Wang, A., Yang, X.: SDXL-lightning: progressive adversarial diffusion distillation (2024). arXiv:2402.13929 [cs.CV]
20. Liu, H., et al.: DisCo: disentangled implicit content and rhythm learning for diverse co-speech gestures synthesis. In: Proceedings of the 30th ACM International Conference on Multimedia, pp. 3764–3773 (2022)
21. Ma, H., et al.: Multi-objective diverse human motion prediction with knowledge distillation. In: Proceedings of the IEEE/CVF Conference on Computer Vision and Pattern Recognition, pp. 8161–8171 (2022)
22. Mor, B., Garhwal, S., Kumar, A.: A systematic review of hidden Markov models and their applications. Arch. Comput. Methods Eng. **28**, 1429–1448 (2021)
23. Mughal, M.H., et al.: ConvoFusion: multi-modal conversational diffusion for co-speech gesture synthesis. In: Proceedings of the IEEE/CVF Conference on Computer Vision and Pattern Recognition, pp. 1388–1398 (2024)
24. Ng, E., et al.: From audio to photoreal embodiment: synthesizing humans in conversations. In: Proceedings of the IEEE/CVF Conference on Computer Vision and Pattern Recognition, pp. 1001–1010 (2024)
25. Plappert, M., Mandery, C., Asfour, T.: The KIT motion-language dataset. Big Data **4**(4), 236–252 (2016). https://doi.org/10.1089/big.2016.0028. ISSN 2167-647X
26. Sauer, A., et al.: Adversarial diffusion distillation (2023). arXiv:2311.17042 [cs.CV]
27. Li, S., et al.: Bailando: 3D dance generation by actor-critic GPT with choreographic memory. In: Proceedings of the IEEE/CVF Conference on Computer Vision and Pattern Recognition, pp. 11050–11059 (2022)
28. Tao, H., et al.: Neural motion graph. In: SIGGRAPH Asia 2023 Conference Papers, SA 2023. Association for Computing Machinery, Sydney, NSW, Australia (2023). https://doi.org/10.1145/3610548.3618181. ISBN 9798400703157
29. Tevet, G., et al.: Human motion diffusion model (2022). arXiv:2209.14916 [cs.CV]
30. Tian, L., et al.: EMO2: end-effector guided audio-driven avatar video generation (2025). arXiv:2501.10687 [cs.CV]
31. Tsai, Y.-H.H., et al.: Multimodal transformer for unaligned multimodal language sequences (2019). arXiv:1906.00295 [cs.CL]
32. Wang, Y., et al.: MotionGPT-2: a general-purpose motion-language model for motion generation and understanding (2024). arXiv:2410.21747 [cs.CV]
33. Xing, W., et al.: Hybrid motion graph for character motion synthesis. J. Vis. Lang. Comput. **25**(1), 20–32 (2014). https://doi.org/10.1016/j.jvlc.2013.10.001. ISSN 1045-926X
34. Xu, S., Wang, Y.-X., Gui, L., et al.: Interdreamer: zero-shot text to 3D dynamic human-object interaction. In: Advances in Neural Information Processing Systems, vol. 37, pp. 52858–52890 (2024)
35. Yi, H., et al.: Generating holistic 3D human motion from speech (2023). arXiv:2212.04420 [cs.CV]
36. Yoon, Y., et al.: Speech gesture generation from the trimodal context of text, audio, and speaker identity. ACM Trans. Graph. (TOG) **39**(6), 1–16 (2020)
37. Zhang, S., et al.: Deep learning-based multimodal emotion recognition from audio, visual, and text modalities: a systematic review of recent advancements and future prospects. Expert Syst. Appl. **237**, 121692 (2024)

WireSculptor: Interactive Guided Bending Workflow for Novice-Friendly Wire Sculpture Fabrication

Runze Xue, Fei Yu, Baohang Zhou, Jialu Wang, Fan Zhong, Qiong Zeng, and Haisen Zhao(✉)

Shandong University, 72 Binhai Highway, Qingdao, China
{zhongfan,qiong.zn,haisenzhao}@sdu.edu.cn

Abstract. This paper presents WireSculptor, an innovative interactive system designed to enable novices to create complex wire sculptures through an interactive guided bending workflow. In wire structure fabrication, manual bending offers flexibility in shaping intricate forms but is mainly suitable for experienced experts. To bridge this gap for novices, we construct a closed-loop guided bending workflow, which organically combines a visualization module for presenting precomputed bending instructions, and a bending error checker module for real-time error detection and feedback. To seek the most comfortable and effective bending setups for beginners, we apply a formative study on novices' bending operations, where we test different bending settings to see how they affect the forming quality and time novices take. Leveraging formative study findings, we craft bending instructions with a coarse-to-fine approach. First, users bend large-scale wire units segmented by bending points of salient curvature change. Following this, they make precise adjustments guided by instructions from a graph-cut-based line-circular segment fitting method. Technical evaluations demonstrate that most first-time users achieve higher accuracy when guided by our method compared to the unguided methods, all while preserving artistic expressiveness. Furthermore, several application areas have been explored in greater depth, namely artistic fonts, line art, and the physicalization of children's line drawing.

Keywords: Wire sculpture · wire fabrication · interactive guidance

1 Introduction

Wire sculpture involves crafting sculptures using wire, with roots in 2nd Dynasty Egypt and the Bronze and Iron Ages in Europe [27]. Today, wire sculpture remains of great significance in various modern contexts, spanning artistic creation, industrial design, handicraft education, and kinetic art installations [40].

R. Xue and F. Yu—Equal contribution.

A. Hinkenjan et al. (Eds.): ICXR 2025, LNCS 16428, pp. 72–99, 2026.
https://doi.org/10.1007/978-981-95-7195-6_5

While manual bending offers artistic flexibility for intricate wire shapes but challenges novices due to limited spatial cues, requiring substantial time and practice to master [31]. Another potential challenge is that this manual process may be error-prone, discouraging artists, especially novices, to shape their ideas with the wire sculpturing. Conversely, automated machines bending offers high precision for industrial applications, it struggles to achieve the geometric complexity and artistic flexibility inherent in manual freehand bending [2]. Furthermore, hybrid approaches, like [41], integrates both strategies by adjusting the target shape to be collision-free for the wire bending machine and then having a human revert it to the target. However, such automated wire bending machines are not easy to afford for a novice users. This paper focuses on empowering *novices* to create wire sculptures with complex geometric features through manual bending. It aims to address the critical gap in guided workflows tailored to their needs in the specific applications. These applications range from creating prototypes of artistic fonts and line arts, to crafting Cloisonné works, and even physicalizing children's line drawings, as depicted in Fig. 2.

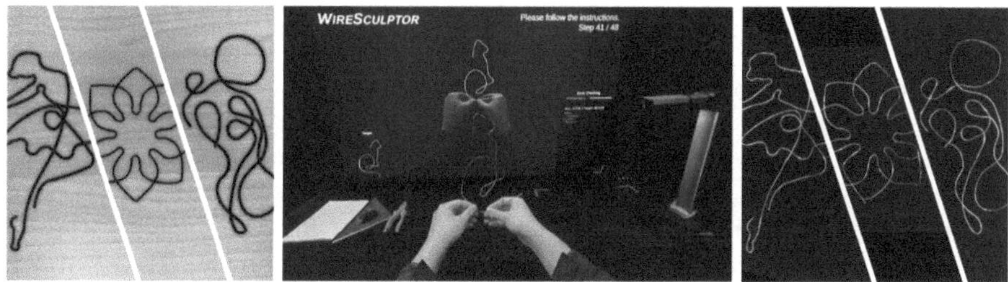

Fig. 1. For the input single-line wire sculptures (left), novice users utilize the proposed WireSculptor system to perform bending operations. The figure on the right demonstrates the resulting fabricated sculptures.

The unique material characteristics of metal wire, including high elasticity and easy deformability, pose significant challenges for manual manipulation due to the inherent complexity and precision required [14]. Existing manual bending workflows rely heavily on expert intuition. Skilled practitioners optimize bending sequences by balancing global structural planning with local precision, leveraging years of experience for mature craftsmanship [13]. Novices, however, often lack such holistic understanding, resorting to trial-and-error approaches and various physical aids for manually aligning. These assistive tools may include 2D paper blueprints [43], or 3D-printed jigs that allow users to wind the wire into the preset cavity channels [19,31,32]. While these methods can enhance the rigid geometric accuracy of wire sculptures with relatively low geometric complexity, they still pose challenges when it comes to wire shapes with a lot of geometric details or many self-intersections [43]. This is because the physical assistance they provide becomes a limiting factor for novices, where it's hard for the novices to determine a feasible bending sequence. These methods fall short of offering clear, step-by-step guidance. As a result, novices lack support in crucial decision-making areas such as step sequencing and error rectification. Moreover, it is extremely challenging for novices to learn from a wire-bending expert, as such experts are rare and often difficult to access (Fig. 1).

Fig. 2. Wire sculptures: Word art wire, 3D Ballerina art, parent-child activities, Cloisonne. [10,16,41].

To tackle the issue of novice wire sculptors lacking sufficient guidance, we aim to further amplify guidance with a step-by-step visual instruction guided bending workflow for novices. As far as we know, the existing research work in this regard is still in its preliminary stage. Interactive guidance based on mixed reality [11] has proven transformative in domains like assembly tasks [37] and training for construction works [28] and team sports [6], yet remains scarcely explored for wire sculpture fabrication via bending operations [8]. We identified Dong et al. [8]'s study as the most relevant to our work, where they introduce ARAWTS, an AR-aided wire-bending training framework for orthodontics. It presents four standard training exercises and delivers feedback and improvement suggestions through gesture recognition [8]. However, ARAWTS is mainly oriented towards specific bending operations in orthodontic treatment and does not generate sequential guidance for arbitrary wire shapes.

To bridge this research gap of providing an interactive guided bending workflow, our key design philosophy prioritizes guiding novice operators through each step of the bending process. In this paper, we propose two fundamental bending operations: the *bend* operation for creating line segments and the *curve* operation for forming circular segments. To learn the novice users' technical limitations and preferences, we conduct a formative study to identify optimal bending configurations by examining how different parameters (such as the length of line segment, length of circular segment) influence both forming quality and operational efficiency. Building on these findings, we propose **WireSculptor**, a closed-loop guided bending workflow (illustrated in Fig. 4), with the following key capabilities:

- a dual-scale decomposition approach using a coarse-to-fine strategy: the input wire is first divided at points of salient curvature change for users to shape

large wire units; in the fine level, a graph-cut algorithm fits line-circular segments to assist users in refining wire bends accurately.
- a visualization module simultaneously presents wire deformation and hand-posture animations during each bending operation. These animations are rendered at a scale identical to the physical setup, ensuring accurate and intuitive guidance.
- a real-time quality detection module, highlighting inaccuracies in the wire with visual feedback to enable quick error identification and rectification. Additionally, it determines whether the user can advance to the next step based on the accuracy assessment.

Our main contribution is WireSculptor, the first guided bending workflow that empowers novices to fabricate intricate wire sculptures through step-by-step visual guidance and real-time error correction. Unlike traditional unguided approaches, in our experiment, we demonstrate its versatility through four application domains: artistic fonts, line art, wire-wrapped jewelry, and physicalized children's drawings. In the comparison, WireSculptor enables that most participants to bend wire sculptures with higher accuracy compared to two unguided approaches (static blueprints and jig-based assisted method). Furthermore, we demonstrate that WireSculptor is flexible to support diverse creative use cases, including artistic fonts, line art, and the physicalization of children's line drawing. WireSculptor's key contribution to HCI is demonstrating that an interactive guided strategy benefits novices in sculpture fabrication. Its system design also inspires other similar applications.

2 Related Work

2.1 Manual Wire Bending Techniques

Traditionally, manual wire bending has depended on skilled artisans' intuitive control of force and spatial reasoning [13], posing challenges for novices due to the absence of spatial and structural indicators [46]. To assist novices, researchers have developed various physical aids ranging from 2D templates [43] to 3D assistive devices, which are well designed for specific wire shapes and fabricated using 3D printing techniques. Garg et al. [15] create a 3D scaffold through laser cutting to assist the manual bending process of wire mesh. Iarussi et al. [19] produce physical jigs by extruding support walls from 2D jewelry drawings to guide wire wrapping operations. Torres et al. [32] propose ProxyPrint, a fabrication and construction proxy that enables a high-fidelity wire bending process. Wang et al. [29] propose FlexTruss with a construction pipeline to assemble truss-shaped objects by threading. [39] generate surface grooves on 3D models to serve as wire molds. More recently, Toji et al. [31] produce 3D-printed jigs for guiding the fabrication of multi-view wire art by humans.

While existing methods assist the manual bending process by providing spatial constraints, allowing novices to wrap wires around physical assistive devices, their utility diminishes significantly for complex shapes. As the target geometry grows intricate, these assistive structures themselves become increasingly elaborate, introducing new cognitive burdens: novices must not only navigate the device's physical complexity but also deduce operation sequences autonomously. Conversely, WireSculptor's intention is to assist novices at each step of the wire bending process.

2.2 Automated and Hybrid Bending Systems

In addition to manual methods, wire-bending machines for automatic bending [2], are extensively utilized in the industrial production of structural wire products. This includes elastically deforming wire structures that act as the skeletons for kinetic wire figures, as described in [24,42]. However, manufacturing most complex wire sculptures, especially those with many self-intersections, directly using wire bending machines poses challenges. Thus, the hybrid strategy combining machine and human wire bending techniques has been suggested: 1) a "decompose-then-assemble" strategy: first split the complex wire sculpture into fabricable sub-wires (planar rods [26] or Eulerian wires [3,23]), then manually assemble them into the final wire sculpture. 2) a "machine-then-human-bending" strategy with two bending stages is proposed in [41]. In the machine-bending stage, the wire bending machine realizes the deformed wire to ensure a collision-free CNC bending process. In the human-bending stage, with human assistance, the deformed wire is bent back to the target shape.

The mentioned automatic bending techniques produce rigid commands while considering the constraints of wire bending machines. Among the hybrid techniques featuring a manually-operated stage, there is a lack of step-by-step dynamic guidance during the human operation process. In contrast, WireSculptor guides novices through the bending steps, considering their skillset and preferences, where we perform an empirical study on novices' bending operations.

2.3 Guidance Assisted Fabrication

Guided workflows play a crucial role in enabling novices to acquire skills in the realm of crafts. Interactive guidance based on mixed reality [11] or online video parsing [37] has demonstrated its revolutionary impact in various fields, including, construction work training [28], team sports [6], rapid prototyping of breadboarded circuits [21], and active assembly [18,37]. For the design and fabrication of wire sculpture, mixed reality technologies have been applied. Examples include Pen2VR [22] and Y-AR [12], two mixed-reality systems for wire art design using a VR controller or hand gestures. WireDraw [46] is an augmented reality system for 3D wire object drawing with a 3D extruder pen. Except for ARAWTS [8], such interactive guidance techniques have rarely been applied to manual bending-based wire sculpture fabrication. ARAWTS uses AR to guide wire bending for dental applications, focusing on gesture recognition and error feedback. However, it is tailored to specific orthodontic wire types and lacks support to generate sequential guidance for arbitrary shapes. To address the above issue, we aim to further enhance the guidance through an interactive guided bending workflow tailored for novices.

2.4 Guidance Workflow Planning

This section presents related works on guidance fabrication workflow planning methods to assist human manual operation. Miguel et al. compute the stability-aware assembly sequence to assemble a set of planar-rod wire contours into a single one [26]. Yu et al. propose LineUp, which generates a collision-free physical transformation motion to guide users in converting a single-line structure into a 3D model [45]. Liu et al. presents a motion planner algorithm for the robot arm to collaborate with a wire-bending machine to perform 3D metal wire curving [25]. Wang et al. propose an integrated design, simulation, and fabrication workflow for self-morphing electronics [38]. Yu et al. develop a process for crafting customizable interactive textiles [44]. For the guided bending workflow planning, Yang et al. [43] breaks a single-line 3D wire shape into near-planar segments, which can be printed into a set of blueprints to guide manual work. Wu et al. first decompose the input wire into a sequence of fabricable bending segments that comply with machine constraints [41], and then generate G-code bending commands for the wire-bending machine. During the manual bending stage, they do not provide specific instructions for users to bend the tuned points to the specified angles.

In conclusion, while prior work has explored manual aids and automated systems, no existing solution provides a closed-loop guided bending workflow that: 1) simplifies wire sculpture shapes into novice-friendly bending operations, 2) delivers sequential interactive guidance, and 3) provides real-time error correction. WireSculptor fills this research gap by combining algorithmic wire decomposition, interactive guidance of animated bending instructions, and feedback mechanisms, enabling novices to create intricate wire sculptures with unprecedented efficiency.

3 Design Exploration

Our core research question is how to design a wire sculpture system that effectively guides novice users in performing bending operations. To address this, we first summarize our design goals and then present our design framework.

3.1 Design Goals

The aim of wire sculpture guidance is to enhance novice users' quality and efficiency during the wire bending workflow. Based on literature review and informal semi-structured interviews with two artists, we identified three design goals:

- **D1. Provide novice-friendly instructions.** As our workflow is intended for novice users, the system should decompose complex wire sculpture designs

into a sequence of simple, manageable steps. Each instruction should be easy to follow and executable with minimal prior experience or training. One of the artists we interviewed pointed out that "I can naturally come up with each subsequent step, but this might be hard for beginners." And another artist pointed out that "Novices often fail to organize global structural planning. But global structural planning remains critical for wire sculptures."
- **D2. Introduce step-by-step guidance via animations.** To help users stay aligned with the design intent and track their progress, the system should incorporate animated visual guidance—such as illustrating the bending process—and highlight the correspondence between each bending operation and the intended target shape. One of the artists we interviewed pointed out that "Novices lack of the ability to observe". And another artist pointed out that "It would be beneficial for beginners to have mentor for teaching handcrafts step-by-step."
- **D3. Present intuitive quality evaluations**. The system should offer real-time, easy-to-understand feedback to help users detect and correct bending inaccuracies. For example, visual cues and performance metrics could be applied to guide users in refining their operations and improving overall fabrication quality. The artist pointed out that "I can't complete my handcrafts without iteratively tuning it according to the goal in my mind."

3.2 Design Framework

Motivated by the design goals identified above, we propose an interactive wire sculpture workflow specifically tailored for novice users. We structure the workflow design around four key aspects. First, we examine and explore fundamental parameter configurations in the human bending process. Next, we derive novice-friendly and executable fabrication instructions from a complex design. Following this, we identify the essential elements for effective guidance visualization and interactive feedback. Together, these components support novice users in sculpting wire structures step by step with improved accuracy and confidence.

Aspect 1: Human Bending Model. A core component of our workflow is a human bending model that captures how novice users perform wire bending under different bending configurations, which is essential for informing the design of fabrication instructions that are both executable and novice-friendly. To construct this model, we first conducted a formative study that systematically evaluated the effects of bending radius and angle on two key performance metrics: bending accuracy and time cost. By analyzing the collected data, we built predictive models that estimate user performance across various radius–angle combinations. These models are fundamental to generating novice-friendly instructions for fabrication steps that minimize error while maximize efficiency.

Aspect 2: Novice-Friendly Instructions. Novice-friendly instructions refer to a sequence of wire bending operations that are automatically translated from an input design. To generate these instructions, we adopt a dual-scale decomposition approach to divide the input wire, which transforms the original design into multi-level geometric primitives (coarse: large wire units; fine: line-circular segments), enabling a quick coarse-to-fine bending operation.

Aspect 3: Augmented Guidance. Augmented visualization provides intuitive, real-time guidance by overlaying key cues—such as bend angles, directions, and sequence—onto a 3D virtual wire model. This visualization module guides novices through the fabrication process by presenting precomputed bending instructions in an interactive and spatially meaningful way. Users align their physical operations with the animated guide, which serves as a dynamic scaffold that supports step-by-step execution.

Aspect 4: Intuitive Feedback. Timely feedback is critical for preventing error accumulation during step-by-step wire fabrication. To address this need, we introduce a bending quality detection module that provides real-time error detection and corrective feedback. This lightweight mechanism continuously monitors deviations between the user's current bending result and the ground-truth geometry. When discrepancies are detected, the system issues intuitive alerts through color-coded visual overlays and concise textual prompts. These feedback cues help users quickly identify and correct errors.

4 Human Bending Model

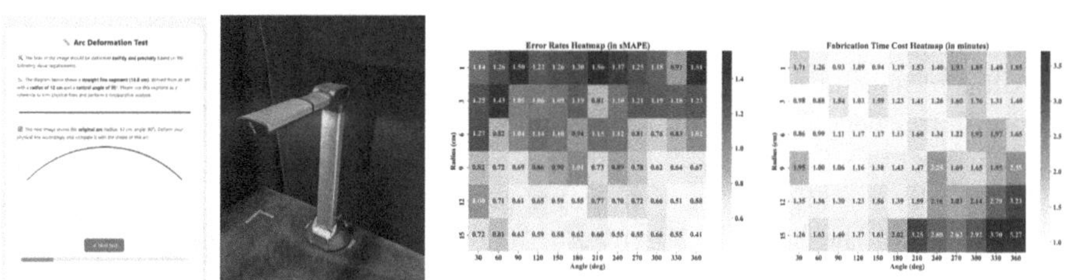

(a) Web-based Interface (b) Photographic Apparatus (c) Error Rates Heatmap The lower the better. (d) Time Cost Heatmap The lower the better.

Fig. 3. An overview of the setups and results of our formative study. (a) The web-based interface to provide instructions for participants, with an example stimulus. (b) The high-speed photographic apparatus we used to capture the manually-bent curves. (c)–(d) The results of our formative study. Results demonstrate that larger radius and angle lead to lower error rates, while ultimate radius ($\geq$12 cm) and angle ($\geq$180°) lead to sharp increase in the fabrication time cost.

We aim to construct a human bending model that can identify optimal bending configurations for achieving high-quality and high-efficiency, novice-friendly operations. To this end, we first explore the research question: *how the accuracy and time cost for novice users to bend a simple wire segment under different bending radii and angles?* This question guided the design of a formative study to collect bending data from human subjects and to build a fitting model that interpolates between the tested values, enabling generalization across different combinations of bending radii and angles.

Table 1. The analysis result of the effects of bending radius and angle on error rates and time cost, using the ANOVA method. All P values < 0.05, indicating that both bending radius and angle show significant effects on both error rates and time cost. *: $p < 0.05$, **: $p < 0.01$, ***: $p < 0.001$.

Factor	Error Rates		Time	
	F	p	F	p
Radius	152.85	***	127.11	***
Angle	4.97	*	168.94	***

4.1 Formative Study

We conducted a formative study using a two-factor mixed design to examine the effects of bending radii and angles on the error rates and time costs of human bending operations. The two factors in the study are bending radius and bending angle, with a between-subjects design for bending radius and a within-subjects design for bending angle. Participants were required to bend a straight wire according to specific bending radii and angles. To mitigate learning effects, the presentation order of stimuli was randomized. The primary dependent variables were the quality of the bent wire, measured as the symmetric mean absolute percentage error (sMAPE) and the corresponding ground truth arc curves, and the time cost of the bending operation.

Stimuli. To simplify the bending curve and facilitate analysis, we generated a set of arc curves with varying bending radii and angles. Specifically, we defined the bending radius as the curvature radius of the arc, which was set to 1 and $3 \times n$ $(n = 1, 2, ..., 5)$, with the unit of centimeters. We measured the bending angle using the central angle of the arc, which was set to values $30 \times m$ $(m = 1, 2, \cdots, 12)$ with the unit of degree. In total, we generated a dataset of 72 unique visual stimuli. An example of our stimulus, along with the study interface, is shown in Fig. 3(a).

Participants. We recruited 24 participants with no prior experience in wire sculpture from the local university, majoring in computer science, law, economics, cryptography, and electric engineering. The sample size was determined based on an anticipated effect size of 0.8 and a statistical power of 0.7, equal to the minimum requirement of 12 participants (2 groups × 12 participants). Participant demographics included 17 males and 7 females, aged 18 to 25 years. Each participant was compensated approximately 10.32 dollars for their time, with an average task completion time of 75 min.

Tasks. Each participant was required to bend lines to replicate the shape of an arc curve displayed on the screen as accurately and quickly as possible. For each trial, we recorded the participant's bent curve along with the time taken to complete the task. The manually bent curves were captured using a high-speed photographic apparatus (see Fig. 3(b)).

Procedure. The experiment consisted of three phases. Participants began with a training phase involving three trials. They then proceeded to the line bending phase, which consisted of 36 trials, with a five-minute rest after completing the first 18 trials. After each trial, participants were required to place their bent curve under the photographic apparatus and capture a photo. The stimuli were randomized to minimize ordering and learning effects. Finally, participants completed a demographic information questionnaire. All phases of the experiment were conducted in a controlled, well-lit room, with participants seated approximately 55 cm from a screen with a resolution of 3840 × 1080 pixels.

Collected Data. We retained all data from the participants, resulting in a total of 864 trials. For each combination of bending radius and angle in a trial, we computed the sMAPE and time cost for each participant. Results are shown in Fig. 3(c)–(d).

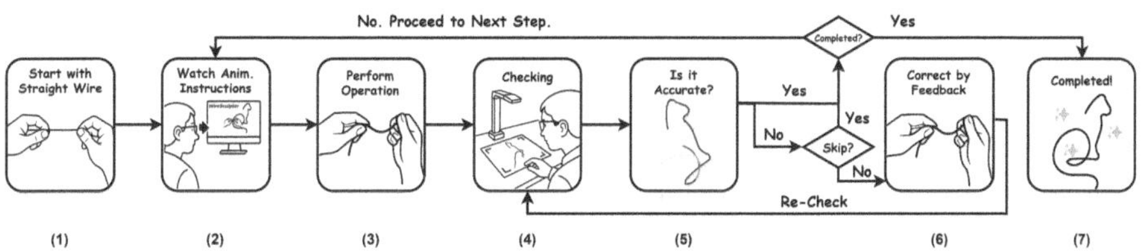

Fig. 4. The overview of our workflow. By watching the animated visualization and follow the instructions (2), the user perform operation (3) to deform the wire in order to fabricate the wire sculpture (7). Along with this process, the real-time error checker with feedback enables the user to make corrections (4)–(6).

4.2 Analysis and Model Construction

Based on the collected data from the user study, we first analyzed the impact of bending radius and angle on error rates and time costs during the bending process, using the ANOVA method. As shown in Table 1, we found significant effects of bending radius and angle on both error rates and time costs.

To construct the human bending models, we begin with two radius–angle metric tables representing error rates and time costs for specific combinations of radius r and angle θ, denoted as $T_e(r,\theta)$ and $T_t(r,\theta)$, respectively. In both tables, rows correspond to bending radii, columns correspond to bending angles, and each cell contains the average sMAPE in T_e or average time costs in T_t. Figure 3(b) presents the averaged error rates (denoted as sMAPE) and time costs. We model both the error rates and time costs for an arbitrary combination of radius and angle using bilinear interpolation [7], which preserves trends and captures smooth transitions across radius-angle values and supports estimation for general combinations.

4.3 Findings

Overall, our results show statistically significant impacts of both bending radii and angles on both error rates and time costs during the bending processes. Based on our statistical analysis and models, we summarize the key findings of the human bending model:

- **Effect of bending radius.** Error rates decrease as the bending radius increases. Sharper curves (i.e., smaller radii) introduce greater difficulty for novice users, resulting in higher error rates.
- **Effect of bending angle.** Error rates decrease as the bending angle increases. However, when the bending radius $\geq$12 cm and the bending angle beyond 180°, the fabrication time cost will sharply increase as the angle increases, where the bending path becomes substantially longer. We find that moderate angles ($60° \sim 120°$) tend to yield lower error rates without causing significant time costs.
- **Novice-friendly design.** We recommend avoiding combinations of small radii and large angles when designing novice-friendly tasks. Wire sculptures can be optimized with radii larger than 6 cm and angles smaller than 120° to maximize accuracy and efficiency.

5 Wire Sculptor

5.1 Workflow Overview

We first provide an overview of the proposed interactive guided bending workflow, which is illustrated in Fig. 4. Given a wire fabrication task, the system first coarsely decomposes the wire design into salient structural units, then finely fits each unit with simple line-circular segments, thus generating novice-friendly instructions with human bending model (Sect. 4) accordingly. Thereafter, animated visualization guides novices through the fabrication process by presenting these instructions. Along with this process, interactive real-time error checking and feedback are provided.

From the user's perspective, in one fabrication task, the user gradually deforms a straight wire into the final desired sculpture by repeating the following closed-loop steps:

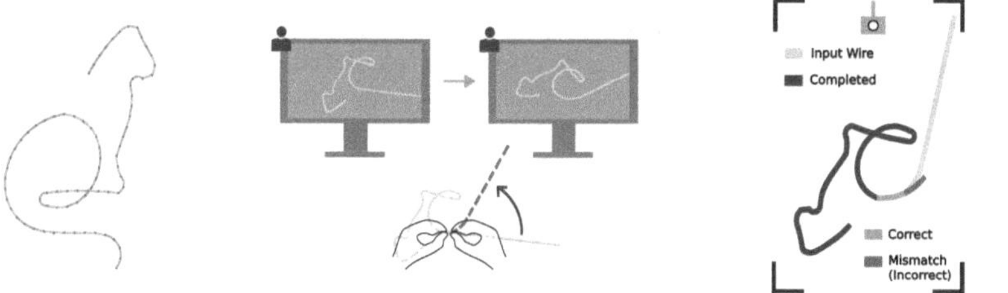

(a) Wire Decomposition (b) Animated Visualization (c) Real-Time Error Checker

Fig. 5. The overview of our modules. Given an wire design as input, we first divide it into a coarse-to-fine bending segments (a). Subsequently, we generate an animated visualization guide for each fabrication step for guidance, demonstrating the operations required (b). Within each operation, an error checker (d) is utilized to check the current progress and provide visual feedback by highlighting inaccuracies.

1. The user starts with a straight piece of wire (Fig. 4(1)).
2. The user watches an animated novice-friendly instruction that demonstrates how to perform a small, localized fabrication operation (Fig. 4(2)).
3. The user then freely performs the operation using any tools or hand techniques they prefer (Fig. 4(3)).
4. At any time during or after the operation, the user can place the wire under the high-speed photographic apparatus to receive feedback (Fig. 4(4)).
5. The workflow automatically checks the accuracy of the current progress (Fig. 4(5)).
   (a) If the progress is sufficiently accurate, the workflow proceeds to the next step (proceeding to step (2)), or reports that all instructions are finished (proceeding to step (7)).
   (b) If inaccuracies are detected, the system highlights the inaccurate regions in an overlaid image, enabling users to easily identify and rectify the issues, then the workflow proceeds to step (6). Alternatively, the user could interactively skip to next step (proceeding to step (2)).
6. The user freely correct the wire sculpture based on the highlighted inaccurate region. At any point during the correction process, the workflow can transition to step (4).
7. If all instructions are finished, the overall fabrication is completed.

We propose three central modules that collaboratively drive the *WireSculptor* workflow, enabling a guided fabrication experience, as shown in Fig. 5:

- **Wire Decomposition**. This module includes a dual-scale decomposition approach to divide the input wire into coarse-to-fine bending segments, enabling generation of structured wire bending instructions.
- **Animated Visualization**. For each step, we generate an animated guide that visually demonstrates the operation required, aiding user comprehension and execution.

- **Real-Time Error Checker.** Within each operation, the system captures images of the current progress and evaluates its alignment with the target, offering visual feedback to assist users in correction.

5.2 Module 1: Wire Decomposition

(a) Input Design (b) Salient Structual Units Decomposition(c) Line-Circular Segments

Fig. 6. The process of our dual-scale wire decomposition. Given a vector graphic as input design (a), we first decompose it into salient structural units (b)–(c). Thereafter, for each unit, we fit it with simple line-circular segments (d). These line-circular segments and units will be utilized in the generation of animated visualization.

This module decomposes complex wire designs in a coarse-to-fine manner, serving as a basis for generating animated wire bending instructions in Sect. 5.3. It employs a dual-scale decomposition approach. Given an input wire design, the dual-scale decomposition approach first decompose it into several salient structural units $\{U_0, U_1, \cdots\}$, and subsequently fit each unit U_i with a sequence of simple line-circular segments $S^{\text{final}} = \{s_0{}^{\text{final}}, s_1{}^{\text{final}}, \cdots\}$. As illustrated in Fig. 6, this dual-scale decomposition approach involves *coarse-level: unit wire decomposition* and *fine-level: graph-cut-based segment fitting.*

Coarse-Level: Unit Wire Decomposition. Given a vector graphic of the wire design as input, the dual-scale decomposition approach aims to divide it into a sequence of units $\{U_0, U_1, \cdots\}$ at points of salient curvature change for users to shape large wire units. First, uniformly sample a sequence of points along the input wire. Then, compute the tangent line at each sampling point, which can be readily converted into a planar angle between the tangent line and the coordinate axis. Starting from one end of these sampling points, a traversal process is executed along the wire to generate each segment U_i with two criteria: 1) a total length is less than 10 cm or 2) the cumulative amount of planar angle change is less than 120°.

Fine-Level: Graph-Cut-Based Segment Fitting. At the fine level, each unit is broken down into line-circular segments to assist users in applying the bending operations and to refine wire bends accurately. We adapt a graph-cut based segment fitting technique originally proposed in [41] for a wire bending machine. This adaptation is feasible because, as shown in [2], the interpolated bending strategy can realize line-segments, and the strike bending strategy can realize circular segments. These two types of bending segments are also essential for novice users. The graph-cut based segment fitting technique starts with generating candidate line-circular segments from each sampling point of a single line curve through a *forward-and-backward traverse* and a line-circular fitting procedure; these produced line-circular segments often overlap, so a graph-cut decomposition helps resolve the overlaps.

In our case, we generate candidate line-circular segments $S^{\text{cand}} = \{s_0{}^{\text{cand}}, s_1{}^{\text{cand}}, \cdots\}$ similarly but make a key change in the second step for resolving overlaps, with the consideration of these findings from Sect. 4. For each unit U_i, we construct a graph $G = (V, E, L)$. Assuming that the unit U_i contains $n+2$ sampling points $P = \{p_0, p_1, \cdots, p_{n+1}\}$, the vertex set V represents a segment set $S^{\text{init}} = \{s_0{}^{\text{init}}, s_1{}^{\text{init}}, \cdots, s_n{}^{\text{init}}\}$, where for each segment $s_i{}^{\text{init}}$, it linearly connects two adjacent points p_i, p_{i+1}. The edge set E is the sampling points P, where each $p_i \in P$ connects segments $s_i{}^{\text{init}}$ and $s_{i+1}{}^{\text{init}}$. For each vertex $s_i{}^{\text{init}} \in S^{\text{init}}$, we aim to allocate a candidate line-circular segment $l_i = s_j{}^{\text{cand}}$ as its label. Our goal is to find an allocation $L = \{l_0, \cdots, l_n\}$ that minimizes the loss term $\mathcal{L}$, which is defined by:

$$\mathcal{L} = \sum_{i=0}^{n} \mathcal{L}_{\text{d}}(s_i{}^{\text{init}}, l_i) + \sum_{i=0}^{n-1} \mathcal{L}_{\text{sm}}(l_i, l_{i+1}) + \mathcal{L}_{\min}(L). \tag{1}$$

$\mathcal{L}_{\text{d}}$ denotes the data term measuring the cost of allocating l_i for $s_i{}^{\text{init}}$ and is defined by:

$$\mathcal{L}_{\text{d}}(s_i{}^{\text{init}}, l_i) = \begin{cases} \lambda_1 \cdot \mathcal{E}\left(l_i; \{s_i{}^{\text{init}}\}\right) \cdot \left(1 + \frac{e(l_i)}{2}\right)^{\lambda_2} & s_i{}^{\text{init}} \text{ in } l_i \\ \infty & \text{otherwise} \end{cases}, \tag{2}$$

where $\mathcal{E}$ denotes the maximum Euclidean distance between l_i and all $s_i{}^{\text{init}}$ covered. λ_1, λ_2 are hyper-parameters, and e denotes the difficulty of novice fabrication, which is calculated via interpolation on a lookup table filled with our formative study data. $e(l_i)$ is defined by:

$$e(l_i) = \begin{cases} \text{interp}\left(T_e; r(l_i), \theta(l_i)\right) & l_i \text{ is a circular segment} \\ 0 & \text{otherwise} \end{cases}, \tag{3}$$

where $r(l_i), \theta(l_i)$ denote the curvature radius and angle of the circular segment l_i, and $\text{interp}\left(T_e; r(l_i), \theta(l_i)\right)$ is calculated via bilinear interpolation on the error rate metric table T_e (see in Sect. 4.2).

$\mathcal{L}_{\text{sm}}$ denotes the smoothness term measuring the cost of allocating different labels (candidate segments $s_j{}^{\text{cand}}$) for the adjacent vertices $s_i{}^{\text{init}}, s_{i+1}{}^{\text{init}}$ and $\mathcal{L}_{\text{sm}}(l_i, l_{i+1})$ is set to 1 if $l_i \neq l_{i+1}$, otherwise, it's set to 0.

$\mathcal{L}_{\min}$ is utilized to minimize the number of final segments and is defined by:

$$\mathcal{L}_{\min}(L) = \sum_{s_i{}^{\text{cand}} \in S^{\text{cand}} \wedge s_i{}^{\text{cand}} \text{ occurs in } L} \lambda_3 t(s_i{}^{\text{cand}}), \tag{4}$$

where λ_3 is one hyper-parameter, and $t({s_i}^{\text{cand}})$ is defined by:

$$t({s_i}^{\text{cand}}) = \begin{cases} \text{interp}\left(T_t; r({s_i}^{\text{cand}}), \theta({s_i}^{\text{cand}})\right) & {s_i}^{\text{cand}} \text{ is a circular segment} \\ 0 & \text{otherwise} \end{cases}, \tag{5}$$

where $r({s_i}^{\text{cand}}), \theta({s_i}^{\text{cand}})$ denote the curvature radius and angle of the segment ${s_i}^{\text{cand}}$, and $\text{interp}\left(T_t; r({s_i}^{\text{cand}}), \theta({s_i}^{\text{cand}})\right)$ is calculated via bilinear interpolation on the time cost metric table T_t (see in Sect. 4.2).

By finding the allocation L that minimizes the loss term $\mathcal{L}$, we resolve overlaps with the consideration from Sect. 4. The final fine-level wire segments $S^{\text{final}} = \{{s_0}^{\text{final}}, {s_1}^{\text{final}}, \cdots\}$ that fit the unit U_i can be obtained then by removing duplicate elements from L. S^{final} will be utilized in the generation of animated visualization.

5.3 Module 2: Animated Visualization

The animated visualization module is engineered to create novice-friendly bending instructions, offering visual guidance to inexperienced users during the bending process. This is accomplished by transforming the decomposed dual-scale segments: the coarse-level structural wire segments $\{U_0, U_1, \cdots\}$ and the fine-level wire segments $S^{\text{final}} = \{s_0^{\text{final}}, s_1^{\text{final}}, \cdots\}$ into animated instructions, as illustrated in Fig. 8. To balance fabrication simplicity with shape fidelity, users are not prompted to start bending immediately after one animation of each individual fine-level line-circular segment; instead, animations are grouped based on coarse-level decomposition. All fine-level animations within each unit U_i are played in sequence, and then users perform the bending operations following the entire set of animations in that group.

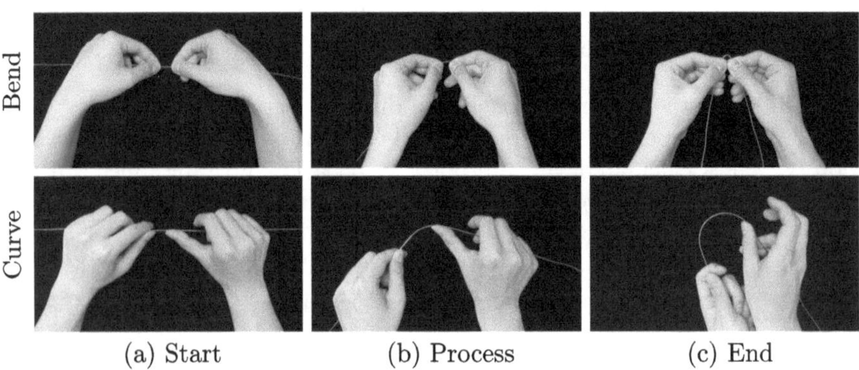

Fig. 7. Illustrations of our two atomic bending operations. With bend or curve operations (a)–(b), novices can easily and conveniently fabricate nice-looking line or circular segments (c).

Therefore, the key technical challenges to realize the animated visualization module are twofold: 1) Determining the appropriate bending operations for the two types of fine-level segments (line segment and circular segment); 2) Developing a method to generate animated instructions that effectively visualize these bending operations.

Determining Bending Operations. To address the first technical challenge, we introduce two fundamental fabrication operations (atomic bending operations): the **bend** operation for creating **line segments** and the **curve** operation for forming **circular segments**, illustrated in Fig. 7.

- In the **bend** operation, the user exerts force at a pre-determined bending point on the wire, resulting in the wire folding at a particular angle.
- In the **curve** operation, the user gradually applies a uniform bending force along a section of the wire, thereby shaping it into a circular arc with the desired curvature.

Generating Animated Visualization. To address the second challenge of generating animated visualization instructions for these atomic bending operations, we generate wire deformation animations to illustrate the wire's deformation procedure, and hand-gesture animations to demonstrate how the designated segment should be manipulated by hands, implemented with the Unity Engine [33].

- To generate the wire deformation animation for each atomic bending operation, we uniformly perform linear interpolation over a specific time period. This interpolation is carried out between the *pre-bending wire shape* and the *post-bending wire shape*. The post-bending wire shape corresponds to the target bending segment, while the pre-bending wire shape represents the wire's configuration prior to applying the bending operations. Specifically, for the bend operation, the initial bending angle is set to zero; for the curve operation, the circular segment initially exists as a straight line segment.
- To generate the hand-gesture animations for each atomic bending operation, we meticulously set the positions of two 3D hand models. This process can be divided into two aspects: 1) For the bend operation, we place the two hand models on the two adjacent line segments connected by the bending point, at a distance of 1/4 of the length of the line segment from the bending point. 2) For the curve operation, we position the right hand models along the bending point throughout the animation. For the left hand, when making the first 5 cm of the segment, it remains at the beginning of the segment. Afterwards, it is positioned 5 cm away from the right hand.

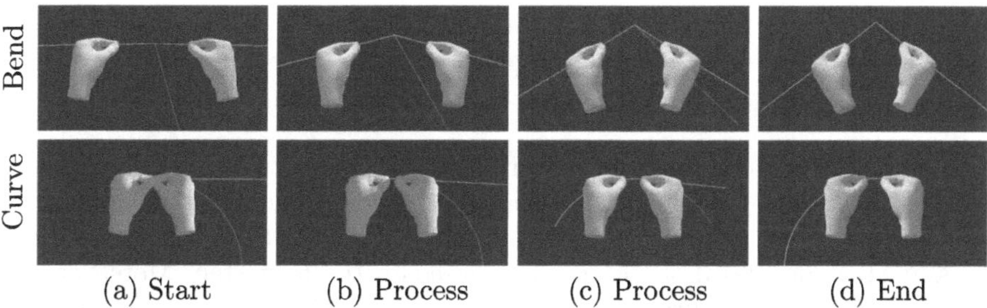

Fig. 8. Visualization of our wire deformation animation and hand-gesture animations. For the wire deformation animation, we uniformly perform linear interpolation over a specific time period.

As illustrated in Fig. 8, these operation-wise animations offers clear, actionable feedback, enabling novices to follow complex fabrication with minimal ambiguity and difficulties. Additionally, the generated 3D wire and hand-gesture are with identical scale to the physical setting, where the length of the wire precisely corresponds to its real-world counterpart, ensuring accurate guidance, and the size of demonstrated hand's model is approximated to the real setting.

5.4 Module 3: Real-Time Error Checker

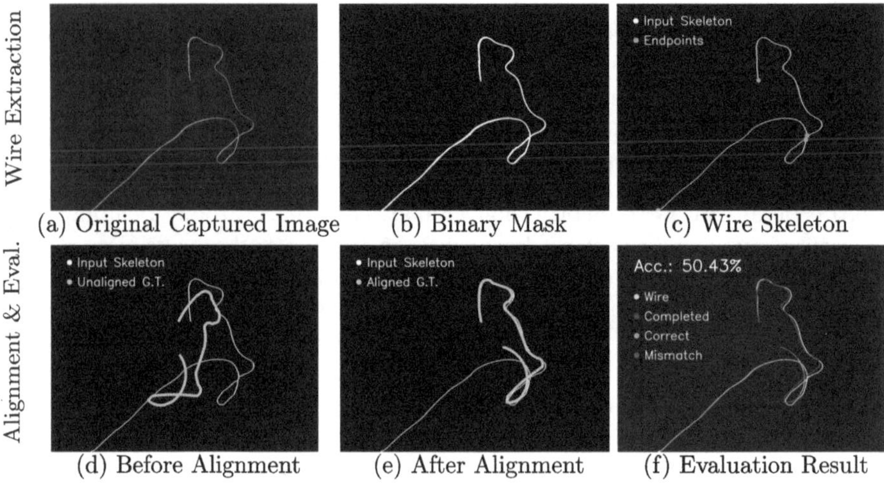

Fig. 9. Illustrations of the processes of our error checker. After capturing the image of the user's progress (a), we first pre-process the image to obtain a binary mask (b), and perform skeletonization to obtain a wire skeleton (c). In the meanwhile, we find all endpoints and intersections (marked as green points in (c)) of the wire skeleton. These points will be used in the following alignment process (d)–(e) to reduce the searching space, thus reducing the computational burden and increase robustness. The alignment process is shown in (d)–(e), where the ground truth are represented as orange curves. After evaluation (f), we provide users with the accuracy of current progress. The user's wire are marked as yellow curves, the completed and accurate (correct) ground-truth are marked as blue and green curves, while the inaccurate (mismatched) parts are highlighted as red curves. (Color figure online)

This module features a real-time error checker to evaluate the user's progress, which captures the real-time sequence of images by a photographic apparatus, and compares it to the target line-circular segments S^{final}. Based on the accuracy assessment, it decides if the user can proceed to the next step. Moreover, the checker highlights inaccuracies in the wire with visual feedback, allowing users to quickly identify and rectify errors. This real-time functionality maintains fabrication accuracy while offering intuitive guidance for corrections.

As depicted in Fig. 9, when provided with a captured image as input, we employ the following processing pipeline:

Green-Blue Region Detection. Recall that users can interactively skip to the next step, even when the current wire product fails to meet the required accuracy threshold. This functionality is enabled by using a printed green-blue cardboard (see Fig. 10. When the user intend to skip to next coarse-level bending segment, they put the cardboard under the photographic apparatus. For each capturing image captured, we detect the green and blue pixels. Once the proportion of these pixels reaches a predefined level, the process will automatically proceed to the next step.

Wire's Skeleton Extraction. This step aims to extract the wire's skeleton from the input image (Fig. 9(a)) with two key steps: 1) first obtain a binary mask with a image pre-processing stage (Fig. 9(b)), including performing gaussian blur to remove small noises, threshold segmentation to strip the wire area, removing connected components with area less than a threshold for further denoising, and binarization; 2) apply Zhang and Suen [47]'s method on the cleaned binary mask to obtain the wire skeleton (Fig. 9(c)). Using a convolution-based neighborhood counting method, we extract all endpoints (degree $= 1$) and intersection points (degree ≥ 3) from the resulting skeleton. These points are then used in the subsequent alignment process.

Optimization-Based Wire Alignment. To match the extracted wire shape with the ground-truth template, we need to align these two shapes (Fig. 9(d)). This task is a classical *rigid registration* problem [1], to minimize the total distance between a transformed ground-truth point set and the extracted input point set. To reduce the computational burden and increase the robustness against to local minima, we propose a key empirical finding: *In nearly all real-world scenarios, the starting point of the fabricated wire shape should closely match that of the ground-truth shape.* Based on this insight, we fix the translation by aligning a chosen input endpoint with the ground-truth starting point, which yields a 1D scalar minimization problem over the rotation angle. To efficiently and robustly solve the 1-DoF optimization problem, we employ a two-stage optimization strategy:

- Coarse Stage: We conduct a grid-search over evenly spaced candidate angles to find a promising initial rotation.
- Fine Stage: A bounded scalar minimization problem is initialized around the best coarse candidate for fine-tuning the alignment, and then optimized using Brent [5]'s method.

For all of these endpoints and intersection points extracting from the wire skeleton, we will try to match it to the endpoint of the ground-truth shape by the above 1-DOF optimization. Then output the one with the minimal matching error, as shown in Fig. 9(e). The above approach enables us to achieve real-time, accurate geometric alignment between the input skeleton and the ground-truth shape.

Wire Accuracy Evaluation. For each ground-truth point, we query its Euclidean distance to the nearest input skeleton point using a *KD-tree* based nearest point query algorithm. Points exceeding a mismatch threshold are labeled as **incorrect**, which are highlighted in red colors, as shown in Fig. 9(f).

5.5 Hardware and Software

In this section, we meticulously elaborate on our hardware and software configurations, encompassing the parameter settings of the three modules.

Software Setups. Our wire decomposition module is developed using C++ and relies on the following third-party libraries: CGAL [30], libhgp [48], libigl [20], Eigen [17] and gco-v3.0 [34] for geometric computations and graph-cut optimization. In the point sequence P, there is a spacing of 1 cm between each two adjacent points. In *Graph-Cut-Based Segment Fitting*, we set the fitting error threshold $\varepsilon = 0.6$, and set the loss weights $\lambda_1 = 30$, $\lambda_2 = 0.2$, $\lambda_3 = 50$.

Our animated visualization module is developed using Unity Engine [33]. Our real-time error checker module is developed using Python, with the following third-party libraries: OpenCV [4] for image capturing and processing, scikit-image [36] for wire skeletonization, SciPy [35] for the scalar optimizer and KD-tree based nearest point query. The resolution of images captured in the checker is set to 1024×768. The proportion of green-blue pixels required as a threshold for skipping to the next step is setting to $80000/(1024 \times 768)$.

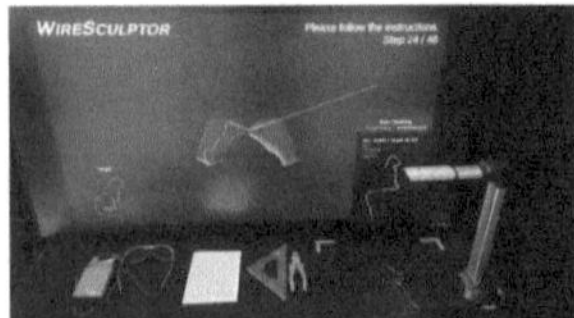

(a) Experimental Setup

(b) Scenario: Operating

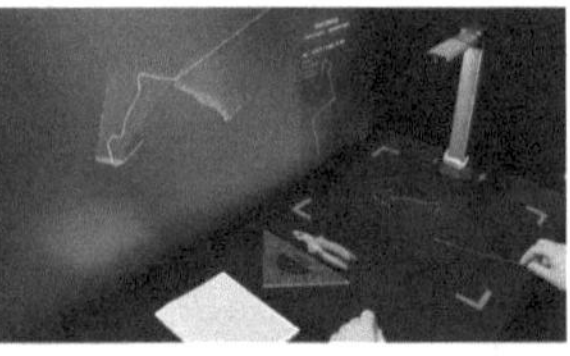

(c) Scenario: Checking

Fig. 10. An overview of our WireSculptor. (a) Experimental setup. Our system is set in a well-lit room with a 65-inch monitor and a high-speed photographic apparatus. (b) The scenario where the user performs a bending operation, following the animated visualization. (c) The scenario where the user checks the progress. The user puts the wire under the photographic apparatus, and the checker provides real-time accuracy calculation and intuitive feedback.

Hardware Setups. Figure 10 presents the hardware setups of our system. We set our system in a well-lit room with a monitor of 65 in., and the high-speed photographic apparatus capture the image with the resolution of 768×1024. We test our program on a PC with an Intel Core i7-14700F CPU operating at 5.3 GHz and 64 GB memory. In experiments, our checker can run at a speed of approximately 12 fps and achieve real-time checking.

6 Results and Discussions

We assess the effectiveness and practicality of WireSculptor by comparing it with alternative methods and conducting an ablation study to analyze the necessity of each system module.

6.1 Comparative Evaluation

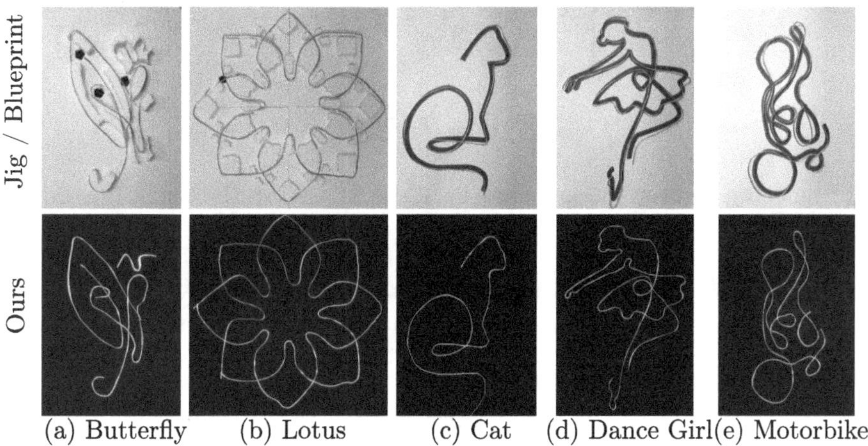

Fig. 11. Fabrication results of the comparative experiment: The first row shows the results of the two alternative approaches (jig and blueprint based methods), while the second row presents the results of our method. From left to right, the sculptures are a butterfly, a lotus, a cat, a dance girl, and a motorbike.

We conducted a user study in a controlled laboratory setting to assess how effectively participants could bend sculptures using our method compared to two alternative approaches: a **blueprint-based manual bending** method and a **physical-model fabrication** method [19]. In the previous approach, users fabricate sculptures by following a paper-printed design. In the latter approach, it provides physical jigs by extruding support walls from 2D jewelry drawings to guide wire wrapping operations [19]. Figure 11 shows the fabrication results of this comparative experiment.

Stimuli. We selected seven wire sculptures from [19,41], encompassing simple shapes like lotus flowers and cats, as well as more complex forms such as human figures and motorbikes. These stimuli were chosen to embody a diverse range of bending challenges in terms of shape complexity and structural detail.

Participants. We recruited 18 participants without any prior wire sculpting experience, consisting of 13 males and 5 females, aged between 19 and 25 years old. During the experiment, participants were seated roughly 60 cm from a 65-inch monitor in a well-lit room. After completing the study, each participant was compensated with a reward of $10.32 per hour for their participation.

Task. Each participant was asked to bend $5 \sim 7$ wire sculptures by following the instructions provided by our method as well as the two alternative approaches. All trials were presented in a randomized order to each participant to mitigate ordering effects. For each sculpture, we recorded the total time the participant spent on the bending process (termed "fabrication time") and, after the experiment, measured the modified Hausdorff distance [9] (MHD) between the user-bent sculpture and the original design (termed "shape accuracy"). In detail, given two point sets A, B, the MHD between them $H(A, B)$ is defined as:

$$H(A,B) = \max(h(A,B), h(B,A)), \tag{6}$$

where

$$h(A,B) = \frac{1}{|A|} \sum_{a \in A} \min_{b \in B} d(a,b), \tag{7}$$

and $|A|$ denotes the number of points in A, $d(a, b)$ denotes the Euclidean distance between point a and b.

Procedure. Our experiment consisted of three main steps: 1) a training session to introduce the task, consisting of one practice trial; 2) the main experiment; and 3) a short post-experiment interview to help analyze the results. During the main experiment, each participant was presented with $5 \sim 7$ wire designs, along with instructions indicating which method to use. Fabrication time was recorded for each design. On average, participants took approximately 39.6 min to complete the main experiment (min: 11.4 min, max: 66.6 min).

Table 2. Quantitative comparison of fabrication methods. MHD: mean Hausdorff distance [9]. The lower the better. Compared with both methods, our workflow shows advantages for novices in accuracy, within an acceptable time trade-off. Regarding the third component of butterfly, it's an antenna of a butterfly, which is of length 67 mm. Since our error checker allows error tolerance, the closed-loop will complete before the participant finishes fabricating, thus resulting in a poor fabrication quality. However, such scenario of "fabricating tiny components" is unlikely to occur in real-world fabrication.

MHD [9] ↓	Butterfly			Lotus	Cat	Dance Girl	Motorbike
	Comp. 1	Comp. 2	Comp. 3				
Jig [19]	1.835	1.662	1.678	2.567	\	\	\
Blueprint	\	\	\	\	2.064	2.765	2.548
Ours	1.528	1.889	2.262	2.296	1.835	2.404	2.625
Time ↓	Butterfly			Lotus	Cat	Dance Girl	Motorbike
	Comp. 1	Comp. 2	Comp. 3				
Jig [19]	115	179	99	253	\	\	\
Blueprint	\	\	\	\	264	613	454
Ours	174	361	68	593	468	1115	1124

Results. We collected 105 valid results from the experiments, summarized in Table 2. As shown in the table, most participants were able to bend sculptures with higher accuracy when guided by our method compared to the alternative approaches. The time increase observed with our method is, we believe, a reasonable and acceptable trade-off. While our visual guidance system may require more fabrication time due to user interaction with the error checker and the need to watch animations before each bending step, this added duration is offset by the benefits it brings. In particular, the system's real-time feedback, error correction, and step-by-step instructions significantly reduce user uncertainty and prevent cumulative mistakes—factors that are especially important for novice users. We argue that the increased time cost reflects a more deliberate and informed fabrication process, rather than inefficiency. Most importantly, participants generally expressed a positive attitude in our post-experiment interview, which will be discussed in the following section.

6.2 Post-experiment Interview

To complement the quantitative evaluation, we conducted a post-experiment interview with all participants. Our interview was carried out in the form of a structured questionnaire, comprising nine questions that investigated participants' subjective experience with the three bending assistance tools. Specifically, the questionnaire asked the following:

1. Compared to our WireSculptor workflow, did you find the blueprint/jig method easier or more comfortable to use?
2. Why did you find your preferred method more effortless or comfortable?
3. After trying all three methods, what advantages do you think our workflow offers?
4. If you could choose one method to continue using, which one would you choose and why?
5. Do you think blueprint-based bending guidance is suitable for beginners? Why or why not?
6. Did you encounter any difficulties when using the blueprint method (e.g., ambiguity at intersections)?
7. Do you think the jig method is suitable for beginners?
8. How would you rate our workflow? (Scale: -5 to 5, higher is better)
9. Do you have any comments or suggestions for our workflow?

We have collected 9 valid responses from participants. The responses provide insights into the subjective experience and usability of these three bending assistance tools.

Ease of Use and Intuitiveness. Most participants (6 of 9 valid interview results) found our system significantly more intuitive and less physically demanding. As one participant noted, *"WireSculptor tells me how far I should bend in each step. It feels like it's bending with me."* Another commented that *"WireSculptor gives feedback and shows what I did wrong, helping me fix it before moving on."* Compared to the paper blueprint, which several participants described as *"confusing at wire intersections"* and *"lacking interaction"*, our system's dynamic, real-time feedback was repeatedly cited as a key advantage. One participant emphasized that *"blueprint-based designs are hard to follow when wires overlap, but the WireSculptor always shows what to do next."*

Effectiveness for Novice Users. A notable theme is how well our method supported novice users. Nearly all participants (8 of 9 valid interview results) believed the visual guidance tool was more suitable for novices than the alternatives (e.g., blueprint and jig). As one participant put it, *"each step gave me feedback and made me confident I could finish the piece."* In contrast, the blueprint and jig-based methods were often described as requiring experience or trial-and-error. One participant noted that *"with the 3D jig, it was hard to know where the wire should go next."*

Engagement and Satisfaction. Participants also found our system more engaging and enjoyable. Several referred to the visual guidance tool as *"more fun"* and *"more interactive"* than the alternatives. One participant praised its ability to guide without breaking immersion: *"It's like the system is folding with me, step by step."* In contrast, some participants mentioned that with blueprint or jig-based methods, *"you often finish the whole shape before realizing something went wrong."*

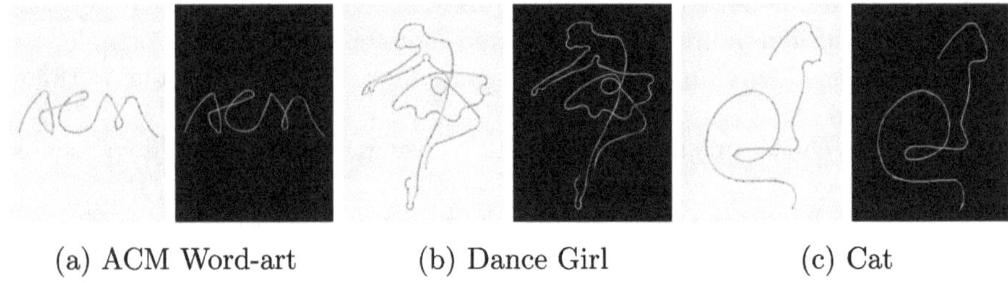

(a) ACM Word-art (b) Dance Girl (c) Cat

Fig. 12. Illustrations of the application of our workflow in wire sculpture fabrication for novices. Whether the design is simple or complex (the first, third, fifth columns), with our workflow, novices are capable of fabricating nice-looking corresponding wire sculpture (the second, fourth, sixth columns).

Rating and Feedback. On a -5 to 5 rating scale (the higher the better), our system received an average score of **3.78**, with most participants (7 of 9) assigning it a 4 or 5. Participants appreciated its precision and interactivity, while also suggesting minor usability improvements. For instance, a few participants noted that *"placing the screen closer to the wire could reduce head movement,"* and that *"being able to replay a bending step would be helpful when catching up."*

These qualitative results reinforce our experimental results: our system not only improves bending accuracy, but also transforms the fabrication experience into a guided, confident, and even enjoyable process, particularly for novices. The integration of animated visualization, real-time checking and interactive feedback distinguishes our system as a more usable and empowering tool for wire sculpting.

7 Applications

We demonstrate that our workflow is flexible to support diverse creative use cases. In this section, we present two key application scenarios.

7.1 Wire Sculpture Fabrication for Novices

Our workflow enables novice users to create aesthetically pleasing and structurally sound wire sculptures with minimal prior experience. We showcase three examples in Fig. 12: a stylized ACM word-art, a dance girl figure, and a sitting cat. Throughout these tasks, novice users benefited from the WireSculptor's coarse-to-fine segmentation of steps, allowing them to focus on one bending operation at a time without being overwhelmed. The integrated error checker provided instant feedback, helping novice users identify and correct errors early before they propagated. By removing much of the guesswork traditionally associated with the craft, our system empowers novice users to achieve professional-looking results with minimal frustration.

7.2 Innovative Educational Hand-Crafting for Children

Beyond regular sculpture fabrication tasks, our workflow also serves as an educational tool for children to engage in hand-crafting with the support of their parents or educators. In this setting, children sketch their desired shapes, and parents then handle the physical bending with the assistance of our interactive animation and visual feedback tools. This collaborative process allows children to participate in both the design and evaluation loop, encouraging creativity and hands-on learning. Figure 13 showcases three sample outcomes produced

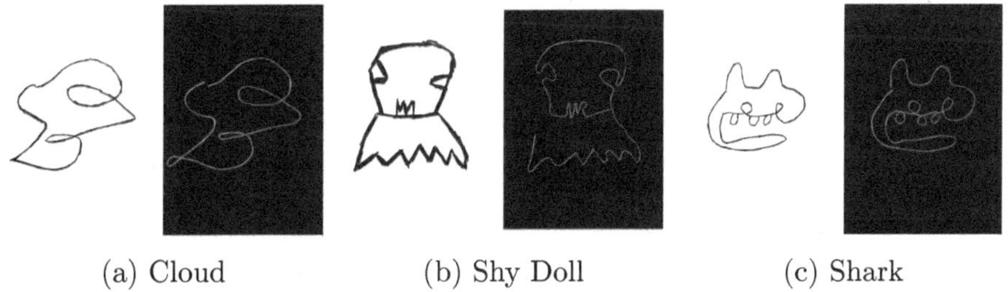

(a) Cloud (b) Shy Doll (c) Shark

Fig. 13. Illustrations of the application of our workflow in innovative educational hand-crafting for children. After children sketching their desired shapes (the first, third, fifth columns), adults can assist in transforming the shapes into wire sculptures (the second, fourth, sixth columns).

through child-parent collaboration. Each of them captures the child's original design while maintaining physical fidelity.

8 Conclusion

In this paper, we present *WireSculptor*, an innovative interactive workflow that enables novices to fabricate wire sculptures through a guided, step-by-step process. Our workflow combines the intuitiveness of human-in-the-loop hand crafting with the precision of visual feedback and error checking. We designed the system around three core modules: wire decomposition with a formative study, interactive animated visualization, and a real-time error checker. Through user experiments, we validated the effectiveness of our workflow in improving fabrication accuracy and accessibility for novices.

Limitations. Our interactive guided animations, being screen-displayed, suffer from the drawback of not being viewable from all directions. Also, in our fabrication, we didn't account for wire characteristics like thickness and hardness, beyond just its length, and future studies could incorporate these. Methodologically, we're restricted to single, non-self-closing wires, topologically limiting the artworks we can guide, so introducing multiple wires and self-closing wires is a future prospect. In terms of time cost, our method consumes excessive time in the fabrication of many shapes, with the analysis revealing the following reasons. Firstly, our system involves the use of multiple operational modules, like animated visualization module and real-time error checker module, resulting in a steeper learning curve compared to other methods. Secondly, our operation module and visualization module are separate entities, requiring users to constantly contrast both modules during tasks, which incurs a time overhead for this comparison process. Finally, the animation playback and demonstration process incurs a time overhead.

Future Work. We plan to expand the 3D wire sculpture fabrication, and the assembly process of multi-wires. To enhance user freedom, we aim to enable the system to dynamically plan operations in response to users' real-time bending actions as their skills develop. We also intend to integrate AI techniques, such as large language models (LLMs), to help generate dynamic bending guidance for wire sculpture fabrication. Furthermore, it would be fascinating to incorporate mixed-reality devices into our system. Using mixed-reality devices can integrate our operation module and visualization module into a unified system, facilitating user learning and operation, thereby reducing the system's time overhead. To achieve this, we need to solve the problem of real-time error detection based on 3D wire reconstruction. Another promising direction is to expand the application domains of WireSculptor. For example, we could investigate its use in creating more complex 3D wire-frame structures for architectural models or in the field of industrial prototyping. And the other direction is to enhance system efficiency. Designing more flexible control strategies such as introducing an adaptive mode that reduces animation playback time and decreases inspection frequency as users become more proficient can enhance system efficiency and reduce time consumption.

Acknowledgments. We thank all reviewers for their valuable comments and constructive suggestions. We would like to express our gratitude to Liang He, Yan Jin, Boya Dong and Ziqian Sheng for their insightful advice on our project, and to Shuai Feng, Shudan Guo, Hao Xu, and many others for their contributions to the user experiment. This work is supported in part by grants from National Key Research and Development Program of China (Grant No. 2024YFB3309500), National Natural Science Foundation of China (Grant No. U23A20312, 62472257, 62372271).

Disclosure of Interests. The authors have no competing interests to declare that are relevant to the content of this article.

References

1. Ashburner, J., Friston, K.J.: Rigid body registration. Statistical parametric mapping: The analysis of functional brain images, pp. 49–62 (2007)
2. Baraldo, A., et al.: Automatic computation of bending sequences for wire bending machines. Int. J. Comput. Integr. Manuf. **35**(12), 1335–1351 (2022)
3. Bhundiya, H.G., Cordero, Z.C.: Bend-forming: a CNC deformation process for fabricating 3D wireframe structures. Additive Manuf. Lett. **6**, 100146 (2023)
4. Bradski, G.: The OpenCV library. Dr. Dobb's J. Softw. Tools (2000)
5. Brent, R.P.: Algorithms for minimization without derivatives. Courier Corporation (2013)
6. Cheng, L., et al.: Viscourt: in-situ guidance for interactive tactic training in mixed reality. In: Proceedings of the 37th Annual ACM Symposium on User Interface Software and Technology, pp. 1–14 (2024)
7. Cohen-Or, D., et al.: A Sampler of Useful Computational Tools for Applied Geometry, Computer Graphics, and Image Processing, 1st edn. A. K. Peters Ltd., USA (2015)
8. Dong, J., Xia, Z., Zhao, Q., Zhao, N.: Human-machine integration based augmented reality assisted wire-bending training system for orthodontics. Virtual Reality **27**(2), 627–636 (2023)
9. Dubuisson, M.P., Jain, A.: A modified Hausdorff distance for object matching. In: Proceedings of 12th International Conference on Pattern Recognition, vol. 1, pp. 566–568 (1994). https://doi.org/10.1109/ICPR.1994.576361
10. Etsy: Wire 'grateful' Sign, Handmade Wire Words, Names, Phrases, Quotes, Lyrics, Metal Wall Art, Cursive Lettering - Etsy UK | Grateful signs, Hanging signs, Handmade wire—kr.pinterest.com (2025). https://kr.pinterest.com/pin/1127659194200817649/. Accessed 01 May 2025
11. Fang, W., Zhang, T., Chen, L., Hu, H.: A survey on Hololens AR in support of human-centric intelligent manufacturing. J. Intell. Manuf. **36**(1), 35–59 (2025)
12. Feng, S., Liu, B., Berman, O., Haraldsson, H., Roumen, T., et al.: Y-AR: a mixed reality cad tool for 3D wire bending. arXiv preprint arXiv:2410.23540 (2024)
13. Firoozabadi, R., Kramer, P.A., Benirschke, S.K.: Kirschner wire bending. J. Orthop. Trauma **27**(11), e260–e263 (2013)

14. France, M.M., Shallit, J.O.: Wire bending. J. Comb. Theory Ser. A **50**(1), 1–23 (1989)
15. Garg, A., et al.: Wire mesh design. ACM Trans. Graph. **33**(4) (2014)
16. GreccoSimone: família wire sculpture Simone Grecco | Esculturas em arame, Esculturas, Artistas—kr.pinterest.com (2025). https://kr.pinterest.com/pin/844493664835104/. Accessed 01 May 2025
17. Guennebaud, G., Jacob, B., et al.: Eigen v3 (2010). http://eigen.tuxfamily.org
18. Gupta, A., Fox, D., Curless, B., Cohen, M.: Duplotrack: a real-time system for authoring and guiding duplo block assembly. In: Proceedings of the 25th Annual ACM Symposium on User Interface Software and Technology, pp. 389–402 (2012)
19. Iarussi, E., Li, W., Bousseau, A.: Wrapit: computer-assisted crafting of wire wrapped jewelry. ACM Trans. Graph. (TOG) **34**(6), 1–8 (2015)
20. Jacobson, A., Panozzo, D., et al.: libigl: a simple C++ geometry processing library (2018). https://libigl.github.io/
21. Lee, W., et al.: Virtualwire: supporting rapid prototyping with instant reconfigurations of wires in breadboarded circuits. In: Proceedings of the Fifteenth International Conference on Tangible, Embedded, and Embodied Interaction, pp. 1–12 (2021)
22. Li, W.: Pen2VR: a smart pen tool interface for wire art design in VR (2021)
23. Lira, W., Fu, C.W., Zhang, H.: Fabricable Eulerian wires for 3D shape abstraction. ACM Trans. Graph. (TOG) **37**(6), 1–13 (2018)
24. Liu, M., Zhang, Y., Bai, J., Cao, Y., Alperovich, J.M., Ramani, K.: Wirefab: mix-dimensional modeling and fabrication for 3D mesh models, pp. 965–976 (2017)
25. Liu, R., Wan, W., Harada, K.: Tamp for 3D curving—a low-payload robot arm works aside a bending machine to curve high-stiffness metal wires. IEEE Trans. Autom. Sci. Eng. (2023)
26. Miguel, E., Lepoutre, M., Bickel, B.: Computational design of stable planar-rod structures. ACM Trans. Graph. (TOG) **35**(4), 1–11 (2016)
27. Ogden, J.M.: Classical gold wire: some aspects of its manufacture and use. Jewellery Stud. **5**, 95–105 (1991)
28. Osti, F., de Amicis, R., Sanchez, C.A., Tilt, A.B., Prather, E., Liverani, A.: A VR training system for learning and skills development for construction workers. Virtual Reality **25**, 523–538 (2021)
29. Sun, L., et al.: Flextruss: a computational threading method for multi-material, multi-form and multi-use prototyping. In: Proceedings of the 2021 CHI Conference on Human Factors in Computing Systems, pp. 1–12 (2021)
30. The CGAL Project: CGAL User and Reference Manual. CGAL Editorial Board, 6.0.1 edn. (2024). https://doc.cgal.org/6.0.1/Manual/packages.html
31. Tojo, K., Shamir, A., Bickel, B., Umetani, N.: Fabricable 3D wire art. In: ACM SIGGRAPH 2024 Conference Proceedings. SIGGRAPH 2024 (2024). https://doi.org/10.1145/3641519.3657453
32. Torres, C., Li, W., Paulos, E.: Proxyprint: supporting crafting practice through physical computational proxies. In: Proceedings of the 2016 ACM Conference on Designing Interactive Systems, pp. 158–169 (2016)
33. Unity Technologies: Unity 6.0 (2025). https://unity.com/releases. Accessed 30 Mar 2025
34. Veksler, O., Delong, A.: GCO-v3.0 (2015). https://github.com/nsubtil/gco-v3.0
35. Virtanen, P., et al.: SciPy 1.0: fundamental algorithms for scientific computing in python. Nat. Methods **17**, 261–272 (2020). https://doi.org/10.1038/s41592-019-0686-2

36. van der Walt, S., et al.: Scikit-image: image processing in Python. PeerJ **2**, e453 (2014). https://doi.org/10.7717/peerj.453
37. Wang, B., et al.: Active assembly guidance with online video parsing. In: 2018 IEEE Conference on Virtual Reality and 3D User Interfaces (VR), pp. 459–466. IEEE (2018)
38. Wang, G., et al.: Morphingcircuit: an integrated design, simulation, and fabrication workflow for self-morphing electronics. Proc. ACM Interact. Mob. Wearable Ubiquit. Technol. **4**(4), 1–26 (2020)
39. Wang, Y., Yang, X., Fukusato, T., Igarashi, T.: Computational design and fabrication of 3D wire bending art, pp. 1–2 (2019)
40. Wikipedia contributors: Wire sculpture—Wikipedia, the free encyclopedia (2025). https://en.wikipedia.org/w/index.php?title=Wire_sculpture&oldid=1272801587. Accessed 27 Mar 2025
41. Wu, Q., et al.: Tune-it: optimizing wire reconfiguration for sculpture manufacturing. In: SIGGRAPH Asia 2024 Conference Papers. SA 2024. Association for Computing Machinery, New York (2024). https://doi.org/10.1145/3680528.3687588
42. Xu, H., Knoop, E., Coros, S., Bächer, M.: Bend-it: design and fabrication of kinetic wire characters. ACM Trans. Graph. (TOG) **37**(6), 1–15 (2018)
43. Yang, Z., Xu, P., Fu, H., Huang, H.: Wireroom: model-guided explorative design of abstract wire art. ACM Trans. Graph. (TOG) **40**(4), 1–13 (2021)
44. Yu, J., et al.: Irontex: using ironable 3D printed objects to fabricate and prototype customizable interactive textiles. Proc. ACM Interact. Mob. Wearable Ubiquit. Technol. **8**(3), 1–26 (2024)
45. Yu, M., Ye, Z., Liu, Y.J., He, Y., Wang, C.C.: Lineup: computing chain-based physical transformation. ACM Trans. Graph. (TOG) **38**(1), 1–16 (2019)
46. Yue, Y.T., Zhang, X., Yang, Y., Ren, G., Choi, Y.K., Wang, W.: Wiredraw: 3D wire sculpturing guided with mixed reality. In: Proceedings of the 2017 CHI Conference on Human Factors in Computing Systems, pp. 3693–3704 (2017)
47. Zhang, T.Y., Suen, C.Y.: A fast parallel algorithm for thinning digital patterns. Commun. ACM **27**(3), 236–239 (1984). https://doi.org/10.1145/357994.358023
48. Zhao, H.: libhgp. Zhao, Haisen (2024). https://github.com/haisenzhao/libhgp

The Effect of Unexpected Visual Stimuli on Short-Term Memory in Immersive Experience

Shoulong Zhang[1], Ming Li[2], Yutian Xiao[1,3], Lu Xuejing[4], Yan Wang[1](✉), and Shuai Li[1,3](✉)

[1] Zhongguancun Laboratory, Beijing, China
{zhangsl,wangyan}@zgclab.edu.cn
[2] Department of Computer Science and Technology, Tsinghua University, Beijing, China
mingli_thu@tsinghua.edu.cn
[3] State Key Laboratory of Virtual Reality Technology and Systems, Beihang University, Beijing, China
{by_ytxiao,lishuai}@buaa.edu.cn
[4] CAS Key Laboratory of Mental Health, Institute of Psychology, Chinese Academy of Sciences, Beijing, China
luxj@psych.ac.cn

Abstract. Virtual reality (VR) can offer unexpected and fictional visual content, thus creating unique experiences and satisfying individual imaginations. Nevertheless, the effect of unexpected stimuli on cognition has yet to be studied in VR, and the existing paradigm is unsuitable for dynamic and flexible configurations. This paper investigates the effects of unexpected visual stimuli on short-term memory in VR experience. Building upon typical static and sequential isolation effect studies, we meticulously designed six VR scenes that cover various perceptual patterns, encompassing static or dynamic, as well as sequential, semi-sequential, or non-sequential elements. We then recruit 24 participants to assess short-term memory after each session through two classic goal-directed tasks: free recall and recognition test. To further enhance the credibility of our findings, we record eye-tracking and EEG data to analyze gaze and neurobiological patterns in the presence of unexpected content. The cognitive task results show a significant average recall gain of 30.92%, a recognition accuracy boost of 12.89%, and a shorter reaction time for unexpected items. Moreover, it can observe a longer gaze duration, significant activation in the frontal and parietal regions of the θ and α bands, and an elevation of δ oscillatory energy in the parietal region in response to unexpected visual stimuli. Our study demonstrates that unexpected visual content has a significant impact on human short-term memory and exhibits distinct physiological patterns in VR. The conclusion offers valuable guidance for VR application design and provides a deeper understanding of the consequences of everyday VR use.

Keywords: Unexpected visual stimuli · Isolation effect · Eye-tracking · EEG

Supplementary Information The online version contains supplementary material available at https://doi.org/10.1007/978-981-95-7195-6_6.

A. Hinkenjan et al. (Eds.): ICXR 2025, LNCS 16428, pp. 100–115, 2026.
https://doi.org/10.1007/978-981-95-7195-6_6

1 Introduction

Virtual reality offers limitless possibilities, encompassing both realistic and lifelike scenarios, while also delivering unforeseen and imaginative immersive experiences to the user. Contemporary 2D and 3D generative methods highlight their inherent capacity for *concept combination* and tend to create fictional and imaginative assets according to user intentions [18,27]. This capacity has the potential to generate fictional content that challenges conventional commonsense knowledge and unforeseen interpretations [4] in VR applications. Therefore, understanding the impact of unexpected content in VR offers valuable guidance for application developers and enhances their comprehension of the potential consequences of daily VR usage. Nevertheless, the effect of unexpected visual stimuli on the human cognitive process in the VR environment remains unexplored.

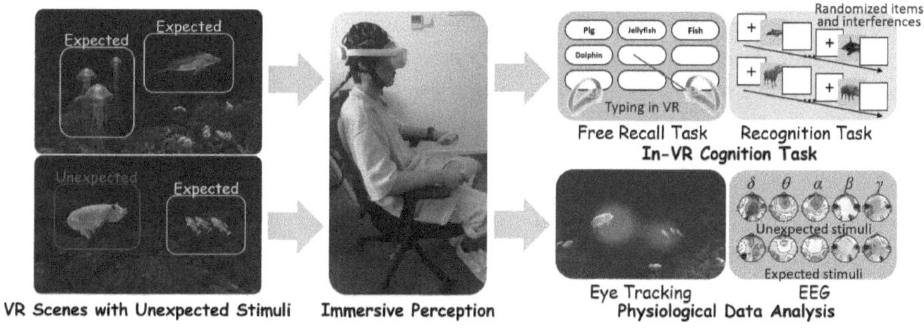

Fig. 1. Overview of experiment framework.

Similar to [10], we refer to the term *expectation* to generate forecasts of upcoming content by utilizing existing knowledge. We primarily focus on schema-driven expectation, which applies commonsense knowledge from the world to predict and interpret sensory inputs [2,13]. In this study, we define *unexpected stimuli* as visual information that contradicts mental schemata, immersive context, and semantic knowledge structured over a significant period and through lived experiences. In prior cognitive science studies, the isolation effect (i.e., von Restorff effect) [38] demonstrated that heterogeneous stimuli presented in a homogeneous sequence are more easily recalled, owing to their intrinsic salience. However, the isolation effect in a laboratory setting can only be studied through conventional methods, such as identifying unexpected words/images through a static sequence (i.e., the oddball paradigm), due to its controllability [38]. These methods, which involve word lists [9], image sequences [39], or human faces [1,19], offer users sequential and static visual information, limiting their ability to assess human cognition performance in dynamic environments with complex perception patterns in real life. This limitation highlights the importance of our work, which leverages the superior immersion, presence, and configuration flexibility of the virtual environment to assess the cognitive abilities of humans in VR when facing unexpected inputs.

In this work, we investigate the impact of unexpected VR content on short-term memory while developing cognitive assessment immersive environments. Through our analysis of existing literature, we expand upon von Restorff's assumptions and formulate the following hypothesis: In addition to the static and sequential stimuli, unexpected visual content can activate the superior functioning of short-term memory in dynamic and natural VR settings. To verify the proposed hypotheses, we meticulously design six VR scenarios encompassing static and dynamic environments, as well as sequential, semi-sequential, and non-sequential perceptual settings. To evaluate the memory performance following VR exposure, we employ conventional free recall [25] and recognition [26] tests in each session. These two assessments can methodically determine how much people can memorize both in-context and unexpected items. Furthermore, we collect physiological data from participants during VR experiences, including eye-tracking data and EEG signals. The experimental framework is illustrated in Fig. 1. Our main contributions are enumerated as follows:

- We conduct the first study to explore the relationship between unexpected visual content and short-term memory performance across various perceptual VR environments. These findings have ramifications for the visual design of VR applications and offer insights into human-computer interface technologies.
- We extend the static linear stimulus hypothesis proposed in our previous research on isolation effects to validate the isolation effects of dynamic and non-linear stimuli within immersive environments.
- We identify stable behavior and neural patterns associated with unexpected visual stimuli in VR. Unexpected stimuli capture longer gaze duration and reveal an elevation in δ oscillatory energy in the parietal region as well as θ and α bands in both the frontal and parietal regions. This essential evidence enhances our understanding of the neural mechanisms implicated in the VR user's unexpected virtual experiences.

2 Related Work

As an interdisciplinary research endeavor, our work simultaneously engages with cognitive science and VR technology. Specifically, we conduct a brief literature review from three perspectives: expectation and memory, memory assessment in VR, and physiological data analysis of memory.

Expectation and Memory. Expectation is a fundamental factor studied in memory research. Upon encountering an unforeseen input, the back-propagation of bottom-up prediction errors refines the top-down predictions. The expectation violation may activate the contextual novelty arising from the unexpected input combination. For instance, oddball [38] is a conventional paradigm used to manipulate contextual novelty in the isolation effect research. The subsequent studies have evolved different stimulus modalities. Schmidt et al. [30] adopted a mixed paradigm of Stoop and word list recall to study the inattentional blindness in von Restorff effect. Frank et al. [11] constructed an image sequence of a single object with 1/3 of the cues violating the semantic consistency and proved that expectation violation specifically aids the disambiguation of overlapping inputs. Wittmann et al. [39] used a novel landscape image in a familiar scene image sequence to study the functionality of a reward system in novelty processing. The experiment supports that the anticipatory activation of the hippocampus, along with the novelty signal, might be essential in memory encoding of novel stimuli. Behaviourally, contextually novel stimuli at encoding are usually associated with enhanced memory performance, measured using recognition [26] and recall [25] tasks. We expand upon the traditional linear experimental paradigm by using VR to create highly immersive, dynamic, and controllable representations.

Memory Assessment in VR. Conventional memory assessments are rigorously designed and have played a crucial role in diagnosing and assessing the extent of cognitive impairments [22]. Moreover, VR technology has recently been demonstrated as qualified to offer a viable option for evaluating memory in ecologically realistic settings with highly immersive, non-laboratory conditions and complete control of the experimental process. Sauzéon et al. [29] developed the Human Object Memory for Everyday Scenes (HOMES) VR test to evaluate episodic memory in a simulated everyday setting in both older adults and those with Alzheimer's disease (AD). Corriveau Lecavalier et al. [8] established an ecological setting named Virtual Shop, wherein the participant was required to commit to memory 12 familiar objects. Coleman et al. [7] examine the assessment of working memory in a virtual classroom setting for children who exhibit inattention and off-task behavior. The participants performed the AX-CPT task [3,5] while being exposed to visual and auditory distractions during the performance. This VR-based assessment can indicate far-transfer effects and provide additional validity in evaluating the effectiveness of training. Jaiswal et al. [15] developed a virtual corridor environment, where Individuals encode spatial information by presenting a navigational route to the target room and recalling the precise route via the corridor. Although our paper utilizes VR's advantages to evaluate cognitive levels, we delve further into the influence of VR's unforeseen visual content on human cognitive abilities.

Physiological Pattern of Memory. Short-term memory serves as a temporary repository for retrieving a restricted quantity of information from the sensory register, where the hippocampus network plays a vital role in the formation and subsequent reactivation of new memories [6]. Kishiyama et al. [16] examined 16 patients who suffered unilateral prefrontal cortex damage using the von Restorff test to assess their recognition of novelty. The results show that the patients did not demonstrate any novelty advantage in recall. Moreover, Løvstad et al. [20] noted that individuals with lesions in the lateral prefrontal regions showed decreased P3 response created by novelty stimulation. EEG signals are conventionally classified into different brain regions and five frequency bands: δ (1–4 Hz), θ (4–7 Hz), α (8–12 Hz), β (13–28 Hz), and γ (29–47 Hz). Shestyuk et al. [32] used EEG to assess cognitive processes related to attention and memory changes when stimulated with media content. The researchers determined that oscillations in the frontocentral alpha band, which is frequently associated with attention processing [12,36], and the memory processing mobilization frequently increase theta power in the frontocentral area [37]. However, there is also a notable lack of research in VR-based cognitive research on the neurophysiological mechanisms. In response to

Fig. 2. Unexpected visual stimuli in VR scenes. The unexpected items are illustrated in the red boxes. All six VR scenes are either static or dynamic, which also cover three perception patterns: sequential (Scene 1–2), semi-sequential (Scene 3–4), and non-sequential (Scene 5–6). (Color figure online)

this research gap, our physiological data related to attention and memory are crucial for a better understanding of the cognitive effects of VR content.

3 Method

In this section, we will detail the experimental procedures involving volunteer participants and the data processing methods. The experimental setup description covers VR scene design, cognitive task selection, participant demographics, and the experimental process. Data analysis methods include eye-tracking data and EEG data analysis.

VR Stimuli Scene Design. We create six immersive virtual environments as visual materials, with each scene consisting of approximately ten visual items that participants need to memorize. Additionally, only one unexpected category is introduced in each session. We report the basic information of the scenarios in Table 1 and illustrate the VR scenes in Fig. 2. Unlike the oddball [38], word list [9], and image sequence [39] paradigms typically employed in classical studies on the isolation effect, our VR scenes offer more immersive and high-presence experiences that closely resemble real-life perception scenarios, including 1) static and dynamic scenes and 2) sequential, csemi-sequential, and non-sequential perceptual patterns. In static scenes, objects remain stationary in physical space, whereas in dynamic settings, objects may exhibit localized action animations and global movements. Within our VR environments, we manipulate the number of memorable items displayed in each time segment to provide various perceptual difficulties. In the sequential configuration, only a single object type is present in the field of view. Semi-sequential scenes exhibit pairs of two categories, with co-occurrent object groups shown in a linear temporal order. In the sequential and semi-sequential settings, the unexpected item appears in the middle positions of the sequence, randomly from 5 to 7. By contrast, all memorable entries are depicted simultaneously

Table 1. VR Scenes designed for the experiment. The unexpectation index (i.e. unexp. index) indicate the position of unexpected stimulus in the sequential and semi-sequential settings. Thus, the index is not accessible in non-sequential setting where all stimuli appear simultaneously.

ID	Scene Name	Items	Unexp. Index	Scene Type	Unexp. Type	Perception Type	Length (s)
1	African Savanna	10	6	Dynamic	Violating biological & physical rules	Sequential	55
2	Supermarket	10	7	Static	Semantic inconsistency	Sequential	58
3	Underwater	10	5	Dynamic	Violating biological rules	Semi-sequential	30
4	Marketplace	10	6	Static	Semantic inconsistency	Semi-sequential	33
5	Park	10	–	Dynamic	Abnormal behavior	Non-sequential	28
6	Room	11	–	Static	Semantic inconsistency	Non-sequential	20

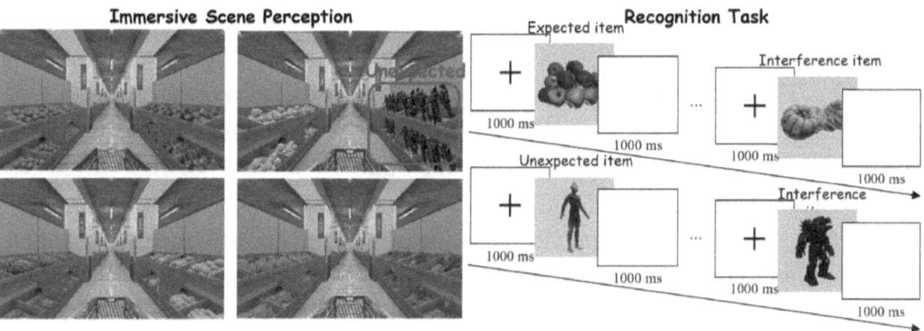

Fig. 3. Recognition task process. The recognition task is the second test after immersive perception in each session. After the mark of concentration lasting 1000 ms, the participants have to judge an image of either a memorable or interference item by pulling the left or right trigger, respectively. There is a rest stage of 1000 ms before the subsequent trial.

in the non-sequential settings. Due to the page limit, please refer to the supplementary material for detailed scene design.

Cognitive Tasks. We utilize *free recall* and *recognition* tests to evaluate the extent to which participants recollect both expected and unexpected objects across various perception settings. In line with prior research on the isolation effect, the free recall task is the primary indicator to determine whether subjects could recollect the target stimulus [25,38]. In order to prevent inattentional blindness in our memory tests [23,30], before the scene exploration, the task introductions explicitly indicate the range of the content to memorize, which includes all the in-context and unexpected categories. Following the end of the scene perception, participants were instructed to input the elements they remembered into the in-VR interface. The free-recall test had no time constraint and did not require participants to respond in the order in which they perceived the items. In the second recognition task, participants are shown snapshots of items. They are asked to determine if they had previously seen the object during the perception phase, as depicted in Fig. 3. At the start of each trial, a VR interface displayed a + sign in the center of the visual field for 1000 ms, indicating the concentration focus point. Then, a question image replaced the + sign as a visual stimulus. Participants were required to indicate whether they had seen the object in the picture by pulling either the left or right trigger without aiming at any target. Immediately after responding, the image vanished, and a 1000-ms interval followed before the subsequent trial. We measured reaction time and judgment accuracy in real-time VR applications during the recognition task to quantify memory performance. Greater accuracy and shorter reaction time indicate better memorization of the object. The recognition task consists of 20 judgment questions in total. Among the 20 alternatives, 10 items represent objects observed in the VR experience, while the remaining 10 items are used as interference items. Two entries are categorized similarly to the unexpected stimulus among the ten distractors, while the remaining eight entries are used as distractors for the in-context stimuli. The order of these 20 questions is randomized. For detailed information on the experiment apparatus and settings, please refer to the supplementary material.

Participants. The experiment was conducted in a controlled indoor environment with a constant temperature of 26 °C. We recruited 24 participants aged 20 to 30 years (M = 25.0, SD = 3.24), consisting of 10 females and 14 males. All individuals exhibit right-handedness and normal visual acuity. All subjects have no prior medical history of heart disease, neurological illnesses, or any other cognitive-related issues. The study received approval from the local ethics commission: Bioethics and Medical Ethics Committee of Beihang University with code BM20240258.

Procedure. All subjects willingly and voluntarily agreed to participate in this study. Before conducting the experiment, the researchers provided the volunteers with detailed information on the study's objectives, procedures, possible risks, and the importance of the cognitive tasks. This thorough preparation is aimed at ensuring the participants' understanding and comfort. The participants were then required to sign a written informed consent form, further solidifying their preparedness. They were also informed that they could terminate the experiment if they encountered any problems. The researcher then fine-tuned and calibrated the distance between the pupils and the sensors that track the participant's movements in the HMD. Ultimately, the participants proceeded to the instructional level in order to engage in basic instructional scenarios and become acquainted with the visual presentation and interface manipulation of the free recall task and the recognition task, ensuring their comprehension of the task's demands. We placed the EEG cap on the participant's head, verified the quality of the signals, and proceeded to initiate the experiment.

The experiment comprises one tutorial session and six experimental sessions. Before the commencement of each session, participants were provided with written information regarding the broad range of object categories that needed to be memorized. While perceiving a scene, the subjects remained stationary in a chair. They were permitted to make little movements of their head and eyes to ensure they could see the objects that needed to be memorized inside the realistic environment. Only one scenario is depicted in each session and performed in the sequence indicated in Table 1. While perceiving scenes, we collected participants' eye movement data and EEG signals in real-time.

After each scene perception is completed, the free recall task and the reproduction task are initiated consecutively. We integrate the user interface of both tests into an

Fig. 4. Pixel-level AOI annotation exemplars of designed VR scenes as 360° videos for gaze pattern analysis. The background objects and decorations are ignored in gaze duration calculation.

empty and dark environment, guaranteeing that users do not need to take off the VR glasses to respond to the questions and preventing any extraneous visual inputs from influencing memory performance. During the free recall task, participants are instructed that they do not need to remember the items in the same order they are presented. Participants must enter the answers to the recalled entries by typing and spelling them out in the input field. In the recognition task, participants are not required to aim. Instead, they have to pull the left and right triggers to indicate whether the content of the picture on the screen has been displayed. Throughout the response, we measured the precise timing of when each photo was displayed and when the participant initiated the trigger, which was then utilized to compute the participant's reaction time.

After each scene, the participants were brought back to a well-lit and neutral area for a 60-second respite. This was done to guarantee that the individuals regained their cognitive abilities. The entire experiment lasted around 1.1 h.

Eye-Tracking Data. Previous research has demonstrated that patterns of eye inspection can provide insights for analyzing aspects of human visual attention and scene perception [14]. To investigate whether individuals allocate more significant visual attention resources when exposed to unexpected stimuli, we collected real-time eye-tracking data by recording the 3D coordinates of participants' gaze points as they perceived their surroundings. Leveraging the operability of synthetic experimental materials, we can generate precise annotations of area of interest (AOI) at the pixel level. We assign distinct colors to items based on their class, with objects in the background belonging to the same class. The AOI exemplars are displayed in Fig. 4. As proposed in article [24], we compute the cumulative number of all gaze points on the AOI of each memorable object to measure the allocation of attentional resources. We empirically allocate a 7-pixel wide square local window as the region of focus centered on the gaze point in each frame. The intersection of the local gaze region and AOI is regarded to receive attention. Given the AOI object-level mask $\mathbf{M}^o \in \mathbb{R}^{F \times W \times H}$ and the attention map $\mathbf{A}^i \in \mathbb{R}^{F \times W \times H}$ of i-th participant of all frames F, we compute the gaze time T^o at the object o by the following equation.

$$T^o = \frac{1}{N} \frac{1}{N_{\text{FPS}}} \sum_i \sum_f \text{sign}(\sum_{w,h} \mathbf{A}^i_{f,w,h} \odot \mathbf{M}^o_{f,w,h}), \quad (1)$$

where $\odot$ is the element-wise production operation, N is the number of participants, and N_{FPS} is the frame rate of the VR scene videos.

EEG Data. EEG signals often contain significant noise, and the likelihood of noise generation can increase in more natural environments like VR. In our experiments, we instruct participants to avoid excessive head movements. In our experiment, the VR scenes are designed to be centrally located, allowing participants to view the panoramic video without turning their heads, ensuring an unimpaired experience and experimental outcomes while maintaining high-quality signal acquisition. We divide the 62 electrodes into four functional regions: the frontal lobe, parietal lobe, temporal lobe, and occipital lobe area, based on existing neuroscience knowledge. We first re-reference the signals to the bilateral mastoid electrodes M1 and M2 for the collected raw EEG data. Subsequently, a band-pass filter from 1 to 47 Hz is applied to the data. Ultimately, Independent Component Analysis (ICA) is conducted to decompose the raw signals into 62 distinct components (ICs). Components associated with blinks, eye movements, muscle activity, and other artifacts are removed based on visual inspection. On average, 9.84 ± 1.79 components are discarded per subject. The entire process was accomplished using the MNE package in Python.

We derive frequency-domain characteristics from the preprocessed EEG data by segmenting it into 1-second intervals. For each channel of the EEG, we employ a short-time Fourier transform to ascertain the power spectral density (PSD) on a per-second basis. Subsequently, we meticulously extract PSD features corresponding to the δ, θ, α, β and γ frequency bands.

4 Data Analysis

For the statistical analysis of both subjective and objective data, we initially employed the Shapiro-Wilk test to assess the normality of the data. If the data are normally distributed, we then utilize the paired-sample t-test to evaluate statistical disparities. In cases where the data do not conform to a normal distribution, we resort to the Wilcoxon signed-rank test. The significance level for all statistical analyses is set at 0.05.

Analysis of Free Recall Results. The free recall task is a primary paradigm in studying the isolation effect. The participants should recall objects they have seen in the VR experience and fill in the answers in an in-VR user interface. The final recall results are independent of the order in which the participants answered. Figure 5 (a) compares the recall of each session's memorized expected and unexpected items. The recall of the expected item is the average value of all recalled in-context items of each session. The overall recall of the unexpected stimuli (M = 0.92, SD = 0.27) is significantly greater than that of the in-context items (M = 0.61, SD = 0.18) with $p < 0.001$. Specifically, in the static scenes, the mean recall of both expected items (M = 0.65, SD = 0.17) and unexpected items (M = 1.00, SD = 0.00) are better than those of the dynamic scenes with statistical results (M = 0.58, SD = 0.18) and (M = 0.85, SD = 0.36), respectively. The results support the conclusion that the isolation effect can be activated in both

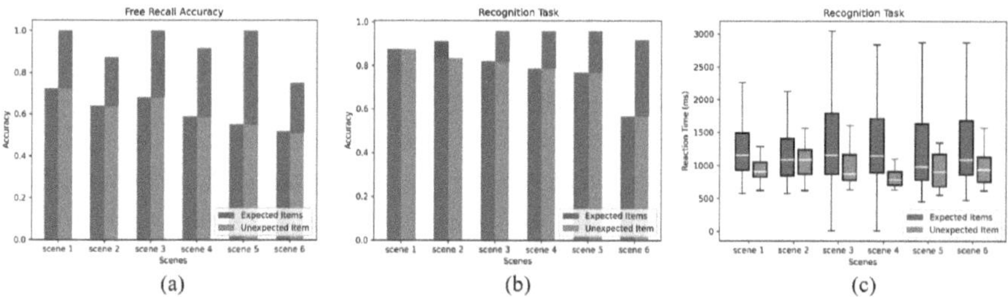

Fig. 5. Free recall and recognition task results. Across all six VR scenes, (a) the participants recalled more categories of unexpected stimuli (red bars) than expected stimuli (blue bars) in the free recall task; In the recognition task, (b) the participants demonstrated higher recognition accuracy for unexpected stimuli in both semi-sequential and non-sequential settings, (c) and exhibited shorter reaction times across all settings. Dark-colored bar segments highlight greater differences in recall and recognition accuracy. (Color figure online)

Table 2. Free recall results and recognition accuracy for three perception patterns, including sequential, semi-sequential, and non-sequential scenarios.

Scene ID	Perception Type	Free Recall	Recognition
1	Sequential	0.75	0.88
2	Sequential	0.66	0.90
3	Semi-Sequential	0.71	0.83
4	Semi-Sequential	0.62	0.80
5	Non-Sequential	0.60	0.79
6	Non-Sequential	0.52	0.60

static and dynamic scenarios and in various perceptional patterns, including sequential, semi-sequential, and non-sequential settings.

Furthermore, we compare the effect of the factors of object mobility and presentation linearity on free recall performances. For the expected entries, participants perform better for dynamic stimuli (M = 0.65, SD = 0.17) than static stimuli (M = 0.58, SD = 0.18) with $p < 0.01$. Furthermore, for the unexpected entries, the difference between dynamic (M = 1.00, SD = 0.00) and static items (M = 0.85, SD = 0.36) is more significant with $p < 0.001$. In addition, Table 2 reports the average recall of all items in the three perception modalities. The sequential scenario illustrates the best average free recall performance with 0.71, and the participants perform worse in the semi-sequential and non-sequential settings with competition of cognitive resources, with average recalls of 0.67 and 0.56, respectively. However, the participants perform less variety in sequential and semi-sequential scenes for expected items ($p = 0.226$) and unexpected items ($p = 0.650$). In the comparison of sequential and non-sequential scenes, the participants perform better in the sequential paradigm (M = 0.68, SD = 0.19) than the non-sequential stimuli (M = 0.53, SD = 0.14) with $p < 0.01$. However, the participants performed less variously for unexpected items in both sequential and non-sequential settings ($p = 0.298$).

Analysis of Recognition Results. We conduct the recognition task as the second test so that the image cues do not impact the free recall task. Due to the image reference, the recognition task is more accessible than the free recall test. We record the recognition accuracy and the reaction time (RT) to measure the short-term memory performance. Figure 5 (b) reports the average accuracy of the presented items of each VR scenario. In sequential settings, in Scene 2, for instance, participants achieve a comparable accuracy of the expected (M = 0.91, SD = 0.19) and unexpected items (M = 0.83, SD = 0.37). The reasons behind this phenomenon could be twofold. Firstly, there is not enough competition for cognitive resources in the sequential setting, so more items are temporally stored in sensory memory. Secondly, the image hint could be an effective reminder so the participant could successfully retrieve more entries that might be forgotten during the free recall task. However, the unexpected items have a more significant advantage than in-context entries in the semi-sequential and non-sequential settings, with accuracy boosts of 13.89%, 17.13%, 18.98%, and 35.19% for Scenes 3–6, respectively. In addition, Table 2 reports the average recognition accuracy of all items in the three perception modalities. The sequential scenario illustrates the best average recognition performance with 0.89, and the participants perform worse in the semi-sequential and non-sequential settings with the competition of cognitive resources, with a recognition accuracy of 0.82 and 0.70, respectively.

Figure 5 (c) reports RT during recognition trials, which indicates the robustness of impression in short-term memory. Since the individual difference in cognition performance and possible external noises, we choose to illustrate the RT results in box plots with outlier elimination. The box plot shows that the median reaction times facing unexpected stimuli are lower than in-context stimuli. Generally, participants respond faster when recalling unforeseen stimuli. Across six sessions, there is a significant performance difference while retrieving unexpected items (M = 1022.17 ms, SD = 374.67 ms) and expected items (M = 1554.14 ms, SD = 566.68 ms) with $p < 0.001$. Moreover, when identifying different types of unexpected stimuli in a scene, participants could identify static objects (M = 1055.44 ms, SD = 710.42 ms) more quickly than dynamic objects (M = 1230.63 ms, SD = 1004.52 ms).

Analysis of Eye-Tracking Data. This subsection analyzes the gaze duration at AOIs in semi-sequential and non-sequential settings in competition with attentional resources. In Scene 3 and Scene 4, the unexpected item and its in-context counterpart appear simultaneously. Specifically, in Scene 3, the gaze duration of the unexpected stimulus is 1073.33 ms while that of the co-occur in-context item is 944.17 ms. In Scene 4, the gaze duration is 1294.17 ms and 1073.33 ms for unexpected and expected ones, respectively. For the non-sequential setting, we compare the unexpected stimulus with all the presented items in the scene. In Scene 5, the average gaze duration of all expected stimuli is 967.59 ms, while the unexpected item obtains more attention time with 1133.33 ms. Similarly, In Scene 6, the unexpected item gaze of 2136.67 ms exceeds the mean gaze duration of in-context items of 1574.33 ms.

Analysis of EEG Data. We examine the variations in EEG features associated with expected versus unexpected visual stimuli. The channels with significant levels of

$p < 0.01$ under two different stimulus conditions are listed in Table 3; for the δ band, channels AF4, Cz, CPz, Pz, P1, and CP1 have lower PSD under expected stimuli compared to unexpected stimuli. For the θ band, the PSD at channels FC2, FP1, AF3, and AF4 is significantly lower under expected stimuli than unexpected stimuli. Similarly, for the α band, the PSD at channels FZ, FC1, FC2, FCZ, CZ, and C2 is significantly lower under expected stimulation than unexpected stimulation. The topographic maps of cerebral activity across different frequency bands are delineated based on the PSD of all electrode channels. As shown in Fig. 6, within the δ band, there is a marked increase in activation within the parietal region under conditions of unexpected stimuli. In the θ band, increased activation is observed in both the frontal and parietal regions in response to the unexpected stimuli. The α band mirrors this pattern, with enhanced activation in the frontal and parietal regions noted during unexpected as opposed to expected stimuli.

Table 3. Channels with significant differences between expected and unexpected stimulus.

Band	Channel	Expected Stimulus	Unexpected Stimulus
δ	AF4	0.71	0.86
	Cz	0.62	0.79
	CPz	0.60	0.78
	Pz	0.58	0.82
	P1	0.55	0.83
	CP1	0.56	0.81
θ	FC2	0.58	0.84
	FP1	0.67	0.98
	AF3	0.48	0.85
	AF4	0.51	0.76
α	Fz	0.37	0.72
	FC1	0.31	0.69
	FC2	0.32	0.67
	FCz	0.26	0.69
	Cz	0.28	0.68
	C2	0.30	0.66

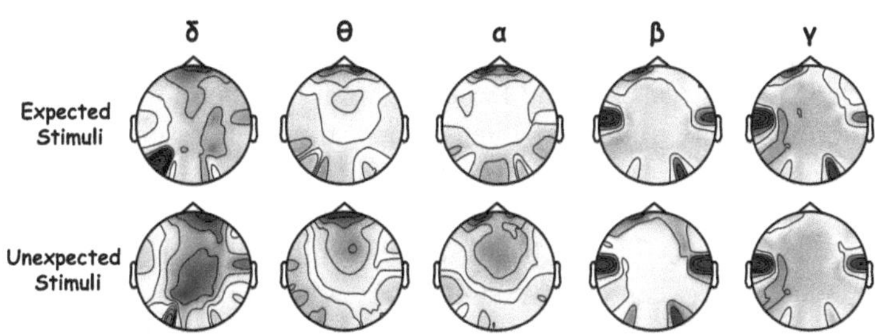

Fig. 6. EEG topography of five bands under two types of stimulation.

5 Discussion

Based on the conventional study framework in the isolation effect and the static linear paradigm, our experiments explore the effects of unexpected stimuli on short-term memory performance under dynamic and nonlinear perceptual conditions with the advantages of VR. In addition, we study potential physiological mechanisms influencing this relationship with the analysis of eye-tracking and EEG information. In this section, we summarise and discuss the obtained findings and analyze them alongside insights from neuroscience studies.

Cognitive Task Results of Isolation Effect in VR. The analysis in Sect. 4.1 validates that unforeseen stimuli can successfully elicit the isolation effect, irrespective of the dynamism or staticity of the objects in the VR environment or the presence of attentional resource rivalry. These findings provide a foundation for investigating the impact of VR material on short-term memory. Compared to the easier recognition task, the more challenging free recall task results exhibit a more prominent isolation effect. Furthermore, the recognition task shows that more challenging semi-sequential and non-sequential perceptual scenarios result in more noticeable isolation effects. The derived theory from these results is that individuals have enough cognitive resources to complete memory tasks when the complexity of memory material and perceptual patterns is low. Consequently, they are capable of reliably recalling unexpected and in-contextual stimuli. Nevertheless, restricted cognitive resources are insufficient to facilitate the performance of memory tasks in dynamic and cognitively competitive scenarios. Under these circumstances, the inherent importance of the unforeseen stimuli will be more readily remembered in short-term memory.

Physiological Patterns of Isolation Effect in VR. Neuroscience research has previously demonstrated that brain regions associated with attention, sensory processing, and integration include the frontal and parietal lobes [33,35]. Furthermore, θ waves have been linked to subconscious processes [31], while α waves are related to the transition from a resting state to a state of attention [17]. Consequently, we speculate that subjects' attention must be redirected and adapted to the stimulus when an unexpected stimulus occurs, leading to increased activation of the frontal and parietal lobes. Integrating the eye-movement data, the participants had extended periods of gazing in the area where the unexpected stimulus was present. Furthermore, it may be shown that elevated levels of short-term memory triggered by unexpected stimuli are associated with a shift in attentional resources. This conclusion coincides with the theory of Rundus [28], where the isolated items receive additional attention, causing an advantage in the memory process. Furthermore, for the β and γ bands, no discernible differences in regional brain activity are detected between the two stimulus conditions. Since these two bands are typically associated with higher-intensity stimuli such as excitement [21] or anxiety [34], the unexpected stimuli do not elicit high-intensity fluctuations in the subjects.

Limitations. While our findings can adequately substantiate hypothesis testing and serve as an expansion of the isolation effect research methodology, its limitations persist. The VR scenarios examined in this study showcase only several perceptual modalities and visual contents. Choosing common object categories as memorable content, we acknowledge that the context of VR immersive experience encompasses additional elements such as sound, sense of touch, narrative, and emotional induction for stimuli control. Hence, further research should be conducted using more ample and diverse material modalities to yield more thorough findings regarding unexpected stimuli. Additionally, time consumption and cost limit the number of participants, thereby hindering the validation of results on a larger scale.

6 Conclusion and Future Work

In this work, we explore the unexpected visual stimuli on short-term memory in VR by designing six specialized scenes and an immersive cognition evaluation platform. With conventional free recall and recognition cognitive tasks, we demonstrate the activation of the isolation effect in static and dynamic scenarios and in sequential, semi-sequential, and non-sequential perceptual modalities in VR. Additionally, it can observe a longer gaze duration and significant frontal and parietal region activation in δ, θ, and α oscillatory energy with unexpected visual stimuli. The results prove that humans' attention must be redirected and adapted to unexpected stimuli. The increased attention to the unexpected object showed a positive correlation with the higher level of short-term memory. The β and γ bands have no significant fluctuation across brain regions. Our study on short-term memory can provide valuable guidance in VR applications that need to emphasize and highlight specific visual contents. Otherwise, the conclusion also reveals short-term cognitive consequences of daily use of VR.

Our near-term research efforts are geared towards immediate improvement with physiological information analysis for more detailed conclusions. Other aspects of VR content and cognitive impact could be researched long-term. For example, we could expand the evaluation platform to explore multi-modal VR content on high-level cognition abilities, such as executive function, reasoning, and social cognition. Additionally, it would be of interest to researchers to explore the cognitive impact of AI-generated content, including immersive 3D scenes and virtual human agents.

Acknowledgments. This paper is supported by National Natural Science Foundation of China (62525204, 62502469). This work is also supported by Zhongguancun Laboratory.

References

1. Axmacher, N., et al.: Intracranial EEG correlates of expectancy and memory formation in the human hippocampus and nucleus accumbens. Neuron **65**(4), 541–549 (2010)
2. Bar, M.: The proactive brain: using analogies and associations to generate predictions. Trends Cogn. Sci. **11**(7), 280–289 (2007)
3. Barch, D.M., et al.: Cntrics final task selection: working memory. Schizophr. Bull. **35**(1), 136–152 (2009)

4. Bitton-Guetta, N., et al.: Breaking common sense: whoops! a vision-and-language benchmark of synthetic and compositional images. In: Proceedings of the IEEE/CVF International Conference on Computer Vision, pp. 2616–2627 (2023)
5. Braver, T.S.: The variable nature of cognitive control: a dual mechanisms framework. Trends Cogn. Sci. **16**(2), 106–113 (2012)
6. Cascella, M., Al Khalili, Y.: Short-Term Memory Impairment. StatPearls Publishing, Treasure Island (2023)
7. Coleman, B., Marion, S., Rizzo, A., Turnbull, J., Nolty, A.: Virtual reality assessment of classroom-related attention: an ecologically relevant approach to evaluating the effectiveness of working memory training. Front. Psychol. **10**, 1851 (2019)
8. Corriveau Lecavalier, N., Ouellet, É., Boller, B., Belleville, S.: Use of immersive virtual reality to assess episodic memory: a validation study in older adults. Neuropsychol. Rehabil. **30**(3), 462–480 (2020)
9. Elhalal, A., Davelaar, E.J., Usher, M.: The role of the frontal cortex in memory: an investigation of the von restorff effect. Front. Hum. Neurosci. **8**, 410 (2014)
10. Frank, D., Kafkas, A.: Expectation-driven novelty effects in episodic memory. Neurobiol. Learn. Mem. **183**, 107466 (2021)
11. Frank, D., Montemurro, M.A., Montaldi, D.: Pattern separation underpins expectation-modulated memory. J. Neurosci. **40**(17), 3455–3464 (2020)
12. Frey, J.N., Ruhnau, P., Weisz, N.: Not so different after all: the same oscillatory processes support different types of attention. Brain Res. **1626**, 183–197 (2015)
13. Friston, K.: The free-energy principle: a rough guide to the brain? Trends Cogn. Sci. **13**(7), 293–301 (2009)
14. Huddleston, P., Behe, B.K., Minahan, S., Fernandez, R.T.: Seeking attention: an eye tracking study of in-store merchandise displays. Int. J. Retail Distrib. Manag. **43**(6), 561–574 (2015)
15. Jaiswal, N., Ray, W., Slobounov, S.: Encoding of visual-spatial information in working memory requires more cerebral efforts than retrieval: evidence from an eeg and virtual reality study. Brain Res. **1347**, 80–89 (2010)
16. Kishiyama, M.M., Yonelinas, A.P., Knight, R.T.: Novelty enhancements in memory are dependent on lateral prefrontal cortex. J. Neurosci. **29**(25), 8114–8118 (2009)
17. Klimesch, W.: Alpha-band oscillations, attention, and controlled access to stored information. Trends Cogn. Sci. **16**(12), 606–617 (2012)
18. Liu, R., Wu, R., Van Hoorick, B., Tokmakov, P., Zakharov, S., Vondrick, C.: Zero-1-to-3: zero-shot one image to 3d object. In: Proceedings of the IEEE/CVF International Conference on Computer Vision, pp. 9298–9309 (2023)
19. Long, N.M., Lee, H., Kuhl, B.A.: Hippocampal mismatch signals are modulated by the strength of neural predictions and their similarity to outcomes. J. Neurosci. **36**(50), 12677–12687 (2016)
20. Løvstad, M., et al.: Contribution of subregions of human frontal cortex to novelty processing. J. Cogn. Neurosci. **24**(2), 378–395 (2012)
21. Machizawa, M.G., et al.: Quantification of anticipation of excitement with a three-axial model of emotion with eeg. J. Neural Eng. **17**(3), 036011 (2020)
22. Mancuso, V., et al.: Systematic review of memory assessment in virtual reality: evaluating convergent and divergent validity with traditional neuropsychological measures. Front. Hum. Neurosci. **18**, 1380575 (2024)
23. Martin, D., Sun, X., Gutierrez, D., Masia, B.: A study of change blindness in immersive environments. IEEE Trans. Visual Comput. Graph. **29**(5), 2446–2455 (2023)
24. Peters, C., Pelachaud, C., Bevacqua, E., Mancini, M., Poggi, I.: A model of attention and interest using gaze behavior. In: International Workshop on Intelligent Virtual Agents, pp. 229–240. Springer, Heidelberg (2005)

25. Rajaram, S.: The effects of conceptual salience and perceptual distinctiveness on conscious recollection. Psychon. Bull. Rev. **5**, 71–78 (1998)
26. Ranganath, C., Rainer, G.: Neural mechanisms for detecting and remembering novel events. Nat. Rev. Neurosci. **4**(3), 193–202 (2003)
27. Rombach, R., Blattmann, A., Lorenz, D., Esser, P., Ommer, B.: High-resolution image synthesis with latent diffusion models. In: Proceedings of the IEEE/CVF Conference on Computer Vision and Pattern Recognition, pp. 10684–10695 (2022)
28. Rundus, D.: Analysis of rehearsal processes in free recall. J. Exp. Psychol. **89**(1), 63 (1971)
29. Sauzéon, H., N'Kaoua, B., Pala, P.A., Taillade, M., Auriacombe, S., Guitton, P.: Everyday-like memory for objects in ageing and Alzheimer's disease assessed in a visually complex environment: the role of executive functioning and episodic memory. J. Neuropsychol. **10**(1), 33–58 (2016)
30. Schmidt, S.R., Schmidt, C.R.: Inattentional blindness and the von restorff effect. Memory Cogn. **43**, 151–163 (2015)
31. Shaari, N., Syafiq, M., Amin, M., Mikami, O.: Electroencephalography (eeg) application in neuromarketing-exploring the subconscious mind. J. Adv. Manuf. Technol. (JAMT) **13**(2 (2)) (2019)
32. Shestyuk, A.Y., Kasinathan, K., Karapoondinott, V., Knight, R.T., Gurumoorthy, R.: Individual EEG measures of attention, memory, and motivation predict population level tv viewership and twitter engagement. PLoS ONE **14**(3), e0214507 (2019)
33. Simpson, G.V., et al.: Dynamic activation of frontal, parietal, and sensory regions underlying anticipatory visual spatial attention. J. Neurosci. **31**(39), 13880–13889 (2011)
34. Sporn, S., Hein, T., Herrojo Ruiz, M.: Alterations in the amplitude and burst rate of beta oscillations impair reward-dependent motor learning in anxiety. Elife **9**, e50654 (2020)
35. Szczepanski, S.M., Konen, C.S., Kastner, S.: Mechanisms of spatial attention control in frontal and parietal cortex. J. Neurosci. **30**(1), 148–160 (2010)
36. Thut, G., Nietzel, A., Brandt, S.A., Pascual-Leone, A.: α-band electroencephalographic activity over occipital cortex indexes visuospatial attention bias and predicts visual target detection. J. Neurosci. **26**(37), 9494–9502 (2006)
37. Vecchiato, G., et al.: Changes in brain activity during the observation of tv commercials by using eeg, gsr and hr measurements. Brain Topogr. **23**, 165–179 (2010)
38. Von Restorff, H.: Über die wirkung von bereichsbildungen im spurenfeld. Psychol. Forsch. **18**, 299–342 (1933)
39. Wittmann, B.C., Bunzeck, N., Dolan, R.J., Düzel, E.: Anticipation of novelty recruits reward system and hippocampus while promoting recollection. Neuroimage **38**(1), 194–202 (2007)

Model-Guided 3D Cranial Open Surface Reconstruction Based on Euler's Elastica and Optimal Transport

Lijun Zhu[1], Junli Zhao[1](✉), Pengbo Zhou[2], Guodong Wang[1], Huiqin Niu[1], and Zhenkuan Pan[1]

[1] College of Computer Science and Technology, Qingdao University, Qingdao 266071, China
zjl@qdu.edu.cn
[2] School of Arts and Communication, Beijing Normal University, Beijing 100875, China

Abstract. Cranial reconstruction is a key technology in fields such as forensic science and archaeology. However, existing methods still face two major challenges for reconstructing a high-genus cranial open surface from computed tomography (CT) scan data: the inaccurate segmentation of complex anatomical structures, and the insufficient fidelity, which is often accompanied by loss of detail and topological errors. In this paper, we propose a cranial open surface reconstruction framework that fuses Optimal Transport (OT) theory and Unsigned Distance Fields (UDF). In the segmentation stage, we designed a novel segmentation network (EGCA-Net) that combines a graph convolutional attention mechanism (GCAM) and variational theory. This network utilizes graph convolution to capture global long-range dependencies and introduces a loss function based on Euler's Elastica model as a geometric constraint, significantly improving the smoothness and anatomical accuracy of the segmentation results. In the reconstruction stage, we sample point clouds from the precise segmentation results and propose an enhanced unsigned distance field learning strategy. This strategy, by introducing OT-based geometric regularization and a projection consistency constraint, combined with an advanced surface extraction algorithm, can generate high-fidelity 3D mesh models that are topologically accurate and rich in detail. Experimental results demonstrate that our framework exhibits significant advantages in both segmentation accuracy and reconstruction quality, achieving excellent results in Cranial Open Surface reconstruction.

Keywords: Euler's Elastica · Medical Image Segmentation · Unsigned Distance Field · Optimal Transport · Open-Surface Reconstruction

1 Introduction

As the most morphologically complex structure in the human skeleton, the precise 3D cranial reconstruction holds significant application value in numerous fields, including forensic medicine, archaeology, anthropology, and clinical

A. Hinkenjan et al. (Eds.): ICXR 2025, LNCS 16428, pp. 116–132, 2026.
https://doi.org/10.1007/978-981-95-7195-6_7

medicine. Reconstructing the skull surface from CT scan data provides a crucial basis for craniofacial reconstruction, identity verification, and injury analysis in fields like archaeology and criminal investigation [23,34]. In clinical medicine, precise skull models are equally indispensable for the planning of craniomaxillofacial surgery, implant design, and postoperative evaluation [6]. Especially when combined with extended reality (XR) technologies [33], the immersive interactive experience provided in scenarios such as surgical training, pre-operative planning, and real-time intra-operative guidance can greatly improve the overall accuracy and safety of surgery [25].

However, reconstructing high-fidelity cranial open surface from raw medical scan data (such as CT) still faces two core bottlenecks. First, in the segmentation stage, it is challenging for existing methods to balance the accuracy of global structure and local details simultaneously. Due to the limitations of their local receptive field [21], traditional convolutional networks have difficulty capturing long-distance dependencies when processing CT data, resulting in topological errors; at the same time, they lack effective geometric constraints, which makes the segmentation boundaries often have non-smooth artifacts in complex structures. Second, in the reconstruction stage, generating high-fidelity open-surface models from segmentation results is also extremely challenging. In particular, advanced methods based on UDF, although suitable for open surfaces, are susceptible to the vanishing gradient problem near the zero level set during learning [8], and lack strong geometric regularization methods, resulting in the final model being often too smooth, losing the fine anatomical features that are crucial for forensic or archaeological research. Finally, reconstructing high-quality 3D surfaces from segmentation results (point clouds), especially for structures with open boundaries and complex topology, such as the skull, is difficult for their high-genus structure and without a closed surface.

Inspired by the advantages of variational theory in maintaining geometric regularity in image processing, the powerful capabilities of graph neural networks in processing non-Euclidean spatial data and long-range relationships, and the application of optimal transport theory to geometric metrics, in this paper, we propose a model-guided 3D cranial Open Surface reconstruction framework. We integrate Euler's Elastica-guided graph convolutional attention segmentation networks and OT-guided UDF reconstruction networks to address the topological and boundary issues in segmentation and reconstruct high-fidelity open surfaces. Our main contributions are as follows:

- We propose a novel geometric guided segmentation network, EGCA-Net, which effectively captures global context and long-range dependencies by integrating a graph convolutional attention mechanism (GCAM) combined with a geometric loss function based on Euler's elastic model. It ensures smoothness and anatomical plausibility of segmentation boundaries.
- We innovatively designed an optimal transport (OT)-guided UDF reconstruction strategy. By introducing an OT geometric regularization term and projection consistency constraints, we ensure that the point cloud distribution of the reconstructed surface is geometrically consistent with the original sam-

pled point cloud. And we also design a staged optimization strategy from coarse to fine to accurately recover fine structures and complex topology.
- We integrate Euler's Elastica-guided graph convolutional attention segmentation networks and OT-guided UDF reconstruction networks and propose a model-guided CT surface reconstruction framework, which can reconstruct high-fidelity open-surface 3D cranial models from raw CT images. Extensive experiments demonstrate that this framework exhibits significant advantages in segmentation accuracy and reconstruction quality.

2 Related Works

This chapter will review two areas closely related to our research: medical image segmentation based on deep learning and 3D surface reconstruction technology using implicit neural representation.

2.1 Medical Image Segmentation

Accurate skull contour segmentation is the basis for subsequent 3D reconstruction. Traditional segmentation methods, such as thresholding, region growth, and active contour models [11], are often sensitive to initialization and noise and have difficulty coping with complex anatomical structures. In recent years, deep learning-based methods, especially convolutional neural networks (CNNs), have become the mainstream of medical image segmentation.

U-Net Based Segmentation Network. U-Net [24] and its numerous variants are the cornerstones of the current field of medical image segmentation. Its classic encoder-decoder structure and skip connection design effectively integrate deep semantic information and shallow detail features, and have achieved great success in various segmentation tasks. Subsequent studies have further optimized the network information flow and gradient propagation by introducing residual connections (such as Res-UNet [5]) and dense connections (such as Dense-UNet [1]). However, these models mainly rely on the local receptive field of convolution and have limited ability to capture global context and long-range dependencies, which is a challenge for skull segmentation that requires general morphological constraints.

Attention-Based Segmentation Networks. In the field of medical image segmentation, attention-based networks have made significant progress. Early representative works such as Attention U-Net [20]introduced attention gates in skip connections, enabling the network to focus on key local feature areas. Later, in order to more directly establish a global context model, researchers further introduced the Transformer architecture with strong long-distance dependency modeling capabilities into the segmentation task. For example, TransUNet

[2]innovatively combined CNN with Transformer, using CNN powerful local feature extraction capabilities and Transformer global information capture capabilities to model local and global dependencies effectively; DS-TransUNet [15] uses a dual-scale encoder based on Swin Transformer [16], which can not only efficiently process multi-scale inputs, but also deeply encode local and global feature representations from different semantic levels through the self-attention mechanism. Similarly, UNETR [7] successfully applied this idea to 3D medical image segmentation. These models demonstrate that whether through attention gates or self-attention, attention-based mechanisms are effective at capturing long-range dependencies, yet they primarily learn these relationships implicitly from data.

The classical U-Net network effectively fuses multi-scale local features through its encoder-decoder structure, while the subsequent Attention and Transformer-based architectures make up for its shortcomings in capturing global context and long-range dependencies. In recent years, large-scale base models represented by SAM [13] have further demonstrated powerful generalized segmentation capabilities, but their common limitation is that as purely data-driven methods, they generally lack explicit constraints on the geometrical shape of segmented targets. To this end, we introduce the Eulerian elasticity loss as a model-guided geometric prior, aiming to impose explicit regularization on the network and thus ensure the smoothness and anatomical soundness of the segmentation boundaries.

2.2 3D Surface Reconstruction

3D surface reconstruction algorithms can be classified into two categories: explicit and implicit. Among explicit methods, the classic Marching Cubes (MC) [18] algorithm directly extracts iso-surfaces on a voxel grid but is prone to generating stair-step artifacts. Poisson Surface Reconstruction [12] is another popular method that can generate smooth watertight surfaces by solving the Poisson equation, but it requires accurate normal vector information and forces the generation of closed surfaces, which makes it unsuitable for reconstructing natural open surfaces such as the skull.

Implicit methods learn a continuous function to represent geometric shapes and have received widespread attention in recent years. Among them, the signed distance field (SDF) [22] is good at representing closed, watertight surfaces, but it is not suitable for open surfaces such as skull defects. The UDF [4] is an ideal choice to represent open surfaces because it does not distinguish between inside and outside. Work such as NUDF [28] has demonstrated the feasibility of learning UDF directly from images. However, UDF learning faces its challenges, namely the problem of vanishing or non-differentiable gradients near the zero-level set, which severely impacts reconstruction quality.

Recent works have tackled this from different perspectives; for instance, NeuralUDF [17] proposes a novel volume rendering scheme to learn UDFs directly from multi-view images, while LoSF-UDF [9] presents a lightweight framework that learns from a synthetic dataset of local geometric patches to reconstruct surfaces from point clouds. Other works, including CAP-UDF [35], LevelSetUDF [36], and DEUDF [32], have been dedicated to alleviating this issue. In our work, we use OT to provide a holistic and geometrically-aware signal, guiding the network to learn a high-quality open-surface representation by comparing entire distributions of point clouds, thus enhancing the reconstruction of complex cranial geometries.

3 Method

This section details our proposed framework for model-guided 3D cranial open-surface reconstruction based on Euler's Elastica and Optimal Transport. As shown in Fig. 1, the entire framework consists of two core stages: first, accurate skull segmentation using EGCA-Net; then, based on the segmentation result (point cloud), open-surface reconstruction is achieved by OT-guided UDF reconstruction networks.

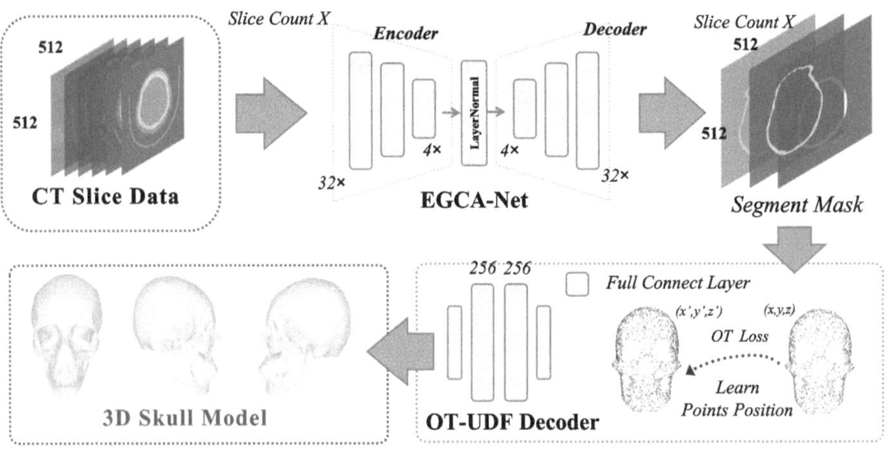

Fig. 1. Cranial Open surface reconstruction framework that integrates Euler's Elastica-guided graph convolutional attention segmentation networks (EGCA-Net) and OT-guided UDF reconstruction networks.

3.1 EGCA-Net: CT Segmentation Based on Euler's Elastica-Guided Graph Convolutional Attention Networks

We designed a novel segmentation network, EGCA-Net (Euler's Elastica-guided Graph Convolutional Attention networks) which introduces the Graph Convolutional Attention Model (GCAM) and Euler's Elastica loss function based on variational theory, enabling it to effectively capture long-range dependencies and retain global information to achieve more robust and more accurate segmentation.

CT Segmentation Network Based on Graph Convolutional Attention Mechanism. The EGCA-Net proposed in this study adopts a classic encoder-decoder structure as its backbone network, aiming to achieve precise segmentation of cranial CT images. The core of this network consists of two parts: First, we employ the Pyramid Vision Transformer (PVT) [31] as the encoder, which efficiently extracts hierarchical features at four different scales from CT slices using the self-attention mechanism. Second, we design a four-stage cascaded decoder. At each decoding stage, the module first fuses the features from the corresponding scale of the encoder through skip connections, then refines the fused features with the key module, which embeds the Graph Convolution Attention Module (GCAM) for global context enhancement, and finally performs upsampling to restore the high-resolution segmentation map gradually. The specific network architecture is shown in Fig. 2.

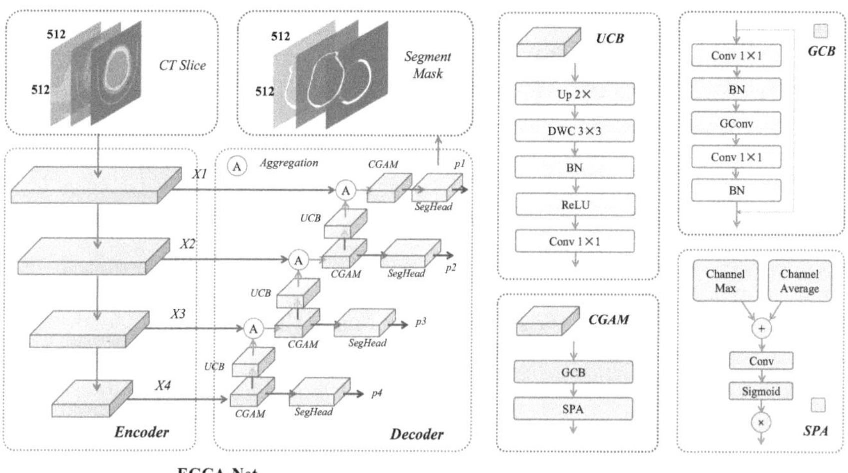

Fig. 2. EGCA-Net network structure diagram

The Graph Convolutional Attention Module (GCAM), which is central to the cranial segmentation task, synergistically refines features through a cascade of two submodules: the Graph Convolutional Block (GCB) and the Spatial Attention (SPA) module. First, the feature graph is fed into the GCB, which considers each spatial location in the feature graph as a graph node and establishes topological relationships among the nodes through a dynamically constructed K-Nearest Neighbor Graph (KNN) [29]. By using graph convolution operations, GCB can effectively aggregate non-local contextual information. Through this module, it can capture the global dependencies of the skull as a whole structure. Even if some skull structures appear blurred or discontinuous in the image, GCB can infer and maintain their structural integrity through their association with clear bone structures in the distance, thereby effectively avoiding unreasonable phenomena in the segmentation results.

After its global context is enhanced by the GCB, the feature map is then fed into the SPA module for spatial focusing. The SPA module operates by performing max-pooling and average-pooling in parallel along the channel dimension of the feature map. This process generates a descriptor that outlines the importance of spatial regions, which is then used to compute a two-dimensional attention map. This map quantifies the importance of each spatial position for identifying the cranial contour. Ultimately, by performing an element-wise multiplication of this attention map with the GCB output feature map, the model focuses its computational resources on segmenting the complex cranial contours, thereby achieving precise segmentation of local boundary details while preserving global structural integrity.

Euler's Elastica Segmentation Constraint. To produce smoother and more anatomically plausible segmentation boundaries, we employ Euler's Elastica [3] [37] as a regularization term to guide network segmentation results. Based on variational principles, this term incorporates curvature, length, and area information as natural geometric constraints for the segmentation task. This approach leads to a more robust and accurate segmentation. The loss function is defined as:

$$L(u,f) = \int_{\Omega} (\alpha + \beta\kappa^2) \mathrm{d}s + \lambda \int_{\Omega} u(c_1 - f)^2 \mathrm{dx} + \lambda \int_{\Omega} (1-u)(c_2 - f)^2 \mathrm{dx} \quad (1)$$

Among them, the first term is Euler's Elastica regular term, while the second and third terms represent the inner and outer regions of the contour line, respectively. α and β are positive parameters that control the balance between the curvature and length of the segmentation boundary. κ is the average curvature of the segmentation contour. c_1 and c_2 are the average intensity values of the foreground and background regions, respectively. $\mathrm{d}s = |\nabla u| \, \mathrm{dx}$ is the length of the segmentation boundary, $\mathrm{x} = (x, y)$, f is the true segmentation, and u is the predicted segmentation. The average curvature $\overline{\kappa}$ is defined as:

$$\overline{\kappa} = \frac{(1+u_x^2)u_{yy} + (1+u_y^2)u_{xx} - 2u_x u_y u_{xy}}{2(1+u_x^2+u_y^2)^{3/2}} \quad (2)$$

where u_x, u_y is the first-order derivative of u in the x and y directions, and u_{xx}, u_{xy}, and u_{yy} are the corresponding second-order derivatives. To use this in neural network training, we need to discretize it. For a two-dimensional image with a pixel grid of (i, j), $L(u, f)$ discrete format is as follows:

$$\sum_{i=1}^{\Omega}\sum_{j=1}^{\Omega}(\alpha+\beta\kappa_{i,j}^2)|\nabla u_{i,j}| + \lambda\sum_{i=1}^{\Omega}\sum_{j=1}^{\Omega} u_{i,j}(c_1 - f_{i,j})^2 + \lambda\sum_{i=1}^{\Omega}\sum_{j=1}^{\Omega}(1-u_{i,j})(c_2 - f_{i,j})^2 \quad (3)$$

The derivatives of each order required for the gradient ∇u and the curvature κ are approximated by the Sobel operator [10]. The entire discrete formula is differentiable. Therefore, the parameters of the segmentation network can be optimized end-to-end during the training process through the back-propagation algorithm, guiding the network to learn the segmentation capability with geometric smoothness characteristics.

3.2 OT-UDFR: OT-Guided UDF Open-Surface Reconstruction

After obtaining the accurate cranial segmentation result, we first perform a neighborhood topology-based analysis on the original grayscale CT data to generate an over-complete set of boundary candidates. Then, through a single four-directional projection scan, we extract a single external contour from this candidate set, thereby obtaining the initial point cloud P. Our goal is to learn a continuous geometric representation capable of accurately capturing its complex topology and open boundary. To this end, we adopt the UDF representation and design a reconstruction framework based on Optimal Transport theory.

Unsigned Distance Field Prediction. Unlike traditional SDFs, UDFs only represent the distance from any point in space to the nearest surface, without considering whether the point is inside or outside the object. Therefore, they are more suitable for handling complex skull structures with open boundaries or internal cavities. We train a small multi-layer perceptron (MLP) network f_θ to map spatial coordinates (x, y, z) to UDF values:$f_\theta(x, y, z) \rightarrow d$, the network architecture diagram is shown below (see Fig. 3):

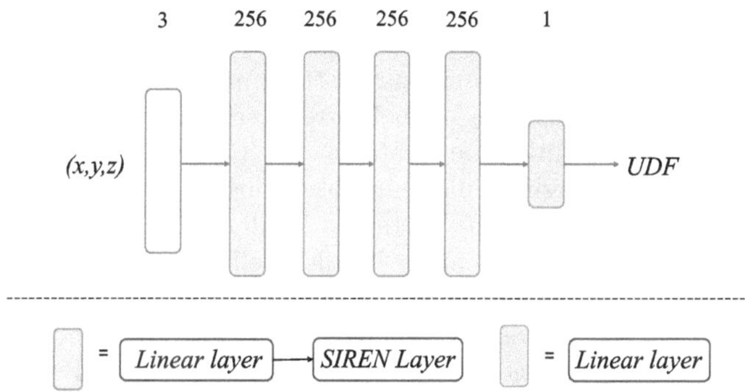

Fig. 3. UDF Network Architecture

To accurately capture high-frequency details on the skull surface, we chose SIREN (Sinusoidal Representation Network) [27] as the backbone network for the parameterized UDF function f_θ. SIREN uses sine functions as activation functions, which are well suited for expressing complex geometric signals.

Projection Consistency. For any given point q in the space defined by a UDF $f_\theta(x, y, z)$, the local gradient $\nabla f_\theta(q)$ indicates the direction of the fastest increase in distance, which is away from the surface. Consequently, the normalized gradient direction can be defined as the implicit normal vector at that point:

$$n(q) = \frac{\nabla f_\theta(q)}{\|\nabla f_\theta(q)\|_2} \tag{4}$$

Based on this, we can construct a differentiable projection operation from any spatial point to its corresponding target surface point. Specifically, for a query point q, we move along the reverse direction of its implicit normal vector by the distance value $f_\theta(q)$ predicted by the network, thereby projecting it onto the point z on the zero level set:

$$z = q - f_\theta(q) \cdot n(q) = q - f_\theta(q)\frac{\nabla f_\theta(q)}{\|\nabla f_\theta(q)\|_2} \tag{5}$$

After projecting the spatial query point set $\{q_i\}$ to obtain the predicted surface point set $\{z_i\}$, the network calculates the chamfer distance between $\{z_i\}$ and the input target surface. This loss function directly penalizes points that deviate from the true surface after projection. To minimize this loss, the network must simultaneously adjust the distance prediction $f_\theta(q_i)$ and the gradient prediction $\nabla f_\theta(q_i)$ so that the projected point $\{z_i\}$ can fall accurately on the target point cloud P, thereby ensuring projection consistency.

Geometric Regularization and Phased Optimization Based on Optimal Transport. In order to reconstruct a surface from the projected point set $Z = \{z_i\}_{i=1}^M$ that is highly consistent with the real skull point cloud $P = \{p_j\}_{j=1}^N$ in both geometric details and topological structure, we introduce the optimal transport theory [30] as the core geometric regularization method and design a corresponding staged optimization strategy.

Traditional nearest-neighbor matching-based losses, such as the chamfer distance, only penalize point-to-point distances locally. While this ensures the correct local positions of generated points, it fails to effectively constrain the overall geometric distribution of the point cloud, which can easily lead to topological errors. To overcome this limitation, we innovatively introduce the optimal transport (OT) loss as a global geometric regularization term. OT theory takes a macroscopic view of distributions, calculating the minimum cost required to transport one point cloud distribution to another. Consequently, it is highly sensitive to the overall shape, topology, and density distribution. This regularization term enforces that the global geometry of the predicted surface remains consistent with the true surface. Specifically, in each training iteration, we sample a predicted point cloud $Z = \{z_i\}_{i=1}^M$ from the near-zero isosurface of the current UDF and compare it with the ground truth $P = \{p_j\}_{j=1}^N$.

We consider these two point sets as empirical measures sampled from two underlying probability distributions μ_Z and μ_P respectively. The optimal transmission loss $\mathcal{L}_{\text{OT}}$ between them is defined as the squared Wasserstein-2 distance:

$$\mathcal{L}_{\mathrm{OT}}(P, Z) = W_2^2(\mu_P, \mu_Z) = \inf_{\gamma \in \Pi(\mu_P, \mu_Z)} \int_{\mathbb{R}^3 \times \mathbb{R}^3} \| \mathbf{x} - \mathbf{y} \|_2^2 \, d\gamma(\mathbf{x}, \mathbf{y}) \tag{6}$$

Among them, $\Pi(\mu_P, \mu_Z)$ represents the set of all joint probability measures (i.e., transmission plans) with μ_P and μ_Z as marginal distributions Given the extremely high computational complexity of directly solving this problem, we adopted the Sinkhorn algorithm [14] based on entropy regularization to perform efficient and differentiable approximate calculations.

Our total loss function is a weighted sum of the Chamfer Distance loss and the Optimal Transport regularization term, with a weighting coefficient that is dynamically adjusted according to the training phase.

$$\mathcal{L}_{total} = \mathcal{L}_{CD} + \lambda_{OT} \cdot \mathcal{L}_{OT} \tag{7}$$

L_{CD} is defined as follows:

$$\mathcal{L}_{CD} = \frac{1}{|M|} \sum_{i=1}^{|M|} \min_{j=1,\ldots,N} ||z_i - p_j||_2 + \frac{1}{|N|} \sum_{j=1}^{|N|} \min_{i=1,\ldots,M} ||p_j - z_i||_2 \tag{8}$$

The Optimal Transport loss term introduces a powerful global structural prior to the UDF learning process, which effectively avoids topological defects arising from local overfitting.

Staged Optimization Strategy. Directly imposing a strong distribution consistency constraint $\mathcal{L}_{OT}$ at the beginning of training may lead to an unstable optimization process, as the network has not yet developed a knowledge of the basic shape of the object at this point. For this reason, we design a staged optimization strategy from coarse to fine.

Phase 1 (Global Shape Alignment): At the beginning of training (the first 40,000 iterations), our main goal is to allow the network to learn the general outline of the skull quickly. In this phase, we mainly rely on a chamfer distance loss $\mathcal{L}_{CD}$, which is simpler to compute and more robust. At the same time, we set the weight λ_{OT} of the Optimal Transport regularization term $\mathcal{L}_{OT}$ to 0.2, enabling it to serve as a supporting function.

Phase 2 (Detail Distribution Fine-tuning): After 40,000 training iterations, once the network has achieved a good fit for the basic shape of the skull, we enter the second phase. Here, we raise λ_{OT} to its full weight, making $\mathcal{L}_{OT}$ the dominant force in the optimization process. Based on the macroscopic shape, it fine-tunes the distribution of projection points to recover rich surface details.

Through this learning strategy, from macro-alignment to fine-tuning, our framework can converge stably and ultimately learn a high-quality UDF that can not only accurately fit the input point cloud but also generate uniform, smooth, and richly detailed ones.

4 Experiments

To systematically evaluate the effectiveness of our proposed framework, we conducted comprehensive experiments. Acknowledging the current scarcity of public datasets suitable for open-surface skull reconstruction from raw CT data, we utilized a private dataset of 483 clinical CT scans. The experimental design in this chapter aims to rigorously evaluate two key aspects, both qualitatively and quantitatively: 1) the accuracy of our EGCA-Net on skull segmentation; and 2) the precision and fidelity of the OT-UDFR method, which incorporates Optimal Transport, for open-surface 3D reconstruction.

4.1 Implementation Details

We use Pytorch to implement our network and conduct experiments. The model is trained on a single NVIDIA 4090 GPU with 24 GB of memory. During the training of the model segmentation stage, we conducted a total of 200 epochs of training with a batch size of 4. We used the AdamW optimizer [19], setting the initial learning rate to 1×10^{-4} and implementing a stepwise decay strategy, reducing the learning rate to 10% of its original value every 100 epochs. To enhance the model's robustness, we also introduced a multi-scale training strategy, randomly scaling the input images to 0.75, 1.0, and 1.25 times their original size in each iteration. During the training process of the reconstructed network, we adopted a phased strategy with a total of 80,000 iterations. The initial learning rate of the optimizer was set to 1×10^{-3}, and the learning rate warm-up was conducted for the first 1000 iterations.

This research was carried out on a database of whole-head CT scans from volunteers, primarily belonging to the Han ethnic group in the North of China. The scans were acquired at Xianyang Hospital using a clinical multislice CT scanner system (Siemens Sensation 16). Our research was approved by the Institutional Review Board (IRB) of the Image Center for Brain Research, National Key Laboratory of Cognitive Neuroscience and Learning, Beijing Normal University. All participants gave written informed consent.

4.2 Framework Overall Performance

This section demonstrates the reconstruction data pipeline and the results of our proposed framework. Figure 4 visually illustrates the complete reconstruction process from the original CT scan to the final 3D model. The high-quality segmentation result Fig. 4(b) lays a solid foundation for subsequent reconstruction, ultimately generating a high-fidelity skull model with rich details and smooth surfaces (Fig. 4(c)).

In order to comprehensively evaluate the reconstruction performance of our framework, we conducted a series of 3D reconstruction experiments using the dataset. Figure 5 visually illustrates the reconstruction results of our framework on the dataset from various viewpoints, and the results intuitively demonstrate that our method is able to generate high-fidelity skull models with accurate morphology and complete details when dealing with different individuals.

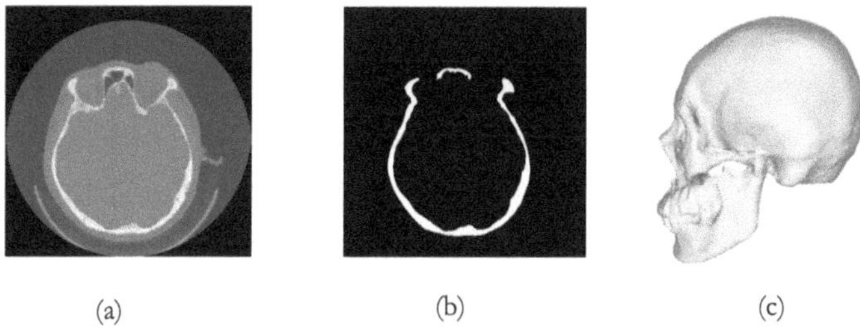

Fig. 4. The data reconstruction process of this framework. (a) Input original CT axial slice. (b) Segmentation result generated by EGCA-Net. (c) Final 3D skull model reconstructed by the OT-UDFR method.

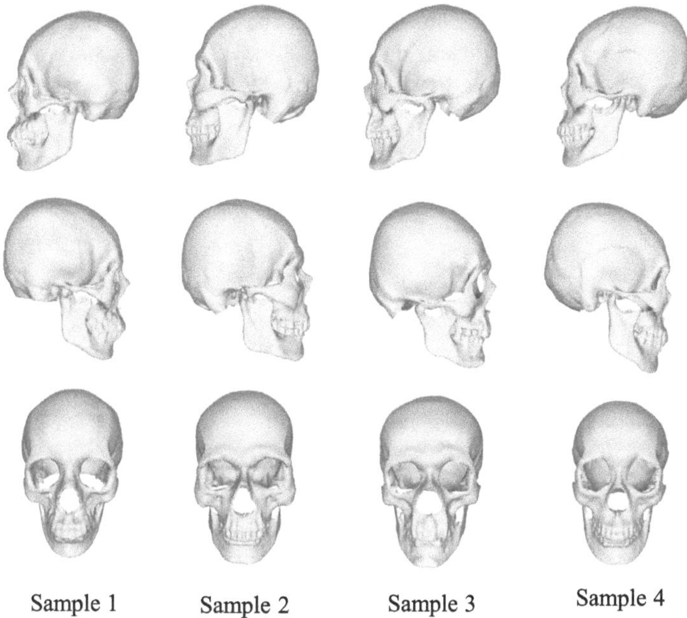

Fig. 5. Reconstruction results of the framework on some samples in the dataset.

4.3 Comparative Analysis

In terms of segmentation effects, we compare our approach with U-Net [24], Attention U-Net [20] and CSCA-U-Net [26], and we obtain quantitative comparison results in Table 1.

Table 1. Quantitative evaluation results of different segmentation methods

Method	Dice ↑	HD ↓
U-Net	0.8074	12.279
Attention U-Net	0.8216	9.796
CSCA-U-Net	0.8309	9.358
EGCA-Net	**0.8515**	**8.671**

We compare our approach with the state-of-the-art shape reconstruction methods LevelSetUDF [36] and CAP-UDF [35]. The qualitative comparison in Fig. 6 visually demonstrates the superiority of our method, which produces more continuous and precise geometric shapes than the other approaches. For a quantitative analysis, we report the comparison results in Table 2, where our approach achieves the best performance in all indicators.

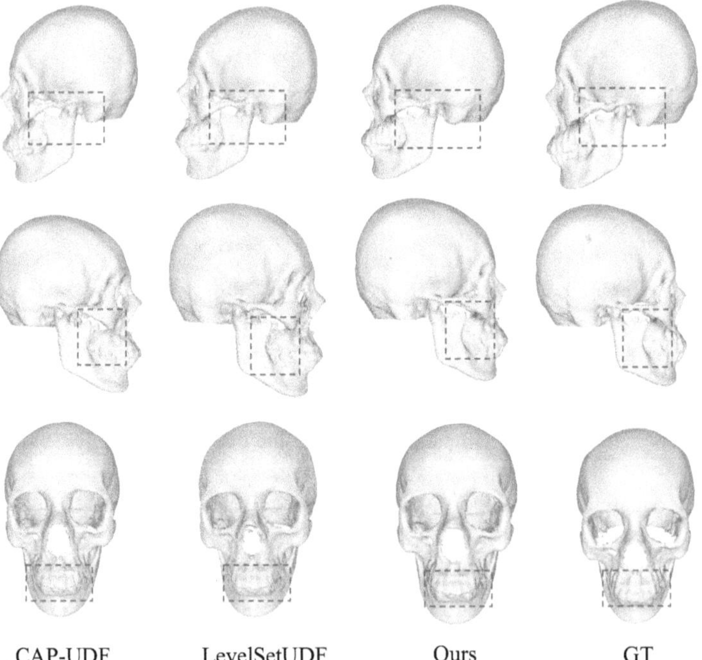

Fig. 6. Qualitative comparison of reconstruction results from different methods.

Table 2. Quantitative comparison of different 3D reconstruction methods. Lower Chamfer-L1 is better, while a higher F1-Score is better.

Method	Chamfer-L1 ↓	F1-Score-0.005 ↑	F1-Score-0.01 ↑
CAP-UDF	0.071	91.07	99.23
LevelSetUDF	0.073	90.23	99.17
Ours	**0.069**	**92.11**	**99.31**

4.4 Ablation Study

To validate the effectiveness of our proposed components, we conducted a series of ablation studies as detailed in Table 3. Our methodology starts with the full model and systematically removes one key component at a time: the Graph Convolutional Attention Mechanism (GCAM), the Euler's Elastica loss, and the Optimal Transport (OT) loss. The results show that removing any of these components leads to a degradation in performance (higher Chamfer-L1 and lower F1-Score), which confirms the significant contribution of each part to the final reconstruction quality.

Table 3. Ablation study on the impact of each component on the final reconstruction performance.

Method	GCAM	Euler's Loss	OT Loss	Chamfer-L1 ↓	F1-Score-0.005 ↑
Ours	✓	✓	✓	**0.069**	**92.11**
w/o GCAM	×	✓	✓	0.079	88.52
w/o Euler's Loss	✓	×	✓	0.072	90.56
w/o OT Loss	✓	✓	×	0.075	89.25

5 Conclusion

This paper proposes a novel two-stage framework to address the two major challenges of inaccurate segmentation and distorted reconstruction in skull open surface reconstruction. In the segmentation stage, our designed EGCA-Net achieves high-precision and smooth segmentation of complex skull structures by combining graph convolutional attention and Euler's Elastica loss. In the reconstruction stage, our proposed enhanced UDF learning strategy effectively overcomes the limitations of traditional UDF by introducing projection consistency and innovative optimal transport geometry regularization, generating high-fidelity 3D models with accurate topology and rich details. Experimental results fully verify the excellent performance of our framework, which outperforms existing advanced methods in both segmentation accuracy and reconstruction quality.

This provides a powerful and reliable technical tool for practical applications in fields such as criminal investigation and archaeology.

Future work will focus on improving the model's computational efficiency and generalization capabilities. To this end, we will research more efficient Optimal Transport algorithms to improve computational efficiency. We will also expand this approach to a wider range of application scenarios, such as reconstructing complex anatomical structures and preserving cultural heritage.

Acknowledgments. The authors gratefully appreciate the anonymous reviewers for all of their helpful comments. We also thank the support of Xianyang Hospital and People's Hospital of Toxon County for providing CT images. This research is supported in parts by the National Natural Science Foundation of China under Grant (Nos. 62172247,62271393,12472040), Natural Science Foundation of Shandong Province (Nos. ZR2024MF087, ZR2025MS1088).

References

1. Cai, S., Tian, Y., Lui, H., Zeng, H., Wu, Y., Chen, G.: Dense-unet: a novel multiphoton in vivo cellular image segmentation model based on a convolutional neural network. Quant. Imaging Med. Surg. **10**(6), 1275 (2020)
2. Chen, J., et al.: Transunet: transformers make strong encoders for medical image segmentation. arXiv preprint arXiv:2102.04306 (2021)
3. Chen, X., Luo, X., Zhao, Y., Zhang, S., Wang, G., Zheng, Y.: Learning Euler's elastica model for medical image segmentation. arXiv preprint arXiv:2011.00526 (2020)
4. Chibane, J., Pons-Moll, G., et al.: Neural unsigned distance fields for implicit function learning. Adv. Neural. Inf. Process. Syst. **33**, 21638–21652 (2020)
5. Diakogiannis, F.I., Waldner, F., Caccetta, P., Wu, C.: Resunet-a: a deep learning framework for semantic segmentation of remotely sensed data. ISPRS J. Photogramm. Remote. Sens. **162**, 94–114 (2020)
6. Du, R., et al.: A systematic approach for making 3d-printed patient-specific implants for craniomaxillofacial reconstruction. Engineering **6**(11), 1291–1301 (2020)
7. Hatamizadeh, A., et al.: Unetr: transformers for 3d medical image segmentation. In: Proceedings of the IEEE/CVF Winter Conference on Applications of Computer Vision, pp. 574–584 (2022)
8. Hou, F., Chen, X., Wang, W., Qin, H., He, Y.: Robust zero level-set extraction from unsigned distance fields based on double covering. ACM Trans. Graph. (TOG) **42**(6), 1–15 (2023)
9. Hu, J., et al.: A lightweight UDF learning framework for 3D reconstruction based on local shape functions. arXiv preprint arXiv:2407.01330 (2024)
10. Kanopoulos, N., Vasanthavada, N., Baker, R.L.: Design of an image edge detection filter using the sobel operator. IEEE J. Solid-State Circuits **23**(2), 358–367 (1988)
11. Kass, M., Witkin, A., Terzopoulos, D.: Snakes: active contour models. Int. J. Comput. Vision **1**(4), 321–331 (1988)
12. Kazhdan, M., Bolitho, M., Hoppe, H.: Poisson surface reconstruction. In: Proceedings of the fourth Eurographics Symposium on Geometry Processing, vol. 7 (2006)

13. Kirillov, A., et al.: Segment anything. In: Proceedings of the IEEE/CVF International Conference on Computer Vision, pp. 4015–4026 (2023)
14. Knight, P.A.: The Sinkhorn-Knopp algorithm: convergence and applications. SIAM J. Matrix Anal. Appl. **30**(1), 261–275 (2008)
15. Lin, A., Chen, B., Xu, J., Zhang, Z., Lu, G., Zhang, D.: Ds-transunet: dual swin transformer u-net for medical image segmentation. IEEE Trans. Instrum. Meas. **71**, 1–15 (2022)
16. Liu, Z., et al.: Swin transformer: hierarchical vision transformer using shifted windows. In: Proceedings of the IEEE/CVF International Conference on Computer Vision, pp. 10012–10022 (2021)
17. Long, X., et al.: Neuraludf: learning unsigned distance fields for multi-view reconstruction of surfaces with arbitrary topologies. In: Proceedings of the IEEE/CVF Conference on Computer Vision and Pattern Recognition, pp. 20834–20843 (2023)
18. Lorensen, W.E., Cline, H.E.: Marching cubes: a high resolution 3D surface construction algorithm. In: Seminal Graphics: Pioneering Efforts that Shaped the Field, pp. 347–353 (1998)
19. Loshchilov, I., Hutter, F.: Decoupled weight decay regularization. arXiv preprint arXiv:1711.05101 (2017)
20. Oktay, O., et al.: Attention u-net: learning where to look for the pancreas. arXiv preprint arXiv:1804.03999 (2018)
21. O'shea, K., Nash, R.: An introduction to convolutional neural networks. arXiv preprint arXiv:1511.08458 (2015)
22. Park, J.J., Florence, P., Straub, J., Newcombe, R., Lovegrove, S.: Deepsdf: learning continuous signed distance functions for shape representation. In: Proceedings of the IEEE/CVF Conference on Computer Vision and Pattern Recognition, pp. 165–174 (2019)
23. Rinchon, S., Arpita, S., Mahipal, S., Rajeev, K.: 3D forensic facial reconstruction: a review of the traditional sculpting methods and recent computerised developments. Int. J. Forens. Sci. **3**(1), 1–8 (2018)
24. Ronneberger, O., Fischer, P., Brox, T.: U-net: convolutional networks for biomedical image segmentation. In: Navab, N., Hornegger, J., Wells, W.M., Frangi, A.F. (eds.) MICCAI 2015. LNCS, vol. 9351, pp. 234–241. Springer, Cham (2015). https://doi.org/10.1007/978-3-319-24574-4_28
25. Shi, H., Zhang, K., Li, Y., Shi, H., Wen, X., Qian, T.: The efficacy of augmented reality technology assisted by 3D-CT reconstruction in microvascular decompression for hemifacial spasm craniotomy. BMC Surg. **25**(1), 382 (2025)
26. Shu, X., Wang, J., Zhang, A., Shi, J., Wu, X.J.: CSCA U-Net: a channel and space compound attention CNN for medical image segmentation. Artif. Intell. Med. **150**, 102800 (2024)
27. Sitzmann, V., Martel, J., Bergman, A., Lindell, D., Wetzstein, G.: Implicit neural representations with periodic activation functions. Adv. Neural. Inf. Process. Syst. **33**, 7462–7473 (2020)
28. Sørensen, K., Camara, O., De Backer, O., Kofoed, K.F., Paulsen, R.R.: Nudf: neural unsigned distance fields for high resolution 3d medical image segmentation. In: 2022 IEEE 19th International Symposium on Biomedical Imaging (ISBI), pp. 1–5. IEEE (2022)
29. Steinbach, M., Tan, P.N.: knn: k-nearest neighbors. In: The Top Ten Algorithms in Data Mining, pp. 165–176. Chapman and Hall/CRC, Boca Raton (2009)
30. Villani, C., et al.: Optimal Transport: Old and New, vol. 338. Springer, Heidelberg (2008)

31. Wang, W., et al.: Pyramid vision transformer: a versatile backbone for dense prediction without convolutions. In: Proceedings of the IEEE/CVF International Conference on Computer Vision, pp. 568–578 (2021)
32. Xu, C., et al.: Details enhancement in unsigned distance field learning for high-fidelity 3d surface reconstruction. In: Proceedings of the AAAI Conference on Artificial Intelligence, vol. 39, pp. 8806–8814 (2025)
33. Zhang, J., Lu, V., Khanduja, V.: The impact of extended reality on surgery: a scoping review. Int. Orthop. **47**(3), 611–621 (2023)
34. Zhang, N., et al.: An end-to-end conditional generative adversarial network based on depth map for 3D craniofacial reconstruction. In: Proceedings of the 30th ACM International Conference on Multimedia, pp. 759–768 (2022)
35. Zhou, J., Ma, B., Li, S., Liu, Y.S., Fang, Y., Han, Z.: CAP-UDF: learning unsigned distance functions progressively from raw point clouds with consistency-aware field optimization. IEEE Trans. Pattern Anal. Mach. Intell. **46**(12), 7475–7492 (2024)
36. Zhou, J., Ma, B., Li, S., Liu, Y.S., Han, Z.: Learning a more continuous zero level set in unsigned distance fields through level set projection. In: Proceedings of the IEEE/CVF International Conference on Computer Vision, pp. 3181–3192 (2023)
37. Zhu, W., Tai, X.C., Chan, T.: Image segmentation using Euler's Elastica as the regularization. J. Sci. Comput. **57**(2), 414–438 (2013)

Calibration-Free Multi-view 3D Hand Pose Estimation for XR Cockpit Interactions

Hanling Zhan[1], Xiaolong Liu[2], Baojun Chen[1], Meng Gai[3], Jun Cao[4], Liang Xie[2], Haoyang Zhang[2(✉)], and Erwei Yin[2]

[1] School of Mechanical Engineering, Tianjin University, Tianjin 300354, China
{hanlingzhan,baojun_chen}@tju.edu.cn

[2] Defense Innovation Institute, Academy of Military Sciences, Beijing 100071, China
haoyang@tju.edu.cn

[3] School of Computer Science, Peking University, Beijing 100871, China
gaimeng@pku.edu.cn

[4] Nanjing Ruiyue Technology Co., Ltd., Nanjing 210012, China
april.li@inibiru.com

Abstract. Extended Reality (XR) is increasingly integrated into cockpits, where gesture interaction is the fundamental method of immersive human-computer interaction. However, there are three challenges to reliable 3D hand pose estimation in cockpits: (1) restricted hand observability based on egocentric field of view, (2) infeasibility of cockpit motion-induced calibration, and (3) self-occlusion induced by hand-object interaction. To address these challenges, we propose a calibration-free multi-view pipeline that fuses the egocentric XR headset with external third-person cameras. Our framework comprises two explicit modules: the guidance-driven fusion stage mitigates 3D pose ambiguity by constructing a global reference for feature interaction, and the hypothesis-driven alignment stage models extrinsic parameter uncertainty via multi-hypothesis spatial alignment. Extensive experiments on Dex-YCB and HanCo under uncalibrated setups demonstrate that our approach outperforms existing both calibrated and uncalibrated state-of-the-art methods in accuracy and robustness.

Keywords: Extended Reality · Cockpit Interactions · 3D hand pose estimation · Uncalibrated multiple views

1 Introduction

Extended Reality (XR) is increasingly integrated into cockpits [4,10,25,35], where gesture interaction is the fundamental method of immersive human-computer interaction. And accurate 3D hand pose estimation is the basic technology for gesture interaction. Existing 3D hand pose methods fall into two categories: direct 3D estimation and 2D-to-3D lifting. Direct 3D estimation methods [1,11,18,27,40] regress joint locations directly from images, while 2D-to-3D lifting methods [7,9,13,33] infer the 3D pose from intermediate 2D key-

A. Hinkenjan et al. (Eds.): ICXR 2025, LNCS 16428, pp. 133–150, 2026.
https://doi.org/10.1007/978-981-95-7195-6_8

point estimates. Compared to direct 3D estimation, 2D-to-3D lifting demonstrates enhanced flexibility by effectively adapting to various 2D pose estimators [3,8,20,29,36], and benefits from high-quality 2D annotations obtained from training on massive datasets [29,43]. However, these methods cannot be directly applied in cockpits, where 2D-to-3D lifting from single-view RGB images remains an ill-posed problem due to inherent depth ambiguity and occlusions.

Recent works have adopted calibrated multi-view frameworks [31,34,39] to combine information from multiple cameras, enabling more complete hand coverage. However, achieving reliable 3D hand pose estimation in cockpits still faces three main challenges: (1) cockpit-induced motion, which renders multi-view calibration infeasible (Fig. 1 a), (2) the egocentric field-of-view (FoV) constraint, which limits the observable hand workspace (Fig. 1 b), and (3) severe self-occlusion caused by hand–object interactions (Fig. 1 c). Thus, multi-view camera parameters in cockpits are susceptible to disturbance and degradation, making calibration-based methods impractical, which motivates the exploration of calibration-free designs suited for such environments.

Although calibration-free methods can eliminate cumbersome calibration, the absence of camera parameters introduces a challenge for cross-view correspondence. Without known stereo cues between the XR headset and third-person cameras, mapping 2D detections to unique 3D configurations becomes geometrically ambiguous. Meanwhile, continuous changes in viewpoint caused by XR headset motion and camera displacement mean that each frame of 2D observations corresponds to a multi-distribution of valid 3D hand poses. However, most existing methods in human pose estimation [2,16] sidestep the ambiguity by performing a deterministic regression and producing a single estimate, thereby collapsing the solution space and ignoring pose uncertainty. Specifically, occluded fingertips exhibiting identical projections across views permit geometrically valid yet contradictory 3D configurations, while deterministic regression forces disambiguation by arbitrary selection, inducing spatiotemporal instability.

To address instability caused by dynamic extrinsic disturbances in cockpit systems, combining XR headset and external multi-view cameras, we propose a calibration-free framework rooted in explicit modeling. Our approach resolves multi-view reconstruction ambiguities by structuring feature interaction and pose alignment into two dedicated modules. To this end, our approach introduces two complementary components: (1) an explicit guidance for multi-view feature fusion, which leverages a unified representation to directly fuse view-specific features, thereby mitigating implicit feature entanglement, (2) an explicit probabilistic extrinsic estimation for pose alignment, which models each camera's transform as a mixture of candidate hypotheses, thereby enabling principled reasoning over plausible spatial configurations. By modeling both the cross-view structural interactions and latent geometric relationships explicitly, our method constrains the ill-posed nature of the problem, leading to significantly more robust and accurate 3D hand pose estimation under dynamic platform perturbations. We conduct experiments on challenging multi-view hand-object interaction datasets (Dex-YCB [5] and HanCo [42]), where our method signif-

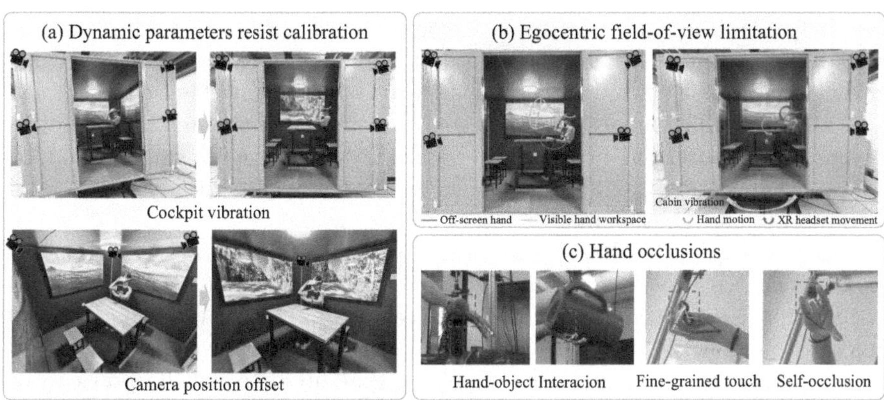

Fig. 1. Cockpits equipped with XR and in-cabin cameras aim to support natural, gesture-based interaction in immersive human-computer environments. Three main challenges in XR cockpit 3D hand estimation: (a) dynamic parameters resist calibration, where cockpit vibrations induce continuous camera position offsets; (b) egocentric field-of-view limitation, restricting visible hand workspace; (c) hand occlusions, arising from hand–object interactions, fine-grained touch and self-occlusion.

icantly outperforms state-of-the-art (SOTA) methods by a large margin and maintains consistent robustness across calibration-free camera configurations. Furthermore, the experimental results demonstrate that even under different multi-view counts and camera configurations, our method maintains uniformly accurate and robust 3D pose estimation, highlighting its strong resilience to diverse configurations.

The contributions of our paper can be summarized as follows:

- We propose a cockpit-adaptive framework for uncalibrated multi-view hand pose estimation, achieving vibration-robust 3D hand pose estimation in dynamic XR-cabin systems despite persistent drift.
- We introduce a guidance-driven interaction strategy that leverages the cross-view consistency of hand structure to achieve explicit multi-view feature fusion, alleviating implicit entanglement and correspondence ambiguity.
- We develop a hypothesis-based alignment module that models per-view extrinsic as a mixture of candidate transformations, enabling explicit physical alignment and mitigating parameter uncertainty.

2 Related Work

With the rapid integration of XR into cockpits [4,10,25,35], gesture-based control has emerged as a primary modality for immersive human–computer interaction. Caputo et al. [4] demonstrated XR's potential for pilot training but used predefined gestures. Yang et al. [35] introduced multi-view fusion aids recognition, yet required stable calibration. Ren et al. [25] proposed a multi-task XR cockpit system integrating gesture, gaze, and object state recognition, achieving robustness in controlled environments but depending on fixed sensor layouts, limiting adaptability to reconfigurable setups. Gao et al. [10] focused on interaction efficiency while employing single-view estimation that remains susceptible to depth ambiguity and occlusions. However, these methods can not support accurate, calibration-free 3D hand pose estimation under the dynamic conditions inherent in the cockpits.

In XR cockpits, 3D hand pose estimation from RGB remains challenging due to egocentric FoV restrictions and depth ambiguity. Early single-view RGB-based 3D pose estimation has been extensively explored through two categories: direct 3D estimation approaches that map pixels to 3D coordinates via end-to-end frameworks, and two-stage pipelines that lift detected 2D poses to 3D space. Although direct 3D estimation methods [1,11,18,27,40] better preserve low-level visual cues, such as photometric textures and implicit geometric patterns, through dense feature learning, they inevitably entangle pose-relevant features with extraneous visual features, including background clutter and illumination variations. In contrast, the 2D-to-3D lifting methods [7,9,13,33] benefits from training on large-scale datasets with high-quality 2D annotations. These methods further demonstrate superior flexibility by decoupling pose estimation from visual encoding, enabling compatibility with diverse off-the-shelf 2D detectors [3,8,20,29,36] and achieving lightweight deployment through sparse keypoint processing. However, RGB-based single-view approaches remain limited by the inherent depth ambiguity of monocular observation and persistent sensitivity to occlusions, as single-view constraints provide insufficient geometric evidence to resolve these physically ill-posed scenarios.

To mitigate issues like single-view depth uncertainty and occlusion-induced structural gaps, recent studies [31,34,39] adpot multi-view complementary stereo cues to refine 3D pose. Such works are categorized into calibration-required and calibration-free approaches. Calibrated methods utilize explicit extrinsics to enforce geometric consistency through triangulation or epipolar constraints [14,15,38], achieving high accuracy but failing under conditions where static calibration is disrupted, such as cockpit vibrations. Uncalibrated approaches remove the calibration burden by embedding camera parameters into learned representations [2,16,21,32], or by modeling uncertainty with statistical priors [17]. While more adaptable to reconfigurable camera layouts, these methods still rely on implicit fusion or hand-crafted assumptions, leading to unstable cross-view correspondence and degraded performance in dynamic, occlusion-heavy cabin environments. The success of transformer [30] in capturing global dependencies has inspired its application to multi-view fusion without explicit camera geometry. Ma et al. [21] prune redundant image tokens for efficient attention-based fusion but underperform in occlusion-heavy scenes due to weak geometric cues. Cai et al. [2] enhance this by integrating deformable attention for adaptive feature sampling, improving articulation handling, yet their implicit geometric reasoning remains unstable in sparse-view setups. In a different vein, Zhu et al. [41] further introduce multi-view mixture experts to

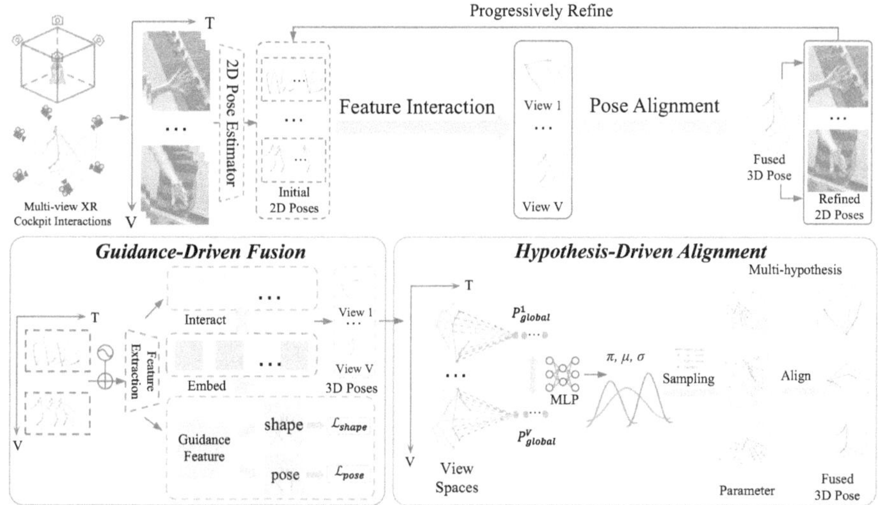

Fig. 2. Overall framework of our method for calibration-free multi-view 3D hand pose estimation in dynamic headset-cockpit settings. Specifically, Guidance-Driven Fusion (GDF) for explicit cross-view feature interaction, and Hypothesis-Driven Alignment (HDA) for probabilistic pose alignment. It achieves robust multi-view fusion by integrating structure-guided feature interaction and hypothesis-based pose alignment, explicitly establishing cross-view correspondences, and significantly alleviating the difficulty of learning complex cross-view relations without camera parameters.

dynamically weight view contributions, but complex optimization spaces persist, echoing issues in Shuai et al. [28]. However, these methods overlook explicit cross-view alignment and still rely on single-hypothesis regression, resulting in unstable correspondence and unstable training. Different from prior methods, our method achieves robust 3D hand pose estimation in dynamic cockpit environments by explicitly aligning multi-view features with structural guidance and hypothesis-based parameters.

3 Method

3.1 Preliminary

For input multi-view image sequences $\mathcal{I} = \{\mathrm{I}_i\}_{i=1}^{T\times V}$ with T frames and V views, each frame in each view is an image $\mathrm{I} \in \mathbb{R}^{W\times H\times 3}$, with width W and height H. We first employ an offline 2D hand pose estimator to obtain the 2D pose $\mathcal{P}_{2D} \in \mathbb{R}^{T\times V\times J\times 2}$, where J denotes the number of hand keypoints in each image. Following this, feature extraction initially reshapes and processes the multi-view 2D pose sequences $\mathcal{P}_{2D} \in \mathbb{R}^{T\times V\times J\times 2}$, which transforms the input into a more suitable representation for further processing:

$$x_{emb} = Embed\left(\mathcal{P}_{2D}\right), \tag{1}$$

where $x_{emb} \in \mathbb{R}^{T \times V \times C}$ represents the embedded 2D pose features, with C being the dimension of the embedding space. We integrate task-aware positional encoding P_{pos} into x_{emb} inspired by FusionFormer [2] and replacing fixed patterns with learned spatial relations [30] to form the combined feature $x \in \mathbb{R}^{T \times V \times C}$. This is fed through encoder blocks with multi-head attention, capturing intra-frame, inter-frame, and cross-view dependencies. By flattening into $x_{flat} \in \mathbb{R}^{(T \times V) \times C}$, self-attention builds a global $(T \times V) \times (T \times V)$ matrix. Decoder blocks then yield view-specific features $x_{view} \in \mathbb{R}^{T \times V \times C}$. FE encompasses a series of encoder and decoder blocks and can be formulated as follows:

$$x_{view} = FE\left(x_{emb} + P_{pos}\right). \tag{2}$$

3.2 Guidance-Driven Fusion

Conventional fusion methods depend on the network to infer cross-view correspondences implicitly, a requirement that complicates optimization and undermines convergence stability. We note that, at each time step, all cameras capture the same dynamic hand pose, and, throughout a sequence, they observe identical morphological characteristics such as finger lengths and palm geometry. Based on this insight, we introduce a global guidance feature that encodes both per-frame pose and sequence-wide shape information, and use it to explicitly steer interactions among view-specific feature maps. By supplying this unified feature to every camera branch, we eliminate the need for implicit correspondence learning, reducing ambiguity and stabilizing multi-view feature fusion.

To ensure the consistency of hand across views and frames, we adopt information from a parametric hand model as global guidance, which consists of shape parameters capturing the overall hand morphology and pose parameters encoding joint rotations. These parameters provide a compact representation of the hand, maintaining consistency in hand morphological features across views and frames. Specifically, shape parameters enforce cross-view consistency in anthropometric characteristics with finger lengths and palm width by embedding multi-view observations into a biomechanically constrained global space. Meanwhile, pose parameters guarantee the kinematic validity of joint rotations with finger articulation angles and wrist orientation through synchronized optimization in a motion-constrained configuration space. This consistency is essential for improving the robustness of the 3D pose estimation, as it mitigates the challenges arising from view-specific variations.

As shown in Fig. 2, the initialization of the global guidance feature begins with view-specific features $x_{view} \in \mathbb{R}^{T \times V \times C}$. These features are first processed through a learnable Fully Connected Layer (FC), which serves as a parameterized module to dynamically derive view-weighting coefficients $w \in \mathbb{R}^{T \times V \times 1}$. Each element in w adaptively scales the contribution of views using the sigmoid function σ as follows:

$$w = \sigma\left(FC\left(x_{view}\right)\right), \tag{3}$$

where w indicates the learned weight, it then performs view-adaptive adjustment on the view-specific features $x_{view} \in \mathbb{R}^{T \times V \times C}$ through channel-wise importance reweighting, generating initial weighted features $x_{view}^{w} \in \mathbb{R}^{T\times 1\times C}$, which can be described by the following equation:

$$x_{view}^{w} = w \otimes x_{view}, \tag{4}$$

where $x_{view}^{w} \in \mathbb{R}^{T\times 1\times C}$ serves as the foundation for deriving the parametric hand model MANO features $x_{mano} \in \mathbb{R}^{T\times 1\times M}$ (M as the guiding dimension), which are jointly supervised through both the shape and pose losses. Although the global guidance is supervised with MANO shape and pose parameters, the resulting representation should be regarded as an explicit guidance rather than a direct copy of MANO vectors. The supervision anchors the embedding to a biomechanically meaningful space, enforcing cross-view and temporal consistency, but the learned code remains a flexible latent feature that can capture additional view-specific variations beyond the strict MANO parameterization. In this way, the explicit encoding functions as anchor that guides multi-view feature interaction, rather than being identical to the MANO parameters themselves.

These features $x_{mano} \in \mathbb{R}^{T\times 1\times M}$ are then embedded back into the feature space through a learnable linear transformation, effectively transforming the initial weighted feature $x_{view}^{w} \in \mathbb{R}^{T\times 1\times C}$ to facilitate shared semantic interaction with per-view features. This representation is broadcast along the view dimension through the expansion as the global guidance feature $x_{guide}^{re} \in \mathbb{R}^{T\times V\times C}$. The multi-view 3D hand poses $\mathcal{P}_{3D} \in \mathbb{R}^{T\times V\times J\times 3}$ are then computed by passing the concatenated feature through the decoder, i.e.,

$$\mathcal{P}_{3D} = Decoder\Big(Concat\big(x_{view}, Repeat(Linear(x_{view}^{w}), V)\big)\Big). \tag{5}$$

3.3 Hypothesis-Driven Alignment

In this section, we introduce our multi-hypothesis based extrinsic estimation framework for multi-view 3D hand pose estimation under uncalibrated camera setups. Our method is designed to explicitly model the uncertainty in multi-view geometry by generating a distribution of plausible camera extrinsics conditioned on predicted 3D poses. We then perform hypothesis fusion via a learnable consistency-driven mechanism to obtain robust extrinsic alignment and global 3D hand estimation. To handle the ill-posed problem of extrinsic estimation from multi-view hand pose observations under uncalibrated settings, we propose a multi-hypothesis extrinsic modeling framework that explicitly captures geometric uncertainty through a distributional representation of pose-to-camera relationships. Our goal is to derive accurate camera extrinsics and a consistent global 3D hand pose by leveraging the statistical regularities in multi-view predictions, without relying on ground-truth camera calibration. Given per-view predicted 3D hand poses $\mathcal{P}_{3D} \in \mathbb{R}^{T\times V\times J\times 3}$, we aim to infer the extrinsic transformation $T_v \in SE(3)$ for each view v that aligns local poses to a canonical space. Instead of committing to a single transformation, we model the posterior distribution over possible extrinsics via Mixture Density Network (MDN) as shown in Fig. 2. This design parametrizes a weighted set of hypotheses over the six-dimensional axis-angle plus translation space $\theta = (\omega, t) \in \mathbb{R}^6$, where ω encodes rotation via its direction (rotation axis) and norm (rotation angle in radians), and t is a 3D translation vector:

$$p(T_v \mid \mathcal{P}_{3D}) = \sum_{m=1}^{M} \pi_v^{(m)} \cdot \mathcal{N}(\theta_v; \mu_v^{(m)}, \Sigma_v^{(m)}), \tag{6}$$

where each component $\mu_v^{(m)} \in SE(3)$ represents a plausible rigid transformation hypothesis that conforms to the Special Euclidean group SE(3), with corresponding mixing weight $\pi_v^{(m)}$. The MDN is implemented as a lightweight MLP that takes $\mathcal{P}_{3D}$ as input and outputs the parameters of the mixture. This design captures multiple feasible solutions of extrinsic alignment per view, especially under self-similarity, depth ambiguity, and occlusion. For each hypothesis $T_v^{(m)}$, we transform the local pose $\mathcal{P}_v$ to the global space:

$$\hat{\mathcal{P}}_v^{(m)} = T_v^{(m)} \cdot \mathcal{P}_v, \tag{7}$$

where the transformation applies both rotation and translation. This results in a set of aligned poses $\hat{\mathcal{P}}_v^{(m)}$, which are then fused across views and hypotheses to obtain a consensus global pose $\mathcal{P}_{fused}$.

This multi-hypothesis formulation effectively accounts for ambiguities such as depth uncertainty, occlusions, and left–right symmetry, enabling the network to select geometrically consistent hypotheses for robust extrinsic alignment. Importantly, the entire pipeline is differentiable and end-to-end trainable, allowing gradients to backpropagate through hypothesis selection and pose fusion modules. This empowers the model to learn to resolve ambiguity based on spatial consistency and statistical regularity over the training corpus. Traditional approaches often suffer from the inability to differentiate reliable observations across views due to occlusions or sensor noise, and the irreversible propagation of errors from initial 2D keypoint detections. The proposed framework addresses inherent challenges in multi-view 3D hand pose estimation by integrating geometric fusion with a self-correcting feedback loop. Specifically, our framework introduces a two-stage mechanism that dynamically fuses multi-view predictions while iteratively refining both 3D outputs and 2D inputs through closed-loop optimization. The core lies in an uncertainty-aware fusion strategy, which computes the 3D pose ensemble as a weighted sum of aligned predictions from multiple cameras.

Unlike existing methods that rely on independent regression followed by simple averaging or heuristic fusion, our framework dynamically integrates geometric and semantic consistency across views, exploiting their complementary strengths to resolve ambiguities and suppress outliers:

$$\mathcal{P}_{fused} = \sum_{v=1}^{V} w_v \cdot \mathcal{P}_{align3D}, \tag{8}$$

where w_v represents the confidence weight for the v-th view from equation3 in Sect. 3.3. This module dynamically evaluates spatial coherence and temporal consistency across frames, allowing it to suppress occluded or low-quality views and leverage high-quality information. The iterative refinement establishes a bidirectional relationship between 3D and 2D representations. After initial fusion, the 3D pose is reprojected onto the 2D plane of each view:

$$\hat{\mathcal{P}}_{2D}^{v} = Project\left(K_v\left(R_v \cdot \mathcal{P}_{fused} + t_v\right)\right), \tag{9}$$

where K_v is the intrinsic matrix, R_v is a 3×3 orthogonal rotation matrix and t_v is a 3×1 translation vector from the learned extrinsic matrices $E_v \in \mathbb{R}^{T\times V\times 4\times 4}$. These reprojected 2D keypoints $\hat{\mathcal{P}}_{2D}^{v}$ are concatenated with the original detections $\mathcal{P}_{2D}$ along the joint dimension, forming an augmented representation. This combined input is processed through a lightweight MLP that outputs refined 2D coordinates, which are then fed back into the system for the next fusion cycle. By iteratively optimizing both the 2D inputs and the fused 3D pose $\mathcal{P}_{fused}$, the method progressively reduces detection noise and geometric inconsistencies through self-correcting feedback.

3.4 Loss Functions

The loss function integrates three components to ensure geometric consistency between 3D predictions and multi-view constraints.

Multi-view 3D Consistency Loss. We enforce geometric coherence both before and after alignment by penalizing the L2-norm error between the predicted and ground-truth 3D poses. Specifically, for the intermediate multi-view estimates in camera coordinates:

$$\mathscr{L}_{view3D} = \left\|\hat{p}_{3D} - p_{3D}\right\|_2, \tag{10}$$

and for the aligned poses in the unified canonical space:

$$\mathscr{L}_{align3D} = \left\|\hat{p}_{align3D} - p_{align3D}\right\|_2. \tag{11}$$

Shape and Pose Loss. For global guidance feature, we supervise the shape parameter M_{shape} and the pose parameter M_{pose} by L2 loss. The shape loss $\mathscr{L}_{shape}$ ensures the predicted feature aligns with the ground-truth shape parameters, while the pose loss $\mathscr{L}_{pose}$ ensures that the predicted pose parameters align with the ground-truth pose parameters:

$$\begin{aligned} \mathscr{L}_{shape} &= \|\hat{M}_{shape} - M_{shape}\|_2, \\ \mathscr{L}_{pose} &= \|\hat{M}_{pose} - M_{pose}\|_2, \end{aligned} \tag{12}$$

where $\hat{M}_{shape}, \hat{M}_{pose}$ and M_{shape}, M_{pose} represent the ground truth and the prediction of the two parameters, respectively.

Multi-view 2D Keypoint Projection Loss. Minimizes the discrepancy between projected 2D coordinates across all views p_{2D} and their ground truths $\hat{p}_{2D}$, promoting cross-view geometric consistency:

$$\mathcal{L}_{2D} = \|\hat{p}_{2D} - p_{2D}\|_2. \tag{13}$$

Fused 3D Pose Loss. The fused 3D pose loss computes the mean per joint position error (MPJPE) between the predicted $\hat{p}_{fuse3D}$ and the ground-truth 3D pose p_{fuse3D} after the root joint (wrist) alignment:

$$\mathcal{L}_{fuse3D} = \frac{1}{J}\sum_{j=1}^{J}\left\|\hat{p}^{j}_{fuse3D} - p^{j}_{fuse3D}\right\|. \tag{14}$$

Therefore, the total loss function is defined as:

$$\begin{aligned}\mathcal{L}_{total} &= \lambda_1\mathcal{L}_{view3D} + \lambda_2\mathcal{L}_{fuse3D} + \lambda_3\mathcal{L}_{align3D} \\ &+ \lambda_4(\mathcal{L}_{shape} + \mathcal{L}_{pose}) + \lambda_5\mathcal{L}_{2D},\end{aligned} \tag{15}$$

where λ_{1-5} are used to balance the loss magnitudes of different terms, λ_1, λ_2 and λ_3 are set to 1, and λ_4 as well as λ_5 are set to 0.1.

4 Experimental Results

4.1 Experiment Setting

We evaluate the proposed approach using representative hand-object interaction datasets and standard metrics, as detailed below.

Datasets. Dex-YCB [5] is a large-scale dataset for 3D hand-object reconstruction, comprising 1,000 sequences (over 582,000 frames) of 10 subjects interacting with 20 objects captured from 8 synchronized views. It provides annotations for 2D and 3D poses across all views. We use the default "S0" train/test split for training and testing respectively. HanCo [42] is a multi-view extension of the widely used FreiHand dataset [43], designed to capture complex hand gestures and hand-object interactions. Compared to Dex-YCB, HanCo features more intricate hand-object interactions, a wider variety of objects, and richer gesture poses. It also provides annotations, including 2D and 3D hand keypoints and MANO parameters. It contains 107,538 time steps recorded from 8 synchronized views, resulting in over 860,000 RGB images. We implement a 9:1 train-test split on HanCo to preserve temporal continuity while ensuring evaluation robustness.

Metrics. Our evaluation employs two principal metrics: procrustes-aligned mean per joint position error (P-MPJPE) and its non-aligned counterpart MPJPE. These metrics quantify the spatial discrepancy by computing the Euclidean distance in millimeters between the ground-truth joint coordinates and the model predictions. The P-MPJPE metric employs procrustes analysis [12] to remove global rigid transformations (translation, rotation, isotropic scaling) between skeletal predictions and references, thereby establishing scale- and rotation-invariant error assessment. This alignment isolates local pose estimation accuracy from global coordinate system variations.

2D Pose Estimator. To align with established evaluation protocols, we initialize 2D hand poses using OpenPose [3] on the HanCo dataset, consistent with the HaMuCo benchmark methodology [39]. For the Dex-YCB dataset, we also use OpenPose as the 2D estimator. Meanwhile, MediaPipe [20] as another prevalent 2D pose estimator is employed for comparison. In succeeding tables, OP and MP denote the two 2D pose estimators respectively.

Implementation Details. We implement our method using the PyTorch framework [23]. All experiments are conducted on an NVIDIA RTX 4080 Super GPU. We train our network using AdamW optimizer [19] with an initial learning rate of 1e-4. Note that learning decay is executed after the end of every 30 epochs. The whole training process takes 90 epochs with batch size of 30.

4.2 Comparisons with the SOTAs

We evaluate our calibration-free framework on the HanCo [42] dataset focusing on egocentric hand-object interactions and the Dex-YCB [5] dataset focusing on dexterous manipulations, comparing against single-view, calibrated multi-view and calibration-free baselines, as summarized in Table 1. Compared to single-view methods, our explicit multi-view integration reduces mean joint error by over 50% among HandOccNet [22], MobRecon [6], H2ONet [33] and WiLoR [24], confirming the power of complementary multiple views. For calibrated multi-view methods, we compare to Voxel [15], MvP [37], MMI [26], and HaMuCo [39]. For calibration-free multi-view baselines, we evaluate PPT [21], SiMA-Hand [32], and FusionFormer [2]. Quantitative results demonstrate that our method achieves the lowest MPJPE on HanCo and Dex-YCB datasets under egocentric and third-person hand-object interaction scenarios. Our pipeline outperforms the calibration-required methods by roughly 35.1% and the calibration-free approaches by about 38.8%, validating the strength of explicit global guidance fusion and hypothesis-driven alignment.

Table 1. The comparison with the SOTAs on the HanCo and Dex-YCB datasets. Best and second-best results are marked in bold and underlined.

Method	Venue	HanCo		Dex-YCB	
		MPJPE↓	P-MPJPE↓	MPJPE↓	P-MPJPE↓
Single-view methods					
HandOccNet [22]	CVPR'22	8.09	–	14.04	5.80
MobRecon [6]	CVPR'22	7.95	–	14.20	6.36
H2ONet [33]	CVPR'23	6.78	–	14.02	5.65
WiLoR [24]	CVPR'25	8.13	6.90	10.46	4.79
Multi-view methods with calibrated cameras					
Voxel [15]	ICCV'19	4.92	3.63	7.81	4.34
MvP [37]	NIPS'21	–	–	6.23	<u>4.26</u>
MMI [26]	CVPR'22	5.54	3.90	7.93	4.71
HaMuCo [39]	ICCV'23	5.80	<u>3.40</u>	–	–
Multi-view methods without calibrated cameras					
PPT [21]	ECCV'22	6.61	6.10	9.22	4.97
SiMA-Hand [32]	AAAI'24	–	6.55	–	5.16
FusionFormer [2]	AAAI'24	<u>4.90</u>	3.78	<u>5.98</u>	4.43
Ours(OP [3])	–	**3.55**	**3.28**	**4.98**	**3.88**
Ours(MP [20])	–	**3.49**	**3.22**	**4.15**	**3.67**

4.3 Ablation Study

In the ablation study, we aim to evaluate each module in the proposed framework. We conduct ablation studies for different frames, views, and the explicit interaction and alignment on the HanCo dataset [42] with OpenPose [3], while different 2D estimators are adapted and compared on OpenPose and Mediapipe [20]. In addition, we further compare the runtime efficiency of different configurations to assess the trade-off between accuracy and computational cost.

Table 2. Ablation study of different 2D pose estimators.

Method	2D Estimator	MPJPE↓	P-MPJPE↓
FusionFormer	OpenPose	4.90	3.78
	MediaPipe	4.32	3.53
Ours	OpenPose	**3.31**	**2.97**
	MediaPipe	**3.29**	**2.91**

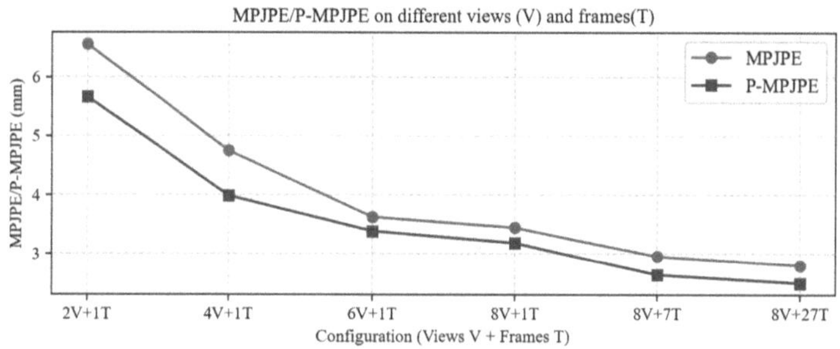

Fig. 3. The ablation study on different views (V) and frames(T).

Adaptability of Different Frames and Views. Our comprehensive evaluation demonstrates the robust adaptability of our method across varying view configurations and temporal sequences in Fig. 3. It achieves consistent performance gains under different view selections (T = 1 with 2/4/6/8 views) and frames (V = 8 with 1/7/27 frames). Notably, our approach attains 3.62/3.40 mm MPJPE/P-MPJPE with only 6 views, outperforming existing 8-view SOTA results of 4.90/3.78 mm as shown in Table 1, highlighting its effective strength in resolving pose ambiguity via guidance-driven global feature interaction with view-specific features, while modeling camera parameter uncertainty through hypothesis-driven multi-view spatial alignment.

Adaptability of Different 2D Estimators. We evaluate our framework and SOTA with diverse 2D pose estimators in Table 2. The results demonstrate the strong adaptability and stability of our method across estimators (MediaPipe [20] and OpenPose [3]) with consistent performance improvements. As shown in Fig. 4, our iterative refinement pipeline robustly corrects degraded 2D inputs, such as misaligned keypoints under severe occlusion, and yields visually plausible 3D poses even from unreliable initial observations. Our framework demonstrates compatibility with diverse 2D estimators while inherently compensating for their limitations, particularly in possible occlusions.

Efficiency Analysis. We analyze the computational characteristics of our framework in Table 3. The results indicate that Guidance-Driven Fusion (GDF) introduces moderate overhead, while Hypothesis-Driven Alignment (HDA) scales its cost with the mixture size K in the MDN. Smaller K values yield faster inference with minor loss in accuracy, whereas larger K values slightly improve robustness but with considerable growth in FLOPs. The iterative refinement module further improves accuracy, with performance gains saturating after two iterations. Overall, two refinement stages with a moderate mixture size

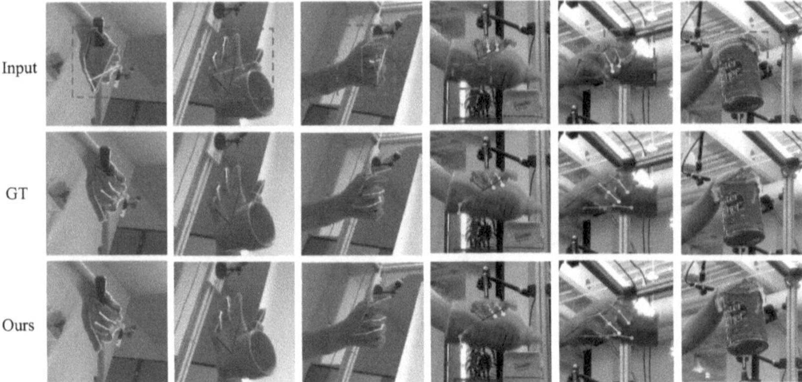

Fig. 4. Comparative visualization of 2D pose on HanCo and Dex-YCB datasets, contrasting the initial 2D estimator inputs, our refined 2D results and ground-truth 2D poses.

(K=6) provide the best balance between efficiency and accuracy, showing that our method can flexibly adapt to different deployment scenarios ranging from resource-constrained XR devices to high-accuracy offline settings.

Table 3. Runtime and efficiency breakdown of the proposed pipeline. Latency is measured on a single RTX 4080 GPU with $V = 8$ views. FLOPs are theoretical estimates. "Refinement $\times n$" denotes the number of iterative refinement stages, and "HDA (K)" indicates the mixture size used in the MDN for multi-hypothesis extrinsic modeling. Increasing either the number of refinement stages or the mixture size improves accuracy but also increases FLOPs, with diminishing returns beyond two refinements or large K.

Module/Setting	Params (M)	FLOPs (G)	MPJPE↓ (mm)
Guidance-Driven Fusion (GDF)	8.2	18.5	–
Hypothesis-Driven Alignment (HDA, K=1)	1.0	3.5	–
Hypothesis-Driven Alignment (HDA, K=6)	1.5	6.2	–
Hypothesis-Driven Alignment (HDA, K=12)	2.1	11.8	–
Refinement $\times 1$	0.8	0.59	4.56
Refinement $\times 2$	0.8	1.18	3.55
Refinement $\times 3$	0.8	1.78	3.57
Total (2 iters, K=6)	11.3	26.0	3.55

Effectiveness of the Explicit Interaction and Alignment. As shown in Table 4, our systematic module-wise analysis quantifies the contributions of each module in our method. The baseline of FusionFormer [2] achieves 4.90 mm

MPJPE, while integrating Guidance-Driven Fusion (GDF) reduces errors by 6.9% to 4.56 mm through the explicit guidance. This improvement stems from GDF's effectiveness in resolving feature-level inconsistencies across views by enforcing semantic consensus, particularly under occluded regions where single-view estimators fail. Hypothesis-Driven Alignment (HDA) further enhances performance by 12.9% to 3.89 mm, replacing conventional Singular Value Decomposition (SVD)-based camera parameter inference with coordinate space constraints. HDA with iterative refinement drives an additional 15.9% improvement to 3.55 mm by dynamically integrating complementary multi-view observations through reprojection error correction. Progressive optimization in HDA (Iteration) maintains the theoretical advantages of combining independent estimators, where fused 3D predictions systematically outperform by mitigating view-specific biases and amplifying consensus signals.

Table 4. Ablation of different modules. FusionFormer is set as the baseline. GDF and HDA represent key modules of our framework. SVD serves as a conventional method for camera parameter inference, used for comparison with our HDA.

Baseline	GDF	SVD	HDA	HDA(Iteration)	MPJPE ↓	P-MPJPE ↓
✔					4.90	3.78
✔	✔				4.56	3.72
✔	✔	✔			4.54	3.85
✔	✔		✔		3.89	3.39
✔	✔		✔	✔	**3.55**	**3.28**

5 Conclusion, Limitation, and Future Work

In this paper, we propose a calibration-free framework for robust 3D hand pose estimation in a dynamic XR headset and external camera arrays within cockpits. Our method transforms the multi-view correspondence challenge into explicit global guidance feature fusion and hypothesis-driven extrinsic alignment to mitigate instability from continuous parameter drift. We evaluate our method on a simulated headset and third-person camera scenario and show superior accuracy, robustness, and adaptability to variable view configurations. Our method has a limitation that the current simulation fails to capture real cockpit lighting variations and vibration spectra, which may introduce unmodeled noise. Future work will mitigate this limitation by conducting in-cabin experiments under realistic vibrations, lighting changes, and user behaviors could adapt the framework to operational conditions and enhance robustness.

Acknowledgments. This work was supported in part by the grants from the National Natural Science Foundation of China under Grant (62332019), the National Key

Research and Development Program of China (2023YFF1203900, 2023YFF1203903), sponsored by Beijing Nova Program (20240484513).

References

1. Boukhayma, A., Bem, R.D., Torr, P.H.: 3D hand shape and pose from images in the wild. In: Proceedings of the IEEE/CVF Conference on Computer Vision and Pattern Recognition, pp. 10843–10852 (2019)
2. Cai, Y., Zhang, W., Wu, Y., Jin, C.: Fusionformer: a concise unified feature fusion transformer for 3D pose estimation. In: Proceedings of the AAAI Conference on Artificial Intelligence, vol. 38, pp. 900–908 (2024)
3. Cao, Z., Hidalgo Martinez, G., Simon, T., Wei, S., Sheikh, Y.A.: Openpose: realtime multi-person 2d pose estimation using part affinity fields. IEEE Trans. Pattern Anal. Mach. Intell. (2019)
4. Caputo, A., Jacota, S., Krayevskyy, S., Pesavento, M., Pellacini, F., Giachetti, A.: Xr-cockpit: a comparison of VR and AR solutions on an interactive training station. In: 2020 25th IEEE International Conference on Emerging Technologies and Factory Automation (ETFA), vol. 1, pp. 603–610. IEEE (2020)
5. Chao, Y.W., et al.: Dexycb: a benchmark for capturing hand grasping of objects. In: Proceedings of the IEEE/CVF Conference on Computer Vision and Pattern Recognition, pp. 9044–9053 (2021)
6. Chen, X., et al.: Mobrecon: mobile-friendly hand mesh reconstruction from monocular image. In: Proceedings of the IEEE/CVF Conference on Computer Vision and Pattern Recognition, pp. 20544–20554 (2022)
7. Chen, X., Song, Z., Jiang, X., Hu, Y., Yu, J., Zhang, L.: Handos: 3D hand reconstruction in one stage. arXiv preprint arXiv:2412.01537 (2024)
8. Contributors, M.: Openmmlab pose estimation toolbox and benchmark (2020). https://github.com/open-mmlab/mmpose
9. Cui, Y., et al.: Camera distance helps 3D hand pose estimated from a single RGB image. Graph. Models **127**, 101179 (2023)
10. Gao, F., Ge, X., Li, J., Fan, Y., Li, Y., Zhao, R.: Intelligent cockpits for connected vehicles: taxonomy, architecture, interaction technologies, and future directions. Sensors **24**(16), 5172 (2024)
11. Gao, K., et al.: Progressively global-local fusion with explicit guidance for accurate and robust 3d hand pose reconstruction. Knowl.-Based Syst. **304**, 112532 (2024)
12. Gower, J.C.: Generalized procrustes analysis. Psychometrika **40**, 33–51 (1975)
13. Guleryuz, O.G., Kaeser-Chen, C.: Fast lifting for 3d hand pose estimation in AR/VR applications. In: 2018 25th IEEE International Conference on Image Processing (ICIP), pp. 106–110. IEEE (2018)
14. He, Y., Yan, R., Fragkiadaki, K., Yu, S.I.: Epipolar transformers. In: Proceedings of THE IEEE/CVF Conference on Computer Vision and Pattern Recognition, pp. 7779–7788 (2020)
15. Iskakov, K., Burkov, E., Lempitsky, V., Malkov, Y.: Learnable triangulation of human pose. In: Proceedings of the IEEE/CVF International Conference on Computer Vision, pp. 7718–7727 (2019)
16. Jia, K., Zhang, H., An, L., Liu, Y.: Delving deep into pixel alignment feature for accurate multi-view human mesh recovery. In: Proceedings of the AAAI Conference on Artificial Intelligence, vol. 37, pp. 989–997 (2023)

17. Jiang, B., Hu, L., Xia, S.: Probabilistic triangulation for uncalibrated multi-view 3d human pose estimation. In: Proceedings of the IEEE/CVF International Conference on Computer Vision, pp. 14850–14860 (2023)
18. Jiang, C., et al.: A2j-transformer: anchor-to-joint transformer network for 3d interacting hand pose estimation from a single RGB image. In: Proceedings of the IEEE/CVF Conference on Computer Vision and Pattern Recognition, pp. 8846–8855 (2023)
19. Loshchilov, I., Hutter, F.: Decoupled weight decay regularization. In: International Conference on Learning Representations (2017)
20. Lugaresi, C., et al.: Mediapipe: a framework for building perception pipelines. arXiv preprint arXiv:1906.08172 (2019)
21. Ma, H., et al.: PPT: token-pruned pose transformer for monocular and multi-view human pose estimation. In: European Conference on Computer Vision, pp. 424–442. Springer, Heidelberg (2022). https://doi.org/10.1007/978-3-031-20065-6_25
22. Park, J., Oh, Y., Moon, G., Choi, H., Lee, K.M.: Handoccnet: occlusion-robust 3d hand mesh estimation network. In: Proceedings of the IEEE/CVF Conference on Computer Vision and Pattern Recognition, pp. 1496–1505 (2022)
23. Paszke, A., et al.: Automatic differentiation in pytorch. In: Advances in Neural Information Processing Systems (2017)
24. Potamias, R.A., Zhang, J., Deng, J., Zafeiriou, S.: Wilor: end-to-end 3d hand localization and reconstruction in-the-wild. In: Proceedings of the Computer Vision and Pattern Recognition Conference, pp. 12242–12254 (2025)
25. Ren, M., Fan, J., Yu, C., Zheng, P.: Cockpitgemini: a personalized design framework for smart vehicle cockpits integrating generative model-based multi-agent systems and human digital twins. Int. J. AI Mater. Des. **1**(3), 4–19 (2024)
26. Ren, P., Sun, H., Hao, J., Wang, J., Qi, Q., Liao, J.: Mining multi-view information: a strong self-supervised framework for depth-based 3D hand pose and mesh estimation. In: Proceedings of the IEEE/CVF Conference on Computer Vision and Pattern Recognition, pp. 20555–20565 (2022)
27. Ren, P., et al.: Decoupled iterative refinement framework for interacting hands reconstruction from a single RGB image. In: Proceedings of the IEEE/CVF International Conference on Computer Vision, pp. 8014–8025 (2023)
28. Shuai, H., Wu, L., Liu, Q.: Adaptive multi-view and temporal fusing transformer for 3D human pose estimation. IEEE Trans. Pattern Anal. Mach. Intell. **45**(4), 4122–4135 (2022)
29. Simon, T., Joo, H., Matthews, I., Sheikh, Y.: Hand keypoint detection in single images using multiview bootstrapping. In: CVPR (2017)
30. Vaswani, A., et al.: Attention is all you need. In: Advances in Neural Information Processing Systems, vol. 30 (2017)
31. Wang, H., Sun, M.: Smart-vposenet: 3D human pose estimation models and methods based on multi-view discriminant network. Knowl.-Based Syst. **239**, 107992 (2022)
32. Wang, Y., Xu, H., Heng, P.A., Fu, C.W.: Sima-hand: boosting 3D hand-mesh reconstruction by single-to-multi-view adaptation. In: Proceedings of the AAAI Conference on Artificial Intelligence, vol. 38, pp. 5704–5712 (2024)
33. Xu, H., Wang, T., Tang, X., Fu, C.W.: H2onet: hand-occlusion-and-orientation-aware network for real-time 3d hand mesh reconstruction. In: Proceedings of the IEEE/CVF Conference on Computer Vision and Pattern Recognition, pp. 17048–17058 (2023)

34. Xu, M., Qin, L., Chen, W., Pu, S., Zhang, L.: Multi-view adversarial discriminator: mine the non-causal factors for object detection in unseen domains. In: Proceedings of the IEEE/CVF Conference on Computer Vision and Pattern Recognition, pp. 8103–8112 (2023)
35. Yang, D., et al.: Aide: a vision-driven multi-view, multi-modal, multi-tasking dataset for assistive driving perception. In: Proceedings of the IEEE/CVF International Conference on Computer Vision (ICCV), pp. 20459–20470 (2023)
36. Yang, Z., Zeng, A., Yuan, C., Li, Y.: Effective whole-body pose estimation with two-stages distillation. In: Proceedings of the IEEE/CVF International Conference on Computer Vision, pp. 4210–4220 (2023)
37. Zhang, J., Cai, Y., Yan, S., Feng, J., et al.: Direct multi-view multi-person 3d pose estimation. Adv. Neural. Inf. Process. Syst. **34**, 13153–13164 (2021)
38. Zhang, Z., Wang, C., Qiu, W., Qin, W., Zeng, W.: Adafuse: adaptive multiview fusion for accurate human pose estimation in the wild. Int. J. Comput. Vision **129**, 703–718 (2021)
39. Zheng, X., Wen, C., Xue, Z., Ren, P., Wang, J.: Hamuco: hand pose estimation via multiview collaborative self-supervised learning. In: Proceedings of the IEEE/CVF International Conference on Computer Vision, pp. 20763–20773 (2023)
40. Zhou, Y., Habermann, M., Xu, W., Habibie, I., Theobalt, C., Xu, F.: Monocular real-time hand shape and motion capture using multi-modal data. In: Proceedings of the IEEE/CVF Conference on Computer Vision and Pattern Recognition, pp. 5346–5355 (2020)
41. Zhu, Y., et al.: MUC: mixture of uncalibrated cameras for robust 3D human body reconstruction. arXiv preprint arXiv:2403.05055 (2024)
42. Zimmermann, C., Argus, M., Brox, T.: Contrastive representation learning for hand shape estimation. In: Bauckhage, C., Gall, J., Schwing, A. (eds.) DAGM GCPR 2021. LNCS, vol. 13024, pp. 250–264. Springer, Cham (2021). https://doi.org/10.1007/978-3-030-92659-5_16
43. Zimmermann, C., Ceylan, D., Yang, J., Russell, B., Argus, M., Brox, T.: Freihand: a dataset for markerless capture of hand pose and shape from single RGB images. In: Proceedings of the IEEE/CVF International Conference on Computer Vision, pp. 813–822 (2019)

Geometry-Aware Global Feature Aggregation for Real-Time Indirect Illumination

Meng Gai[1,2], Guoping Wang[1,2], and Sheng Li[1,2(✉)]

[1] School of Computer Science, Peking University, Beijing, China
{gaimeng,wgp,lisheng}@pku.edu.cn
[2] National Key Laboratory of Intelligent Parallel Technology, Beijing, China

Abstract. Real-time rendering with global illumination is crucial to afford the user realistic experience in virtual environments. We present a learning-based estimator to predict diffuse indirect illumination in screen space, which is then combined with direct illumination to synthesize globally-illuminated high dynamic range (HDR) results. Our approach tackles the challenges of capturing long-range/long-distance indirect illumination when employing neural networks and is generalized to handle complex lighting and scenarios. From the neural network thinking of the solver to the rendering equation, we present a novel network architecture to predict indirect illumination. Our network is equipped with a modified attention mechanism that aggregates global information guided by spatial geometry features, as well as a monochromatic design that encodes each color channel individually. We conducted extensive evaluations, and the experimental results demonstrate our superiority over previous learning-based techniques. Our approach excels at handling complex lighting, such as varying-colored lighting and environment lighting. It can successfully capture distant indirect illumination and simulate the interreflections between textured surfaces well (i.e., color bleeding effects); it can also effectively handle new scenes that are not present in the training dataset.

Keywords: global illumination · neural network · real-time rendering

1 Introduction

Visual realism with global illumination is a key demand of immersive virtual reality (VR) applications to intrigue users' immersion arousal and respond realistically to virtual environments and events [48]. However, realistic rendering of such globally-illuminated scenarios in real time remains a big challenge, especially in handling complex lighting situations like dynamic changes of illumination and environment lighting [31]. While photo-realistic rendering techniques (e.g., Monte Carlo path tracing) can synthesize images with global illumination, they are often extremely time-consuming and may take hours to render. Meanwhile, various works attempt to use approximations along with classical rasterization-based rendering, thus approximating global illumination effects at interactive or real-time performance. They generally operate in either image or 3D space and adopt different precomputation techniques to reduce runtime

A. Hinkenjan et al. (Eds.): ICXR 2025, LNCS 16428, pp. 151–174, 2026.
https://doi.org/10.1007/978-981-95-7195-6_9

cost [22,38]. Recently, learning-based techniques for photo-realistic rendering were proposed, some of which combine data-driven methods with classic rendering pipeline, resulting in improved image quality or rendering speedup [6,45]. These techniques, namely neural rendering [43], usually provide stronger supervision to generative models by applying the prior knowledge in classical rendering techniques to neural networks.

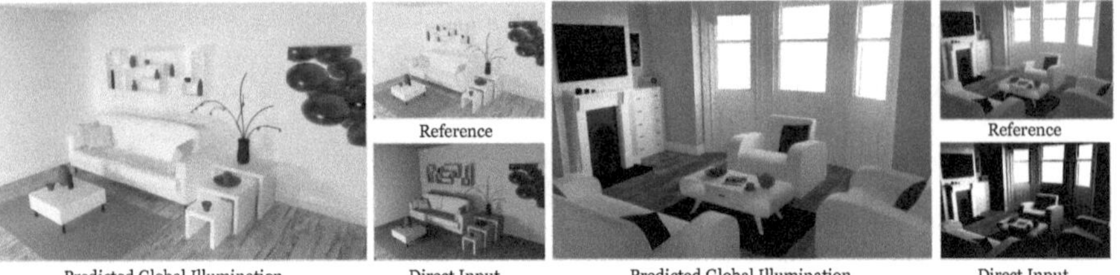

Fig. 1. Our model efficiently synthesizes HDR results with global illumination predicted in around 12 ms. We highlight that our model is well generalized to handle complex dynamic lighting in scenes, such as varying-colored lighting (left) and environment lighting (right), which are new scenes that have not been present in the training dataset.

Predicting indirect illumination is, nonetheless, a challenging task. Prior works generally regard this as a special case of image-to-image translation, and use convolutional neural networks (CNN) for indirect/global illumination prediction. The auxiliary geometry features are provided as inputs to predict global illumination, further conditioned on input the direct lighting [32,47] or emission maps [6]. However, several major challenges remain:

- Poor generalization. Various lighting conditions, geometries, and surface textures jointly result in diversified scenes, inflicting high demands on both training data and model capacity. However, synthetic datasets have limited coverage; and the need for real-time performance restricts model capacity/complexity.
- Difficult to model long-distance indirect illumination due to narrow-range dependencies. Prior works generally use stacks of convolutional operations within their model, where the processing of inputs is limited to a local neighborhood.
- Inaccurate color when predicting indirect illumination. We find that the generative models easily fall into predicting the average of the distribution within the training data, resulting in inconsistency between direct and indirect illumination.

To address these issues, we adopt a learning-based approach to address the issue of global illumination, following the principles of the rendering equation [20]. Our approach includes a learnable module that aggregates global features while utilizing geometry supervision. This module incorporates a modified multi-head attention mechanism [44] to calculate the distribution based on geometry features, which guides the global aggregation of spatial features. This non-local process can be analogized to an integral over screen space, where the geometry-aware attention works as a learnable counterpart of the geometry term. Our proposed module overcomes the network bottleneck of the deep stack of convolutional layers, requiring less computation and fewer parameters while better capturing the long-range dependencies. Moreover, it can be applied to other tasks where geometry supervision is available and long-range dependency modeling is preferred.

Second, we present a monochromatic model design, where each RGB channel is independently processed using a shading generator conditioned on shared features from a geometry encoder. The redundant inter-channel interactions (introduced by the interconnections of convolutional filters) can be eliminated, and this relieves the burden of training data and network capacity, and enforces the network to learn the accurate color of indirect light. Furthermore, this makes our model immune to color variations, therefore allowing better generalization to novel and complex scenes and dynamic lighting, which are not present in the training data. Since HDR images can provide a much wider range of brightness and contrast for the high sensitivity of the human visual system to enhance the user's perception of immersion and presence in the immersive virtual environment [7,28], our model is trained to synthesize HDR global illumination.

Finally, we created a novel synthetic HDR dataset of indoor scenes for network training based on the public indoor layout dataset 3D-Front [11]. Our dataset comes with well-annotated lighting, texture, and geometry features; the surfaces are also assigned with physically based materials, providing sufficient diversity for geometry features and visual appearances. We design an adversarial training framework to directly optimize our network on HDR data, where the discriminator and the perceptual loss are jointly used for network optimization.

Our model can produce plausible indirect illumination at real-time performance, handling global effects, accurately predicting indirect shading with good generalization, as shown in Fig. 1. To summarize, our main contributions include:

- We propose a neural network for indirect illumination prediction that leverages a global feature aggregation module for geometry features to model long-range dependencies, thereby synthesizing realistic HDR images with high performance.
- We present a monochromatic design featuring the independent processing of each color channel, which benefits our model in terms of efficiency, compactness, and explainability.
- We create a photo-realistic synthetic HDR dataset with pixel-wise annotated features, including factorized lighting, material, and geometry. Our dataset can offer significant potential as a resource for learning-based rendering algorithms to facilitate diverse benchmarks of real-time global illumination, supporting high presence in immersive virtual reality applications.

2 Related Work

2.1 Real-Time Global Illumination

Numerous works seek to acquire global illumination effects at a low time budget. Classical methods adopt different approximations to reduce performance costs. Some of them operate in 2D screen space, such as screen space ambient occlusion (SSAO) [1] and screen space directional occlusion (SSDO) [35], using rasterized direct lighting and g-buffer features to approximate inter-reflections between surfaces. While some others operate in 3D space, usually achieving more realism with higher computational costs and storage, such as voxel cone tracing (VXGI) [5] and light propagation volumes (LPV) [21]. Lastly, precomputation-based methods like precomputed radiance transfer (PRT) [38] reduce the runtime cost by computing pre-integrations on the environment and BRDFs. Recently, with the advances in deep learning, data-driven methods have also been adopted to improve rendering quality efficiently. For example, training CNNs to denoise low sample-count images [3], or predicting the proper sample count for real-time raytracing [26].

2.2 Image-to-Image Translation

The task of image-to-image translation converts images from one domain to another, e.g., image style translation, colorization, etc. The architecture of convolutional neural networks (CNN) has been the most commonly used technique for image-to-image tasks, such as U-Net [36] and ResNet [15]. After the generative adversarial network (GAN) proposed by Goodfellow et al. [13], it has been further extended to conditional generative models and introduced to image-to-image tasks as well [18]. Recently, there has been another trend of using pre-trained models (e.g., VGG-19 [37]) to capture structurally correlated high-level image features for network optimization, namely the perceptual loss [19]. We show that a model's output quality and robustness could be enhanced by jointly introducing adversarial loss and perceptual loss into network optimization.

2.3 Network Conditioning

Image-to-image translation could also be regarded as conditional synthesis, where networks learn to generate images conditioned on input geometry or semantic labels. Most of the early works simply provide conditioning data as the input of the network [18]. In contrast, many recent works focus on finding better ways to condition the image generation process, e.g., using a depth map to explicitly guide the convolution [46], using learned transformations to modulate convolutional features [33]. While these works have achieved great success, they are mainly used along with convolution layers, and thus remain local conditioning methods.

Inspired by the great success of attention mechanisms in modeling global dependencies [44,49] and motivated by our task formulation, we propose a feature aggregation method that models long-range dependencies guided by geometry features, where the aggregation weights are obtained from a modified multi-head attention mechanism. Different from the prior work on integrating attention to CNN [49], we 1) explicitly use geometry features to guide the aggregation of global features; then 2) extend it into multi-head attention [44], and find it sufficient to equip only bottleneck layers with attention. Both bring a significant reduction of computational overhead, with no observable performance degradation in our experiments.

2.4 Global Illumination Prediction

Several recent works use neural networks to predict global illumination given auxiliary shading and geometry features. Nalbach et al. [32] first introduced CNN into global illumination prediction. They use a U-shaped CNN, taking pixel-wise features as inputs and predicting globally illuminated images. Bi et al. [2] train GANs to predict global illumination, and Dai et al. [6] use the perceptual loss for network optimization. Then Xin et al. [47] used a lightweight CNN and predicted the indirect component similar to the task setup in our work. However, Nalbach et al. [32] used global illumination computed in screen space as their ground truth, and Dai et al. excluded textures in their ground truth data generation. Most prior works used LDR data for training or took no special care in training in linear HDR space. Moreover, they generally use stacked convolutional operations for shading learning, limiting the receptive fields to local neighborhoods, and thus it is difficult to predict global effects like indirect illumination.

Our approach focuses on capturing more accurate long-range indirect illumination while better handling the inter-reflections between differently textured surfaces (i.e., color-bleeding effects).

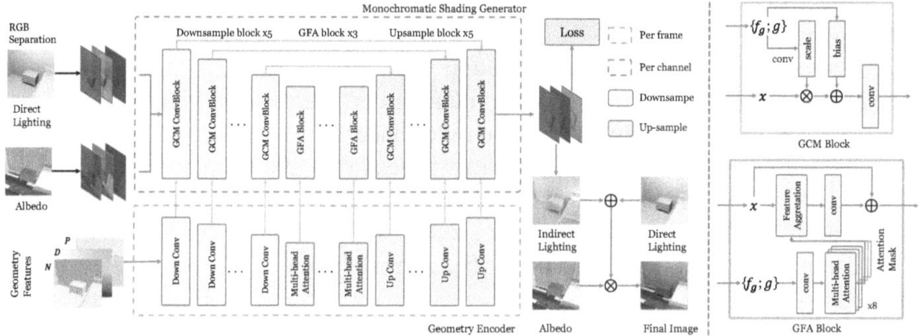

Fig. 2. Overview of our model architecture. GCM: geometry-aware conditional modulation; GFA: geometry-aware feature aggregation. The geometry encoder takes in the auxiliary geometry information of each frame as input and provides geometry conditional features (GCM) and attention weights (GFA) to the generator. The monochromatic shading generator then independently predicts each color channel of the indirect illumination, given the lighting and reflectance of the corresponding channel as input.

3 Our Method

We first outline the neural network thinking of the solver for rendering equations. Then, we present our network architecture, including the feature aggregation module and the monochromatic design. Finally, we discuss the technical details, practical considerations about performance and optimization, and the adversarial training framework.

3.1 Task Formulation

We aim to predict indirect lighting given direct lighting and auxiliary geometry features, including surface normal, depth, reflectance, etc. All these inputs can be efficiently computed using a rasterization-based rendering pipeline in real time. For simplicity, we assume all Lambertian surfaces within the scene, i.e., the BRDF term $f(\mathrm{p}, \omega_i, \omega_o)$ is a constant for arbitrary ω_i and ω_o. We first briefly review the concepts of rendering equation [20] and physically based rendering; by splitting the incident radiance L_i into direct and indirect terms, we derive an alternative form of the surface rendering equation:

$$\begin{aligned} L_o(\mathrm{p}, \omega_o) &= \int_A \left(L_i^{\mathrm{d}}(\mathrm{p}, \omega_i) + L_i^{\mathrm{ind}}(\mathrm{p}, \omega_i)\right) f_r(\mathrm{p}) G(\mathrm{p}, \mathrm{p}')\,\mathrm{d}A(\mathrm{p}') \\ &= L_o^{\mathrm{d}}(\mathrm{p}, \omega_o) + L_o^{\mathrm{ind}}(\mathrm{p}, \omega_o)\ , \end{aligned} \tag{1}$$

where $L_{\mathrm{o}}^{\mathrm{d}}$ and $L_{\mathrm{o}}^{\mathrm{ind}}$ are the direct and indirect components of the scattering radiance, respectively. $G(\mathrm{p}, \mathrm{p}') = \frac{V(\mathrm{p}' \leftrightarrow \mathrm{p}) \cos\theta \cos\theta'}{\|\mathrm{p}-\mathrm{p}'\|}$ is the geometry term where $V(\mathrm{p}' \leftrightarrow \mathrm{p})$ indicates the visibility between two vertices. We can obtain the direct lighting term $L_{\mathrm{o}}^{\mathrm{d}}$ by integrating over all light sources or by real-time alternatives [10,16,38]. We then feed $L_{\mathrm{o}}^{\mathrm{d}}$ into the network and predict the indirect component $L_{\mathrm{o}}^{\mathrm{ind}}$.

To apply fine-grained supervision to the network, we first decompose the direct and indirect components of the final illumination, letting the network focus on predicting the indirect component instead of global illumination. We then use reflectance factorization to demodulate shading and diffuse reflectance, thus effectively tasking the network with learning the demodulated shading (instead of scattered radiance), which has a relatively low frequency after multiple bounces within the scene. The final rendering is obtained by multiplying the predicted shading with the reflectance. Moreover, we propose a feature aggregation module for better modeling global dependencies, which is intuitively similar to an integral over screen space. We employ the modified attention mechanism [44] to impose the effects of distance and visibility on network models, which intuitively works like a learnable counterpart of the geometry term, as is discussed later.

Summarization. To predict indirect illumination, the geometry information (surface normals $\mathbf{N}$, depth $\mathbf{D}$, diffuse reflectance $\mathbf{R}$, bold type indicates image data) and direct lighting $\mathbf{L}_{\mathrm{d}}$ are provided as conditioning features. The network is expected to predict the indirect shading component $\mathbf{S}_{\mathrm{ind}}$, from which we can obtain the full indirect illumination $\mathbf{L}_{\mathrm{ind}}$ by multiplying the reflectance, i.e., $\mathbf{L} = \mathbf{R} \cdot \mathbf{S}$. The final global illumination $\mathbf{L}$ is acquired by adding direct illumination $\mathbf{L}_{\mathrm{d}}$ (provided as inputs) to the predicted indirect illumination, i.e., $\mathbf{L} = \mathbf{L}_{\mathrm{d}} + \mathbf{L}_{\mathrm{ind}}$. Note that all the above computations are pixel-wise operations in linear space; thus, all the components should be represented with linear values and stored as HDR images.

3.2 Model Design

Overview. Our model contains a shading generation branch and a geometry encoding branch, both using a U-shaped network with skip-connections [36]. We integrate 1) our feature aggregation module into the shading generator to model long-range dependencies; 2) the monochromatic design for a more consistent deep rendering process. We also utilize conditional modulation techniques [33] for better geometry-aware supervision. The overview of our network architecture is shown in Fig. 2.

Geometry Encoder. We use an additional geometry encoder that encodes geometry properties (i.e., positions **P**, normals **N**, and depth **D**), leaving the other inputs to the shading encoder. The encoded geometry features are provided to condition the synthesis process of the shading generator. The separation of the encoding process splits the task into spatial structure modeling and light transport simulation, thus alleviating the requirements on training data and network complexity. Instead of simply concatenating the geometry features to the inputs of the generator layers, we use a more effective method, namely geometry-aware conditional modulation (GCM) similar to [33]. Specifically, the conditional geometry features are transformed into scaling and biasing factors through learnable convolution layers as:

$$\mathbf{GCM}(x) = \left(\gamma(\hat{f}_g) \otimes x\right) \oplus \beta(\hat{f}_g), \tag{2}$$

where $\oplus$ and $\otimes$ denote element-wise addition and multiplication, respectively. $\hat{f}_g = \{f_g; g\}$ denotes the layer-wise encoded geometry features concatenated with original geometry inputs (i.e., $\mathbf{N}, \mathbf{D}$, etc.), while γ and β are learnable transformations implemented with convolution layers. Experimentally, this is more effective and computationally saving when jointly used with our monochromatic network, as discussed below.

Geometry-Aware Feature Aggregation. Fully convolutional networks (FCN) will result in a limited-sized receptive field [6,32,47], i.e., the output pixel value is conditioned only on a local region. While deep stacks of convolutional operations can enlarge the receptive field, they also bring prohibitive computational costs, making network optimization difficult. In this work, we expect the network to generate indirect illumination from features of all locations within the image space. A learnable module is needed that can efficiently aggregate global features guided by geometry.

We use a modified multi-head attention mechanism [44] to acquire the weights for the feature aggregation module based on geometry features (i.e., positions, depth, and surface normals). For each spatial location, the module first calculates the attention weights based on the encoded geometry features f_g, then obtains the response of that position as a weighted combination of the features from all locations. The attention weights $\text{Attn}(j \mid i)$ for location i are computed as:

$$\text{Attn}(j \mid i) = \text{Softmax}_j \left(\text{Dot}\left(Q(\hat{f_g}^i), K(\hat{f_g}^j)\right)\right), \tag{3}$$

where i and j are indices to the features within image space, Q and K are linear transformations (implemented as 1×1 convolutions). Specifically, F and G correspond to these two transformations in the geometry encoder, representing the Query (Q) and Key (K) projections applied to geometry features, as shown in Fig. 3. The encoded features $\hat{f}_g$ are again concatenated with original geometry inputs (down-sampled to the current size) to preserve them from being washed away. The attention distribution of i is normalized for all spatial location j using softmax, and is then used to get the aggregated global feature $\hat{x}^i$ for location i as:

$$\hat{x}^i = x^i + \Sigma_{j=1}^{N} \left(V(x^j)\,\text{Attn}(j \mid i)\right), \tag{4}$$

where x^i is the residual connection applied to outputs, and V is an extra linear transformation applied to the original features while preserving their original dimensionality. Intuitively, this process is similar to the process of integrating over screen space, where the attention mechanism calculates some sort of mutual contribution between two points for shading based on their geometry features (just like a learnable counterpart of the geometry term, Eq. 1). By attending to the projected subspace of geometry features, it learns to determine whether the feature x_j of location j is useful and thus should be aggregated into the current location i (see Fig. 3).

In addition, we find it beneficial to use multiple learnable linear transformations within attention computation, i.e., obtain multiple attention distributions Attn_k using different sets of linear transformations Q_k, K_k, and V_k, where $k = 1...h$ is the index of attention head and $h = 8$ in our experiments. The aggregated features $\hat{x_k}$ are then concatenated to produce the final output $\hat{x}$, resulting in the multi-head version [44] of the aggregation module. This allows the network to simultaneously attend to different subspaces of the spatial features, resulting in a better capacity for modeling long-range dependencies.

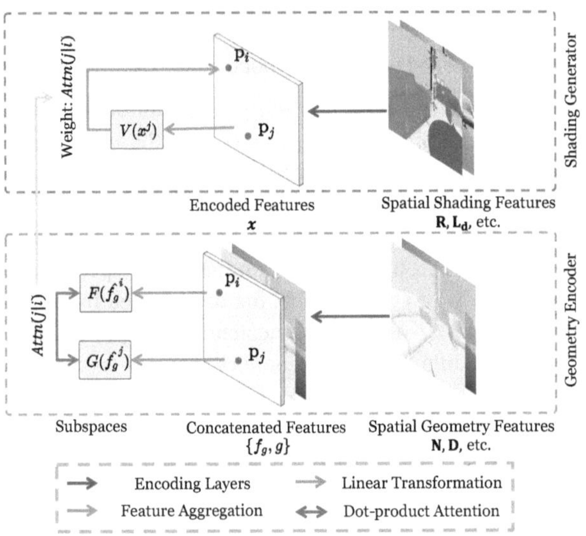

Fig. 3. Geometry-aware feature aggregation operation. p_i and p_j could be any two 2D locations of the input features, thus effectively modeling global dependencies within screen space.

Monochromatic Shading. The key insight of the monochromatic design is from the difference between the convolutional neural networks (CNN) and a typical rendering pipeline. The CNN generally encodes an RGB image in one pass, where the features in different color channels could interact via the inter-channel connections in convolutional filters. However, this is inconsistent with a typical rendering pipeline, where the rendering process of each color channel (or the light transport of a specified wavelength) is handled independently.

Specifically, we interpret the rendering process as a mapping $F : \mathscr{X} \rightarrow \mathscr{Y}$, where $\mathscr{X}$ is the high-dimensional inputs encoding the scene geometry, camera, materials, etc., and

$\mathscr{Y}$ is the rendered 2D image, thus, rendering can be viewed as evaluating the function $Y = F(X)$. Since the rendering process is wavelength-independent (thus is channel-independent if the RGB color model is used), this function can be further written in a channel-independent way, i.e., $Y^c = F^c(X^c)$, where $c \in \{\mathrm{r,g,b}\}$ indicates the specific channel. However, in the general learning-based methods, the mapping between inputs and outputs is written as $\hat{Y} = G(X;\theta)$, where θ is the model parameter, and $\hat{Y}$ is the predicted indirect illumination. Note that each color channel of the RGB inputs (i.e., reflectance and lighting) contributes to all three channels of $\hat{Y}$ via the interconnections within the convolutional filters, which is redundant and inconsistent with the typical rendering process.

Based on this observation, our monochromatic shading generator processes each color channel independently, i.e., for each input with RGB channels, the shading network takes in each channel in parallel and predicts the shading of that channel. Note that the same shading network is shared between different color channels. We could thus interpret the prediction process as:

$$\hat{\mathbf{L}}^c_{\mathrm{ind}} = \mathbf{Generator}(\mathbf{L}^c_{\mathrm{d}}, \mathbf{R}^c, f_g; \theta)\;, \tag{5}$$

where c indicates the current color channel and $\mathbf{f}_g$ is the encoded features from the geometry encoder. This channel-independent process is consistent with the typical rendering process, freeing our network from the inequalities in the color distribution in training data. Moreover, the RGB feature of each pixel is not considered helpful in our task, where we seek to simulate light transportation only, which is channel-wise independent. We will discuss its superiority in Sect. 5.

3.3 Optimizations

Minimizing Computational Overhead. The conditional feature modulation (CFM) modules are carefully designed to enhance the data reusing/sharing between channels, thus minimizing the extra computational overhead introduced by the monochromatic design. Specifically, the conditional features ($\gamma(\hat{f}_g)$ and $\beta(\hat{f}_g)$ by GCM Block), as well as the attention distribution ($\mathrm{Attn}(j\,|\,i)$ by GFA Block) are both only dependent on the geometry features (see Fig. 2), thus are shared and reused by different color channels. While a per-channel process is still needed(instead of directly reconstructing RGB outputs), we later justify this potential loss of efficiency by showing that a smaller monochromatic model can still perform better with similar computational complexity and fewer parameters than a normal model.

Optimizing on HDR Images. Most image generation tasks use tone-mapped low dynamic range (LDR) images for training and directly render tone-mapped images in LDR space. We note that multiple benefits could be obtained by optimizing the model directly using linear HDR data, including 1) preserving details in both dark bright areas of high contrast images; 2) preserving the zero-mean distribution of noise (introduced by unbiased Monte Carlo sampling), which may be beneficial for the learning process; and 3) allowing for more flexible post-processing applications on outputs, such as re-exposure or refocus. Moreover, if we use tone-mapped LDR images for both input and output, the physical correctness (i.e., the linearity between direct and indirect components) would be lost in our training data.

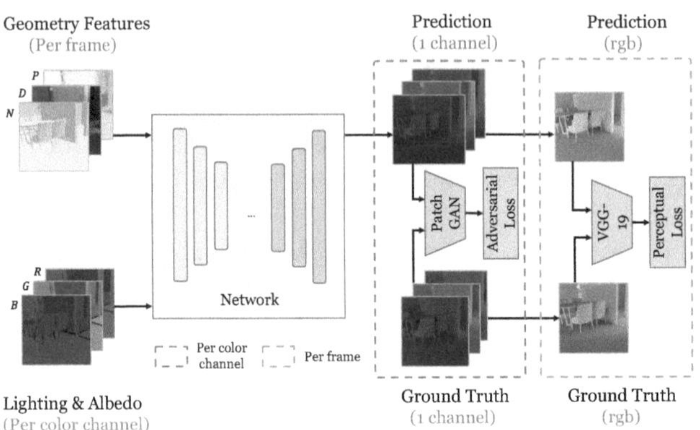

Fig. 4. Our adversarial training framework. We use a PatchGAN as the discriminator for adversarial training, and the perceptual loss is acquired using a pre-trained VGG-19. The computation of adversarial loss is in a per-color-channel manner, whereas the perceptual loss is computed on the final RGB image.

To better parameterize the linear radiance values, we use an exponential activation for the generator output rather than a sigmoid function commonly used for reconstructing LDR images. Furthermore, the linearity between direct illumination and indirect illumination could be utilized with HDR training. Specifically, for the direct $\mathbf{L}_\mathrm{d}$ and indirect $\mathbf{L}_\mathrm{ind}$ components within a rendered frame, if we perturb the direct illumination with a random factor, i.e., $\hat{\mathbf{L}}_\mathrm{d} = \alpha \cdot \mathbf{L}_\mathrm{d}$ (equivalent to re-exposure or scaling all light sources within the scene), we will have its corresponding indirect illumination as $\hat{\mathbf{L}}_\mathrm{ind} = \alpha \cdot \mathbf{L}_\mathrm{ind}$. We exploit this fact by adding random perturbations to the exposure of each frame while training, which improves the model's robustness to illumination variations. This could also be regarded as an effective data augmentation technique.

3.4 Adversarial Training and Loss Function

We present an adversarial training framework using a weighted combination of losses for network optimization, including a content loss $\mathscr{L}_\mathrm{c}$, a perceptual loss $\mathscr{L}_\mathrm{p}$, and an adversarial loss $\mathscr{L}_\mathrm{a}$. As illustrated in Fig. 4, our final loss function $\mathscr{L}$ can be written as:

$$\mathscr{L} = \omega_\mathrm{a}\mathscr{L}_\mathrm{a} + \omega_\mathrm{c}\mathscr{L}_\mathrm{c} + \omega_\mathrm{p}\mathscr{L}_\mathrm{p}\,, \tag{6}$$

where ω_c, ω_p, and ω_a are the hyperparameters controlling the weight of each loss term, we use empirical values where $\omega_\mathrm{c} = 0.7$, $\omega_\mathrm{p} = 0.28$, $\omega_\mathrm{a} = 0.02$ in our experiments. We use smooth L1 loss [34] as our content loss. While the L1 loss could not capture the inter-pixel correlations or the structural information of the image, we thus additionally introduced a PatchGAN [18] as the discriminator to obtain the adversarial loss term, which helps recover high-frequency local details. Moreover, it is an ill-posed problem to predict indirect illumination given direct lighting in screen space only (instead of in 3D solutions). While classic pixel-wise loss (e.g., L1, L2) generally tends to predict the average value over all possible solutions [27], we hope the adversarial training can guide the generator to approximate one particular solution, thus being more consistent with human perception.

Fig. 5. Some indoor scenes rendered in our synthetic dataset.

Furthermore, to bridge the gap between the generative model and human perception, we introduce the perceptual loss [19], which captures the structurally correlated high-level features and thus is robust to noise and local artifacts. Specifically, we compute the perceptual loss $\mathscr{L}_{\mathrm{p}}$ based on the L1 distance of different convolutional layers within a pre-trained VGG-19 [37]:

$$\mathscr{L}_{\mathrm{p}}(X,Y,\theta) = \sum_{l}^{N} \lambda_i \left\| \Phi_l(Y) - \Phi_l(\mathbf{G}(X,\theta)) \right\|_1 , \tag{7}$$

where Φ_l is the l-th layer of VGG-19 and λ_i is the weight of each layer. Note that while the content loss and the adversarial loss are computed and averaged for each color channel, the perceptual loss, however, is applied to the composited RGB image (see Fig. 4), making the final output coherent with human perception and maintaining the visual consistency across independently processed channels.

4 Synthetic Dataset

We created a novel synthetic dataset of indoor scenes (see Fig. 5) to train our network, which is based on the 3D-Front [11] public interior dataset with over 60k distinct house layouts. To the best of our knowledge, there is no publicly available dataset containing completely annotated lighting (with factorized shading and reflectance, separated direct/indirect and diffuse/specular components) and geometry features that adapt well to our task. Our dataset will be released publicly online upon publication to fill the absence of a high-quality dataset for learning-based shading prediction tasks.

Our synthetic dataset contains over 30,000 high dynamic range (HDR) images rendered from 1.5k indoor layouts from 3D-Front, each with pixel-wise annotations of lighting, texture, and geometry features. While all textures in 3D-Front are restricted to diffuse materials, and some surfaces have no materials, we also assign physically based materials to the surfaces, which provide highly diverse visual effects and improve visual realism compared to similar synthetic datasets as [39,51]. Note that our dataset also applies to many other computer vision tasks, such as indoor scene understanding, inverse rendering, intrinsic decomposition, etc. Please see the supplementary document for more details and illustrations about material assignment and dataset generation.

To create photo-realistic rendered images with less manual effort, we use a custom data generation pipeline based on Blender Cycles [4], which can be summarized as the following steps:

Texture Assignment. To achieve more realism on our synthetic dataset, we use an open-source CC0 texture library [8] which includes over 1,300 types of physically based materials covering various surfaces such as wood, metal, glass, etc. We randomly assign certain materials based on the object type in a rule-based style, using a similar strategy with [9]. For example, for each wall surface, we uniformly sample one material among all wood, marble, or concrete-type materials. This rule-based technique for random texture assignment significantly reduces the effort of manually assigning the textures for each object while preserving sufficient consistency and diversity for indoor layouts.

Light Sources Placement. We randomly sample the placement of light sources. To approximate direct lighting at real-time performance, we use directional and point/spherical light sources only. We place point and spherical light sources for each room at random positions near the ceiling, and let all spherical light sources' radius and intensity vary within a certain range to acquire more diverse visual appearances.

Viewpoint Sampling. We uniformly sample camera poses within the scene, then heuristically filter those that are considered to be of low quality. Specifically, we examine the statistics of depth distribution within each image, particularly thresholding the mean $\mathrm{E}(\mathbf{D})$ and variance $\mathrm{Var}(\mathbf{D})$ of depth values. Part of images with incorrect statistics (e.g., a low $\mathrm{E}(\mathbf{D})$ or too many dark pixels) will be discarded, which is often the case where cameras are partially/completely occluded by surfaces or nearby objects.

5 Experiments and Evaluations

5.1 Implementation Detail

We implement our network model using PyTorch. For the output of each convolutional layer, we apply Leaky ReLU activation, except for the last layer where an exponential activation is used. For both the generator and discriminator, we use Adam optimizer [23] for optimization and Xavier [12] for network initialization. Dropout [40] is used in up-sampling layers to avoid over-fitting. The model is trained for 80 epochs using over

50 h. Model performance is measured on an RTX 3090, using 768 × 512 (3:2 ratio) as the standard resolution for network inference to synthesize image. Please refer to the supplemental material for our code implementation and the pre-trained model, which will be released online along with the training dataset.

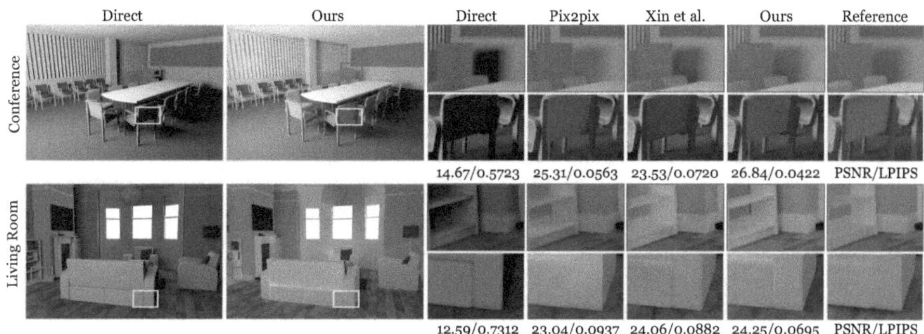

Fig. 6. With regard to global illuminations, our approach outperforms other methods in terms of PSNR and LPIPS, and our approach produces results that are visually closer to the reference.

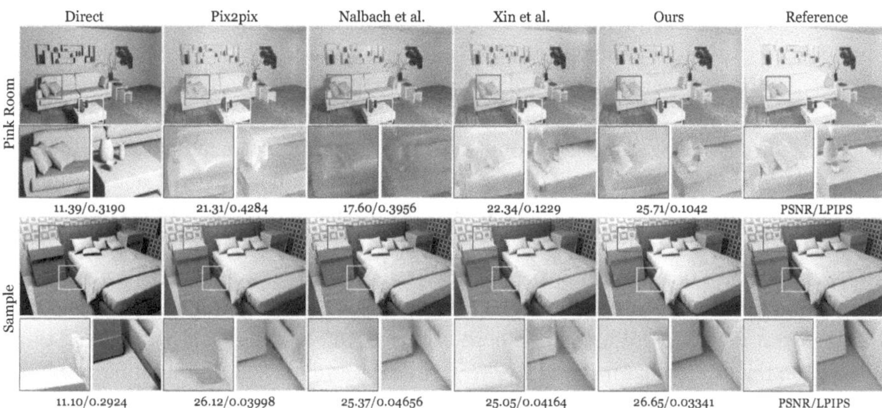

Fig. 7. Upper of each scene: full rendering (direct + indirect + texture); lower of each scene: untextured indirect component with zoom-in regions (demodulated from reflectance). our approach outperforms other methods in terms of PSNR and LPIPS.

Fig. 8. Capability of capturing long-range indirect light of different methods. A green wall on the left is treated as an indirect light source, lit by an area light facing the wall. Our approach synthesizes the better result closer to the reference. (Color figure online)

5.2 Results and Discussions

We use three evaluation metrics to compare the performance of different methods, including SSIM, PSNR, and LPIPS [50]. The LPIPS metric calculates perceptual similarity based on high-level features in a pre-trained AlexNet [25], which is more robust to noise and better resembles human choice. We compare two recent works on global illumination prediction, including Nalbach et al. [32] and Xin et al. [47]. Our method adopts a neural rendering approach based on shading space, predicting indirect illumination from screen space to achieve real-time HDR global illumination estimation. Its core idea is to efficiently simulate long-range indirect light transport through an image-to-image learning paradigm, without relying on explicit geometric modeling or physical path integration, thus belonging to a fast, screen-space neural rendering framework. In contrast, [52] focuses on 3D explicit scene modeling and object-level light transport representation. It implicitly models the illumination contribution of each object in the scene, superposing them in latent space to solve for global illumination. These methods differ fundamentally in technical routes, input spaces, and problem formulations. Therefore, such scene-space neural rendering methods [14,41,42,52] are not included for direct comparisons.

Note that Nalbach et al. [32] directly reconstructs the global illumination image, while Xin et al. [47] predicts the indirect component, similar to our task setup. For Nalbach et al.'s implementation, we use the "mono" version they described. We train all models on our dataset since the dataset they used is not publicly available. We also compare our method with the commonly used models in image-to-image translation or image style transfer tasks, including Pix2pix [18] and ResNet [15] with the same training setup and loss function as our model. All evaluation results are obtained on our test set, including 1000 rendered frames from our synthetic dataset and about 200 frames from public scenes we collected, e.g., **PinkRoom**, **LivingRoom**, **Gallery** and **Conference**. The averaged results of the evaluation metrics are shown in Table 1.

As can be seen, our model consistently outperforms all previous works and different network models on the three metrics. While the SSIM metric has a somewhat smaller difference among different methods, there is a huge gap between our method and other methods on the perceptual metric LPIPS, implying more natural illumination produced by our method. Visualizations of the whole predicted illumination are shown in Fig. 6. We further look into the predicted indirect component (demodulated from texture) in Fig. 7, which is more intuitive for comparing the performance of different methods. As observed, Xin et al.'s method used a lightweight model and tended to produce over-smoothed illumination on high-frequency regions, while the deeper models (Pix2pix and ResNet) using more parameters sometimes produced noisy and distorted results. Our method strikes a balance between model complexity and image quality, producing more plausible results at a reasonable time budget (12ms at 768×512), compared to the methods of Nalbach et al. [32] (6 ms) and Xin et al. [47] (13 ms).

Table 1. Validation on our test set demonstrates that our method achieves superior performance compared to existing approaches. "Ambient" refers to applying a constant, uniform incident radiance to approximate indirect light.

	Params.	**SSIM ↑**	**PSNR ↑**	**LPIPS ↓**
Direct Illumination	-	0.8676	22.17	0.0804
Ambient	-	0.9455	26.15	0.0832
Pix2pix [18]	41.83M	0.9611	28.88	0.0352
Nalbach et al. [32]	7.75M	0.9564	27.95	0.0391
Xin et al. [47]	3.95M	0.9658	30.28	0.0312
Ours	14.42M	**0.9743**	**31.88**	**0.0203**

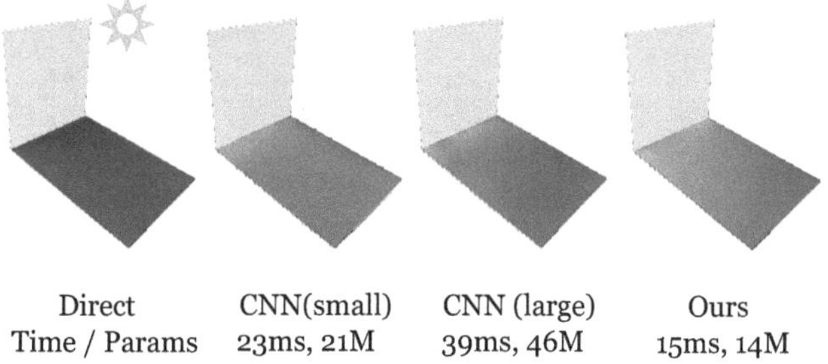

Fig. 9. Our GFA module effectively captures distant indirect light compared to stacks of convolution operations. The object covers an area of about 512×512 pixels, larger than the receptive field of the *CNN(small)* model.

Another observation is that our model can accurately handle the color of indirectly reflected light, while all other methods cannot in most cases. In our experiments, smaller networks (e.g., Xin et al.'s method) tend to produce over-smoothed results. Whereas, the deeper generative models (e.g., Pix2pix and ResNet), however, are easy to overfit and produce the averaged color (i.e., the most frequently occurred one) within training data, resulting in erroneously predicted colors. This problem remains if other color models are used, e.g., CIE XYZ or HSV. We further verify this by selecting frames that feature interreflections between differently textured surfaces (see Fig. 11). We attribute this success to the design of the monochromatic generator, which will be further discussed in the next section.

5.3 Validation

To verify the effectiveness of the design choices in our model, we conduct ablation studies by modifying different components of our model and comparing their performance with the full model.

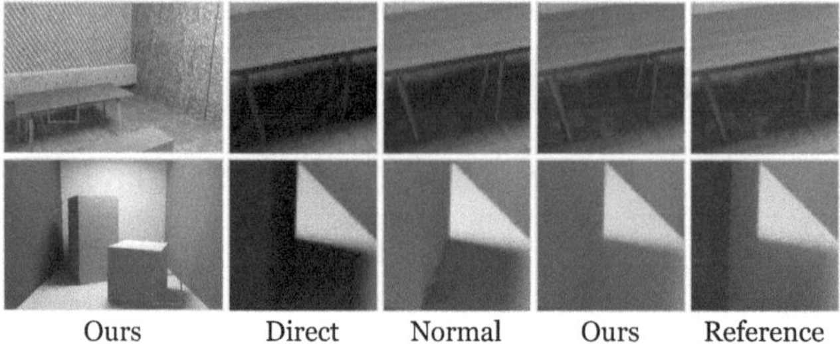

Fig. 10. Validation of our monochromatic design. Our approach handles the colored indirect illumination better, especially in the shadowed regions. "Normal" refers to the generally used network with RGB inputs.

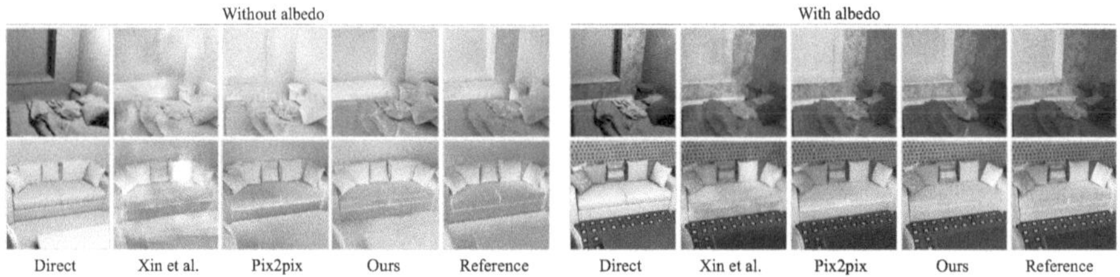

Fig. 11. Diffuse interreflections. Both the untextured (left) and textured (right) indirect components are shown. Our model can accurately capture the colored indirect light reflected from nearby surfaces, while the other methods cannot.

Effectiveness of Global Geometry-Aware Feature Aggregation. As discussed in Sect. 3, we exploit the modified multi-head attention mechanism for guiding global feature aggregation based on geometry features. This allows modeling long-range dependencies for any two locations in the image space, which is inherently impractical for fully convolutional networks (FCN) that prior works used. We validate this with a simple scene containing one major indirect light source (see Fig. 8), whose horizontal span exceeds the receptive field of the compared models. We show that previous works have difficulty capturing distant indirect light sources due to the locality of convolution operations, whereas our method efficiently models long-range dependencies with a feature aggregation module. Please refer to our supplemental video for more comparisons under dynamic lighting.

We also validate the efficiency of our method by simply stacking more convolutional layers using a similar setup (see Fig. 9). We compare our method to the variants that use convolutional layers to replace the feature aggregation module within the network bottleneck (i.e., two models with 7/9 layers in both their encoders and decoders). All variants use the monochromatic design and the same training strategy for a fair comparison. We show that the 7-layer model is unable to capture distant indirect lighting. While it is possible to enlarge the receptive field by using a deeper stack of convolutional operations (e.g., the 9-layer model), it brings extra computational overhead and optimization difficulty while still performing worse than our proposed feature aggregation method. We also note that the prior works generally perform worse than the 7-layer model in capturing long-range dependencies since they all have smaller receptive fields.

We then investigate the effectiveness of the multi-head extension by changing the number of attention heads (see the middle section of Table 2). We show that the model performs better by increasing the number of heads, while introducing little computational overhead or extra parameters (0.024 million parameters per head). We thus believe it important to attend to different subspaces of the features in bottleneck layers, where the features have a down-sampled spatial resolution but with high dimensionality.

Effectiveness of Monochromatic Design. We regard the monochromatic design as the main reason that helps the model capture the correct color from indirectly reflected light (see Fig. 11). To further validate this, we implement an alternate version of our model, taking in the RGB inputs and directly reconstructing the RGB output, namely the **Normal** network. Both versions of the network use the same architecture except for the image reconstruction process. As shown in Fig. 10, our model is significantly more capable of capturing the colored indirect lighting. This is most visible in the regions consisting of indirect illumination only (e.g., the shadowed areas in CornellBox). Note that while Nalbach et al. [32] also suggested the independent inference for each channel, they simply take it in a completely independent manner, resulting in visual artifacts like color-shifting (see Fig. 8 in the main text and also Fig. 5 in Nalbach et al. [32]) due to their network's poor ability to preserve linearity (i.e., $\mathbf{Net}(\alpha x) \neq \alpha\mathbf{Net}(x)$). In contrast, our network design takes several strategies to avoid this downside, including reusing shared geometry features, applying an inter-channel perceptual loss, and an effective data augmentation strategy for HDR training (see Sect. 3).

Moreover, to justify the potential performance loss of the monochromatic design (introduced by the parallel inference of three channels, see Sect. 3), we implement a mini version of the monochromatic network **Ours (mini)**, using the same network architecture as **Ours**'s but reducing the number of channels in intermediate layers to roughly half the model size. As shown in the first section of Table 2, the **Ours (mini)** still performs better than **Normal** with similar computational cost and a much smaller amount of parameters. As discussed in Sect. 1, we believe the success of the monochromatic network may result from three major reasons: 1) eliminating the redundant connections (correlations) between different color channels; 2) reducing the high-dimensional space of RGB input/output by introducing the prior that the rendering process of each color channel (or wavelength) is independent; thus 3) making the network more robust to the inequality and bias in the color distribution of training data. To further verify the superiority of our monochromatic model, we introduce scenes illuminated with colored lights that are not present in our training data (see Fig. 1 and Fig. 13). Our monochromatic model can still produce plausible outputs without further training or fine-tuning, whereas the normal models generally cannot achieve this with no (or only a few) training data in this domain.

Table 2. We use ablation experiments to show the effectiveness of the multi-head attention mechanism (via changing the number of attention heads) and the monochromatic design, respectively.

	Params.	Time(ms)	SSIM ↑	PSNR ↑	LPIPS ↓
Normal	15.17M	**9.15**	0.9625	31.49	0.0316
Ours(mini)	**8.76M**	9.76	0.9663	31.62	0.0271
Ours-1Head	14.29M	11.55	0.9545	31.13	0.0247
Ours-4Heads	14.35M	11.73	0.9419	30.92	0.0237
Ours (No $\mathscr{L}_p$)	14.42M	12.17	0.9705	31.52	0.0232
Ours (No $\mathscr{L}_a$)	14.42M	12.17	0.9688	31.42	0.0240
Ours	14.42M	12.17	**0.9743**	**31.88**	**0.0203**

Effectiveness of Perceptual and Adversarial Loss. We validate the effectiveness of the perceptual and adversarial components in our loss function by removing each of them and comparing their performance with the full model. As shown in Fig. 12, the model produces color-shift artifacts without the perceptual term, whereas the outputs are blurry without the adversarial term. We thus assert that the adversarial loss helps reconstruct the high-frequency details, and the perceptual loss improves the visual consistency across channels. Moreover, we found that the perceptual metric (e.g., LPIPS) becomes much worse when removing either of the loss terms, since both the adversarial discriminator and the pre-trained VGG can capture the structurally correlated image patterns at a higher abstract level. In contrast, classic metrics like L1 and L2 simply assume no interconnections between pixels, which are usually vulnerable to noise and local artifacts. We thus use a mixture of pixel-wise loss and perceptual loss, along with the adversarial training strategy, to guide our model to produce more plausible indirect illumination.

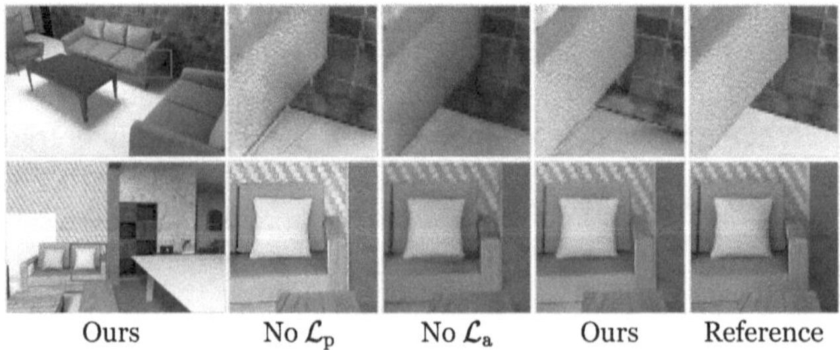

Fig. 12. Using different loss functions (indirect component). The predicted color tends to be erroneous without perceptual loss (No $\mathscr{L}_p$), and the results are blurry without adversarial training (No $\mathscr{L}_a$). Both variants tend to produce more visual artifacts.

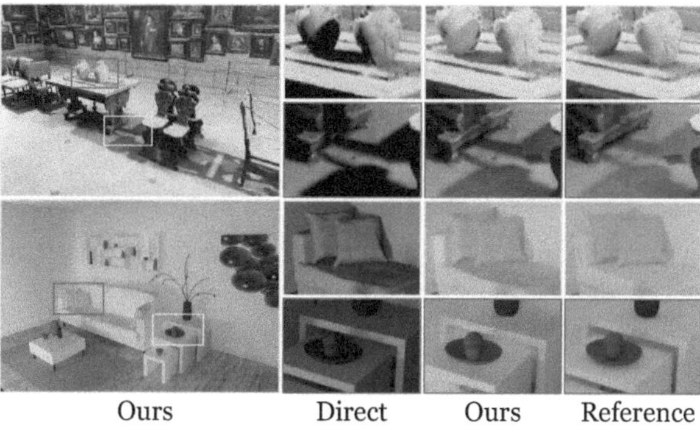

Fig. 13. Scenes lit by the colored light source that are not in the training data. Our approach is well generalized to colored lights due to the independent prior of each color channel.

5.4 Discussion

Network Generalization. As discussed in Sect. 5.2, our model can be generalized to the publicly collected scenes, as well as the colored light sources, which are not present in our training data. Based on this, we further show that our model can also generalize to dynamic lighting with more complex light sources, such as area lights and image-based environment lighting (acquired using Monte Carlo integration since they cannot be effectively approximated), with no obvious downgrade of performance. We regard this success of generalization as a result of multiple reasons, including 1) the use of the monochromatic design makes the network unaffected by color shifting and color variances; 2) the training setup of learning shading instead of scattered radiance makes the learning process easier; and 3) the diversity of our synthetic training data in terms of materials, geometry, and viewpoints. Please see our supplemental video for network performance under continuous frames and dynamic lighting.

GPU-Accelerated Ray Tracing Alternatives. While there are multiple existing methodologies for efficient specular or glossy reflections in different use cases [17,29], the diffuse indirect illumination needs more sophisticated processing due to its uniform scattering nature (resulting by its hemispherical diffuse BRDF lobe, instead of glossy or Dirac delta ones). Recently, the development of GPU ray tracing acceleration offered new capability for real-time indirect illumination, among which sparsely traced results with denoising is a promising technique.

Thereby, we compare our method with the GPU-accelerated ray tracing+denoising alternative, which often uses larger time consumption than our method. As shown in Fig. 14, we found that the denoised results suffer from loss of high-frequency details, implying that our method might still be beneficial for modern rendering applications. Nonetheless, we think that the ray tracing techniques could be used to compensate for the absence of the out-of-screen features in our method, which might be an interesting avenue for future work.

Rendering Pipeline Integration. Our model can be integrated into an interactive rendering pipeline, given that the direct illumination is relatively simple and can be approximated with real-time algorithms [10,16]. By doing this, all the inputs are generated on-the-fly within GPU memory, which can be immediately sent to the neural networks without the additional cost of memory transfer operations. However, the practicality of our method is limited in the following aspects, which could be improved straightforwardly:

- *Performance.* Since the image's resolution will heavily affect the time cost for inference, our model works at 768×512 and can generate outputs in 12 ms. For those VR applications with a higher resolution requirement (e.g., monocular at 1800×1920 on Meta Quest), We can accelerate the inference by bilateral up-sampling techniques like [24] at an even lower resolution, which could upscale the predicted indirect illumination at a low time budget since the indirect component has few high-frequency details.
- *Temporal coherence.* Our method may produce perceivable flickering under drastic viewpoint or geometry changes, which is common when applying learning-based methods to video. This can be alleviated with temporal anti-aliasing (TAA) techniques.

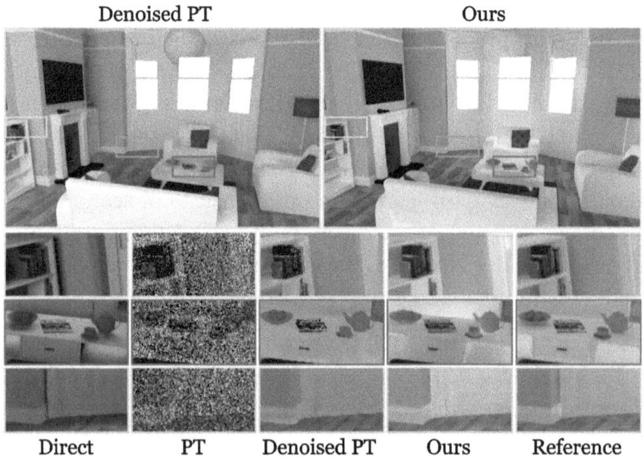

Fig. 14. Our method vs. denoised path-tracer (PT). Path tracing (1 spp) with next event estimation (NEE) is used, which is then denoised with the AI-Accelerated denoiser in OptiX™ [3]. Our method is closer to the reference in many scenarios in terms of the predicted indirect component while using less time consumption than the Denoised PT.

6 Conclusion, Limitation, and Future Works

We present a screen-space global illumination method based on a novel network design for indirect illumination prediction for any newly-constructed scenarios with complex lighting conditions. Our learning-based method can synthesize realistic images using a time budget close to the real-time rendering of local illumination. Therefore, it paves a feasible path to highly-efficient realistic rendering and can be affordable to many VR/AR applications for realism enhancement.

While our method could predict plausible indirect illumination, it has several limitations. First, our method has similar limitations to other screen-space methods due to the lack of layered depth features. Second, our method cannot handle those highly glossy or specular surfaces well, which other orthogonal solutions might compensate for in future work. This jointly implies limited practicality for current real-time rendering pipelines, which additional strategies may improve, as discussed in Sect. 5.4.

In the future, we will investigate more effective techniques for indirect illumination prediction while maintaining a relatively lightweight and efficient network architecture for VR applications, especially binocular rendering. Meanwhile, better exploiting 3D spatial features or implicit scene representation (e.g., via multi-view images or temporal coherence) may also be helpful for illumination prediction. Our proposed approaches are also potentially beneficial for other tasks. Specifically, the geometry-aware aggregation module might be preferred when geometry-supervised long-range modeling is needed. Moreover, while the monochromatic design is hardly seen in computer vision tasks, it would be interesting to see if it could be applied to various neural rendering tasks, e.g., learning-based Monte Carlo denoising [3] or neural radiance fields [30].

Acknowledgments. This work was supported by Southern Marine Science and Engineering Guangdong Laboratory (Zhuhai) (No. SML2021SP101) and Shenzhen Science and Technology Program (KJZD20230923114114028).

References

1. Bavoil, L., Sainz, M., Dimitrov, R.: Image-space horizon-based ambient occlusion. In: ACM SIGGRAPH 2008 Talks, pp. 1 (2008)
2. Bi, S., Sunkavalli, K., Perazzi, F., Shechtman, E., Kim, V.G., Ramamoorthi, R.: Deep cg2real: synthetic-to-real translation via image disentanglement. In: Proceedings of the IEEE/CVF International Conference on Computer Vision, pp. 2730–2739 (2019)
3. Chaitanya, C.R.A., et al.: Interactive reconstruction of Monte Carlo image sequences using a recurrent denoising autoencoder. ACM Trans. Graph. (TOG) **36**(4), 1–12 (2017)
4. Community, B.O.: Blender - a 3D modelling and rendering package. Blender Foundation, Stichting Blender Foundation, Amsterdam (2018). http://www.blender.org
5. Crassin, C., Neyret, F., Sainz, M., Green, S., Eisemann, E.: Interactive indirect illumination using voxel cone tracing. In: Computer Graphics Forum, vol. 30, pp. 1921–1930 (2011)
6. Dai, P., Li, Z., Zhang, Y., Liu, S., Zeng, B.: PBR-net: imitating physically based rendering using deep neural network. IEEE Trans. Image Process. **29**, 5980–5992 (2020)
7. Debevec, P.: Rendering synthetic objects into real scenes: bridging traditional and image-based graphics with global illumination and high dynamic range photography. In: ACM SIGGRAPH 2008 Classes, SIGGRAPH 2008. Association for Computing Machinery, New York, NY, USA (2008). https://doi.org/10.1145/1401132.1401175
8. Demes, L.: Cc0 textures (2021). `CC0textures.com`
9. Denninger, M., et al.: Blenderproc. arXiv preprint arXiv:1911.01911 (2019)

10. Fernando, R.: Percentage-closer soft shadows. In: ACM SIGGRAPH 2005 Sketches, SIGGRAPH 2005, p. 35–es. Association for Computing Machinery, New York (2005). https://doi.org/10.1145/1187112.1187153
11. Fu, H., et al.: 3D-front: 3D furnished rooms with layouts and semantics. arXiv preprint arXiv:2011.09127 (2020)
12. Glorot, X., Bengio, Y.: Understanding the difficulty of training deep feedforward neural networks. In: Proceedings of the Thirteenth International Conference on Artificial Intelligence and Statistics, pp. 249–256. JMLR Workshop and Conference Proceedings (2010)
13. Goodfellow, I.J., et al.: Generative adversarial networks. arXiv preprint arXiv:1406.2661 (2014)
14. Hadadan, S., Chen, S., Zwicker, M.: Neural radiosity. ACM Trans. Graph. (TOG) **40**(6), 1–11 (2021)
15. He, K., Zhang, X., Ren, S., Sun, J.: Deep residual learning for image recognition. In: Proceedings of the IEEE Conference on Computer Vision and Pattern Recognition, pp. 770–778 (2016)
16. Heitz, E., Dupuy, J., Hill, S., Neubelt, D.: Real-time polygonal-light shading with linearly transformed cosines. ACM Trans. Graph. (TOG) **35**(4), 1–8 (2016)
17. Hirvonen, A., Seppälä, A., Aizenshtein, M., Smal, N.: Accurate real-time specular reflections with radiance caching. In: Ray Tracing Gems, pp. 571–607. Apress, Berkeley, CA (2019). https://doi.org/10.1007/978-1-4842-4427-2_32
18. Isola, P., Zhu, J.Y., Zhou, T., Efros, A.A.: Image-to-image translation with conditional adversarial networks. In: Proceedings of the IEEE Conference on Computer Vision and Pattern Recognition, pp. 1125–1134 (2017)
19. Johnson, J., Alahi, A., Fei-Fei, L.: Perceptual losses for real-time style transfer and super-resolution. In: Leibe, B., Matas, J., Sebe, N., Welling, M. (eds.) ECCV 2016. LNCS, vol. 9906, pp. 694–711. Springer, Cham (2016). https://doi.org/10.1007/978-3-319-46475-6_43
20. Kajiya, J.T.: The rendering equation. SIGGRAPH Comput. Graph. (1986)
21. Kaplanyan, A.: Light propagation volumes in cryengine 3. ACM SIGGRAPH Courses **7**, 2 (2009)
22. Keller, A.: Instant radiosity. In: Proceedings of the 24th Annual Conference on Computer Graphics and Interactive Techniques, pp. 49–56 (1997)
23. Kingma, D.P., Ba, J.: Adam: a method for stochastic optimization. arXiv preprint arXiv:1412.6980 (2014)
24. Kopf, J., Cohen, M.F., Lischinski, D., Uyttendaele, M.: Joint bilateral upsampling. ACM Trans. Graph. (ToG) **26**(3), 96–es (2007)
25. Krizhevsky, A., Sutskever, I., Hinton, G.E.: Imagenet classification with deep convolutional neural networks. In: Advances in Neural Information Processing Systems, vol. 25, pp. 1097–1105 (2012)
26. Kuznetsov, A., Kalantari, N.K., Ramamoorthi, R.: Deep adaptive sampling for low sample count rendering. In: Computer Graphics Forum, vol. 37, pp. 35–44. Wiley Online Library (2018)
27. Ledig, C., et al.: Photo-realistic single image super-resolution using a generative adversarial network. In: Proceedings of the IEEE Conference on Computer Vision and Pattern Recognition, pp. 4681–4690 (2017)
28. Matsuda, N., Zhao, Y., Chapiro, A., Smith, C., Lanman, D.: HDR VR. In: ACM SIGGRAPH 2022 Emerging Technologies, SIGGRAPH 2022. Association for Computing Machinery, New York, NY, USA (2022). https://doi.org/10.1145/3532721.3535566
29. McGuire, M., Mara, M.: Efficient GPU screen-space ray tracing. J. Comput. Graph. Tech. (JCGT) **3**(4), 73–85 (2014)
30. Mildenhall, B., Srinivasan, P.P., Tancik, M., Barron, J.T., Ramamoorthi, R., Ng, R.: Nerf: representing scenes as neural radiance fields for view synthesis. In: ECCV (2020)

31. Mortensen, J., et al.: Real-time global illumination for VR applications. IEEE Comput. Graph. Appl. **28**(6), 56–64 (2008)
32. Nalbach, O., Arabadzhiyska, E., Mehta, D., Seidel, H.P., Ritschel, T.: Deep shading: convolutional neural networks for screen space shading. In: Computer Graphics Forum, vol. 36, pp. 65–78 (2017)
33. Park, T., Liu, M.Y., Wang, T.C., Zhu, J.Y.: Semantic image synthesis with spatially-adaptive normalization. In: Proceedings of the IEEE/CVF Conference on Computer Vision and Pattern Recognition, pp. 2337–2346 (2019)
34. Ren, S., He, K., Girshick, R., Sun, J.: Faster R-CNN: towards real-time object detection with region proposal networks. arXiv preprint arXiv:1506.01497 (2015)
35. Ritschel, T., Grosch, T., Seidel, H.P.: Approximating dynamic global illumination in image space. In: Proceedings of the 2009 Symposium on Interactive 3D Graphics and Games, pp. 75–82 (2009)
36. Ronneberger, O., Fischer, P., Brox, T.: U-net: convolutional networks for biomedical image segmentation. In: International Conference on Medical Image Computing and Computer-Assisted Intervention (2015)
37. Simonyan, K., Zisserman, A.: Very deep convolutional networks for large-scale image recognition. arXiv preprint arXiv:1409.1556 (2014)
38. Sloan, P.P., Kautz, J., Snyder, J.: Precomputed radiance transfer for real-time rendering in dynamic, low-frequency lighting environments. In: Proceedings of the 29th Annual Conference on Computer Graphics and Interactive Techniques, pp. 527–536 (2002)
39. Song, S., Yu, F., Zeng, A., Chang, A.X., Savva, M., Funkhouser, T.: Semantic scene completion from a single depth image. In: Proceedings of the IEEE Conference on Computer Vision and Pattern Recognition, pp. 1746–1754 (2017)
40. Srivastava, N., Hinton, G., Krizhevsky, A., Sutskever, I., Salakhutdinov, R.: Dropout: a simple way to prevent neural networks from overfitting. J. Mach. Learn. Res. **15**(1), 1929–1958 (2014)
41. Su, R., Dong, H., Jin, H., Chen, Y., Wang, G., Li, S.: Vertex features for neural global illumination. In: ACM SIGGRAPH Asia 2025 Conference Papers, SA 2025, Hong Kong, China (2025). https://doi.org/10.1145/3757377.3763826
42. Su, R., et al.: Dynamic neural radiosity with multi-grid decomposition. In: ACM SIGGRAPH Asia 2024 Conference Papers, SA 2024, Tokyo, Japan (2024). https://doi.org/10.1145/3680528.3687685
43. Tewari, A., et al.: State of the art on neural rendering (2020)
44. Vaswani, A., et al.: Attention is all you need. In: Advances in Neural Information Processing Systems, vol. 30 (2017)
45. Vicini, D., Koltun, V., Jakob, W.: A learned shape-adaptive subsurface scattering model. ACM Trans. Graph. (TOG) **38**(4), 1–15 (2019)
46. Wang, W., Neumann, U.: Depth-aware CNN for RGB-D segmentation. In: Proceedings of the European Conference on Computer Vision (ECCV), pp. 135–150 (2018)
47. Xin, H., Zheng, S., Xu, K., Yan, L.Q.: Lightweight bilateral convolutional neural networks for interactive single-bounce diffuse indirect illumination. IEEE Trans. Visualization Comput. Graph. (2021)
48. Yu, I., Mortensen, J., Khanna, P., Spanlang, B., Slater, M.: Visual realism enhances realistic response in an immersive virtual environment-part 2. IEEE Comput. Graph. Appl. **32**(6), 36–45 (2012)
49. Zhang, H., Goodfellow, I., Metaxas, D., Odena, A.: Self-attention generative adversarial networks. In: International Conference on Machine Learning, pp. 7354–7363. PMLR (2019)
50. Zhang, R., Isola, P., Efros, A.A., Shechtman, E., Wang, O.: The unreasonable effectiveness of deep features as a perceptual metric. In: Proceedings of the IEEE Conference on Computer Vision and Pattern Recognition, pp. 586–595 (2018)

51. Zhang, Y., et al.: Physically-based rendering for indoor scene understanding using convolutional neural networks. In: Proceedings of the IEEE Conference on Computer Vision and Pattern Recognition, pp. 5287–5295 (2017)
52. Zheng, C., et al.: Neural global illumination via superposed deformable feature fields. In: SIGGRAPH Asia 2024 Conference Papers, pp. 1–11 (2024)

Neural Global Illumination via HoloMap and AdaptMap

Shi Huang, Guangzheng Fei(✉), and Sihao Li

School of Animation and Digital Arts, Communication University of China, Beijing, China
{huangshi,gzfei}@cuc.edu.cn

Abstract. We present a neural rendering framework for real-time global illumination, composed of a Neural Baker and a Neural Renderer. The Neural Baker transforms G-Atlas into a UV-space feature atlas, HoloMap, encoding static geometry and material information. The Neural Renderer takes HoloMap along with view and lighting parameters to learn a dynamic neural field, AdaptMap. Training occurs in two phases: first, both modules are jointly optimized to construct a consistent HoloMap; then, the Neural Baker is detached, HoloMap is fixed, and AdaptMap is initialized from it and refined to capture view- and lighting-dependent effects. At inference, the Neural Renderer uses both HoloMap and AdaptMap to produce global illumination. Experiments show that our staged training design reduces model complexity and memory footprint, while achieving high-quality, real-time rendering with improved efficiency. Furthermore, our optimized training strategy, combining multi-threaded asynchronous rendering with an adaptive sampling policy, reduces the total training time by approximately 50% compared to baseline methods.

Keywords: real time global illumination · staged training · neural rendering · adaptive sampling · dual-map representation

1 Introduction

Real-time global illumination (GI) remains a fundamental yet challenging problem in computer graphics. Traditional rasterization-based approximations often struggle to capture complex light transport phenomena such as multi-bounce interreflections and glossy indirect shadows, especially in scenes with detailed geometry and diverse materials. Recent neural rendering techniques have shown promising results by learning to approximate global illumination from data. However, most existing approaches adopt monolithic, end-to-end architectures that entangle static scene content with dynamic rendering parameters (e.g., view and lighting), resulting in large model sizes, increased training cost, and limited flexibility during inference. This motivates a more modular and interpretable solution that can separately model static appearance and dynamic variation in a unified rendering framework.

A key challenge lies in designing a representation that cleanly separates static scene priors from dynamic rendering, while still supporting high-quality global illumination.

A. Hinkenjan et al. (Eds.): ICXR 2025, LNCS 16428, pp. 175–190, 2026.
https://doi.org/10.1007/978-981-95-7195-6_10

Such a decoupled representation should allow for efficient reuse of static information across frames, enable fast adaptation to dynamic inputs, and maintain a compact memory footprint. Addressing this challenge opens the door to more scalable and generalizable neural rendering frameworks.

To address these challenges, we propose a staged neural rendering framework that decouples static and dynamic components of the rendering process. In the first stage, a Neural Baker and Neural Renderer are jointly trained to map G-buffer features and dynamic scene parameters (e.g., view, lighting, object transformations) to ground truth images, generating a HoloMap encoding static scene priors. In the second stage, AdaptMap, a dynamic neural field initialized from HoloMap, is introduced to capture dynamic effects, refining only the Neural Renderer and AdaptMap while freezing HoloMap. This dual-map representation and staged training scheme significantly reduce model complexity and training costs. At inference, the framework achieves high-fidelity real-time global illumination using solely the Neural Renderer with precomputed maps, matching monolithic end-to-end networks in quality with substantially lower inference costs and improved flexibility.

We demonstrate that our decoupled representation and staged training scheme not only achieve high-fidelity real-time rendering but also significantly improve training efficiency. A comprehensive evaluation shows our framework converges faster and reduces total training time by half, while matching or exceeding the quality of larger, monolithic networks.

2 Related Work

2.1 Inverse Rendering and Neural Textures

Inverse rendering, a core application of neural rendering, aims to recover accurate scene representations (geometry, materials, lighting) from images, enabling novel view synthesis. Key advancements include geometry-aware reconstruction [1, 2], neural interpolation for view synthesis [3], and geometry-guided networks supporting free-viewpoint lighting editing [4]. The field evolved toward neural field representations: Srinivasan et al. predicted multiplane images [5] and introduced reflectance/visibility fields [6], culminating in Mildenhall et al.'s NeRF [7] for scene illumination encoding.

Neural textures emerged as a pivotal technique within this domain. Thies et al. [8] encoded scene appearance into feature maps, effectively mitigating artifacts from imperfect geometry. This approach was later extended to material modeling [9]. While successful for static scenes, these methods inherently couple static appearance with the underlying representation. Unlike conventional neural textures, our Dual-Map framework explicitly decouples static and dynamic components, enabling efficient reuse of static information through HoloMap across frames and rapid adaptation to dynamic parameters via AdaptMap.

2.2 Radiance Regression Frameworks

Radiance Regression Functions (RRFs) [10] established the groundwork for neural real-time global illumination. Ren et al. [10] first utilized neural networks to map local attributes to indirect illumination values, enabling global illumination computation in dynamic scenes. Subsequent research expanded this framework across multiple dimensions: Qin et al. [11] added transparent object support, Thomas et al. [12] integrated generative adversarial networks to enhance detail reconstruction, Gao et al. [13] achieved real-time computation for dynamic area lights. Although these works improved rendering adaptability, their end-to-end architectures maintained tight coupling between static scene attributes and dynamic parameters, resulting in substantial model complexity. Our work overcomes this limitation through a two-stage training mechanism that fundamentally decouples components.

2.3 Pixel Generator Architectures

Pixel generator architectures demonstrate unique advantages in view consistency. The per-pixel Multi-Layer Perceptrons (MLP) framework proposed by Sitzmann et al. [14], by avoiding the local dependencies inherent in convolutional operations, exhibits consistent mapping from 3D coordinates to color values during camera viewpoint changes and supports arbitrary-resolution output without retraining. This characteristic makes it particularly suitable for dynamic scenes with free-viewpoint rendering requirements. Compared to convolutional architectures like U-Net [15] which preserve high-frequency details through skip connections but suffer from neighborhood sensitivity during viewpoint transformations, the pixel generator maintains strict spatial consistency. Granskog et al. [16] subsequently provided rigorous experimental comparisons between these architectures, confirming that U-Net's convolutional nature fundamentally limits its ability to handle continuous viewpoint variations. The pixel generator's invariance to camera movement stems from its coordinate-based mapping paradigm, ensuring identical 3D positions always yield consistent outputs regardless of viewing angles. This architectural property aligns precisely with our requirement for stable global illumination under dynamically changing viewpoints, motivating our adoption of the pixel generator as the core architecture for the neural renderer.

2.4 Adaptive Sampling Strategies

Adaptive sampling strategies are crucial for training efficiency in high-dimensional parameter spaces. Traditional uniform sampling proves prohibitively expensive when capturing complex lighting effects like caustics and specular reflections. Diolatzis et al. [17] introduced active exploration using Markov Chain Monte Carlo (MCMC) to dynamically generate samples, calculating weights based on training loss to guide samplers toward high-value regions. We enhance this methodology through three optimizations: (a) Parallelized regional sampling, (b) Error-driven importance weighting, and (c) Incremental sampling density allocation for dynamic elements. This optimization significantly reduces training sample requirements and lowers computational burdens.

2.5 Dynamic Scene Neural Rendering

Recent advances in neural rendering for dynamic scenes demonstrate innovative approaches to feature compression. Müller et al. [18] pioneered multiresolution hash encoding, a breakthrough technique that accelerates neural graphics primitives training by orders of magnitude through efficient GPU-friendly hash tables. This framework supports diverse applications including neural radiance fields and signed distance functions, achieving real-time rendering at 1080p resolution with just milliseconds of latency. Building upon this foundation, Coomans et al. [19] developed a specialized architecture for dynamic light field rendering, integrating spatial, temporal, and surface-space encodings to enable 40 volume updates per second at 1283 resolution. While achieving 20 times faster inference than prior methods, their approach focuses specifically on temporal variations within rigid scenes and does not address geometric topology changes. Complementary innovations include Raghavan et al.'s neural-wavelet PRT for high-frequency indirect illumination [20] and Zhang et al.'s neural baking for refractive materials [21, 22]. In contrast to Su et al. [23]'s dynamic neural radiosity, which employs a unified multi-grid decomposition for high-dimensional scenes but lacks explicit static-dynamic decoupling, our HoloMap/AdaptMap framework introduces a staged training pipeline. This design explicitly bakes static geometry into a reusable HoloMap and adapts dynamic effects via AdaptMap, largely reducing training time and achieving real-time inference with minimal overhead for superior fidelity in static-scene-dominated dynamic lighting scenarios. Furthermore, Zheng et al. [24] introduced NeLT, an object-oriented neural light transfer technique that decomposes scenes into object-level neural representations. Their approach enables complex light interactions between objects but requires pre-segmented objects and does not address the unified rendering of integrated scene geometry under arbitrary viewpoint and lighting changes, which is a key strength of our HoloMap/AdaptMap framework.

Unlike these specialized solutions, our AdaptMap supports arbitrary combinations of dynamic parameters including geometric transformations, material variations, and lighting modifications, providing comprehensive flexibility for complex interactive scenes.

3 Staged Neural Rendering with Dual-Map Representation

Our framework proposes a dual-map neural rendering approach for dynamic global illumination, extending the pixel generator architecture from Active Exploration [17]. The system builds upon the deferred rendering paradigm, which decouples geometry processing from lighting calculations through several core concepts essential to understanding our method: **G-buffer (Geometry Buffer)** serves as a screen-space repository storing per-pixel geometric and material attributes, including world position, surface normal, albedo color, texture coordinates, and additional material properties rendered in an initial pass. **G-Atlas** represents our extension of the standard G-buffer into a globally parameterized texture atlas. This involves unwrapping the entire scene's geometry into UV space, creating a unified atlas that aggregates G-buffer data for every surface point, serving as the primary input for baking our neural representations. **UV-Space Feature Atlas** moves beyond conventional attribute storage by utilizing UV parameterization to store learned neural features.

Building upon these foundations, our system fundamentally decouples static scene representation from dynamic adaptation through two specialized neural atlases. The hierarchical design enables real-time photorealism under varying conditions through a three-phase process of baking, adaptation, and inference.

3.1 Framework Overview and Rendering Pipeline

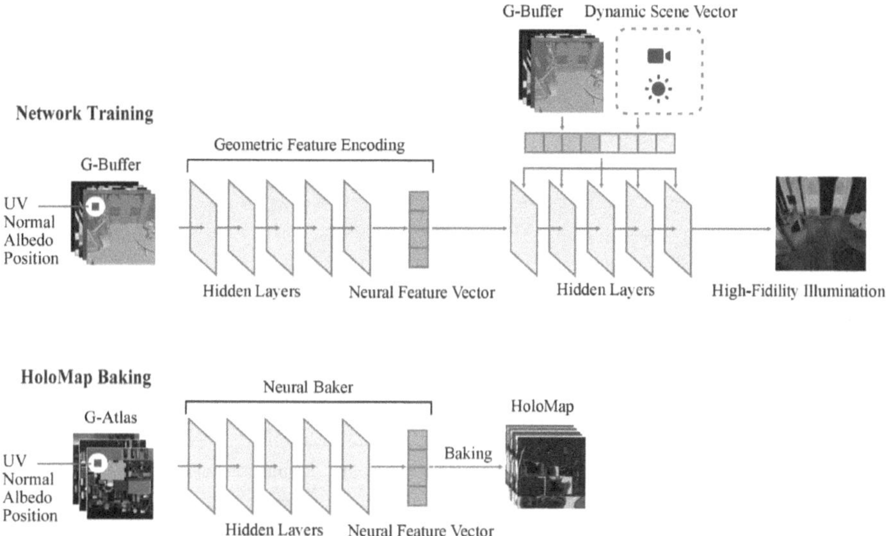

Fig. 1. Network Training & HoloMap Baking: Static feature generation from G-buffer inputs (position, normal, albedo, and UV) via neural processing and atlas storage for rendering reuse.

Building upon Active Exploration's pixel generator [17], our baseline architecture processes screen-space pixels through Multi-Layer Perceptrons (MLPs). As illustrated in Fig. 1, the system first executes a training process where geometric feature encoding network transforms G-buffer vector $\mathbf{g}_p$ (comprising position, normal, albedo, and UV) into latent features. The encoding network employs L hidden layers with LeakyReLU activations φ [25]. The output of the l-th layer is given by:

$$h^{(l)} = \varphi(\mathbf{W}_l h^{(l-1)} + \mathbf{b}_l) \quad (1)$$

where $h^{(0)}$ is defined as the input G-buffer vector $\mathbf{g}_p$.

The neural renderer begins with feature fusion integrating three inputs, namely the geometric feature encoding output $h^{(L)}$, original G-buffer vector $\mathbf{g}_p$, and dynamic parameters $\mathbf{v}$ encoding all variable scene state parameters, such as view direction, lighting conditions (e.g., intensity, position), object transformations (e.g., position, rotation), and other dynamic scene properties (e.g., window states).

For fusion layer k:

$$\mathbf{h}^{(k)} = \varphi(\mathbf{W}_k[\mathbf{h}^{(k-1)} \oplus \mathbf{g}_p \oplus \mathbf{v}] + \mathbf{b}_k) \quad (2)$$

where $\mathbf{h}^{(0)}$ is initialized as $h^{(L)}$, and where $\oplus$ denotes channel-wise concatenation.

The fused features are transformed to radiance in RGB space at output layer n:

$$RGB(p) = \varphi(\mathbf{W}_n[\mathbf{h}^{(n)} \oplus \mathbf{g}_p \oplus \mathbf{v}] + \mathbf{b}_n) \tag{3}$$

Following the completion of network training, the baking process traverses the entire scene, i.e. G-Atlas, to generate a HoloMap $\mathcal{H}$ that stores these precomputed latent features. The HoloMap is then reused in all subsequent stages, including the adaptation stage for AdaptMap training and the inference stage for real time rendering.

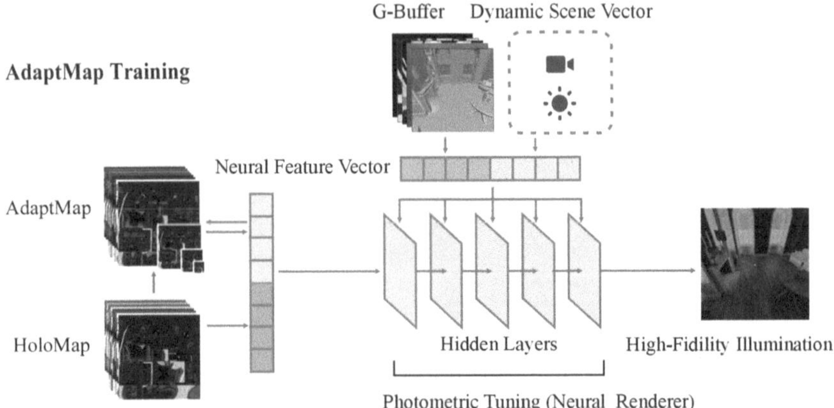

Fig. 2. AdaptMap Training Pipeline: Joint backpropagation updates to Neural Renderer weights and AdaptMap features using fused inputs (static HoloMap $\mathcal{H}$, G-buffer vector $\mathbf{g}_p$, dynamic vectors $\mathbf{v}$). HoloMap features remain fixed during training.

Leveraging the precomputed HoloMap $\mathcal{H}$, the system advances to the dynamic optimization phase shown in Fig. 2. This prebaked feature atlas now completely substitutes the encoding network: during Neural Renderer training, static features are directly sampled from $\mathcal{H}$ using texture coordinates $\mathbf{uv}_p$. To model scene dynamics, we introduce a trainable neural feature atlas AdaptMap $\mathcal{A}$ initialized from $\mathcal{H}$ for delivering photometric compensation parameters. The Neural Renderer $\mathcal{R}$ processes the fused input with $\mathbf{f}_p^H = \mathcal{H}(\mathbf{uv}_p)$ and $\mathbf{f}_p^A = \mathcal{A}(\mathbf{uv}_p)$:

$$RGB(p) = \mathcal{R}(\mathbf{f}_p^H \oplus \mathbf{f}_p^A \oplus \mathbf{g}_p \oplus \mathbf{v}) \tag{4}$$

During backpropagation, the Neural Renderer's weights are optimized through its hidden layers while the feature vector $\mathbf{f}_p^A$ undergoes concurrent updates. These modified features are directly written to their corresponding atlas positions in $\mathcal{A}$ through a synchronized write-back mechanism. This co-optimization achieves three critical objectives: the Neural Renderer $\mathcal{R}$ attains photometric accuracy in illumination synthesis; the AdaptMap $\mathcal{A}$ effectively encodes dynamic scene variations; and spatial coherence is rigorously maintained across all updates via the shared atlas parameterization. Upon convergence of this joint optimization process, the final rendering equation integrates both frozen feature maps and operates as:

$$\mathrm{RGB}(p) = \mathcal{R}(\mathcal{H}(\mathbf{uv}_p) \oplus \mathcal{A}(\mathbf{uv}_p) \oplus \mathbf{g}_p \oplus \mathbf{v}) \tag{5}$$

Both $\mathcal{H}$ and $\mathcal{A}$ are stored in atlases with identical parameterization to the G-Atlas. The detailed generation processes of these two maps, along with their real-time rendering inference procedure, are elaborated in the subsequent sections.

3.2 Baking Stage: Geometric Feature Encoding

As mentioned in Sect. 3.1, in the first stage, we jointly train two neural networks, the Neural Baker and the Neural Renderer. The Neural Baker takes as input per-pixel G-buffer features extracted from a 3D scene and processes them to produce latent neural features. The transformation is formally defined by:

$$\mathbf{b}_p = F_B(\mathbf{g}_p; \theta_B) \tag{6}$$

where $\mathbf{b}_p$ denotes neural feature vector at point p, θ_B is the trainable parameters of the Neural Baker, and F_B is the feature encoding function.

These neural features are then passed through an intermediate hidden layer and combined with the original G-buffer features alongside dynamic parameters to form the input for the Neural Renderer. The Neural Renderer predicts a rendered image, supervised by ground truth images generated via path-traced global illumination. Through this process, the Neural Renderer learns a generalizable mapping from G-buffer features and dynamic parameters to high-fidelity appearance representations.

Following the joint training of the Neural Baker and Neural Renderer, we perform a comprehensive baking pass over the entire scene geometry to generate our compressed neural feature representation. This process executes the fully optimized Neural Baker network across the complete G-Atlas in a single forward pass. The resulting output constitutes the final HoloMap, formally defined as:

$$\mathcal{H} = F_B(\mathcal{G}; \theta_B) \tag{7}$$

where $\mathcal{H}$ denotes HoloMap, $\mathcal{G}$ represents the integrated G-Atlas containing all scene geometry, and θ_B denotes the frozen weights of the trained HoloMap Baker. This precomputed feature atlas encapsulates the scene's intrinsic appearance properties in a memory-efficient format, serving as the geometric foundation for subsequent adaptation stages. The baking process completes the static scene representation workflow, enabling real-time rendering through efficient feature retrieval rather than computational reprocessing during inference.

3.3 Adaptation Stage: Photometric Tuning

This stage aims to introduce adaptability to dynamic scenes for our neural rendering architecture, while also attempting to preserve the trained dynamic neural features in an atlas format. To achieve this, we abandon the geometric feature encoding network and instead feed precomputed HoloMap features directly into the Neural Renderer via a hidden layer. Concurrently, we introduce AdaptMap, a trainable feature atlas initialized from HoloMap data, whose evolving features provide dynamics-aware adaptation during optimization.

The Neural Renderer synthesizes pixel-accurate illumination through fusion of four complementary inputs: static features $\mathbf{f}_p^H$ from HoloMap; multi-resolution adaptive features $\mathbf{f}_p^A$ from AdaptMap (see Sect. 4.2 for hierarchical fusion details); geometric buffer vector $\mathbf{g}_p$; and dynamic parameters $\mathbf{v}$ (a normalized high-dimensional vector encoding the complete state of all dynamic elements, including view direction, lighting parameters, object positions/orientations, and scene configuration states like window openness). Formally, this process is defined by:

$$L(p, v) = F_R(f_p^H, f_p^A, g_p, v; \theta_R) \tag{8}$$

where θ_R constitutes the Neural Renderer's trainable weights. Through backpropagation supervised by path-traced ground truth, we jointly optimize AdaptMap features and θ_R to capture illumination variations while maintaining HoloMap features as frozen geometric anchors, yielding two deployable components: an adapted Neural Renderer for dynamic illumination synthesis, and an optimized AdaptMap encoding dynamics-specific photometric properties.

However, it is important to note that the current design of AdaptMap accommodates only continuous variations of predefined dynamic parameters (encoded in $\mathbf{v}$) and cannot handle arbitrary changes beyond the scope of these parameters, such as object deformation or scene reconfiguration. Extending AdaptMap to model such topological variations through neural skinning or implicit deformation fields remains a promising direction for future work.

3.4 Inference Stage: Real-Time Rendering

During inference, the system leverages only the optimized Neural Renderer for real-time synthesis. The pipeline executes four efficient operations per frame: sampling static features $\mathbf{f}_p^H$ from HoloMap; sampling multi-resolution dynamic features $\mathbf{f}_p^A$ from AdaptMap; concatenating features with current G-buffer vector $\mathbf{g}_p$ and dynamic parameters $\mathbf{v}$; and processing the composite tensor through the Neural Renderer's MLP architecture. Formally, the final pixel color is calculated through the rendering function:

$$RGB(p) = F_R(\mathbf{f}_p^H \oplus \mathbf{f}_p^A \oplus \mathbf{g}_p \oplus \mathbf{v}; \theta_R) \tag{9}$$

where θ_R contains trained weights produced by the former adaptation procedure. By eliminating neural feature precomputations and leveraging pre-optimized representations in HoloMap and AdaptMap, the pipeline achieves real-time performance while maintaining photorealistic quality across various dynamic conditions defined by the preset parameters in $\mathbf{v}$ (e.g., view, lighting, object transformations).

4 Implementation Detail

4.1 Adaptive Sampling of Training Space

Dynamic scenes involve numerous variables such as object positions, light sources, and camera angles, leading to an exponential increase in the number of training samples required for neural network training. Moreover, generating each global illumination training sample demands significant computational resources. Uniform sampling, though easy to implement, often produces redundant or uninformative data, resulting in longer training times without noticeable improvements in image quality. To overcome these limitations, we propose an active sampling method inspired by Active Exploration [17] strategies. Our approach leverages Markov Chain Monte Carlo (MCMC) techniques combined with an importance weighting strategy to prioritize the most informative samples. By focusing on regions with the highest prediction errors, our method effectively reduces the sample space while maintaining or even enhancing rendering performance.

MCMC Sampling: The MCMC method allows the system to explore the sample space by transitioning from one sample to another based on the likelihood of the sample improving the network's performance. At each step of the MCMC process, the importance of the new sample is evaluated based on how much it reduces the training loss. If the new sample improves the network's performance significantly, it is accepted; otherwise, it is discarded. The use of MCMC ensures that the network is sampling efficiently by avoiding the redundancy inherent in uniform sampling methods. It focuses computational resources on the most critical parts of the scene. To further improve sampling efficiency, we complement our sampling strategy with a parallelized implementation. Specifically, we leverage a multi-threaded setup that allows simultaneous sampling from multiple regions of the scene. Each thread operates independently, sampling specific regions identified as critical by the network. The results are then aggregated and used to update the network's parameters.

Importance Weighting: To guide the network toward more effective learning, we calculate a weight for each sample based on its initial prediction error. Samples from regions with higher errors are assigned greater importance in the sampling process, ensuring that the network focuses its learning capacity where improvement is most needed. To reinforce this strategy, we modify the loss function to incorporate a weighting factor that emphasizes these high-error samples, allowing the network to prioritize correcting its mistakes during training. Regions exhibiting complex lighting phenomena, such as caustics, specular reflections, and shadows, are flagged for higher sampling density. These areas often contain subtle yet crucial lighting details that uniform sampling methods may miss. By increasing the sampling resolution in such regions, the network gains a richer understanding of challenging lighting interactions. Furthermore, we account for the scene's dynamic elements, including moving light sources or rotating objects. These components introduce time-varying visual changes, which require the network to continuously adapt. By assigning additional sampling attention to these dynamic regions, our method ensures that the network remains responsive and accurate under real-time scene variations.

Multi-threaded Asynchronous Rendering: We implement a producer-consumer architecture where a dedicated pool of 12–16 worker threads executes Mitsuba 3 rendering jobs asynchronously. A main thread continuously consumes the generated samples to train the neural networks. This design ensures the GPU is fully utilized, hiding the latency of path tracing by leveraging computational gaps for training, thereby drastically reducing idle time.

4.2 Multi-resolution Representation of Feature Space

Fixed-resolution neural maps face inherent limitations when rendering complex scenes with varying depth. Distant regions underutilize texture memory due to insufficient screen coverage, while close surfaces exceed texture capacity, where each texel must represent multiple screen pixels, causing critical detail loss. Moreover, training stability suffers from a fundamental dichotomy: Oversized maps require impractical sample counts per texel, leading to under-trained parameters and high-frequency noise artifacts; conversely, undersized maps force parameter sharing across screen-space blocks. This quantization creates discontinuous transitions between adjacent blocks, manifesting as aliasing artifacts along geometric edges. These dual challenges of spatial inefficiency and training instability necessitate hierarchical representations that adapt to scene depth while maintaining optimal parameter conditioning.

Inspired by techniques analogous to Mipmapping in classical computer graphics, as well as the works of Thies et al. [8] and Müller et al. [18], we employ a multi-resolution hierarchy with K levels to address challenges related to scene depth and texture scale. Each level in this hierarchy contains a neural map whose resolution increases exponentially with the level index.

Multi-level Feature Fusion: To capture multi-scale dynamics representations, we implement a hierarchical feature sampling approach across K resolution levels (Fig. 3). Using normalized texture coordinates and nearest-neighbor interpolation, features are sampled simultaneously from all hierarchical levels. These multi-resolution features undergo channel-wise concatenation to form a unified feature vector, which is subsequently fused with static HoloMap features through additional channel-wise concatenation. This composite representation serves as input to the MLP-based Neural Renderer, enabling the network to autonomously learn optimal feature fusion strategies across resolution scales during rendering.

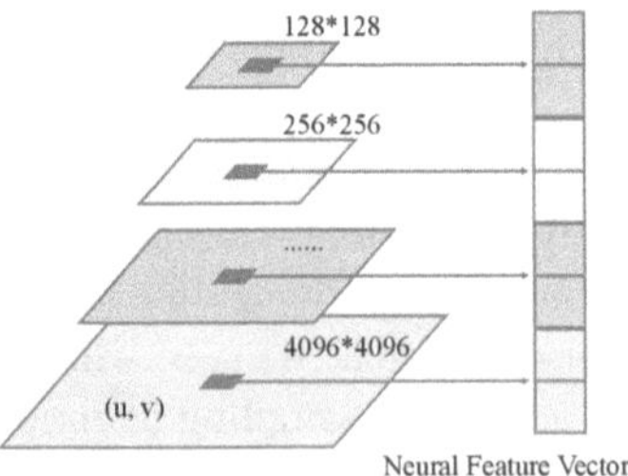

Fig. 3. Multi-level feature sampling hierarchy (K = 6 levels, D = 16 feature dimensions per level). Resolution progression: base level = 128 × 128 pixels, doubling at each subsequent level.

Weight Decay Regularization: To mitigate overfitting-induced high-frequency noise in high-resolution levels and underfitting-induced excessive blurring in low-resolution levels (Fig. 4), we employ level-dependent weight decay during AdaptMap optimization. This is critical because higher-resolution levels exhibit sparser texel coverage per pixel, amplifying sensitivity to sampling noise.

The weight decay factor λ_i for level i is defined by:

$$\lambda_i = \begin{cases} 0 & , i = 0 \\ 10^{-4} \times 2^{i-1} & , i > 0 \end{cases} \quad (10)$$

The exponential term 2^{i-1} scales regularization strength to match the quadratic growth of texel density in higher levels, enforcing smoother feature transitions where spatial samples are scarce.

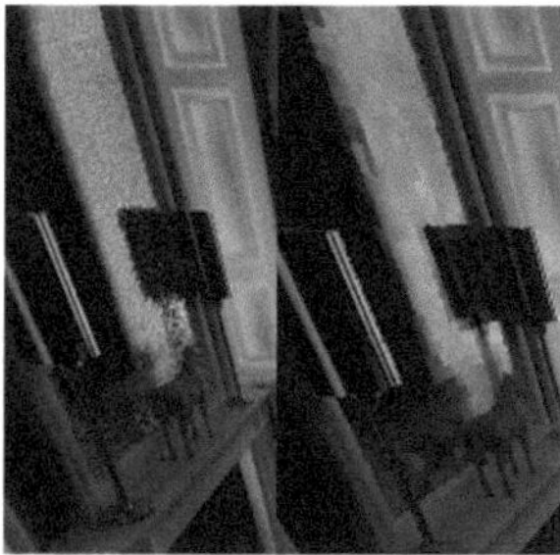

Fig. 4. Artifacts from non-adaptive regularization: (Left) High-frequency noise due to over-regularized high-res levels; (Right) Excessive blurring due to under-regularized low-res levels.

5 Experimental Results

We evaluated our framework on three dynamic scenes featuring diverse interactive elements. The Living Room scene incorporated two additional dynamic parameters beyond the base camera controls: a 1D chandelier light intensity parameter enabling variable illumination simulation, and a 1D surrounding blinds state parameter controlling openness to modulate indoor light distribution and spatial perception. The Veach Egg scene centered on dynamic light-material interactions through a transparent glass egg (designed for caustic learning evaluation), introducing movable components including a 1D glass egg position parameter and a 3D spotlight position parameter, collectively testing the network's adaptability to light-object interplay. The Veach Ajar scene focused on rotational geometry challenges with a partially open-door leaf governed by a 1D rotation parameter, primarily assessing the network's capacity to handle object rotation and spatial relationship changes.

All scenes featured a dynamic camera parameterized by 5D pose (position and orientation). After normalization, all dynamic parameters were aggregated into a unified high-dimensional state vector $\mathbf{v}$, comprehensively representing the full configuration of the variable scene.

All experiments were conducted on a system with an NVIDIA RTX 3090 GPU. Training data were generated using Mitsuba 3 path tracing (600–8000 SPP, 9–12 bounces) with OptiX AI denoising. We implemented our networks in PyTorch and trained them using the Adam optimizer with a learning rate of 1e-4 and LeakyReLU activations. Our optimized training pipeline (multi-threaded rendering, adaptive sampling) achieved roughly half the total training time required by the implementation without these optimizations.

Network Configurations. The study compares five network configurations, as shown in Table 1. The baseline Pixel128/256 architectures serve as pixel generators with 5 hidden layers and 128/256 features. Holo128 extends Pixel128 by incorporating a HoloMap precomputed using a 5 × 512 generator. Adapt128 similarly builds upon Pixel128 but integrates an AdaptMap with a 6-level hierarchical structure and 16 features per level. Finally, Dual128 combines both approaches by fusing the HoloMap and AdaptMap within the Pixel128 framework.

Table 1. Inference Time and Rendering Quality Comparison Across Network Configurations.

Network	Params	Inference (ms)	SSIM
Pixel128	5 layers × 128 features	20.56	0.9397
Pixel256	5 layers × 256 features	42.35 (+106%)	0.9606
Holo128	Pixel128 + HoloMap	21.59 (+5.0%)	0.9488
Adapt128	Pixel128 + AdaptMap	21.68 (+5.4%)	0.9480
Dual128	Pixel128 + HoloMap + AdaptMap	23.56 (+14.6%)	0.9585

Quantitative results demonstrate significant performance differences across the evaluated configurations. Regarding rendering quality, neural feature map variants substantially outperformed the equivalently sized Pixel128 baseline. The Dual128 configuration achieved particularly notable results, reaching 99.78% of Pixel256's SSIM improvement (scoring 0.9585 versus Pixel256's 0.9606). In terms of inference speed, all neural feature map variants introduced only minimal runtime overhead, adding <15% compared to Pixel128. Dual128 showed exceptional efficiency, operating 1.8× faster than Pixel256 despite delivering near-identical rendering quality.

As shown in Fig. 5, the baseline architecture Pixel128 exhibits early saturation of its learning capacity around 18k steps, negligible improvement thereafter. In contrast, Holo128, Adapt128, and Pixel256 continue to reduce loss well beyond this point. This accelerated and sustained convergence is a direct result of our efficient training strategy. The adaptive sampling policy ensures the network is continually fed the most informative samples, while the multi-threaded architecture maximizes throughput, allowing for this more effective optimization within a reduced timeframe.

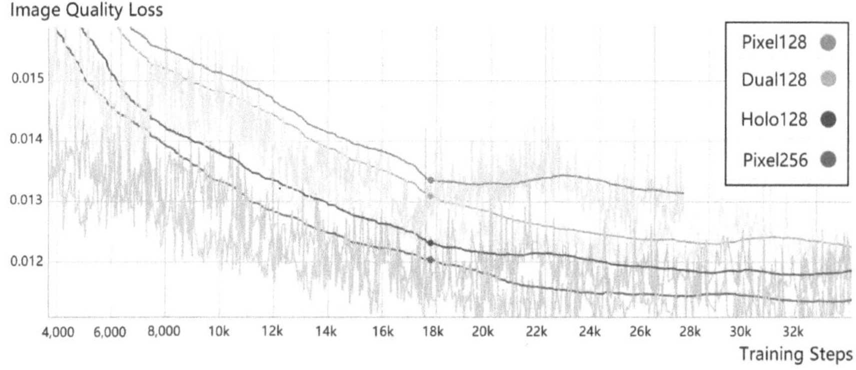

Fig. 5. Training Performance Comparison. Performance saturation observed in Pixel128 at 18k steps, while Adapt128, Holo128, and Pixel256 exhibit loss reduction beyond this point.

Qualitative analysis of critical regions in the Living Room scene (Fig. 6) reveals distinct performance variations. For glass refraction effects, both Holo128 and Adapt128 accurately reconstructed the distorted table edges visible through glass surfaces, while Dual128 achieved near-perfect alignment with the ground truth reference. In contrast, Pixel128 exhibited significant blurring in this region. Regarding specular reflection, Dual128 demonstrated superior fidelity in reconstructing the glossy horse figurine, effectively preserving fine geometric details in the head region while suppressing noise artifacts, a limitation observed in Adapt128's output. Furthermore, Dual128 avoided visual artifacts present in alternative methods, such as the erroneous translucency manifesting in Pixel256's rendering.

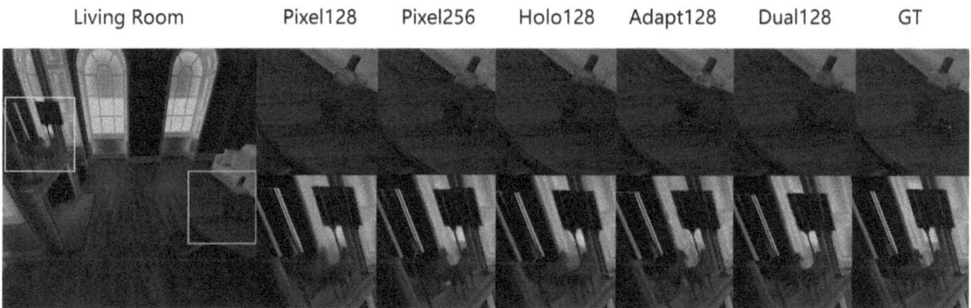

Fig. 6. Rendering Quality Comparisons of Living Room. Dual128 achieves near-ground-truth quality in refraction (glass bottle) and reflection (mirrored horse).

Performance validation in complex dynamic scenes employed standardized benchmarks: the Veach Egg scene (featuring movable light sources, translocatable glass, and dynamic caustics) and Veach Ajar scene (with rotating door leaf). As demonstrated in Fig. 7, our method maintains consistent rendering robustness across both scenarios. Quantitative results further validate the efficacy: Dual128 achieved high SSIM scores of

0.982 (Veach Egg) and 0.977 (Veach Ajar), confirming strong generalization capabilities in handling dynamic scene elements.

Fig. 7. Performance validation on dynamic scenes: (a) Veach Egg scene with movable lights/translocatable glass; (b) Veach Ajar scene with rotating door leaf.

6 Conclusions

We introduced a novel neural rendering framework for real-time global illumination that effectively decouples static scene representation from dynamic illumination and view-dependent effects. Our core contributions include: (a) A two-stage pipeline separating geometric baking from photometric adaptation; (b) A memory-efficient dual-map representation enabling efficient reuse of neural features; and (c) A modular training scheme that reduces network complexity while enhancing rendering quality.

Experimental validation across complex dynamic scenes demonstrates that our Dual128 configuration achieves near-reference quality with $<15\%$ inference overhead compared to baseline pixel generators, outperforming monolithic networks with $1.8\times$ faster inference than equivalent-quality alternatives. Crucially, the staged design reduces sample complexity during dynamic adaptation by leveraging pre-baked scene priors, while our multi-resolution feature encoding and adaptive sampling strategies ensure robust handling of high-frequency lighting effects under constrained resources. In conclusion, we presented a novel neural rendering framework for real-time global illumination that decouples static and dynamic components.

There are several avenues to further improve our approach. Cross-scene generalization could be enhanced through transfer learning mechanisms, enabling HoloMap/AdaptMap representations trained on reference scenes to bootstrap adaptation for structurally similar environments, thereby drastically reducing per-scene training costs. Another critical direction involves extending AdaptMap's capabilities to handle topological changes, such as deformable objects or scene reconfiguration, through integration of neural skinning or implicit deformation fields. This would overcome current limitations where non-rigid transformations restrict applicability to rigid scenes. Furthermore, adopting multiresolution hash encoding techniques [18] could significantly compress AdaptMap storage while accelerating feature retrieval, potentially unlocking 4K real-time performance on consumer hardware.

Acknowledgments. This work was supported by the Beijing Municipal Science and Technology Commission under grant Z251100006125002.

References

1. Hedman, P., Philip, J., Price, T., et al.: Deep blending for free-viewpoint image-based rendering. ACM Trans. Graphics **37**(6), 1–15 (2018). Article 257
2. Riegler, G., Koltun, V.: Free view synthesis. In: Proceedings of 16th European Conference on Computer Vision, Part XIX 16, pp. 623–640. Springer (2020)
3. Bemana, M., Myszkowski, K., Seidel, H.P., et al.: X-fields: implicit neural view-, light-and time-image interpolation. ACM Trans. Graphics **39**(6), Article 257 (2020)
4. Philip, J., Gharbi, M., Zhou, T., et al.: Multi-view relighting using a geometry-aware network. ACM Trans. Graphics **38**(4), 1–14 (2019). Article 78
5. Srinivasan, P.P., Tucker, R., Barron, J.T., et al.: Pushing the boundaries of view extrapolation with multiplane images. In: Proceedings of the IEEE Conference on Computer Vision and Pattern Recognition, pp. 175–184 (2019)
6. Srinivasan, P.P., Deng, B., Zhang, X., et al.: NeRV: neural reflectance and visibility fields for relighting and view synthesis. In: Proceedings of the IEEE Conference on Computer Vision and Pattern Recognition, pp. 7495–7504 (2021)
7. Mildenhall, B., Srinivasan, P.P., Tancik, M., et al.: NeRF: representing scenes as neural radiance fields for view synthesis. Commun. ACM **65**(1), 99–106 (2021)
8. Thies, J., Zollhfer, M., Niener, M.: Deferred neural rendering: image synthesis using neural textures. ACM Trans. Graphics **38**(4), 1–12 (2019). Article 66
9. Zeltner, T., et al.: Real-time neural appearance models. ACM Trans. Graphics **43**(3), 1–17 (2024)
10. Ren, P., Wang, J., Gong, M., et al.: Global illumination with radiance regression functions. ACM Trans. Graphics **32**(4), 1–12 (2013)
11. Qin, X., Xiao, S.: Transparent-supported radiance regression function. In: Proceedings of the 13th ACM VRCAI, pp. 197–200. ACM (2014)
12. Thomas, M., Forbes, G.: Deep illumination: approximating dynamic global illumination with generative adversarial network (2017). https://doi.org/10.48550/arXiv.1710.09834
13. Gao, D., Mu, H., Xu, K.: Neural global illumination: interactive indirect illumination prediction under dynamic area lights. IEEE Trans. Vis. Comput. Graphics (2022)
14. Sitzmann, V., Zollhöfer, M., Wetzstein, G.: Scene representation networks: continuous 3D-structure-aware neural scene representations. In: Proceedings of the Conference on Neural Information Processing Systems (NeurIPS) (2019)
15. Ronneberger, O., Fischer, P., Brox, T.: U-net: convolutional networks for biomedical image segmentation. In: Proceedings of the 18th International Conference on Medical Image Computing and Computer-Assisted Intervention, pp. 234–241. Springer (2015)
16. Granskog, J., Rousselle, F., Papas, M., Novåk, J.: Compositional neural scene representations for shading inference. ACM Trans. Graphics **39**(4), Article 135 (2020)
17. Diolatzis, S., Philip, J., Drettakis, G.: Active exploration for neural global illumination of variable scenes. ACM Trans. Graphics **41**(5), Article 171 (2022)
18. Müller, T., Evans, A., Schied, C., et al.: Instant neural graphics primitives with a multiresolution hash encoding. ACM Trans. Graphics **41**(4) (2022)
19. Coomans, A., Dominci, E.A., Döring, C., et al.: Real-time neural rendering of dynamic light fields. Comput. Graphics Forum **43**(2), e15014 (2024)
20. Raghavan, N., Xiao, Y., Lin, E., et al.: Neural free-viewpoint relighting for glossy indirect illumination. Comput. Graphics Forum **42**(4), e14885 (2023)

21. Zhang. Z., Simo-Serra, E.: Neural scene baking for permutation invariant transparency rendering with real-time global illumination. arXiv preprint arXiv:2405.19056 (2024)
22. Zhang, Z., Simo-Serra, E.: CrystalNet: texture-aware neural refraction baking for global illumination. Comput. Graphics Forum **43**(7), e15227 (2024)
23. Su, R., et al.: Dynamic neural radiosity with multi-grid decomposition. In: ACM SIGGRAPH Asia 2024 Conference Proceedings (2024)
24. Zheng, C., et al.: NeLT: object-oriented neural light transfer. ACM Trans. Graphics **42**, 5 (2023). Article 163
25. Maas, A.L., Hannun, A.Y., Ng, A.Y.: Rectifier nonlinearities improve neural network acoustic models. In: Proceedings of the 30th International Conference on Machine Learning, vol. 28, no. 3 (2013)

RBTFusion: Region-Based Tracking for Real-Time Reconstruction from RGB-D Data

Shiyi Lu[1,2], Panpan Zhao[1,2], Xin Cao[1,2], Ming Li[3], Xiaolong Yuan[4], and Xueying Qin[1,2](✉)

[1] School of Software, Shandong University, Jinan, People's Republic of China
{lsy_sdu,zhaopanpan,sdu_cx}@mail.sdu.edu.cn, qxy@sdu.edu.cn
[2] Engineering Research Center of Digital Media Technology, Ministry of Education, Shandong University, Jinan, People's Republic of China
[3] Shandong Inspur Database Technology Co., Ltd., Jinan, People's Republic of China
liming2017@inspur.com
[4] Inspur Software Group Ltd., Jinan, People's Republic of China
yuanxiaolong@inspur.com

Abstract. Real-time 3D reconstruction with consumer-level RGB-D cameras is an essential task in the field of augmented reality. Using hand-held RGB-D cameras for scene and object depth modeling can assist computers in quickly locating space and achieving virtual-real interaction. Currently, state-of-the-art methods often rely on color features for spatial localization and reconstruction. While these methods achieve impressive results in sequences with rich color features, they struggle to track sequences with weak textures. To tackle this issue, we propose RBTFusion, a real-time 3D reconstruction system that performs spatial registration through region-based implicit segmentation. We employ color distributions and point cloud distances as posterior probabilities, implicitly segmenting both 2D images and 3D space to estimate camera poses. Experimental results on the TUM, Scannet, and our proposed RBTObj dataset demonstrate that our method has a broader applicability range, superior tracking robustness, and better reconstruction accuracy compared to existing methods, particularly in object reconstruction sequences where it exhibits significant advantages. Additionally, RBTFusion exhibits excellent efficiency throughout the tracking and point cloud fusion process, maintaining a stable frame rate of over 35 Hz from tracking to fusion.

Keywords: 3D reconstruction · camera tracking · Region-based registration

1 Introduction

Real-time 3D reconstruction based on consumer-level RGB-D cameras has been a key challenge in augmented reality. By reconstructing real-world 3D scenes,

A. Hinkenjan et al. (Eds.): ICXR 2025, LNCS 16428, pp. 191–209, 2026.
https://doi.org/10.1007/978-981-95-7195-6_11

virtual elements can be seamlessly integrated with the real world, providing users with a more immersive augmented reality experience. In scenarios with a demand for intelligent interaction, systems often require high-speed and high-precision reconstruction. The reconstruction of 3D space can visually demonstrate the intelligent system's understanding of the scene, aiding in accomplishing various challenging intelligent tasks. Since the pioneering work of KinectFusion [26], numerous real-time 3D reconstruction methods have been proposed. Despite the considerable advancements in this field, due to the limitations of existing registration methods, there are still many issues to be addressed in achieving high-precision 3D model reconstruction using consumer-level RGB-D cameras.

Currently, various mainstream dense 3D reconstruction systems typically rely on extracting and matching color features from consecutive frames, followed by using ICP and its variations for camera tracking [1,31]. For instance, methods using SIFT or ORB feature descriptors for point cloud matching and registration [23,30]. However, these methods heavily rely on color features and struggle to handle sequences with no or weak textures. Such sequences lack sufficient color features, leading to significant errors in matching and registration.

In response to the aforementioned challenges, we introduce RBTFusion, drawing inspiration from tracking strategies used in 3D object tracking, particularly for textureless objects. Specifically, we implicitly divide the image into regions, which do not necessarily have to be closed, by counting the color probabilities of local regions. We use this probability model to iteratively optimize and estimate the camera pose. Implicit segmentation refers to the process of distinguishing foreground and background by calculating posterior probabilities during the tracking optimization, without actually performing pixel-level segmentation. Furthermore, following the region-based tracking concept, we apply a similar approach to the depth point cloud. We partition the point cloud into regions based on point cloud distance cues and construct probability models accordingly. By integrating this depth-based strategy with the color-based approach, we achieve a more robust camera pose estimation. This method not only effectively addresses registration challenges posed by textureless or weakly textured sequences but also demonstrates excellent performance in general reconstruction sequences. It's worth mentioning that if using segmentation networks like SAM [21] to replace implicit segmentation with explicit segmentation, theoretically, better tracking accuracy could be achieved. However, this approach is not feasible in real-time due to its computational demands. As a result, we did not adopt this solution.

Building upon the proposed region-based tracking approach, we have integrated a point-based fusion module [18] as well as local and global optimization modules to create a real-time 3D reconstruction system. Furthermore, to showcase RBTFusion's superiority in object reconstruction, we introduce a new object reconstruction dataset named RBTObj. This dataset comprises reconstruction sequences and scan models of various objects, including those with weak textures, strong textures, large sizes, and small sizes. We extensively evaluated our method on various RGB-D sequences and demonstrated our advantages in both tracking and reconstruction.

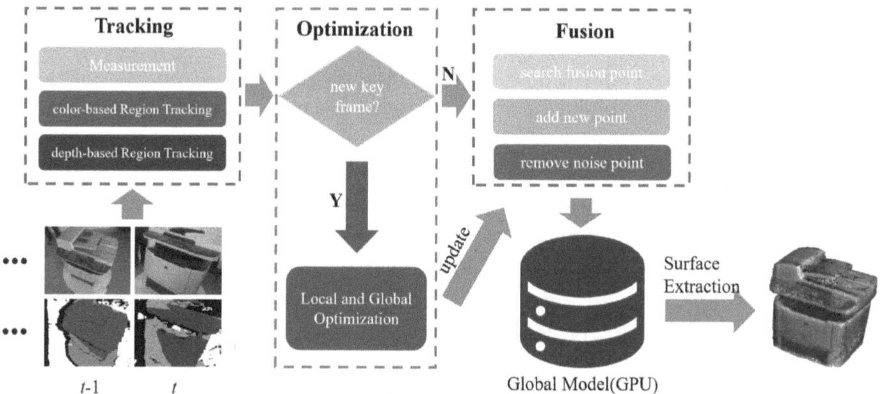

Fig. 1. System Overview. Our method takes an RGB-D image stream as input, which pass through three modules: Tracking, Optimization, and Fusion. These modules collectively estimate the camera pose for each frame and produce the final reconstructed model. **Tracking:** The input images are transformed into point clouds with color and normal vector. The camera pose can be estimated based on our region-based tracking method. **Optimization:** This module conducts feature extraction, keyframes maintenance, local and global optimization processes, refining the camera poses further. **Fusion:** Associating data with GPU, merging newly input point clouds into the global model, or modifying existing point clouds based on new poses.

In summary, the contributions of this work are:

- We propose RBTFusion, an end-to-end real-time dense reconstruction system that robustly and stably performs real-time reconstruction even in sequences containing images with weak or no texture.
- We propose a region tracking method based on color and depth. By utilizing color and depth point clouds for implicit region segmentation in both 2D images and 3D space, our method robustly tracks camera poses.
- To demonstrate the effectiveness of RBTFusion, we have introduced a new object reconstruction dataset called RBTObj. This dataset comprises scan sequences and accurate models of 10 textured objects and 10 textureless objects. It enables comprehensive evaluation and validation of our method's performance.

2 Related Works

In this section, we will provide an overview of real-time 3D reconstruction, region tracking algorithms, and deep learning to 3D reconstruction. Due to space limitations, we will focus on presenting works closely related to our study.

2.1 Online RGB-D Reconstruction

The earliest real-time reconstruction system based on voxel fusion was proposed by Newcombee et al., known as KinectFusion. However, voxel-based methods impose limitations on the size of the reconstructed space and require significant memory usage. To address this issue, techniques utilizing spatial hierarchies [8] and hashing schemes for voxel organization were introduced [17,27]. On the other hand, point-based reconstruction methods have also been considered as an alternative solution. These methods do not require the partitioning of the reconstruction space, resulting in lower memory consumption. The density of the generated model is solely dependent on the image resolution. This technique has been applied in various works, such as RGB-D Mapping, ElasticFusion, and Staticfusion [15,33,43].

As research progressed, the focus of reconstruction shifted gradually from model representation to camera pose estimation. More accurate pose estimation leads to better model reconstruction, prompting subsequent reconstruction methods to propose various solutions for pose optimization. BundelFusion [12] introduced a GPU-based global point cloud registration method. It aligns sparse features of each frame through matching and applies Bundle Adjustment (BA) iteratively to optimize poses, mitigating cumulative errors. ROSEFusion [46] employs an optimization objective function based on depth-to-TSDF [5]. Utilizing a strategy of stochastic optimization, it achieves featureless camera tracking and addresses the challenge of reconstructing rapidly moving sequences. HRBF-Fusion [44], on the other hand, incorporates the geometric implicit representation of Hermite radial basis functions as a novel cue for point cloud matching in its approach to camera tracking.

2.2 Region-Base Object Tracking

Region-based object tracking methods primarily target tracking of textureless objects. These methods typically require an accurate model of the tracked object. They divide the image into regions based on the projected contour of the model, and utilize color statistics to simulate the probability of each pixel belonging to the object or background. By using these probabilities, the tracked object is segmented, and subsequent pose optimization is performed. In earlier works, segmentation and optimization were handled separately [4,29,32], but later efforts efficiently combined these two steps [13]. Subsequently, Charles Bibby and others introduced the concept of per-pixel posterior probabilities, which became a foundational theory in this field. Based on this theory, various methods capable of robustly tracking textureless objects emerged, such as PWP3D, SLOT, ROBT, SRT3D, and more [2,16,28,34,38].

The tracking algorithm in this article mainly draws inspiration from ROBT's local color histogram model. This approach equips RBTFusion with the capability to handle both single-color and rich-color sequences. Furthermore, our work also incorporates ideas from SLOT, utilizing search lines for per-pixel weighting, allowing more pixels to be involved in the calculation.

2.3 Learning-Based Multi-View Stereo

Early depth learning-based reconstruction methods predominantly relied on regression techniques. By constructing two-dimensional and three-dimensional convolutional networks, these methods regressed the truncated distance for each voxel, thereby obtaining a generative model. [3,25,37]. In the view synthesis and field of feedforward architecture-based 3D reconstruction, a series of significant research efforts have emerged in recent years. NeRF [24] combines neural fields with volume rendering to generate high-quality novel views from a small number of 2D images. However, it suffers from high training and rendering time and cost, is limited to exhibits degraded performance with fewer input views, and has poor generalization. 3D Gaussian Splatting [19] represents scenes using Gaussian distributions, achieving a certain level of rendering efficiency. Nevertheless, it tends to produce artifacts when observational data is insufficient, has poor scalability for large-scale scenes, suffers from visibility algorithm flaws in the rendering pipeline, generates aliasing artifacts when handling variable resolutions, ignores underlying geometric structures, and performs poorly in complex scenes and under varying lighting conditions across different viewpoints. Feedforward networks [22,39,40] enable end-to-end learning for fast output. However, deep networks face challenges such as gradient vanishing or explosion during back-propagation, making training difficult; they are prone to overfitting with limited data, involve complex hyperparameter tuning, have limited capability in processing sequential data, and offer poor interpretability. Thus, utilizing deep learning technology for achieving real-time, high-precision 3D reconstruction remains a significant challenge.

3 Method

We present an overview of our method in Fig. 1, which encompasses the three major modules: Tracking, Optimization, and Fusion. As Fusion and Optimization are implemented with reference to ElasticFusion and ORB-SLAM3 [6], respectively, the specific methods are not outlined in this paper. This section begins by introducing the parameterized objectives for estimation, followed by a focused introduction to the color-based and depth-based region tracking algorithms.

3.1 Preliminaries

When inputting the t-th frame image, the algorithm proposed in this paper needs to estimate the camera pose from frame t-1 to frame t. This can be represented using a 4×4 homogeneous matrix:

$$\boldsymbol{T} = \begin{bmatrix} \boldsymbol{R} & \boldsymbol{t} \\ \mathbf{0}^\top & 1 \end{bmatrix} \in \mathbb{SE}(3), \text{ with } \boldsymbol{R} \in \mathbb{SO}(3) \text{ and } \boldsymbol{t} \in \mathbb{R}^3 \tag{1}$$

For pose optimization, the update perturbation $\Delta\boldsymbol{T}$ is expressed using a six-dimensional twist vector $\boldsymbol{\theta} = [w_1, w_2, w_3, v_1, v_2, v_3]^\top$, which is parameterized using Lie algebra.

3.2 Color-Based Region Registration Method

This registration algorithm primarily relies on the color distribution of sampled points near the image edge contours for pose estimation. The basic algorithmic principle is illustrated in Fig. 2. To estimate the pose of frame t , our method first extracts the Canny edges of frame t-1 and randomly samples L_c edge points. For the i-th sampled point $\boldsymbol{c}_i \in \mathbb{R}^2$, we compute the local color histogram in the color space of frame t-1 for the region centered at the point with a radius of R_c. We also use the color gradient $\boldsymbol{n}_i \in \mathbb{R}^2$ at that point as a normal vector to construct a search line r_i on frame t for pixel-wise searching, aiming to find the corresponding edge point in frame t for $\boldsymbol{c}_i$. To quantify the likelihood of each point on the search line as being part of the edge contour, we adopt the following cost function, as inspired by SLOT:

$$\begin{aligned} E_c(\boldsymbol{\theta}) = -\sum_{\boldsymbol{x}_{ij}} \log \left[H_e\left(d\left(\boldsymbol{x}_{ij}\right)\right) P_f^c\left(\boldsymbol{x}_{ij}\right)\right. \\ \left. + \left(1 - H_e\left(d\left(\boldsymbol{x}_{ij}\right)\right)\right) P_b^c\left(\boldsymbol{x}_{ij}\right)\right] \end{aligned} \tag{2}$$

where $\boldsymbol{x}_{ij} \in \mathbb{R}^2$ represents the j-th pixel along the i-th search line, $P_f^c\left(\boldsymbol{x}_{ij}\right)$ and $P_b^c\left(\boldsymbol{x}_{ij}\right)$ denote the posterior probabilities of each pixel's membership to the foreground and background regions, respectively, computed from the local color histogram of $\boldsymbol{c}_i$. The function $d\left(\boldsymbol{x}_{ij}\right) = \boldsymbol{n}_i^\top\left(\boldsymbol{x}_{ij} - \boldsymbol{c}_i\right)$ calculates the signed Euclidean distance between the search point and the sampled point. The Heaviside function is defined as follows:

$$H_e\left(d\left(\boldsymbol{x}_{ij}\right)\right) = \frac{1}{\pi}\left(-\operatorname{atan}\left(d\left(\boldsymbol{x}_{ij}\right) s_h\right) + \frac{\pi}{2}\right) \tag{3}$$

where $s_h \in \mathbb{R}$ is a parameter controlling the smooth transition width. In an ideal scenario, pixels with $d\left(\boldsymbol{x}_{ij}\right) < 0$ are classified as foreground region, while pixels with $d\left(\boldsymbol{x}_{ij}\right) > 0$ are classified as background region. Therefore, using the piecewise function F_e instead of H_e to constrain the edge points would theoretically be more effective. F_e is defined as:

$$F_e\left(d\left(\boldsymbol{x}_{ij}\right)\right) = \begin{cases} 1 & d\left(\boldsymbol{x}_{ij}\right) < 0 \\ 0 & d\left(\boldsymbol{x}_{ij}\right) > 0 \end{cases} \tag{4}$$

however, since F_e is not differentiable at $d\left(\boldsymbol{x}_{ij}\right) = 0$, the Heaviside function is used for smoothing instead. By applying constraints to the edge points, this method gradually aligns the edges between the two frames during the optimization process, enabling highly accurate pose estimation.

3.3 Depth-Based Region Registration Method

The color-based registration method operates solely in the image space, lacking constraints in the third dimension. Hence, we introduce depth-based constraint equations. Similar to the color-based approach, we begin by applying a method

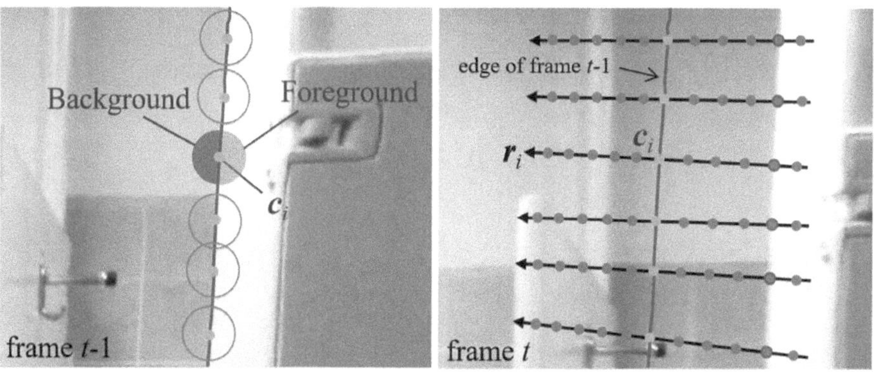

Fig. 2. Color-based region segmentation method schematic. **left:** Extract edges from the RGB image of frame t-1 (red lines) and obtain sampling points on the edges (green points). Based on the edge information and color gradient direction, the local region around the sample points is divided into foreground and background regions, and local color histograms are constructed within these regions. The circular region around sample point $\boldsymbol{c}_i$ represents the result of local region segmentation for that sample point, with purple indicating the background region and blue indicating the foreground region. **Right:** We project the sampling points from frame t-1 onto frame t and construct search lines. By using local color histograms to compute the posterior probability for region segmentation and performing pixel-wise search, our method progressively aligns the edge sampling points from frame t-1 to the edges of frame t.

akin to KinectFusion to compute the vertex map and normal map from the input depth image. Subsequently, we randomly sample L_d points on the t-1-th frame's depth map space and construct three-dimensional search lines.

For the search line R_i, with the center point being the sampled point $\boldsymbol{C}_i \in \mathbb{R}^3$ and the normal vector $\boldsymbol{N}_i \in \mathbb{R}^3$, where $\boldsymbol{X}_{ij} \in \mathbb{R}^3$ represents the j-th point on R_i with line coordinate $R_i(j)$, thus $\boldsymbol{X}_{ij}$ can be defined as:

$$\boldsymbol{X}_{ij} = \boldsymbol{C}_i + R_i(j)\boldsymbol{N}_i \tag{5}$$

The cost function defined based on depth-region is:

$$\begin{aligned} E_d(\boldsymbol{\theta}) = -\sum_{\boldsymbol{X}_{ij}} \log \big[& H_e\left(D\left(\boldsymbol{X}_{ij}\right)\right) P_f^d\left(\boldsymbol{X}_{ij}\right) \\ & + \left(1 - H_e\left(D\left(\boldsymbol{X}_{ij}\right)\right)\right) P_b^d\left(\boldsymbol{X}_{ij}\right)\big] \end{aligned} \tag{6}$$

$$D\left(\boldsymbol{X}_{ij}\right) = \boldsymbol{N}_i^\top\left(\boldsymbol{X}_{ij} - \boldsymbol{C}_i\right) \tag{7}$$

similar to color method, this cost function employs H_e as the smoothing function. $D\left(\boldsymbol{X}_{ij}\right)$ represents the signed Euclidean distance between the search point and the sampled point. Unlike the method in previous Section, the foreground and background posterior probabilities of the search points need to be determined based on the distance relationship between point clouds. Figure 3 illustrates the

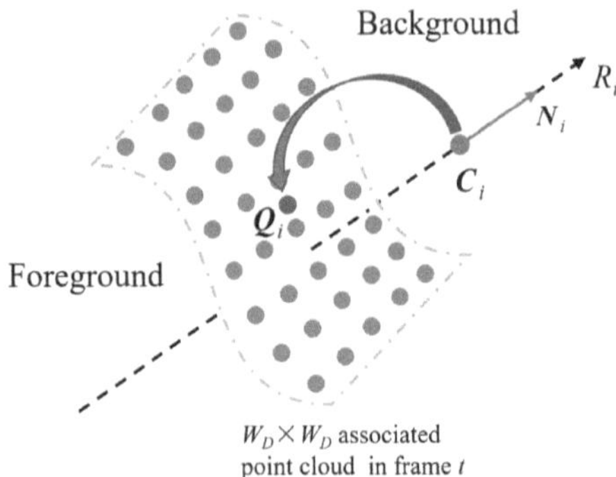

Fig. 3. Illustration of a 3D search line. Using the sample point from frame t-1 as the center, three-dimensional search lines are constructed in the direction of the sample point's normal vector. Through point-by-point search along the lines, the sample point is gradually brought closer to the centroid of the associated point cloud on frame t.

concept of 3D search lines. Based on the sampled points and search lines in the camera space of frame t, we seek surfaces composed of associated point clouds, which partition the camera space into regions. Specifically, we project the sampled point cloud from frame t-1 onto the depth image of frame t, taking a region around the projected pixel of size $W_D \times W_D$ as the associated point cloud. We then compute the center $\boldsymbol{Q}_i \in \mathbb{R}^3$ of this point cloud. Referring to the smoothing function of hyperbolic tangent curve from SRT3D [34], the formula for calculating foreground and background posterior probabilities in this algorithm is:

$$P_f^d\left(\boldsymbol{X}_{ij}\right) = \frac{1}{2} - \frac{1}{2}\tanh\left(\boldsymbol{N}_i^\top\left(\boldsymbol{X}_{ij} - \boldsymbol{Q}_i\right)s_a\right) \tag{8}$$

$$P_b^d\left(\boldsymbol{X}_{ij}\right) = \frac{1}{2} + \frac{1}{2}\tanh\left(\boldsymbol{N}_i^\top\left(\boldsymbol{X}_{ij} - \boldsymbol{Q}_i\right)s_a\right) \tag{9}$$

where $s_a \in \mathbb{R}$ is the parameter controlling the slope. According to the definition of the probability formula, when $D\left(\boldsymbol{X}_{ij}\right) < 0$, the foreground probability is greater than the background probability. The region where the search point is located is considered foreground, representing the interior of the reconstructed surface. When $D\left(\boldsymbol{X}_{ij}\right) > 0$, the search point is considered a background point, representing the exterior of the reconstructed surface. As per the definition of the cost function, when the sampled point precisely lies on the reconstructed surface, the points on this 3D search line will be perfectly separated. Consequently, in the optimization iteration process, the sampled points will automatically align with the closest associated surface and consistently move in that direction.

By combining these two methods, the final cost function is:

$$E(\boldsymbol{\theta}) = \omega E_c(\boldsymbol{\theta}) + (1-\omega)E_d(\boldsymbol{\theta}) \tag{10}$$

where ω is a user-defined weight parameter. We use the Gauss-Newton algorithm for iterative optimization of the problem. For relevant derivative formulas, please refer to the supplementary material.

3.4 Implementation

We used the Canny function from the OpenCV library to extract image edges. During random point sampling, points lacking depth, having exceptional depth values, or lacking normal vectors were discarded to ensure smooth optimization. In the point-based fusion module, we leveraged the code framework related to point cloud fusion referenced in ElasticFusion to achieve implementation, primarily facilitating data communication between CPU and GPU through OpenGL library and Shader code. Meanwhile, in the optimization module, we mainly adopted techniques outlined in ORB-SLAM3, including ORB feature extraction, keyframe detection and generation, maintenance of feature point maps, and bundle adjustment based on reprojection error, to optimize all input frames. Optimization module aims to address the issue of accumulated tracking errors. However, as this method relies heavily on color features, RBTFusion selectively continues with optimization based on the performance of this module. When the module struggles to identify features effectively, it is turned off.

4 Experiments

We evaluated our reconstruction framework on a diverse range of datasets, including various object and scene datasets. Additionally, we conducted ablation experiments to validate the effectiveness of our method.

4.1 Experimental Setup

Datasets. We primarily use three datasets: ScanNet [11], TUM RGB-D dataset [36], and our self-captured RBTObj dataset. The TUM RGB-D dataset's scan sequences consist of RGB-D images for each frame along with their corresponding ground truth poses, making it highly suitable for evaluating tracking accuracy. ScanNet primarily comprises scan sequences for scenes, with provided ground truth models for each scene. Therefore, the experiments regarding scene reconstruction in this paper are primarily conducted on this dataset. The RBTObj dataset, constructed by us, comprises reconstruction sequences of various objects. It is primarily utilized for experimental comparisons regarding object reconstruction, as detailed in Subsect. 4.3.

4.2 Tracking Robustness

Baselines. We perform performance comparisons against various 3D reconstruction or Simultaneous Localization and Mapping (SLAM) systems, including

Table 1. ATE RMSE [m] (↓) on the TUM benchmark.

	fr1/desk	fr2/xyz	fr3/office	fr3/nst
DVO SLAM	0.021	0.018	0.035	0.018
RGBD SLAM	0.023	0.008	0.032	0.017
MRSMap	0.043	0.020	0.042	2.018
Kintinuous	0.037	0.029	0.030	0.031
ElasticFusion	0.020	0.011	0.017	0.016
BundleFusion	0.016	0.011	0.022	**0.012**
Redwood	0.027	0.091	0.030	1.929
UncertaintyAware	0.015	0.006	0.009	0.014
HRBFFusion	**0.014**	0.005	**0.007**	0.016
RBTFusion	0.016	**0.003**	0.009	0.013

Table 2. Reconstruction accuracy [m](↓) on the ScanNet dataset.

	BundleFusion	ROSEFusion	HRBFFusion	**RBTFusion**
scene0036_00	0.023	0.091	0.062	**0.013**
scene0038_01	0.056	0.135	0.023	**0.016**
scene0042_02	0.025	0.025	0.052	**0.013**
scene0045_00	0.071	0.050	0.038	**0.032**
scene0047_00	0.145	0.147	0.145	**0.096**
scene0053_00	0.051	0.055	0.037	**0.035**
scene0060_00	0.168	0.156	0.059	**0.030**
scene0064_00	0.122	0.190	0.086	**0.049**
scene0065_01	0.015	0.071	0.014	**0.010**
scene0092_00	0.033	0.060	0.029	**0.025**

DVO SLAM [20], RGBD SLAM [14], MRSMap [35], Kintinuous [42], ElasticFusion, BundleFusion, Redwood [9], UncertaintyAware [7], HRBFFusion, and ROSEFusion. Additionally, we will specifically focus on comparing the reconstruction accuracy against BundleFusion, ROSEFusion, and HRBFFusion.

Metrics. We use the absolute trajectory error (ATE) and root-mean-square error (RMSE) to assess the performance of the reconstruction system's camera pose tracking. Surface reconstruction accuracy is measured by the average distance from the reconstructed model to the ground truth surface. Reliable ground truth data is essential for both of these metrics. For tracking accuracy, we will utilize the evo library. For reconstruction accuracy, we will first perform high-precision ICP registration between the reconstructed and ground truth models, followed by computing the Chamfer distance based on this alignment.

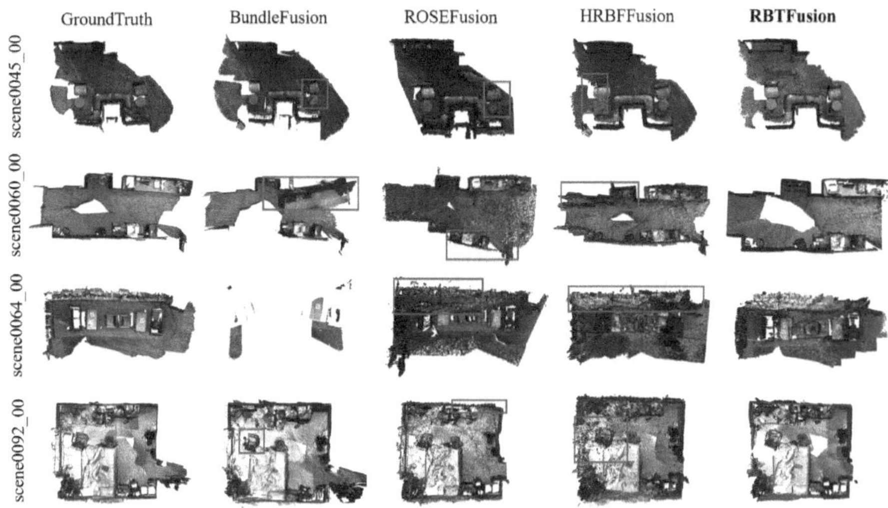

Fig. 4. Comparison of Reconstruction Results on ScanNet. The red boxes highlight areas with reconstruction errors. (Color figure online)

Implementation Details. All experimental reconstruction processes were ran on a laptop equipped with an AMD Ryzen 7 4800H CPU and an NVIDIA RTX 2060 GPU. In all our experiments, we configured the number of color and depth sampling points as $L_c = L_d = 400$. The radius R_c was set to 20 to compute the local color histograms, and $W_D = 9$ was used for locating associated point clouds. s_h in Eq. 3 was set to 8, s_a in Eq. 8 and Eq. 9 was set to 100, and ω in the Eq. 10 was set to 0.5.

4.3 The RBTObj Dataset

To validate the performance of RBTFusion, we aim to conduct thorough testing in both scene and object application scenarios. While there are many suitable public datasets available for scene-level reconstruction, current public datasets for object-level reconstruction suffer from some deficiencies. For example, the ground truth models provided by Object Scans [10] are reconstructed and registered using the ICP method, which isn't reliable for object reconstruction tasks. While the CuFusion dataset [45] does offer accurate models, its data type is more suitable for methods reliant on depth-based reconstruction. The data acquisition for the CoRBS benchmark [41] is currently closed. Therefore, we have constructed the RBTObj dataset, which comprises two parts: textured and textureless object datasets.

For the textured object dataset, we selected 10 common objects and captured sequences using the RealSense d415 camera. To ensure reliability and referenceability of the reconstruction error metrics, we used the Artec Leo laser 3D scanner to reconstruct models while building the ground truth models. Additionally, we

Table 3. Reconstruction accuracy [m](↓) of textured objects on the RBTObj dataset.

	BundleFusion	ROSEFusion	HRBFFusion	**RBTFusion**
Container	0.034	0.014	0.010	**0.007**
Computer	0.014	0.022	0.014	**0.009**
Vintage Computer	0.006	0.016	0.013	**0.004**
Large Printer	0.005	0.015	0.014	**0.003**
Large Server	0.009	0.016	0.012	**0.003**
Suitcase	0.005	0.008	0.012	**0.004**
Printer	0.008	0.016	0.009	**0.006**
Laptop	0.025	0.013	0.011	**0.006**
Fridge	0.019	0.019	0.015	**0.010**
Cushion	0.025	0.009	0.009	**0.007**

Table 4. Reconstruction accuracy [m](↓) of textureless objects on the RBTObj dataset.

	BundleFusion	ROSEFusion	HRBFFusion	**RBTFusion**
Untex1	0.00712	0.00187	0.00683	**0.00146**
Untex2	0.01527	0.00251	0.00222	**0.00149**
Untex3	0.00941	0.00212	0.00147	**0.00107**
Untex4	0.00488	0.00237	0.00171	**0.00126**
Untex5	0.00942	0.00413	0.00194	**0.00118**
Untex6	0.01122	0.00423	0.00123	**0.00122**
Untex7	0.00614	0.00197	0.00234	**0.00151**
Untex8	0.00803	0.00431	0.00474	**0.00130**
Untex9	0.00475	0.00230	0.00214	**0.00142**
Untex10	0.00472	0.00164	0.00136	**0.00130**

utilized professional 3D model repair software to perform precise repairs on the reconstructed models, resulting in high-precision real object 3D models. On the other hand, for the textureless object dataset, we selected 10 CAD models and obtained high-precision real models using 3D printing technology. These models were ensured to have no texture by applying a single color to the surface. Finally, data was captured using the RealSense d415 camera.

We initially conducted comparative experiments on camera pose tracking accuracy using the TUM dataset, which is widely employed for assessing tracking precision. We selected four commonly used sequences, namely fr1/desk, fr2/xyz, fr3/office, and fr3/nst. These sequences capture scenes with a variety of color features. The experimental results are shown in Table 1. The metrics of our method rank third, first, second, and second across the four sequences, respectively. Overall, our approach shows comparable tracking performance to state-of-the-art methods, with slight variations in metrics for sequences where it isn't the

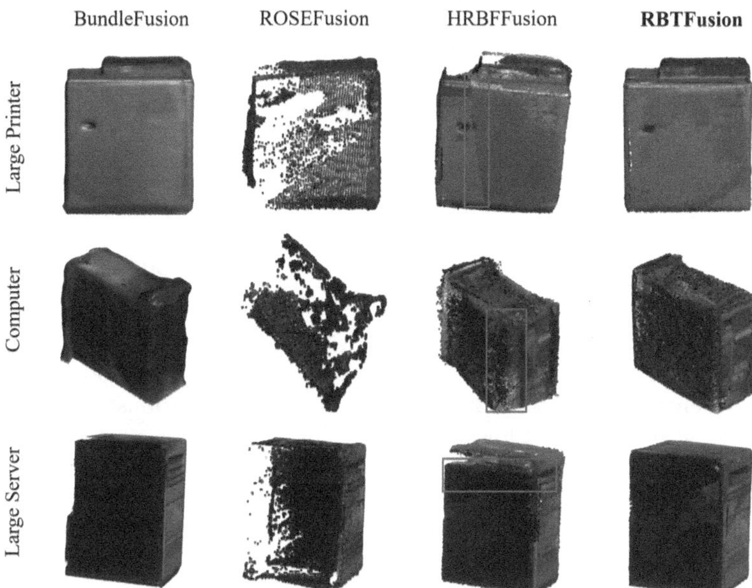

Fig. 5. Comparison of textured object reconstruction on the RBTObj dataset. The red boxes highlight areas where HRBFFusion exhibits significant reconstruction errors. (Color figure online)

top performer. The results indicate that despite our method's design for handling weak-textured objects, it still performs well on feature-rich sequences like those from TUM. This is likely due to the effectiveness of the local color histogram even in color-rich images. Regions with more unique color distributions tend to generate more distinctive color histograms, resulting in more accurate color foreground-background separation during optimization alignment. The experimental results from TUM demonstrate that our method has broader applicability across various scenarios.

4.4 Reconstruction Accuracy

Next, we evaluate RBTFusion on three tasks: scene reconstruction, textured object reconstruction, and textureless object reconstruction. For scene reconstruction, we use the ScanNet dataset, which contains over 1500 scan sequences with high-quality reconstructed models. These models are initially reconstructed using BundleFusion and VoxelHashing, then refined through geometric optimization, IMU-constrained alignment, and manual inspection to ensure reliability. We randomly select 10 sequences for evaluation and compare our method against state-of-the-art systems—BundleFusion, ROSEFusion, and HRBFFusion. Table 2 presents the reconstruction accuracy results, with all data obtained by running the respective source codes on the same device.

The results show that RBTFusion achieves the highest reconstruction accuracy across all 10 sequences. It performs well in diverse conditions—uniform or

Table 5. Ablation Study on the TUM benchmark. **Only CR:** Solely utilizing the color-based region tracking method. **Only DR:** Solely utilizing the depth-based region tracking method. **CR+DR:** Simultaneously employing both color and depth methods. **Full:** Simultaneously employing both color and depth methods along with the optimization module for optimization.

ATE RMSE(↓)	Only CR	Only DR	CR+DR	Full
Mean	0.013	0.015	0.010	**0.009**
Std.	0.009	0.009	0.006	**0.005**

rich colors, weak textures (e.g., scene0060_00, scene0065_01), and strong lighting (e.g., scene0053_00, scene0092_00)—demonstrating robustness and superiority over state-of-the-art methods. This highlights its strong capability in large-scale scene reconstruction. Visual comparisons in Fig. 4 further confirm RBTFusion's improved completeness and accuracy. Notably, BundleFusion fails in weakly textured sequences (e.g., scene0060_00, scene0064_00) due to feature-poor regions causing tracking drift, while RBTFusion maintains stable tracking and minimizes cumulative errors for high-quality results.

Experiments on textured and textureless object reconstruction were done on the RBTObj dataset. RBTFusion and other state-of-the-art systems were tested here, with results compared to ground truth models. 3 shows textured object reconstruction accuracy results, where RBTFusion led in all cases. This is due to its region tracking algorithm for textureless objects, which distinguishes foreground and background well, using them as anchors for precise results. Figure 5 compares RBTFusion's visual results with BundleFusion, ROSEFusion, and HRBFFusion. BundleFusion handles medium-to-large objects but has rough textures. ROSEFusion is for fast motion and poor at textured objects. HRBFFusion and RBTFusion use point cloud fusion, but HRBFFusion has errors while RBTFusion's constraints work better, especially for textured objects.

Table 4 shows RBTFusion achieves the best reconstruction accuracy across all textureless object sequences, highlighting the advantage of region-based tracking. It implicitly segments textureless objects, enables high-precision surface registration via depth data, and models small objects' shape and texture well through point-based fusion for accurate 3D reconstruction. Figure 6 displays reconstruction results: BundleFusion produces blurry contours and fails the task; ROSEFusion reconstructs general contours but with sparse point clouds; HRBFFusion has modeling errors and detail omissions, yielding low-quality models. In contrast, RBTFusion's models have good visuals, are complete with no obvious errors, and achieve the highest quality among the methods.

4.5 Ablation Study

To validate the effectiveness of our proposed region tracking method, we conducted ablation experiments to compare the tracking accuracy of RBTFusion under different conditions. In these experiments, our system ran the fr1/desk,

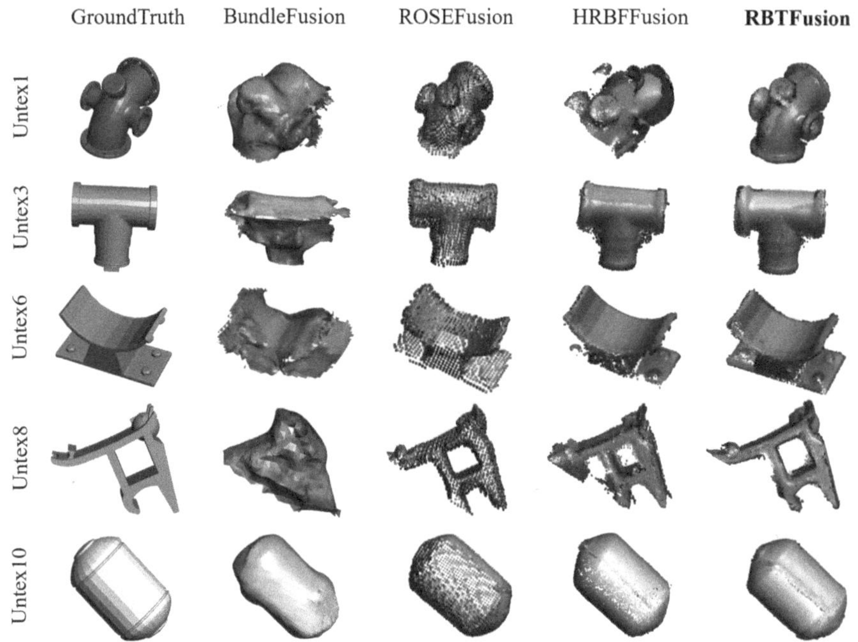

Fig. 6. Comparison of textureless object reconstruction on the RBTObj dataset.

fr2/xyz, fr3/office, and fr3/nst sequences from the TUM dataset under various conditions. We recorded the ATE RMSE metric for each run and calculated the mean and variance of this metric for each condition. The results are summarized in Table 5.

The table indicates that while both tracking methods exhibit some effectiveness when used individually, their combined use significantly improves accuracy. This suggests the correctness of our method's theoretical design, as neither method comprehensively considers all three dimensions of the camera coordinate system on its own. Additionally, the inclusion of an optimization module further enhances accuracy, albeit marginally. This underscores the strong performance of algorithms based on region tracking theory in camera tracking, indicating that the accumulation of pose errors is not too rapid when handling typical sequences.

4.6 Limitations

Despite its advancements, RBTFusion has limitations: it only handles static scenes, struggles in featureless color regions or uniform depth conditions due to segmentation challenges, and employs a frame-to-frame region tracking method that cannot establish global frame associations. Thus, it relies heavily on graph-based optimization to correct accumulated errors.

5 Conclusion

We have presented RBTFusion, a dense reconstruction system based on a region tracking algorithm. By implicitly dividing both image space and three-dimensional space into regions using color and depth information separately, we achieve inter-frame pose alignment by registering the edges of these regions. Furthermore, our designed optimization and point cloud fusion modules allow real-time elimination of accumulated errors and incremental improvement of the reconstruction model. The algorithm demonstrates high efficiency in execution. Refer to the supplementary materials for runtime speed. Experimental results demonstrate that our method adapts well to sequences with both uniform and diverse color distributions, and it performs effectively in tracking and reconstructing various sequences. Moreover, our approach exhibits significant advantages over state-of-the-art reconstruction systems in object reconstruction tasks.

Acknowledgements. This work is partially supported by the NSF of China (No. 62172260), and Technological Innovation and Enhancement Project for Small and Medium-sized Sci-tech Enterprises of Shandong Province (No.2025TSGCCZZB0004).

References

1. Besl, P.J., McKay, N.D.: A method for registration of 3-d shapes. IEEE Trans. Pattern Anal. Mach. Intell. **14**(2), 239–256 (1992). https://doi.org/10.1109/34.121791
2. Bibby, C., Reid, I.: Robust real-time visual tracking using pixel-wise posteriors. In: Forsyth, D., Torr, P., Zisserman, A. (eds.) ECCV 2008. LNCS, vol. 5303, pp. 831–844. Springer, Heidelberg (2008). https://doi.org/10.1007/978-3-540-88688-4_61
3. Bozic, A., Palafox, P.R., Thies, J., Dai, A., Nießner, M.: Transformerfusion: monocular RGB scene reconstruction using transformers. In: Ranzato, M., Beygelzimer, A., Dauphin, Y.N., Liang, P., Vaughan, J.W. (eds.) Advances in Neural Information Processing Systems 34: Annual Conference on Neural Information Processing Systems 2021, NeurIPS 2021, December 6-14, 2021, virtual, pp. 1403–1414 (2021). https://proceedings.neurips.cc/paper/2021/hash/0a87257e5308197df43230edf4ad1dae-Abstract.html
4. Brox, T., Rosenhahn, B., Gall, J., Cremers, D.: Combined region and motion-based 3d tracking of rigid and articulated objects. IEEE Trans. Pattern Anal. Mach. Intell. **32**(3), 402–415 (2010). https://doi.org/10.1109/TPAMI.2009.32
5. Bylow, E., Sturm, J., Kerl, C., Kahl, F., Cremers, D.: Real-time camera tracking and 3d reconstruction using signed distance functions. In: Newman, P., Fox, D., Hsu, D. (eds.) Robotics: Science and Systems IX, Technische Universität Berlin, Berlin, Germany, June 24 - June 28, 2013 (2013). https://doi.org/10.15607/RSS.2013.IX.035, http://www.roboticsproceedings.org/rss09/p35.html
6. Campos, C., Elvira, R., Rodríguez, J.J.G., Montiel, J.M.M., Tardós, J.D.: ORB-SLAM3: an accurate open-source library for visual, visual-inertial and multi-map SLAM. CoRR **abs/2007.11898** (2020). https://arxiv.org/abs/2007.11898

7. Cao, Y., Kobbelt, L., Hu, S.: Real-time high-accuracy three-dimensional reconstruction with consumer RGB-D cameras. ACM Trans. Graph. **37**(5), 171 (2018). https://doi.org/10.1145/3182157
8. Chen, J., Bautembach, D., Izadi, S.: Scalable real-time volumetric surface reconstruction. ACM Trans. Graph. **32**(4), 113:1–113:16 (2013). https://doi.org/10.1145/2461912.2461940
9. Choi, S., Zhou, Q., Koltun, V.: Robust reconstruction of indoor scenes. In: IEEE Conference on Computer Vision and Pattern Recognition, CVPR 2015, Boston, MA, USA, June 7-12, 2015, pp. 5556–5565. IEEE Computer Society (2015). https://doi.org/10.1109/CVPR.2015.7299195
10. Choi, S., Zhou, Q., Miller, S., Koltun, V.: A large dataset of object scans. CoRR **abs/1602.02481** (2016). http://arxiv.org/abs/1602.02481
11. Dai, A., Chang, A.X., Savva, M., Halber, M., Funkhouser, T.A., Nießner, M.: Scannet: richly-annotated 3d reconstructions of indoor scenes. In: 2017 IEEE Conference on Computer Vision and Pattern Recognition, CVPR 2017, Honolulu, HI, USA, July 21-26, 2017, pp. 2432–2443. IEEE Computer Society (2017). https://doi.org/10.1109/CVPR.2017.261
12. Dai, A., Nießner, M., Zollhöfer, M., Izadi, S., Theobalt, C.: Bundlefusion: real-time globally consistent 3d reconstruction using on-the-fly surface reintegration. ACM Trans. Graph. **36**(3), 24:1–24:18 (2017). https://doi.org/10.1145/3054739
13. Dambreville, S., Sandhu, R., Yezzi, A., Tannenbaum, A.: Robust 3D pose estimation and efficient 2D region-based segmentation from a 3D shape prior. In: Forsyth, D., Torr, P., Zisserman, A. (eds.) ECCV 2008. LNCS, vol. 5303, pp. 169–182. Springer, Heidelberg (2008). https://doi.org/10.1007/978-3-540-88688-4_13
14. Endres, F., Hess, J., Engelhard, N., Sturm, J., Cremers, D., Burgard, W.: An evaluation of the RGB-D SLAM system. In: IEEE International Conference on Robotics and Automation, ICRA 2012, 14-18 May, 2012, St. Paul, Minnesota, USA, pp. 1691–1696. IEEE (2012). https://doi.org/10.1109/ICRA.2012.6225199
15. Henry, P., Krainin, M., Herbst, E., Ren, X., Fox, D.: RGB-D mapping: using depth cameras for dense 3d modeling of indoor environments. In: Khatib, O., Kumar, V., Sukhatme, G.S. (eds.) Experimental Robotics - The 12th International Symposium on Experimental Robotics, ISER 2010, December 18-21, 2010, New Delhi and Agra, India. Springer Tracts in Advanced Robotics, vol. 79, pp. 477–491. Springer, Cham (2010). https://doi.org/10.1007/978-3-642-28572-1_33
16. Huang, H., Zhong, F., Qin, X.: Pixel-wise weighted region-based 3d object tracking using contour constraints. IEEE Trans. Vis. Comput. Graph. **28**(12), 4319–4331 (2022). https://doi.org/10.1109/TVCG.2021.3085197
17. Kähler, O., Prisacariu, V.A., Ren, C.Y., Sun, X., Torr, P.H.S., Murray, D.W.: Very high frame rate volumetric integration of depth images on mobile devices. IEEE Trans. Vis. Comput. Graph. **21**(11), 1241–1250 (2015). https://doi.org/10.1109/TVCG.2015.2459891
18. Keller, M., Lefloch, D., Lambers, M., Izadi, S., Weyrich, T., Kolb, A.: Real-time 3d reconstruction in dynamic scenes using point-based fusion. In: 2013 International Conference on 3D Vision, 3DV 2013, Seattle, Washington, USA, June 29 - July 1, 2013, pp. 1–8. IEEE Computer Society (2013). https://doi.org/10.1109/3DV.2013.9
19. Kerbl, B., Kopanas, G., Leimkühler, T., Drettakis, G.: 3d gaussian splatting for real-time radiance field rendering. ACM Trans. Graph. **42**(4) (2023). https://repo-sam.inria.fr/fungraph/3d-gaussian-splatting/

20. Kerl, C., Sturm, J., Cremers, D.: Dense visual SLAM for RGB-D cameras. In: 2013 IEEE/RSJ International Conference on Intelligent Robots and Systems, Tokyo, Japan, November 3-7, 2013, pp. 2100–2106. IEEE (2013). https://doi.org/10.1109/IROS.2013.6696650
21. Kirillov, A., et al.: Segment anything. CoRR **abs/2304.02643** (2023). https://doi.org/10.48550/arXiv.2304.02643
22. Leroy, V., Cabon, Y., Revaud, J.: Grounding image matching in 3d with mast3r (2024)
23. Lowe, D.G.: Distinctive image features from scale-invariant keypoints. Int. J. Comput. Vis. **60**(2), 91–110 (2004). https://doi.org/10.1023/B:VISI.0000029664.99615.94
24. Mildenhall, B., Srinivasan, P.P., Tancik, M., Barron, J.T., Ramamoorthi, R., Ng, R.: NeRF: representing scenes as neural radiance fields for view synthesis. In: Vedaldi, A., Bischof, H., Brox, T., Frahm, J.-M. (eds.) ECCV 2020. LNCS, vol. 12346, pp. 405–421. Springer, Cham (2020). https://doi.org/10.1007/978-3-030-58452-8_24
25. Murez, Z., van As, T., Bartolozzi, J., Sinha, A., Badrinarayanan, V., Rabinovich, A.: Atlas: end-to-end 3D scene reconstruction from posed images. In: Vedaldi, A., Bischof, H., Brox, T., Frahm, J.-M. (eds.) ECCV 2020. LNCS, vol. 12352, pp. 414–431. Springer, Cham (2020). https://doi.org/10.1007/978-3-030-58571-6_25
26. Newcombe, R.A., et al.: Kinectfusion: real-time dense surface mapping and tracking. In: 10th IEEE International Symposium on Mixed and Augmented Reality, ISMAR 2011, Basel, Switzerland, October 26-29, 2011, pp. 127–136. IEEE Computer Society (2011). https://doi.org/10.1109/ISMAR.2011.6092378
27. Nießner, M., Zollhöfer, M., Izadi, S., Stamminger, M.: Real-time 3d reconstruction at scale using voxel hashing. ACM Trans. Graph. **32**(6), 169:1–169:11 (2013). https://doi.org/10.1145/2508363.2508374
28. Prisacariu, V.A., Reid, I.D.: PWP3D: real-time segmentation and tracking of 3d objects. Int. J. Comput. Vis. **98**(3), 335–354 (2012). https://doi.org/10.1007/s11263-011-0514-3
29. Rosenhahn, B., Brox, T., Weickert, J.: Three-dimensional shape knowledge for joint image segmentation and pose tracking. Int. J. Comput. Vis. **73**(3), 243–262 (2007). https://doi.org/10.1007/s11263-006-9965-3
30. Rublee, E., Rabaud, V., Konolige, K., Bradski, G.R.: ORB: an efficient alternative to SIFT or SURF. In: Metaxas, D.N., Quan, L., Sanfeliu, A., Gool, L.V. (eds.) IEEE International Conference on Computer Vision, ICCV 2011, Barcelona, Spain, November 6-13, 2011, pp. 2564–2571. IEEE Computer Society (2011). https://doi.org/10.1109/ICCV.2011.6126544
31. Rusinkiewicz, S., Levoy, M.: Efficient variants of the ICP algorithm. In: 3rd International Conference on 3D Digital Imaging and Modeling (3DIM 2001), 28 May - 1 June 2001, Quebec City, Canada, pp. 145–152. IEEE Computer Society (2001). https://doi.org/10.1109/IM.2001.924423
32. Schmaltz, C., Rosenhahn, B., Brox, T., Weickert, J.: Region-based pose tracking with occlusions using 3d models. Mach. Vis. Appl. **23**(3), 557–577 (2012). https://doi.org/10.1007/s00138-010-0317-5
33. Scona, R., Jaimez, M., Petillot, Y.R., Fallon, M.F., Cremers, D.: Staticfusion: background reconstruction for dense RGB-D SLAM in dynamic environments. In: 2018 IEEE International Conference on Robotics and Automation, ICRA 2018, Brisbane, Australia, May 21-25, 2018, pp. 1–9. IEEE (2018). https://doi.org/10.1109/ICRA.2018.8460681

34. Stoiber, M., Pfanne, M., Strobl, K.H., Triebel, R., Albu-Schäffer, A.: SRT3D: a sparse region-based 3d object tracking approach for the real world. Int. J. Comput. Vis. **130**(4), 1008–1030 (2022). https://doi.org/10.1007/s11263-022-01579-8
35. Stückler, J., Behnke, S.: Multi-resolution surfel maps for efficient dense 3d modeling and tracking. J. Vis. Commun. Image Represent. **25**(1), 137–147 (2014). https://doi.org/10.1016/j.jvcir.2013.02.008
36. Sturm, J., Engelhard, N., Endres, F., Burgard, W., Cremers, D.: A benchmark for the evaluation of RGB-D SLAM systems. In: 2012 IEEE/RSJ International Conference on Intelligent Robots and Systems, IROS 2012, Vilamoura, Algarve, Portugal, October 7-12, 2012, pp. 573–580. IEEE (2012). https://doi.org/10.1109/IROS.2012.6385773
37. Sun, J., Xie, Y., Chen, L., Zhou, X., Bao, H.: Neuralrecon: real-time coherent 3d reconstruction from monocular video. In: IEEE Conference on Computer Vision and Pattern Recognition, CVPR 2021, virtual, June 19-25, 2021, pp. 15598–15607. Computer Vision Foundation / IEEE (2021). https://doi.org/10.1109/CVPR46437.2021.01534, https://openaccess.thecvf.com/content/CVPR2021/html/Sun_NeuralRecon_Real-Time_Coherent_3D_Reconstruction_From_Monocular_Video_CVPR_2021_paper.html
38. Tjaden, H., Schwanecke, U., Schömer, E., Cremers, D.: A region-based gauss-newton approach to real-time monocular multiple object tracking. IEEE Trans. Pattern Anal. Mach. Intell. **41**(8), 1797–1812 (2019). https://doi.org/10.1109/TPAMI.2018.2884990
39. Wang, J., Chen, M., Karaev, N., Vedaldi, A., Rupprecht, C., Novotny, D.: Vggt: visual geometry grounded transformer. In: Proceedings of the IEEE/CVF Conference on Computer Vision and Pattern Recognition (2025)
40. Wang, S., Leroy, V., Cabon, Y., Chidlovskii, B., Revaud, J.: Dust3r: geometric 3d vision made easy. In: CVPR (2024)
41. Wasenmüller, O., Meyer, M., Stricker, D.: Corbs: comprehensive RGB-D benchmark for SLAM using kinect v2. In: 2016 IEEE Winter Conference on Applications of Computer Vision, WACV 2016, Lake Placid, NY, USA, March 7-10, 2016, pp. 1–7. IEEE Computer Society (2016). https://doi.org/10.1109/WACV.2016.7477636
42. Whelan, T., Johannsson, H., Kaess, M., Leonard, J.J., McDonald, J.: Robust tracking for real-time dense rgb-d mapping with kintinuous (2012)
43. Whelan, T., Leutenegger, S., Salas-Moreno, R.F., Glocker, B., Davison, A.J.: Elasticfusion: Dense SLAM without A pose graph. In: Kavraki, L.E., Hsu, D., Buchli, J. (eds.) Robotics: Science and Systems XI, Sapienza University of Rome, Rome, Italy, July 13-17, 2015 (2015). https://doi.org/10.15607/RSS.2015.XI.001, http://www.roboticsproceedings.org/rss11/p01.html
44. Xu, Y., Nan, L., Zhou, L., Wang, J., Wang, C.C.L.: Hrbf-fusion: accurate 3d reconstruction from RGB-D data using on-the-fly implicits. ACM Trans. Graph. **41**(3), 35:1–35:19 (2022). https://doi.org/10.1145/3516521
45. Zhang, C., Hu, Y.: Cufusion: accurate real-time camera tracking and volumetric scene reconstruction with a cuboid. Sensors **17**(10), 2260 (2017). https://doi.org/10.3390/s17102260
46. Zhang, J., Zhu, C., Zheng, L., Xu, K.: Rosefusion: random optimization for online dense reconstruction under fast camera motion. ACM Trans. Graph. **40**(4), 56:1–56:17 (2021). https://doi.org/10.1145/3450626.3459676

Learning A Deep Second-Order Unfolding Model for Arbitrary-Scale Depth Map Super-Resolution

Hao Ren[1], Lijun Zhao[1(✉)], Jinjing Zhang[2], Huihui Bai[3], and Anhong Wang[1]

[1] Taiyuan University of Science and Technology, Taiyuan 030024, China
leejun@tyust.edu.cn, s202315110476@stu.tyust.edu.cn

[2] North University of China, Jiancaoping District, Taiyuan 030051, China
zjj_ginger@nuc.edu.cn

[3] Institute of Information Science, Beijing Jiaotong University, Beijing 100044, China
hhbai@bjtu.edu.cn

Abstract. Depth map Super-Resolution (DSR) is a pivotal foundation for spatial computing in virtual-real fusion scenarios, with deep unfolding networks being a promising research approach. However, most existing deep unfolding methods rely on first-order optimization algorithms, suffering from slow convergence and sub-optimal learning efficiency. To tackle these issues, we propose a Second-order semi-smooth Newton Unfolding Network (SNU-Net) for arbitrary-scale DSR, which is formed by expanding DSR optimization model via the second-order semi-smooth Newton algorithm. SNU-Net adopts a two-stage progressive reconstruction framework, comprising two main parts: augmented Lagrange multiplier update network and Depth map reconstruction Network (DNet) which is build upon First-order reconstruction Network (FNet) and Second-order reconstruction Network (SNet). Here, the FNet handles initial feature mapping and shallow structure recovery, while the SNet conducts multi-scale feature transformation and fusion to progressively refine depth features. To achieve arbitrary-scale DSR, we introduce a decoupled semi-scale sampling mechanism to resolve structural information loss in previous unfolding networks caused by the mapping relationships at different resolutions merely involving a single-stage up and down sampling process. This mechanism divides the up-sampling process into two consecutive sub-stages: semi-scale sampling and fine sampling. Comprehensive experiments have demonstrated that the proposed SNU-Net outperforms several methods, achieving superior reconstruction fidelity and structural consistency.

Keywords: Depth map super-resolution · Deep Unfolding · Arbitrary-scale up-sampling · Semi-scale sampling

A. Hinkenjan et al. (Eds.): ICXR 2025, LNCS 16428, pp. 210–222, 2026.
https://doi.org/10.1007/978-981-95-7195-6_12

1 Introduction

Guided Depth map Super-Resolution (GDSR) task is one of the core supporting technologies for Augmented Reality (AR) and Mixed Reality (MR) applications, which aims to recover High-Resolution (HR) depth map from Low-Resolution (LR) one with the help of a paired HR color image, and its performance directly determines the accuracy and user experience of downstream tasks. In MR hand tracking, LR depth maps can cause blurry gesture edges, resulting in interaction delays or misidentification. High quality GDSR can reduce depth edge localization errors and ensure real-time response to gesture commands [15,16]. If there is a lack of efficient GDSR solutions, the above system will need to rely on higher cost depth sensors, or reduce the interaction frame rate to be compatible with LR data. Therefore, developing a high-performance GDSR is of great significance for downstream tasks such as AR and MR. In GDSR, let $L \in \mathcal{R}^{1\times m\times n}$ and $H \in \mathcal{R}^{1\times M\times N}$ denote the acquired LR and corresponding HR depth maps respectively. The degradation model can be mathematically formulated as:

$$\arg\min_{H} \frac{1}{2}\|L - QKH\|_2^2 + \lambda\, g(H), \tag{1}$$

where λ denotes the trade-off parameters and g is a regularization function. Q and K denote down-sampling operators and blurring kernels.

Within the early model-based depth recovery methods, adaptive auto-regressive optimization model [1] uses bilateral filters to get adaptive weights of auto-regressive term to better mine contextual information. Although traditional model-based methods are interpretable, they have high computational complexity. The latest advances in deep learning algorithms have completely changed the field of GDSR due to their powerful representation capabilities. For instance, Ye et al. [3] introduced a progressive multi-branch aggregation network, named PMBA-Net, which strategically leveraged iterative up-sampling and down-sampling residual operations and multi-stage attention mechanisms to progressively enhance the boundary features of depth maps. Unlike the PMBA-Net, Tang et al. [4] proposed a multi-task learning framework to achieve depth map SR. However, the CNN-based reconstruction methods are inherently lacking in interpretability due to their network black box properties.

Recently, some researchers have tried to combine traditional mathematical models with deep networks to construct different deep unfolding models. For instance, Zhou et al. [5] established local and non-local priors and embedded them into the deep extension network, thereby enhancing the performance of image SR results. The above GDSR methods only consider super-resolution with fixed integer-scale factors (×4, ×8, ×16). In the real world, people need to continuously zoom in and out to view the details of specific areas, so using arbitrary-scale SR for reconstruction is of great significance for the practical application. But few previous works discuss how to implement DSR of arbitrary scale factor. Recently, Wang et al. [6] proposed to construct the continuous representation of depth map through geometric space aggregator, and realized the DSR based on RGB guidance at arbitrary-scale. Zhang et al. [7] proposed to insert high-low frequency prior information into an optimization model to get an arbitrary-scale DSR unfolding network. Although the existing deep unfolding based networks are constructed by unfolding mathematical optimization model, most prevalent deep unfolding methods rely on the first-order algorithm, such as Half Quadratic Splitting (HQS) and Alternating Direction Method of Multiplier (ADMM) to solve the optimization problem. The first-order optimization algorithms typically exhibit slower convergence rate and are more prone to being trapped in local optimal solutions. All of the above problems hinder the efficiency of deep unfolding networks, so it is essential to further study it.

Departing from traditional first-order models, the second-order semi-smooth Newton optimization algorithm can enable faster convergence and enhanced recovery accuracy. We leverage this algorithm to build up an arbitrary-scale DSR method. The main contributions of the proposed method are summarized as follows:

1. We propose a deep second-order unfolding model by expanding GDSR optimization model via the second-order Semi-smooth Newton (SN) algorithm for arbitrary-scale DSR, named SNU-Net, breaking through the bottlenecks traditional first-order optimization algorithms, e.g., HQS, ADMM, such as slow convergence and tendency to get trapped in local of optima.
2. The proposed SNU-Net adopts a two-stage progressive reconstruction approach, which is composed of two main parts: augmented Lagrange Multiplier Update (LMU) and Depth map reconstruction Network (DNet). DNet is build upon the First-order reconstruction sub-Network (FNet) and the Second-order reconstruction sub-Network (SNet). The FNet takes charge of initial feature mapping and shallow structure recovery, while the SNet conducts multi-scale feature transformation and fusion to progressively refine depth features.
3. A semi-scale sampling strategy is proposed to decouple the projection process into two consecutive sub-stages, which can suppress the information loss caused by single-stage sampling in previous DSR unfolding methods. This mechanism divides the upsampling process into two consecutive sub-stages: semi-scale sampling and fine sampling.

We organize the rest as follows. First, we will present the proposed method in Sect. 2. Secondly, experimental results are provided and analyzed in Sect. 3. Finally, conclusions are given in Sect. 4.

2 The Proposed Method

2.1 Problem Formulation

The goal of image super-resolution (SR) is to solve the inverse operation of Eq. (1), to find the mapping relationship between low-resolution LR and HR images. In practical applications, due to the typically complex degradation conditions of SR, which is usually an ill-posed problem. Moreover, previous unfolding network-based depth map SR methods [5] generally perform unfolding in the image domain. In contrast, we impose constraints on the image and map H to the feature domain via the feature transformation matrix $E \in \mathcal{R}^{C\times M\times N}$, thereby formulating the following optimization problem:

$$\arg\min_{H} \frac{1}{2}\|L - QKH\|_2^2 + \lambda g(Z) \qquad \text{s.t. } Z = EH. \tag{2}$$

Next, we leverage the augmented Lagrangian method to turn Eq. (2) to the following optimization problem:

$$\mathcal{L}(H, Z, \Lambda) = \arg\min_{H}\frac{1}{2}\|L - QKH\|_2^2 + \lambda g(Z) + \langle \Lambda, Z - EH\rangle + \frac{\rho}{2}\|Z - EH\|_2^2. \tag{3}$$

where Λ is the Lagrangian multiplier and ρ stands for penalty parameters. $\langle \Lambda, Z-EH\rangle$ denotes the inner product of Λ and $Z - EH$. The above optimization problem can be efficiently solved by decomposing it into the following two sub-problems, that is the alternating update of (H^n, Z^n) and Λ^n, which can be written as:

$$(H^n, Z^n) = \arg\min_{H,Z}\mathcal{L}(H, Z, \Lambda^{n-1}), \tag{4}$$

$$\Lambda^n = \Lambda^{n-1} + \rho(EH^n - Z^n). \tag{5}$$

First, we concentrate on solving the sub-problem in Eq. (4). Consequently, to obtain the minimum values for H and Z, we set $\frac{\partial\mathcal{L}}{\partial Z} = 0$ and $\frac{\partial\mathcal{L}}{\partial H} = 0$, which constitutes the solution conditions for the sub-problem in Eq. (4). These conditions can be mathematically formulated as follows:

$$\alpha\partial g(Z) - \Lambda + \rho(Z - EH) = 0, \tag{6}$$

$$(QK)^T(QKH - L) + E^T(\Lambda + \rho(EH - Z)) = 0, \tag{7}$$

in which $\partial g(Z)$ represents the sub-derivative of $g(Z)$ and $g(\cdot)$ is the L1-norm. By introducing the soft-thresholding function $S(\cdot)$ with the threshold as (λ/ρ), the update of Z derived from Eq. (6) can be written as:

$$Z = S\left(\frac{\Lambda}{\rho} + EH\right). \tag{8}$$

Next, by substituting Eq. (8) into Eq. (7) and only treating H as the unknown variable, we can obtain the following equation:

$$(QK)^T(QKH - L) + E^T\left\{\Lambda + \rho\left[EH - S\left(\frac{\Lambda}{\rho} + EH\right)\right]\right\} = 0. \tag{9}$$

Subsequently, let's define the left-hand side of Eq. (9) as $F(H)$. The semi-smooth Newton method treats Eq. (9) as a set of nonlinear equations, entailing intricate calculations. Due to $F(H)$ being both convex and non-negative with respect to H, solving $F(H) = 0$ is equivalent to solving $\|F(H)\|_2^2$. Hence, we employ gradient-descent algorithm to derive the solution of Eq. (9), which can be written as:

$$F(H^{n-1}) = (QK)^T(QKH^{n-1} - L) + E^T\{\Lambda^{n-1} + \rho[EH^{n-1} - S(\frac{\Lambda^{n-1}}{\rho} + EH^{n-1})]\}, \tag{10}$$

$$G(H^{n-1}) = (QK)^T F(H^{n-1})(QK) + \rho E^T\left\{[EF(H^{n-1})] \odot \left[1 - S\left(\frac{\Lambda^{n-1}}{\rho} + EH^{n-1}\right)\right]\right\}, \tag{11}$$

$$H^n \leftarrow H^{n-1} - \eta G(H^{n-1}), \tag{12}$$

where $n \in \{1, 2, 3, \ldots\}$ represents the n-th gradient-descent iteration, 1 represents a matrix with all elements being 1. $F(H^{n-1})$ denotes the sub-derivative and $G(H^{n-1})$ the second-derivative of $\|F(H)\|_2^2$ with respect to H^{n-1}. η denotes the learnable step-size. After substituting the Eq. (8) into Eq. (5), the Lagrangian multiplier Λ^n can be written as follows:

$$\Lambda^n = \Lambda^{n-1} + \rho\left(EH^n - S\left(\frac{\Lambda^{n-1}}{\rho} + EH^n\right)\right). \tag{13}$$

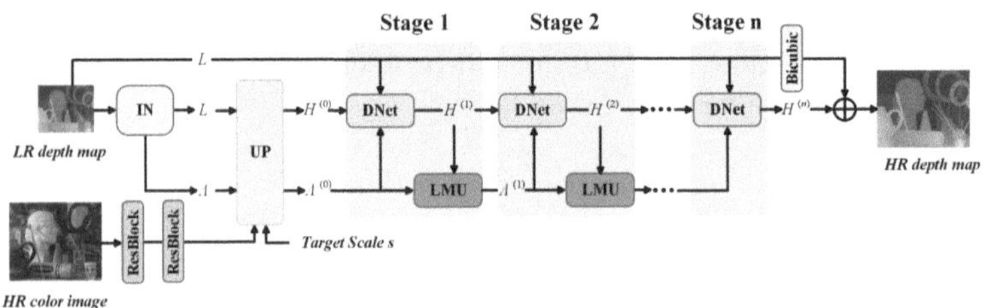

Fig. 1. The diagram of the proposed SNU-Net.

2.2 Deep Unfolding

According to joint alternative updating of Eq. (10), Eq. (11), Eq. (12) and Eq. (13), the iterative optimization procedures are expanded into the FNet, SNet, and LMU, which constitute the interpretable SNU-Net for solving the arbitrary-scale DSR problem. Here, FNet and SNet are combined together to form the DNet for depth map reconstruction. The overall framework of SNU-Net is shown in Fig. 1. Specifically, given the degraded image L and color image $C \in \mathcal{R}^{3\times M\times N}$, some basic variables including L, the HR image H, and the multiplier $\Lambda \in \mathcal{R}^{1\times M\times N}$ are initialized through the INitialization (IN) module. Some initialized variables first reach the target resolution through an up-sampling module and then go through iterative update of DNet and LMU with n stages to

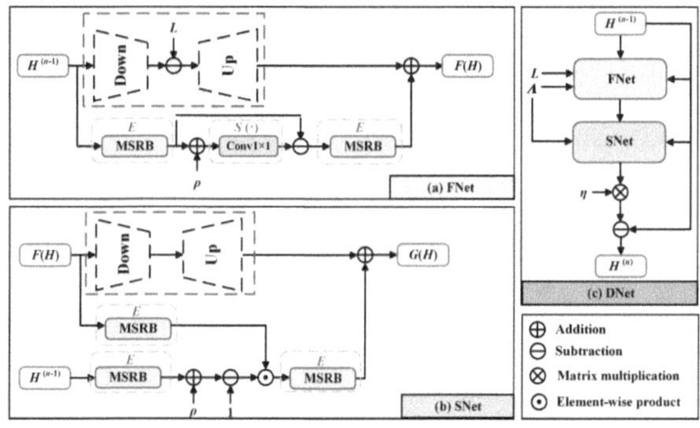

Fig. 2. The structures of the FNet (a), SNet (b), DNet (c).

obtain the final restored image $D_{SR} \in \mathcal{R}^{1 \times M \times N}$. Each stage corresponds to one SN iteration in the SN algorithm by solving Eq. (3). Additionally, the IN module plays a role in expanding the number of channels and preliminary feature extraction, including one 1×1 convolution layer and two Residual Blocks, denoted as ResBlock. The up-module directly adopts the fusion module of DASUNet [7]. To prevent information loss, the bypass with Bicubic interpolation is used to assist LR image reconstruction. Next, we introduce these sub-networks in detail.

Depth Map Reconstruction Sub-Network (DNet). The DNet is designed by following Eq. (10), Eq. (11) and Eq. (12) in the SN algorithm. As shown in Fig. 2(c), the inputs of the DNet in the n-th stage include the multiplier Λ, LR depth map $L \in \mathcal{R}$, and the updated image H^{n-1} from the previous stage. The output of the DNet is the new updated image H^n. We use a single step of gradient descent. In addition, to improve the learning capacity, the original feature transformation matrix E and its transpose are substituted with learnable layer f_e, which is a Multi-Scale Residual Block (MSRB), as shown in Fig. 3(c). While the nonlinear function $S(\cdot)$ and its sub-gradient $S_d(\cdot)$ are approximated by the 1×1 convolution layer f_s. As a result, the DNet is designed according to the following steps.

Step 1: The First-order reconstruction sub-Network (FNet). As shown in Fig. 2(a), to obtain first-order reconstruction result, Eq. (10) can be expanded as the following equations:

$$\begin{cases} F_a^n = Up[L - Down(H^{n-1})], \\ F_b^n = f_s(\Lambda + f_e(H^{n-1})), \\ F_c^n = f_e(\Lambda + \rho[f_e(H^{n-1}) - F_b^n]), \\ F^n = F_a^n + F_a^n, \\ F^n = Res(F^n), \end{cases} \tag{14}$$

in which F_a^n represents the mapping between the depth map feature in the previous stage and the LR depth features L. We use one down-sampling operation and two ResBlocks to replace QK. $(QK)^T$ is the reverse representation of DK. F_b^n reflects the integration and transformation of feature information by the auxiliary variable Z during the iterative process. It is an intermediate quantity used to connect the depth map features of the preceding and succeeding stages. Finally, ResBlock is introduced to further optimize and disseminate information.

Step 2: The Second-order reconstruction sub-Network (SNet). As shown in Fig. 2(b), after the FNet, the SNet can obtain the first-order reconstruction results $F(H^{n-1})$, which are the key conditions for SNet. The Eq. (11) can be re-written as:

$$\begin{cases} G_a^n = Up(DownF(H^{n-1})), \\ G_b^n = f_e[f_e(F(H^{n-1}))] \odot [1 - f_s(\Lambda + f_e(H^{n-1}))], \\ G_c^n = G_a^n + G_b^n, \\ G^n = Res(G_c^n). \end{cases} \tag{15}$$

The SNet is got by entirely unfolding the given equations. It performs feature transformation, fusion, and optimization on the first-order reconstruction results from various aspects. Firstly, the upsampling and downsampling operations are applied on G_a^n to adjust the resolution of feature maps at different scales, aiming to align features for subsequent processing. Secondly, G_b^n leverages different functions (f_s, f_e) for feature extraction, screening, and weighting, which can effectively fuse diverse features to enhance representation ability. Then, the *ResBlock* is utilized to learn feature changes, enabling high-throughput information transfer between stages and preventing information loss, thus ensuring the integrity of the reconstruction process. Finally, the update of Eq. (12) can be written as:

$$H^n = H^{n-1} - \eta G^n. \tag{16}$$

In summary, DNet is mainly composed of FNet and SNet. Through a progressive reconstruction process, it can effectively extract and fuse different scales features.

Lagrange Multiplier Update (LMU). The Lagrange multiplier update is got in accordance with Eq. (13) of the SN algorithm. For the LMU in the n-th restoration stage, H^n and Λ^{n-1} are the inputs, and the output is Λ^n. In line with Eq. (13), the LMU can be written as follows:

$$\Lambda^n = \Lambda^{n-1} + f_e H^n - f_s(\Lambda^{n-1} + f_e H^n). \tag{17}$$

Analogous to the DNet, we employ learnable network layers $f_e(\cdot)$ and $f_s(\cdot)$ to replace the feature transformation E and the nonlinear function $S(\cdot)$. As shown in Fig. 3(b), the architecture of the LMU module utilizes the MSRB and 1×1 convolution to respectively implement $f_e(\cdot)$ and $f_s(\cdot)$ within the network.

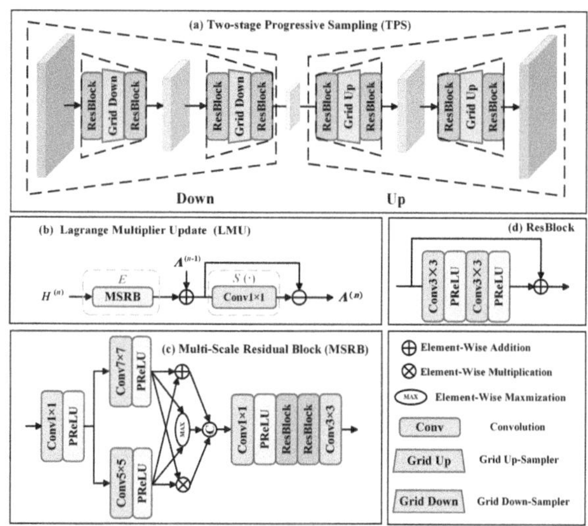

Fig. 3. The structures of TPS (a), LMU (b), MSRB (c) and ResBlock (d).

Two-Stage Progressive Sampling (TPS). Among interpretable depth map super-resolution methods [5,17], when modeling the mapping relationship between the target resolution and the low resolution in existing depth map degradation models, a single-stage up-sampling kernel with a fixed sampling ratio is often used for feature space mapping. However, this kind of method is prone to cause the loss of structural information of the depth map due to the overly-large single-scale up-sampling factor. When directly mapping to the target scale, the drastic change in the feature space will trigger local geometric structure distortion. Especially around complex edge areas of the depth map, grid distortion and abnormal fluctuations of depth values are likely to occur.

To address the above challenges, we propose a two-stage progressive grid up-down sampling framework, as shown in Fig. 3(a). This method decouples the traditional single sampling process into two consecutive stages of operations. Firstly, half-scale sampling is adopted to increase the resolution of the LR feature map to half of the target scale. Then, based on the half-scale feature map, the secondary fine sampling is carried out to reach the target scale. Each sampling stage is combined with a *ResBlock* block to learn the feature representations at different resolutions.

2.3 Loss Function

As done in previous GDSR works [6,17], the data loss with the L_1 norm is employed to regularize the learning of the proposed SNU-Net, which can be written as:

$$Loss_H = \frac{1}{N}\sum_{i=1}^{N} \|H_{SR,i} - H_{GT,i}\|_1, \tag{18}$$

in which H_{GT} is the GT depth map. i denotes the i-th pixel of the depth map, and N is the total pixel number.

Table 1. Objective performance comparison of different DSR approaches on fixed factors from NYU-v2, Middlebury and Lu RGB-D dataset in term of the average RMSE (**Cont** indicate whether networks have continuous up-sampling).

Methods	Cont	NYU-v2			Middlebury			Lu			Average		
		4×	8×	16×	4×	8×	16×	4×	8×	16×	4×	8×	16×
Bicubic	✓	4.28	7.14	11.58	2.28	3.98	6.37	2.42	4.54	7.38	2.99	5.22	8.44
DJFR [8]	×	2.80	5.33	9.46	1.68	3.24	5.62	1.65	3.96	6.75	2.04	4.18	7.28
PAC [9]	×	1.89	3.33	6.78	1.32	2.62	4.58	1.20	2.33	5.19	1.47	2.76	5.53
DMSG [10]	×	3.02	5.38	9.17	1.88	3.45	6.28	2.30	4.17	7.22	2.40	4.33	7.17
FDKN [11]	×	1.86	3.58	6.96	1.08	2.17	4.50	0.82	2.10	5.05	1.25	2.62	5.50
DKN [11]	×	1.62	3.26	6.51	1.23	2.12	4.24	0.96	2.16	5.11	1.27	2.51	5.29
DCTNet [12]	×	1.59	3.16	5.84	1.10	2.05	4.19	0.88	1.85	4.39	1.19	2.35	4.80
JIIF [13]	×	**1.37**	2.76	5.27	1.09	1.82	3.31	0.85	1.73	4.16	1.10	2.10	4.24
AHMF [14]	×	1.40	2.89	5.64	1.07	**1.63**	3.14	0.88	1.66	3.71	1.11	2.06	4.16
MADUNet [5]	×	1.51	3.02	6.23	1.15	1.69	3.23	0.90	1.74	3.86	1.18	2.15	4.44
GeoDSR [6]	✓	1.42	2.62	4.86	1.04	1.68	3.10	0.82	1.59	3.92	1.09	1.96	3.96
DASU-Net [7]	✓	1.44	2.58	4.79	1.03	1.71	3.05	0.81	**1.43**	3.52	1.09	**1.90**	3.78
SNU-Net(our)	✓	1.40	**2.57**	**4.70**	**1.02**	**1.63**	**2.92**	**0.80**	1.50	**3.49**	**1.07**	**1.90**	**3.71**

3 Experimental Results

3.1 Implementation Details

The proposed SNU-Net is implemented using the Pytorch framework and run on the GPU of an NVIDIA GeForce RTX 3090. The proposed method is optimized by the popular Adam optimizer. During the training phase, we randomly crop images to a size of 256 × 256 from the NYU-v2 RGB-D dataset as the GT depth map H_{GT}. Then, we use Bicubic interpolation to degrade H_{GT} by m times, where $m \in (1, 16)$, to obtain the LR depth map L. The fixed 8× up-sampling model is trained in the last 200 epochs, while the initial learning rate is 0.0001 and decays with a factor of 0.2 every 60 epochs. The default iteration number of the proposed SNU-Net is three.

3.2 Comparison with the Latest Different DSR Methods

We utilize the initial 1000 pairs of RGB-D images from the NYU-v2 dataset [18] for training the proposed method, and evaluate the performance of the proposed SNU-Net by testing it with the final 499 pairs of RGB-D images from the NYU-v2 dataset and 30 pairs of RGB-D images from the Middlebury dataset [19]. Six

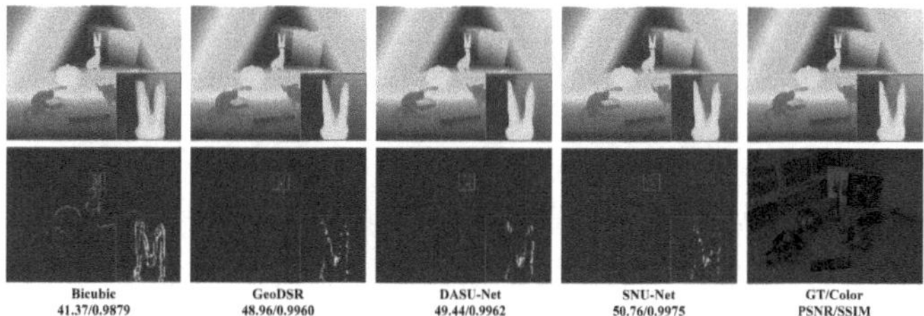

Fig. 4. Comparison of 3.75× up-sampling visualization, error map results and color image of 1-st image of the Lu RGB-D dataset (The brighter the area in the error map, the greater the pixel error).

pairs of RGB-D images from the Lu dataset [20] is used for validation. We employ Structural Similarity (SSIM), Peak Signal-to-Noise Ratio (PSNR), and Root Mean Square Error (RMSE) to assess the performance of the proposed SNU-Net for arbitrary-scale DSR task. Several excellent methods are used to compare with our methods, including DMSG [10], FDKN [11], DKN [11], PAC [9], DCTNet [12], AHMF [14], DJFR [8], MADUNet [5], JIIF [13], GeoDSR [6], and DASU-Net [7]. In certain tables, black and underlined fonts signify the top-performing and second-best performing results respectively. As shown in Table 1, our method has remarkable superiority. When three datasets at three upsampling factors are tested, it achieves optimal results in the ten cases, and attains sub-optimal results in the remaining two cases. In fixed-scale super-resolution tasks, across the NYU-v2, Middlebury, and Lu datasets, our method shows excellent overall performance, only obtaining a sub-optimal value at the 4× scale on the NYU-v2 dataset. Regarding arbitrary-scale super-resolution tasks, it fails to reach the optimal value only at the 8× scale on the Lu dataset.

Table 2. Objective performance comparison of different DSR approaches on non-integer factors on NYU-v2, Middlebury and Lu RGB-D dataset in term of average RMSE.

Methods	NYU-v2		Middlebury		Lu		Average	
	14.60×	17.05×	14.60×	17.05×	14.60×	17.05×	14.60×	17.05×
Bicubic	10.90	11.93	6.00	6.52	7.20	7.96	8.03	8.80
GeoDSR [6]	4.56	5.18	2.77	3.17	3.54	4.24	3.62	4.19
DASU-Net [7]	4.51	5.12	2.75	3.16	3.21	3.88	3.49	4.05
SNU-Net(our)	**4.43**	**5.05**	**2.63**	**3.02**	**3.15**	**3.83**	**3.40**	**3.97**

Furthermore, to demonstrate the advancement of our method for arbitrary-scale DSR tasks, Table 2 gives the RMSE values of up-sampling with non-integer factors for three datasets. The proposed SNUnet achieves state-of-the-art performance across all up-sampling factors. Specifically, at the 14.60× up-sampling

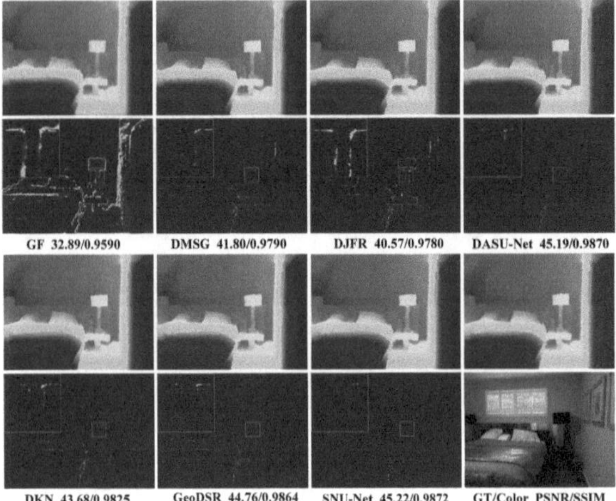

Fig. 5. Comparison of 8× visualization results and error maps of 1012-nd image from the NYU-v2 RGB-D dataset (The brighter the area in the error map, the greater the pixel error).

factor on the Middlebury dataset, our RMSE value is decreased by 0.12, corresponding to 4.5% performance improvement. This indicates that our method possesses extremely strong generalization ability. For an intuitive demonstration of the advantages of our method, we display the visualization results and error maps of the Lu dataset under 3.75× up-sampling, as shown in Fig. 4.

To visually highlight the superiority of our proposed method, we provide the 1012-th visualization result and corresponding error map from the NYU-v2 dataset under 8× upsampling in Fig. 5. Traditional methods like DMSG [10] and DJFR [8] leverage deep learning frameworks. Their simplistic network architectures result in structural distortions in the upsampled outputs. DKN [11] introduces a deformable convolution kernel, which allows it to flexibly adjust to spatial shifts in feature map positions. GeoDSR [6] and DASU-Net [7] adopts a color-depth feature fusion mechanism analogous to a logical "AND" operation, which effectively suppresses texture noise but inadvertently compromises boundary reconstruction fidelity.

In summary, these quantitative results strongly prove the performance superiority of our method in traditional integer-scale factor super-resolution tasks. Moreover, it can effectively achieve super-resolution at arbitrary-scales with a single model.

3.3 Ablation Study

In this section, we train various variants on the NYU-v2 RGB-D dataset and validate them on the Lu RGB-D dataset to assess the proposed method's effectiveness. To demonstrate the TPS module's efficacy, we replace it with single-step projection via grid-sampling, and the results are shown in Table 3.

Table 3. The ablation study of SNU-Net in the Lu RGB-D dataset.

TPS	RMSE		PSNR		SSIM	
	14.60×	17.05×	14.60×	17.05×	14.60×	17.05×
×	3.25	3.99	38.40	36.68	0.9828	0.9785
✓	**3.14**	**3.82**	**38.75**	**37.14**	**0.9834**	**0.9796**

4 Conclusion

In this paper, we propose a novel GDSR model based on the second-order semi-smooth Newton algorithm, and unfold its optimization process as the SNU-Net. The FNet and SNet jointly form the DNet to achieve hierarchical feature refinement. Additionally, the proposed SNU-Net employs a two-stage progressive grid upsampling/downsampling framework, decomposing single-step projection into semi-scale sampling and secondary fine sampling, thereby enhancing feature information complementarity and reducing geometric distortion in complex edge regions. Experimental results show that the proposed SNU-Net outperforms many methods in reconstruction accuracy, and arbitrary-scale generalization, e.g., non-integer factors like 14.60× and 17.05×. Future work will focus on lightweight design and multi-modal adaptation to improve practical application efficiency.

Acknowledgements. This work was supported by National Natural Science Foundation of China (62202323, 62331003), Shanxi Scholarship Council of China (2024-130), Shanxi Province Science Foundation for Youth (202203021222047), The Shanxi Province Third Batch of Outstanding Doctoral Research Initial Funding in 2022 (98001836), and The First Batch of Doctoral Research Initial Funding in 2023 (110136051).

References

1. Yang, J., Ye, X., Li, K., Hou, C., Wang, Y.: Color-guided depth recovery from RGB-D data using an adaptive autoregressive model. IEEE Trans. Image Process. **23**(8), 3443–3458 (2014)
2. Ferstl, D., Reinbacher, C., Ranftl, R., Rüther, M., Bischof, H.: Image guided depth upsampling using anisotropic total generalized variation. In: Proceedings of the IEEE International Conference on Computer Vision, pp. 993–1000 (2013)
3. Ye, X., et al.: PMBANet: progressive multi-branch aggregation network for scene depth super-resolution. IEEE Trans. Image Process. **29**, 7427–7442 (2020)
4. Tang, Q., et al.: Bridgenet: a joint learning network of depth map super-resolution and monocular depth estimation. In: Proceedings of the 29th ACM International Conference on Multimedia, pp. 2148–2157 (2021)
5. Zhou, M., Yan, K., Pan, J., Ren, W., Xie, Q., Cao, X.: Memory-augmented deep unfolding network for guided image super-resolution. Int. J. Comput. Vision **131**(1), 215–242 (2023)

6. Wang, X., Chen, X., Ni, B., Tong, Z., Wang, H.: Learning continuous depth representation via geometric spatial aggregator. In: Proceedings of the AAAI Conference on Artificial Intelligence, vol. 37, no. 3, pp. 2698–2706 (2023)
7. Zhang, J., Zhao, L., Zhang, J., Chen, B., Wang, A.: Deep arbitrary-scale unfolding network for color-guided depth map super-resolution. In: Chinese Conference on Pattern Recognition and Computer Vision (PRCV), pp. 225–236. Springer, Singapore (2023)
8. Li, Y., Huang, J.B., Ahuja, N., Yang, M.H.: Joint image filtering with deep convolutional networks. IEEE Trans. Pattern Anal. Mach. Intell. **41**(8), 1909–1923 (2019)
9. Su, H., Jampani, V., Sun, D., Gallo, O., Learned-Miller, E., Kautz, J.: Pixel-adaptive convolutional neural networks. In: Proceedings of the IEEE/CVF Conference on Computer Vision and Pattern Recognition, pp. 11166–11175 (2019)
10. Hui, T.W., Loy, C.C., Tang, X.: Depth map super-resolution by deep multi-scale guidance. In: European Conference on Computer Vision, pp. 353–369. Springer, Cham (2016)
11. Kim, B., Ponce, J., Ham, B.: Deformable kernel networks for joint image filtering. Int. J. Comput. Vision **129**(2), 579–600 (2021)
12. Zhao, Z., Zhang, J., Xu, S., Lin, Z., Pfister, H.: Discrete cosine transform network for guided depth map super-resolution. In: Proceedings of the IEEE/CVF Conference on Computer Vision and Pattern Recognition, pp. 5697–5707 (2022)
13. Tang, J., Chen, X., Zeng, G.: Joint implicit image function for guided depth super-resolution. In: Proceedings of the 29th ACM International Conference on Multimedia, pp. 4390–4399 (2021)
14. Zhong, Z., Liu, X., Jiang, J., Zhao, D., Chen, Z., Ji, X.: High-resolution depth maps imaging via attention-based hierarchical multi-modal fusion. IEEE Trans. Image Process. **31**, 648–663 (2021)
15. Voynov, O., et al.: Perceptual deep depth super-resolution. In: Proceedings of the IEEE/CVF International Conference on Computer Vision, pp. 5653–5663 (2019)
16. Mueller, F., Mehta, D., Sotnychenko, O., Sridhar, S., Casas, D., Theobalt, C.: Real-time hand tracking under occlusion from an egocentric RGB-D sensor. In: Proceedings of the IEEE International Conference on Computer Vision, pp. 1154–1163 (2017)
17. Zhao, L., Zhang, J., Zhang, J., Bai, H., Wang, A.: Joint discontinuity-aware depth map super-resolution via dual-tasks driven unfolding network. IEEE Trans. Instrum. Meas. **73**, 1–14 (2024)
18. Silberman, N., Hoiem, D., Kohli, P., Fergus, R.: Indoor segmentation and support inference from RGBD images. In: European Conference on Computer Vision, pp. 746–760. Springer, Heidelberg (2012)
19. Scharstein, D., Pal, C.: Learning conditional random fields for stereo. In: 2007 IEEE Conference on Computer Vision and Pattern Recognition, pp. 1–8. IEEE (2007)
20. Lu, S., Ren, X., Liu, F.: Depth enhancement via low-rank matrix completion. In: Proceedings of the IEEE Conference on Computer Vision and Pattern Recognition, pp. 3390–3397 (2014)

A 3D Simulation Platform for Fuel Handling and Storage Systems

Qixiang Ma[1], Zhiqiang Zhang[2], Zhikai Wen[1], Min Zhang[2], Jian Wu[1], Bo Li[2], Lili Wang[1(✉)], and Peng Zhang[2(✉)]

[1] State Key Laboratory of Virtual Reality Technology and Systems, Beihang University, Beijing 100191, China
wanglily@buaa.edu.cn

[2] Instrumentation and Control Institute, China Nuclear Power Engineering Co., Ltd., Beijing 100840, China
zhangpeng@cnpe.cc

Abstract. The Fuel Handling and Storage System (designation code: PMC) is a critical subsystem in nuclear power plants, responsible for the safe loading, transfer, storage, and retrieval of fuel and core components during refueling. Conventional PMC systems rely heavily on manual visual inspection, and while 2D monitoring based on sensor signals offers supplementary support, it lacks integration of multi-device, multi-viewpoint, and cross-temporal information, limiting safety and efficiency. We present a 3D simulation platform, built with a industrial quasi-digital twin strategy, that combines high-fidelity modeling with spatiotemporal data from industrial encoders to reconstruct and synchronize equipment states. A dedicated hardware–software architecture and control algorithms convert operational data into unified flows driving real-time simulation and 3D rendering. The visualization results are delivered to multiple touchscreen terminals, offering interactive feedback and user-controlled viewpoints that improve coordination among personnel and equipment. The platform enhances information clarity, spatial awareness, and interference or collision avoidance compared with conventional systems. Besides online simulation, the platform also supports offline simulations using historical logs and procedural files, enabling repeated training and reducing potential operational errors in live environments. A built-in spatial mapping algorithm adapts the virtual environment to plants of varying scales. Validation via gripper vibration evaluation and system error analysis confirms spatiotemporal consistency and high simulation accuracy between real and virtual environments, providing a practical foundation for future PMC enhancements.

Keywords: 3D Simulation · Fuel Handling and Storage · Industrial Digital Twin · Interactive Visualization

1 Introduction

The Fuel Handling and Storage System (designation code: PMC, also referred to as RFH in certain updated nomenclature) is a mission-critical subsystem in

A. Hinkenjan et al. (Eds.): ICXR 2025, LNCS 16428, pp. 223–242, 2026.
https://doi.org/10.1007/978-981-95-7195-6_13

nuclear power plants, responsible for the secure receipt, transfer, storage, and retrieval of nuclear fuel and core components during reactor refueling [1]. In current practice, three major devices form the operational core of the PMC: the spent fuel pit crane (SPC), the fuel transfer device (FTD), and the manipulator crane (MC). These components work in sequence to move fuel assemblies between the spent fuel pit, transfer pit, and core pit, strictly following predefined operational procedures. The operational environment imposes stringent constraints. Fuel assemblies must be handled with high positional accuracy under complex conditions involving path planning, mechanical characteristics of the handling devices, and segmented work areas distributed across separate plant buildings to minimize radiation exposure and account for elevated water temperatures. Many tasks take place underwater, often requiring synchronized actions between teams operating in physically isolated zones.

Conventional PMC implementations still rely heavily on manual visual judgment to tolerate positional deviations. Although 2D graphical interfaces based on sensor feedback are used as auxiliary aids, they fail to provide an integrated operational picture that fuses multi-device, multi-view, and cross-temporal information. End-to-end refueling procedures often lack embedded spatiotemporal path-planning capabilities, making it difficult to foresee mechanical interference or procedural conflicts. Furthermore, the underwater working environment restricts the ability to inspect potential collisions from multiple angles in real time, which constrains operational safety. Current procedure validation is often limited to simplified, single-building simulations, reducing applicability to plants with differing structural layouts. The main limitations can be summarized as: (1) fragmented real-time data from independent devices remain unintegrated; (2) operational verification relies on procedural documents and operator experience, with procedure validation rarely accounting for structural variations across facilities; (3) the absence of multi-view, collaboratively controllable, interactive monitoring of equipment status and environmental conditions makes it difficult to detect potential issues in time.

To address these challenges, we develop a PMC 3D Simulation Platform that integrates a complete hardware–software architecture with a industrial quasi-digital twin (DT) strategy. The platform combines detailed 3D models with spatiotemporal data streams from industrial PLC-connected encoders. These measurements are converted into unified control instructions that drive real-time simulation and rendering. In addition to online real-time visualization, the platform offers offline simulation using archived historical operation logs and procedural files, enabling operators to rehearse complex maneuvers and repeat training without disrupting live operations. A suite of control algorithms, including sensor data dropout mitigation to stabilize communication between hardware and software layers, a heuristic early-warning mechanism derived from on-site motion data for collision prediction, and an adaptive speed control model, ensures the robustness of both online and offline simulations. To support deployment in plants with varying layouts, the system incorporates retargeting (or redirection) [6,11,19] techniques from virtual reality (VR) and a multi-stage spatial mapping algorithm that adapts the unified virtual workspace to facilities of different scales. Simulation results are delivered to multiple interactive touchscreen terminals, enabling adjustable viewpoints and coordinated operation among multiple users and devices. This design improves spatial clarity, strengthens situational awareness, and provides actionable feedback beyond the capabilities of traditional systems.

In summary, the main contributions of this work are:

- A complete hardware–software architecture for PMC 3D simulation, inspired by a industrial quasi-DT strategy;
- A suite of control algorithms enhancing simulation robustness, precision, adaptability, and portability;
- A multi-user, touch-enabled 3D visualization interface designed for collaborative fuel-handling and storage operations.

2 Project Background

This section introduces the related work of the project and outlines the physical structure of the PMC on which the 3D simulation platform is modeled.

2.1 Related Work

Digitalization technologies have been increasingly adopted in nuclear power plant subsystems to enhance safety, operational efficiency, and training effectiveness. As the International Atomic Energy Agency (IAEA) has noted, beyond the primary power generation systems, auxiliary subsystems such as the Chemical and Volume Control System [12] and the Reactor Cavity and Spent Fuel Pit Cooling and Treatment System [21] have been early targets for digital integration. These developments reflect a broader trend toward incorporating real-time sensing, advanced simulation, and intelligent control into plant-wide digital infrastructures. Fuel assembly handling, transfer, and storage are core functions of the PMC, ensuring the safe movement of fuel between the spent fuel pit, transfer pit, and reactor core pit [9]. The IAEA has emphasized that digital tools, VR, and robotic systems can accelerate tasks such as fuel unloading and facility decommissioning while improving coordination and safety [10]. Industrial practices increasingly deploy 3D simulation, VR visualization [3], and DT [20] architectures to optimize refueling workflows, support multi-equipment collaboration, and enable predictive fault detection [2,16]. Recent research has advanced DT solutions for nuclear systems [14,18], addressing both physics-informed and data-driven modeling. Examples include reduced-order modeling for reactor physics [7] and hybrid algorithms for parameter identification and state estimation in reactor operation DTs [8]. Other studies have developed hybrid physics– and data-driven DT models for nuclear power plants [4], while prognostic DTs have been explored for auxiliary systems such as NAMAC [13]. Specific DT applications include environmental assisted fatigue assessment for plant components [5].

These works highlight the adaptability of DT frameworks to diverse operational contexts, ranging from heavy mechanical handling to structural health monitoring. The educational and training dimension of VR is also gaining recognition. The Nuclear Institute's Nuclear Reactor Simulator [15] and the IAEA's VR-based research reactor models [17] demonstrate the utility of immersive simulations for both operator training and safeguards education. Scenario-driven VR environments support experiential learning, promote procedural compliance, and can be potentially coupled with DT backends for realistic physics behavior.

2.2 Structural Overview of the Facility

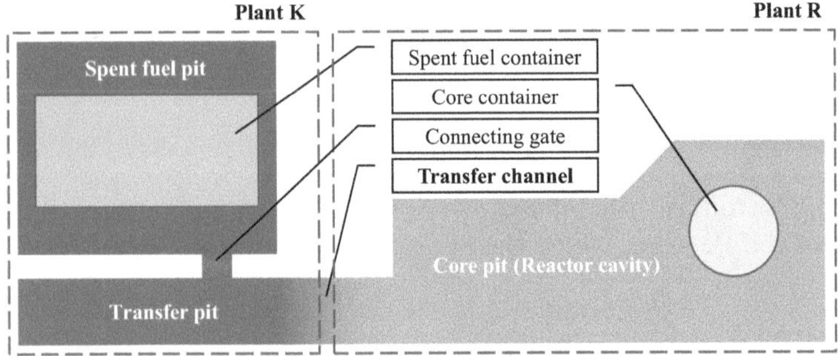

Fig. 1. Abstracted physical layout of PMC-related plant facilities, illustrating the spatial arrangement of three pits across Plant K and Plant R.

The PMC system is designed to handle nuclear fuel assemblies during reactor refueling outages, with a focus on safe and efficient fuel handling and storage operations. As shown in Fig. 1, the overall layout consists of multiple interconnected facility zones that operate in coordination, often with underwater interfaces. Structurally, the system can be abstracted into three primary pits: (1) **Spent fuel pit** – equipped with racked containers for storing non-fissioning (spent or fresh) fuel assemblies; (2) **Core pit** (reactor cavity) – housing the core container (pressure vessel) where nuclear fission reactions occur during plant operation; (3) **Transfer pit** – serving as an intermediate connection between the two. To ensure radiation shielding and operational safety, the spent fuel pit and transfer pit are located in the same reinforced-concrete building, designated as Plant K, and are linked internally by a *connecting gate*, which allows controlled transfer of fuel between the two areas. The core pit is located in a separate reinforced-concrete building, Plant R. The two buildings are joined indirectly via a *transfer channel* extending from the end of the transfer pit.

Figure 2 illustrates the primary handling equipment. Operations in Plant K are mainly performed by: (1) the **spent fuel pit crane** (SPC), while operations in Plant R are handled by (2) the **manipulator crane** (MC). The two buildings are connected by (3) the **fuel transfer device** (FTD), which transports fuel

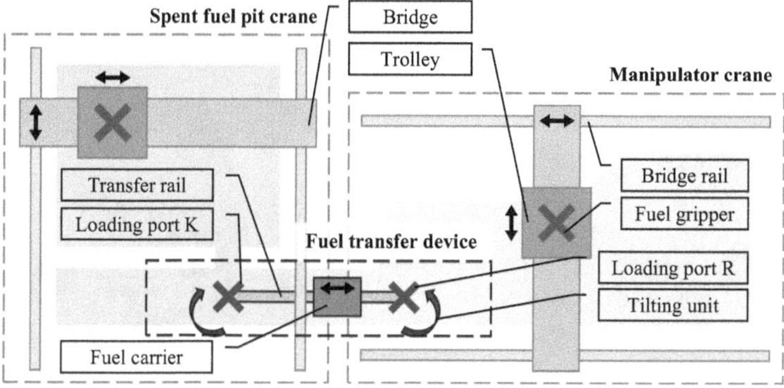

Fig. 2. Abstracted mobility and coordination of PMC-related handling equipment, showing the operational ranges and cooperative workflow of the SPC, FTD, and MC.

between the pits along the transfer channel. Each crane comprises three main components: the *bridge* (large cart), which travels along ceiling-mounted *bridge rails*; the *trolley* (small cart), which moves perpendicularly along the bridge; and the *fuel gripper*, which raises and lowers vertically to engage the fuel assemblies. In the diagram, the vertical position of the gripper is indicated by a dark orange "X." In the SPC, the gripper is suspended by pulleys, steel cables, and hooks, with on-site personnel applying manual damping to prevent excessive swing. The MC instead uses a rigid telescopic sleeve and a pneumatically actuated gripper, enabling precise vertical movement and secure handling during core operations. The FTD consists mainly of a *tilting unit* and a *fuel carrier*. During loading, the SPC delivers a fuel assembly to the tilting unit at *Loading Port K*, marked with a dark gray "X," which is initially vertical. Once positioned, the tilting unit rotates 90° to align the assembly horizontally under controlled hoist slackening (located above). The fuel carrier then moves the assembly along the *transfer rail* to *Loading Port R*, where the hoist tightens to return the tilting unit to a vertical position. The MC then retrieves the assembly for core loading. Unloading follows the same sequence in reverse.

3 Platform Architecture Design

This section presents the detailed architectural hardware-software design of the 3D simulation platform, along with its embedded control algorithms.

3.1 Hardware Architecture

Taking the facility layout described in Subsect. 2.2 as a reference, the hardware architecture shown in Fig. 3 is designed to capture spatiotemporal signals from the field, track the status of equipment and fuel assemblies across Plants K, R, and the transfer channel, and stream data to the rendering terminals.

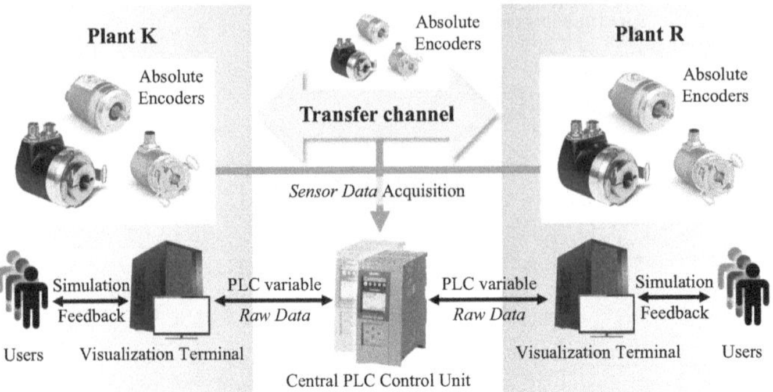

Fig. 3. Overview of the hardware architecture. The central PLC control unit functions as the core hub, relaying raw data from absolute encoders deployed in Plant K and Plant R to the visualization terminals. This real-time data acquisition chain enables simulation feedback to be presented to end users for interactive monitoring and control.

Absolute rotary encoders (see Fig. 4) with PROFINET-IO RT interfaces are installed on key equipment motion axes across Plants K, R, and the transfer channel. Enclosed in stainless-steel housings, these encoders provide 13-bit single-turn and 14-bit multi-turn resolution, with repeatability within ± 1 bit. Their support for real-time industrial Ethernet communication makes them well-suited for continuous position monitoring in nuclear fuel handling. Encoder configurations are selected to match the mechanical characteristics of each subsystem. Bridge and trolley motions in both cranes use rack-and-pinion–driven encoders, which convert linear displacement into rotary motion and are ideal for high-precision linear travel measurement. Main hoisting systems and tilting mechanisms use cable-drum–driven encoders, providing a measurement precision of $\pm 0.05\%$, travel ranges up to 15 m, and operating speeds up to 6 m/s. This configuration enables compact vertical measurement assemblies while supporting long-travel applications.

For safety and reliability, all critical axes employ dual-redundant encoders, with a differential comparison mechanism to detect faults. In the bridge drive, dual encoders are mounted on one side; when their readings differ beyond a set threshold, an alarm is raised but movement continues, allowing operators to switch to the backup channel. If both sides fail, the bridge is brought to a stop. For the trolley, a threshold exceedance triggers an immediate halt, again with backend switching capability. For the main hoist and tilting winch, any excessive discrepancy between the two encoders causes the axis to stop, after which operation can be resumed via backend channel switching.

The PLC control system continuously samples encoder values to perform closed-loop monitoring. For horizontal motion (bridge and trolley), measurement uncertainty is maintained within ± 0.5 mm, with absolute positional accuracy better than 1 mm. For vertical motion (hoisting and tilting), the system achieves an overall control accuracy within ± 5 mm, meeting the strict displace-

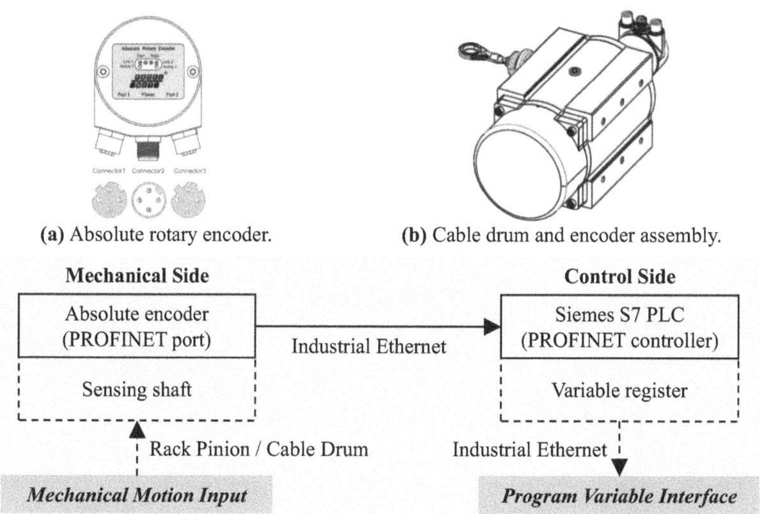

(c) Signal flow diagram from mechanical motion to PLC variable interface.

Fig. 4. PROFINET-based integration of absolute encoders with the facility front-end and the central PLC core hub.

ment tolerances required for nuclear fuel handling. As shown in Fig. 5, all encoder data are transmitted via PROFINET industrial Ethernet to a dual-redundant PLC control unit, and then mapped into program variable tables for use by the graphical workstation. This workstation drives the 3D simulation rendering and user interaction terminals, forming a closed-loop chain of *sensing* → *control* → *simulation* → *interaction* that improves process visibility, fault tolerance, and safety margins during both live operations and training.

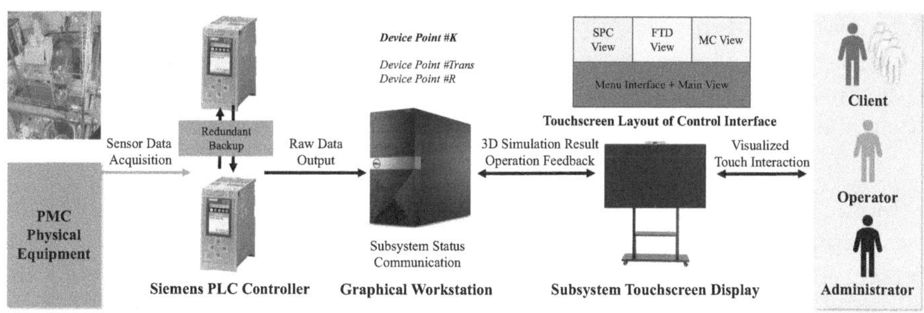

Fig. 5. Macro-level data flow and the hardware design for a representative device point.

Figure 5 illustrates the downstream hardware configuration for a representative equipment point under encoder integration. Taking Plant K as an example, the graphical workstation reads the PLC variable table, processes the data through the software system (Subsect. 3.2), and generates an interactive 3D simulation view. The output is presented on a front-end touchscreen that supports multi-level user interaction. The PLC system is based on Siemens S7-1500 series 4 MB ROM controllers in a dual-redundancy setup. The graphical workstation is equipped with an Intel i9-12900 CPU @ 3.90 GHz, 32 GB RAM, and an RTX 3080 Ti GPU. The front-end display is a 55-inch 4K (16:9) multi-touch screen, enabling high-fidelity visualization and responsive multi-user interaction.

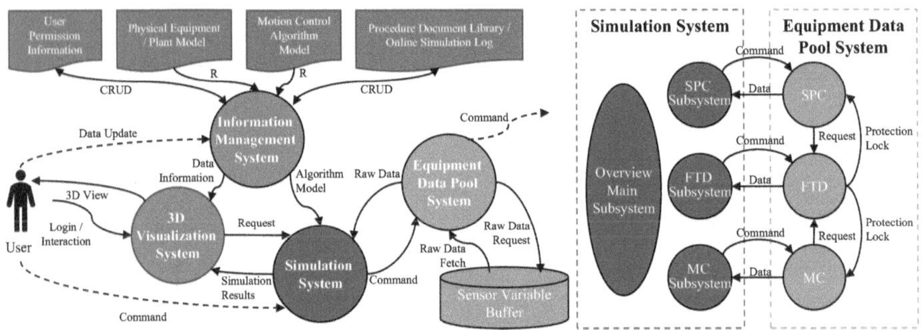

Fig. 6. Software architecture of the PMC 3D simulation platform. The left diagram illustrates the interactions among the four core systems. The right diagram details the internal subsystem structure of the Simulation System, showing bidirectional command–data exchanges with the corresponding physical devices via the Data Pool.

3.2 Software Architecture

The software architecture of the platform, illustrated in Fig. 6, is organized into four core systems: the **Information Management System**, the **Equipment Data Pool System**, the **Simulation System**, and the **3D Visualization System**. These adopt a modular design and operate in close coordination to enable quasi-DT modeling of PMC equipment operating states, command dispatch, simulation-driven reasoning, and interactive 3D visualization.

Information Management System. Situated at the upstream end of the software workflow, the Information Management System provides unified ingestion, storage, scheduling, and updating of all structured data. It interfaces with multiple data sources, including: (1) User permissions and role definitions; (2) PMC plant structure and equipment models; (3) Motion control algorithms and logic models; (4) Online simulation historical operation logs and procedural file repositories. The system integrates permission data, geometric models, and control rules to supply the Simulation and Visualization subsystems with the necessary datasets, while also archiving simulation results from repositories. Administrators can perform full CRUD (create, read, update, delete) operations on user permissions, simulation models, logic rules, and scheduling plans. Operators can manage equipment status. Regular users, in accordance with their access rights, can browse or execute procedural files and review historical logs.

Equipment Data Pool System. The Equipment Data Pool System functions as an intermediary buffer and abstraction layer between the Simulation System and on-site equipment, providing a unified interface for accessing equipment information. Leveraging the PLC Ethernet interface described in Subsect. 3.1, it uses TCP/IP to query sensor variable buffer addresses within the local network, polling at 20 Hz to continuously retrieve raw data. These data include encoder positions, motion feedback, load measurements, and deflection angles of on-site devices. Once acquired, the data are normalized and forwarded to the Simulation System for quasi-DT computations. The Data Pool supports concurrent requests and includes packet-loss mitigation (see Sect. 3.3) to ensure stable, real-time acquisition. It also supports reverse command dispatch (for example, sending emergency stop signals) by relaying alerts or anomaly-based stop commands from the Simulation System back to the equipment control layer. This capability forms the foundation for a preliminary "virtual–physical closed loop" for coordinated control.

Simulation System. The Simulation System is the computational core of the platform, supporting two primary operational modes:

- **Online Simulation**: Reads real-time sensor variables from the Equipment Data Pool to maintain synchronous DT simulations with the physical PMC system. It supports real-time motion computation, rendering, and state prediction, along with command dispatch, emergency stop handling, and simulation log recording for later analysis and traceability.
- **Offline Simulation**: Loads either (1) historical operation logs or (2) procedural files to reconstruct simulation sequences through playback, or uses algorithmic models to predict the outcomes of alternative motion paths. This mode is valuable for operator training, scenario validation, and virtual prototyping. Operation logs share the same raw data format as online simulations, while procedural files define end-to-end path sequences used by nuclear power operators for refueling planning or training.

To enhance modularity and reuse, the Simulation System is organized into four subsystems: (1) **Main Overview Subsystem** handles global simulation modeling, main loop control, time progression, module scheduling, and spatial alignment (Sect. 3.3); (2) **SPC Subsystem** manages the lifting structures and motion logic of the Plant K spent fuel pit crane, including the bridge, trolley, hoist, and encoder components visualization; (3) **FTD Subsystem** models motion control for the transfer channel and associated devices, including transportation paths and posture changes of fuel assemblies between the two plants, while monitoring or simulating protection locks to avoid conflicts between the bridge crane and the fuel handling machine; (4) **MC Subsystem** simulates the telescoping, loading, and unloading operations of the Plant R manipulator crane, ensuring virtual–physical consistency at critical reactor core locations. Each subsystem can operate independently for local testing or be integrated for full-system simulation.

3D Visualization System. The 3D Visualization System serves as the primary interface for user interaction with the Simulation System, offering multiple view modes, parameter displays, and an interactive dashboard. Users log in via a touch-enabled terminal and operate within the privileges granted to their role:

- **Regular Users**: View 3D scenes, observe simulation processes, adjust viewpoints to inspect equipment states, and monitor parameters and trends.
- **Operators**: In addition to the above, perform interactive simulation control, load and import logs or procedural files, edit training paths, trigger emergency stops in online mode, and start or pause offline simulations.
- **Administrators**: In addition to the above, update datasets, manage user accounts, and modify simulation configurations.

The layout follows the four-section dashboard shown in Fig. 5, corresponding to the four Simulation System subsystems. It supports real-time rendering, multi-user synchronized interactions, and automated camera tracking of points of interest. Users can search and highlight specific PMC components, trigger close-up camera views, and preview disassembly animations, providing an intuitive and immersive interaction experience.

3.3 System Control Algorithms

Sensor Data Dropout Mitigation. Short network glitches or PLC jitter can momentarily drop encoder packets, causing state desynchronization or visual popping in the simulation. We use a lightweight hybrid correction that blends the latest valid measurement with constant-velocity extrapolation from recent frames. Let $\delta_{\eta_{i+1}} \in \{0, 1\}$ indicate whether sensor η returns a value at step $i+1$; φ is the inferred parameter and ω the measured parameter:

$$\varphi_{i+1} = \delta_{\eta_{i+1}}\, \omega_{i+1} + \left(1 - \delta_{\eta_{i+1}}\right)\left(\varphi_i + \frac{\varphi_i - \varphi_{i-1}}{\Delta t_i}\, \Delta t_{i+1}\right). \tag{1}$$

When a packet arrives ($\delta=1$), the stream is snapped to the measured update parameter. Otherwise, a smooth prediction is produced by linear extrapolation from the last two frames. This keeps the virtual and physical timelines aligned and suppresses rendering jumps without introducing model-specific parameters.

Collision Detection. In Plant K, the SPC gripper is cable-suspended (four cables, pulleys, hook, gripper). When the trolley brakes from maximum speed to rest, the gripper exhibits post-stop swing whose trajectory is well approximated by a Lissajous-like ellipse. In the ideal undamped case with identical initial kinetic energy, the swing-end amplitude δ scales with the square root of the cable length l, i.e., $\delta \propto \sqrt{l}$, where $l = 8.0 - h$, h is the gripper height (meters). Fitting recorded trajectories with principal-component analysis yields the height-dependent safety margin:

$$\epsilon(h) = k\,(8.0 - h)^{0.5} + b, \tag{2}$$

with k and b obtained from the vibration-fitting study in Subsect. 5.1. Because raw PLC variables do not encode instantaneous swing, the collision checker inflates the fuel-assembly bounding volume by $\epsilon(h)$ before testing against surrounding geometry, thereby reflecting on-site safety envelopes in the DT.

Adaptive Speed Control. The simulation advances component transforms by discrete display integration. For a step from x_k to x_{k+1} over Δt, the physics engine generates an interpolated sequence $S_{x_k} = \mathrm{interp}(x_k, x_{k+1}, \Delta t)$ with $|S_{x_k}| = f\,\Delta t$ at frame rate f. Offline runs driven by procedural files lack timing between anchors x_s and x_t, so we reconstruct temporal states with rule-based speeds derived from site drawings. Motions outside constrained areas use $v_{\mathrm{high}} \approx 0.20 \pm 0.05\,\mathrm{m/s}$; slow zones use $v_{\mathrm{low}} = 0.10\,\mathrm{m/s}$. As shown in Fig. 7(a), the slow-speed region $\mathcal{Z}_{\mathrm{slow}}$ is dilated by the swing margin $\epsilon(h)$ to form $\mathcal{Z}_{\mathrm{slow}} \oplus \epsilon(h)$; the plant boundary $\mathcal{Z}_{\mathrm{bd}}$ and its dilation $\mathcal{Z}_{\mathrm{bd}} \oplus \epsilon(h)$ serve as emergency-stop and warning regions, respectively. When crossing a high/low boundary, we model joystick latency ($\approx 0.5\,\mathrm{s}$) with bounded acceleration $0.2\,\mathrm{m/s^2}$ until the target speed is reached. For a sampling density γ, anchors are linearly subdivided into $\{x_i\}_{i=0}^{\gamma}$ and each segment duration is set by its target speed v_i:

$$S_{x_i} = \mathrm{interp}\left(x_i, x_{i+1}, \frac{\|x_{i+1} - x_i\|}{v_i}\right), \tag{3}$$

then concatenated to yield the full trajectory. Warning regions execute at v_{low} with alerts; emergency regions halt the run with abnormal-state feedback.

Multi-stage Motion Retargeting. In VR, the *translation gain* is:

$$g_t = \frac{\|\Delta \mathbf{X}\|}{\|\Delta \mathbf{P}\|}, \tag{4}$$

where $\Delta \mathbf{P}$ is a displacement in the physical plant and $\Delta \mathbf{X}$ the corresponding displacement in the virtual space. Adjusting g_t allows spatial scaling within perceptual limits. Our multi-stage retargeting maps heterogeneous PMC layouts to a common virtual environment by dividing the plant into semantic regions, each with physical anchors $\mathbf{p}_n^{(i)}, \mathbf{p}_f^{(i)}$ and virtual anchors $\mathbf{x}_n^{(i)}, \mathbf{x}_f^{(i)}$:

$$\mathbf{g}_t^{(i)} = \frac{\mathbf{x}_f^{(i)} - \mathbf{x}_n^{(i)}}{\mathbf{p}_f^{(i)} - \mathbf{p}_n^{(i)}}, \tag{5}$$

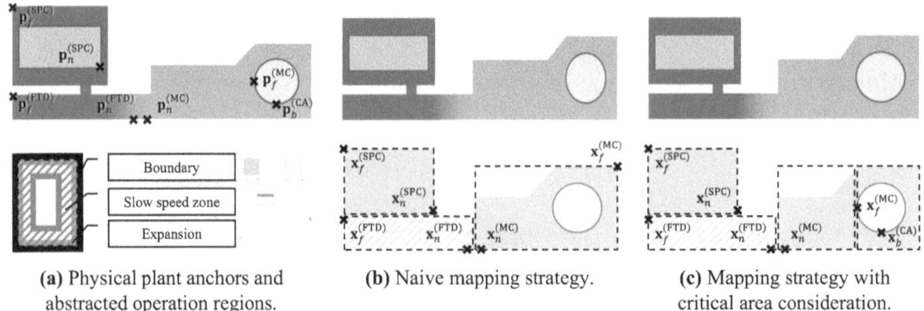

(a) Physical plant anchors and abstracted operation regions.

(b) Naive mapping strategy.

(c) Mapping strategy with critical area consideration.

Fig. 7. Illustration of adaptive speed control zones and facility size retargeting. The diagrams show physical plant anchors, operational regions, and corresponding virtual plant anchors under different mapping strategies. In the naive mapping approach, distortion occurs in the pressure vessel area, whereas incorporating critical area constraints eliminates the distortion. The operational zones shown are illustrative abstractions and do not represent the actual zoning specifications defined in proprietary plant design.

and

$$f_i(\mathbf{p}) = \mathbf{x}_n^{(i)} + \mathbf{g}_t^{(i)} \odot \left(\mathbf{p} - \mathbf{p}_n^{(i)}\right), \tag{6}$$

with $\odot$ the Hadamard product. In the core pit, naive near–far mapping distorts the cylindrical pressure vessel, misaligning feed points and causing pseudo-interpenetration in the DT. To fix this, *critical anchors* ($\mathbf{p}_b^{(\mathrm{CA})}, \mathbf{x}_b^{(\mathrm{CA})}$) are added. Outside the critical zone, Eq. 6 applies as usual; inside, a strict 1:1 mapping preserves geometry integrity (see Fig. 7).

4 Interactive Graphical Interface

The interactive graphical interface serves as the primary human–computer interaction layer of the 3D simulation platform, integrating scene visualization, gesture-based interaction, and multi-perspective camera control. It enables users to intuitively access and manipulate simulation in both online and offline modes.

4.1 Scene Visualization and Gesture Interaction

The 3D scene is reconstructed from CAD models provided by the PMC plant owner, covering both civil structures and major equipment layouts. Original CAD drawings are converted into `.fbx` format via a standardized processing pipeline, preserving geometry hierarchies and texture mapping to ensure accurate digital representation. The finalized plant assets are shown in Fig. 8(a).

To enhance spatial comprehension and maintain rendering efficiency, the visualization system integrates the following features:

- **Level of Detail (LOD) rendering**: As shown in Fig. 8(b), static fuel elements in the pits are rendered with simplified meshes, reducing polygon count and improving frame rates without sacrificing operational context.

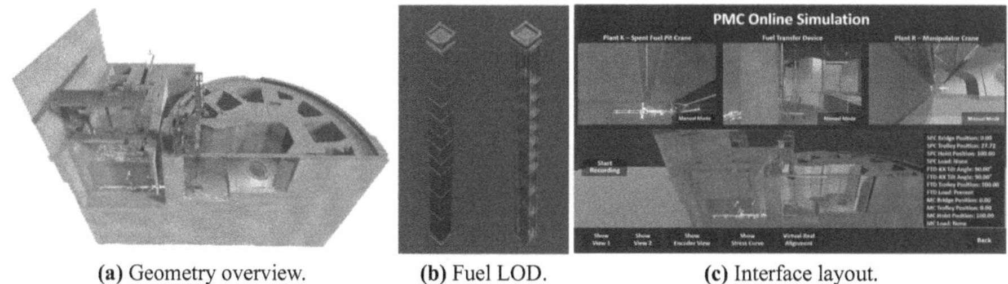

(a) Geometry overview. **(b)** Fuel LOD. **(c)** Interface layout.

Fig. 8. Examples of 3D asset rendering details and an overview of the online simulation visualization interface. (b) shows the full rendered fuel on the left, with 10% simplified meshes for static elements rendering on the right.

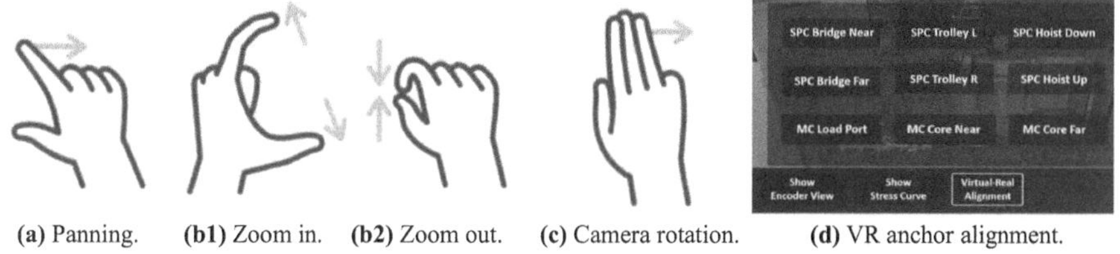

(a) Panning. **(b1)** Zoom in. **(b2)** Zoom out. **(c)** Camera rotation. **(d)** VR anchor alignment.

Fig. 9. Three manual touch-based camera interaction modes and the virtual–real anchor alignment interface.

- **Section view rendering**: Enables cross-sectional cuts of buildings and equipment to reveal internal structures for inspection and training in real-time.
- **Surface for water bodies**: Simulates dynamic water surfaces using a spring system to provide realistic depth cues and physical responses to interactions.
- **Multi-camera architecture**: Comprises three interactive subsystem cameras of SPC, FTD, and MC, along with a fixed global main overview camera for continuous scene monitoring.

Gesture-based interaction is implemented for intuitive control on touch-enabled devices (Fig. 9(a–c)). Users can manually pan, zoom, and rotate the viewport, select interactive components, switch to a director mode for automatic tracking of objects of interest, or perform keyword-based searches to focus on specific components with detailed close-up views. Before system operation, to ensure proper visualization without model interpenetration, users must move the gripper to a designated real-world position and perform manual virtual–real alignment using the anchor alignment interface shown in Fig. 9(d).

4.2 Functional Layout of the Interface

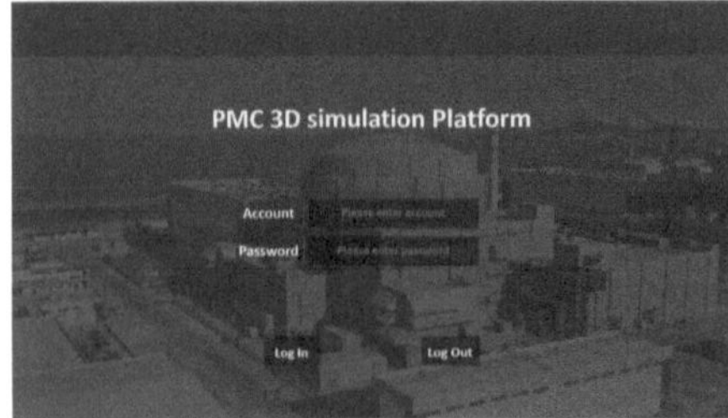

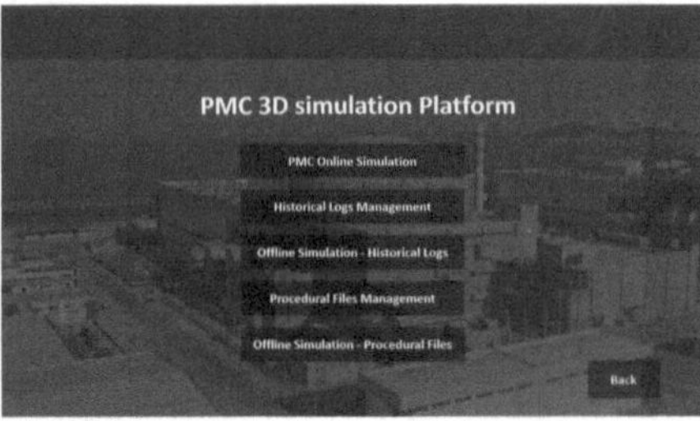

(a) Initialization interface.

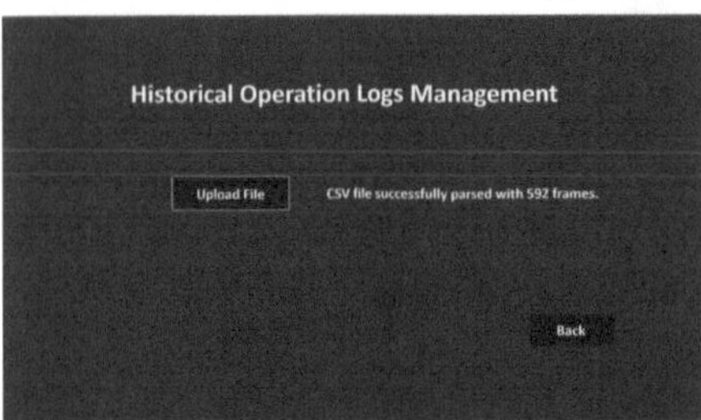

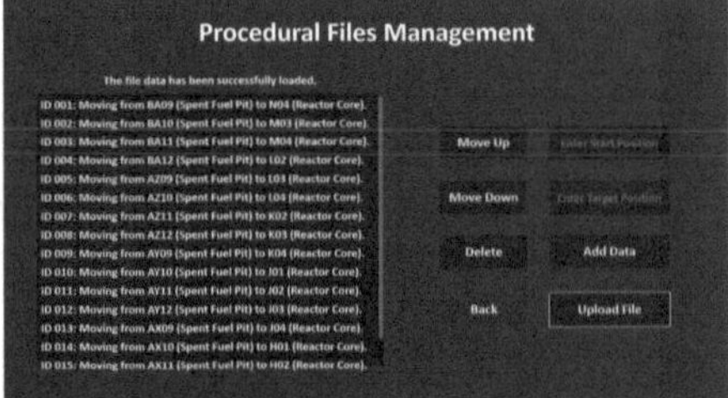

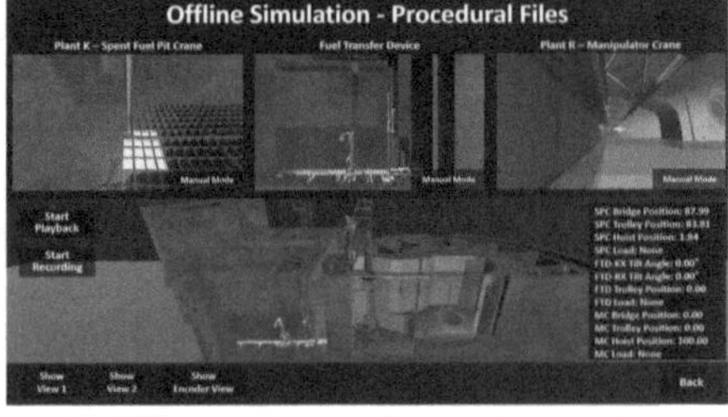

(b) Offline simulation with playback interface. (c) Offline simulation with procedure interface.

Fig. 10. Interface layouts for key platform functions, including initialization, historical log playback, and procedural file-based offline simulation.

The functional layout of the interface, shown in Fig. 10, comprises a login screen, a main menu, and dedicated views for each operational mode:

- **Initialization interface:** Handles user authentication and role-based access control, ensuring secure operation and mode management (Fig. 10(a)).
- **Online simulation interface:** Displays real-time PMC equipment status synchronized with physical devices, supporting live simulation (Fig. 8(c)).
- **Playback interface:** Enables loading and replaying of historical operation logs for offline simulation (Fig. 10(b)).
- **Procedure interface:** Supports loading, editing, training, and execution of procedural files for offline simulation (Fig. 10(c)).

5 System Validation

This section presents the experimental validation of the proposed system, focusing on the gripper vibration fitting process and the analysis of system-level errors. All tests were conducted under realistic operating conditions to ensure the results are representative of actual PMC refueling scenarios.

5.1 Gripper Vibration Fitting Evaluation

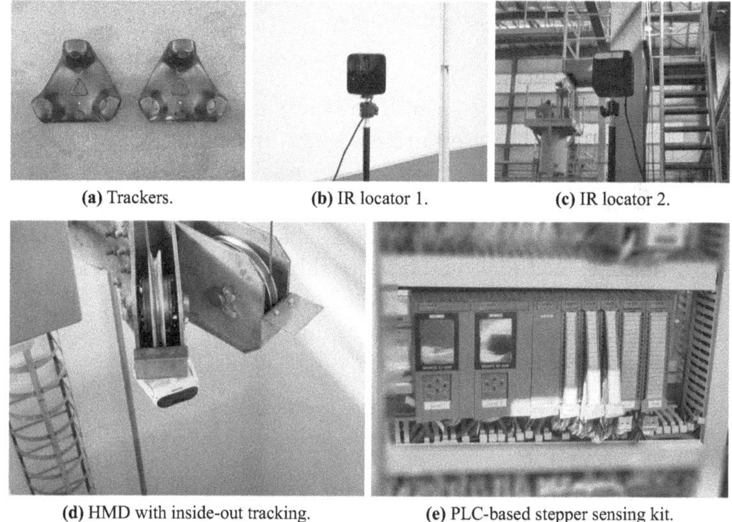

(a) Trackers. **(b)** IR locator 1. **(c)** IR locator 2.

(d) HMD with inside-out tracking. **(e)** PLC-based stepper sensing kit.

Fig. 11. Overview of equipment used for on-site experimental data acquisition.

To characterize the oscillatory behavior of the gripper and to determine collision-related parameters for subsequent error analysis, we recorded motion trajectories under a range of operating conditions. Two complementary acquisition methods were used: (1) optical positioning with the *tracker* setup shown in Fig. 11(a–c); and (2) a novel approach in which an XR headset with *inside-out tracking* capability (Fig. 11(d)) was physically mounted on the gripper to record trajectories using its onboard IMU and visual–inertial fusion algorithms. The latter method effectively addressed the limitation of conventional trackers, which cannot capture trajectories inside the pit at ground level (0 m), thereby enabling complete motion data coverage. In addition, the central PLC control unit illustrated in Subsect. 3.1 has its corresponding stepper sensing kit shown in Fig. 11(e).

Trajectory data were collected at a maximum rate of 60 Hz, theoretically resulting in more than 120,000 points spanning oscillations at multiple heights. The test procedure was as follows: the gripper was positioned at a specified height, the crane's trolley and bridge were accelerated to maximum speed,

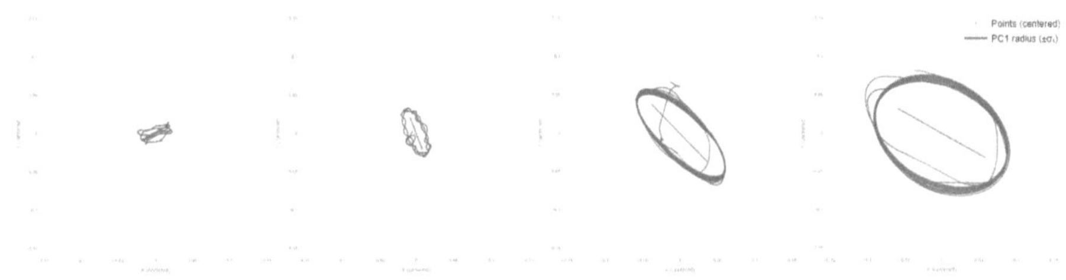

(a) Gripper at height 3m. **(b)** Gripper at height 1m. **(c)** Gripper at height -1m. **(d)** Gripper at height -3m.

Fig. 12. End-effector oscillation trajectories (blue) of the gripper after emergency stops at different heights, with PCA results (principal axis σ_1 in red). The ground level is taken as the 0 m reference. (Color figure online)

and then brought to an abrupt stop. The subsequent free-swing trajectory was recorded in its entirety. Representative results are shown in Fig. 12. For each height, principal component analysis (PCA) was applied to extract the swing eccentricity. The primary axis length σ_1 was taken as the target ϵ for curve fitting, in accordance with Eq. 2. The fitted parameters were $k = 0.0882$ and $b = -0.1721$, yielding the functional relationship $\epsilon(h)$. This model is directly integrated into the simulation platform's collision-warning module to enable early prediction and risk assessment of potential interference events.

5.2 System Error Analysis

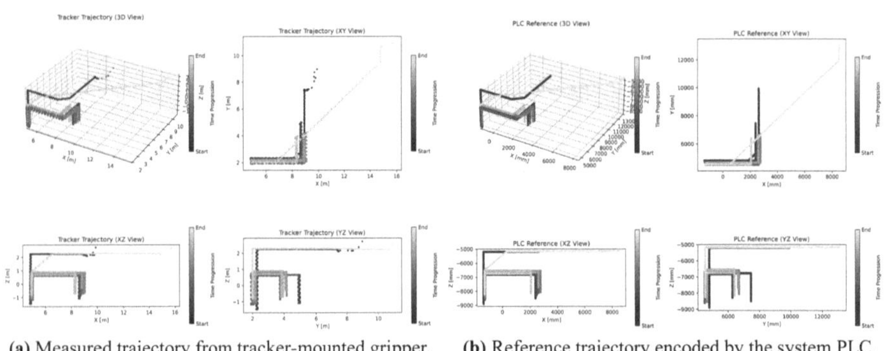

(a) Measured trajectory from tracker-mounted gripper. **(b)** Reference trajectory encoded by the system PLC.

Fig. 13. Pseudo-color visualization of the gripper end-effector trajectory over time, comparing (a) tracker-based measurements and (b) PLC-encoded reference data.

Building on the tracking strategy in Subsect. 5.1, we recorded the gripper's zero-point motion trajectory during continuous fuel-loading operations of the PMC system to analyze the distribution and influencing factors of system error. The dataset covers multiple consecutive loading sequences over a one-hour period.

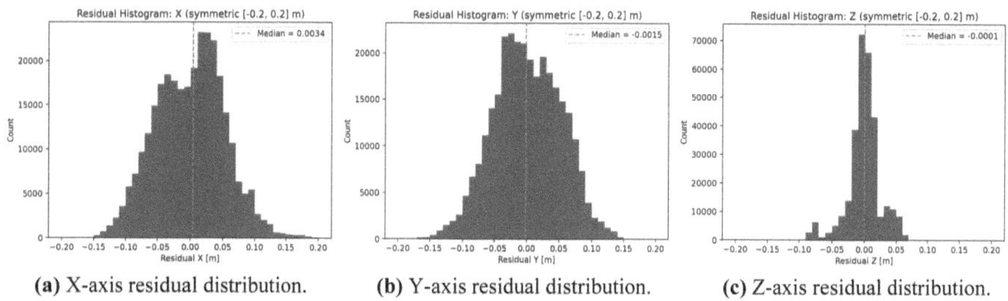

(a) X-axis residual distribution. **(b)** Y-axis residual distribution. **(c)** Z-axis residual distribution.

Fig. 14. Statistical distributions of system residuals along the X, Y, and Z axes.

After 10× uniform downsampling, Fig. 13(a) shows the ground-truth trajectory from the tracker, while Fig. 13(b) shows the corresponding PLC-encoded trajectory retrieved from the Equipment Data Pool System. Qualitatively, the trajectories align closely, indicating consistent motion between the physical and virtual environments, and providing preliminary validation of the 3D simulation platform.

To quantify the effect of fine-scale motion jitter and mechanical characteristics, residuals were computed between the two trajectories. After converting encoder outputs from millimeters to meters and applying a uniform coordinate bias correction, the median residuals in x, y, and z were $m_x = 0.0034$, $m_y = -0.0015$, and $m_z = -0.0001$, respectively. The histogram of these residuals is shown in Fig. 14. Mean residuals for all components were below the vertical motion tolerance of 0.005 m specified in the hardware architecture (see Subsect. 3.1). A joint t-test over all three components yielded $p = 0.9954$, indicating no statistically significant deviation from zero and thus no evident cumulative systematic error. The absolute residual values were $a_x = 0.0438 \pm 0.0537$, $a_y = 0.0428 \pm 0.0523$, and $a_z = 0.0177 \pm 0.0254$, all within the 0.05 m cumulative error tolerance defined in the software architecture. Skewness analysis showed $\gamma_x = 0.070$ and $\gamma_y = -0.036$, both below the industrial threshold of 0.1, indicating good symmetry and minimal tail bias. For z, $\gamma_z = -0.561$ suggested mild negative skewness, likely caused by slight cable elongation under fuel load, manifesting as a small downward drift when loaded.

Table 1. Summary of residual statistics over segmented speed bins.

Speed bin	Count	Residual							
		R_n ($abs \downarrow$)	R_n^{max} ($\downarrow$)	R_x ($abs \downarrow$)	R_x^{max} ($\downarrow$)	R_y ($abs \downarrow$)	R_y^{max} ($\downarrow$)	R_z ($abs \downarrow$)	R_z^{max} ($\downarrow$)
$[0.00, 0.05)$	71887	0.0708 ± 0.0335	0.2165	0.0024 ± 0.0508	0.2031	-0.0025 ± 0.0540	0.1658	-0.0031 ± 0.0250	0.0902
$[0.05, 0.10)$	161679	0.0707 ± 0.0340	0.2171	-0.0016 ± 0.0534	0.2062	**-0.0017** ± 0.0510	0.1794	**0.0006** ± 0.0263	0.0903
$[0.10, 0.15)$	59459	0.0750 ± 0.0356	0.2136	**0.0001** ± 0.0579	0.2054	0.0093 ± 0.0537	0.1702	0.0025 ± 0.0237	0.0950
$[0.15, 0.20)$	7391	**0.0646** ± 0.0343	0.1924	0.0050 ± 0.0543	0.1900	-0.0081 ± 0.0433	0.1374	-0.0015 ± 0.0210	0.0955
$[0.20, 0.25)$	894	0.0702 ± 0.0237	0.1619	0.0421 ± 0.0421	0.1305	-0.0340 ± 0.0229	0.0814	-0.0015 ± 0.0163	0.0874
$[0.25, 0.30)$	12	0.0847 ± 0.0305	**0.1226**	0.0537 ± 0.0214	**0.0948**	-0.0388 ± 0.0304	**0.0631**	-0.0412 ± 0.0274	**0.0849**

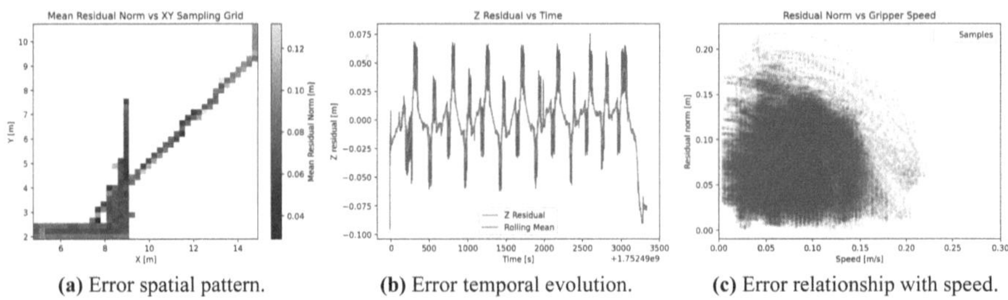

(a) Error spatial pattern. **(b)** Error temporal evolution. **(c)** Error relationship with speed.

Fig. 15. Spatiotemporal characterization of system errors, covering spatial pattern, temporal evolution, and speed correlation.

We further analyzed the spatio-temporal characteristics of the residuals. Figure 15(a) shows a top-view heatmap of mean residual norms, highlighting concentration in critical areas such as the spent fuel rack and connecting gate, with larger deviations in unloaded zones (e.g., near cell (14, 8)). Figure 15(b) plots the z-axis residual time series over the one-hour run, which included seven loading events. The residual exhibits a periodic rise–fall pattern, with peaks largely within the 0.05 m design tolerance; this periodicity is consistent with load-induced cable stretching and oscillations. Finally, Fig. 15(c) shows residual magnitude versus velocity, obtained by differentiating trajectories by timestamp. The $[0, 0.3)$ m/s velocity range was discretized into 0.01 m/s steps. Table 1 further summarizes the residual statistics across different speed bins. It reveals an empirical envelope that decreases with speed, suggesting that at higher velocities, anisotropic effects tend to align error vectors with the motion direction, compressing the residual spread.

6 Conclusion, Limitations, and Future Work

This work presented the design, implementation, and validation of a PMC-oriented 3D simulation platform that integrates hardware sensing, PLC-based control, and multi-level software subsystems for quasi-digital twin modeling. The platform enables real-time visualization, procedural offline simulation, adaptive control algorithms, and motion retargeting, while supporting both operator training and system analysis under realistic plant constraints. Comprehensive experiments, including gripper vibration fitting and system-level error evaluation, demonstrated close correspondence between the virtual and physical systems.

Several limitations remain. First, the digital twin representation focuses on geometric and kinematic fidelity rather than full physical-process coupling, limiting its predictive depth. Second, the current implementation does not provide comprehensive on-site command execution; direct control over critical mechanical subsystems is intentionally restricted for safety reasons. Third, long-term drift or load-induced bias in mechanical components is monitored but not yet addressed through automated correction. Finally, the system lacks intelligent data-driven analytics for long-horizon operational patterns, such as fatigue-induced deviations.

Future work will address these limitations by: (1) extending the DT framework to incorporate higher-fidelity physical and thermal models; (2) enhancing secure bidirectional control channels to support supervised execution of key mechanical actions; (3) developing automated compensation strategies for cumulative drift based on statistical and learning-based approaches; and (4) introducing intelligent analysis modules for predictive maintenance, ergonomic assessment, and multi-scenario optimization of refueling operations.

Acknowledgments. This work is supported by the National Natural Science Foundation of China through Project 61932003, 62372026, by Beijing Science and Technology Plan Project Z221100007722004, by National Key R&D plan 2019YFC1521102, and by the fundamental research funds for the central universities.

References

1. International Atomic Energy Agency: Design of fuel handling and storage systems for nuclear power plants. International Atomic Energy Agency (2003)
2. Bandala, M., et al.: Digital twin challenges and opportunities for nuclear fuel manufacturing applications. Nucl. Eng. Des. **420**, 113013 (2024)
3. Berg, L.P., Vance, J.M.: Industry use of virtual reality in product design and manufacturing: a survey. Virtual Reality **21**(1), 1–17 (2017)
4. Chen, F., et al.: A study on the development of digital model of digital twin in nuclear power plant based on a hybrid physics and data-driven approach. Appl. Therm. Eng. **271**, 126289 (2025)
5. Chen, M., et al.: Development of the environmental assisted fatigue assessment method for nuclear plants in digital twin. Nucl. Eng. Technol. **57**(6), 103402 (2025)
6. Clarence, A., Knibbe, J., Cordeil, M., Wybrow, M.: Stacked retargeting: combining redirected walking and hand redirection to expand haptic retargeting's coverage. In: Proceedings of the 2024 CHI Conference on Human Factors in Computing Systems, pp. 1–13 (2024)
7. Gong, H., Cheng, S., Chen, Z., Li, Q.: Data-enabled physics-informed machine learning for reduced-order modeling digital twin: application to nuclear reactor physics. Nucl. Sci. Eng. **196**(6), 668–693 (2022)
8. Hong, L.Z., Gong, H.L., Ji, H.J., Lu, J.L., Li, H., Li, Q.: Optimizing near-carbon-free nuclear energy systems: advances in reactor operation digital twin through hybrid machine learning algorithms for parameter identification and state estimation. Nucl. Sci. Tech. **35**(8), 135 (2024)
9. IAEA: Design of Fuel Handling and Storage Systems for Nuclear Power Plants: Specific Safety Guide. International Atomic Energy Agency (2021)
10. International Atomic Energy Agency: Digital tools, virtual reality and robots to help in accelerating dismantling of retired nuclear facilities, IAEA survey shows (2022). https://www.iaea.org/newscenter/news/digital-tools-virtual-reality-and-robots-to-help-in-accelerating-dismantling-of-retired-nuclear-facilities-iaea-survey-shows. Accessed 08 Aug 2025

11. Kim, D., Shin, J., Lee, J., Woo, W.: Adjusting relative translation gains according to space size in redirected walking for mixed reality mutual space generation. In: 2021 IEEE Virtual Reality and 3D User Interfaces (VR), pp. 653–660. IEEE (2021)
12. Lew, R., Ulrich, T.A., Boring, R.L.: Nuclear reactor crew evaluation of a computerized operator support system HMI for chemical and volume control system. In: Schmorrow, D.D., Fidopiastis, C.M. (eds.) AC 2017. LNCS (LNAI), vol. 10285, pp. 501–513. Springer, Cham (2017). https://doi.org/10.1007/978-3-319-58625-0_36
13. Lin, L., Gurgen, A., Dinh, N.: Development and assessment of prognosis digital twin in a NAMAC system. Ann. Nucl. Energy **179**, 109439 (2022)
14. Nguyen, T.N., Ponciroli, R., Bruck, P., Esselman, T.C., Rigatti, J.A., Vilim, R.B.: A digital twin approach to system-level fault detection and diagnosis for improved equipment health monitoring. Ann. Nucl. Energy **170**, 109002 (2022)
15. Nuclear Institute: Nuclear reactor simulator (2024). https://nuclearinst.com/nuclear-reactor-simulator. Accessed 09 Aug 2025
16. Park, S.Y., et al.: Digital twin and deep reinforcement learning-driven robotic automation system for confined workspaces: a nozzle dam replacement case study in nuclear power plants. Int. J. Precision Eng. Manuf.-Green Technol. **11**(3), 939–962 (2024)
17. Rossa, R., Borella, A., Kochetkov, A., Meer, K., Vittiglio, G.: Developing a virtual reality research reactor in support of safeguards education and training. In: Symposium on International Safeguards: Reflecting on the Past and Anticipating the Future, p. 7. No. IAEA-CN-303 (2022)
18. Song, H., Song, M., Liu, X.: Online autonomous calibration of digital twins using machine learning with application to nuclear power plants. Appl. Energy **326**, 119995 (2022)
19. Steinicke, F., Bruder, G., Hinrichs, K., Jerald, J., Frenz, H., Lappe, M.: Real walking through virtual environments by redirection techniques. J. Virtual Reality Broadcasting **6** (2009)
20. Tao, F., Zhang, H., Liu, A., Nee, A.Y.: Digital twin in industry: state-of-the-art. IEEE Trans. Industr. Inf. **15**(4), 2405–2415 (2018)
21. Ye, C., Zheng, M., Wang, M., Zhang, R., Xiong, Z.: The design and simulation of a new spent fuel pool passive cooling system. Ann. Nucl. Energy **58**, 124–131 (2013)

Learning Disentangled Speech- and Expression-Driven Blendshapes for 3D Face Animation

Yuxiang Mao[1,2], Zhijie Zhang[2], Zhiheng Zhang[1,2], Jiawei Liu[3], Chen Zeng[3], and Shihong Xia[1,2(✉)]

[1] Institute of Computing Technology, Chinese Academy of Sciences, Beijing, China
{maoyuxiang22z,zhangzhiheng20g,xsh}@ict.ac.cn
[2] University of Chinese Academy of Sciences, Beijing, China
[3] Huadian (Beijing) Co-Generation Co., Ltd., Beijing, China

Abstract. Expressions are fundamental to conveying human emotions. With the rapid advancement of AI-generated content (AIGC), realistic and expressive 3D facial animation has become increasingly crucial. Despite recent progress in speech-driven lip-sync for talking-face animation, generating emotionally expressive talking faces remains underexplored. A major obstacle is the scarcity of real emotional 3D talking-face datasets due to the high cost of data capture. To address this, we model facial animation driven by both speech and emotion as a linear additive problem. Leveraging a 3D talking-face dataset with neutral expressions (VOCAset) and a dataset of 3D expression sequences (Florence4D), we jointly learn a set of blendshapes driven by speech and emotion. We introduce a sparsity constraint loss to encourage disentanglement between the two types of blendshapes while allowing the model to capture inherent secondary cross-domain deformations present in the training data. The learned blendshapes can be further mapped to the expression and jaw pose parameters of the FLAME model, enabling the animation of 3D Gaussian avatars. Qualitative and quantitative experiments demonstrate that our method naturally generates talking faces with specified expressions while maintaining accurate lip synchronization. Perceptual studies further show that our approach achieves superior emotional expressivity compared to existing methods, without compromising lip-sync quality.

Keywords: Speech-Driven · 3d facial animation · Expression-Controllable

1 Introduction

In recent years, speech-driven 3D facial animation has found wide applications in fields such as entertainment [17], XR [15], and video conferencing [30]. This technology enables the generation of high-quality 3D talking faces from arbitrary speech inputs. With the rapid advancement of deep learning, the

A. Hinkenjan et al. (Eds.): ICXR 2025, LNCS 16428, pp. 243–259, 2026.
https://doi.org/10.1007/978-981-95-7195-6_14

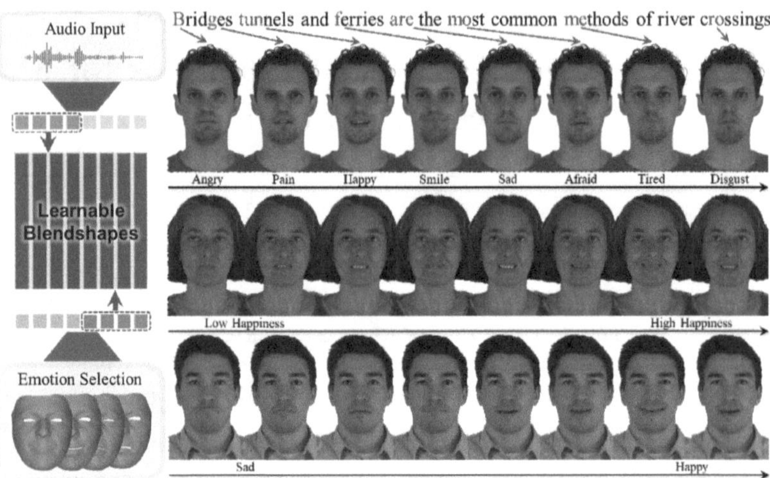

Fig. 1. We regress the weights of the learned speech- and expression-driven blendshapes respectively, remove the secondary cross-domain deformations, and then combine them to produce realistic, emotionally expressive talking avatars.

field has achieved remarkable progress [3–5,8,20,22,25–28,31,33]. Recent studies [4,9,10,20,22] have extended beyond lip synchronization, emphasizing the role of facial expressions as crucial non-verbal cues.

The core challenge in emotional talking-face animation lies in accurately conveying emotion while ensuring that lip motion remains synchronized with the input audio. However, in 3D facial animation, datasets that contain speech-driven 3D talking faces with diverse emotional expressions are scarce, making relevant research difficult. Existing methods [4,8,9,22,27] often reconstruct 3D pseudo ground-truth data from emotional 2D video datasets [19,29,32] to train emotion-enhanced speech-driven facial animation models. Yet, such pseudo ground-truth data falls short of real 3D scans in quality, leading to decreased lip-sync accuracy [20], and making it difficult to learn well-disentangled and accurate facial deformations driven by both speech and emotion. We observe that while no single dataset simultaneously contains both factors, real 3D scan datasets for each individual factor are accessible [3,23]. This motivates us to adopt a data-driven approach to learn realistic facial motion patterns from these high-quality 3D scan datasets.

Blendshape [2] is a widely used technique in 3D facial animation [18], representing facial motion as a linear combination of a neutral base mesh and multiple predefined deformation targets weighted by adjustable coefficients to generate complex expressions and lip movements. We model speech- and expression-driven animation as a linear additive problem, jointly learning a set of disentangled speech- and expression-driven blendshapes from two real scan datasets: the audio-driven 3D facial animation dataset VOCAset [3] and the 3D facial expression dataset Florence4D [23]. These blendshapes naturally embed emotional deformations into talking faces and can be further mapped to the parameter space of FLAME [15], enabling the animation of Gaussian-based head avatars [24] (Fig. 1).

However, the training data in each domain inevitably contains certain deformations that originate from the other factor. In VOCAset, for instance, speakers seldom maintain a perfectly neutral expression during speech; in Florence4D, emotional expressions often affect lip articulation. We refer to these interfering components as *secondary deformations*—domain-specific deformations that should ideally be attributed to the other domain. Due to the presence of such secondary deformations, directly combining speech- and expression-driven deformations can lead to artifacts, such as the lips failing to fully close (Fig. 6).

To address this, we introduce a sparsity constraint loss that encourages the disentanglement of speech and expression factors while still allowing the model to account for secondary deformations during training. During inference, our deformation fusion module regresses blendshape weights for speech and expression deformations respectively, removes the cross-domain components, and then combines the two to synthesize talking faces with accurate lip synchronization and emotional expressiveness (Fig. 3).

In summary, the main contributions of our work are as follows:

- We present a data-driven approach to learn disentangled speech- and expression-driven blendshapes from real 3D face scan datasets, enabling the capture of realistic lip motion and emotional facial deformations with high fidelity.
- We introduce a sparsity constraint loss that removes secondary cross-domain deformations, achieving clean separation between speech and expression effects and preventing artifacts when combining the two factors.
- The learned blendshape coefficients are mapped to the FLAME parameter space, enabling our deformation fusion module to further animate Gaussian head avatars in real-time, producing natural, emotionally expressive 3D talking faces with accurate lip synchronization.

2 Related Work

Currently, a number of efforts [3–5,8,20,22,25,26,28,31,33] have developed methods for generating speech-driven 3D talking faces.

VOCA [3] presents a speaker-independent method for 3D facial animation that captures diverse speaking styles. FaceFormer [5] is the first to adopt a transformer-based model that autoregressively produces facial motion from vocal inputs. CodeTalker [31] develops a discrete codebook for general facial movements and employs a framework similar to FaceFormer to synthesize these animations. However, these approaches mainly emphasize lip movements while overlooking the subtle non-verbal cues that occur during speech.

Karras et al. [10] incorporates a trainable emotional state vector, assigning one vector to each training sample to construct an emotion database. However, the learned vectors lack explicit semantic interpretation, and the architecture does not include a disentanglement mechanism to separate the influence of speech and emotion signals. MeshTalk [25] decouples voice and non-voice factors by introducing a novel cross-modality loss, encouraging the model to learn upper-face movements independent of audio and accurate mouth movements that depend solely on audio. However, emotional cues can also manifest in the lower face region, such as in the corners of the mouth, making the assumption of strict upper – lower face disentanglement potentially too strong.

Currently, to the best of our knowledge, there is no publicly available real 3D scan dataset for talking-face animation with diverse emotions. Several studies [4,8,9,22,27] extract pseudo ground-truth 3D data from emotional 2D video datasets such as MEAD [29], HDTF [32], and RAVDESS [19]. However, experiments [20] show that this reconstructed data still falls short of real scan data in terms of geometric detail and lip accuracy.

EmoVOCA [20] leverages the widely used real 3D scan dataset with paired audio (VOCAset [3]) and the 3D facial expression dataset (Florence4D [23]), synthesizing a new 3D dataset that combines the effects of speech and expressions on facial deformations via a double-encoder-shared-decoder architecture. However, this method assumes that the features in the two datasets are perfectly disentangled into speech and expression deformations, which differs from our view. We argue that both datasets inevitably contain subtle deformations attributable to the other domain, which should be disentangled during training.

Unlike the above methods, our approach learns a set of explicitly disentangled blendshapes for the two driving factors from VOCAset and Florence4D. By applying a sparsity constraint loss to the regressed blendshape weights, we separate the secondary cross-domain deformations present in each dataset, thereby achieving better disentanglement.

3 Method

Our method involves first training a speech-driven facial animation model to generate speech-driven deformations from the input audio. Then, our deformation fusion module regresses a set of learned blendshape weights for both the speech and specified expression (sequence) deformations respectively. By removing cross-domain artifacts and combining these two sets of weights, we achieve natural and realistic emotional talking face animation.

3.1 Data Preparation and Geometric Mapping

Unlike point clouds, mesh models have explicit topology that encodes neighborhood relationships in 3D space. However, representing mesh vertex coordinates as simple column vectors fails to preserve this local connectivity, and is not naturally compatible with CNN architectures, which are designed to exploit such spatial locality. To address this, we adopt the method of Fan et al. [6], which represents 3D shapes on a square image grid while preserving the adjacency relationships of 3D vertices.

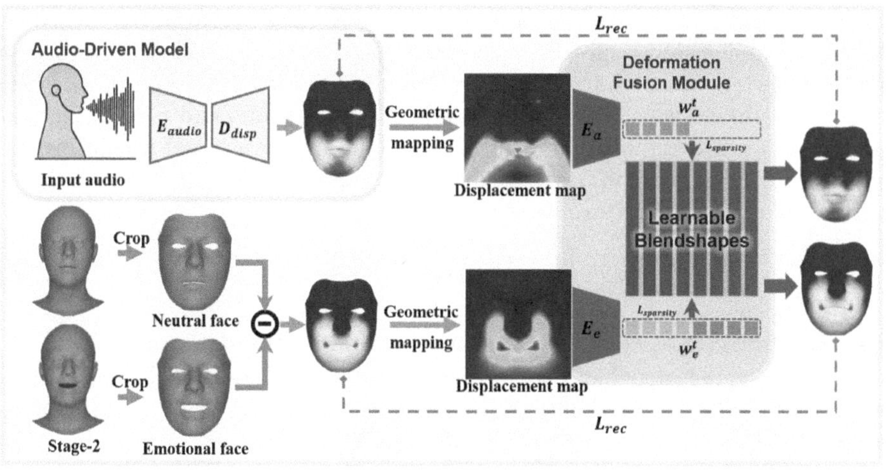

Fig. 2. Architecture. Our model comprises two stages. In the first stage, an audio-driven talking face model is employed to generate speech deformations from the input audio. In the second stage, we jointly learn the blendshapes for speech- and expression-driven deformations, with the encoders E_a and E_e trained simultaneously to regress their corresponding weights.

Specifically, for a speech-driven mesh M_a from VOCAset or a expression-driven mesh M_e from Florence4D, we first crop the frontal face region. Following the procedure of Fan et al. [6], we apply a dense registration method [7] to align them with the provided face template, resulting in meshes with unified topology, denoted as $V_a \in \Re^{n_v \times 3}$ and $V_e \in \Re^{n_v \times 3}$, where $n_v = 10857$. We then subtract their corresponding canonical face to obtain per-vertex displacements ΔV_a and ΔV_e representing speech- and expression-driven deformations. As shown in Fig. 2, these displacements are subsequently mapped, via interpolation, to geometry displacement maps $D_a \in \Re^{H \times W \times 3}$ and $D_e \in \Re^{H \times W \times 3}$ on a square image grid [6]:

$$D_{i,j} = w_{i,j,1} \Delta V_{I_{i,j,1}} + w_{i,j,2} \Delta V_{I_{i,j,2}} + w_{i,j,3} \Delta V_{I_{i,j,3}}, \tag{1}$$

where $I_{i,j,*}$ and $w_{i,j,*}$ denote the indices of the three corresponding vertices in V and their barycentric interpolation weights for each vertex (pixel) $D_{i,j}$ in the resulting square image grid.

3.2 Audio-Driven Model

First, we construct a speech-driven model to generate corresponding mesh deformations from input audio. Following FaceFormer [5], we train this model on the registered VOCAset meshes $\{V_a\}$. The audio encoder E_{audio} in FaceFormer adopts the wav2vec 2.0 model [1], which includes an audio feature extractor based on a Temporal Convolutional Network (TCN) [12–14] to transform raw audio into features, which are then processed by a Transformer encoder to produce higher-level speech representations. The decoder D_{disp} leverages a causal self-attention mechanism to learn temporal motion representations, along with a cross-modal attention mechanism to align the audio and motion modalities, thereby achieving accurate synchronization. This process of predicting the current-frame deformation based on the input audio $A^{1:T}$ and the previous deformations $\Delta\hat{V}_A^{1:t-1}$ can be formulated as:

$$\Delta\hat{V}_A^t = D_{\text{disp}}\left(E_{\text{audio}}(A^{1:T}), \Delta\hat{V}_A^{1:t-1}\right). \tag{2}$$

3.3 Learning Speech and Expression-Driven Blendshapes

Formulation We model speech and expression as two additive driving factors in a linearly additive problem. By linearity, the resulting deformation can be formulated as:

$$\Delta V = f_A(A) + f_E(E) = B_A \boldsymbol{w_A} + B_E \boldsymbol{w_E}, \tag{3}$$

where B_A and B_E are the blendshapes for speech and expression, and w_A and w_E are the corresponding weights.

Given speech- and expression-driven deformation data ΔV_a and ΔV_e (or D_a and D_e), our goal is to learn the blendshape sets B_A and B_E. We assume that each domain's deformation data inevitably contains secondary deformations from the other domain. For example, for an expression-driven deformation ΔV_{E_0} in the training set, where E_0 denotes an arbitrary expression, we have:

$$\Delta V_{E_0} = B_E \boldsymbol{w_{E_0}} + B_A \boldsymbol{\epsilon}, \tag{4}$$

where $\boldsymbol{\epsilon}$ represents the non-negligible secondary speech-related deformation.

If $\boldsymbol{\epsilon}$ is ignored, then for a speech input A_0 and expression E_0 we have:

$$\Delta V_{A_0} = B_A w_{A_0} + B_E \cdot \mathbf{0}, \quad \Delta V_{E_0} = B_A \cdot \mathbf{0} + B_E w_{E_0}. \tag{5}$$

The resulting combined deformation for the target talking face with expression would be:

$$\Delta V_{O_0} = B_A \boldsymbol{w_{A_0}} + B_E \boldsymbol{w_{E_0}} = \Delta V_{A_0} + \Delta V_{E_0}, \tag{6}$$

which degenerates into a naive sum (or interpolation) of the two input deformations.

Our ablation study demonstrates that such naive composition degrades lip articulation, particularly for closed-mouth phonemes (Fig. 6), because certain expression deformations introduce undesired mouth openings that are not compensated for. Therefore, $\boldsymbol{\epsilon}$ should also be regressed and removed during the fusion of speech and expression deformations.

Specifically, for the speech-driven deformation ΔV_{A_0} and the expression-driven deformation ΔV_{E_0}, we have:

$$\Delta V_{A_0} = B_A \boldsymbol{w_{A_0}} + B_E \boldsymbol{\epsilon_{A_0}}, \quad \Delta V_{E_0} = B_A \boldsymbol{\epsilon_{E_0}} + B_E \boldsymbol{w_{E_0}}. \tag{7}$$

The fused output deformation is then given by:

$$\Delta V_{O_0} = B_A w_{A_0} + B_E w_{E_0} = (\Delta V_{A_0} - B_E \boldsymbol{\epsilon_{A_0}}) + (\Delta V_{E_0} - B_A \boldsymbol{\epsilon_{E_0}}). \tag{8}$$

Architecture We jointly learn the blendshapes for speech- and expression-driven deformations within our **deformation fusion module**, which consists of two independent CNN encoders, E_a and E_e, and a linear layer as the decoder. The weight matrix of this linear decoder serves as the learnable blendshapes, while the latent vectors encoded by the encoders serve as the blendshape weights. We partition the blendshapes such that the first half B_A corresponds to speech-driven deformations and the second half B_E corresponds to expression-driven deformations, as illustrated in Fig. 2.

Specifically, in our implementation, each encoder consists of six blocks of convolutional layers, instance normalization layers, and ReLU activation functions. The input speech-driven deformation ΔV_{A_0} and expression-driven deformation ΔV_{E_0} are first interpolated to geometry displacement maps D_{A_0} and D_{E_0}, respectively. These are then encoded by their corresponding encoders E_a and E_e into blendshape weights, which are subsequently passed through the linear decoder to produce the predicted per-vertex displacements $\Delta\hat{V}_{A_0}$ and $\Delta\hat{V}_{E_0}$. By supervising $\Delta\hat{V}_{A_0}$ and $\Delta\hat{V}_{E_0}$ to match the input ΔV_{A_0} and ΔV_{E_0}, we self-supervise the regression of both the learnable blendshapes and their corresponding weights.

Sparsity Constraint Loss To encourage disentanglement between the learned speech- and expression-driven blendshapes, we introduce a sparsity constraint loss to suppress the cross-domain blendshape weights produced by the encoders. Specifically, the output of the speech encoder E_a is split into two halves, $\boldsymbol{w}_{\boldsymbol{A}_0}$ and $\boldsymbol{\epsilon}_{\boldsymbol{A}_0}$, where $\boldsymbol{w}_{\boldsymbol{A}_0}$ corresponds to the weights of speech-driven blendshapes B_A, and $\boldsymbol{\epsilon}_{\boldsymbol{A}_0}$ corresponds to the weights of expression-driven blendshapes B_E. We impose a sparsity constraint on $\boldsymbol{\epsilon}_{\boldsymbol{A}_0}$ to encourage its values to be small. Similarly, the output of the expression encoder E_e is split into $\boldsymbol{w}_{\boldsymbol{E}_0}$ and $\boldsymbol{\epsilon}_{\boldsymbol{E}_0}$, where $\boldsymbol{\epsilon}_{\boldsymbol{E}_0}$ corresponds to the weights of speech-driven blendshapes B_A. A sparsity constraint is also applied to $\boldsymbol{\epsilon}_{\boldsymbol{E}_0}$ to minimize the cross-domain influence:

$$\mathcal{L}_{\text{sparsity}} = \|\epsilon_{A_0}\|_1 + \|\epsilon_{E_0}\|_1, \tag{9}$$

It is worth noting that this loss does not enforce $\boldsymbol{\epsilon}_{\boldsymbol{A}_0}$ and $\boldsymbol{\epsilon}_{\boldsymbol{E}_0}$ to be exactly zero, but allows them to take small nonzero values.

Overall Losses. We jointly train the speech encoder E_a, the expression encoder E_e, and the blendshape bases B_A and B_E on the speech- and expression-driven datasets VOCAset and Florence4D. In total, we optimize:

$$\mathcal{L}_{\text{overall}} = \lambda_{\text{rec}}\mathcal{L}_{\text{rec}} + \lambda_{\text{sparsity}}\mathcal{L}_{\text{sparsity}} + \lambda_{\text{Laplace}}\mathcal{L}_{\text{Laplace}} + \lambda_{\text{reg}}\mathcal{L}_{\text{reg}}, \tag{10}$$

where $\mathcal{L}_{\text{reg}}$ is an ℓ_2 regularization loss applied to the output deformations, and:

$$\mathcal{L}_{\text{rec}} = \frac{1}{n_v}\sum_{k=1}^{n_v} \omega_k \|\Delta\hat{V}_k - \Delta V_k\|_2 \tag{11}$$

is the reconstruction loss, which minimizes the weighted mean squared error between the predicted deformation and the ground truth.

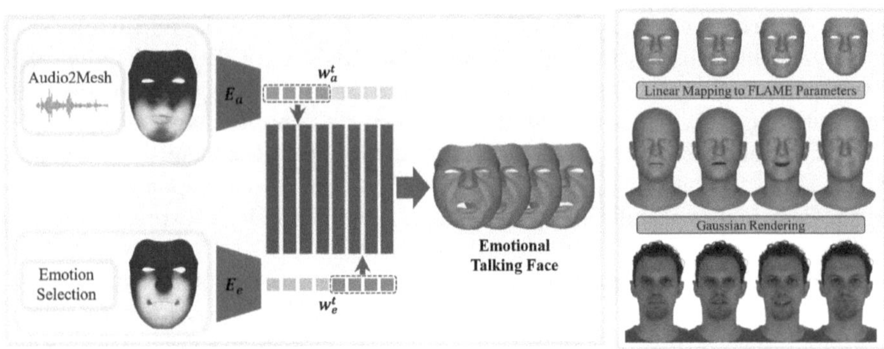

Fig. 3. Left: Given the speech and expression deformations as input, we combine their respective blendshape weights to generate talking-face animations with expressions. **Right**: The learned blendshapes can be linearly mapped to the FLAME parameter space, enabling the animation of Gaussian head avatars.

The Laplace smoothing term is defined as:

$$\mathcal{L}_{\text{Laplace}} = \sum_{i=1}^{n_v} \left\| \hat{V}_i - \frac{1}{\sum_j A_{ij}} \sum_j A_{ij} \hat{V}_j \right\|_2, \tag{12}$$

where A_{ij} denotes the adjacency matrix of the facial mesh: $A_{ij} = 1$ if vertices i and j are connected by an edge, and $A_{ij} = 0$ otherwise. This term enforces local smoothness of the mesh surface, thereby reducing visual artifacts.

3.4 3D Emotional Talking Face Generation

During inference (Fig. 3, left), we generate 3D emotional talking faces by combining the speech blendshape weights $\boldsymbol{w}_{\boldsymbol{A}_0}$ and the expression blendshape weights $\boldsymbol{w}_{\boldsymbol{E}_0}$. Given the input speech deformation ΔV_{A_0} and expression deformation ΔV_{E_0}, the fused deformation is computed as:

$$\Delta V_{O_0} = B_A \boldsymbol{w}_{\boldsymbol{A}_0} + B_E \boldsymbol{w}_{\boldsymbol{E}_0}. \tag{13}$$

This per-vertex deformation is then added to the canonical template mesh to produce the final talking face with the specified expression.

In addition, we learn a linear mapping $\mathrm{L}_{\mathcal{G}}$ from the learned blendshapes to the FLAME model's expression and jaw pose parameters [15] through an optimization process with the following loss:

$$\mathcal{L}_{\text{mapping}} = \lambda_{\text{fit}} \mathcal{L}_{\text{fit}} + \lambda_{\text{reg}} \mathcal{L}_{\text{reg}}, \tag{14}$$

where $\mathcal{L}_{\text{reg}}$ is an ℓ_2 regularization loss applied to the output deformations, and:

$$\mathcal{L}_{\text{fit}} = \frac{1}{n_v} \sum_{k=1}^{n_v} \omega_k \| \Delta \tilde{V}_k - \Delta \hat{V}_k \|_2 \tag{15}$$

is the fitting loss, which minimizes the weighted mean squared error between the vertex deformations corresponding to the FLAME model's expression and jaw pose parameters and those generated by our deformation fusion module. This allows our method to further animate Gaussian head avatars [24] parameterized by FLAME, producing realistic, natural, and emotionally expressive talking faces (Fig. 3, right).

4 Experiments

4.1 Implementation Details

We train our models using the publicly available datasets VOCAset [3] and Florence4D [23]. VOCAset contains 29 min of paired audio and 3D scans from 12 speakers, while Florence4D provides dynamic sequences of 3D faces covering a wide range of expressions. Specifically, the speech-driven model is trained on VOCAset, while our deformation fusion module jointly learns the speech- and expression-driven blendshapes from both VOCAset and Florence4D. We implement our models in Pytorch [21], and employ the Adam optimizer [11] with a learning rate of 3*e*-4. We use a batch size of 128 and optimize the models for 4000 epochs. Additional implementation details are provided in the materials.

4.2 Quantitative Evaluation

Since our audio-driven model adopts the FaceFormer architecture [5], we quantitatively evaluate the impact of our deformation fusion module on lip-sync accuracy. Specifically, we assess the lip vertex error (LVE), defined as the maximum ℓ_2 error among all lip vertices, on 119 audio samples from three subjects in our VOCAset test set. We compare the lip-sync accuracy of our audio-driven model (i.e., FaceFormer retrained on the registered VOCAset training data) against the output after applying the deformation fusion module. As reported in Table 1, the LVE increases by only 0.002134 mm after the deformation fusion module, which is imperceptible to the human eye. This demonstrates that the learned speech-driven blendshapes can accurately capture the lip deformations for speech articulation.

Table 1. Quantitative evaluation results on VOCAset. The loss in lip-sync accuracy, as measured by LVE, caused by our deformation fusion module (DFM) is negligible.

Method	LVE (mm) ↓
FaceFormer	4.9298
FaceFormer+DFM	4.9319

Table 2. Inference Speed. The inference speed is measured in frames per second (FPS). Our emotional talking-face animation model, which consists of the FaceFormer-based audio-driven module and our deformation fusion module (DFM), runs at 177.62 FPS on an NVIDIA GeForce RTX 3090 GPU. After incorporating the linear mapping $L_{\mathcal{G}}$ from the learned blendshapes to the FLAME parameters, the model still achieves 168.63 FPS.

Method	Driving FPS
FaceFormer+DFM	177.62
FaceFormer+DFM+$L_{\mathcal{G}}$	168.63

4.3 Inference Speed and Efficiency

We implement our framework in Python using the PyTorch library. The trained weights of the deformation fusion module occupy 17.89 MB of storage. As shown in Table 2, our full model runs at over 165 FPS on a commercial GPU (NVIDIA GeForce RTX 3090), enabling efficient real-time generation of emotionally expressive talking-face animations in scenarios such as live video conferencing.

4.4 Perceptual Studies

Since it is challenging to find an appropriate metric to automatically evaluate both the synchronization between lip articulation and input speech and the quality of emotional expression, we conducted two perceptual experiments to compare our method with previous state-of-the-art approaches. We generated 3D facial mesh sequences using different methods, rendered the outputs, and then displayed them side-by-side. Twenty-five participants rated the animations on a 5-point Likert scale [16], evaluating both lip-sync accuracy and the quality of emotional expression. All audio – visual stimuli were randomized independently for each participant to avoid order and position bias. Each stimulus was evaluated under all compared methods, ensuring a fully balanced design across methods.

Evaluation of Lip Articulation and Emotion. The first part of this evaluation compares our approach with publicly available 3D talking-face animation methods, including VOCA [3], FaceFormer [5], CodeTalker [31], EmoTalk [22], and EMOTE [4]. For testing, we randomly select 8 neutral voice sequences from the MEAD dataset [29]. This round of evaluation focuses on the synchrony of mouth shapes for neutral expressions. The participants rate the rendered videos from different methods, resulting in 200 paired observations (25 participants $\times$ 8 audio – visual stimuli). For each comparison between our method and another approach, we perform one-sided paired t-tests on the paired ratings. Specifically, for each participant – stimulus pair, we compute the score difference, and test the alternative hypothesis $H_1 : \mu_d > 0$, where μ_d denotes the

Table 3. Perceptual study evaluating the lip-synchronization performance of our method against state-of-the-art approaches. Subjective lip-sync quality scores (Mean Opinion Score, MOS; higher is better) are reported as mean ± standard deviation (SD), along with one-sided paired t-tests comparing each approach against our method. Reported p-values and Cohen's d_z indicate statistical and practical significance, respectively.

Method	Training Set	MOS ↑	Significance vs. Ours	
		Score ± SD	p-value	Cohen's d_z
VOCA [3]	VOCA	3.64 ± 0.87	1.8×10^{-10}	0.47
CodeTalker [31]	VOCA	3.81 ± 0.94	4.8×10^{-4}	0.24
EmoTalk [22]	RAV/HDTF	3.78 ± 0.95	8.5×10^{-5}	0.27
EMOTE [4]	MEAD	3.22 ± 1.10	1.7×10^{-20}	0.73
FaceFormer [5]	VOCA	$\mathbf{4.02 \pm 0.81}$	0.25	0.05
Ours	VOCA	$\mathbf{4.06 \pm 0.82}$	–	–

Table 4. Perceptual study evaluating the lip-synchronization and expression quality of our method against state-of-the-art emotional talking face approaches. Mean Opinion Scores (MOS) are reported as mean ± standard deviation (SD) for both aspects, along with one-sided paired t-tests comparing each approach against our method.

Aspect	Method	Training Dataset	MOS ↑	Significance vs. Ours	
			Score ± SD	p-value	Cohen's d_z
Lip-Sync	EmoTalk [22]	RAV/HDTF	3.17 ± 1.03	1.4×10^{-22}	0.78
	EMOTE [4]	MEAD	3.00 ± 1.04	1.0×10^{-30}	0.97
	Ours	VOCA&Flr-4D	$\mathbf{4.08 \pm 0.84}$	–	–
Expression	EmoTalk [22]	RAV/HDTF	2.71 ± 1.09	1.0×10^{-38}	1.15
	EMOTE [4]	MEAD	2.70 ± 1.05	5.9×10^{-37}	1.11
	Ours	VOCA&Flr-4D	$\mathbf{4.20 \pm 1.01}$	–	–

population mean of these paired differences. A significant positive mean difference indicates that our method was consistently rated higher. The resulting p-values quantify the statistical significance of the observed score improvements over previous approaches, while the effect sizes (Cohen's d_z) measure their practical significance. As shown in Table 3, our model, which employs the retrained FaceFormer as the audio-driven backbone, performs on par with FaceFormer (no statistically significant difference, $p = 0.25$) and significantly outperforms VOCA, CodeTalker, EmoTalk, and EMOTE ($p < 0.001$) according to one-sided paired t-tests. The corresponding effect sizes (Cohen's $d_z = 0.24 - 0.73$) indicate small-to-large practical improvements, confirming that our model produces perceptually more synchronized and natural lip movements.

The second part of the evaluation compares the proposed approach with publicly available emotional 3D talking-face animation methods, including

EmoTalk [22] and EMOTE [4]. We randomly select 8 audio sequences from the MEAD dataset, each accompanied by exemplar videos as emotion references (e.g., happiness, sadness, anger, and disgust). This round of evaluation assesses both lip articulation and emotional expressiveness. The participants rate the rendered videos from different methods, resulting in 200 paired observations (25 participants × 8 audio – visual stimuli) for each aspect. As in the first part, we perform one-sided paired t-tests on the paired ratings to examine whether our method is rated significantly higher than the previous methods. As shown in Table 4, our model outperforms previous emotional 3D talking-face animation methods by approximately 1 MOS point in both evaluation aspects. One-sided paired t-tests show that the improvements over EmoTalk and EMOTE are statistically significant ($p < 10^{-22}$ and $p < 10^{-30}$ for lip-sync, $p < 10^{-37}$ for expression), with large effect sizes (Cohen's $d_z = 0.78 - 1.15$). These results demonstrate that our approach achieves a substantial perceptual advantage in the mixed driving of speech and emotion. This improvement is attributed to our explicitly disentangled speech- and expression-driven blendshapes, together with the sparsity constraint loss, which reduces cross-domain interference and preserves both lip-sync accuracy and emotional expressiveness.

Table 5. Ablation study results. The full model achieves the highest scores in both lip synchronization and expression quality.

Configurations	MOS (Lip-Sync)↑	MOS (Expression)↑
w/o $\mathcal{L}_{\text{Laplace}}$	3.38 ± 0.72	3.52 ± 0.85
w/o $\mathcal{L}_{\text{sparsity}}$	2.90 ± 0.87	2.67 ± 1.21
w/o Geometric Mapping	2.95 ± 0.98	2.90 ± 1.06
Interpolation of Inputs	2.71 ± 1.08	2.76 ± 0.97
Ours	$\mathbf{4.57 \pm 0.58}$	$\mathbf{4.19 \pm 0.66}$

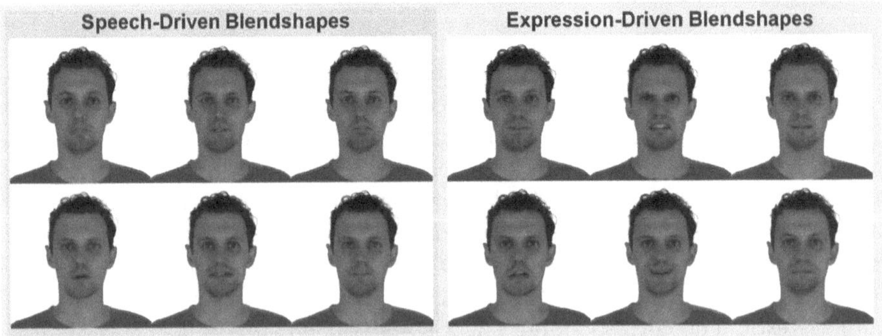

Fig. 4. Visualization of **learned blendshapes**. The blendshapes are linearly mapped to the FLAME parameter space and used to animate Gaussian head avatars for intuitive visualization.

Ablation Study: Perceptual Evaluation. This study aims to assess the contribution of each component within our model. We conducted comparisons among: (1) without Laplace smoothing loss, (2) without sparsity constraint loss, (3) without geometric mapping, (4) with the interpolation method, where the output of our audio-driven model is directly interpolated with expressions, and (5) our full model. The experimental setup is identical to that used in the perceptual study for 3D emotional talking-face animation evaluation. The results (Table 5) demonstrate the necessity of each component in our method. In particular, our approach significantly outperforms the direct interpolation of speech-driven and expression-driven deformations, indicating that our deforma-

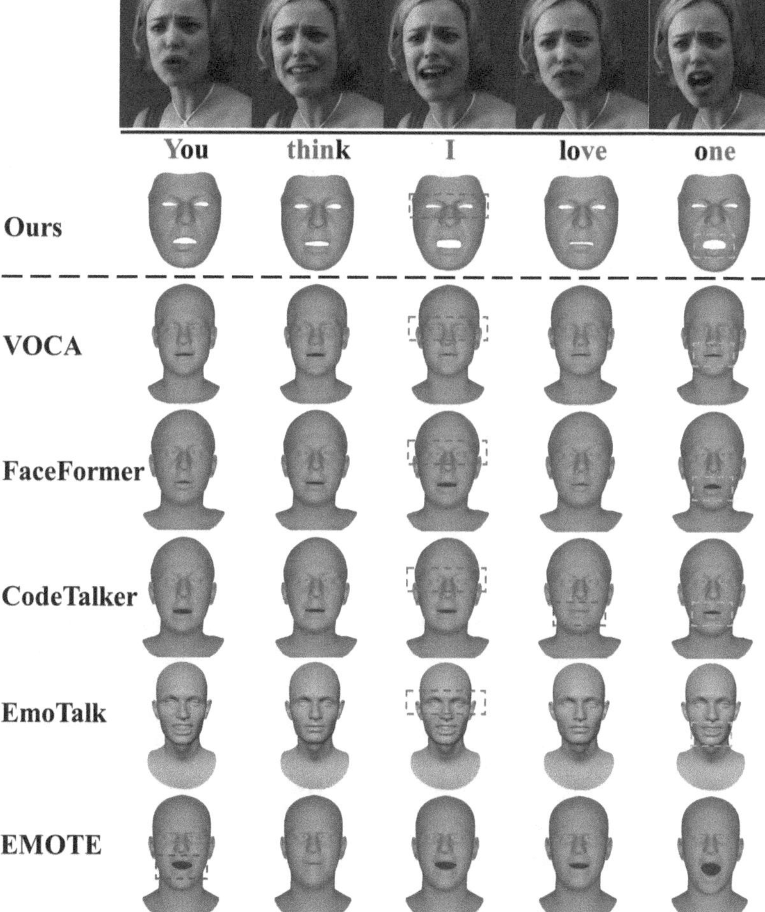

Fig. 5. Qualitative Comparison with Existing Methods. For reference, the first row shows the corresponding RGB frames. The subsequent rows present corresponding frames synthesized by our method and previous state-of-the-art methods (VOCA [3], FaceFormer [5], CodeTalker [31], EmoTalk [22], and EMOTE [4]).

tion fusion module can effectively regress and remove cross-domain deformations present in the inputs. Furthermore, the significant performance drop without the sparsity constraint loss validates the effectiveness of our soft disentanglement strategy during blendshape learning, which allows the model to capture minor cross-domain deformations inherent in the training data.

4.5 Qualitative Evaluation

Visualization of Learned Blendshapes. We visualize a subset of the speech- and expression-driven blendshapes learned in the deformation fusion module. For more intuitive presentation, the blendshapes are linearly mapped to the FLAME parameter space to animate Gaussian head avatars [24]. As shown in Fig. 4, our model learns disentangled speech-driven and expression-driven deformations. The learned speech-driven blendshapes primarily focus on variations in mouth articulation, while the expression-driven blendshapes capture distinct emotional expressions.

Visual Comparison. In Fig. 5, we compare our method with state-of-the-art approaches [3–5,22,31]. While most methods produce natural lip movements, they sometimes fail to align perfectly with the ground truth. For example, CodeTalker and EMOTE occasionally struggle to synchronize lip movements accurately with verbal signals on certain syllables (indicated by the blue dashed lines). In addition, except for EMOTE, other methods exhibit less effective performance in the upper facial region compared to ours (indicated by the red dashed lines). In the last column, while most methods are able to reflect lip movements matching the speech, they seldom account for emotional expression, as indicated by the green dashed lines. This highlights that our fusion strategy can generate high-quality facial animations in both speech and expression domains.

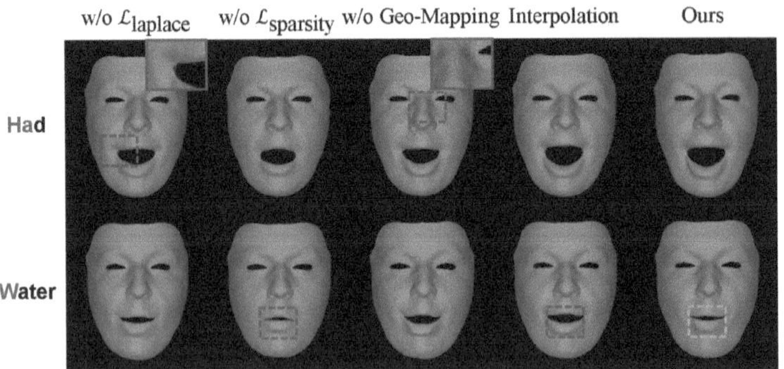

Fig. 6. Visual ablation study results. From left to right: (1) without Laplace smoothing loss, (2) without sparsity constraint loss, (3) without geometric mapping, (4) with the interpolation method, where the speech- and expression-driven deformations are directly interpolated, and (5) our full model.

Ablation Study: Visual Comparison. As shown in Fig. 6, the model without the Laplace smoothing loss exhibits spiky artifacts around the mouth corners due to the absence of local smoothness constraints. The model without the sparsity-constrained loss fails to produce correct emotional expressions, as speech- and expression-driven deformations are not disentangled during training. The model without geometric mapping produces uneven artifacts because it cannot leverage the locality of 3D mesh deformations through the CNN architecture. Finally, directly interpolating speech- and expression-driven deformations disregards the inherent secondary cross-domain deformations in the inputs, which can cause issues such as the lips failing to close properly for phonemes like /w/ due to the influence of a smiling expression. This supports our hypothesis that cross-domain deformations should be regressed and removed during the fusion of speech- and expression-driven deformations.

5 Conclusion

We presented a novel approach for 3D emotional talking-face animation that learns disentangled speech-driven and expression-driven deformations. By modeling facial animation as a linear combination of two blendshape sets learned from high-quality 3D scans, our method captures realistic lip motions and rich emotional expressions. Our main contribution lies in the deformation fusion module trained with the sparsity constraint loss, which effectively separates the two driving factors while accommodating subtle cross-domain effects. Experiments demonstrate that our approach improves emotional expressiveness without sacrificing speech articulation accuracy. Furthermore, the learned blendshape parameters can be mapped to the FLAME model, enabling the animation of high-quality Gaussian head avatars.

We present a novel approach for 3D emotional talking-face animation that learns disentangled speech-driven and expression-driven deformations. By modeling facial animation as a linear combination of two blendshape sets learned from high-quality 3D scans, our method effectively captures both realistic lip motions and rich emotional expressions. Our main contribution lies in the deformation fusion module trained with the sparsity constraint loss, which effectively separates the two driving factors while accommodating subtle cross-domain effects. Experiments demonstrate that our approach improves emotional expressiveness without sacrificing speech articulation accuracy. Our model is lightweight and achieves a frame rate of over 165 FPS on a commercial GPU (NVIDIA GeForce RTX 3090). Furthermore, the learned blendshape parameters can be mapped to the FLAME model, enabling the animation of high-quality Gaussian head avatars. This allows for the generation of more realistic, emotionally expressive talking faces, with potential applications in real-time interactive environments such as XR, where improved expression-speech alignment can enhance user engagement, social presence, and immersion.

References

1. Baevski, A., Zhou, Y., Mohamed, A., Auli, M.: wav2vec 2.0: a framework for self-supervised learning of speech representations. Adv. Neural Inf. Process. Syst. (NeurIPS) **33**, 12449–12460 (2020)
2. Chuang, E., Bregler, C.: Performance driven facial animation using blendshape interpolation. Comput. Sci. Tech. Rep. Stanford Univ. **2**(2), 3 (2002)
3. Cudeiro, D., Bolkart, T., Laidlaw, C., et al.: Capture, learning, and synthesis of 3D speaking styles. In: Proceedings of the IEEE/CVF Conference on Computer Vision and Pattern Recognition (CVPR), pp. 10101–10111 (2019)
4. Daněček, R., Chhatre, K., Tripathi, S., et al.: Emotional speech-driven animation with content-emotion disentanglement. In: Proceedings of SIGGRAPH Asia 2023 Conference Papers, pp. 1–13 (2023)
5. Fan, Y., Lin, Z., Saito, J., et al.: Faceformer: Speech-driven 3D facial animation with transformers. In: Proceedings of the IEEE/CVF Conference on Computer Vision and Pattern Recognition (CVPR), pp. 18770–18780 (2022)
6. Fan, Z., Zhang, Z., Yang, S., et al.: Unpaired multi-domain attribute translation of 3D facial shapes with a square and symmetric geometric map. In: Proceedings of the IEEE/CVF International Conference on Computer Vision (ICCV), pp. 20828–20838 (2023)
7. Fan, Z., Peng, S., Xia, S.: Towards fine-grained optimal 3D face dense registration: An iterative dividing and diffusing method. Int. J. Comput. Vision 1–21 (2023)
8. He, S., He, H., Yang, S., et al.: Speech4mesh: Speech-assisted monocular 3D facial reconstruction for speech-driven 3D facial animation. In: Proceedings of the IEEE/CVF International Conference on Computer Vision (ICCV), pp. 14192–14202 (2023)
9. K., S.B., L., H., Hong, D.H., et al.: Laughtalk: expressive 3D talking head generation with laughter. In: Proceedings of the IEEE/CVF Winter Conference on Applications of Computer Vision (WACV), pp. 6404–6413 (2024)
10. Karras, T., Aila, T., Laine, S., et al.: Audio-driven facial animation by joint end-to-end learning of pose and emotion. ACM Trans. Graphics (TOG) **36**(4), 1–12 (2017)
11. Kingma, D.P., Ba, J.: Adam: A method for stochastic optimization. In: 3rd International Conference on Learning Representations, ICLR 2015, San Diego, CA, USA, May 7-9, 2015, Conference Track Proceedings (2014)
12. Lea, C., Flynn, M.D., Vidal, R., Reiter, A., Hager, G.D.: Temporal convolutional networks for action segmentation and detection. In: Proceedings of the IEEE Conference on Computer Vision and Pattern Recognition (CVPR), pp. 156–165 (2017)
13. Lea, C., Reiter, A., Vidal, R., Hager, G.D.: Temporal convolutional networks: a unified approach to action segmentation. In: European Conference on Computer Vision Workshops (ECCV Workshops), pp. 47–54. Springer (2016)
14. Lea, C., Reiter, A., Vidal, R., Hager, G.D.: Temporal convolutional networks for action segmentation. In: IEEE Conference on Computer Vision and Pattern Recognition (CVPR) Workshops, pp. 1–10. IEEE (2017)
15. Li, T., Bolkart, T., Black, M.J., Li, H., Romdhani, J.: Learning a model of facial shape and expression from 4D scans. ACM Trans. Graphics (TOG) **36**, 194:1–194:17 (2017)
16. Likert, R.: A technique for the measurement of attitudes. Archives of psychology (1932)

17. Liu, C.: An analysis of the current and future state of 3D facial animation techniques and systems. Master's thesis, Simon Fraser University (2009)
18. Liu, X., Mao, T., Xia, S., Yu, Y., Wang, Z.: Facial animation by optimized blendshapes from motion capture data. Comput. Animat. Virtual Worlds **19**(3–4), 235–245 (2008)
19. Livingstone, S.R., Russo, F.A.: The ryerson audio-visual database of emotional speech and song (ravdess): a dynamic, multimodal set of facial and vocal expressions in north american english. PLoS ONE **13**(5), e0196391 (2018)
20. Nocentini, F., Ferrari, C., Berretti, S.: Emovoca: Speech-driven emotional 3D talking heads. In: 2025 IEEE/CVF Winter Conference on Applications of Computer Vision (WACV), pp. 2859–2868. IEEE (2025)
21. Paszke, A., et al.: Pytorch: an imperative style, high-performance deep learning library. Adv. Neural Inf. Process. Syst. **32** (2019)
22. Peng, Z., Wu, H., Song, Z., et al.: Emotalk: Speech-driven emotional disentanglement for 3D face animation. In: Proceedings of the IEEE/CVF International Conference on Computer Vision (ICCV), pp. 20687–20697 (2023)
23. Principi, F., Berretti, S., Ferrari, C., et al.: The florence 4D facial expression dataset. In: Proceedings of the 2023 IEEE 17th International Conference on Automatic Face and Gesture Recognition (FG), pp. 1–6. IEEE (2023)
24. Qian, S., et al.: Gaussianavatars: Photorealistic head avatars with rigged 3D gaussians. In: Proceedings of the IEEE/CVF Conference on Computer Vision and Pattern Recognition, pp. 20299–20309 (2024)
25. Richard, A., Zollhöfer, M., Wen, Y., et al.: Meshtalk: 3D face animation from speech using cross-modality disentanglement. In: Proceedings of the IEEE/CVF International Conference on Computer Vision (ICCV), pp. 1173–1182 (2021)
26. Shen, S., Zhao, W., Meng, Z., et al.: Difftalk: Crafting diffusion models for generalized audio-driven portraits animation. In: Proceedings of the IEEE/CVF Conference on Computer Vision and Pattern Recognition (CVPR), pp. 1982–1991 (2023)
27. Sun, Z., et al.: Diffposetalk: Speech-driven stylistic 3D facial animation and head pose generation via diffusion models. ACM Trans. Graphics (TOG) **43**(4), 1–9 (2024)
28. Thambiraja, B., Habibie, I., Aliakbarian, S., et al.: Imitator: personalized speech-driven 3d facial animation. In: Proceedings of the IEEE/CVF International Conference on Computer Vision (ICCV), pp. 20621–20631 (2023)
29. Wang, K., Wu, Q., Song, L., et al.: Mead: a large-scale audio-visual dataset for emotional talking-face generation. In: Proceedings of the European Conference on Computer Vision (ECCV), pp. 700–717. Springer International Publishing, Cham (2020)
30. Wang, T.C., Mallya, A., Liu, M.Y.: One-shot free-view neural talking-head synthesis for video ,pp. 10039–10049 (2021)
31. Xing, J., Xia, M., Zhang, Y., et al.: Codetalker: Speech-driven 3D facial animation with discrete motion prior. In: Proceedings of the IEEE/CVF Conference on Computer Vision and Pattern Recognition (CVPR), pp. 12780–12790 (2023)
32. Zhang, Z., Li, L., Ding, Y., et al.: Flow-guided one-shot talking face generation with a high-resolution audio-visual dataset. In: Proceedings of the IEEE/CVF Conference on Computer Vision and Pattern Recognition (CVPR), pp. 3661–3670 (2021)
33. Zhou, Y., Han, X., Shechtman, E., et al.: Makeittalk: speaker-aware talking-head animation. ACM Trans. Graphics (TOG) **39**(6), 1–15 (2020)

3DOPT-SLAM: Robust SLAM via Joint Optimization with 3D Object Pose Tracking

Yufan Zhang[1,2], Shanhao Yang[1,2], Hui Zhang[3], Ning Jin[3], Xueying Qin[1,2(✉)], and Xiangxu Meng[1,2]

[1] School of Software, Shandong University, Jinan, People's Republic of China
qxy@sdu.edu.cn
[2] Engineering Research Center of Digital Media Technology, Ministry of Education, Beijing, People's Republic of China
[3] Shandong Inspur Database Technology Co., Ltd., Jinan, People's Republic of China

Abstract. We propose 3DOPT-SLAM, a robust monocular SLAM method that leverages 3D object pose tracking to address feature scarcity in challenging environments. By incorporating known 3D object models as priors, any detectable object—regardless of its texture richness—can serve as a 6DoF pose anchor. Capitalizing on advances in object pose tracking, these methods robustly estimate object poses in real-time, even in textureless or weakly textured scenes. Based on these methods, we present a novel framework where point-based SLAM and 3D object poses mutually complement each other. Initially, camera localization is achieved solely through object tracking. Following the extraction of a sufficient number of feature point pairs, we establish a joint optimization framework between objects and feature points in both front-end and back-end threads. Simultaneously, we indicate that scene feature points can integrate with 3D object tracking constraints across multiple frames. The experiment results on the public dataset YCB-Video and TUM RGB-D cabinet sequence demonstrate significant improvements in the accuracy of camera trajectory estimation and the accuracy of object tracking. These results underscore that the collaboration between feature points and objects enhances camera localization and object tracking.

Keywords: SLAM · 3D object tracking · Camera trajectory estimation

1 Introduction

Visual Simultaneous Localization and Mapping (SLAM) is a fundamental technology in Augmented Reality (AR) and Mixed Reality (MR). Although monocular visual SLAM has made significant advancements, it still faces challenges in textureless environments. This can result in prolonged SLAM initialization times and instability caused by limited feature point matches. Introducing additional constraints in the form of object priors has emerged as a novel solution.

A. Hinkenjan et al. (Eds.): ICXR 2025, LNCS 16428, pp. 260–279, 2026.
https://doi.org/10.1007/978-981-95-7195-6_15

Some Object SLAM methods [14,21,23,26,30,37,42,53,56,60] employed individual objects in the scenes to replace the pose estimation of SLAM, establish additional constraints in SLAM, and showed benefits in relocation [60] or loop detection [21]. However, these methods can not estimate the precise poses of individual objects, so they are limited in their ability to improve the accuracy of camera pose estimation. In some cases [30,37,60], they may even have a negative impact on the accuracy of the estimated camera poses.

Therefore, accurate observations of object poses become crucial for improving the accuracy of camera localization when introducing objects as constraints. Fortunately, 3D object tracking methods are great advanced recently, which can robustly track the poses of an object with its 3D model between objects and cameras. However, alternative replacement of the camera pose only in case of camera localization fails like [23] may cause worse instable.

In this paper, we propose a novel SLAM method via joint optimization that combines point features and object features in the scene, achieving mutual enhancement between SLAM and 3D object tracking. Our contributions are as follows:

- An improved optimization framework of SLAM, fusing the object shape and object position into the map points reprojection error, capable of improving the accuracy of camera pose estimation.
- We introduce 3D object tracking to treat scene objects as 6DoF anchors. Proposing camera localization constraints relying solely on objects enhances the robustness of SLAM in scenarios where feature points are not operational.
- We perform joint optimization across multiple views with objects and map points, leveraging the relative static relationships in the static scene, which enhances the accuracy and stability of 3D object tracking for static objects.

2 Related Work

This section provides an overview of Visual SLAM (2.1), Object SLAM (2.2), and 3D Object Tracking (2.3). We also discuss existing approaches on potential extensions and the various challenges faced by SLAM and 3D Object Tracking in diverse scenarios.

2.1 Visual SLAM

Visual SLAM has made significant advancements in the past decades, there are mainly two traditoinal approaches in monocular RGB SLAM: direct methods, feature-based matching methods, and learning-based methods.

Direct methods use directly the pixel intensities in the images to do optimization. DSO [13] is capable of accurately computing camera poses in situations where point detectors perform poorly, enhancing robustness in low-texture areas. But in all cases, the lack of integration of more reliable data features and scene information in the environment results in lower accuracy and robustness compared to our proposal. In feature-based matching methods, the pioneering work PTAM [24] splits camera tracking and mapping into two parallel threads: one thread deals with tracking erratic motion, while the other produces 3D map points from previously observed video frames. This framework, which ensures both system runtime and accuracy, has becomes the gold standard in visual SLAM. Inheriting the principles of PTAM [24], ORB-SLAM2 [35] uses oriented fast and rotated brief (ORB) features, enabling real-time online estimation of camera pose and reconstruction of the corresponding 3D positions of feature points in multi-view RGB images. However, these methods often lead to camera localization failures or instability in textureless environments. Therefore, it necessitates the exploration of new scene features to augment the constraints of SLAM.

The previous works mentioned above have adopted line [27,39] and plane [9, 57] features to compensate the missing of textures, which achieves obvious improvements in textureless environments. However, due to the instability to extract and match lines and planes, these methods are still sensitive to the initialization condition and can achieve limited accuracy in many situations. Since there are always objects present in the scene, utilizing objects to enhance the camera localization accuracy and robustness of SLAM has become an important approach.

Recently, learning-based SLAM methods have developed rapidly, using deep learning approaches such as semantic features [59], object detection [1], and online reconstruction priors [36], to enhance their adaptability to weak features. However, despite their potential, learning-based SLAM methods have yet to achieve an advantage in accuracy due to the lack of determinism in semantic constraints. The methods of obtaining generalizable priors driven through large amounts of data has become an important trend. However, it is the disadvantage of neural networks to represent the constraints generated by precise properties like 6DoF poses. Additionally, GS-SLAM [55]leverages 3D Gaussian Splatting for dense visual SLAM, achieving efficient map optimization and RGB-D rendering via real-time differentiable splatting, which provides a new direction for scene representation in challenging environments.

2.2 Object SLAM

Object SLAM utilizes constraints established by objects to enhance the performance of SLAM. The representation of objects in Object SLAM mainly includes CAD models, reconstructed models, and geometric representations.

Object pose tracking has been applied for SLAM with CAD model priors. [23] leveraged object pose tracking to initialize the scale of SLAM, and take over only when SLAM fails. SLAM++ [42] employs CAD model representation and establishes constraints through ICP [3]. [26] focuses on pose estimation for symmetric objects. Some methods reconstruct models from image sequences, [41] combines ICP and photometric error, and [31] establishes constraints through contour alignment. However, these methods require RGB-D input. For RGB input, [14] uses 3D-2D correspondences to map extracted keypoints on the objects onto space as anchor points for SLAM optimization. This approach may not be effective when dealing with textureless objects.

Some works use geometric representations for object modeling. CubeSLAM [56] recovers cuboid representation from line information and 2D bounding box, but it is not suitable for irregular objects. Another category of methods employs dual quadrics as object representation from 2D bounding box. They jointly estimate the camera pose and the dual quadrics parameters by their optimazation framework. In some studies [30,37,60], it has been observed that incorporating this representation into SLAM optimization, while performing well in loop closure [21] and relocation [60], can lead to a decrease in camera trajectory accuracy. We think that the decrease is from imprecise object localization.

Scale constraints, symmetry constraints, and planar support constraints are explored in [30]. [53] uses RGB-D data input with edge constraints. The addition of these new constraints does not fundamentally address the errors introduced by dual quadrics representations, which arise from inaccurate object pose estimation. Instead, it introduces new constraints to compensate for these errors. Therefore, we focus on addressing the problem fundamentally by employing a 3D object tracking module to estimate object pose in monocular RGB SLAM.

2.3 Textureless 3D Object Tracking

3D object tracking technology involves estimating the pose of an object relative to the camera in an image sequence, forming a crucial foundation for understanding the relationship between scene objects and the camera. When an object has sufficient distinctive features, its tracking problem is similar to the traditional feature-based SLAM camera tracking problem. For tracking textureless or weakly textured objects, CAD models are often used as support, providing good speed and accuracy. These methods typically rely on image edges [6,8,12,16,20,33,44, 52] or region [4,5,7,10,18,22,34,38,40,43,46,47,51,58] information or combine both types of features [19]. They commonly use the object shape information and optimize along the contour points of textureless objects, aligned with the direction of the contour normals. Edge-based methods extract edges as candidates for object edges, while region-based methods essentially maximize the likelihood of foreground and background during the optimization process.

Currently, the most accurate methods in 3D object tracking methods include ICG+ [46], SLOT [19], and [50]. ICG+ [46] significantly improves computational speed using pre-rendered templates, making it a benchmark for our 3D object tracking. Newly progress includes that the object pose can be tracked without 3D model priors [45], or estimated based on deep learning with limited priors [11, 15,29,32,54]. However, their computation speed and accuracy typically do not meet the precision requirements for real-time tracking and are usually used for tracking initialization or recovery from failures.

Moreover, although 3D object tracking does not necessarily require objects to be in motion, in a static scene, there exist stationary object pose relationships across multiple frames. Furthermore, we establish object pose constraints across multiple frames with object shape and map points in a static scene can yield more accurate object tracking results.

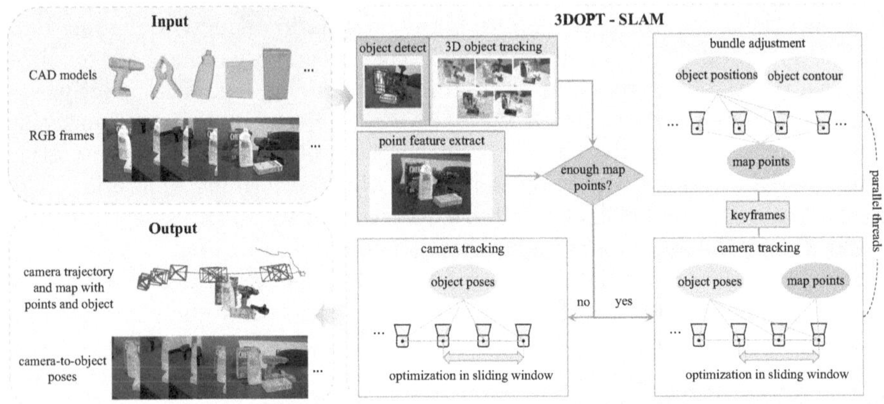

Fig. 1. The overview of our proposed SLAM system. Inputting known textureless object models and RGB frames, the initial pose of the object is obtained using a detection network. For each frame, we observe the 6DoF object poses by 3D object tracking module and attempt to establish map points. When the object is continuously visible, the 3D object tracking module provides stable tracking of the object, potentially addressing object matching issue. When there are not enough map points in the scene, the localization relies solely on object poses in the sliding window frames. As soon as enough map points are established, the front-end depends on points from adjacent frames and object poses in sliding window frames for localization. In the back end, optimization is performed on objects and map points on keyframes. Finally, the output includes camera trajectories and a map containing objects and map points. At the same time, in the optimization framework, leveraging the static constraints of both scene feature points and objects across multiple frames resulted in more accurate 3D object tracking results.

3 Method

In this section, we give an overview of our pipeline. This system is based on the ORB-SLAM2 [35] comprising a camera tracking front-end and a bundle adjustment (BA) back-end. Our primary modifications in the front-end involve the addition of a object-only camera localization. For the BA process, we incorporates both object and points to enhance SLAM performance.

As shown in Fig. 1, we establish the camera coordinate system of the first frame as the world coordinate system. Given the CAD model of an object, we obtain the initial pose of the object by detection module. The initial pose is then refined using a 3D object tracking module. For each frame in the RGB video stream, we perform 3D object tracking, as described in 3.1, and extract image feature points. Transforming the object into a 6DoF anchor in the scene using the object-world-camera relationship described in 3.2, we establish an optimization framework involving points and objects. In the camera tracking process as described in 3.3, we introduce the 6DoF anchor and points for camera localization. Once a reliable set of map points is established, both the camera tracking and BA threads run simultaneously. The back-end BA thread, as described in 3.4, conducts joint optimization based on points and objects across multiple keyframes. Finally, the g2o [25] optimization library is employed to obtain the results for 3DOPT-SLAM.

Notations: the main symbols are listed in Table 1, followed by a brief explanation with some examples. Specifically, for example, $\boldsymbol{T}_{c_j o_k}$ represents the transformation from object k coordinate system to camera coordinate system of frame j. $\boldsymbol{X}_{o_k}^{e_{ki}}$ represents the i-th contour point of the object k in the object coordinate system o_k. $\boldsymbol{X}_{w}^{m_i}$ represents the i-th map point in the world coordinate system.

Table 1. The main symbols in our paper.

Symbol	Meaning
$\boldsymbol{T}$	transformation, belonging to $\mathbb{SE}(3)$
$\boldsymbol{X}$	3D point, belonging to $\mathbb{R}^3$
subscript o, w, c	object, world, camera coordinate system
subscript i, j, k	3D point, frame, object index
superscript m, e	map point, contour point
$\mathcal{O}_j$	the index set of objects tracked in frame j
$\mathcal{E}_k$	the index set of contour points for object k

3.1 3D Object Pose Tracking

The 3D object tracking module obtains 6DoF object-to-camera pose. We opted for the state-of-the-art region-based method ICG+ [46] as the baseline for obtaining individual object poses. ICG+ [46] utilizes a pre-known CAD model to create a pre-rendered template of the foreground, sampling corresponding lines along the foreground contour. It achieves the object pose of a single object in the current frame by maximizing the foreground-background probability along these lines. For more detailed implementation, please refer to [46]. It is worth noting that ICG+ [46] tends to provide stable object tracking when the object is continuously visible. This characteristic addresses our object matching challenge.

Building upon ICG+ [46], we incorporate spatiotemporal static relationships in the static scene. In scenarios where feature points are not operational, we perform joint optimization of multiple objects across a sliding window of frames. Once reliable map points can be established, we combine scene map points and objects across multiple keyframes for 3D object tracking optimization.

3.2 Object-World-Camera Relationship

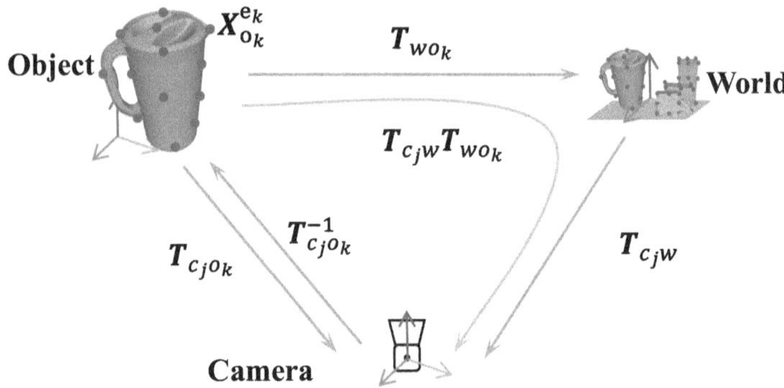

Fig. 2. Object-world-camera relationship. The transformation relationships between the object coordinate system, world coordinate system, and camera coordinate system. The red points represent sampled model points that may correspond to the object contour points of the frame. (Color figure online)

To transform objects in the scene into 6DoF anchors, we define the object-world-camera relationship, describing the relationship between the world coordinate system, camera coordinate system, and object coordinate system as illustrated in Fig. 2. The estimated pose $\boldsymbol{T}_{c_j o_k}$ from the 3D object tracking is treated as an observation. Theoretically, this pose can also be derived by $\boldsymbol{T}_{c_j o_k} = \boldsymbol{T}_{c_j w}\boldsymbol{T}_{wo_k}$, transforming the object pose in the world coordinate system $\boldsymbol{T}_{wo_k}$ into the camera coordinate system with $\boldsymbol{T}_{c_j w}$.

The object-to-camera pose obtained from 3D object tracking makes textureless objects in the scene become 6DoF anchors, providing a more comprehensive and generalized feature compared to feature points.

3.3 Camera Tracking

Our camera tracking process provides real-time pose estimation in the front-end. At the beginning of the sequence, when reliable map points cannot be established due to a lack of scene feature points or small disparities, our camera tracking process estimates the camera pose using the 6DoF anchors in a sliding window on frames. Once reliable map points are successfully established in the scene, camera tracking performs real-time pose estimation using both 6DoF anchors and map points, concurrently initiating the BA thread. We propose a unified optimization formulation that incorporates camera motion model errors, object 6DoF pose errors, and point reprojection errors, addressing both scenarios.

Camera Motion Model Constraint. From the previous frames motion changes $\Delta \boldsymbol{T}_{c_{j-1}w} = \boldsymbol{T}_{c_{j-1}w}\boldsymbol{T}_{c_{j-2}w}^{-1}$, we derive the initial pose of the current frame j ($j > 1$):

$$\boldsymbol{T}_{c_j w} = \Delta \boldsymbol{T}_{c_{j-1}w}\boldsymbol{T}_{c_{j-1}w} \tag{1}$$

In the meanwhile, the camera motion model error $e_{c\_mot_j}$ is established as follows:

$$\hat{\boldsymbol{r}}_{c\_mot_j} = ln(\Delta \boldsymbol{T}_{c_{j-1}w}\boldsymbol{T}_{c_{j-1}w}\boldsymbol{T}_{c_j w}^{-1}) \tag{2}$$

$$e_{c\_mot_j} = \boldsymbol{r}_{c\_mot_j}^{\top} diag(\boldsymbol{\lambda}_{c\_mot}^{\top})\boldsymbol{r}_{c\_mot_j} \tag{3}$$

where $\boldsymbol{\lambda}_{c\_mot}$ represents different wights to measure each component in $\boldsymbol{r}_{c\_mot_j}$, $diag(.)$ creates a diagonal matrix from a vector. A pose $\boldsymbol{T} \in \mathbb{SE}(3)$ can be mapped to $\hat{\boldsymbol{r}} \in \mathbb{R}^{4\times 4}$ by the logarithmic mapping $ln(.)$, and $\boldsymbol{r} \in \mathbb{R}^6$ is the Lie algebra corresponding to $\hat{\boldsymbol{r}}$ by $\hat{\boldsymbol{r}} = ln(\boldsymbol{T})$, for further details of Lie algebra, please refer to [2].

Object 6DoF Pose Constraint. Our goal in the camera tracking process is the camera-world pose, so we incorporate the object pose into the optimization. For the same object, the pose obtained through the object-world-camera transformation should remain consistent. We use the logarithm to map the $\mathbb{SE}(3)$ error to the tangent space of 6DoF, the object pose error $e_{o\_pos_j}$ on the j-th frame is:

$$\hat{\boldsymbol{r}}_{o_k} = ln(\boldsymbol{T}_{c_j o_k}^{-1}\boldsymbol{T}_{c_j w}\boldsymbol{T}_{w o_k}) e_{o\_pose_j} = \sum_{k\in\mathcal{O}_j} \hat{\boldsymbol{r}}_{o_k}^{\top} diag(\boldsymbol{\lambda}_k^{\top})\hat{\boldsymbol{r}}_{o_k} \tag{4}$$

where $\boldsymbol{\lambda}_k$ are different wights to measure each component in object k.

As the number of objects in a single frame is limited, we perform camera pose optimization in the sliding window. With the map point reprojection error, object pose error, and camera motion model error for the current frame q, here is our camera tracking formulation:

$$\{\boldsymbol{T}_{c_j w} | j \in \mathcal{W}\}^* = \underset{\boldsymbol{T}_{c_j w}}{\arg\min}\, e_{point_q} + \sum_{j\in\mathcal{W}} (\lambda_{o\_pose} e_{o\_pose_j} + \lambda_{mot} e_{c\_mot_j}) \tag{5}$$

where $\mathcal{W}$ represents the set of frames index in the sliding window $(q-s,\ q]$, s represents the window size. The e_{point_j} is the map point reprojection error in the frame j:

$$e_{point_j} = \sum_{\boldsymbol{X}_w^{m_i}\in\mathcal{P}_j} \left\|\boldsymbol{x}_i - \pi(\boldsymbol{T}_{c_j w}\boldsymbol{X}_w^{m_i})\right\|^2 \tag{6}$$

where $\pi(.)$ can project a 3D point in the camera coordinate system onto the image, $\mathcal{P}_j$ represents the map points in frame j, $\boldsymbol{x}_i$ represents the corresponding point of map point $\boldsymbol{X}_w^{m_i}$ on the image.

With the camera tracking, we can still perform camera-to-world pose estimation based on objects, in scenes where establishing map points is challenging.

3.4 Bundle Adjustment

In our back-end optimization, we propose constraints based on object position and shape in addition to the map point errors.

Object Position Constraint. To save optimization time, we use object position error instead of object poses error during back-end optimization. According to the object-world-camera relationship, the object observed by the 3D object tracking module and the object transformed into the world coordinate system should have the same spatial position. For frame j, we establish the object center point error $e_{o\_position_j}$ as follows:

$$e_{o\_position_j} = \sum_{k \in \mathcal{O}_j} \left\| trans(\boldsymbol{T}_{c_j o_k}) - trans(\boldsymbol{T}_{c_j w}\boldsymbol{T}_{wo_k}) \right\|^2 \tag{7}$$

where $\mathcal{O}_j$ represents the objects tracked on the j-th frame, $trans(.)$ represents the translation component of the object pose.

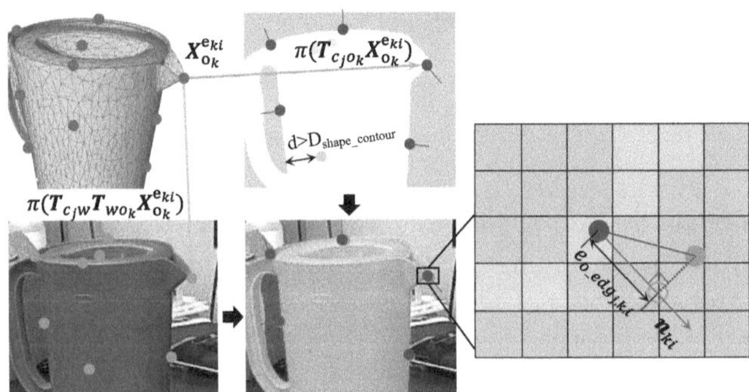

Fig. 3. 2D object contour error along the normal. By projecting object points (red points) through 3D object tracking (process on the gray arrow), when the distance between the contour and the projected point exceeds $D_{shape\_contour}(Color figure online)$, we consider that the point (yellow points) is not on the contour of the current frame. When it's less than $D_{shape\_contour}$, we consider the object point to be on the object contour of the current frame (blue points). The error is calculated between the blue points and the corresponding green points projected by $\boldsymbol{T}_{c_j w}\boldsymbol{T}_{wo_k}$ along the normal (red line). The same object point naturally forms a pair of matching points.

Object Shape Constraint. We discretize the shape of the CAD model into object points. By randomly sampling these points and applying the object-world-camera transformation relationship, the same object point should also map to the same position. Different mappings from the same object point naturally form matching point pairs. In the meanwhile, the 3D object tracking module optimizes along the normals of the object contour, establishing constraints in 3D space would lead to large errors along the viewing direction. Therefore, we also establish errors in the 2D image. We simply use distance-based criteria to find object points in the current frame object contour. When the projection of a 3D object point is less than $D_{shape\_contour}$, we consider this point to be on the contour of the current frame, as shown in Fig. 3.

For frame j, as shown in Fig. 3, the 3D object contour points transformed in various ways into the camera coordinate are projected onto the image first, followed by projecting their distance along the normal direction. The object contour error $e_{o\_contour_j}$ can be calculated as follows:

$$e_{o\_contour_j} = \sum_{k \in \mathcal{O}_j} \sum_{i \in \mathcal{E}_{k,j}} \left\| \left\langle \hat{\boldsymbol{n}_{ki}} \left(\pi(\boldsymbol{T}_{c_j o_k} \boldsymbol{X}_{o_k}^{e_{ki}}) - \pi(\boldsymbol{T}_{c_j w} \boldsymbol{T}_{w o_k} \boldsymbol{X}_{o_k}^{e_{ki}}) \right) \right\rangle \right\|^2 \tag{8}$$

where $\mathcal{E}_{k,j}$ represents the set of contour points index of the k-th object on the j-th frame, $\pi(.)$ can project a 3D point in the camera coordinate system onto the image, $\hat{\boldsymbol{n}_{ki}}$ represents the corresponding unit contour normals for the i-th contour point of the k-th object.

We use map points and objects to describe the scene. When map points are established, we perform joint optimization on keyframes in the back-end, incorporating constraints based on map point reprojection error, object position error and object shepe error. Finally, here is our BA formulation:

$$\begin{aligned} &\{\boldsymbol{T}_{c_j w}, \boldsymbol{X}_w^{m_i} | j \in \mathcal{K}, \boldsymbol{X}_w^{m_i} \in \mathcal{P}\}^* = \\ &\mathop{\arg\min}_{\boldsymbol{T}_{c_j w}, \boldsymbol{X}_w^{m_i}} \sum_{j \in \mathcal{K}} (e_{point_j} + \lambda_{o\_position} e_{o\_position_j} + \lambda_{o\_shape} e_{o\_contour_j}) \end{aligned} \tag{9}$$

where $\mathcal{K}$ represents the set of keyframes index, and $\mathcal{P}$ represents the set of map points.

The back-end optimization involves joint optimization across multiple keyframes, optimizing the observations of 3D objects from various perspectives. After optimization by g2o [25], the object-to-camera pose can be calculated from the object-world-camera relationship. In this way, both the front-end and back-end, built upon the original SLAM framework, are enhanced in robustness and accuracy through the pose information provided by the 3D object tracking module.

Fig. 4. The workflow and SLAM results comparison on the YCB-Video 52 sequence (low texture). ORB-SLAM2 [35]* fails to track due to the inability to extract features. Our method, using the objects as anchors (blue area), achieves camera localization.

4 Experiment

4.1 Setup

The equipment used in our experiments was a desktop computer with an Intel i7-8700 CPU 3.20 GHz, a Nvidia GeForce GTX 1060 3GB GPU, and 16GB of RAM. The optimization is solved using the g2o [25] optimization library.

Datasets. As our experiments require CAD models, we evaluate our system on the YCB-Video [54] dataset. Following the experimental setup as ICG+ [46], we test on sequences 48–59 while adjusting parameter choices on other sequences. Given the evident inaccuracies on the YCB-Video data, we use calibrated data [28] as ground truth. Additionally, as show in Table 2, we evaluate our system on the TUM RGB-D [48] cabinet sequence. This weak feature scene is challenging for SLAM. We roughly reconstruct the model of the cabinet and use RGB data as experiment input.

Metrics. In the camera tracking evaluation, we assess the Root Mean Square Error (RMSE) of Absolute Trajectory Error (ATE). The results represent the average over ten runs. In the 3D object tracking evaluation, metrics are performed as defined by [51]. We calculate the translation error e_t and rotation error e_r between the estimated pose and the ground truth pose and then evaluate the success rates of $e_t < Th_t$, $Th_t \in \{1cm, 2cm, 5cm, 10cm\}$ or $e_r < Th_r$, $Th_r \in \{1^\circ, 2^\circ, 5^\circ, 10^\circ\}$ on each object. Since a sequence contains multiple objects, we calculate the average success rate of multiple objects.

Parameters. For the front-end sliding window frame optimization, we set the window size to $s = 20$. This ensures a balance between efficiency and accuracy. λ_{c_mot}=[0.3, 0.3, 0.3, 0.3, 0.3, 0.3], λ_k=[0.35, 0.35, 0.35, 0.35, 0.35, 0.35]. For back-end BA, because our framework integrates objects and feature points. We employ dynamic weights related to the number of optimization terms for objects and points and fixed weights to control the optimization. For object position constraint, $\lambda_{o_{position}}$ is related to op_num_weight.

$$op\_num\_weight = size(points)/size(objects\_position)$$

$$\lambda_{o\_position} = \begin{cases} 0.3 \times op\_num\_weight & \text{if } op\_num\_weight < 80.0 \\ 0.15 \times op\_num\_weight & \text{if } op\_num\_weight \geq 80.0 \end{cases}$$

For object shape constraint, $\lambda_{o_{shape}}$ is related to os_num_weight.

$$os\_num\_weight = size(points)/size(objects\_shape)$$

$$\lambda_{o\_shape} = \begin{cases} 3.0 \times os\_num\_weight & \text{if } os\_num\_weight < 1.0 \\ 1.5 \times os\_num\_weight & \text{if } os\_num\_weight \geq 1.0 \end{cases}$$

For each CAD model, the number of sampled object points is set to 400. The threshold $D_{shape\_contour}$ for the distance from model points to contour points is 0.8 pixels. The object pose of the first frame can be obtained using a detection network [17, 49]. In our experiments, we simulate them by applying perturbations to the ground truth.

Table 2. RMSE of camera trajectories ATE(cm) on the YCB-Video dataset and TUM RGB-D(RGB input only) cabinet sequence. The results are the average of 10 runs for each sequence, with the best results shown in bold. * indicates the algorithm reproduced on our local computer. Ours(BA) denotes the error on frames optimized jointly with objects after successful map point establishment, evaluating the performance of our back-end framework. Ours(o+BA) includes the error on frames which are all frames in the test sequence optimized jointly with objects after relying solely on object localization and map point establishment.

Seq.	CubeSLAM* [56]	DSO* [13]	ORB-SLAM2* [35]	Ours (BA)	Ours (o+BA)
YCB-Video / 48	7.0999	5.8057	6.8772	**1.0799**	1.1049
YCB-Video / 49	0.9701	2.1127	0.7423	**0.5594**	0.5740
YCB-Video / 50	3.1747	4.0587	1.3840	**0.7305**	0.7490
YCB-Video / 51	5.1720	5.1793	1.3425	**0.4908**	0.5399
YCB-Video / 52	N/A	2.8291	N/A	N/A	**0.7849**
YCB-Video / 53	N/A	3.1257	N/A	N/A	**2.0937**
YCB-Video / 54	3.1729	3.4811	1.9252	**0.8470**	1.3827
YCB-Video / 55	1.5718	3.6053	1.0455	**0.3108**	2.7073
YCB-Video / 56	N/A	2.1189	N/A	N/A	**1.3906**
YCB-Video / 57	5.7724	5.7086	2.3196	**1.4303**	**1.4303**
YCB-Video / 58	2.0553	4.1952	1.2808	**0.7196**	0.7396
YCB-Video / 59	3.1983	3.8574	3.3780	**1.1927**	1.2914
TUM / cabinet	17.0000	N/A	N/A	N/A	**14.9994**

4.2 Camera Pose Estimation Results

We compare the accuracy of camera trajectory with the SOTA monocular RGB SLAM methods ORB-SLAM2 [35], DSO [13], and representative work in object SLAM CubeSLAM [56], in Table2. The symbol * represent reproductions in our computer of the respective algorithm. The results for CubeSLAM [56]* on TUM RGB-D cabinet sequence are taken from the [56]. N/A indicates that there are 5 or more failures out of 10 attempts in the tests on these sequences, suggesting that SLAM for these sequences could not be successfully completed.

Ours(BA) represents our back-end BA optimization framework using constraints on the map point, object position and object shape. The results in this column consistently outperform all other methods, demonstrating the effectiveness of our back-end BA optimization framework. CubeSLAM [56]* models objects using the representation of cubes and combines them with points for optimization. However, compared to ORB-SLAM2 [35]*, CubeSLAM [56]* exhibits a decrease in accuracy on the YCB-Video dataset. We attribute this to the limitations in accurately describing object poses on the YCB-Video dataset using prior knowledge and cube representations. This is also validating our hypothesis that more accurate object pose estimation can improve the accuracy of camera pose estimation.

In 52, 53, and 56 sequences, due to failed to establish map points, CubeSLAM [56]*, ORB-SLAM2 [35]* and Ours(BA) relying on points and objects are unable to operate. Ours(o+BA) includes the part where the camera is positioned solely relying on objects, complementing SLAM in these situation, highlighting the robustness of our system in low-texture environments.

Figure 4 present a qualitative and quantitative comparison of the workflow and experimental outcomes between our system and ORB-SLAM2 [35]*.

Table 3. Success rate(%) of 3D object tracking on the YCB-Video dataset.

	1.0 cm↑		2.0 cm↑		5.0 cm↑		10.0 cm↑		1.0° ↑		2.0°↑		5.0° ↑		10.0°↑	
Seq.	Ours	ICG+ [46]*	Ours	ICG+ [46]*	Ours	ICG+ [46]*	Ours	ICG+ [46]*	Ours	ICG+ [46]*	Ours	ICG+ [46]*	Ours	ICG+ [46]*	Ours	ICG+ [46]*
48	**27.32**	21.50	**58.74**	36.00	**100.00**	63.96	**100.00**	84.53	**54.68**	6.11	**94.19**	16.76	**99.89**	38.85	**100.00**	59.58
49	**99.08**	43.46	**99.37**	53.07	**99.96**	57.83	**100.00**	63.83	**75.28**	7.85	**99.29**	33.51	**99.44**	49.66	**100.00**	58.32
50	**98.91**	32.35	**99.88**	58.86	**100.00**	84.99	**100.00**	86.95	**73.82**	30.31	**96.01**	53.30	**99.89**	68.32	**100.00**	82.95
51	**99.33**	30.62	**99.90**	59.62	**99.99**	83.66	**100.00**	96.82	**89.41**	9.70	**99.52**	24.44	**99.76**	55.51	**99.80**	73.40
52	**75.14**	74.98	**98.89**	98.86	**100.00**	**100.00**	**100.00**	**100.00**	**29.20**	26.97	**57.09**	55.45	**73.67**	70.42	**97.37**	96.74
53	**49.84**	48.55	**80.21**	74.36	**90.54**	86.49	**98.90**	98.63	**17.13**	16.73	**33.78**	33.74	**51.90**	51.42	**81.30**	78.80
54	**51.12**	44.97	**66.30**	62.28	**95.64**	91.45	**100.00**	98.08	**12.98**	12.55	**60.53**	38.40	**89.50**	78.81	**93.09**	92.18
55	**39.93**	36.42	**67.26**	66.66	**79.73**	78.77	**91.54**	88.28	**6.16**	5.45	**29.11**	28.22	**57.64**	53.52	**67.65**	63.88
56	**58.06**	57.18	**72.27**	70.55	**85.68**	85.06	**96.35**	96.18	**30.71**	29.87	**62.67**	60.94	**83.56**	82.34	**88.88**	87.87
57	**81.91**	25.72	**98.05**	46.95	**99.75**	69.01	**99.86**	78.77	**59.26**	3.51	**89.30**	19.31	**99.39**	51.50	**99.55**	65.98
58	**99.19**	67.98	**99.51**	74.21	**99.87**	76.11	**99.89**	76.38	**88.03**	11.24	**98.89**	37.56	**99.86**	67.07	**99.87**	73.63
59	**91.25**	14.36	**98.99**	30.69	**99.65**	59.75	**99.97**	65.33	**26.05**	1.76	**63.48**	5.97	**98.82**	28.08	**99.83**	47.26
AVG.	**72.59**	41.51	**86.61**	61.01	**95.90**	78.09	**98.87**	86.15	**46.89**	13.50	**73.65**	33.97	**87.51**	58.23	**93.94**	73.38

In our experiment on the TUM RGB-D cabinet sequence, as shown in the last row of Table 2. ORB-SLAM2 [35]* and DSO [13]* failed. Furthermore, our performance surpasses CubeSLAM [56] as we leverage more regional information from images, as shown in Table 2. QISO-SLAM [53] is an Object SLAM algorithm utilizing dual quadric representation with RGB-D input. QISO-SLAM

Fig. 5. Our results (middle) of 3D object tracking on the YCB-Video dataset, compared with groundtruth (top) and ICG+ [46] (bottom). The red arrow indicates objects with a larger pose estimation error by our 3D object tracking benchmark ICG+ [46]. Our method leverages the joint optimization of multiple objects and map points in the scene from various viewpoints, effectively improving the 3D object tracking results.

Table 4. Runtime (mSec) of different system components on the YCB-Video dataset.

Components	Runtime
Track an object (per object)	3.44 ms
Tracking (per frame)	32.87 ms
BA (per round)	170.18 ms

published the ATE RMSE between frames 850 and 1100 with a value of 4.8 cm, and ours is 3.0 cm in these frames. It's noteworthy that despite using RGB input, our results outperform QISO-SLAM.

The results on the YCB-Video dataset and TUM cabinet sequence demonstrate that our proposed sliding window object localization and optimization framework based on feature points, object shape, and object position can enhance the robustness of SLAM and improve camera localization accuracy. It even compares favorably with some RGB-D methods.

4.3 3D Object Tracking Results

We replicated the current state-of-the-art method for region-based object tracking, our 3D object tracking baseline ICG+ [46]. Table 3 shows the comparison results of 3D object tracking evaluation sequences on the YCB-Video dataset, where ICG+* denotes the algorithm replication of ICG [46]+ on a local machine. There is even a 40% increase in success rates for 1 cm or 1°. Within 5 cm or within 5°, over 90% of frames in most sequences are successfully tracked. This indicates that introducing optimization involving multiple frames and feature points, in addition to constraints based on object shape and position, significantly improves the stability and accuracy of 3D object tracking. Figure 5 shows that our method has achieved more accurate 3D object tracking results qualitatively.

4.4 Time Analysis

We provide a time evaluation of our system. As shown in Table 4, 3D object tracking for each object takes approximately 3.44 ms, and the tested sequences typically involve 3–6 objects. The tracking process, including tracking multiple objects and camera tracking, operates at approximately 30 Hz, meeting real-time requirements. BA runs in a separate back-end thread and is not constrained by real-time limitations. Additionally, we can adjust the sliding window size for object-based front-end camera tracking to meet real-time performance. All experiments are conducted with a sliding window size of 20.

4.5 Ablation Study

To validate the effectiveness of the constraints proposed in our current work on the back-end BA, we conducted ablation study on the different constraints in the back-end, as shown in Table 5. In the first case, only the point constraint is equivalent to our baseline ORB-SLAM2 [35]. The second case involves map point and object position constraints. The third case involves map point and object shape constraints. In both of these cases, object constraints improve the baseline accuracy. In the end, with map points, object position and shape, our system effectively utilizes object information. This leads to promising results across various sequences.

4.6 Limitations and Future Work

While our system has demonstrated good results on public datasets and sequences, there are still some challenges to address for further improvement in quality and generality.

In our current 3D object tracking module, our pipeline relies on known 3D models. This is because textureless 3D object tracking often requires knowledge of the object shape. Although this aligns well with certain industrial scenarios where models are known, this restricts the application of our approach in more diverse scenes. We believe that simultaneously reconstructing, tracking,

Table 5. RMSE of camera trajectories ATE (cm) on the YCB-Video dataset with different constraint in the back-end.

Seq.	point	point+position	point+shape	point+position +shape
48	6.8772	1.2827	1.5307	**1.0799**
49	0.7423	0.5647	0.5631	**0.5594**
50	1.3840	0.7328	1.0239	**0.7305**
51	1.3425	0.7302	0.4966	**0.4908**
54	1.9252	0.8942	0.8796	**0.8470**
55	1.0455	0.4776	0.5800	**0.3108**
57	2.3196	1.6471	**1.3006**	1.4303
58	1.2808	0.7227	0.7253	**0.7196**
59	3.3780	1.2402	1.2036	**1.1927**
AVG.	2.2550	0.9214	0.9226	**0.8179**

and optimizing object shapes will be an interesting direction. Additionally, in the sequences tested so far, objects are visible in all frames. When the object becomes temporarily invisible or reappears, our system relies on the object detection network and 3D object tracking modules to estimate the initial pose. However, this is constrained by the accuracy of the detection network. Furthermore, the current pipeline does not incorporate loop closure and relocation, which suggests that tracking performance could be further enhanced.

5 Conclusions

We propose a monocular RGB SLAM approach called 3DOPT-SLAM, which leverages 6DoF object pose constraints to overcome the problems of SLAM in weak feature environments. By the stable continuous textureless object pose tracking, our SLAM framework establishes constraints based on map points, object position and object shape. Simultaneously, by incorporating map points from multiple keyframes due to static scene constraints, our approach also enhances 3D object tracking. Evaluations on the public dataset demonstrate that our method improves the accuracy and robustness of camera trajectory estimation, indirectly leading to more precise tracking of static objects.

Acknowledgements. This work is partially supported by the NSF of China (No. 62172260), and the National Key R&D Program of China under grant (No. 2022YFB3303203).

References

1. Adkins, A., Chen, T., Biswas, J.: Obvi-slam: long-term object-visual SLAM. IEEE Robotics Autom. Lett. **9**(3), 2909–2916 (2024)

2. Alexander Kirillov, J.: An Introduction to Lie Groups and Lie Algebras. Cambridge Studies in Advanced Mathematics, Cambridge University Press (2008)
3. Besl, P.J., McKay, N.D.: Method for registration of 3-D shapes. In: Sensor fusion IV: control paradigms and data structures. vol. 1611, pp. 586–606. Spie (1992)
4. Bibby, C., Reid, I.: Robust real-time visual tracking using pixel-wise posteriors. In: Computer Vision–ECCV 2008: 10th European Conference on Computer Vision, Marseille, France, October 12-18, 2008, Proceedings, Part II 10, pp. 831–844. Springer (2008)
5. Brox, T., Rosenhahn, B., Gall, J., Cremers, D.: Combined region and motion-based 3D tracking of rigid and articulated objects. IEEE Trans. Pattern Anal. Mach. Intell. **32**(3), 402–415 (2009)
6. Bugaev, B., Kryshchenko, A., Belov, R.: Combining 3D model contour energy and keypoints for object tracking. In: Proceedings of the European Conference on Computer Vision (ECCV), pp. 53–69 (2018)
7. Chan, T.F., Vese, L.A.: Active contours without edges. IEEE Trans. Image Process. **10**(2), 266–277 (2001)
8. Comport, A.I., Marchand, E., Pressigout, M., Chaumette, F.: Real-time markerless tracking for augmented reality: the virtual visual servoing framework. IEEE Trans. Visual Comput. Graphics **12**(4), 615–628 (2006)
9. Concha, A., Civera, J.: Dpptam: Dense piecewise planar tracking and mapping from a monocular sequence. In: 2015 IEEE/RSJ International Conference on Intelligent Robots and Systems (IROS), pp. 5686–5693. IEEE (2015)
10. Dambreville, S., Sandhu, R., Yezzi, A., Tannenbaum, A.: Robust 3D pose estimation and efficient 2d region-based segmentation from a 3D shape prior. In: Computer Vision–ECCV 2008: 10th European Conference on Computer Vision, Marseille, France, October 12-18, 2008, Proceedings, Part II 10. pp. 169–182. Springer (2008)
11. Deng, X., Mousavian, A., Xiang, Y., Xia, F., Bretl, T., Fox, D.: Poserbpf: A rao-blackwellized particle filter for 6-D object pose tracking. IEEE Trans. Rob. **37**(5), 1328–1342 (2021)
12. Drummond, T., Cipolla, R.: Real-time visual tracking of complex structures. IEEE Trans. Pattern Anal. Mach. Intell. **24**(7), 932–946 (2002)
13. Engel, J., Koltun, V., Cremers, D.: Direct sparse odometry. IEEE Trans. Pattern Anal. Mach. Intell. **40**(3), 611–625 (2017)
14. Gálvez-López, D., Salas, M., Tardós, J.D., Montiel, J.M.: Real-time monocular object slam. Robot. Auton. Syst. **75**, 435–449 (2016)
15. Garon, M., Lalonde, J.F.: Deep 6-dof tracking. IEEE Trans. Visual Comput. Graphics **23**(11), 2410–2418 (2017)
16. Harris, C., Stennett, C.: Rapid-a video rate object tracker. In: BMVC, pp. 1–6 (1990)
17. He, X., Sun, J., Wang, Y., Huang, D., Bao, H., Zhou, X.: Onepose++: keypoint-free one-shot object pose estimation without cad models. Adv. Neural. Inf. Process. Syst. **35**, 35103–35115 (2022)
18. Hexner, J., Hagege, R.R.: 2D–3D pose estimation of heterogeneous objects using a region based approach. Int. J. Comput. Vision **118**, 95–112 (2016)
19. Huang, H., Zhong, F., Qin, X.: Pixel-wise weighted region-based 3D object tracking using contour constraints. IEEE Trans. Visual Comput. Graphics **28**(12), 4319–4331 (2021)
20. Huang, H., Zhong, F., Sun, Y., Qin, X.: An occlusion-aware edge-based method for monocular 3D object tracking using edge confidence. In: Computer Graphics Forum. vol. 39, pp. 399–409. Wiley Online Library (2020)

21. Ji, X., Liu, P., Niu, H., Chen, X., Ying, R., Wen, F.: Loop closure detection based on object-level spatial layout and semantic consistency. arXiv preprint arXiv:2304.05146 (2023)
22. Kass, M., Witkin, A., Terzopoulos, D.: Snakes: active contour models. Int. J. Comput. Vision **1**(4), 321–331 (1988)
23. Kempter, T., Wendel, A., Bischof, H.: Online model-based multi-scale pose estimation. NA (2011)
24. Klein, G., Murray, D.: Parallel tracking and mapping for small ar workspaces. In: 2007 6th IEEE and ACM International Symposium on Mixed and Augmented Reality, pp. 225–234 (2007). https://doi.org/10.1109/ISMAR.2007.4538852
25. Kümmerle, R., Grisetti, G., Strasdat, H., Konolige, K., Burgard, W.: g 2 o: A general framework for graph optimization. In: 2011 IEEE International Conference on Robotics and Automation, pp. 3607–3613. IEEE (2011)
26. Lee, T., Jang, Y., Kim, H.J.: Object-based slam utilizing unambiguous pose parameters considering general symmetry types. arXiv preprint arXiv:2303.07872 (2023)
27. Lemaire, T., Lacroix, S.: Monocular-vision based slam using line segments. In: Proceedings 2007 IEEE International Conference on Robotics and Automation, pp. 2791–2796. IEEE (2007)
28. Li, Y., Zhong, F., Wang, X., Song, S., Li, J., Qin, X., Tu, C.: For a more comprehensive evaluation of 6dof object pose tracking (2023)
29. Li, Y., Wang, G., Ji, X., Xiang, Y., Fox, D.: Deepim: Deep iterative matching for 6D pose estimation. In: Proceedings of the European Conference on Computer Vision (ECCV), pp. 683–698 (2018)
30. Liao, Z., Hu, Y., Zhang, J., Qi, X., Zhang, X., Wang, W.: So-slam: semantic object slam with scale proportional and symmetrical texture constraints. IEEE Rob. Autom. Lett. **7**(2), 4008–4015 (2022)
31. Lin, S., Wang, J., Xu, M., Zhao, H., Chen, Z.: Contour-slam: a robust object-level slam based on contour alignment. IEEE Trans. Instrum. Meas. **72**, 1–12 (2023)
32. Manhardt, F., Kehl, W., Navab, N., Tombari, F.: Deep model-based 6D pose refinement in RGB. In: Proceedings of the European Conference on Computer Vision (ECCV), pp. 800–815 (2018)
33. Marchand, E., Bouthemy, P., Chaumette, F.: A 2D–3D model-based approach to real-time visual tracking. Image Vis. Comput. **19**(13), 941–955 (2001)
34. Mumford, D.B., Shah, J.: Optimal approximations by piecewise smooth functions and associated variational problems. Commun. Pure Appl. Math. (1989)
35. Mur-Artal, R., Tardós, J.D.: Orb-slam2: an open-source slam system for monocular, stereo, and RGB-D cameras. IEEE Trans. Rob. **33**(5), 1255–1262 (2017)
36. Murai, R., Dexheimer, E., Davison, A.J.: Mast3r-slam: Real-time dense SLAM with 3D reconstruction priors. In: CVPR, pp. 16695–16705. Comput. Vision Found. / IEEE (2025)
37. Nicholson, L., Milford, M., Sünderhauf, N.: Quadricslam: dual quadrics from object detections as landmarks in object-oriented slam. IEEE Robo. Autom. Lett. **4**(1), 1–8 (2018)
38. Prisacariu, V.A., Reid, I.D.: Pwp3D: real-time segmentation and tracking of 3D objects. Int. J. Comput. Vision **98**, 335–354 (2012)
39. Pumarola, A., Vakhitov, A., Agudo, A., Sanfeliu, A., Moreno-Noguer, F.: Pl-slam: real-time monocular visual slam with points and lines. In: 2017 IEEE International Conference on Robotics and Automation (ICRA), pp. 4503–4508. IEEE (2017)
40. Rosenhahn, B., Brox, T., Weickert, J.: Three-dimensional shape knowledge for joint image segmentation and pose tracking. Int. J. Comput. Vision **73**, 243–262 (2007)

41. Runz, M., Buffier, M., Agapito, L.: Maskfusion: real-time recognition, tracking and reconstruction of multiple moving objects. In: 2018 IEEE International Symposium on Mixed and Augmented Reality (ISMAR), pp. 10–20. IEEE (2018)
42. Salas-Moreno, R.F., Newcombe, R.A., Strasdat, H., Kelly, P.H., Davison, A.J.: Slam++: simultaneous localisation and mapping at the level of objects. In: Proceedings of the IEEE Conference on Computer Vision and Pattern Recognition, pp. 1352–1359 (2013)
43. Schmaltz, C., Rosenhahn, B., Brox, T., Weickert, J.: Region-based pose tracking with occlusions using 3D models. Mach. Vis. Appl. **23**(3), 557–577 (2012)
44. Seo, B.K., Park, H., Park, J.I., Hinterstoisser, S., Ilic, S.: Optimal local searching for fast and robust textureless 3D object tracking in highly cluttered backgrounds. IEEE Trans. Visual Comput. Graphics **20**(1), 99–110 (2013)
45. Song, X., et al.: Prior-free 3D object tracking. In: Proceedings of the IEEE Conference on Computer Vision and Pattern Recognition (CVPR). IEEE (2025)
46. Stoiber, M., Elsayed, M., Rechert, A.E., Steidle, F., Lee, D., Triebel, R.: Fusing visual appearance and geometry for multi-modality 6dof object tracking (2023)
47. Stoiber, M., Pfanne, M., Strobl, K.H., Triebel, R., Albu-Schaeffer, A.: Srt3D: a sparse region-based 3D object tracking approach for the real world. Int. J. Comput. Vision **130**(4), 1008–1030 (2022)
48. Sturm, J., Engelhard, N., Endres, F., Burgard, W., Cremers, D.: A benchmark for the evaluation of rgb-d slam systems. In: Proceeding of the International Conference on Intelligent Robot Systems (IROS) (2012)
49. Sun, J., et al.: Onepose: one-shot object pose estimation without cad models. In: Proceedings of the IEEE/CVF Conference on Computer Vision and Pattern Recognition, pp. 6825–6834 (2022)
50. Tian, X., Lin, X., Zhong, F., Qin, X.: Large-displacement 3D object tracking with hybrid non-local optimization. In: European Conference on Computer Vision, pp. 627–643. Springer (2022)
51. Tjaden, H., Schwanecke, U., Schömer, E., Cremers, D.: A region-based gauss-newton approach to real-time monocular multiple object tracking. IEEE Trans. Pattern Anal. Mach. Intell. **41**(8), 1797–1812 (2018)
52. Wang, G., Wang, B., Zhong, F., Qin, X., Chen, B.: Global optimal searching for textureless 3D object tracking. Vis. Comput. **31**, 979–988 (2015)
53. Wang, Y., Xu, B., Fan, W., Xiang, C.: Qiso-slam: object-oriented slam using dual quadrics as landmarks based on instance segmentation. IEEE Robo. Autom. Lett. **8**(4), 2253–2260 (2023)
54. Xiang, Y., Schmidt, T., Narayanan, V., Fox, D.: Posecnn: a convolutional neural network for 6d object pose estimation in cluttered scenes. arXiv preprint arXiv:1711.00199 (2017)
55. Yan, C., et al.: GS-SLAM: dense visual SLAM with 3D gaussian splatting. In: CVPR, pp. 19595–19604. IEEE (2024)
56. Yang, S., Scherer, S.: Cubeslam: Monocular 3-D object slam. IEEE Trans. Rob. **35**(4), 925–938 (2019)
57. Yang, S., Song, Y., Kaess, M., Scherer, S.: Pop-up slam: semantic monocular plane slam for low-texture environments. In: 2016 IEEE/RSJ International Conference on Intelligent Robots and Systems (IROS), pp. 1222–1229. IEEE (2016)
58. Zhong, L., Zhao, X., Zhang, Y., Zhang, S., Zhang, L.: Occlusion-aware region-based 3D pose tracking of objects with temporally consistent polar-based local partitioning. IEEE Trans. Image Process. **29**, 5065–5078 (2020)

59. Zhu, S., et al.: SNI-slam: Semantic neural implicit slam. In: Proceedings of the IEEE/CVF Conference on Computer Vision and Pattern Recognition, pp. 21167–21177 (2024)
60. Zins, M., Simon, G., Berger, M.O.: Oa-slam: leveraging objects for camera relocalization in visual slam. In: 2022 IEEE International Symposium on Mixed and Augmented Reality (ISMAR), pp. 720–728. IEEE (2022)

RainMirror: An Immersive VR System for Dance Learning and Real-Time Co-dancing with Digital Dancer

Tong Xue(✉), Han Zhang, Zekai Liao, and Mingyi Tong

Beijing Film Academy, Haidian District West TuCheng Road 4, Beijing, China
xuetong@bfa.edu.cn

Abstract. This paper presents RainMirror, an immersive virtual reality dance system that bridges dance education and artistic experience through psychologically informed design. Inspired by the iconic rain scene in *Singin' in the Rain* (1952), RainMirror integrates motion capture, cinematic aesthetics, and a three-phase learning framework to guide users from passive observation to embodied expression. Grounded in the principles of emotional engagement, progressive learning, and low-interference immersion, our system enables non-expert users to develop kinesthetic confidence and expressive freedom in a non-evaluative virtual environment. Users wear a Meta Quest Pro HMD and interact via handheld controllers, engaging with a virtual world built in Unreal Engine. The system architecture comprises three modules, including motion capture & processing, virtual scene construction & rendering, and interaction & logic control. In addition, user experience design emphasizes the flow of interaction, role transformation from learner to performer, and environmental influence on user's behavior By blending real-time motion-driven dancer with affective audiovisual design, RainMirror transforms dance into an accessible, emotionally resonant, and self-directed experience, with potential applications in education, cultural heritage, and well-being. Future work will explore multi-user co-presence and adaptive feedback to enhance immersion and inclusivity.

Keywords: The RainMirror System · Virtual Reality · Motion Capture

1 Introduction

With the rapid development of virtual reality (VR) technology, its applications in artistic expression, cultural heritage preservation, and human-computer interaction have become increasingly profound. Dance, as an art form highly dependent on bodily perception and spatial interaction, has long been constrained by physical environments and high barriers to participation. The integration of VR technology opens new pathways for dance experiences, enabling cross-temporal and cross-spatial co-dancing through virtual avatars, motion capture, and real-time animation [1]. By leveraging audiovisual synchronization within immersive environments, such systems can guide users into the emotional and rhythmic flow of dance, reduce psychological barriers for beginners, and enhance engagement and freedom of bodily expression [2] (Fig. 1).

A. Hinkenjan et al. (Eds.): ICXR 2025, LNCS 16428, pp. 280–286, 2026.
https://doi.org/10.1007/978-981-95-7195-6_16

Fig. 1. Introduction to the RainMirror system: (a) Demonstration phase: a live dancer provides dance instruction; (b) Rainy night street scene; (c) UI Panel: the user selects an experience mode; (d) Follow-along phase: the user follows a digital dancer to practice Latin dance; (e) Follow-along phase: the user follows a digital dancer to practice Modern dance; (f) Co-dancing phase: the user synchronizes movements with a digital dancer in the virtual environment, where the digital dancer is driven in real time by a live dancer via motion capture.

We present RainMirror, a VR dance system that combines instructional learning with immersive co-dancing, inspired by the iconic rain scene from the classic film "*Singin' in the Rain*" (1952). Built in Unreal Engine with a focus on low interference and high immersion, RainMirror features a cinematic virtual streetscape enhanced by dynamic rain, atmospheric lighting, and spatial audio. The user experiences via a Meta Quest Pro head-mounted display (HMD) and a controller. The experience begins with a learning phase guided by a live dancer and digital cues, followed by a co-dancing mode where the user synchronizes with a virtual partner driven by real-time motion capture [3]. RainMirror bridges real-world instruction and virtual immersion, supporting non-experts in transitioning from passive observation to active participation [4]. It offers an innovative approach to embodied dance learning and immersive cultural engagement.

2 Related Work

Recent research on VR applications in dance has primarily focused on three directions: professional choreography tools (e.g., Digital Dance Studio VR [5]), VR-based dance training systems that rely on performance evaluation (e.g., VR Dance Training System [6]), and clinical or artistic practices in dance therapy. The first category of systems enables choreographers to freely orchestrate dancers, timing, and environments within a three-dimensional space. The second employs multi-camera setups and motion capture technologies to achieve high-precision movement assessment. Despite significant technical advancements in both approaches, their design paradigms are centered on professionalism or standardization, often overlooking the needs of non-expert users, particularly with regard to emotional safety, freedom of movement, and intrinsic motivation. Moreover, their emphasis on evaluative feedback and correctness can inadvertently induce performance anxiety among casual participants. In contrast, dance therapy has been formally integrated into clinical care pathways, such as at the University of Rochester

Medical Center, with extensive studies demonstrating that regular dance-based interventions not only stimulate endorphin release and regulate psychophysiological states but also slow motor decline in Parkinson's patients, increase hippocampal volume in individuals with mild cognitive impairment, and significantly enhance executive function and cognitive flexibility in children [7, 8]. Recently, this therapeutic philosophy has being reimagined through digital media. For example, "*Collective Body*", which is selected for the Venice Immersive 2025 program [9], uses algorithmically generated natural-element avatars to represent users' inner states, guiding participants through a wordless, non-judgmental collective dance that fosters emotional resonance, embodying the therapeutic principle of using the body as a medium and shared movement as connection.

Nevertheless, current VR dance experiences designed for the general public still face critical challenges: they lack accessible, structured guidance; emotionally resonant narrative frameworks; and seamless transitions from passive learning to active co-creation. Particularly in therapeutic contexts, creating a safe, relaxing, and expressive environment that encourages spontaneous movement remains an urgent need. To address this gap, we propose an innovative VR system that integrates emotional narrative, instructional guidance, and social co-dancing, which directly responds to the core tenets of dance therapy—non-judgment, joy, and bodily autonomy. This approach offers a scalable new paradigm for future VR applications at the intersection of artistic expression and mental well-being.

3 Design Philosophy

Inspired by the iconic rain scene from the classic film "*Singin' in the Rain*", the RainMirror system is grounded in a design philosophy focused on emotional engagement, progressive learning, and low-interference immersion.

3.1 Emotional Engagement

Rather than prioritizing technical precision or instructional efficiency, RainMirror emphasizes on fostering an emotional atmosphere. By incorporating contrasting warm and cool lighting, dynamic rain effects, nostalgic architectural elements, and a curated classical soundtrack within the virtual environment, the system is designed to evoke users' emotional resonance with the imagery of dancing in the rain. When users put on the HMD, accompanied by the opening melody of "*Beautiful Girl*" and the ambient sounds of raindrops hitting buildings, their psychological role subtly shifts from a learner to a performer, achieving the simultaneous construction of self-identification and emotional immersion.

3.2 Progressive Learning

Dance learning often induces anxiety among novices due to the perceived complexity of movements. To reduce cognitive load and enhance motivation, the RainMirror system adopts a three-phase progressive learning framework.

- Demonstration phase: the user observes a live dancer's performance to form an initial visual representation of the choreography.
- Follow-along phase: the User repeatedly practices fundamental movements by following a digital dancer in the virtual environment, gradually developing procedural and muscle memory.
- Co-dancing phase: the user enters a non-evaluative co-dancing mode, synchronizing movements with a virtual character driven by real-time motion capture.

Our system maintains low-latency bidirectional interaction without performance assessment or corrective feedback, thereby minimizing performance anxiety. By allowing users to first experience the sensation of free movement before focusing on correctness, the system aims to cultivate intrinsic motivation and kinesthetic pleasure. Thus, RainMirror provides a positive and self-directed approach to dance participation.

3.3 Low-Interference Immersion

Traditional dance instruction is often subject to external distractions, such as being observed by others, spatial constraints, and technical pressure, which can easily trigger anxiety in learners. The RainMirror system leverages VR technology to create an immersive environment with minimal interference.

- Environmental Isolation: the HMD provides a fully enclosed virtual scene, preventing users from seeing their own bodies or the reactions of others, thereby reducing self-evaluation.
- Auditory Guidance: the music and rain sounds form a consistent auditory landscape, establishing a stable rhythmic filed.
- Visual Simplification: the virtual scene eliminates redundant information, retaining only streetlights, building silhouettes, and raindrop trajectories, allowing users to focus their attention on the digital dancer's movements.

Through a minimalist design approach to the virtual environment, our system establishes a psychological safe space, enabling users to explore the possibilities of bodily expression in a low-pressure setting.

4 Technical Implementation

In the RainMirror system, users wear a Meta Quest Pro HMD to experience immersive interaction and use handheld controllers for navigation. The system architecture is shown in Fig. 2.

4.1 Motion Capture and Processing

The RainMirror employs the Noitom Perception Neuron Studio system, which utilizes a hybrid inertial-optical approach for high-fidelity motion recording. The system enables full-body motion tracking with a data computation frequency of 750 Hz and an output frequency of 90 Hz. Two professional dancers performed Latin and Modern in a standardized motion capture studio. Audio and motion data were recorded synchronously to

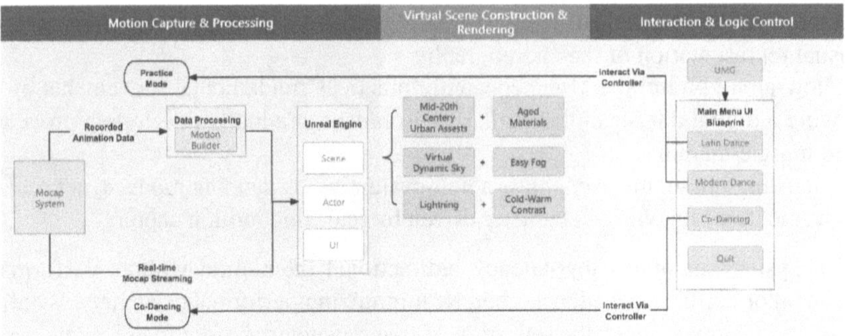

Fig. 2. RainMirror system architecture.

ensure temporal alignment. In the real-time co-dancing phase, motion data is streamed into Unreal Engine with low latency via the Axis Unreal Live Link Plugin. When the live dancer performs in the capture studio, her movements are instantaneously applied to a digital dancer within the virtual environment, enabling live-driven interaction.

4.2 Virtual Scene Construction & Rendering

The virtual environment includes urban elements characteristic of mid-20th century cityscapes, such as lampposts, bicycles, wrought-iron trash cans, and brick-faced buildings. All 3D models were created using Blender and Maya, while materials were textured in Substance Painter with aged effects to enhance historical authenticity and visual realism. Nighttime rainfall effects are achieved using the Ultra Dynamic Sky V2 plugin, combined with volumetric fog generated by the Easy Fog plugin to enrich spatial depth and atmospheric perspective. Lighting design employs a dual-tone strategy: a rectangular light simulates moonlight as the primary source, casting cool-toned shadows, while the point lights simulate streetlamps and warm indoor lighting, creating a deliberate contrast between warm and cool hues. Final color grading is applied through Unreal Engine's Post Process Volume to reinforce the cinematic mood.

4.3 Interaction and Logic Control

The user experience is structured into three states: main menu, learning phase, and real-time co-dancing phase. All state transitions are user-triggered, ensuring autonomy and control over the interaction flow. RainMirror's UI panel is implemented using Unreal Motion Graphics and rendered in world space. It includes dance style selection (Latin/Modern), co-dancing mode, and quit. All interactions are performed via the VR controller, with logic governed by blueprint scripts. We choose the original soundtrack "*Beautiful Girl*" from "*Singin' in the Rain*" as the background music, and the professional dancers have choreographed the dance movements based on that. Additionally, environmental audio is spatialized using 3D audio techniques to enhance immersion and environmental presence.

5 User Experience

This section systematically outlines the design logic of the user experience from three perspectives.

5.1 Experience Flow Design

The RainMirror system follows the psychological model of perception—imitation—participation—release. First, users establish visual cognition and trust by watching live dancer demonstrating movements. They can then choose between Latin or Modern dance mode and follow digital dancer to practice, with the system offering flexible control and a pressure-free environment. When ready, users enter the co-dancing mode, synchronizing their movements with a virtual character driven by live dancer motion capture. This stage emphasizes rhythmic immersion and emotional flow, facilitating the transition from learning to expressive performance.

5.2 User Role Transformation

The RainMirror system guides users through a process of role transformation from learner to performer. First users act as learners, focusing on imitating movements. Then they gradually relax their bodies through repeated practice. Finally, the users transition into the role of performers by immersed into a cinematic audiovisual atmosphere. Although there is no external audience, the imagery of dancing in the rain awakens users' desire for self-expression, shifting their focus from movement accuracy to experiencing the free rhythm of their bodies. Within this non-judgmental environment, users rebuild a positive relationship with their own bodies.

5.3 Environmental Influence on Behavior

The RainMirror system employs multiple design strategies to reduce cognitive load, such as using a VR headset to isolate users from the feeling of being watched, and utilizing rain sounds and background music to guide rhythm perception. These elements help focus users' attention on the coordination between movement and music, enabling focused immersion and enhancing the naturalness and fluidity of bodily engagement.

6 Conclusion

This paper presents the design and implementation of an immersive VR-based dance experience system RainMirror, which is inspired by the iconic rainy street scene from "Singin' in the Rain". Through a three-phase framework with demonstration, follow-along, and co-dancing, our system establishes a low-interference, highly immersive environment for dance engagement in VR. By emphasizing emotional guidance and psychological safety, RainMirror supports non-expert users in gradually building bodily confidence and transitioning from imitation to free expression within a non-evaluative virtual space. Technically, the system integrates motion capture technology with Unreal

Engine to enable real-time, performer-driven co-dancing. Our system offers an accessible and innovative approach to dance education. Future work may incorporate personalized feedback, multi-user interaction, and cross-modal sensory integration to further enhance experiential depth and inclusivity.

Acknowledgements. This research was supported by R&D Program of Beijing Municipal Education Commission (KM202410050001).

References

1. Liu, S.: Research on the construction of a dance simulation training system using VR technology. In: 2023 International Conference on Educational Knowledge and Informatization (EKI), Guangzhou, China, pp. 106–109. IEEE, Piscataway (2023)
2. Wu, S.-H., Wang, K.-T., Chiang, C.-C., Chang, H.-Y., Yeh, C.-Y., Hu, M.-C.: DanceOnStage: positioning training of dancing stage performance in virtual reality. In: 2024 IEEE International Conference on Artificial Intelligence and eXtended and Virtual Reality (AIxVR), Los Angeles, CA, USA, pp. 270–274. IEEE, Piscataway (2024)
3. Akbas, S., et al.: Virtual dance mirror: a functional approach to avatar representation through movement in immersive VR. In: Proceedings of the 8th International Conference on Movement and Computing (MOCO 2022), Article 25, pp. 1–4. ACM, New York (2022)
4. Zhang, F., Li, M., Chang, X., Fu, K., Allen, R.W., LC, R.: Becoming my own audience: how dancers react to avatars unlike themselves in motion capture-supported live improvisational performance. In: Proceedings of the 2025 CHI Conference on Human Factors in Computing Systems (CHI 2025), Article 1057, pp. 1–24. ACM, New York (2025)
5. Whitley, A., Kirchhof, S., Strutt, D.: Digital Dance Studio VR (DDS-VR): an innovative user-focused immersive software application for digital choreographic composition, planning, teaching, learning, and rehearsal. In: ACM SIGGRAPH 2023 Immersive Pavilion (SIGGRAPH 2023), Article 5, pp. 1–2. ACM, New York (2023)
6. Esaki, K., Nagao, K.: VR dance training system capable of human motion tracking and automatic dance evaluation. Presence: Virtual Augmented Reality **31**, 23–45 (2022)
7. University of Rochester Medical Center: Dance therapy. https://www.urmc.rochester.edu/encyclopedia/content?ContentTypeID=85&ContentID=p07338. Accessed 25 Sept 2025
8. Cox, L., Youmans-Jones, J.: Dance is a healing art. Curr. Treat. Options Allergy **10**, 184–195 (2023). https://doi.org/10.1007/s40521-023-00332-x
9. Collective Body: Venice Immersive 2025. https://www.labiennale.org/en/cinema/2025/venice-immersive/collective-body. Accessed 25 Sept 2025

Learning Hanzi Character Through VR-Based Mortise-Tenon

Conglin Ma[1], Jiatong Li[1], Sen-Zhe Xu[2], Ju Dai[3], Jie Liu[1], and Feng Zhou[1](✉)

[1] North China University of Technology, Beijing, China
{conglin04,lijiatong}@mail.ncut.edu.cn, zhoufeng@ncut.edu.cn

[2] University of Science and Technology Beijing, Beijing, China
senzhe@ustb.edu.cn

[3] Peng Cheng Laboratory, Shenzhen, China
daij@pcl.ac.cn

Abstract. This paper introduces a novel VR-based system that redefines the acquisition of Hanzi character literacy by integrating traditional mortise-tenon joinery principles (HVRMT). Addressing the challenge of abstract character memorization in digital learning, our system deconstructs Hanzi components into interactive "structural radicals" akin to wooden joint modules. Leveraging PICO's 6DoF spatial tracking and LLM's morphological analysis, learners assemble stroke sequences with haptic feedback simulating wood-to-wood friction. Our system also supports multiplayer online experiences, enhancing engagement and memory retention while preserving intangible cultural heritage. This innovative approach not only enhances engagement and memory retention but also reconstructs the craft wisdom embedded in Chinese writing systems, offering new pathways for preserving intangible cultural heritage in digital ecosystems. For the demo, please refer to this link.

Keywords: Mortise-Tenon · Virtual Reality · Hanzi Character · LLM

1 Introduction

In the field of digital education, the acquisition of Hanzi character literacy represents a unique and intricate learning task. Previous research has made substantial contributions to this domain, with traditional teaching methods providing systematic instruction in reading and writing [3,8]. Nevertheless, these approaches are typically characterized by a "disembodied" nature, in which learners have limited opportunities for hands-on engagement or interactive exploration. As a result, it can be challenging to meaningfully connect the process of character learning with real-world contexts and cultural backgrounds, potentially leading to difficulties in retention and in developing a deep structural understanding of Hanzi [4]. Currently, Chinese character education remains mired in traditional models. While methods such as memory reinforcement and emotional connection

A. Hinkenjan et al. (Eds.): ICXR 2025, LNCS 16428, pp. 287–293, 2026.
https://doi.org/10.1007/978-981-95-7195-6_17

can improve short-term memorization, they remain constrained by the limitations of flat, book-based training and struggle to showcase the three-dimensional nature of Chinese characters as cultural vehicles. Some studies have attempted to incorporate gamification, such as the "Kanji Industry" system, which simulates an industrial assembly line through component assembly. However, these systems remain focused on the static display of Chinese characters, failing to establish a dynamic connection between their structure and traditional culture. In recent years, virtual learning environments have emerged as promising tools to address some of these challenges. These platforms have introduced elements of interactivity and immersion, enriching the learning process beyond the static delivery of content. However, despite these advances, existing systems often face limitations in fully engaging learners with the cultural heritage and structural complexity embedded within Hanzi characters [9]. For example, immersive, hands-on experiences—which have the potential to enhance spatial cognition and cultural understanding—are still relatively uncommon in current implementations [4].

To further advance this field, the present study proposes a novel VR-based Hanzi learning system inspired by the ancient principles of mortise–tenon joinery. As illustrated in Fig. 1, the system reimagines abstract Hanzi components as interactive "structural radicals," analogous to the precise and functional wooden joint modules used in traditional Chinese carpentry. This design draws on the enduring craftsmanship of mortise–tenon structures, offering learners a tangible metaphor that bridges the gap between abstract character memorization and embodied, interactive learning.

Unlike traditional learning methods, the mortise–tenon joinery requires learners to carefully consider the shape and connection points of each component while assembling the mortise and tenon joints. This deeply engaging and interactive approach deepens their memory of the structure and form of Chinese characters. Furthermore, through engaging with the mortise and tenon joints of Chinese characters, learners not only learn about Chinese characters but also appreciate the charm and wisdom of this ancient craft.

Within this framework, learners physically assemble stroke sequences in a manner akin to architectural construction. Leveraging PICO's advanced 6DoF spatial tracking technology, the system enables users to manipulate virtual components through natural hand movements, while a large language model (LLM)–driven morphological analysis module provides accurate interpretation and guidance. To enhance immersion, haptic feedback simulates the tactile sensation of wood-to-wood contact during component assembly, creating a multisensory learning environment that promotes engagement, improves memory retention, and deepens understanding of Hanzi's structural logic. Furthermore, the system incorporates a virtual community feature, enabling multi-user collaboration and cultural exchange, thereby transforming character literacy learning into a socially enriched experience of cultural heritage transmission.

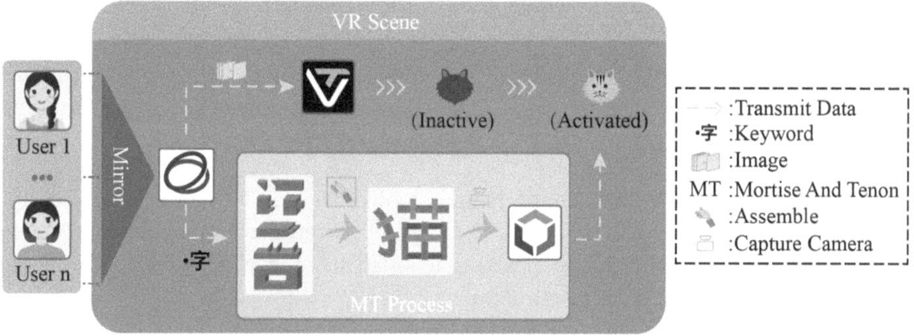

Fig. 1. Overview of our HVRMT application.

2 Related Work

Digital technologies are transforming the ways in which education and cultural heritage are preserved, and the emergence of LLMs has provided new avenues in this domain. A growing body of research is emerging in this area [1,6], and below we will focus on some methods that are directly related to our work.

LLM Application in Educational Technology: Recent applications of LLM in education have shown their potential in delivering personalized feedback and adaptive learning strategies. For example, the LEAP platform by Steinert et al. (2024) employs LLMs to generate formative feedback that supports self-regulated learning through text-based prompts such as self-explanation cues and motivational scaffolds [7]. However, these systems remain limited to textual interactions and metacognitive guidance, lacking tangible or interactive outcomes. In contrast, our system applies LLMs to a distinct functional role—understanding learner speech, performing morphological analysis, and generating corresponding 2D/3D interactive models. This bridges semantic comprehension with embodied interaction, enabling learners to construct and explore Chinese characters through immersive, model-driven experiences in VR.

Cultural Heritage Preservation through Digital Interaction: Many studies in human–computer interaction leverage digital technologies to revitalize traditional skills. For instance, Lee (2019) used AR to teach the three-dimensional structure and projection principles of mortise–tenon joints [5], showing that component-based visual teaching can enhance spatial cognition. However, this work focuses on process understanding and does not establish a semantic mapping between mortise–tenon structures and Chinese characters. Our study reconstructs these traditional principles as an interactive literacy module, systematically translating the idea of "using wood to build characters" into a virtual learning environment. Drawing on Yilmaz's (2022) concept of cloud-based collaborative writing communities [10], we extend this framework into a VR context by enabling multi-user interaction with mortise–tenon components, enhancing group participation and shared knowledge construction.

3 System Design

Our HVRMT is founded on the harmonious fusion of traditional mortise-tenon and Hanzi character literacy acquisition. The following provides a detailed depiction of the system design:

Core Concept: The system maps Hanzi strokes to mortise-tenon components, transforming abstract characters into tangible, interactive modules. Learners assemble Hanzi radicals as if constructing wooden frameworks, bridging language learning with traditional craftsmanship.

Technical Framework: 1. Leverages PICO's 6DoF spatial tracking to capture voice and movements, converting speech to text and extracting core characters. 2. Utilizes LLM for morphological analysis and guidance. Based on user input, it generates 2D images and 3D models of corresponding objects. 3. Provides mortise-tenon parts in the virtual space. A recognition camera captures the assembly process, verifies the formed character against the extracted core character, and activates the 3D model upon matching. 4. Utilizes the features of the mirror plugin to achieve synchronization and interaction among multiple users in VR scenes. Users use the VR thumbstick to move and turn, the trigger to complete UI interactions and other relevant operations, and the grip to pick up parts.

4 Experiments

Multi User System Design: When multiple users wish to experience the system together,the system sets the first logged in user as the homeowner role. Subsequently, other users can utilize the system's built-in network multicast receiving function to enter the same scene as clients, thereby achieving a collaborative interaction experience among multiple users, as shown in Fig. 2.

Fig. 2. Two users scene design.

User Interaction and Data Flow: The virtual space is divided into three functional areas: 1. Speech Area (a): Speech recognition, keyword extraction, and image generation. 2. Model Area (b): 3D modeling and display. 3. Character Area (c): mortise-tenon assembly and OCR, as shown in Fig. 3.

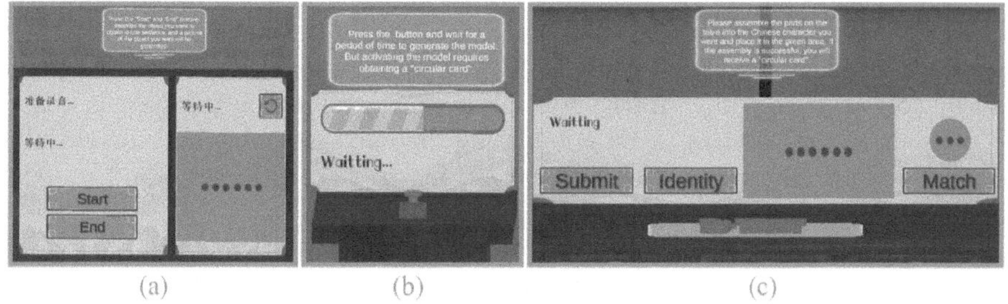

Fig. 3. System area design diagram.

Data flows from voice input to text conversion, core character extraction, image generation, and 3D model creation. Users assemble mortise-tenon parts in the virtual environment. The system captures the assembly, recognizes the character, compares it with the extracted core character, and activates the 3D model if they match.

Experimental Procedure: The user first logs in to the scene, then enters the voice area and describes the object they want to generate. For example, say"a cute cat". The system understands voice and text based on ChatGLM [2]. The Prompt is constructed as follows: *\"model":"glm-4-flash"\, \"messages"\:[\"role"\:"user"\,\"content"\:" + text + ", extract the main object described in this sentence, ignore color and other modifiers, and require the result to be one character\"]"\"]*. Then construct *\"model":"cogView-4-250304"\, \"prompt"\:" + text + ", simple background, no complex environment, solid color background, clear subject"\, \"size"\:"*512×512*"* to generate the corresponding image data.

Afterwards, the user can choose to enter the model area or the parts splicing area. In the model area, after the user clicks the "Generate" button, the system will call the image data generated by the voice module and use it as a basis to start the model generation process. The generated model is initially in the "unactivated" state and does not have interactive capabilities. After obtaining the round card in the subsequent stage, it can be activated and interactive functions can be realized. Use the Tripo interface to trigger the image generation model process by setting imagePath and calling Image_to_Model_func(). After the generation is complete, listen to the OnDownloadComplete callback to obtain the download link (URL) of the model, and then use the GltfAsset component to load the model and display it in the scene.

After the user enters the parts splicing area, he selects the appropriate parts, splices them into the corresponding Chinese characters and places them in the green area. The system captures the image of the area through the fixed-angle recognition camera (CaptureCamera) configured above the desktop and recognizes it. The recognition result will be compared with the core characters previously extracted and stored. If the match is successful, the user will get a round card for subsequent model activation. When the user picks up two parts to splice, the system will identify their numbers (Part ID) and check whether there are equivalent substitutes, and classify them into the same equivalent set (Equivalent Table). Then the recipe table is used to determine whether the two parts can be paired. If they match, the splicing is successful and a new part is generated, as shown in Fig. 4(a). After completing the parts assembly and successfully obtaining the round plate, the user can return to the model area and use the round plate to activate the previously generated model.

In the above stages,multiple users are supported to participate in the experience together,and each user can propose their own methods and suggestions to modify the data flow in each stage.

In this study, we recruit 16 participants to validate our system. Sixteen participants were divided into four groups. Each group was given the same test: first, they learned Chinese characters using the system, and then they learned the same characters using other methods. After the test, the participants rated the two learning methods based on four dimensions: immersion, convenience, fun, and information acquisition efficiency. Each dimension used a Likert scale of 1–5, with 1 indicating very dissatisfied and 5 indicating very satisfied. The average satisfaction of the testers (AVG-SI) was calculated for comparative analysis, as shown in Fig. 4(b).

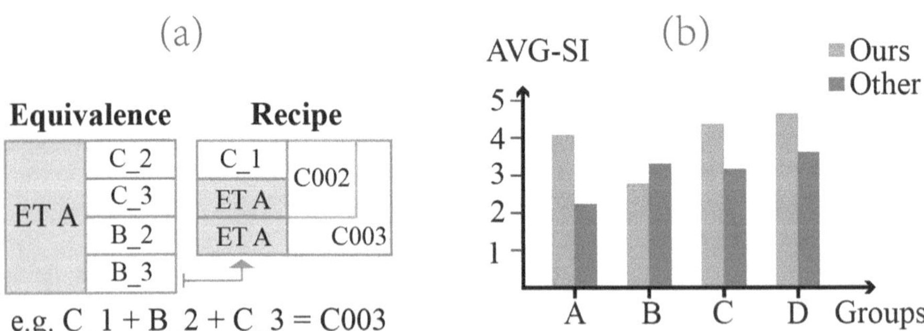

Fig. 4. (a) Recipe table created based on the reusability of parts, (b) Results of user studies.

5 Result and Future Work

Our HVRMT effectively combines Hanzi character acquisition with mortise-tenon joinery through VR. The mapping of strokes to components provides a tangible way to understand Hanzi structure.At the same time,the system's feature of allowing multiple people to participate together further enhances the interaction between users and improves the richness of the learning experience.Experimental results confirm the system's effectiveness in improving memory retention and comprehension, with positive user feedback validating its technical feasibility and educational value. We plan to expand the content library with more Hanzi characters and mortise-tenon types. Further experiments with larger participant groups will assess the system's impact on Hanzi literacy acquisition.

Acknowledgments. This work is supported by Beijing Natural Science Foundation (4232023), R&D Program of Beijing Municipal Education Commission (KM202310009 002), Humanities and Social Science Fund of Ministry of Education (24YJCZH458), Yuxiu Innovation Project of NCUT (2024NCUTYXCX202) and National College Student Innovation and EntrepreneurshipTraining Program(2025).

References

1. Bu, F., Wang, Z., Wang, S., Liu, Z.: An investigation into value misalignment in LLM-generated texts for cultural heritage. arXiv preprint arXiv:2501.02039 (2025)
2. GLM, T., et al.: Chatglm: a family of large language models from GLM-130b to GLM-4 all tools. arXiv preprint arXiv:2406.12793 (2024)
3. Hong, Y., Shi, L., Ying, F.: Hanzi lamp: an intelligent guide interface for Chinese character learning. In: Adjunct Proceedings of the 26th Annual ACM Symposium on User Interface Software and Technology, pp. 75–76 (2013)
4. Hsiao, H.S., Chang, C.S., Chen, C.J., Wu, C.H., Lin, C.Y.: The influence of Chinese character handwriting diagnosis and remedial instruction system on learners of Chinese as a foreign language. Comput. Assisted Language Learn., 306–324 (2015)
5. Lee, I.J.: Using augmented reality to train students to visualize three-dimensional drawings of mortise–tenon joints in furniture carpentry. Interact. Learn. Environ. (2019)
6. Rao, J., Zhou, F., Dai, J., Li, C., Hu, Y.: Formationcreator: designing a VR dance formation system for intangible cultural heritage dance. In: Extended Abstracts of the CHI Conference on Human Factors in Computing Systems, pp. 1–7 (2024)
7. Steinert, S., Avila, K.E., Ruzika, S., Kuhn, J., Küchemann, S.: Harnessing large language models to enhance self-regulated learning via formative feedback. Smart Learn. Environ. (2024)
8. Vogel, D., Schmidt, S., Steinicke, F.: Interactive Chinese character learning in virtual reality. In: SIGGRAPH Asia 2022 XR, pp. 1–2 (2022)
9. Wang, S.h.C.: A study on the learning and teaching of Hanzi-Chinese characters. Working Papers Educ. Linguistics **14**(1), 69–101 (1998)
10. Yilmaz, Y.: A guide to writing within a virtual community of practice. PMC National Library Med. (2022)

BraveQuest: Designing a Mixed Reality Game to Support Exposure Therapy for Children with Zoophobia

Jiajia Li[1(✉)], Xiu Zhang[1], Hongbo Chen[1], Jingyi Zhao[1], Xinwei Yuan[1], Lian Xue[2], and Junyu Jiang[1]

[1] Qingdao University, Shandong, China
jiajiali@qdu.edu.cn
[2] Qingdao Tongde Primary School, Shandong, China

Abstract. During their development, children often experience a rational fear of certain animals, such as spiders and bats, which may, if left unaddressed, gradually escalate into irrational phobias, significantly affecting their mental well-being, daily activities, and social participation. While traditional exposure therapy has been proven effective in treating such fears, it can be challenging to implement in real-world contexts and may cause considerable discomfort or resistance in children, potentially reducing its overall effectiveness. Hence, we present BraveQuest, a mixed reality game that combines virtual agents, gamification elements, and mixed reality-based exposure therapy techniques to help gradually reduce these fears in a safe, controlled, and engaging environment. Preliminary results from initial trials show that BraveQuest not only boosts children's confidence in facing their fears but also offers an enjoyable and immersive interactive experience. This work informs the design of adaptive and inclusive interactive interface systems for interventions to address childhood phobias.

Keywords: Mixed Reality Exposure Therapy · Virtual Agent · Game Design · Childhood Phobias · Child–Computer Interaction

1 Introduction

During childhood, fears or anxieties—such as fear of spiders, bats, or dark-environment monsters—are common, often arising from imaginative thinking and sensitivity to uncertainty, and usually diminish with cognitive maturity [1]. Without timely guidance or intervention, some children may develop persistent irrational fears, that is, phobias, with panic or loss of control negatively affecting their daily life [2].

Traditional interventions mainly include talk and exposure therapies, with the latter using repeatedly confronting real stimuli in efforts to reduce fear, which has proved to be highly effective [3]. However, face-to-face exposure therapy imposes heavy emotional burdens on young children, lowers compliance, and limits flexible adjustment of stimuli. Recently, virtual (VR) and mixed reality (MR) technologies have offered controllable, safe, multisensory environments for fear interventions, reducing stress and improving

A. Hinkenjan et al. (Eds.): ICXR 2025, LNCS 16428, pp. 294–300, 2026.
https://doi.org/10.1007/978-981-95-7195-6_18

participation. Virtual reality exposure therapy (VRET) allows children to face their fears in controlled virtual settings while easing their psychological load [4, 5], but the lack of physical spatial perception and real-life interaction limits experience transfer and long-term therapeutic effects.

Mixed reality exposure therapy (MRET) shows promise for treating phobias and anxiety by overlaying virtual elements onto real environments to enhance immersion and presence, improving therapeutic outcomes [6]. While effective for phobias like fear of spiders or snakes, current MRET systems rely on direct exposure with limited interactivity and engagement, making them less suitable for children. To address this limitation, BraveQuest introduces a novel integration of mixed reality, gamification elements, and socially intelligent virtual agents. Unlike prior systems, BraveQuest emphasizes cooperative storytelling, mentor-guided exposure, and personalized interactive experiences designed specifically to enhance children's engagement and emotional regulation.

2 Related Work

Specific phobias are a common childhood disorder, as children in the preoperational stage struggle to distinguish reality from imagination and often fear darkness, animals, or imaginary entities [7, 8]. Exposure therapy promotes desensitization by presenting fear stimuli in controlled settings [9]; however, traditional methods suffer from low adherence and limited flexibility due to emotional resistance, difficulty in adjusting stimuli, and high demands on therapists.

Following advances in digital technologies, VRET offers innovative approaches for childhood phobia interventions, as VRET reconstructs fear-inducing environments virtually, protecting children from real-world threats while enhancing their immersion through multisensory stimulation. This method has been shown to be efficient in treating animal phobias, social anxiety, and school-related anxiety. For instance, Su and Yan developed *NoPhobiar*, a VR game for 4–6-year-olds with fear of darkness, simulating bedroom and park nighttime scenes, and using gesture and virtual object interactions to facilitate gradual desensitization [10]. Similarly, Thanh et al. used immersive graphics and sound to reduce presleep anxiety [11], while Wechsler et al. created an eye-tracking VR game that alleviates children's spider phobia through gaze interaction [12]. However, fully immersive VR lacks physical spatial perception and real interaction [13], limiting the long-term efficacy of therapeutic experience transfer and offering low engagement for young children. MR exposure shows potential in treating childhood social and animal phobias; for instance, "HoloPhoByeMR" employs multilevel tasks to gradually build courage and reduce fear among users [14]. Despite extensive VR research, MR applications remain scarce.

Based on this corpus, we developed BraveQuest, a MRET game combining virtual agents and gamification in a three-dimensional (3D) cartoon style, enabling children aged 7–11 to reduce their fears by collaborating with virtual characters to complete game levels.

3 Design Approach

To enhance children's engagement and reduce their emotional burden in fear exposure training, we developed BraveQuest, an MRET game integrating gamification, virtual mentors, and gradual exposure to provide a safe and engaging intervention.

3.1 Preliminary Research

We surveyed the fear stimuli preferences of 42 children (20 boys, 22 girls, 7–9 years old) when playing MR games, identifying spiders, bats, and ghosts as primary fears. Subsequently, six children participated in 1-hour semi-structured interviews exploring their fear emotions, scene and character preferences, and emotional support needs. The parents of all participating children provided informed consent, and the children assented to participate. The interview design was based on Su and Yan's *NoPhobiar* protocol [10]. Research shows that children often exhibit tension and avoidance toward fear stimuli, indicating MR interventions must balance challenges with safety. BraveQuest employs a gradual exposure strategy by initially providing support via cartoon characters and progressively increasing the intensity of the stimulus while incorporating contextual tasks like treasure collection to enhance engagement based on the children's preferences. The insights from our preliminary user research directly informed the design of BraveQuest and led to three core design decisions: **(1) Scene Design.** Based on children's cartoon preference, scenes and characters were designed as 3D anthropomorphic cartoons. **(2) Fear Character Designs.** Spiders, bats, and ghosts were selected as core stimuli and were designed with rounded bodies and exaggerated eyes to enhance acceptance among the children. **(3) Virtual Mentor Design.** To support children emotionally, a virtual mentor, appearing as a cartoon anthropomorphic lion (Fig. 1d) inspired by the courageous Cowardly Lion from *The Wizard of Oz*, provides real-time encouragement and rewards through verbal and simulated physical interactions [15].

Fig. 1. Three scary game characters: (a) spider, (b) bat, (c) ghost, and (d) lion (virtual mentor).

3.2 Game Mechanics Design

BraveQuest is a virtual game for the HoloLens 2 (Microsoft, Redmond, WA, USA) MR device, which is designed to help children overcome their animal-related fears through story-driven progressive exposure therapy. In BraveQuest, the children complete adventurous tasks set in a forest, supported by a lion avatar as a virtual guide. Based on initial surveys, the BraveQuest game features three fear stimuli: spiders (Fig. 1a), bats (Fig. 1b), and ghosts (Fig. 1c). The BraveQuest narrative focuses on "saving animals and building friendships," emphasizing cooperation and emotional growth over confrontation. Children engage in three task-based minigames within the MR environment, supporting multimodal interactions like voice and gestures.

In Game 1 "Silky's Way Home," the children meet a frightened spider, build trust by collecting nectar and touching it, and see its appearance shift from cartoonish to realistic and fearsome for gradual exposure. After escorting it home, it shows gratitude and gives them a prop for the next level (Fig. 2a).

In Game 2 "Guardians of Moonshade," the children help a bat shunned for its appearance. Initially trapped in a magical bubble, it prompts them to find a crystal key to free it. They then join the bat to repel mice destroying its home, unlocking the next level. The bat's appearance gradually changes from cute and cartoon-like to fearsome, with pointed ears, sharp teeth, and dark textures, enabling gradual exposure (Fig. 2b).

In Game 3 "Light Up Shadow Hollow," the children collect glowing items in a dark forest to illuminate their path. They encounter a personified "shadow monster" that emits occasional threatening audio cues. By collecting and placing glowing stones, the children gradually brighten their environment, causing the shadow monster to fade and disappear (Fig. 2c).

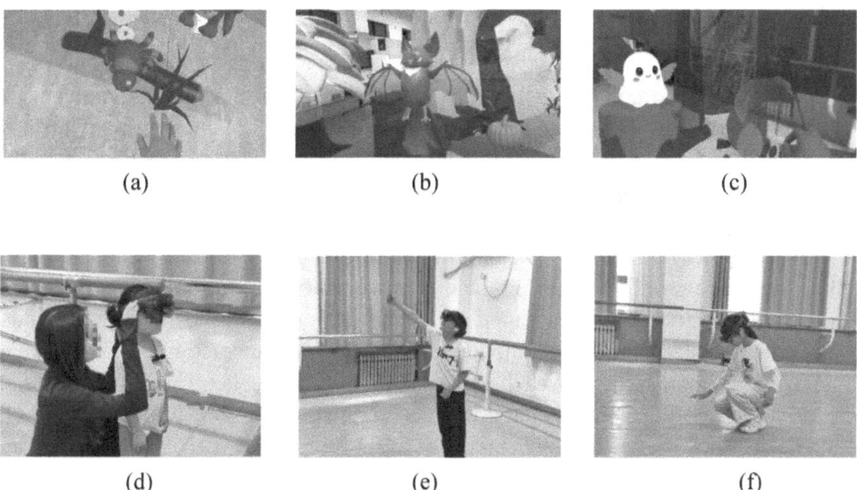

Fig. 2. (a) Silky's Way Home; (b) Guardians of Moonshade, and (c) Light Up Shadow Hollow. (d) debugging equipment; (e) Scene 1; and (f) Scene 2.

When the children approach or touch virtual fear stimuli, the system gradually intensifies visual feedback. For example, the appearance of the spider changes from abstract to realistic following repeated interactions, facilitating controlled desensitization. To reduce emotional tension and boost engagement, the virtual lion mentor guides the children in their tasks and offers emotional support via verbal encouragement, facial expressions, and body language. This combination of narrative, gradual exposure, and socioemotional support aims to enhance the children's safety, emotional regulation, and active participation in the MR experience.

3.3 Technical Support

Developed with Unity 3D (Unity Technologies, San Francisco, CA, USA) and deployed on HoloLens 2, the BraveQuest system employs a modular architecture to deliver child-friendly interactions. Cinema 4D (Maxon Computer GmbH, Bad Homburg vor der Höhe, Germany) was used to create the 3D scenes and character models. The system supports multimodal interactions, including gestures and voice. Processing is distributed to optimize performance: HoloLens 2 handles graphics rendering and gesture recognition, while voice interaction—including recognition, semantic processing, and virtual assistant responses—is processed on a local PC. Expert educators crafted the virtual assistant's dialogue to ensure natural interaction and enhance child engagement.

3.4 User Evaluation

We recruited five children (P1–P5; two boys, three girls) aged 7–11 years (mean = 9.0, standard deviation [SD] = 1.27) for a pilot study. The Ethics Review Board of our university approved this study, and all participants and guardians provided their written informed consent.

We conducted an exploratory evaluation of the MR system's usability and user experience. All children completed the tasks independently and four of the children enjoyed BraveQuest. However, P1 felt the task duration was too long. She was initially afraid of bats and stepped back instinctively but later overcame her fear and touched the bat. P2 and P3 showed high engagement and actively interacted with the agents. As P3 noted, "I thought lions were supposed to be kings of beasts and very fierce, but this one is really cute and keeps helping me." P2 was not afraid of the dark and used hand gestures to "strike" the shadows in Game 3. In Game 2, however, he showed a fear of heights and sought assistance from the virtual mentor. In particular, his parents had not previously been aware of his acrophobia. P4 enjoyed the storyline and interactions, and he gave the virtual agent a thumbs-up after each level. P5 initially struggled to interact unless she was close to the virtual elements but gradually adapted to the game until she could play at a distance from the virtual elements. These findings suggest that BraveQuest may help reduce the children's anxiety toward animals, while also fostering their curiosity and confidence during fear-related tasks.

4 Discussion and Future Work

Our findings indicate that BraveQuest's design is well aligned with children's cognitive characteristics. The 3D cartoon style significantly enhances attention and immersion, consistent with studies on children's preference for cartoon aesthetics. The unique advantages of MR increased their engagement; although they were initially unfamiliar with the system, they quickly adapted and actively interacted with virtual mentors. Notably, natural interactions effectively stimulated their spontaneous exploration, as seen in P4's non-task gestures, such as "thumbs-up."

However, this study has limitations. The small sample size restricts generalizability and the brief avoidance behaviors observed at the start of tasks suggest that the system requires improved personalization to accommodate individual differences.

Future work will expand the sample size to validate the system's applicability and effectiveness across developmental stages. Interactions and task design will be optimized by incorporating adaptive difficulty, personalized guidance, and emotion monitoring to better address individual differences and extend experiments to real-world settings, such as homes and schools.

5 Conclusion

This study introduced BraveQuest, an MR-based system integrating virtual agents, gamification, and progressive exposure therapy to provide a safe, engaging setting for children. Using cartoon-style fear stimuli, anthropomorphic mentors, and multimodal interactions (e.g., gestures, voice, body movements), it helps children gradually overcome fears of animals (e.g., spiders, bats, ghosts) with emotional support and task guidance.

Preliminary results show children could complete tasks independently, reduce anxiety, and gain confidence. Most participants responded positively, suggesting BraveQuest's feasibility and potential to improve emotional regulation and fear acceptance.

Acknowledgments. This work was supported by the National Social Science Fund of China Art Program (grant number: 23CG198). We thank all the parents and children who participated in our studies.

References

1. Bauer, D.H.: An exploratory study of developmental changes in children's fears. J. Child Psychol. Psychiatry **17**(1), 69–74 (1976)
2. LeBeau, R.T., Glenn, D., Liao, B., et al.: Specific phobia: a review of DSM-IV specific phobia and preliminary recommendations for DSM-V. Depress. Anxiety **27**(2), 48–167 (2010)
3. Janecký, D., Kučera, E., Haffner, O., et al.: The use of mixed reality for exposure therapy to improve phobia handling. Int. J. Cogn. Behav. Therapy **18**(2), 201–240 (2025)
4. Garcia-Palacios, A., Hoffman, H.G., Kwong See, S., et al.: Redefining therapeutic success with virtual reality exposure therapy. Cyber Psychol. Behav. **4**(3), 341–348 (2001)
5. Bouchard, S.: Could virtual reality be effective in treating children with phobias? Expert Rev. Neurother. **11**(2), 207–213 (2011)
6. Takazawa, S., Yasuda, K., Sabu, R., et al.: Development of a mixed reality rehabilitation system for real-life environment in stroke patients with unilateral spatial neglect. In: 2022 IEEE International Conference on Systems, Man, and Cybernetics (SMC), pp. 3379–3383. IEEE (2022)
7. Broeren, S., Muris, P.: The relation between cognitive development and anxiety phenomena in children. J. Child Fam. Stud. **18**(6), 702–709 (2009)
8. Piaget, J., Cook, M.: The Origins of Intelligence in Children. International Universities Press, New York (1952)
9. Craske, M.G., Treanor, M., Conway, C.C., et al.: Maximizing exposure therapy: an inhibitory learning approach. Behav. Res. Ther. **58**, 10–23 (2014)

10. Su, X., Yan, S.: NoPhobiar: designing a VR game to prevent childhood dark phobia with children and stakeholders. In: Extended Abstracts of the 2023 CHI Conference on Human Factors in Computing Systems, pp. 1–6 (2023)
11. Thanh, V.D.H., Pui, O., Constable, M.: Room VR: a VR therapy game for children who fear the dark. In: SIGGRAPH Asia 2017 Posters, pp. 1–2 (2017)
12. Wechsler, T.F., Brockelmann, M., Kulik, K., et al.: SpEYEders: adults' and children's affective responses during immersive playful gaze interactions transforming virtual spiders. In: Extended Abstracts of the 2021 Annual Symposium on Computer-Human Interaction in Play, pp. 74–79 (2021)
13. Jiajia, L., Zixia, Z.: DianTea: an augmented performance VR system for enhancing Chinese youth learning about tea-making as an intangible cultural heritage. Int. J. Hum. Comput. Stud. **203**, 1–15 (2025)
14. Janecký, D., Kučera, E., Haffner, O., et al.: The use of mixed reality for exposure therapy to improve phobia handling. Int. J. Cogn. Behav. Therapy **18**, 201–240 (2025)
15. Jiajia, L., Yaqing, C., Zixia, Z.: Yum-Yum! A social game using tangible interaction with a virtual agent for cognitive training in children with low-functioning autism. Int. J. Hum. Comput. Stud. **212**, 1–23 (2026)

Robotic Arm Augmented Reality Control System

Mingyu Ma and Xueying Qin(✉)

Shandong University, Jinan, China
qxy@sdu.edu.cn

Abstract. The traditional robotic arm control mode is relatively cumbersome, and its operation process is not intuitive for users. Complex interaction logic design increases the learning cost for operators. In conventional control approaches, there is a disconnect between the robotic arm's planned movements and the real environment, making it difficult for users to visually determine whether the planned actions will collide with objects in the real scene. This limitation is unfavorable for collision detection and poses potential safety risks. Compared with traditional control methods, the fusion of virtual and real elements brought by augmented reality technology introduces a novel means for monitoring the robotic arm's path planning. The Rokid-based Virtual Robotic Arm Augmented Reality Control System leverages AR to present a virtual robotic arm within an augmented scene that mirrors the real arm's real-time status, allowing users to intuitively obtain joint state information. Users can interact with the AR environment to specify target positions, verify the feasibility of planned paths, and then execute the robotic arm's movements. This effectively prevents potential collisions between the robotic arm and real-world objects during operation, helping users efficiently complete a wide range of robotic arm control tasks.

Keywords: Robot arm · Augmented reality · Virtual-real fusion

1 Introduction

1.1 Background of System Development

With the rapid development of embodied intelligence technology, collaborative robots are extending from industrial scenarios into more diversified fields such as healthcare, households, and service industries [1,2]. It is foreseeable that with further progress in artificial intelligence, materials science, and sensor technology, future collaborative robots will become increasingly intelligent, adaptive, and affordable, finding widespread applications across production and daily life scenarios. Currently, robotic arm control primarily relies on teach pendant operation and virtual simulation environments. However, teach pendants are often cumbersome and complex, requiring a certain level of expertise to operate. Virtual simulations may also have positional deviations from real-world environments,

A. Hinkenjan et al. (Eds.): ICXR 2025, LNCS 16428, pp. 301–307, 2026.
https://doi.org/10.1007/978-981-95-7195-6_19

and mismatches between the two can lead to operational failures. Demonstrating internal parameters of a robotic arm in a purely virtual environment can consume most of the user's attention, leaving less capacity to address unexpected events in the real world. If a user misses the occurrence of a problem, even with extra cameras recording the event, considerable time is still required to review and process the footage. Such issues significantly increase the operational cost of robotic arm control. The Rokid-based Augmented Reality Robotic Arm Control System emerges in this context, leveraging AR technology to empower robotic arm operation and provide users with more intuitive and simplified interaction feedback. The system can overlay a virtual robotic arm on top of the real arm to dynamically display its current status in real time, helping users easily understand its internal data and states, quickly identify operational errors or deviations, and assist in calibrating sensor data. It can also simulate planned robotic arm motions in an AR environment, allowing users to identify potential operational errors before real execution, prevent collisions with real-world objects, and assist in verifying and finalizing feasible manipulation trajectories. Once confirmed, users can safely execute the corresponding actions on the robotic arm.

1.2 Related Work

With the widespread adoption of augmented reality (AR) technology in various human–computer interaction domains, applications leveraging AR to enhance interaction experiences have emerged in industrial settings, service robotics, medical projects, remote communication, and education and training [3]. These diverse application scenarios fully demonstrate the great potential of AR technology in optimizing human–computer interaction. In [4], a series of AR applications in the manufacturing industry are introduced, covering the full production process of industrial products, including design, production, assembly, and maintenance, and mentioning the use of AR user interfaces and AR-based solutions for teleoperation of remote semi-autonomous robots. In modern production and daily-life scenarios, robotic arms are increasingly prevalent, and their deployment has greatly improved industrial productivity. Robotic arm control technology is currently developing rapidly; however, traditional control methods exhibit obvious limitations, such as complex interaction modes and high user learning costs. Consequently, more user-friendly and natural teleoperation methods for robotic arms have shown great development potential, becoming an important control mode in robotic arm applications. They have played significant roles in fields such as search and rescue [5], medicine [6], and aerospace [7]. The emergence of robotic arm teleoperation has greatly enriched its application scenarios, providing more possibilities for its future development. To fully demonstrate the interactive advantages of combining AR technology with robotic arm teleoperation, a systematic engineering integration of the two is required. In [8], AR is introduced into robotic operation as a human–computer interaction method, enhancing the visual feedback of information systems, with application cases combining AR and robotics in medicine, manufacturing, and gaming. In [9], an AR-based robotic arm control system was developed using HoloLens glasses, enabling users to create, modify, simulate, and execute robotic arm trajectories through gesture and voice interaction in the AR headset's view.

2 System Overview Design

2.1 System Architecture Diagram

The system architecture of this project is illustrated in Fig. 1.

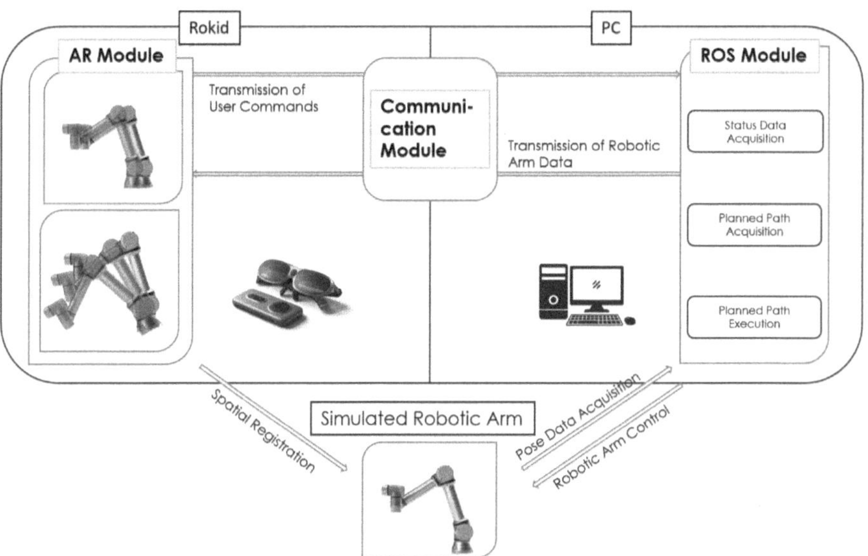

Fig. 1. System Architecture Diagram

2.2 AR Module

The AR module implements functions directly associated with the AR scene and provides the project with a concise, efficient, and user-friendly human–computer interaction interface, responsible for the overall interaction tasks. The main functions of the AR module include:

Interactive Functions Within the AR Scene. Users need to interact with the system within the AR environment, so the AR module designs and implements interaction methods that are easy to use and learn. This system adopts raycast-based interaction for UI buttons. The advantage of raycast interaction is its simplicity and directness, closely resembling the familiar point-and-click method. Supported by Rokid glasses hardware, the raycasting effect is stable and accurately indicates the pointing position. Additionally, the system uses a more straightforward gesture-based drag interaction to control the robotic arm's target position.

Data Calibration. After determining the virtual robotic arm's coordinate in the AR scene, the AR module maps the real robotic arm's real-time state onto the virtual arm. This helps users detect and diagnose potential sensor errors in the robotic arm.

Motion Planning Visualization. Once the user specifies the robotic arm's target point, the AR module animates the planned trajectory on the virtual robotic arm within the AR scene in real time. This simulates the real robotic arm's motion along the planned path, enabling users to identify potential environmental conflicts or path errors and avoid operational mistakes.

2.3 ROS Module

With The ROS module runs on the Ubuntu system and is directly connected to the robotic arm. It is responsible for acquiring detailed sensor data from the robotic arm, performing motion planning based on specific commands, and driving the robotic arm to execute designated actions. The main functions implemented by the ROS module include:

Simulation Environment Visualization. The robotic arm control program depends on the ROS-side simulation environment. This system maps real-time sensor state data from the robotic arm to the ROS simulation environment via the official driver. Using the RViz framework integrated in ROS, the simulation environment is visualized to support subsequent tasks such as data acquisition, motion planning, and robotic arm control.

Data Acquisition. The ROS module establishes a local area network connection with the robotic arm. It obtains all necessary sensor data from the robotic arm through ROS topics communication built on the ROS platform and the official robotic arm driver. The acquired data is saved within the system for further use.

Motion Planning. The ROS module implements the motion planning functionality. After receiving the robotic arm's target coordinates and user planning commands, it analyzes and processes the data to generate specific path planning solutions. The planned path data is stored within the system for subsequent robotic arm control.

Robotic Arm Control. MoveIt is combined with the official robotic arm driver to achieve remote control of the real robotic arm. Once the user confirms the feasibility of the planned path and issues a control command, the AR module invokes the stored planned path data within the system to drive the robotic arm to perform the specified movements.

2.4 Communication Module

The Communication Module's primary function is to enable network communication between the ROS module and the AR module. It operates as a middleware attached to both the AR module and ROS module, running respectively on the Unity platform and the ROS platform. The main functions of the Communication Module include:

AR Module Data Transmission. Planning and execution commands issued by users in the AR module are transmitted to the ROS module through the communication module. Additionally, the communication module collects the robotic arm's real-time dynamic data and planned path data required by the AR module, performing preliminary data processing to ensure the received data format is compatible with the AR module for further processing and use.

ROS Module Data Transmission. The ROS module obtains and analyzes user-issued planning commands, drive commands, and robotic arm target coordinate data via the communication module. After completing tasks such as real-time dynamic data acquisition and path planning, the ROS module further processes these data through the communication module to facilitate data transmission and ensure compatibility with the communication module on the AR client side.

3 System Function Testing

After completing the system environment setup and code development, an overall functional test was conducted on each module of the system to ensure that all modules achieve the expected performance defined in the requirements analysis, and that the system can correctly execute all user commands during operation.

Figure 2 illustrates the real-time status demonstration of the virtual robotic arm corresponding to the real robotic arm. Figure 3 shows the path planning process demonstrated by the virtual robotic arm. Figure 4 depicts the driving process of the real robotic arm based on the path planned by the virtual robotic arm. Through the functional testing of the entire process, the system has been proven capable of correctly executing a series of user-issued commands and successfully fulfilling the specified functional requirements of the project. The overall functionality of the project meets the expected outcomes of the project design.

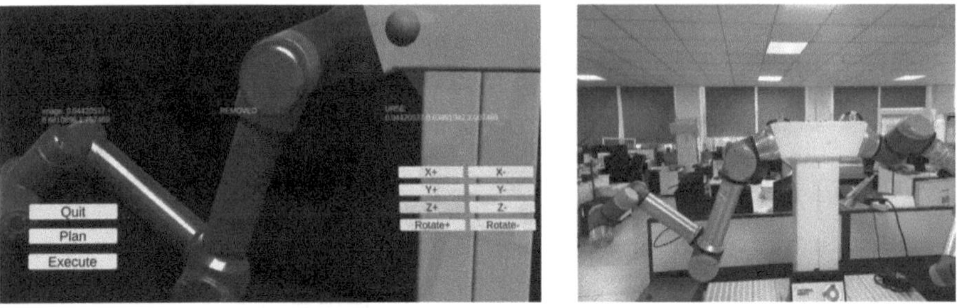

Fig. 2. Real-time status demonstration

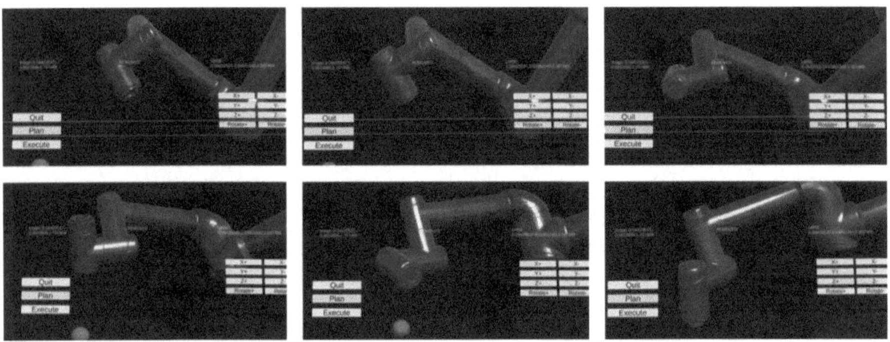

Fig. 3. Path planning demonstration

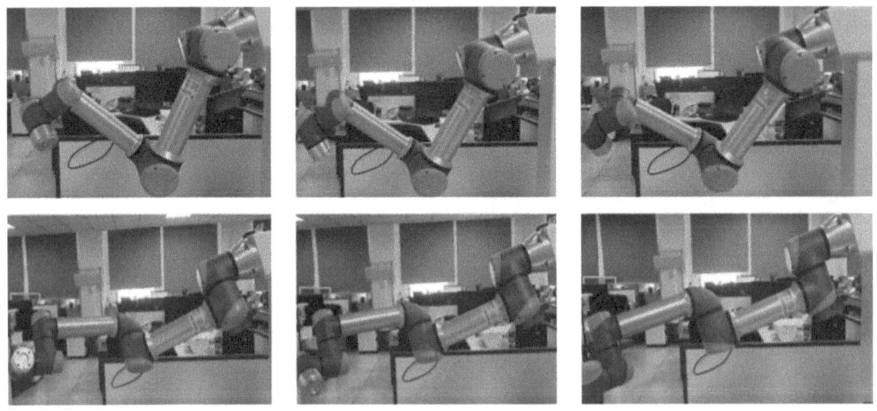

Fig. 4. Robotic arm driving process

References

1. Liu, Y., et al.: Aligning cyber space with physical world: a comprehensive survey on embodied AI. arXiv preprint arXiv:2407.06886 (2024)

2. Ma, Y., Song, Z., Zhuang, Y., Hao, J., King, I.: A survey on vision-language-action models for embodied AI. arXiv preprint arXiv:2405.14093 (2024)
3. Billinghurst, M., Clark, A., Lee, G.: A survey of augmented reality. Found. Trends Hum. Comput. Int. **8**(2–3), 73–272 (2015). https://doi.org/10.1561/1100000049
4. Bottani, E., Vignali, G.: Augmented reality technology in the manufacturing industry: a review of the last decade. IISE Trans. **51**(3), 284–310 (2019)
5. Norton, A., Ober, W., Baraniecki, L., McCann, E., Scholtz, J., Shane, D., et al.: Analysis of human-robot interaction at the darpa robotics challenge finals. Int. J. Robot. Res. **36**(5–7), 483–513 (2017)
6. Zhuang, K.Z., Sommer, N., Mendez, V., Aryan, S., Formento, E., D'Anna, E., et al.: Shared human–robot proportional control of a dexterous myoelectric prosthesis. Nat. Mach. Intell. (2019)
7. Diftler, M., Ahlstrom, T., Ambrose, R., Radford, N., Joyce, C., De La Pena, N., et al.: Robonaut 2 initial activities on-board the ISS. In: 2012 IEEE Aerospace Conference, pp. 1–12. IEEE (2012)
8. Makhataeva, Z., Varol, H.A.: Augmented reality for robotics: a review. Robotics **9**(2), 21 (2020)
9. Quintero, C.P., Li, S., Pan, M.K.X.J., et al.: Robot programming through augmented trajectories in augmented reality. In: 2018 IEEE/RSJ International Conference on Intelligent Robots and Systems (IROS), pp. 1838–1844. IEEE (2018)

Design of an Immersive VR Experience for Awakening Responsibility from an Embodied Cognition Perspective: A Case Study of School Bullying Intervention

Xibei Zhang, Rui Zhang, and Shuo Yan(✉)

School of New Media Art and Design, Beihang University, Beijing 100191, China
shuoyan@buaa.edu.cn

Abstract. This article focuses on the practical challenge of "awakening bystander responsibility" in campus bullying intervention, and based on embodied cognition theory, proposes and constructs an immersive VR experience design framework. Through the narrative structure and embodied interaction mechanism of the three chapters "HALT-HUG-HEAL", emotional empathy, spatial metaphor, and task guidance are deeply integrated, breaking through the bottleneck of insufficient emotional reach and behavioral transformation in traditional intervention methods, and providing a new path based on VR and cognitive theory for campus bullying prevention and control.

Keywords: Embodied cognition · interactive narrative · immersive experience · VR experience design · campus bullying

1 Main Content

1.1 Research Background

Campus bullying, as a recurring, covert, and far-reaching social problem, has become a focus of attention in the global education field. This phenomenon not only causes serious harm to the physical and mental health of victims, leading to damaged self-esteem, depression and anxiety, and even triggering suicidal behavior, but also distorts the essence of school education and destroys the safe campus environment. Specifically, campus bullying is mainly composed of bullies, victims of bullying, assistants, and bystanders. Among them, the "bystander" group in bullying incidents often falls into a gray area of moral contradiction - their silence or inaction invisibly promotes the occurrence of bullying behavior.

Traditional bullying intervention methods often use one-way indoctrination models such as propaganda and education, themed class meetings, etc. Although they can improve students' awareness of bullying at the cognitive level, they are difficult to truly touch the emotional depth, internalize responsibility awareness, and transform behavior. With the rapid development of immersive technology, virtual reality (VR) technology

A. Hinkenjan et al. (Eds.): ICXR 2025, LNCS 16428, pp. 308–317, 2026.
https://doi.org/10.1007/978-981-95-7195-6_20

provides new possibilities for campus bullying intervention due to its unique immersion, interaction, and imagination features. VR technology can create a safe and controllable simulation environment, allowing users to experience the role of bystanders from a first person perspective, providing an unprecedented platform for "responsibility awakening" and "empathy cultivation".

1.2 Theoretical Overview

The embodied cognition theory emphasizes the crucial role of the body in cognitive processes. This theory goes beyond the traditional "disembodied" perspective of cognitive science, emphasizing that cognitive processes do not occur in isolated calculations in the brain, but rather stem from the entire process of interaction between the body and the environment. In VR environments, the three dimensions of the user's body, perception, and cognition together form the foundation of embodied immersion. This theory provides direct theoretical guidance for the VR experience design in this study.

The term 'immersive experience' originated from the flow theory of American psychologist Mihaly Csikszentmihalyi. This theory emphasizes the use of sensory and spiritual experiences to create an environment that fully immerses individuals in a specific context, thereby achieving the optimal state of mind. Based on this, the Halt Hug Heal immersive experience has emerged, using VR technology as a carrier and immersive experience as the core, creating a real campus bullying experience through the perspective of bystanders.

1.3 Design Specifications

This study is based on embodied cognition theory and innovatively proposes and develops an immersive VR responsibility awakening experience design, aiming to break through the limitations of one-way preaching in traditional campus bullying intervention. The system focuses on the key role in bullying incidents - bystanders. Through embodied interaction technology, a highly immersive virtual environment is constructed to transform the potential harm caused by bystanders' unconscious behavior and the resulting cognitive dissonance of responsibility into perceivable and modifiable embodied experiences. Users enter the "psychological world" of the bullied from an observer's perspective, and their behavior directly affects the development of virtual situations, intuitively "causing" the escalation of bullying and triggering strong cognitive dissonance. The system guides users to engage in deep empathy by concretizing the victim's psychology. Ultimately, users participate in the process of "healing" victims through embodied actions.

2 Creative Methods

2.1 Development of Creative Concepts

The creative concept of this experience originates from a profound insight into the dilemma of campus bullying intervention, and has undergone an iterative process from defining core propositions and finding core metaphors to concretizing narrative structures and interaction mechanisms under the systematic guidance of embodied cognition theory.

Definition of Core Propositions

At the beginning of the project, we found through literature review and case analysis of existing campus bullying intervention models that traditional methods such as lectures and posters often focus on one-way imparting of knowledge and moral preaching. However, this has limited effect on the group of "bystanders" who account for the highest proportion of bullying incidents. Because what they often lack is not cognition, but the courage and sense of responsibility to step forward. This sense of responsibility does not stem from external preaching, but from firsthand experience of the relationship between one's own behavior and the consequences of the event.

Therefore, we have redefined the core design proposition of this study: how to create a safe environment where bystanders can "safely make mistakes" and personally experience the direct consequences of their "inaction" or "unconscious behavior", thereby stimulating their sense of responsibility from within? This proposition shifts the design goal from education to awakening, establishing a clear direction for subsequent creative development.

Generation of Core Metaphors

Metaphor is the fundamental structure of human thinking [5], which can help people recognize and process complex, abstract, or invisible concepts. Therefore, we turn to metaphorical thinking and strive to transform the complex psychology in bullying incidents into visual symbols and spatial structures that users can directly perceive and intervene in through their bodies.

For example, we are trying to find a carrier that can perfectly symbolize the spread and harm of language violence in a group. Paper is the most common element on campus, and the paper airplane combines the dual properties of transmission and sharpness. By designing to allow users to first unintentionally pick up, then see the paper airplane pierce into the body of the bullied person, and finally intervene by removing it, the entire metaphor completes a complete and highly impactful concrete expression of the chain of "rumor dissemination causing harm actively stopping". In the healing stage, we need a positive symbol that can form a sharp contrast with the preceding damage and be actively controlled by the user. Light generally symbolizes hope, truth, and care. Design a flashlight as an interactive tool that allows users to dispel darkness, restore color, and awaken life through the concrete action of "shining", perfectly transforming abstract acts of caring into a simple and ritualistic embodied action.

Construction of Narrative Perspective

At the level of digital narrative, this experience adopts a first person narrative perspective to replace the traditional omniscient perspective and construct embodied narrative logic. Users are no longer passive third parties watching events, but have transformed into "bystanders" in the context of campus bullying, experiencing the narrative process firsthand. Through this perspective, users are able to explore the complete narrative plot as characters in a safe environment, and intuitively experience the psychological state and emotional changes of the bullied person. The first person perspective not only prompts users to examine bullying incidents from a bystander's perspective, but also strengthens their emotional connection and identity with the bullied through a dynamic emotional feedback mechanism where the plot evolves in real-time with user behavior, thereby achieving deeper internalization of responsibility at the cognitive and emotional levels [6].

From Concept to Experience

After establishing a narrative perspective, we need to organize it into a narrative process that conforms to the laws of psychological transformation. Guided by embodied cognition theory, this study integrates core metaphors into a three-stage narrative framework of "HALT-HUG-HEAL". The HALT stage reveals the association between users' behavior and the consequences of injury through their physical participation in picking up and throwing paper airplanes, triggering cognitive conflicts; The HUG stage guides users into the psychological space of the bullied, using multi sensory immersive experiences to stimulate emotional resonance; In the HEAL stage, embodied interaction such as flashlight illumination is used to empower users psychologically during the active repair process, completing the internal transformation from cognitive dissonance to responsibility. The entire process is based on physical experience as the cognitive construction foundation, gradually deepening the sense of responsibility and shaping behavioral intentions.

2.2 Technical Implementation Path and Core Interactive Functions

This work adopts Unreal Engine 5 as the core development platform, mainly based on its comprehensive advantages in rendering effects, physical simulation, and cross platform support. Use Blender for scene and prop modeling. By integrating Meta XR plugin with Meta Quest series VR devices, high-precision and low latency head and handle tracking can be achieved using its Inside Out positioning technology. To achieve efficient data communication between PC and VR devices, the system adopts a wired Link streaming scheme, which ensures real-time and stable interaction response while ensuring picture quality and rendering accuracy.

All interaction logic is based on component-based design. Taking the "picking paper airplane" as an example, Line Trace by Channel is used to identify interactive objects, and AttachToComponent is used to dynamically connect the object to the handle. Projectile Movement Component is used to simulate the physical flight trajectory of the paper airplane. To enhance immersion, the system integrates a multi-channel feedback mechanism. When users enter different emotional spaces, the dynamic audio system (Audio Component) adjusts the volume, reverberation, and spatial attenuation of spatial sound effects in real time. The particles in the scene follow the sound triggered by interaction to adjust their motion speed, achieving sound visualization and enhancing emotional immersion.

3 User Experience

3.1 Experience Flow

Prologue

In the prologue, the visual image of the bullied person is divided into three areas, corresponding to the psychological and narrative dimensions of the following three chapters, and equipped with core interactive icons for each chapter, enabling users to establish a preliminary understanding of the overall narrative structure.

After clicking "Start", the user enters the interactive process, and the system presents an actionable diary of the bullied person, summarizing the plot of each chapter, helping the user understand the anti bullying theme and task objectives before officially entering the scene, enhancing immersion and clarity of interaction intentions. The last page of the diary displays a partially missing group photo, with a vacant position for the bullied person, prompting users to collect narrative puzzles by completing chapter tasks to complete the image and anchor the core goals and emotional motivations of the experience. After completing the diary interaction, the paper airplane icon is highlighted with a dynamic effect, prompting the user to use the handle ray to trigger transmission and enter the first chapter "HALT". This design not only achieves natural transitions between scenes, but also enhances the unity of overall interaction logic through coherent visual symbols.

Chapter 1- HALT

In the first chapter "HALT", the user enters a surreal classroom scene. The dynamic silhouette on the wall constantly conveys the paper airplane, symbolizing the spread of bullying discourse and the herd mentality of the group. The formation of connections between participants implies the connection of small groups.

After the paper airplane flies out of the wall, users can pick it up by ray through the handle. The virtual guiding character prompts the user to throw the paper airplane towards it, while the ground model highlights to enhance the interactive prompt. After completing the throwing, the character on the wall throws the paper airplane back into the center of the scene, and then a bullied model with a curled up body and pierced by the paper airplane appears. The user needs to click to remove all paper airplanes, which is a metaphor for resisting and resolving bullying behavior. After removing all the paper planes, the "HALT" puzzle is generated, marking the completion of this chapter. The system returns to the prologue, and the puzzle is automatically placed on the right side of the incomplete group photo. At this point, the "heart" icon representing Chapter 2 is highlighted and animated, guiding users to select and enter the "HUG" scene to maintain emotional engagement and narrative coherence (Fig. 1).

Chapter 2- HUG

In Chapter 2 "HUG", users enter a virtual environment that symbolizes the psychological inner space of bullies. Above the scene is a giant tornado composed of insulting words, and users follow the prompts to enter the center of the vortex, experiencing a descent process and entering the memory tunnel.

Objects carrying memory fragments are arranged in the tunnel, and the continuous falling process not only enhances emotional immersion but also achieves natural scene transitions. After reaching the bottom, the user is faced with a huge heart structure, and the bullied person narrates the experience in the first person, guiding the user to explore inside the heart.

In the perspective of embodied cognition, the various senses of the body are the starting point of cognitive processes, and people clarify their own existence and the existence of other things in the environment through sensory experiences [7]. Based

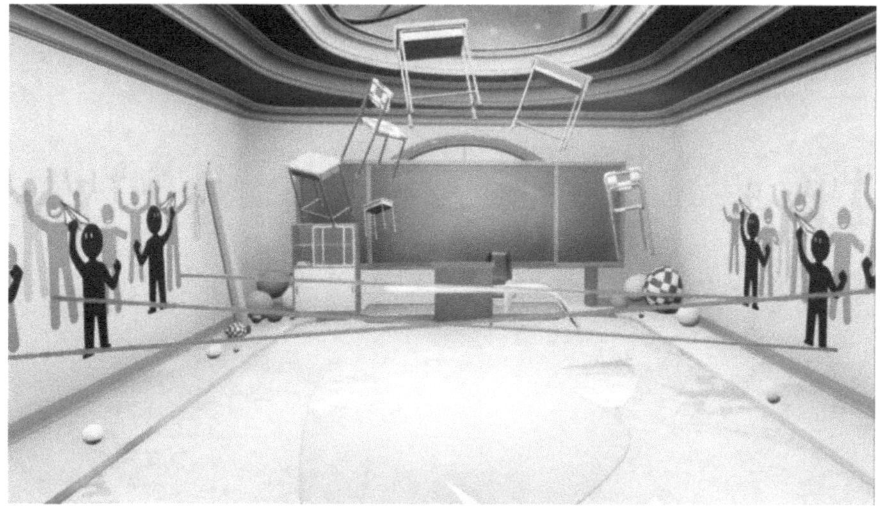

Fig. 1. .

on this theoretical standpoint, this study uses auditory, visual, and somatosensory cues as the core channels for triggering cognitive and emotional transformation when constructing the psychological space within the "heart structure". Specifically, in the first sub scene, the hanging old-fashioned phone creates an auditory dilemma surrounded by verbal violence by playing different types of bullying sound effects, combined with user gaze triggering and particle system sound visualization, allowing users to perceive the isolated situation of the bullied person at the auditory level. The second scene creates a continuous visual pressure with slowly approaching sharp stationery, symbolizing the unavoidable threat of bullying in reality and the psychological reality of victims being in a defensive state for a long time. The third scenario utilizes the collective gaze of a large number of dynamic eyeballs to reinforce the anxiety and inferiority caused by malicious attention in a closed space. The three scenarios work together from the auditory, visual, and somatosensory levels to transform abstract psychological trauma into a multimodal context that can be perceived by the body, enabling users to form a bodily understanding of the victim's situation in sensory experience, thus achieving the design intention of "the body as the cognitive basis" emphasized by embodied cognition theory.

After completing the experience, the user obtains the "HUG" puzzle, and the system returns to the prologue, highlighting the next chapter icon and guiding them to the third chapter "HEAL" (Fig. 2).

Chapter 3- HEAL

In Chapter 3 "HEAL", the user enters a classroom with black, white, and gray tones, metaphorically depicting the repressed state of the bullied person's heart. The flashlight on the podium serves as the core interactive tool, and its beam can restore color to the illuminated area, symbolizing the reconstruction of the psychological world through active intervention.

Fig. 2. .

After the user retrieves the flashlight, follow the prompts to clear the insulting text on the desk, and the system will immediately display motivational statements as positive feedback. Subsequently, based on the 3D audio prompts, the user moves to the water pool and uses a flashlight to illuminate the wet book to virtually pick it up, obtaining motivational text again and reinforcing the positive behavior cycle. Finally, in the dark enclosed scene, the bullied person curls up in the center. When the user shines a flashlight directly on the character, they gradually transition from curling up to standing, symbolizing a change in psychological state and self reconstruction, and submit the "HEAL" puzzle to the user.

After obtaining the puzzle, the system returns to the prologue, and the three pieces of the puzzle are automatically pieced together to fill in the gaps of the bullied person in the group photo, marking the completion of all narrative tasks. This ending not only symbolizes the rescue of the victims, but also achieves the dual goals of education and emotionalization through the active participation and empathy building of users (Fig. 3).

Fig. 3. .

3.2 User Testing

Through user testing, it was found that participants showed the strongest emotional resonance in Chapter 2 (Hug), especially in the "phone room" (the concretization of language bullying) and "eye room" (the feeling of being stared at), where embodied feedback effectively enhanced the sense of immersion in "being isolated" and "being scrutinized". The test feedback also suggests that richer gesture recognition can be introduced in the Heal chapter, such as waving to dispel negative text or using gestures to piece together puzzles, to enhance the naturalness and ritual of interaction. After experiencing it, most users expressed a deeper understanding of bystander responsibility and are more willing to step forward in reality. Preliminary evidence has demonstrated the potential advantages of VR immersive experiences based on embodied cognition in intervening attitudes and behavioral intentions.

4 Innovation and Contribution

This study is a comprehensive exploratory design research project guided by embodied cognitive theory system. Its innovation and contribution are mainly reflected in three aspects: theoretical construction, technical methods, and practical applications, providing replicable paradigms and empirical evidence for using immersive technology for behavior and attitude intervention.

4.1 Theoretical Innovation

Compared with existing research, the theoretical innovation of this project lies in going beyond the simplistic application of viewing VR as an "empathy machine", and instead constructing a systematic, embodied cognition based "responsibility awakening" design framework.

Most existing VR empathy experiences focus on allowing users to "feel" the pain of the victim, which is still a "disembodied" or "shallow embodied" mode centered on emotional reception. This study uses interactive design to make users' physical actions directly the key to narrative progression. For example, in the "HALT" chapter, the user's initial unconscious behavior of "picking up" a paper airplane is revealed in subsequent narratives as participating in the spread of bullying, thereby actively triggering their cognitive dissonance. This design, which links unconscious behavior (Body) → moral cognitive dissonance (Cognition) → remedial action (Action), realizes the internalization process of responsibility from passive acceptance to active assumption, and is a deepening application of embodied cognition theory in the field of moral education.

The three-stage narrative structure of "HALT-HUG-HEAL" proposed in this study is a concrete and structured implementation of the "cognition emotion behavior" theoretical model. The initial experience of behavior intervention and cognitive dissonance during the HALT (prevention) phase; The HUG stage establishes deep emotional empathy by delving into the psychological space of the bullied individual; The HEAL stage provides a pathway for repair through embodied actions. This structure ensures that the experience is not only an emotional impact, but also a complete psychological transformation process that guides positive behavioral intentions.

4.2 Technological and Methodological Innovation

At the level of technology and design methodology, the innovation of this study lies in the development of a embodied interactive language that transforms abstract psychological concepts into perceptible and interactive ones.

Research creatively transforms abstract concepts in campus bullying into a coherent and interactive multisensory metaphorical system. For example, "paper airplane" metaphorically refers to the transmission and harm of rumors and gossip; The "phone room" and "eye room" within the "heart space" respectively metaphorically represent the sustained harm of language bullying and the anxiety of being scrutinized; And 'flashlight' metaphorically represents attention, understanding, and hope. These metaphors are not isolated artistic symbols, but closely coupled with interactive logic and narrative processes. Understanding metaphors through bodily involvement greatly reduces cognitive barriers and enhances the intuitiveness and infectiousness of experiences.

The technical implementation of this study not only pursues visual fidelity, but also focuses on building a dynamic emotional field that responds to user behavior. Its core innovation is the real-time coupling of audio, visual particles, and user behavior. For example, in the "HUG" chapter, the motion speed of the particle system in the scene is adjusted in real time based on the triggered sound intensity and type, achieving "sound visualization". This technological approach transforms intangible emotional fluctuations into tangible visual phenomena, enhancing users' perception of the victim's inner world, and is a key technological contribution to creating a deep sense of immersion and emotional immersion.

At the same time, this design adopts a stylized visual language to transform heavy topics into aesthetically valuable experiences, avoiding psychological shock overload and shaping distinct visual memory points. At the same time, using "jigsaw puzzles" as the thread that runs through the entire process, the fragmented participation of users is integrated into a psychological closed loop of "complete rescue", enhancing the structured level of sense of achievement and responsibility cognition.

4.3 Application and Contribution

The results of this study have clear application value and contribution to relevant academic fields and social practice.

This study demonstrates a complete design research process from problem definition, theoretical mapping, concept development, technical implementation to user testing. Among them, the "embodiment context action" model and the "three-stage" narrative framework have high portability and can be applied to other social issues that require attitude and behavior transformation, providing clear methodological references for similar research.

The user testing feedback, especially the strong emotional resonance felt by participants in the "HUG" chapter and their higher willingness to take responsibility behavior after experiencing it, provides preliminary empirical support for the effectiveness of the theoretical framework and design methods proposed in this study. This demonstrates the potential advantages of embodied cognition based VR experiences in promoting attitude and behavioral intention changes, laying a solid foundation for subsequent empirical research with larger sample sizes and more rigorous controls.

This project expands the application of VR technology from entertainment and skills training to more complex areas of social morality and behavioral intervention. It not only provides a novel intervention tool concept for educators and campus psychologists, but more importantly, it provides an inspiring practical case for using cutting-edge technology to solve social problems.

References

1. Sun, X.B., Liu, H.M.: Rational cognition of school bullying: from school violence to school bullying. Educ. Theory Pract. **35**(31), 26–29 (2015). (in Chinese)
2. Ye, H.S.: Embodied cognition: a new approach to cognitive psychology. Adv. Psychol. Sci. **18**(5), 705–710 (2010). (in Chinese)
3. Xu, X., Kang, J., Yang, L.: Understanding embodied immersion in technology-enabled embodied learning environments. J. Comput. Assist. Learn. **38**(1), 103–119 (2021)
4. Csikszentmihalyi, M.: Flow: The Psychology of Optimal Experience. CITIC Publishing Group, Beijing (2017). (in Chinese)
5. Yang, Y.: Research on multimodal metaphorical representation types in poster discourse. Foreign Lang. Stud. (03), 30–35 (2015). https://doi.org/10.13978/j.cnki.wyyj.2015.03.006
6. Yuan, X., Li, Y.: Physical presence and cognitive extension: digital narrative innovation in digital picture books from the perspective of embodied cognition. Published in Panorama (08), 78–84 (2025). https://doi.org/10.16491/j.cnki.cn45-1216/g2.2025.08.010
7. Li, Z., Zhang, Y.: Cognition, body, and reading: a preliminary discussion on the future development of the publishing industry. Modern Publishing (1), 94–104 (2023)

Journey to Wellness: Motion-Driven VR with 360° Panoramic Environments for Arts-Inspired Relaxation

Wei Gai, Rui Jing, Xiyu Bao, Haitao Li, and Chenglei Yang(✉)

Shandong University, Jinan 250101, China
{gw, baoxiyu,chl_yang}@sdu.edu.cn, jingrui0312@126.com, 270751540@qq.com

Abstract. We present Journey to Wellness, a motion-driven VR art framework that integrates 360° panoramic environments to create an embodied and interactive experience. Its core innovation is a real-time motion-scene coupling technique that synchronizes panoramic transitions with the user's vehicle movement. By translating vehicular dynamics into a panoramic interactive medium, the framework establishes a bidirectional feedback loop between motion and environment. The system comprises three key components: (1) Motion-linked control design, which employs an IMU and ESP32-based vehicle platform for real-time motion sensing and data transmission; (2) Immersive content creation, which uses 360° panoramic capture to reproduce natural and cultural environments with ecological fidelity; and (3) Redirected-mapping spatial expansion, which applies a curvature-gain algorithm to transform limited physical motion into continuous virtual roaming. Through this approach, Journey to Wellness reframes VR spatial cognition by transforming passive cultural tourism into embodied engagement. It offers a mode of technological-artistic integration that connects cultural experience with relaxation, creativity, and holistic well-being.

Keywords: Motion-driven VR · 360° panoramic environments · Embodied interaction · Redirected walking algorithms

1 Introduction

The increasing prevalence of psychological sub-health conditions, with an estimated 301 million cases worldwide in 2019 according to the WHO, highlights the urgent need for innovative approaches to mental well-being. Traditional art-based therapies, although effective in personalized settings, face significant challenges in scalability because of spatial constraints, limited media options, and the shortage of qualified professionals [1].

In recent years, virtual reality (VR) has emerged as a valuable medium for mental health support [2,3]. However, many existing systems remain largely passive and user-centered. Virtual environments often serve only as static backdrops, acting as one-way emotional regulators, while users are confined to fixed

A. Hinkenjan et al. (Eds.): ICXR 2025, LNCS 16428, pp. 318–324, 2026.
https://doi.org/10.1007/978-981-95-7195-6_21

positions with minimal opportunities for embodied interaction. This imbalance weakens the sense of dialogue between individuals and virtual environments, resulting in fragmented experiences that conflict with the ecological principle of mutual responsiveness essential to restorative design.

Technological progress in lightweight VR headsets, intelligent motion vehicles, and low-latency 5G communication has begun to overcome the physical limitations of earlier systems [4–6]. Research in environmental psychology demonstrates that exposure to natural landscapes can promote relaxation, while mindfulness studies emphasize the importance of sensory engagement and present-moment awareness [7].

To address the limitations of current VR applications for well-being, this study presents a motion-driven VR system featuring 360° panoramic environments designed for arts-inspired relaxation. Within this system, a user's physical movement in a compact vehicle directly influences the evolution of panoramic virtual scenes. Static landscapes are transformed into responsive environments, and confined physical spaces are extended into vast virtual horizons through redirected walking algorithms.

The proposed system establishes an initial framework for bidirectional feedback between human movement and virtual environments. It redefines well-being as an active and creative process that integrates technology, culture, and embodied art. Each physical action continuously shapes the virtual narrative, enhancing both relaxation and engagement. While the design draws inspiration from art-therapy principles, it does not claim clinical efficacy. Instead, it provides a conceptual and technological foundation for future studies exploring how motion-coupled panoramic VR experiences can contribute to mental health support.

2 Journey to Wellness: Design and Implementation

The system is based on the concept of panoramic roaming driven by vehicle motion. It comprises three modules: vehicle control, virtual content generation, and redirected roaming (see Fig. 1). These modules operate in a closed loop to achieve three primary goals: (1) real-time synchronization between physical motion and virtual rendering, (2) responsive scene transitions linked to user movement, and (3) expansion of small physical spaces into large-scale virtual roaming environments.

2.1 Motion Vehicles

Hardware Coordination Module Design. The motion vehicle was modified to optimize in-vehicle VR performance, integrating enhanced sensing and control for faster and more precise responses. Two core components enable real-time motion capture and wireless data transmission: the inertial measurement unit (IMU) and the computing core (ESP32).

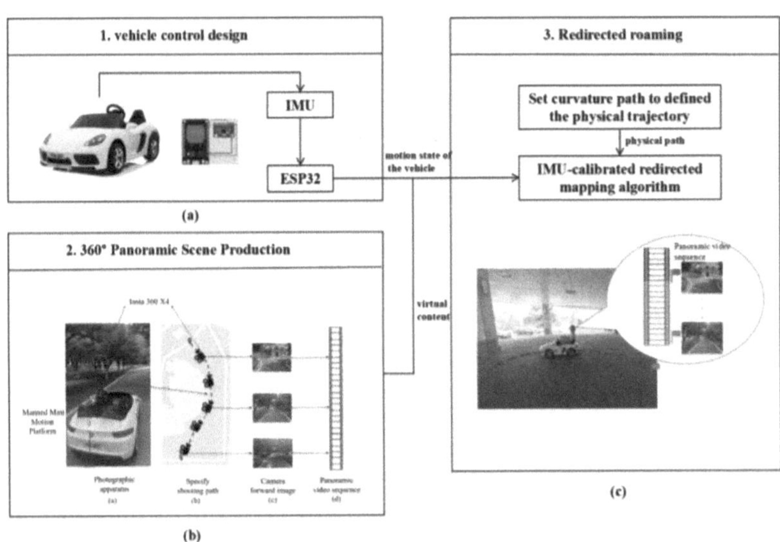

Fig. 1. System Design.

Motion Vehicle. The 12V/14A electric vehicle (Fig. 1a) supports a load of up to 100kg (two passengers) with a maximum speed of 0.3 m/s and minimum turning radius of 3.2 m. It supports both manual and remote-control modes, allowing either independent sessions or guided experiences.

IMU. The MPU-6050, which integrates a gyroscope and an accelerometer, captures real-time acceleration and angular velocity. A Kalman filter minimizes noise and provides accurate 3D estimates, ensuring high-fidelity spatial mapping and a stable immersive experience.

Computing Core (ESP32). Serving as the data hub, the ESP32 integrates, processes, and wirelessly transmits motion data via Wi-Fi. This modular architecture improves scalability and simplifies system maintenance.

Communication and Control. The IMU-ESP32 module attached to the vehicle continuously collects motion data, which are transmitted via Wi-Fi Socket to the VR rendering system for real-time adjustments (Fig. 2). The ESP32, connected to the vehicle's mainboard, also receives control commands from the VR environment, enabling precise bidirectional interaction. Movement control (forward, backward, left, right) is achieved through pin voltage regulation. The modular structure facilitates future upgrades and sensor replacements, balancing efficiency, responsiveness, and user comfort.

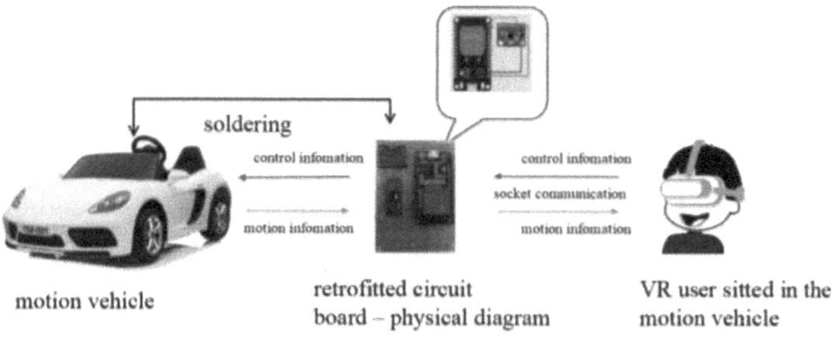

Fig. 2. Schematic Diagram of Vehicle Control Design.

2.2 360° Panoramic Scene Production

360° panoramic media enhances immersion by offering a complete visual field, encouraging autonomous exploration, and stimulating multiple senses through the integration of stereo audio and optional haptic cues. The system supports flexible content customization to suit relaxation-oriented and experiential applications. In addition to self-captured panoramic footage, external 360° materials such as digitally reconstructed cultural artworks (e.g., Along the River During the Qingming Festival), can also be integrated, demonstrating the framework's adaptability to diverse visual sources and its potential for cultural-artistic interpretation.

To achieve optimal motion synchronization and ecological immersion, the present study focuses on self-captured panoramic scenes, produced through a controlled shooting process as illustrated in Fig. 1b. The shooting process is guided by three requirements: natural immersion, motion adaptability, and perspective consistency.

(1) Perspective Alignment: The Insta 360 camera is tightly mounted to the vehicle via a custom bracket, ensuring that its optical axis is aligned parallel to the vehicle's forward direction. This alignment ensures that each panoramic frame corresponds to the virtual path, facilitating later compensation during redirected mapping and avoiding visual discontinuities.

(2) Path Curvature Control: Shooting paths with a curvature radius of at least 5 m are used (Fig. 1b) to minimize motion sickness, since abrupt turns can cause conflicts between visual and vestibular cues. Locations such as bamboo forests, lotus ponds, and botanical gardens are preferred for their high restorative potential as identified in environmental psychology.

(3) Viewpoint Height: The camera is fixed at a height of 1.2 m, simulating the seated eye height of the user. This configuration promotes consistency between physical movement and virtual perspective, thereby minimizing cognitive load.

The camera mounted on the moving vehicle captures continuous frames along the pre-defined path (Fig. 1b(a) – (c)), producing panoramic video sequences for virtual roaming (Fig. 1b(d)).

2.3 IMU-Calibrated Redirected Mapping Algorithm

Although panoramic videos create an immersive virtual path, the physical space available for motion is inherently limited. To overcome this constraint, a curvature-gain redirected mapping algorithm establishes a correspondence between the vehicle's real circular trajectory and a virtual straight-line path. This non-equidistant mapping effectively connects finite physical space with a perceived infinite virtual environment (Fig. 1c).

The algorithm synchronizes the vehicle's real position with the panoramic frame sequence. As the vehicle moves along a circular trajectory, the system selects corresponding panoramic frames to generate a continuous forward-motion perception. The IMU continuously monitors the orientation to correct rotational deviations, ensuring that physical circular movement is perceived as virtual straight-line navigation.

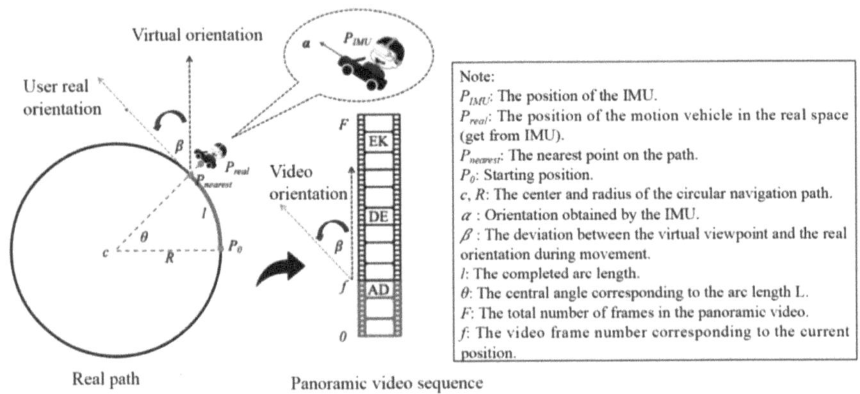

Fig. 3. Mapping relationship diagram.

This process is represented mathematically (refer to Fig. 3). Let the curvature circle radius be R. The vehicle starts from $P_0$and moves along the circular trajectory. The IMU tracks the current position $P_{current}$. Using the previous position P_{prev} and the accumulated distance l_p, the algorithm computes the incremental central angle $\Delta\theta$ and distance Δl, thereby deriving the current travel distance l. The ratio of l to the total path length S equals the ratio of the current frame index f to the total frames F, determining the rendered frame. During motion, the user's actual orientation (green dashed arrow) differs from the virtual forward direction (black dashed arrow). The IMU measures the deviation angle α to align virtual content with the user's forward direction. and adjusts the panoramic video orientation β to maintain alignment.

This redirected mapping algorithm ensures that users perceive natural, continuous motion within confined spaces, achieving high immersion without requiring extensive physical areas.

3 System Applications

The system has been explored through pilot installations in university experiential programs and auxiliary wellness environments. The integration of panoramic virtual scenes with motion vehicles, utilizing synchronized visual, auditory, and vestibular cues, provides an immersive relaxation and reflective experience for young adults and participants experiencing emotional stress (see Fig. 4).

Fig. 4. System Applications.

In university contexts, virtual roaming modules such as Four Seasons Campus and Ecological Botanical Garden enable autonomous VR exploration and creative engagement. Repeated participation has been associated with enhanced relaxation and subjective comfort according to informal user feedback.

In wellness-oriented environments, immersive themes such as Forest Wandering and Serene Waters, are guided by facilitators to encourage emotional balance and sensory immersion rather than formal therapy.

Future developments may extend to community well-being programs and campus mental health promotion, exploring how the integration of cultural tourism content and digital media technologies can support accessible, art-inspired relaxation experiences.

4 Conclusion

This paper presents an artistic VR installation that integrates real-time motion coupling with 360° panoramic visual environments to create an embodied, interactive experience. The system bridges physical movement and virtual perception through a motion-driven feedback loop, transforming limited physical spaces into expansive, responsive environments. While this work is not a clinical study, it offers valuable insights into how immersive, movement-synchronized visuals can support relaxation and emotional reflection. The design framework demonstrates how ecological principles, embodied interaction, and cultural aesthetics can be combined to enhance user well-being and engagement. Moreover, the system provides a solid foundation for future interdisciplinary exploration, offering potential applications in mental health support, rehabilitation design, and experiential education.

Acknowledgments. This work is supported by National Science and Technology Major Project(2022ZD0118002), the National Natural Science Foundation of China under Grant (62332017, 62277035), and Shandong Province Youth Entrepreneurship Technology Support Program for Higher Education Institutions (2022KJN028).

Disclosure of Interests. The authors have no competing interests to declare that are relevant to the content of this article.

References

1. Malchiodi, C.A. (ed.): Handbook of Art Therapy. Guilford Press, New York (2011)
2. Bell, I.H., Nicholas, J., Alvarez-Jimenez, M., Thompson, A., Valmaggia, L.: Virtual reality as a clinical tool in mental health research and practice. Dialogues Clin. Neurosci. **22**(2), 169–177 (2020)
3. Bell, I.H., et al.: Advances in the use of virtual reality to treat mental health conditions. Nat. Rev. Psychol. **3**(8), 552–567 (2024)
4. Bian, Y., Zhou, C., Gai, W., Liu, J., Yang, C.: The effect of embodied interaction designs on flow experience: examination in VR games. Virtual Reality **27**(2), 1549–1565 (2023)
5. Bian, Y., et al.: Exploring the weak association between flow experience and performance in virtual environments. In: Proceedings of the 2018 CHI Conference on Human Factors in Computing Systems, pp. 1–12 (2018)
6. Steinicke, F., Bruder, G., Jerald, J., Frenz, H., Lappe, M.: Estimation of detection thresholds for redirected walking techniques. IEEE Trans. Visual Comput. Graphics **16**(1), 17–27 (2009)
7. Browning, M.H., Mimnaugh, K.J., Van Riper, C.J., Laurent, H.K., LaValle, S.M.: Can simulated nature support mental health? Comparing short, single-doses of 360-degree nature videos in virtual reality with the outdoors. Front. Psychol. **10**, 2667 (2020)

Ebb Within—The Ritual Without Shore: Spatialized VR Reconstruction of the White Snake's Inner World Through Dual-Identity Participation

Liaoruo Liu, Wen Zhou(✉), and Yansong Chen

School of Arts and Communication, Beijing Normal University, Beijing 100875, China
zhouwen@bnu.edu.cn

Abstract. This research proposes a "Chinese Aesthetic Spatial Expression System" (CASES) for cultural heritage contexts, exploring an emotionally spatialized Virtual Reality (VR) narrative model of "Inner Imagery" and its corresponding methodology. Implemented through the VR interactive narrative work *Ebb Within*, developed using Unreal Engine 5, the study reinterprets *The Tale of the White Snake* as an emotion-driven immersive experience. It establishes a "participatory introspection" narrative mechanism, enabling users to adopt a dual identity and delve into seven fragmented inner dreamscapes of Bai Suzhen (White Snake) before her drowning. Through multimodal interactions involving emotional atmospheres, cultural rituals, and Peking Opera soundscapes, users explore the themes of obsession and redemption. The study contributes three core methodologies: a four-layer mapping model of "Inner Emotion → Imagery Space"; a five-element process for the "Embodied Interactive Translation of Cultural Symbols"; and a triple-loop pathway of "Visual-Auditory-Kinesthetic" cross-modal coupling within the CASES framework. This research provides a reusable framework and practical evidence to support the development of Intangible Cultural Heritage VR (ICH-VR) experiences.

Keywords: VR Interactive Narrative · Emotional Spatialization · Cultural Symbol Translation · Peking Opera Soundscape

1 Introduction

Peking Opera and the legend of The Tale of the White Snake, as representatives of China's intangible cultural heritage, face challenges in contemporary dissemination such as homogenized narrative modes and a disconnect with younger generations. Virtual Reality (VR) technology, by virtue of its immersive and embodied interactive characteristics, offers new possibilities for the digital preservation of cultural heritage. In recent years, the academic community has called for a paradigm shift from "technology-oriented" to "culture-oriented." Domestic scholars like Zhou, from an art ontology perspective, have demonstrated the potential of virtual reality as an "ultimate empathy medium" based

A. Hinkenjan et al. (Eds.): ICXR 2025, LNCS 16428, pp. 325–336, 2026.
https://doi.org/10.1007/978-981-95-7195-6_22

on, yet transcending, the body [1]. Xu and Zhou proposed that virtual reality documentary images can serve as auxiliary tools for constructing digital cultural memory and discussed their "hyperreal" aesthetic characteristics and cultural extensions [2]. These studies provide new theoretical perspectives for empowering cultural heritage with VR. However, how to translate these theories into a systematic, implementable artistic creation methodology, particularly in constructing character inner worlds, deep interactive translation of cultural symbols, and integrating Chinese aesthetic systems, remains a persistent research gap.

Addressing these limitations, this study explores, through the work *Ebb Within*, how to use VR technology to build a methodology that breaks through the mere reproduction of the external forms of cultural heritage, achieving the emotional translation and immersive resonance of the character's inner world and deep cultural connotations.

2 Related Work

The integration of ICH and VR is at a stage, shifting from technical reproduction to meaningful depth. This transformation across narrative, spatial, and interactive dimensions remains incomplete in practice.

2.1 Limitations of Narrative Perspective: The Gap from Cultural Memory Transmission to Embodied Experience

At the narrative level, many ICH-VR experiences are designed around an observer-like viewing position, which, in Genette's terms, is heterodiegetic narration with external focalization [3], rather than an internally focalized, first-person immersive perspective. This narrative mode, by positioning the user outside the story, may secure complete information transfer, yet it ultimately compresses rich cultural memory [4] into a one-way narration, blocking the emotional connection between the user and the character's inner world. As Champion argues, virtual heritage should move beyond geometric reconstruction to convey cultural meaning, significance, and social agency [5]. Building on this, narrative design can avoid fixing users in a purely observer-like role by making perspective and interaction structurally consequential. For example, Olaz et al. propose an in-situ mixed-reality heritage visit centered on a conversational avatar, and they explicitly recommend a non-linear, user-controllable narrative structure in which visitors choose what to explore [6]. However, how to design narrative mechanisms and perspectives that guide users towards "participatory introspection," rather than providing predetermined emotional conclusions, remains a challenge in current practice.

2.2 Disconnect in Interactive Semantics: The Disjunction Between Cultural Symbols and Interactive Behaviors

Much of the interaction design in ICH-VR often falls into the "functionalist" trap, where interaction forms merely trigger events or acquire information, becoming detached from profound cultural semantics. Symbolic Interactionism holds that meaning emerges through social interaction with symbols [7]. When "clicking" a prop merely triggers a textual pop-up, the action itself becomes semantically empty and fails to carry cultural narrative. Activity Theory further suggests that human activity is mediated by culturally and historically developed tools, and that meaningful tool use involves the appropriation and internalization of socio-cultural experience [8]; therefore, generic interactions like clicking are often too thin to perform this mediating function. Recent work on ritual design in the digital age argues that embedding ritual-like structures, defined as repeatable sequences of symbolically meaningful actions, can organize participation and strengthen immersion and cultural identification [9]. Similarly, Procedural Rhetoric argues for conveying viewpoints and values through systematic rules and processes [10]. Consequently, a task for current research lies in developing systematic methods to effectively translate cultural symbols into interactive actions imbued with narrative and cultural significance.

2.3 Dilemmas in Spatial Design: The Aphasia of Lyrical Aesthetics in Immersive Environments

In spatial construction, many ICH-VR projects rely on perspective control and 360° panoramic viewing to organize immersion; more broadly, this visual-first approach echoes a long Western lineage of immersive image-making aimed at producing maximal illusion and immersion [11]. While this paradigm can create stunning spectacles, its emphasis on a what-you-see-is-what-you-get mode of visual presence finds it difficult to accommodate the generative path of wandering observation and forming meaning through action emphasized in Chinese aesthetics. As Zong Baihua argues, Chinese aesthetics values "scenery changing with each step," intention guiding form, and the rhythmic vitality of spirit; meaning often emerges through walking, pausing, touching, and choosing, rather than through visual fidelity alone [12]. This paradigm overlooks the core insight of Embodied Cognition, that cognition and emotional depth depend on the body's activities and exploration within the environment [13]. Recent scholarship on immersive theatre suggests that the audience's bodily movement and spatial interaction play a constitutive role in structuring the experience: walking, lingering, and triggering actions shape the order of encounters and redistribute attention across narrative fragments, rather than following a fixed sequence [14, 15]. Although Environmental Storytelling [16] has become an influential approach to narrative space, its application in ICH-VR still tends to prioritize highly realistic visual scene restoration of cultural symbols. How to transform non-representational cultural elements like opera conventions and poetic artistic conception into imagery spatial structures that can be traversed by the body and can evoke specific emotional trajectories remains insufficiently addressed in existing research.

3 System Design and Methodology

The "Inner Imagery" emotionally spatialized VR narrative model proposed in this study is systematically designed and implemented from three dimensions: narrative perspective, interactive semantics, and spatial aesthetics. The systematic design and methodological models of these three dimensions are interconnected and mutually supportive, ultimately realizing the integrated CASES of "Emotion-Space-Narrative-Interaction-Culture."

3.1 Narrative Perspective: Inner Imagery Construction

This study shifts the narrative perspective from "external event/scene restoration" to "mindscape construction/psychological field." To construct the inner imagery, it explores a four-layer mapping methodological model of "Inner Emotion → Imagery Space," translating abstract emotions into specific, traversable imagery space-mechanism combinations through "Narrative Perspective Reconstruction, Emotional Essence Extraction, Emotion-Space Mapping, Spatial Expression Grammar" (Fig. 1).

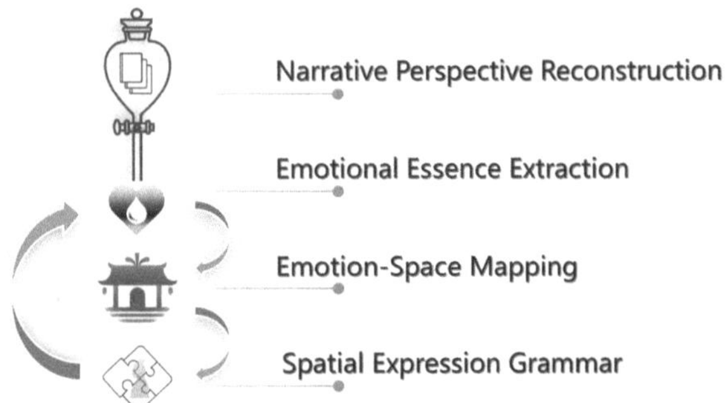

Fig. 1. Four-layer methodological model for emotion-driven spatial mapping

This study reconstructs the script based on the textual context of The Complete Tale of the White Snake [17], shifting the narrative entity from "external events/scene restoration" to "Bai Suzhen's internal emotional experience/mindscape reconstruction." It adopts a dual-identity perspective mechanism in the sense of Brecht's "Verfremdungseffekt" (alienation effect) [18]: on one hand, the user enters Bai Suzhen's dreams as Xiao Qing, an in-situ participant driving the plot; on the other hand, the user is positioned as a reflector in the modern context, making contemporary judgments on emotions and values at key nodes, thus achieving isotopic fusion and a participation–reflection alternation. This mechanism prevents the user from remaining a passive receiver, instead enabling a sensorial discernment of tensions like "fate/agency," "emotion/rationality," "ethics/self" within the experiential inner scenes, thereby initiating the subsequent methodological sequence of "Emotion-Space" mapping. The specific events and interaction anchor points for this dual identity are realized in the work through seven dream chapters.

Centering on the reconstructed script and Peking Opera recitatives, this study extracts a lexicon of Bai Suzhen's core emotions, such as "Inner Abyss," "Obsession as Cage," and "Liberation," forming corresponding relationships between "Core Emotion → Imagery Space," and translating abstract emotions into traversable static spatial prototypes and dynamic field mechanisms. For example, the difficult ascent of the "Marital Journey" is expressed as a circular spiral giant candlestick maze with memory triggers lit level by level; the "inescapable constraint/despair" corresponds to the kinetic field of vertical falling and U-shaped descent; the "Obsession Cage" corresponds to the constricting process of being gradually enclosed by calligraphic Peking Opera monologues in dark space. This mapping ensures a traceable alignment between emotional semantics, spatial geometry, and perceptual cues, making space no longer a narrative background but the co-ontology of narrative and emotion, providing a structured generative basis for target experiences in evaluation, such as "falling sensation/oppression/ascent sensation/relief" (Table 1 and Fig. 2).

Table 1. Example of Emotion-Space Mapping

Core Emotion	Static Spatial Mapping	Dynamic Spatial Mapping	Experience Goal
Inner Abyss	Deep-sea U-shaped space	Boundless falling	Falling sensation, loss
Obsession as Cage	Swords & staffs cage	Enclosure by Peking Opera monologue	Oppression, constraint
Marital Journey	Spiraling ascent space	Ascending around giant red candles	Progression, ascent
Liberation	Temple intact as before	Free movement in shallow water area	Relief, freedom

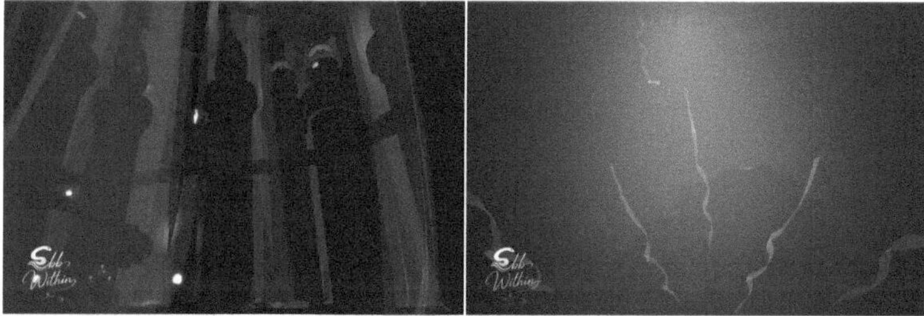

Fig. 2. Spiraling ascent and U-shaped descent spaces, mapping the psychological journey

To fit the chaotic generativity of the inner world and the "emergent" characteristics of memory/dreams, the spatial expression adopts a non-linear, circular, and retrospectively fragmented assembly grammar. Chapters are connected by emotional logic rather than causal linearity, forming a near-fated circular experience through a "leap—backflow—reappearance" organization, encouraging users to complete meaning construction through "puzzle-like understanding." This structure sutures the spatiotemporal and imagery of chapters with emotional threads, making the user's walking, gazing, and triggering actions isomorphic to narrative progression, thereby establishing consistency between subjective internal vision and external performance, ensuring the composability, reusability, and verifiability of the aforementioned "Core Emotion → Imagery Space" mapping at the overall narrative level.

3.2 Interactive Semantics: Cultural Symbol Translation

In translating cultural symbols, this study does not stop at the "superficial application" of Peircean semiotics but attempts to transform native cultural symbols from static representations into narrative interactive predicates and ritualized actions. To this end, it explores an "Embodied Interactive" translation model for cultural symbols, expanding the translation from the static triadic relation of "Sign—Object—Interpretant" to the dynamic five-element process based on Embodied Cognition theory (Fig. 3 and Table 2).

Fig. 3. Five-element process for cultural symbol interactive translation

Table 2. Example of Cultural Symbol Interactive Translation Process

Symbol	Cultural Anchoring	Interactive Ritual	Feedback Design	Meaning Construction
Oil-paper Umbrella	the beginning of Bai- Xu's love/fate	"Return umbrella" during rain at first meeting flashback	Bai dissipates like smoke; Peking Opera monologue	"Beginning and End of Fate" "Letting Go of Obsession"
Lotus Lamp	Xu's wish, liberation	parting "Search for/Hold/Throw" lotus lamp during Xu 's repentance/plea	Xu gradually shatters in darkness; oil-paper umbrella slowly drifts down	"Redemption" "Liberation"
Red Candle	Joy/fulfillment of Bai-Xu wedding	Ascend stairs around giant red candle, light candles level by level	Triggers memory flashback, opens next level door	Marriage's "Joy" & "Sorrow"

This process first extracts and defines core cultural symbols from the classic narrative, specifically the "Lotus Lamp," the "Oil-paper Umbrella," and the "Red Candle." These images not only carry key emotions in The Tale of the White Snake but also refer to the broader spectrum of traditional Chinese culture. Their connotations are then anchored and interpreted within the narrative context and cultural tradition. For example, the "Red Candle" symbolizes the joy and fulfillment in the wedding context of Bai Suzhen and Xu Xian. Subsequently, interactive translation is carried out using the cultural symbols as intermediaries, designing interactive behaviors as embodied rituals that require physical participation to complete. For instance, participants light the "Red Candles" level by level along a spiral path in the "Candlestick Maze." Based on this, user perception and experience targets are set, and a "User Experience Feedback" mechanism is configured, using the environment's dynamic response to reinforce the transmission of emotion and cultural meaning, thus forming a closed-loop experience structure. Thereby, cultural symbols achieve the generation and reproduction of dynamic meaning from static representation; this generative process is triggered by the synergy of the participant's action execution, ritual completion, and feedback reception (Fig. 4).

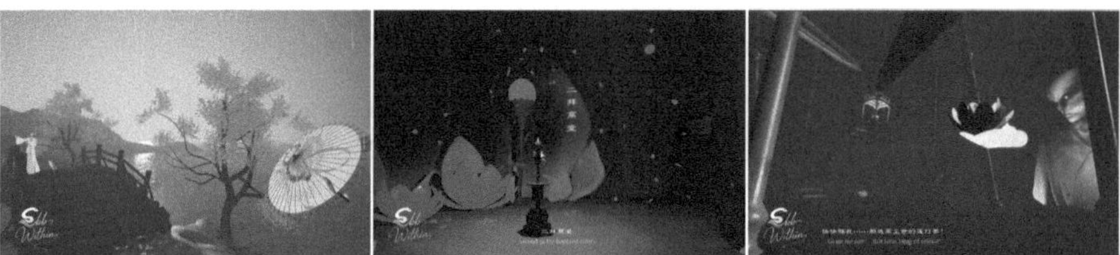

Fig. 4. Cultural symbols for interactive translation in *Ebb Within*—"Oil-paper Umbrella," "Red Candle," "Lotus Lamp"

3.3 Spatial Aesthetics: Chinese Lyrical Expression

This study bases the integration of narrative organization, cultural expression, and emotional effects on VR "presence" as a necessary condition. Accordingly, the aforementioned "spatial mapping of inner emotions" and "interactive translation of cultural symbols" rely on "spatial design" and implementation paths based on "presence." The spatial design of this study is grounded in a synthesis of Chinese artistic traditions, integrating the lyrical aesthetics of Chinese opera, the compositional paradigm of the Three Distances—Level, High, and Deep—from landscape painting theory, and the relational-narrative spatial principle of "scenery changing with every step" derived from garden aesthetics. Based on this, it proposes the CASES. Through multi-centered, diachronic, and suggestive spatial organization, it systematically embeds classical Chinese aesthetics into an immersively explorable VR imagery space coupled with "Inner Imagery—Cultural Symbols—Peking Opera Soundscape" (Fig. 5).

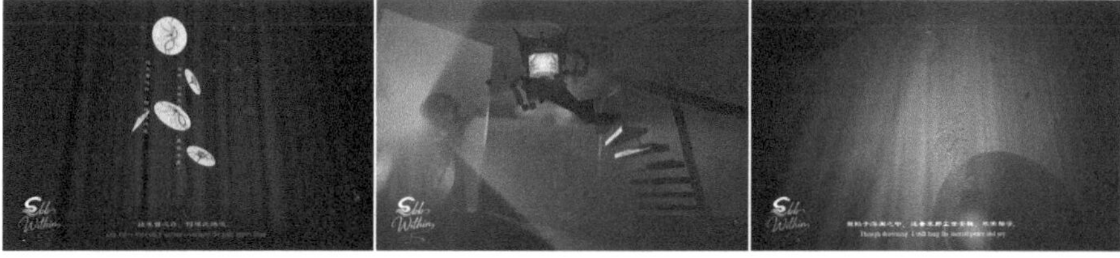

Fig. 5. Chinese lyrical spatial expression in *Ebb Within*

The CASES system is primarily realized through synergistic pathways in three dimensions: visual, kinesthetic, and auditory.

Visual: The visual layer is organized according to "scroll-like segments," pursuing a lyrical expression of dynamic space characterized by the interplay of void and solid, traversability, and perceptibility. It avoids panoramic visibility, creating instead delayed revelation and shifts in foreground/background focus through turns and obstructions. For instance, "Raging Sea" and "Silent Sea" juxtapose compressed and expansive fields of view to emphasize rhythmic transition from confinement to openness; "Overturned Faith" employs non-realistic falling wine vessels and a well-bottom perspective to externalize the imagery of internal conflict; "Umbrella Fades" structures the viewing rhythm through winding paths and post-obstacle unveiling, forming a scroll-like visual experience with sequenced revelation and alternating focal points.

Kinesthetic: Interaction and navigation replace GUI panels with culturally symbolic objects that serve as metaphorical guides and triggers for scene transitions, thereby elevating movement into meaningful action. For example, in "Umbrella Fades," the act of crossing water via a ferry boat translates into the narrative metaphor of "crossing to the other shore"; in "Blade of Liberation," the ritual act of cutting bonds with a double-edged sword embodies the narrative progression of "self-uncovering" (Fig. 6).

Fig. 6. Spirit ribbon and ferry boat navigation in *Ebb Within*

Auditory: The auditory layer integrates Peking Opera vocals with spatialized audio, dynamically adjusting reverb and directionality based on the user's position. Certain vocal passages are further visualized as dynamic calligraphic media, creating a cross-modal coupling of vision, sound, and movement that collectively shapes a complete, traversable, and perceptible Chinese artistic conception (Fig. 7).

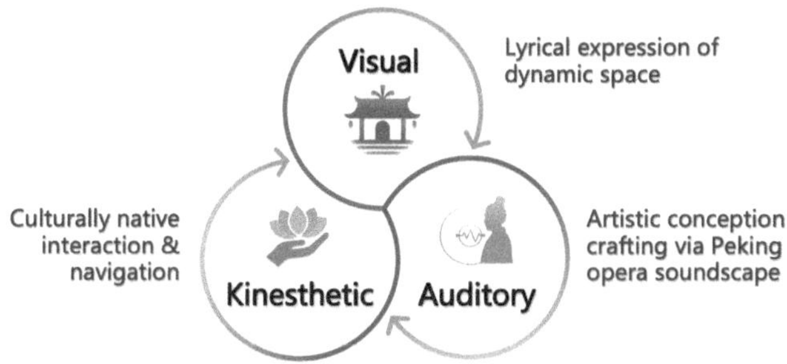

Fig. 7. Three pathways of the CASES system

4 System Implementation

The work was developed using UE5 and Meta XR tools, supplemented by Blender, Maya, Adobe Photoshop, etc., for asset creation. The Lumen real-time global illumination system and Nanite virtualized geometry technology were employed. The interaction system is built upon UE5's Blueprint visual scripting and the Meta XR SDK. Spatial audio technology is utilized, allowing Peking Opera recitatives and environmental sound effects to change dynamically based on the user's position and orientation in the virtual space, enhancing the sense of space. Original music synchronizes with the narrative rhythm. The work is compiled as a C++ project and can run independently on the Meta Quest 3 standalone headset without external PC or network support, ensuring the convenience, smoothness, and accessibility of the immersive experience.

5 User Evaluation and Discussion

5.1 User Evaluation Results

This study collected feedback from 33 users through questionnaires and semi-structured interviews. Participants ranged in age from 18 to 45 years, The gender distribution was 54.55% male and 45.45% female. The sample primarily comprised students, educators, professionals, and enthusiasts in related fields. Quantitative evaluation employed a 5-point Likert scale (1 = Strongly Disagree, 5 = Strongly Agree), with dimensions adapted from established VR narrative experience frameworks to align with characteristics of cultural experiences (Table 3).

Table 3. Core Indicator Scores from User Feedback

Evaluation Dimension	Description	Mean (M)	Std. Dev. (SD)
Aesthetic Perception	The work enhances my perception of the beauty of space, music, and Peking Opera	4.68	0.47

(continued)

Table 3. *(continued)*

Evaluation Dimension	Description	Mean (M)	Std. Dev. (SD)
Cultural Acceptance	The work guides me to more naturally accept Peking Opera art and traditional culture	4.62	0.49
Emotional Immersion	The work makes me feel more immersed in the emotional struggles of Bai Suzhen/Xu Xian	4.62	0.49
Cultural Identity	I can feel and identify with the cultural connotations expressed by the work	4.47	0.50
Interaction Naturalness	I find the interaction with cultural symbols intuitive and natural	4.38	0.49
Narrative Understanding	The experience guides me to understand a new dimension of this story	4.26	0.74

Quantitative data indicated that users gave relatively high ratings across the dimensions of "Aesthetic Perception" (mean 4.68), "Cultural Acceptance" (mean 4.62), and "Emotional Immersion" (mean 4.62). This preliminary suggests that the case study received positive recognition in terms of cultural expression and emotional experience.

Qualitative feedback from the interviews further substantiated and deepened these findings:

Emotional Immersion: Users described the experience as "more like an inner journey than merely viewing scenes" (P22), feeling they "lived" within the story and deeply empathized with Bai Suzhen's internal struggles (P03, P15). Through spatial design, they reported experiencing nuanced emotional shifts such as "oppression, despair, and release" (P08, P11, P24).

Aesthetic Perception: Users noted that the work transformed Peking Opera recitative into spatial elements that could be "actively listened to" (P12, P33), creating an overall "healing and reflective" Chinese aesthetic atmosphere (P32).

Cultural Acceptance: Users emphasized that "through actions like rowing and cutting bonds, [they] could more tangibly understand the cultural metaphors of 'crossing' and 'liberation' (P07, P19). They acknowledged the uniqueness of the narrative perspective originating from the character's inner world (P29) and indicated that this experiential format fostered "active acceptance" of Peking Opera and traditional culture (P29, P33), contributing to the contemporary activation of its spiritual essence (P05).

5.2 Discussion and Future Work

This study proposes a spatialized narrative model that shifts from "external events" to "internal emotions" within a Chinese aesthetic and cultural context, offering a design case for VR cultural heritage applications. Preliminary user feedback supports the effectiveness of this approach, providing a methodological reference for related research.

This study has several limitations. In terms of evaluation, the adopted indicator system, while tailored to cultural experience characteristics, was adapted from existing VR narrative frameworks and has not yet undergone large-scale psychometric validation. Future research should employ scales with established reliability and validity or incorporate objective physiological or behavioral metrics to establish more robust comparative benchmarks. In terms of sample representativeness, initial participants were primarily individuals with higher acceptance of culture, art, or technology. Future testing should include audiences with broader backgrounds and experience levels. The notable individual differences in "Narrative Understanding" indicate a need for improved balance between artistic expression and cognitive load; dynamic difficulty adjustment or personalized narrative guidance mechanisms could be explored. Technically, the current "psychological field" construction still relies on pre-set content design; future work could explore how Artificial Intelligence (AI) technology can generate dynamic inner narrative paths based on user emotions.

6 Conclusion

This paper proposes an Inner Imagery-based VR narrative model. Developed through the case study Ebb Within, it demonstrates a shift in cultural heritage VR from visual scene restoration to emotional and psychological reconstruction. The work contributes to narrative perspective, interactive semantics, and spatial aesthetics, integrating technology and art to reimagine cultural communication. By building an accessible and emotionally engaging inner world, the project transforms cultural heritage into experiential space and value. This approach suggests a viable pathway for the digital development of intangible cultural heritage.

Acknowledgments. This work was supported by the Major Program in Arts of the National Social Science Fund of China (Grant No. 25ZD07).

References

1. Zhou, W.: Virtual reality art: considerations based on four dimensions. Chin. Rev. Art Stud. **8**, 14–28, 125 (2023). https://doi.org/10.19324/j.cnki.zgwypl.2023.08.008
2. Xu, X.T., Zhou, W.: Virtual reality documentary as a tool for constructing digital cultural memory: aesthetic characteristics and cultural extension. J. Beijing Film Acad. **12**, 60–66 (2021)
3. Genette, G.: Narrative Discourse: An Essay in Method. Cornell University Press, Ithaca (1980)
4. Assmann, J.: Cultural Memory and Early Civilization: Writing, Remembrance, and Political Imagination. Cambridge University Press, Cambridge (2011)
5. Champion, E.M. (ed.): Virtual Heritage: A Guide. Ubiquity Press, London (2021). https://doi.org/10.5334/bck
6. Olaz, X., et al.: An interdisciplinary design of an interactive cultural heritage visit for in-situ, mixed reality and affective experiences. Multimodal Technol. Interact. **6**(7), 59 (2022). https://doi.org/10.3390/mti6070059
7. Blumer, H.: Symbolic Interactionism: Perspective and Method. University of California Press, Berkeley (1969)

8. Kaptelinin, V., Nardi, B.A.: Acting with Technology: Activity Theory and Interaction Design. MIT Press, Cambridge (2006)
9. Yue, W., Shen, J., Hsu, C.-C.: Ritual design in digital age: a comprehensive analysis of development and trend. Des. Stud. **100**, 101333 (2025). https://doi.org/10.1016/j.destud.2025.101333
10. Bogost, I.: Persuasive Games: The Expressive Power of Videogames. MIT Press, Cambridge (2007)
11. Grau, O.: Virtual Art: From Illusion to Immersion. MIT Press, Cambridge (2003)
12. Zong, B.: The Walk of Aesthetics. Shanghai People's Publishing House, Shanghai (1981)
13. Varela, F.J., Thompson, E., Rosch, E.: The Embodied Mind: Cognitive Science and Human Experience. MIT Press, Cambridge (1991)
14. White, G.: On immersive theatre. Theatre Res. Int. **37**(3), 221–235 (2012)
15. Machon, J.: Immersive Theatres: Intimacy and Immediacy in Contemporary Performance. Palgrave Macmillan, Basingstoke (2013)
16. Jenkins, H.: Game design as narrative architecture. In: Wardrip-Fruin, N., Harrigan, P. (eds.) First Person: New Media as Story, Performance, and Game, pp. 118–130. MIT Press, Cambridge (2004)
17. Meng, H.G.Z.: The Complete Tale of the White Snake. Yuelu Publishing House, Changsha (2004)
18. Brecht, B.: Brecht on Theatre: The Development of an Aesthetic. Hill and Wang, New York (1964)

MySpace: Metaphor Design of Personal Space Visualization in Social VR

Wen-Tong Shu[1], Yi-Jun Li[2], and Miao Wang[1(✉)]

[1] Beihang University, Beijing 100191, China
{wentongshu,miaow}@buaa.edu.cn
[2] Tsinghua University, Beijing 100084, China
liyijun@mail.tsinghua.edu.cn

Abstract. Personal space plays a critical role in user privacy, safety, and comfort within social virtual reality (VR). While prior work has examined its spatial properties and protective mechanisms, existing systems typically rely on simple geometric boundaries or basic visual indicators that lack expressive and intuitive representation of personal space. We present MySpace, a toolkit that enables users to customize their personal space using expressive, metaphor-based visualizations in immersive environments. MySpace introduces a design framework that combines metaphor and visibility modulation. Users can choose from three metaphor categories—virtual forms (area, bubble), everyday objects (fence, umbrella), and natural phenomena (fog, falling leaves)—each offering a distinct representation style and emotional resonance. Visibility is modulated through properties such as opacity, motion, and spatial extent to suit individual preferences. Implemented in Unity with real-time customization capabilities, our demo showcases multi-user scenarios where users can dynamically adjust their personal space representations. By allowing users to personalize how their personal space is visually expressed and perceived, MySpace supports intuitive communication of spatial boundaries, promotes social awareness, and enables safer, more comfortable interactions in shared virtual environments.

Keywords: Social VR · Personal Space · Metaphor · Visualization · Privacy

1 Introduction

In social VR, personal space is critically interdependent with privacy, comfort, and security. It defines a protective zone around the user that regulates interpersonal distance and social interaction [5]. This space is typically elliptical in shape [1], and its dimensions are influenced by various factors. Prior research has explored the spatial distribution [7], determining factors [2–4], and protective mechanisms [6,8,9] of personal space in virtual environments.

To mitigate discomfort caused by unwanted proximity, existing social VR platforms (e.g., VRChat, Horizon Worlds) typically adopt fixed representations

A. Hinkenjan et al. (Eds.): ICXR 2025, LNCS 16428, pp. 337–343, 2026.
https://doi.org/10.1007/978-981-95-7195-6_23

Fig. 1. Through MySpace, users can express their personal space in social virtual reality environments by utilizing visual metaphors such as umbrella, fog, and falling leaves during their activities.

such as translucent bubbles, circular floor indicators, or simple geometric boundaries. However, these designs lack flexibility and fail to reflect users' diverse preferences for expressing spatial boundaries. More importantly, such "one-size-fits-all" visualizations cannot accommodate different cultural backgrounds, social contexts, or emotional states, potentially limiting user comfort and self-expression in virtual social interactions.

2 Design Overview

We introduce MySpace, a VR personal space visualization toolkit that allows users to select from diverse metaphor-based visualizations and tailor how their personal space is displayed within social VR environments, as shown in Fig 1. The system draws on three metaphor categories—virtual forms (area, bubble), everyday objects (fence, umbrella), and natural phenomena (fog, falling leaves)—to provide six distinct visualization options. Each visualization can be dynamically modulated through properties such as opacity, height, motion, or spatial extent, enabling expressive and personalized representations that adapt to evolving social contexts.

By offering users greater control over how their personal space is presented and perceived, MySpace supports social boundary awareness and fosters safe, immersive, and socially comfortable interactions in shared virtual environments. Our work thus reframes personal space from a passive constraint into an active, expressive resource—one that can be culturally adaptive, emotionally resonant, and socially legible. Our main contributions include:

- A systematic design framework combining metaphor categories with visibility modulation for personal space visualization in VR environments.

- A modular Unity-based toolkit implementing six distinct metaphor-based visualizations with real-time customization capabilities.
- A demonstration of how customizable spatial representations can enhance user agency and social comfort in shared VR environments.

MySpace implements a two-dimensional design framework that combines metaphor categories with visibility modulation to create expressive personal space visualizations. The system architecture consists of three core components: (1) a metaphor selection module offering six distinct visualization options across three categories, (2) a real-time parameter adjustment system for customizing visual properties, and (3) a collision detection and feedback mechanism for boundary interactions.

The metaphor categories are systematically designed to provide different levels of abstraction and emotional resonance. Virtual forms (area, bubble) offer geometric abstractions suitable for minimalistic, universal spatial indication. Everyday objects (fence, umbrella) provide concrete real-world metaphors that explicitly communicate spatial intent and protection. Natural phenomena (fog, falling leaves) create ambient, emotionally resonant cues that maintain approachability while establishing boundaries.

Each visualization supports dynamic parameter adjustment through properties such as opacity, height, motion speed, and spatial extent. A lightweight UI interface overlaid on the left VR controller enables real-time metaphor switching and parameter tuning without breaking immersion. The system is implemented in Unity (v2022.3.17f1) with optimized rendering pipelines to ensure smooth performance across different VR platforms.

2.1 Metaphor Representation

To support expressive and personalized visualization of personal space, we adopt a metaphor-based design approach that moves beyond abstract visual elements commonly used in prior systems. While translucent bubbles or shaded areas can indicate boundaries, these forms often appear impersonal and lack emotional resonance. In contrast, familiar metaphors help users better perceive social boundaries, convey social cues, and feel more comfortable in shared VR spaces.

Our system categorizes visualizations into three metaphor types, each serving different communicative and emotional functions. As shown in Fig 2, the metaphors are organized as follows:

Virtual Forms (Geometric Abstraction):

- **Area:** A flat disk or circular outline on the virtual ground plane, providing a minimalistic, universally recognizable indication of protected area. This draws on established spatial conventions and is especially useful for unobtrusive, low-emotion scenarios.
- **Bubble:** A three-dimensional translucent sphere enveloping the user avatar, echoing the classic "personal bubble" concept. This shape provides a volumetric, immersive sense of boundary, and adjusts in real-time to the user's size and posture.

Fig. 2. Our system enables VR users to choose different metaphors to visualize their personal space. Based on three metaphor categories—virtual forms (area, bubble), everyday objects (fence, umbrella), and natural phenomena (fog, falling leaves)—users can select visualizations that offer distinct representation styles and emotional resonance.

Everyday Objects (Concrete Real-world Metaphors):

- **Fence:** An upright barrier encircling the user at a modifiable height and transparency. The fence explicitly signals a willingness to defend one's personal space—akin to property boundaries or garden fences in real life. This explicitness helps dissuade accidental intrusions and clarifies the user's intent, especially in formal or crowded gatherings.
- **Umbrella:** A domed visual umbrella above the user, metaphorically offering shelter. The umbrella metaphor resonates with themes of privacy, protection, and intimacy; its form can be contextually associated with overhead shelter, and its openness or radius can visually denote the "coverage" or strength of the user's desired boundaries.

Natural Phenomena (Ambient and Emotional Cues):

- **Fog:** A diffuse cloud or haze surrounding the user's space. This metaphor softens spatial cues, creating a sense of gentle separation while remaining approachable and non-confrontational. Fog density, color, and spread can be dynamically tuned.
- **Falling Leaves:** Animated particles (leaves) gently descend around the user's space, evoking natural movement and a sense of calm. This metaphor adds a dynamic, aesthetic, and emotionally warm dimension to personal space, especially suited to informal or playful social settings.

Each visualization can be dynamically switched according to user preference or situational context. Users may make metaphor choices aligned with their current mood, activity, cultural context, or relationship to those nearby. For instance, a user in a collaborative workspace may prefer a subtle area or fog metaphor, while a user seeking solitude in a busy public VR space may opt for a solid fence or dense bubble.

Fig. 3. The visibility of personal space can be adjusted by varying the distinctive properties of its metaphor-based representations—such as the density of fog or the height of a fence.

2.2 Visibility Modulation

Beyond metaphor selection, MySpace provides fine-grained control over the visual prominence and appearance of personal space boundaries through dynamic parameter adjustment. Rather than altering avatar transparency which can reduce presence and immersion, our approach modulates the visibility properties of the spatial metaphors themselves, as shown in Fig 3.

Each metaphor category supports distinct parameter sets tailored to its visual characteristics. Virtual forms (area, bubble) can be adjusted through opacity and scale parameters, allowing users to create subtle hints or prominent boundaries. Everyday objects offer more complex controls: umbrella coverage radius and openness can communicate different levels of accessibility, while fence height and transparency can signal varying degrees of spatial protection. Natural phenomena provide the most dynamic options: fog density, color, and dispersion create ambient boundary effects, while falling leaves can be modulated through particle count, speed, and distribution patterns.

This parametric approach enables nuanced social communication through spatial cues. A highly transparent bubble may invite closer conversation and signal openness, while an opaque, tall fence clearly communicates "busy" or "do not disturb" status. Dense fog creates gentle separation without appearing confrontational, and sparse, slow-moving leaves suggest a relaxed, approachable state. These metaphor-specific adjustments help reduce social ambiguity and support cross-cultural communication in diverse VR environments.

The visibility modulation system operates in real-time through the controller interface, allowing users to adapt their spatial representation as social contexts evolve throughout their VR session.

3 User Experience

Users are equipped with PICO 4 Pro VR head-mounted displays, immersing themselves in a social VR environment designed for spatial interaction exploration. The application maps participants' head and upper body movements to gender-neutral avatars (including only head, VR headset, and shirt) to avoid additional avatar-related effects on personal space perception. The system provides controller-based locomotion through both walking and teleportation modes.

The social virtual environment incorporates diverse contextual settings including multiple lighting conditions (day, dusk, night) and spatial scales (open plaza, intimate rooms, museum hall), enabling users to experience how different metaphors perform across various social contexts. Virtual NPCs with their own visualized personal spaces are positioned throughout the environment, allowing users to engage in social activities.

MySpace enables users to dynamically select and customize their personal space visualization based on immediate social needs and preferences. Users might choose an umbrella metaphor during rainy scenes for thematic consistency, or apply gentle fog in outdoor settings for non-confrontational boundary communication. The real-time customization capabilities allow users to adjust their spatial representation as social contexts evolve, such as increasing boundary visibility in crowded spaces or softening boundaries during intimate conversations.

This approach supports flexible adaptation across diverse social VR scenarios while accommodating different cultural backgrounds and user personalities. By offering multiple visualization options and real-time customization, MySpace encourages users to actively manage their social space, thereby promoting safer, more comfortable, and culturally sensitive interactions in immersive environments.

As an exploratory work, MySpace still presents several avenues for improvement: the visual aesthetics currently lack the refinement and immersive quality desired for rich VR experiences, the repository of metaphors remains limited, and systematic user experiments with accompanying data analyses are absent. Moving forward, we will iteratively refine the system to evolve MySpace into an advanced personal space solution for social VR that integrates aesthetic appeal with scholarly insight.

Acknowledgments. This work was supported by the National Natural Science Foundation of China (Project Number: 62372025 and 62361146854).

References

1. Amaoka, T., Laga, H., Nakajima, M.: Modeling the personal space of virtual agents for behavior simulation. In: 2009 International Conference on CyberWorlds, pp. 364–370 (2009). https://doi.org/10.1109/CW.2009.19
2. Bönsch, A., Radke, S., Ehret, J., Habel, U., Kuhlen, T.W.: The impact of a virtual agent's non-verbal emotional expression on a user's personal space preferences. In: Proceedings of the 20th ACM International Conference on Intelligent Virtual Agents, pp. 1–8 (2020)
3. Buck, L.E., Chakraborty, S., Bodenheimer, B.: The impact of embodiment and avatar sizing on personal space in immersive virtual environments. IEEE Trans. Visual Comput. Graphics **28**(5), 2102–2113 (2022)
4. Bönsch, A., et al.: Social VR: how personal space is affected by virtual agents' emotions. In: 2018 IEEE Conference on Virtual Reality and 3D User Interfaces (VR), pp. 199–206 (2018https://doi.org/10.1109/VR.2018.8446480
5. Hall, E.T.: The hidden dimension. Garden City (1966)
6. LaRubbio, K., Wilson, E., Koppal, S., Jörg, S., Jain, E.: Give me some room please! personal space bubbles for safety and performance. In: 2023 IEEE Conference on Virtual Reality and 3D User Interfaces Abstracts and Workshops (VRW), pp. 897–898. IEEE (2023)
7. Lee, J., Cheon, M., Moon, S.E., Lee, J.S.: Peripersonal space in virtual reality: navigating 3D space with different perspectives. In: Adjunct Proceedings of the 29th Annual ACM Symposium on User Interface Software and Technology, pp. 207–208. UIST '16 Adjunct, Association for Computing Machinery, New York, NY, USA (2016). https://doi.org/10.1145/2984751.2984772
8. Sun, J., Jiang, W., Li, L., Cao, C.: Personal space evaluation and protection in social VR. In: 2021 IEEE Conference on Virtual Reality and 3D User Interfaces Abstracts and Workshops (VRW), pp. 484–485. IEEE (2021)
9. Wang, M., Shu, W.T., Li, Y.J., Li, W.: Can i get there? Negotiated user-to-user teleportations in social VR. IEEE Trans. Visualization Comput. Graphics (2025)

Application Methods and Practices of XR Technology in Virtual Production for Sci-Fi Short Films: A Case Study of "TRIAL"

Xiaowei Liu(✉), Lantian Hou(✉), Yang Liu, and Ziluo Wang

Beijing Film Academy, Beijing 100088, China
smileliu99@163.com, houlantian0521@163.com

Abstract. As an emerging production method in the film and television industry, virtual production is progressively reshaping the workflow of sci-fi filmmaking. This paper systematically examines the application methods and practical experience of XR technology in virtual production, using the competition entry "TRIAL" as a case study. Research indicates that XR technology effectively overcomes limitations in traditional filming regarding scene scale, safety, and cost. It enables efficient real-time pre-visualization, seamless integration of live-action and digital assets, and a true "what you see is what you get" experience, providing a viable production paradigm for complex sci-fi narratives.

Keywords: XR Technology · Virtual Production · Science Fiction Film

1 Introduction

Since its inception, the film industry has been deeply intertwined with technological advancement. Over the past five decades, every facet of film production—from early film cameras to digital cinematography, editing software, sound design, music, and visual effects—has undergone profound transformation. In recent years, cutting-edge technologies continue to drive industry innovation: Extended Reality (XR) technology is reshaping the filmmaking landscape at an unprecedented pace. Its core lies in integrating LED walls with physical sets through real-time 3D rendering. This involves projecting digital scenes onto large virtual studios formed by LED walls while simultaneously filming live performances so as to achieve seamless fusion between virtual and physical worlds [1]. As a technology relying on the coordinated operation of LED walls, camera tracking systems, and real-time rendering engines, XR offers significant advantages—the pixel pitch and brightness of LED walls directly determine background clarity and lighting quality, while camera tracking ensures precise spatial perspective matching between virtual backgrounds and physical performances. This not only offers novel visualization solutions for complex surreal settings in sci-fi films but also empowers creators to design or modify sets and locations more flexibly and cost-effectively. It eliminates the need for time-consuming and expensive physical set construction and location shoots, even shifting substantial post-production work to the pre-production and

A. Hinkenjan et al. (Eds.): ICXR 2025, LNCS 16428, pp. 344–356, 2026.
https://doi.org/10.1007/978-981-95-7195-6_24

on-set phases, significantly boosting efficiency real-time immersion no longer stands in the hands of experts but spreads to creative enthusiasts which result in a huge production of content [2].

Today, XR virtual production has gradually become a vital production method in the film and television industry. This approach not only effectively overcomes limitations imposed by weather, location, and safety factors during on-location shoots but also offers a groundbreaking visualization solution for highly complex, surreal scenes in sci-fi films. In recent years, numerous global sci-fi productions have pioneered the use of XR technology, demonstrating its unique potential for innovation in both visual language and production workflows. For instance, The Mandalorian utilized real-time digital scene projection on LED walls to immerse actors in their performances, demonstrating XR's transformative potential in visual storytelling and production workflows. The rise of Artificial Intelligence (AI) has further elevated this technological revolution, boosting production efficiency, reducing costs, and vastly expanding creative expression possibilities.

XR technologies are a promising technology that can create similar experiences that are comparable to real experiences in the physical world [3]. The short film "TRIAL", the focus of this article, is an experimental work produced with XR technology. Set against a future energy crisis, the narrative revolves around the fictional energy source "Blue Crystal," presenting visually striking scenes such as factory explosions, forest hallucinations, and crystal mines. Under traditional production methods, these scenes would typically require large-scale physical sets and complex post-production compositing—processes that are not only costly but also pose safety risks. During the production of "TRIAL", the team utilized an XR virtual production studio. By building a real-time rendering environment with Unreal Engine and integrating LED walls, camera tracking systems, physical props, and virtual assets, they efficiently captured challenging sequences like forest fires and crystal erosion within a limited physical space.

Thus, "TRIAL" stands not only as an artistic endeavor but also as a practical case study demonstrating XR technology's application in sci-fi production. It reveals how XR technology balances visual spectacle with production efficiency in short filmmaking, optimizes cross-departmental collaboration through virtual asset reuse and real-time previews, and explores new pathways for integrating XR with AIGC technologies. Building upon this case study, this paper systematically examines the application value and developmental potential of XR technology in sci-fi virtual production from the perspectives of technical workflows and methodologies.

2 Related Work

Virtual production harnesses the power of virtualising technologies to create digital environments in, and through which film and television can be made. In combination, these technologies offer more flexibility to filmmakers and the potential to cut carbon emissions. But while the technologies at the centre of virtual production are not new, their application in combination with each other is generating new approaches to production which are evolving fast [4]. The core of virtual production lies in achieving real-time interaction between "virtual environment—actor—camera" through XR technology, enabling complex scenes to be instantly visible on set. Compared to traditional green screen methods, XR's primary advantage lies in projecting virtual environments directly onto LED walls on set. Camera tracking systems dynamically adjust visual parallax in real time, ensuring spatial consistency between actors and virtual scenes. This approach significantly reduces post-production compositing workloads while providing actors with an immersive performance environment, eliminating the reliance on imagination that often leads to inaccuracies in pure green screen shoots.

2.1 System Architecture

The XR virtual production system comprises three core modules—a real-time rendering engine, camera tracking system, and LED display matrix [5], forming a highly integrated technological ecosystem. This architecture represents the cutting-edge integration of current virtual production technologies. Real-time rendering engines like Unreal Engine generate dynamic digital assets and synchronize data with camera tracking systems (e.g., Mo-Sys StarTracker) via NDI protocol. The LED walls matrix must meet high refresh rate requirements (typically $\geq$120 Hz) and low gray-scale response times ($<$1 ms) to eliminate motion blur effects. This technical framework breaks away from the traditional post-production compositing paradigm of green-screen filming, achieving a "near-live-action filming" effect on set and significantly enhancing the production efficiency of camera-to-final-output workflows.

2.2 Technical Solution

During the practical implementation of XR virtual production technology in the sci-fi short film "TRIAL", the production team designed a comprehensive XR virtual production solution. The most distinctive feature was the pre-production technical rehearsal in Unreal Engine, which confirmed the construction of a 13.3-m-long, 7-m-high curved LED wall for filming. Its 1.5 mm pixel pitch and $\geq$120 Hz refresh rate ensured display precision and fluidity, while the $<$1 ms gray-to-gray response time effectively eliminated motion blur. This display system integrates with Disguise media servers and Unreal Engine 5 real-time rendering, utilizing an Display cluster rendering architecture to achieve stable output driven by three parallel servers, guaranteeing 60fps real-time rendering performance.

For cinematography and tracking, the team employed a dual-camera system comprising Sony Venice 2 and RED Komodo 6K cameras. Paired with the Mo-Sys optical camera tracking system, this setup achieves tracking accuracy of $\pm 0.1°$ rotation and $\pm$0.5 mm translation. Combined with the MoCo motion control system, it enables high-precision camera movement control. The lighting control system demonstrates deep integration between virtual and physical illumination. A lighting console synchronizes color temperature and brightness, while the ACES color management pipeline ensures consistent color reproduction. This technical architecture not only achieves seamless fusion of virtual and live-action elements but also innovatively shifts significant post-production workloads to the pre-production phase.

2.3 Research Methodology and Process

This study adopted a methodological framework combining technical process analysis with practical case reviews. It first systematically dissected the technical components and collaborative mechanisms of the XR virtual production studio, establishing data flow and synchronization relationship models between subsystems. In specific scenario analysis, the team examined representative environments like the "Blue Crystal Forest" and "Crystal Mine," delving into virtual asset modeling workflows and optimization strategies, as well as methods for integrating digital assets with physical set construction. For performance optimization, the team developed multiple innovative technical solutions: LOD hierarchical management technology enabled chunked merging of distant assets, reducing GPU utilization by 35%; Nanite technology achieved a 60% compression rate for per-frame polygon counts; and virtual texture technology enabled partitioned loading of 8K textures, Texture-mapping hardware has been successfully exploited for volume rendering [6]. These innovations not only boosted production efficiency but also laid the groundwork for integrating AIGC technologies.

Methodologically, the team prioritized synergistic XR-AI workflows, establishing a closed-loop "Generate-Validate-Regenerate" process. Quantitative evaluations demonstrated this approach shortened asset preparation cycles by 60–75%, significantly boosting production efficiency. The entire research process focused on both optimizing technical component performance and systematically integrating workflows, establishing a replicable technical paradigm and methodological framework for XR technology application in sci-fi film production. This comprehensive research perspective not only addresses current technical challenges in virtual production but also provides valuable reference for future XR technology development.

3 Applications Through Practical Case Studies

In the virtual production practice for "TRIAL", the team successfully addressed core XR production challenges through a systematic technical solution. Digital assets were constructed using Unreal Engine and combined with physical set builds to establish spatial matching benchmarks. The XR virtual production system calibrated proportions, while asset integration optimization strategies shaped the sci-fi atmosphere. The team overcame bottlenecks in achieving consistency between real and virtual lighting and spatial immersion through dynamic tracking management, distributed cluster rendering, and synchronized physical/virtual lighting techniques. In post-production, an AI-generated collaborative workflow established a "generation-validation" closed-loop process. AI-generated assets accelerated iteration, resolving challenges in XR shot expansion and surreal scene construction, thereby validating an efficient co-driven creative pathway for AI and XR.

3.1 Scene Construction and Virtual Assets

Shooting sci-fi scenes with XR technology presents unprecedented challenges in integrating real-world sets with digital assets. These challenges extend beyond physical implementation to encompass visual presentation, technical workflows, and team collaboration models.

During the production of "TRIAL", virtual asset construction served as both the foundation for XR filming and a pivotal element in shaping the sci-fi atmosphere. Real-time rendering engines like Unreal Engine generated dynamic digital assets, synchronizing data with camera tracking systems (e.g., Mo-Sys StarTracker) via NDI protocol. LED walls arrays required high refresh rates (typically ≥120 Hz) and low gray-scale response times (<1 ms) to eliminate motion blur effects [7]. This technical framework broke away from traditional green-screen post-production compositing, achieving "near-live-action" effects on set and significantly boosting the efficiency of camera-to-final-product workflows.

This is the first distinctive feature that sets this film apart from other XR works.For digital asset creation, the team integrated Quixel and Fab asset libraries. In the "Blue Crystal Forest" scene, Unreal's Foliage system was initially used to scatter luminous particles simulating crystals. However, this approach caused severe rendering stuttering on the XRLED wall. Consequently, luminous decals were adopted in digital assets, significantly reducing computational load while enhancing visual depth. For further performance optimization, the team implemented HLOD (Hierarchical Level of Detail) management. By chunking and merging distant assets, they reduced draw call counts, achieving an average 35% reduction in GPU utilization. Simultaneously, Virtual Texture technology was enabled in material management, enabling zoned loading of 8K-level textures at varying distances. This ensured smooth operation at 60fps, meeting XR filming requirements. Additionally, for Nanite model implementation, the team applied Nanite processing to the high-polygon crystal clusters in the "Blue Crystal Mine." achieving a 60% reduction in per-frame polygon count. This preserves the authenticity of crystal light refraction in real-time rendering without risking system crashes. These optimization methods align with Unreal's official real-time rendering performance strategies, including LOD model hierarchy management and judicious use of the Nanite system, which controls the rendering time by collecting run-time performance statistics and performing dynamic LOD selections [8] (Fig. 1).

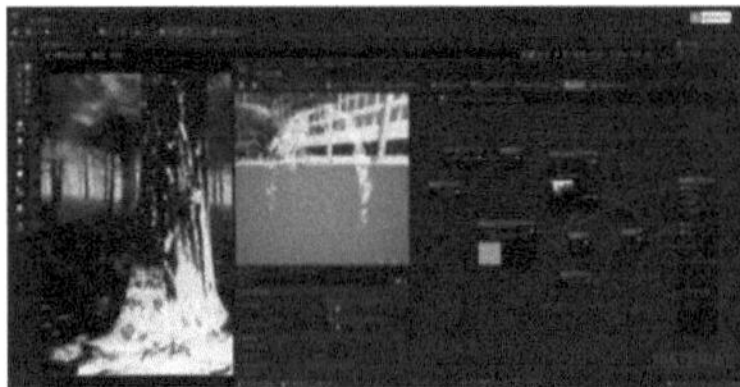

Fig. 1. Optimized implementation results

For spatial and perspective matching, the virtual space projected by the XR studio's LED wall serves as an extension of the physical set, requiring seamless integration with the real-world environment. To achieve this, the team precisely calculated the spatial relationships between the LED walls, physical sets, and cameras beforehand. This organically integrated the physical construction with digital assets. For instance, the team first built a "white box environment" in Unreal Engine, establishing standardized scale references—such as 1.7-m-tall cubes representing human height—to ensure consistency between actors and the virtual space. This approach prevented post-production rework due to scale discrepancies, providing a stable spatial framework for XR filming. Subsequently, the physical "Blue Crystal Glare Forest" foreground was combined with its digitally rendered background counterpart, unified through consistent material textures and lighting effects. This achieved a natural transition between real and virtual elements, eliminating the audience's perception of a "staged" feel in the live-action scenes (Fig. 2).

Fig. 2. White box environment and rendering effect

Thus, digital asset construction is a critical component in XR production methodology. Through asset optimization and virtual-physical integration strategies, this project demonstrates an efficient and cost-effective path for sci-fi virtual production enabled by XR technology.

3.2 Lighting Matching and Optimization Strategies for XR Virtual Production Systems

The material integration between live-action and digital assets is equally critical. Accurate reproduction of surface characteristics significantly impacts visual realism. While LED virtual production eliminates color bleeding, all naturally occurring reflections must be seamlessly coordinated with the virtual environment during filming. Subtle material texture differences exist between physical props and digital assets, including details like glossiness and wear marks. Precise matching is essential to enhance visual authenticity, particularly for highly reflective objects such as metal or glass surfaces. To achieve this matching, production teams must pay special attention to material characteristics during pre-production. They must calculate the interaction between light sources and various materials, accounting for optical phenomena like specular reflection, diffuse reflection, and ambient occlusion. For highly reflective objects, special configurations of the LED display wall's brightness distribution and color temperature parameters are also required to prevent unnatural highlights or overexposure.

In XR virtual production technology, lighting condition matching represents a critical challenge for achieving high-quality integration between real-world sets and digital assets. The core issue lies in reconciling the physical limitations of LED displays with the demand for real-time lighting synchronization in dynamic scenes. LED displays exhibit color gamut differences compared to natural light sources. Particularly in dynamic environments, the reflectance and shadow/light response of digital assets must synchronize in real-time with real-world lighting parameters, highlighting the inadequacies of current color management systems. While LUT calibration achieves $\Delta E < 3$ color difference control in static scenes, under dynamic lighting, the pulse width modulation (PWM) characteristics of LEDs cause color decay curves to deviate from real light sources. For instance, when simulating sunset warm light with a 5600K color temperature LED system, the red channel saturation may be 15%–20% lower than the actual scene.

Simultaneously, the inherent characteristics of LED walls introduce multiple technical challenges. First, screens composed of LED arrays emit diffused light, making it difficult to reproduce hard light effects and resulting in inadequate performance under large-area hard light sources like direct sunlight. Second, the color rendering capabilities of RGB primary-color LEDs are limited, with discontinuous spectral distributions. Excessive energy in the 620 nm to 660 nm wavelength band often causes red channel color spillage, affecting the color reproduction of skin tones and other scenes containing red components. Third, The screen panel's reflectivity limits tonal rendering, resulting in insufficient contrast and loss of shadow detail. This creates a "screen-like" appearance and causes the panel to interfere with virtual scenes when illuminated. Lighting must strictly control the direction, range, and intensity of real-world light sources to minimize this effect.

To address these bottlenecks, our research team developed three optimization strategies through practical filming of the short film "TRIAL", combined with literature and case analysis, also another distinctive feature of the production of this film. First, in the lighting matching phase, we replaced traditional color adaptation methods with color gamut correction algorithms, reducing color difference ΔE to within 1.5 to restore delicate, true-to-life colors. Second, for scenes with perspective distortion, we optimized the adaptive model for virtual-real depth of field, intelligently adjusting matching parameters to reduce distortion rates below 2% and restore natural perspective. Third, to address physical interaction latency during filming, we employed robotic arm data back-calculation technology to directly connect devices and systems, reducing latency from 120 ms to under 15 ms, enabling seamless real-time synchronous interaction.

Simultaneously, the team leveraged screen material properties during physical lighting setup: avoiding direct light projection onto screens to prevent glare contamination of the foreground, using BarnDoors and Diffusion to control light diffusion and ensure natural actor lighting; A layered lighting strategy was adopted: LED walls provided primary ambient lighting for background layers, while adjustable-color-temperature film lights supplemented foreground and midground layers. This ensured consistent spatial illumination while preventing facial and costume detail distortion caused by insufficient screen brightness. To maintain visual authenticity, the team synchronized physical lighting consoles with virtual light sources via Unreal Engine, unifying color temperature and brightness logic. This solution not only resolves the "lighting consistency" challenge in XR production but also demonstrates that virtual production requires establishing collaborative logic and dynamic control mechanisms between virtual and physical lighting at the technical level to achieve high-quality visual output (Fig. 3).

Furthermore, to enhance the physical consistency between virtual and physical lights, the lighting team adopted the ACES color management workflow and loaded LUTs (Look-Up Tables) into the Disguise system. This ensured consistent color reproduction across different cameras (Sony Venice 2 and Komodo 6K). The team also dynamically monitored and calibrated lighting consistency and stability. For lighting control, the response difference between virtual light source latency and physical DMX fixtures was

Fig. 3. On-site Lighting Integration Example

precisely calibrated to within 30ms, enabling natural lighting logic to persist even during actors' rapid movements.

3.3 Perspective Matching in XR Virtual Production Systems

For spatial and perspective matching, the virtual space rendered on LED walls—extending the physical set—must seamlessly integrate with the real-world environment. This requires precise calculation of the spatial relationships between LED walls, physical sets, and cameras. LED display quality is influenced by pixel pitch, display area, and camera shooting distance. Among these factors, pixel pitch determines screen resolution and clarity, display area dictates visual impact, and camera distance affects perspective depth and layering. Any deviation in perspective relationships can diminish audience immersion. For instance, the physical properties of the screen create a sharp, right-angled junction between vertical surfaces and horizontal physical planes, making natural transitions difficult and potentially introducing an unnatural sense of discontinuity in the image. Furthermore, precision errors in camera tracking systems (typically $\pm 0.1°$ rotation/± 0.5 mm translation) can distort asset perspective relationships, particularly noticeable during wide-angle lens shots. Consequently, every detail must be meticulously handled with the final presentation in mind to ensure viewers are fully immersed in the created virtual world.

That the ability to induce this sense of presence and illusion of place is one of the features, which when implemented properly within XR design can greatly increase its usefulness. The immersiveness experience must investigate all facets of immersion to elicit a sense of spatial presence and an emotional connection to the environment in order to develop ways to engage space users in XR and spatial knowledge [9].

Thus, the "TRIAL" production team adopted ILM StageCraft's approach by deploying Display cluster rendering. Three servers drive XR scene rendering in parallel, forming a distributed GPU rendering architecture that eliminates single-machine computational bottlenecks. During camera movement, when tracking a forest scene at 3 m/s, enabling multi-node synchronized rendering reduced frame drops from 12% to 3%. For camera operations, the team dynamically adjusted XR system parameters based on shot movement. For minor camera shifts, they disabled the Mo-Sys StarTracker tracking system to maintain image stability and accommodate dual-camera setups. During extensive movements, the camera tracking system was reactivated to maintain consistent spatial perspective between foreground and background while reducing rendering load. Aperture control typically utilized the T2.8–T4 range to balance depth of field and background clarity. T4 was employed for mid-range shots to preserve background detail, while T2.8 was used for close-ups and extreme close-ups to separate subjects from their environment.

The activation and deactivation of camera tracking serves not only to stabilize footage but also to balance rendering load with optical consistency. Within the Unreal Engine rendering pipeline, when camera movement expands, the system must load more real-time virtual assets. Enabling tracking at this point helps mitigate the risk of background misalignment. Conversely, disabling tracking during small-scale movements avoids unnecessary GPU utilization and enhances output stability (Fig. 4).

Fig. 4. Digital assets and on-set construction for "TRIAL"

3.4 Collaborative Generation of XR and AIGC

With the advancement of AI (artificial intelligence) technology, AI has become a tool for cost reduction and efficiency enhancement in XR production. Artificial Intelligence Generated Content (AIGC) technology, through automated content creation, real-time interactive processing, and personalized experience adjustments, demonstrates significant potential in optimizing immersive imaging experiences [10]. For instance, Neural Radiance Fields (NeRFs) technology provides robust support for LED virtual production in rapid 3D object and virtual environment creation [11]. It leverages generative AI to infer 3D representations from 2D images, enabling filmmakers to swiftly construct virtual elements for LED virtual scenes using simple devices like mobile phones. Tools like Nvidia, Luma.AI, and Volinga simplify complex 3D capture processes, eliminate the high barriers of traditional 3D modeling, and accelerate the production workflow for digital assets in LED virtual scenes. They efficiently generate complex assets such as characters, props, and entire virtual worlds, presenting rich virtual content on LED walls while offering new creative freedom and flexibility [12].

Next, the most distinctive features and innovations of this work will be revealed. During production, the "TRIAL" team leveraged XR technology and AI-generated imagery (AIGC) working in tandem, creating a significant breakthrough in special effects and scene construction while substantially boosting production efficiency and visual impact. Scenes depicting the growth of blue crystals and crystal erosion would have demanded immense manpower and rendering time if relying solely on traditional modeling and post-production compositing. The team employed AIGC-generated reference images and video clips, combined with Unreal Engine's real-time rendering and the Disguise system for iterative testing. This approach rapidly yielded materials and forms aligned with the script's atmosphere. Through this method, AIGC not only provided conceptual visualization support in the early stages but also acted as an "accelerator" during mid-production asset creation, boosting the iteration efficiency of digital assets required within the XR virtual production system.

In the collaborative workflow between XR and AIGC, the team emphasized a "generate-validate-regenerate" iterative cycle. For instance, Stable Diffusion and Midjourney were first used to generate form references for crystal growth. These were then used in Houdini to build foundational volumetric growth meshes based on point cloud simulations. These meshes were imported into Unreal Engine to validate their feasibility under 60 fps real-time rendering. If GPU utilization exceeded 80%, the team reverted to low-poly proxy models and employed Decal replacements for visual compensation. This approach enabled real-time previews of the blue crystal growth effects on the XR set, reducing reliance on post-production compositing. This workflow significantly reduced iteration time, cutting the average asset preparation cycle per shot from 3–4 days to just 1 day. This dramatically enhanced the controllability and completion level of the sci-fi short film within its limited production timeline.

During on-set production, the film showcased three representative AIGC application scenarios. For the script's scattered, brief flashback sequences, traditional methods—whether creating digital assets individually or building physical sets—would have been prohibitively costly and inefficient. The team leveraged AIGC technology to sample and integrate digital assets with on-set elements, generating flashback shots that maintained both textural continuity and stylistic consistency. This approach effectively addressed asset cost-effectiveness while providing actors with clear emotional reference points and performance anchors on set (Fig. 5).

Fig. 5. AIGC Flashback Sequences

In the forest chase scene, height restrictions on LED walls prevented full-wide shots, limiting shot variety and pacing. The production team leveraged Midjourney V7's stable image upscaling capabilities to blend live-action stills with digital assets, creating coherent extended shots. Simultaneously, image super-resolution technology (ESRGAN) unified the resolution of these extended shots to match the LED wall's output resolution (2K), ensuring seamless visual continuity. These enhanced shots were rapidly added to the on-set asset library to support subsequent shot planning. The surreal final sequence was achieved through multi-module collaborative generation by Keeling AI, encompassing motion blending, character reshaping, and particle dynamics simulation. By synthesizing multiple static image inputs in real-time, the system portrays the protagonist's bodily metamorphosis and the environment's geometric distortion in symbiotic coexistence, forming a visual metaphor of "self-dissolution and cognitive reshaping."

This practice not only strengthens the film's narrative convergence but also demonstrates AIGC's potential in dynamic character generation, multi-parameter control, and aesthetic integration (Fig. 6).

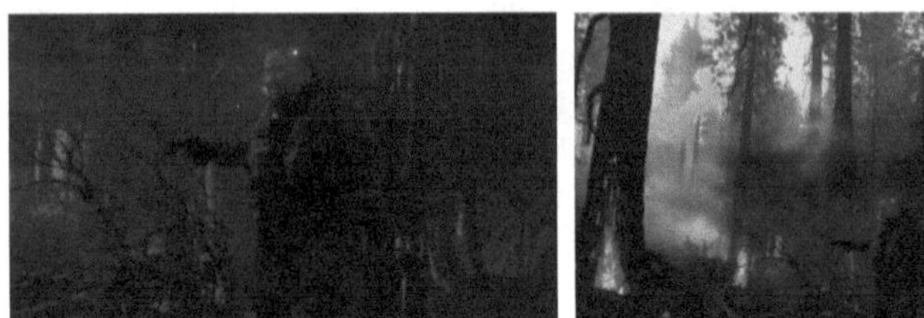

Fig. 6. AIGC Image Expansion Example

Academic and industrial sectors are actively exploring this direction's potential. Research indicates that integrating AIGC significantly reduces reliance on traditional 3D modeling and animation workflows, making XR content creation more efficient and accessible. Drawing from the practical experience of "TRIAL," the synergistic path of XR + AIGC is becoming increasingly clear. AI generates concepts and detailed assets, while XR provides real-time spatial validation, forming a closed-loop system that ensures creative freedom while enhancing production control and cost efficiency.

4 Findings and Limitations

As a significant application of XR virtual production technology in sci-fi short film creation, the "TRIAL" project not only validated the feasibility of current technical solutions but also provided invaluable insights for the industry's future development. By systematically reviewing the technical innovations, practical challenges, and solutions encountered during implementation, we can clearly observe how XR technology is reshaping the fundamental paradigms of sci-fi film production. This technological transformation manifests not only in optimized workflows and enhanced efficiency but also in the unprecedented creative expression it unlocks for filmmakers.

Concurrently, this practice has exposed several critical challenges in XR applications. Despite recent progress in display technology, we are still far from the ultimate goal of creating new virtual environments and augmentations of existing ones that feel and react similarly as their real counterparts [13]. For instance, the LED giant screen serving as the primary light source has inherent limitations in brightness and color reproduction. While it provides stable and accurate ambient lighting, its peak brightness still falls short of professional film lighting equipment. This can lead to underexposure of foreground subjects or overexposure of virtual backgrounds during large-scale scene shoots. Furthermore, significant variations exist among different LED walls in terms of color gamut coverage and color consistency. This can lead to slight discrepancies in color temperature and saturation between the virtual background and real-world props. Such deviations become particularly noticeable in sci-fi films that emphasize contrast between warm and cool lighting and high-saturation visuals. To compensate for these limitations, production teams often need to deploy additional fill lights and perform post-correction using LUTs or ACES color management systems. This inevitably increases production complexity and costs.

Another critical limitation lies in the rendering stability of virtual assets within highly complex scenes, which remains a core constraint on XR technology adoption. When virtual scenes incorporate numerous high-precision geometries and dynamic effects, real-time rendering engines are prone to frame rate drops or even stuttering when GPU load approaches its limit. In high-motion sequences like chase scenes or explosions, dropped frames not only compromise visual fluidity but can also cause spatial misalignment between foreground and background elements, thereby diminishing immersion and narrative tension.

Based on the "TRIAL" project experience, future development of XR virtual production technology in sci-fi filmmaking should focus on these key directions: First, prioritize continuous hardware performance enhancements, including developing new LED walls with brightness exceeding 3000 nits and 95% Rec.2020 color gamut coverage. Further elevate resolution to 8K or higher and optimize refresh rates to achieve smoother dynamic scene rendering. Deep optimization of software algorithms remains central, particularly strengthening distributed computing capabilities in real-time rendering engines to efficiently handle parallel rendering tasks for large-scale virtual scenes. AI-assisted LOD management systems should be introduced, using machine learning algorithms to automatically optimize resource allocation, reduce latency, and enhance the realism of visual details.

As a research case, "TRIAL" demonstrates how XR technology provides practical solutions to challenges in sci-fi film production. Addressing the limitations of LED walls brightness and color reproduction, the film explored unified lighting solutions for virtual and practical environments through synergistic optimization of supplementary lighting systems and color management workflows.

The positive effects or externalities of XR are visible both, for the users and the producers and touch a wide range of activities based on creativity, digital worlds, knowledge or information: from advertising, architecture, design to gaming, software and publishing. Such era can be interpreted as new potential of the XR technologies as the cross-industry discipline [14]. The experience gained from the "TRIAL" project offers invaluable practical insights for this transformation. Achieving this shift requires not only technological breakthroughs but also concerted industry-wide efforts—continuously advancing standardization, talent development, and creative practice—to fully unleash XR technology's transformative potential in cinematic artistry.

Acknowledgements. 2025 Beijing Film Academy Key Project: "Empirical Study on the Integration of Digital Assets and Real-Scene Construction Based on Virtual Production Technology" (Project No.: XZ202508).

References

1. Kadner, A.: The Virtual Production Field Guide (Volume 2). Epic Games (2021)

2. Lescop, L.: Narrative grammar in 360. In: 2017 IEEE International Symposium on Mixed and Augmented Reality (ISMAR-Adjunct), Nantes, France, pp. 254–257 (2017). https://doi.org/10.1109/ISMAR-Adjunct.2017.86
3. Alnagrat, A., Che Ismail, R., Syed Idrus, S.Z., Abdulhafith Alfaqi, R.M.: A review of extended reality (XR) technologies in the future of human education: current trend and future opportunity. J. Hum. Centered Technol. **1**(2), 81–96 (2022)
4. Willment, N., Swords, J.: What is virtual production? An explainer & research agenda (2023)
5. Kadner, N.: Real-time rendering in film production: a technical analysis. ACM SIGGRAPH Comput. Graph. Q. **56**(3), 12–19 (2022)
6. Li, W., Kaufman, A.: Accelerating volume rendering with texture hulls. In: Symposium on Volume Visualization and Graphics, 2002. Proceedings. IEEE/ACM SIGGRAPH, Boston, MA, USA, pp. 115–122 (2002). https://doi.org/10.1109/SWG.2002.1226517
7. Johnsen, K.: Camera tracking accuracy in virtual production. SMPTE Motion Imaging J. **128**(7), 42–49 (2019)
8. Li, X., Shen, H.-W.: Time-critical multiresolution volume rendering using 3D texture mapping hardware. In: Symposium on Volume Visualization and Graphics, 2002. Proceedings. IEEE/ACM SIGGRAPH, Boston, MA, USA, pp. 29–36 (2002). https://doi.org/10.1109/SWG.2002.1226507
9. Khamis, N.E., El-Harairy, Y.: Employing Extended Reality (XR) to Expanding Narratives of Place-Making, Spatial Presence and Immersive Experience (2024)
10. Ma, J., Lei, X.: Exploring the pathways to optimize immersive imaging experiences using AIGC technology. In: 2024 7th International Conference on Artificial Intelligence and Big Data (ICAIBD), pp. 523–529. IEEE (2024)
11. Vitrina. Virtual Production and AI: Changing the Studio Landscape (2024).https://vitrina.ai/blog/ai-in-virtual-production/. Accessed 22 Aug 2025
12. PaulaParisi. AI and the New Era of Creativity (2023). https://scainmotion.org/virtual-production-and-ai. Accessed 22 Aug 2025
13. Hürst, W., Iwai, D., Pucihar, K.Č., Kljun, M.: Multimodal virtual & augmented reality - editorial to the MVAR workshop at ISMAR 2018. In: 2018 IEEE International Symposium on Mixed and Augmented Reality Adjunct (ISMAR-Adjunct), Munich, Germany, p. 265 (2018). https://doi.org/10.1109/ISMAR-Adjunct.2018.00082
14. Novakova, H., ŠTarchoň, P.: Creative industries: challenges and opportunities in XR technologies. SHS web of conferences. EDP Sci. **115**, 03011 (2021)

Interactive 3D Urban Geological Modeling and Visualization with Augmented Reality

Liang He[1,2](✉), Yuxuan Zhu[1], Wenke Liu[1], and Alexander Klippel[2]

[1] School of Environmental Science, Nanjing Xiaozhuang University, Nanjing 211171, China
heliang@njxzc.edu.cn

[2] Cultural Geography Research Group and WANDER XR Experience Lab, Wageningen University and Research, Wageningen, The Netherlands

Abstract. Accurate, timely, and easily interpretable 3D geological information is essential for data-driven urban governance. However, conventional visualisation frameworks cannot dynamically fuse multi-scale subsurface data with rapidly evolving surface urban systems. This study presents an interactive augmented-reality (AR) environment, deployed on Microsoft HoloLens 2 head-mounted displays, that tightly couples high-fidelity geological models with real world cityscapes, enabling simultaneous inspection of surface infrastructure, subsurface utilities and stratigraphic layers in a single immersive scene. Hybrid rendering pipelines combine level-of-detail (LOD) mesh optimisation and GPU-aware adaptive shading, reducing model-loading time by 25%, maintaining Toolbox response times below 1.5 s, and reducing GPU load by 38%. Multimodal voice and gesture interactions significantly lower the expertise threshold for domain specialists and the public. A controlled user study ($n = 35$) yielded an average satisfaction score of 4.4 out of 5 and a System Usability Scale rating of 82.4, confirming high engagement and efficiency. By transforming static geological archives into actionable 3D spatial knowledge, the platform advances participatory planning, risk-aware construction and evidence-based urban management, underscoring AR's role in accelerating sustainable city development.

Keywords: Urban Geology · Augmented Reality · Interactive 3D Modeling · Visualization · HoloLens 2

1 Introduction

Urban geological information is essential for urban planning, construction, and management, covering topography, geological structures, and pipelines [1]. During urban planning, accurate geological information enables planners to rationally zone urban functional areas, avoid geological disaster-prone regions, and optimize utilities construction plans [2]. In urban construction, precise geological information guides construction teams in correctly excavating foundations and laying pipelines, preventing engineering accidents caused by geological issues [3]. In urban management, dynamic monitoring of geological information helps detect geological hazards promptly, enabling corresponding remedial measures to ensure stable urban development.

A. Hinkenjan et al. (Eds.): ICXR 2025, LNCS 16428, pp. 357–368, 2026.
https://doi.org/10.1007/978-981-95-7195-6_25

However, traditional geological information display methods have significant limitations [4]. 2D display methods fail to intuitively represent complex 3D geological structures, requiring users to have professional geological knowledge for comprehension [5]. Field surveys, despite allowing direct geological observation, are restricted by weather, terrain, and other conditions [6]. Moreover, surveying deep-underground geological structures or hazardous areas carries substantial safety risks and operational challenges [7]. Additionally, legacy systems lack spatiotemporal coherence between static geological datasets and evolving urban topologies, resulting in cognitive dissonance during utilities planning, failing to meet the timeliness and convenience requirements of modern urban rapid development.

Augmented Reality (AR) technology integrates virtual information with the real world, which offers new opportunities for geological information display [8]. AR can precisely overlay 3D geological models onto real world scenes, allowing users to intuitively see, for example, the layout of underground pipelines or the distribution of geological structures [9]. This intuitive visualization significantly lowers the threshold for users to understand geological information, making it accessible to both professionals and the general public. Moreover, AR technology supports interactive operations between users and geological models [10]. Users can control the display content and viewpoint of models through gestures or voice, enabling personalized information queries and analyses. Additionally, AR technology can update geological data in real-time, ensuring that users access the latest information, which is crucial for urban geological disaster early-warning and utilities maintenance.

This study aims to develop an augmented reality platform based on HoloLens 2 to address the shortcomings of traditional geological information display methods. As an advanced AR device, HoloLens 2 offers a high-resolution display, precise spatial positioning, and gesture recognition, providing hardware support for efficient geological information visualization [11]. The application of this platform will bring comprehensive improvements to urban planning, construction, and management. Our technical pipeline combines three innovations: (1) a hybrid AR/VR rendering engine for multi-scale geological representation; (2) a proprioceptive interaction framework leveraging HoloLens 2's spatial intelligence; (3) a context-aware data fusion protocol synchronizing virtual models with IoT-enabled urban sensing streams. This integration of real-time data from IoT devices ensures that the platform reflects the most current geological and environmental conditions, enhancing the accuracy and relevance of the information provided to users.

2 Related Work

In the field of urban geological modeling and visualization, traditional 2D visualization methods and 3D modeling technologies have made significant progress, but these methods face significant limitations in dynamic updating and interactivity. In recent years, the development of AR has provided new possibilities for the display and interaction of urban geological information. This section will review the development of these technologies and discuss their applications in urban geological modeling.

2.1 Limitations of Traditional Urban Geological Visualization Techniques

Traditional urban geological visualization relies mainly on 2D geological maps, cross-sections, and tables [12]. While partially meeting the basic needs of urban planning, construction, and management, these methods have notable limitations. First, 2D displays cannot intuitively represent complex 3D geological structures, requiring users to have professional geological knowledge for accurate understanding [13]. Second, traditional methods lack dynamic updating and interactive querying capabilities, failing to reflect geological changes in real-time and making personalized information queries and analyses inconvenient for users[14]. Moreover, field surveys, a key traditional method for obtaining geological information, are restricted by natural conditions like weather and terrain. Surveying deep-underground geological structures or hazardous areas also poses significant safety risks and operational challenges.

2.2 3D Modeling Technology

3D modeling technology is crucial for urban geological visualization, transforming complex geological data into intuitive 3D models [15]. Using common 3D modeling software like 3ds Max, Maya, Blender, and geological data processing tools like ArcGIS and Surfer, high-precision models of surface buildings, underground pipelines, and geological structures can be created [16]. These models realistically reflect geological features and allow for multi-angle observation and analysis. However, 3D modeling technology faces challenges in urban geological visualization [17], such as model simplification, multi-source data fusion, and real-time rendering. To enhance the visualization and interaction of 3D models, researchers are exploring cloud-based rendering and AI-based optimization algorithms.

2.3 Augmented Reality

AR enhances geological information experience by fusing virtual geological models with the real world [18]. Its current applications in geological visualization include: Field geological surveys using AR devices, which overlay virtual geological models to help geologists accurately identify and analyze geological features [19]. AR-based geological education and training systems, enabling students and professionals to observe and study geological phenomena in virtual environments. AR visualization platforms for urban geological information, allowing efficient querying and analysis of geological data and supporting urban planning and management decision-making. Geographic Information System (GIS) is a key supporting technology for urban geological visualization, capable of integrating and managing large volumes of geological data [20]. Combining GIS with AR enhances the visualization and interaction of urban geological information [21]. Combining GIS 3D modeling with VR immersive experiences allows for more realistic geological environment simulation.

The HoloLens 2 is an advanced AR device developed by Microsoft [22]. It has several upgrades and optimizations over the original HoloLens. It has clear advantages in AR applications. Its high-precision spatial positioning and environment-sensing capabilities allow virtual geological models to be accurately combined with real world scenes

[23]. This gives users a more realistic visual experience. In addition, the open development platform of HoloLens 2 supports a variety of programming languages and tools. Developers can create personalized AR applications according to specific needs.

3 Platform Design and Technical Architecture

The See-Through Urban Geology platform aims to create an intuitive and efficient urban geological information visualization tool. By integrating AR and VR technologies, it transforms complex geological data into easily understandable 3D models precisely overlaid onto real world scenes. This allows users to clearly observe details such as surface buildings, underground pipelines, and geological structures. It reduces the threshold for professionals to understand geological information and enables the general public to easily access relevant geological knowledge, enhancing information dissemination efficiency and application value.

The technical roadmap of the platform is shown in Fig. 1, which outlines the key components and their interconnections. The platform's design and technical architecture are structured around four main aspects: Data Acquisition and Processing, 3D Model Construction, AR Function Implementation, and User Interaction Design. Each of these aspects corresponds to a specific layer in the technical roadmap, as detailed below.

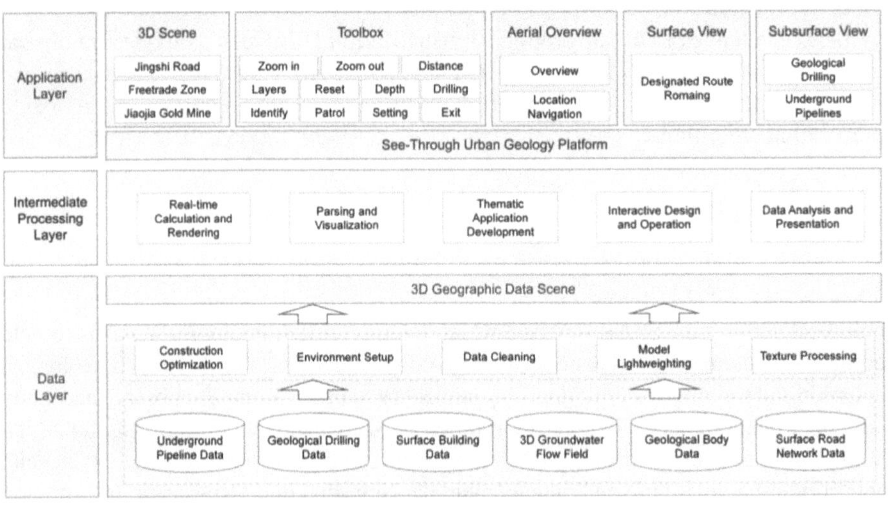

Fig. 1. Technical Roadmap.

3.1 Data Layer

In collaboration with the National Earth Science Data Center, geological survey agencies, and urban planning departments [24], we collect diverse urban geological data, including geological boreholes, seismic waves, and terrain data. These raw data, often in different formats and precisions, require preprocessing and optimization. Data processing involves cleaning, format conversion, coordinate unification, and data fusion to ensure accuracy and consistency. We also optimize data through simplification, compression, and multi-resolution representation to enhance visualization and interaction performance.

3.2 Processing Layer

Using professional 3D modeling software (3ds Max 2021) and algorithms, we construct 3D urban geological models based on processed geological data. The modeling process integrates information on surface buildings, underground pipelines, and geological structures to ensure model completeness and authenticity. To achieve efficient modeling, the platform employs various techniques and tools, such as grid-based, voxel-based modeling, and surface reconstruction algorithms [25]. We also convert and optimize models for compatibility across devices and platforms, like converting them into lightweight 3D formats for quick loading and rendering on HoloLens 2.

3.3 Application Layer

The platform leverages HoloLens 2 spatial positioning and environmental perception to precisely fuse virtual geological models with real world scenes. Utilizing HoloLens 2's sensor fusion pipeline (IMU + depth camera + SLAM) for sub-5cm spatial registration accuracy, it obtains real-time device position and orientation data for accurate virtual model registration and overlay. To enhance the AR experience's stability and fluency, the platform employs spatial mapping and surface reconstruction techniques, enabling virtual models to better adapt to the geometric shapes of the real environment. Additionally, various AR interaction functions, such as gesture recognition and voice control, are developed for natural user interaction with virtual geological models.

The platform supports various interaction methods, including voice, gesture, and controller interactions. For voice interaction, it integrates advanced speech recognition and natural language processing technologies, enabling users to control model operations and query information via voice commands. In gesture interaction, it uses HoloLens 2's gesture recognition to support model selection, movement, and scaling through gestures. For controller interaction, it offers a handheld controller for precise operations via buttons and joysticks. Additionally, the platform focuses on interaction interface design, adopting a simple UI layout and intuitive operation prompts to reduce the user's learning cost.

By thoroughly analyzing geological data, the platform provides users with rich visual charts and statistical information. It supports various data analysis methods, such as spatial, attribute, and trend analyses, helping users understand geological information from different perspectives. In data presentation, geological structures are displayed in 3D models, supplemented by 2D charts, maps, and reports. The platform also supports data export and sharing, facilitating the application of analysis results in other fields and platforms.

4 Platform Implementation

4.1 Development Environment and Tools

The platform is developed using the Unity 3D game engine, which supports 3D model import, scene construction, and interaction feature development. The software environment includes Microsoft HoloLens 2 with the HoloToolkit package for AR features like spatial positioning and gesture recognition. Visual Studio is used for code editing, with C# for module development. The hardware environment consists of a computer with an Intel Core i7, 16GB RAM, and an NVIDIA GeForce RTX 2080 GPU, connected to HoloLens 2 for compatibility. Tools include 3ds Max and Blender for 3D modeling, Photoshop for texture processing, and Unity's Terrain system for terrain building.

We utilized the Basis Universal texture compression format. Basis Universal is a modern, open-source compression format that supports a wide range of platforms and devices. Basis Universal was selected due to its excellent compression ratios and compatibility with various hardware platforms, including HoloLens 2. It allows us to maintain high visual quality while significantly reducing the storage and memory requirements. Asynchronous loading was implemented using Unity's AsyncOperation and Coroutine systems. We created a custom loading manager that handles the background loading of assets and models. We used callback mechanisms to notify the main thread once the loading of each asset is complete. This allows the system to update the user interface and provide feedback on the loading progress.

4.2 Function Design

- **Model Scene.** The platform creates multiple detailed urban geological model scenes, each optimized for performance and user interaction. These scenes cover various urban areas and geological features, including buildings, underground pipelines, and geological bodies. Using Unity's layered scene management and optimized Level of Detail (LOD) techniques, the platform ensures quick loading, smooth display, and high visual quality while reducing computational load. Interactive functions allow users to obtain detailed information by clicking on models, enhancing the overall user experience in diverse urban environments.
- **Toolbox.** The platform offers functions like zooming, resetting, layer management, distance and depth measurement, drilling, recognition, and patrol, as shown in Fig. 2. Users can adjust model display and obtain geological information via gestures or voice commands. For instance, in the Jing Shi Road scene, users can measure building distances using the distance measurement function. They can also use voice commands like Reset model to revert to the initial model state.
- **Aerial Overview.** Using Unity's camera system and transform components, the camera is positioned at a certain height above the model, with rotation angles adjusted for a global bird's-eye view. Users can specify target buildings, areas, or geographic coordinates via voice commands, prompting the system to adjust the view and navigate to the corresponding location. Additionally, users can select target locations on a 2D map, and the system will adjust the 3D view accordingly, allowing users to quickly find and observe the desired area.

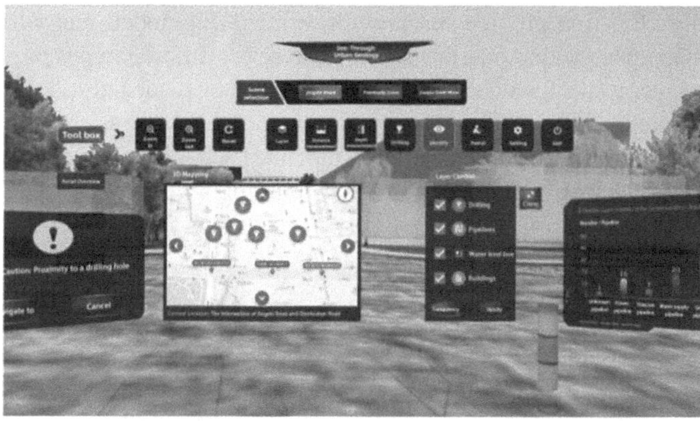

Fig. 2. Toolbox.

- **Surface View.** Based on Unity's animation system and pathfinding algorithms, multiple preset roaming paths are established. After selecting a path, users can control the view to move along it. Users can adjust roaming speed and direction via gestures or voice commands. For example, in the Jing Shi Road scene, users can choose to roam along the main road to observe surface geological features and building distribution.
- **Underground Perspective.** The geological drilling function allows users to perform virtual drilling at specified model locations to explore underground geological structures, as shown in Fig. 3.

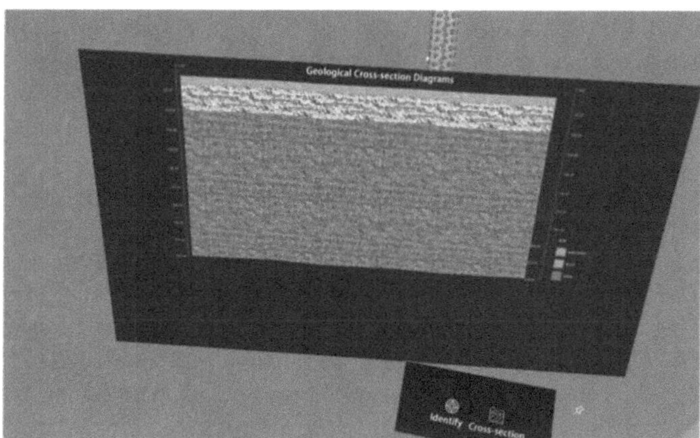

Fig. 3. Geological Cross-Section.

Users can determine drilling locations by clicking on the model using gestures or by specifying drilling coordinates via voice commands. The system simulates the drilling process based on geological model data and real-time displays information on the lithology, thickness, and depth of the strata traversed by the drill hole. The underground pipeline display function provides users with detailed 3D models and attribute information of urban underground pipelines. Users can select different types of pipelines for display using layer control, with each type distinguished by color and style. The platform also supports spatial analysis of underground pipelines, allowing users to query spatial relationships and intersection points between pipelines. Clicking anywhere on a pipeline provides detailed attribute information, as shown in Fig. 4.

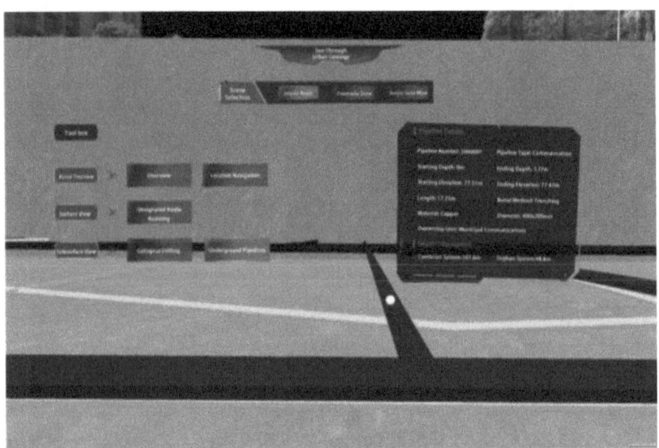

Fig. 4. Underground Pipeline Visualization.

5 Performance Testing and Optimization

To ensure efficient platform operation and high-quality user experience, we conducted comprehensive performance testing followed by optimization measures. During testing, we focused on loading time, response speed, and stability. Toolbox functions like zooming and resetting had response times between 0.5 and 1.0 s, indicating fast overall responsiveness. In stability tests, the platform remained stable for 2 h of continuous use, with a frame rate above 30FPS, providing a smooth visual experience. Performance testing comparison is shown in Table 1.

Based on testing results, we implemented several optimization strategies. For model optimization, simplification and compression reduced rendering load. In the Jing Shi Road scene, building model polygons decreased by 30%, and texture size reduced to 50% of the original, significantly shortening loading time without affecting visual quality. In code optimization, improved algorithm efficiency and resource management reduced unnecessary calculations and consumption, increasing Toolbox function response speed by 20% and enhancing operational fluency. For resource management, asynchronous loading technology decreased loading time by 25%, lowered memory peaks, reduced memory usage, and improved overall platform performance.

Table 1. Performance Comparison Before and After Optimization.

Test Indicator	Before Optimization	After Optimization
Model loading time (Jing Shi Road scene)	20 s	15 s
Model loading time (Free Trade Zone scene)	25 s	20 s
Model loading time (Jiaojia Gold Mine scene)	22 s	18 s
Toolbox function response time (zoom, pan, reset)	0.6–1.2 s	0.5–1.0 s
Toolbox function response time (layer management)	1.2–1.5 s	0.8–1.2 s
Toolbox function response time (distance and depth measurement)	1.8–2.2 s	1.3–1.7 s
Stability (frame rate after 2 h of continuous use)	25–30 FPS	Above 30 FPS
Memory usage	Average 1.2 GB	Average 1.0 GB

6 User Evaluation and Analysis

To comprehensively evaluate platform performance and user experience, we designed a questionnaire to collect feedback on functionality, performance, usability, and immersion. We also invited users for practical operation tests to observe their behavior and reactions. The questionnaire used a Likert scale with five options: Very Satisfied, Satisfied, Neutral, Dissatisfied, and Very Dissatisfied. It focused on specific aspects such as visual effects, natural interaction, functional integrity, and operational convenience. Open-ended questions gathered users' subjective feelings, encountered issues, and suggestions for improvement. In practical operation tests, we observed users completing specific tasks and recorded the fluency of operations, function usage, and encountered issues.

We distributed the questionnaire to six groups: Professional geological staff (geological engineers and explorers) for professional evaluation. Urban planners and architects to assess practical application effectiveness. Construction personnel to evaluate on-site performance. College teachers and students in related fields to assess educational and research value. General public to evaluate public education and knowledge dissemination effectiveness. 100 questionnaires were distributed, with 35 valid responses collected.

Statistical results show a high overall user satisfaction level, with System Usability Scale (SUS) score of 82.4 (SD = 6.7), exceeding the 68.0 threshold for 'good' usability. Visual effects and natural interaction received the highest scores of 4.5 and 4.4, respectively. Usability and immersion scored relatively lower at 4.2 and 4.0. New users, unfamiliar with the operation, initially took longer to adapt, while experienced users utilized the platform more efficiently. In terms of functionality, users affirmed the Toolbox's completeness, meeting diverse geological information query and analysis needs. Experts emphasized the need for subsurface uncertainty visualization (e.g., probabilistic lithology layers), reflecting the epistemic challenges in urban geology. Regarding performance, most users found model loading times reasonable, response speeds fast, and the platform stable. However, a few functions were slightly slow in complex scenes. For usability, most users found gesture and voice operations natural, but some noted unclear operation guidance and insufficient onboarding, complicating the process. In terms of immersion, users highly praised the visual effects, considering the AR function immersive. Yet, some users indicated room for improvement in audio feedback and environmental sound effects.

Based on the above analysis, we have developed targeted improvement measures. We will optimize the interface design, simplify operation, and reduce unnecessary buttons and menus. At the same time, we will enhance operation guidance and onboarding tutorials by providing detailed operation tutorials and prompts for first - time users to help them quickly familiarize themselves with the platform's functions. We will also regularly collect user feedback and adjust the functional layout and operation methods according to user needs and behavior habits. In addition, we will improve audio feedback and environmental sound effects to enhance immersion and explore adding more geological analysis features to expand the platform's application scope and professional depth.

7 Conclusion

The platform, leveraging AR and VR technologies, achieves unified 3D visualization of above-ground and underground urban geological information, significantly enhancing display effects and interactive experiences. Technically, it successfully integrates virtual geological models with the real world urban environment, offering users an immersive experience and pioneering a human-centered cyber-physical framework for urban geological intelligence, where mixed reality serves as a cognitive prosthesis for collaborative spatial reasoning. In practical applications, it strongly supports urban planning, construction, and management, notably improving work efficiency and scientific decision-making.

In the future, the platform will expand and deepen its functionality and applications. it will add more geological analysis features, such as groundwater flow simulation and geological hazard prediction, to meet complex geological research and engineering needs. Additionally, it will establish a real-time data update mechanism, strengthen data sharing with relevant departments, ensure users access the latest geological information, and support continuous platform optimization.

Acknowledgments. We are grateful to the funding support from the National Science Foundation of China (NFSC) (42301487); the General Program for Natural Science Research of Basic Disciplines in Universities of Jiangsu Province (23KJD170004); Jiangsu Provincial Government Scholarship for Studying Abroad. A big thank you to the WANDER XR Experience Lab for its invaluable support in providing the essential technology and resources, and for fostering XR research at Wageningen University & Research.

References

1. Agius, T., Sabri, S., Kalantari, M.: Three-dimensional rule-based city modelling to support urban redevelopment process. ISPRS Int. J. Geo-Inf. **7**(10), 413 (2018)

2. Costa, G.M., Petry, M.R., Martins, J.G., Moreira, A.P.: Assessment of multiple fiducial marker trackers on hololens 2. IEEE Access **12**, 14211–14226 (2024)
3. Di Mitri, M., et al.: Advancing pediatric surgery: the use of HoloLens 2 for 3D anatomical reconstructions in preoperative planning. Child.-Basel **12**(1), 32 (2024)
4. He, L., Han, B.J., Ji, H.J., Mao, G.S., Chen, J.Y.: A method to integrate hydraulic structure models into 3D terrain models for irrigation infrastructure visualization. Sci. Rep. **14**(1), 21255 (2024)
5. Buyukdemircioglu, M., Kocaman, S.: Reconstruction and efficient visualization of heterogeneous 3D city models. Remote Sens. **12**(3), 2128 (2020)
6. Guo, J., et al.: GeoPDNN: a semisupervised deep learning neural network using pseudolabels for three-dimensional urban geological modelling and uncertainty analysis from borehole data. Geosci. Model Dev. **17**(3), 957–973 (2023)
7. Hwang, J.W., Park, J., Park, R.H., Park, H.M.: Audio-visual speech recognition based on joint training with audio-visual speech enhancement for robust speech recognition. Appl. Acoust. **11**(7), 1733 (2023)
8. Xu, H., Wang, C.C., Shen, X.S., Zlatanova, S.: 3D tree reconstruction in support of urban microclimate simulation: a comprehensive literature review. Buildings **11**(9), 417 (2021)
9. Kerkhof, E., et al.: Depth-based registration of 3D preoperative models to intraoperative patient anatomy using the HoloLens 2. Int. J. Comput. Assist. Radiol. Surg. **25**(5), 901–912 (2025)
10. Kinnen, T., Blut, C., Effkemann, C., Blankenbach, J.: Thermal reality capturing with the Microsoft HoloLens 2 for energy system analysis. Energy Build. **288**, 113020 (2023)
11. LaBianca, A., Mortensen, M.H., Sandersen, P., Sonnenborg, T.O., Jensen, K.H., Kidmose, J.: Impact of urban geology on model simulations of shallow groundwater levels and flow paths. Hydrol. Earth Syst. Sci. **27**(8), 1645–1666 (2022)
12. Lentini, A., et al.: The urban geo-climate footprint approach: enhancing urban resilience through improved geological conceptualisation. Cities **155**, 105287 (2024)
13. Herfort, B., Lautenbach, S., de Albuquerque, J.P., Anderson, J., Zipf, A.: A spatio-temporal analysis investigating completeness and inequalities of global urban building data in OpenStreetMap. Nat. Commun. **14**(1), 39698 (2023)
14. O'Meara, J., Szita, K.: AR cinema: visual storytelling and embodied experiences with augmented reality filters and backgrounds. Presence-Virtual Augmented Reality **30**, 99–123 (2021)
15. Fleming, Z.: Using virtual outcrop models and google earth to teach structural geology concepts. J. Struct. Geol. **156**, 104537 (2022)
16. Salloum, S., Huang, J.Z., He, Y.: Exploring and cleaning big data with random sample data blocks. J. Big Data **6**(1), 45 (2019)
17. Saravanavel, J., Ramasamy, S.M., Palanivel, K., Kumanan, C.J.: GIS based 3D visualization of subsurface geology and mapping of probable hydrocarbon locales, part of Cauvery Basin, India. J. Earth Syst. Sci. **129**(1), 36 (2019)
18. Montes, H., Hijón-Neira, R., Pérez-Marìn, D., Montes, S.: Refine results for the design and evaluation of an AR-based serious game to teach programming. IEEE Access **9**, 12567–12578 (2021)
19. Skurowski, P., Myszor, D., Paszkuta, M., Moroń, T., Cyran, K.A.: Energy demand in AR applications—a reverse ablation study of the HoloLens 2 device. Energies **17**(3), 553 (2024)
20. Sun, J., Mi, S.Y., Olsson, P.O., Paulsson, J., Harrie, L.: Utilizing BIM and GIS for representation and visualization of 3D cadastre. ISPRS Int. J. Geo-Inf. **8**(11), 503 (2019)
21. Dieck, M., Krey, N., Cranmer, E.: The value of augmented reality: exploring hedonic and utilitarian augmented reality experiences. Internet Res. **35**(3), 1252–1273 (2024)
22. Wang, D.: Gamified learning through unity 3D in visualizing environments. Neural Comput. Appl. **29**(5), 1399–1404 (2017)

23. Xinping, H., Yang Miang, G., Alexander, L.: Educational impact of an Augmented Reality (AR) application for teaching structural systems to non-engineering students. Adv. Eng. Inform. **50**, 101436 (2021)
24. Yun, S.H., Lee, D.K., Piao, Z.G., Park, C.Y., Kim, S.H., Kim, E.S.: Developing a three-dimensional urban surface model for spatiotemporal analysis of thermal comfort with respect to street direction. Sustain. Cities Soc. **97**, 104721 (2023)
25. Zhao, L., Liu, X., Xu, X., Liu, C., Chen, K.: Three-dimensional simulation model for synergistically simulating urban horizontal expansion and vertical growth. Remote Sens. **14**(6), 1503 (2022)

TongueBCI: An Interaction Method Based on EEG Signals from Tongue Movement Direction

Dingming Tan[1], Zifeng Ni[1], Baiqiao Zhang[1], Chao Zhou[2], Tianshuo Bai[1], Juan Liu[1], Xiangxian Li[1], and Yulong Bian[1](✉)

[1] Shandong University, Weihai, China
202000800489@mail.sdu.edu.cn
[2] Institute of Software, Chinese Academy of Sciences, Beijing, China

Abstract. Computer control based on tongue gestures has been shown to be a potentially accessible interaction method for patients with paralyzing injuries. Considering the advantages of nonintrusive brain-computer interfaces (BCIs), this study explored novel tongue-computer interaction methods by analyzing the electroencephalogram (EEG) signals of tongue gestures. We developed TongueBCI, a nonintrusive tongue-computer interface that could recognize a user's interaction intention using EEG signals from two types of tongue gestures-that is, Motor Imagery (MI) and Motor Execution (ME). We first constructed an EEG dataset that included both types of tongue gestures and then developed a deep-learning model, which achieved an accuracy of 94.1%. We then implemented two corresponding real-time interaction technologies based on MI/ME tongue gestures and designed an experimental system to test their effectiveness. The results showed that MI is a more suitable approach for facilitating accessible interactions than ME.

Keywords: Brain-computer interface · Tongue-Machine Interface(TMI) · accessible interaction · non-intrusive · hands-free · Motor Imagery (MI)

1 Introduction

Accessible interaction is an important theme in human-computer interaction research, providing solutions for people with disabilities or illnesses. Among these, the brain-computer interface (BCI) has garnered much attention. For example, patients with neurological disorders (such as Amyotrophic lateral sclerosis (ALS) or high-level paraplegia) often suffer severe motor-function loss for pathological reasons [5] and a loss of linguistic capabilities [25]. Despite this, most individuals-even in advanced stages of motor impairment-retain cognitive functions and remain non-demented [15]. In such cases, a BCI-based solution allows for communication without muscular control [21].

A. Hinkenjan et al. (Eds.): ICXR 2025, LNCS 16428, pp. 369–380, 2026.
https://doi.org/10.1007/978-981-95-7195-6_26

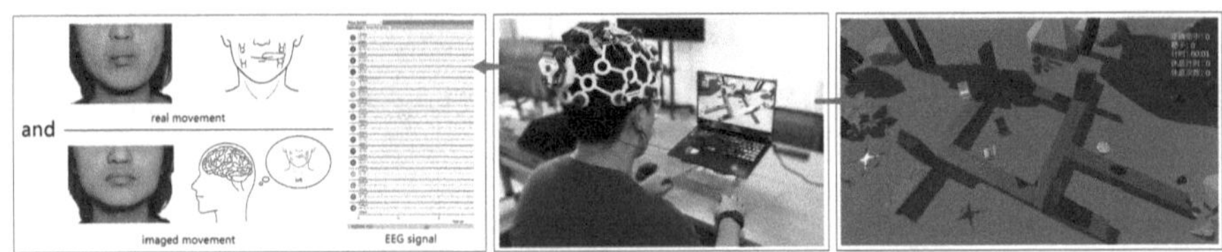

Fig. 1. Tongue movement recognized by EEG (left), User using our system (mid), Our system in experiment.

Since patients can often retain their cognitive function as well as control over muscles such as the tongue, several researchers have begun to explore tongue-machine interaction as a potentially accessible interaction method. Early tongue machines were mainly wearable devices that required mechanical operation [7, 11, 16, 22–24, 26],which require actual muscle-driven tongue movement (Fig. 1).

Tongue movements have its corresponding neural responses, activating various brain regions [17]. Some studies have successfully classified real tongue movements using linear classifiers [12]. Consequently, both Motor Imagery(MI) and Motor Execution(ME) of tongue movements offer methods for extracting useful control information from EEG signals [1]. To the best of our knowledge, previous systems using tongue-machine interactions only used EEG signals to improve system classification accuracy, and none were based solely on the EEG signals themselves.

Accordingly, this research conceived and realized an accessible tongue-machine interaction method based on EEG signals from both actual and imagined tongue movements. The investigation entailed three critical phases: developing a deep learning model for MI/ME recognition, engineering a simple yet effective system for daily use, and conducting a user study to evaluate the entire framework.

The main contributions of this study include:

- We collected a baseline dataset and an interaction dataset on the tongue movement MI and ME paradigms. We achieved up to 94.1% (MI) and 88.4% (ME) accuracy on the former dataset and up to 88.7% (MI) and 92.4% (ME) on the latter.
- A straightforward interactive system was devised that employs tongue gestures for manipulation. The user is afforded the option of using either MI or ME for control.
- The results of experiments conducted in this study demonstrate that MI is a more suitable approach for facilitating accessible interactions than ME.

2 Related Work

2.1 Accessible Interaction and Brain-Computer Interface: Foundations and Challenges

Accessible interaction is designed to provide patients with neuromuscular diseases with interaction methods they can adapt to [3], requiring low-fatigue and reliable input methods [4].

Against this backdrop, brain-computer interfaces (BCIs) have gained attention as a transformative technology for accessible interaction. BCIs enable communication and control without relying on peripheral muscle activity, directly translating neural signals into actionable commands. Classified into invasive and non-invasive systems [13,14], non-invasive BCIs (e.g., electroencephalography [EEG]-based) are particularly suitable for daily use due to their safety and ease of deployment.

A key distinction in BCI research lies in the neural paradigms of Motor Execution (ME) and Motor Imagery (MI). ME refers to the physical performance of a movement, while MI involves the mental simulation of movement without overt muscle activity. Both paradigms elicit distinct yet overlapping neural signatures, such as movement-related cortical potentials (MRCPs) and sensorimotor rhythms (SMRs) [5,8,20]. While ME has been widely used in interaction systems, MI eliminates the need for physical movement–an attribute critical for individuals with severe motor impairment.

2.2 Current Interaction Technologies Based on Tongue Movements

Among potential input modalities of BCIs, tongue movements have emerged as a promising candidate. Unlike limb muscles, tongue muscles are resistant to fatigue and are typically preserved even in advanced stages of motor impairment, making them a stable and sustainable control source for individuals with severe disabilities. Early attempts to leverage tongue movements for interaction included mechanical devices (e.g., tongue-operated joysticks [22]) and invasive/implantable sensors [7,26]., but these approaches suffered from limitations such as high cost, maintenance complexity, and discomfort. Non-invasive alternatives, such as electromyography (EMG)-based systems [7,16,26], have since been developed, but they still require actual muscle contraction, which may be challenging for users with severe motor deficits.

Traditional approaches include intraoral sensors [11,24], inertial measurement units (IMUs) [7], radar arrays [16], and EMG [26]. For example, Zhang et al. [26] achieved 94.17% accuracy in recognizing tongue gestures via submental EMG, while Li et al. [16] developed a non-contact radar-based system with 95% accuracy. These methods, however, either require physical tongue movement (limiting applicability for severe impairments) or fuse multiple signals (increasing system complexity).

2.3 Neural Mechanisms and Recognition of Tongue Movements Based on EEG Signals

Early research established the feasibility of decoding tongue motor execution (ME) from EEG using linear classifiers, achieving up to 93.7% accuracy. However, these efforts largely overlooked motor imagery (MI), despite its significance for users with severe motor impairments. Existing technologies often rely on invasive or multi-modal sensing (e.g., EMG, intraoral sensors), highlighting the need for a non-invasive, EEG-only solution integrating both MI and ME. To address this, we developed TongueBCI, the first system to establish tongue MI as a standalone paradigm using a 16-channel dry-electrode EEG. This work encompasses the construction of an MI/ME dataset, an optimized EEG-GCN model (achieving up to 94.1% accuracy), the design of a real-time interactive system, and user validation demonstrating MI's superior practicality for accessible interaction.

3 Research Design and Methodology

3.1 Theoretical Foundations for Interaction Design

In the field of accessible interaction technologies, the movements used for interaction should be simple and easy to perform. Therefore, we chose forward, left, and right movements as the primary tongue movements for interaction.

- Selection of Interaction Movements: We focus on three basic tongue movements: forward protrusion, left deviation, and right deviation, and a resting state.
- Interaction Mechanism: We adopted a scenario-based interaction paradigm: controlling a virtual drone to land in predefined target zones, to motivate user.
- System Orientation: The interaction targets were derived from six core daily needs (drinking, eating, toileting, sleeping, washing, dressing) identified in Mohamed et al. [18]. To improve flexibility, "eating" and "drinking" were grouped under a "food area" as subcategories.
- Enhanced User Experience via Auxiliary Design: We introduced an automatic switching function: relaxing the tongue (rest state) triggers the drone to switch to the next target, reducing the need for prolonged control.

3.2 Hardware Configuration for EEG Data Acquisition

We used the OpenBCI "MARK IV" EEG headset and Cython Daisy board to acquire 16-channel EEG data opted for electrode placements FC1, FC2, C3, C4, P7, P8, Fz, Cz, FC5, FC6, F3, F4, T7, T8, CP1, and CP2 based on the 10–20 system [9].

3.3 Dataset Construction and Preprocessing

As shown in the previous section, we collect two datasets, each comprising seven distinct data types. These included three slices of action data for each of MI or ME, as well as slices of resting action data. We have two types of datasets:

Baseline tongue movement datasets: Three standard data collection participants each provided 200 samples: 50 static and 150 imagined/actual movement samples (subdivided into 25-direction sets). Each 1-s sample captured movement initiation and maintenance, yielding a total of 600 tongue movement samples.

Interaction tongue movement datasets: Prior to formal interaction, tongue movement data were collected in pre-training mode. The system prompted direction changes every 10 s (mode duration: 3 min). Each participant provided 150 samples (75 MI, 75 ME), yielding a total of 1650 tongue movement samples.

3.4 Deep Learning Model for Tongue Movement Recognition

We improved EEG_GCN [6], a deep model constructed using graph neural networks (GNNs), transform techniques, and full connectivity, by adding convolutional neural networks (CNNs) to integrate various types of features. The input data is initially processed through a CNN for feature extraction, and commonly utilized features in EEG, such as the differential entropy (DE) and the power spectral density (PSD), are extracted. We replicated the multi-view EEG-GCN from the paper to achieve the integration of all features, we used 10 EEG-GCN in our model. Using this approach, we achieved accuracy rates of up to 94.1% (MI) and 88.4% (ME) on the former dataset, and up to 88.7% (MI) and 92.4% (ME) on the latter dataset. After 10-fold cross-checking, the average accuracy for recognizing the former dataset was 88.1% (MI) and 82.9% (ME), and the average accuracy for recognizing the latter dataset was 81.1% (MI),89.7% (ME). Due to the small dataset, the training process directly used all subjects' data.

3.5 Real-Time Interaction System Implementation

Based on the developed tongue movement recognition technique, we implemented a prototype interaction system in which users control a virtual drone to land in specific selection areas. The interface comprises three area types: a resting area, single-category selection areas, and multi-category selection areas.

System Control Mechanism: Drone movement is governed by tongue activity: detected movement propels the drone forward, while a resting state triggers landing, with the landing location determining the user's selection. An integrated anti-shake mechanism maintains drone stability during ambiguous or transitional movement states to prevent erroneous inputs.

Area Definitions: Resting Area: Serves as the interaction starting point. The drone remains here during non-interaction or under weak signal conditions. An optional auxiliary scanning mode enables automated area switching.

Single-Category Selection Areas: Each area is accompanied by an auditory cue and a symbolic visual reference (e.g., a bed for "sleep"). Landing the drone in one of these areas confirms the corresponding choice.

Multi-Category Selection Areas: Landing in these zones navigates the drone into a sub-menu containing single selection areas, the options of which belong to a common category.

Personalization: To improve usability, the system allows customization of interaction scenarios and visual block styles. For subsequent experiments, wooden blocks and a cartoon-inspired natural style were adopted as default settings.

4 Simulate User-Case Study

4.1 Purpose

This study aimed to empirically validate the efficacy of tongue movement-based interaction paradigms (Motor Imagery [MI] vs. Motor Execution [ME]) and the utility of an auxiliary design in enhancing accessible interaction. Specifically, two hypotheses were tested:

- H1:MI is more effective than ME in facilitating accessible interaction, as measured by lower task burden and higher usability.
- H2:The auxiliary design (automatic switching to the nearest option) improves interaction performance, as reflected by increased one-hit accuracy.

4.2 Participants

A total of 11 university students with normal motor function (10 males, 1 female; age range: 19-24 years) were recruited. None of the participants had been involved in the baseline dataset collection and haven't use our project before study begin.

The study was conducted in accordance with the Declaration of Helsinki and approved by the Human Research Ethics Committee of a local hospital. Written informed consent was obtained from all participants prior to the experiment.

4.3 Experimental Design

Two single-factor within-subjects designs were performed, with two independent variables:

BCI Interaction Mode: Two levels were tested:

- ME: Participants physically executed tongue movements (left, right, forward) as instructed.

- MI: Participants imagined executing tongue movements without physical action.

Variable Control:

- To mitigate practice effects and fatigue, the order of interaction modes (ME first vs. MI first) and auxiliary design states (ON first vs. OFF first) was range by ABBA paradigm for each participant.

4.4 Experimental Task and Equipment

Equipment: The equipment used included an OpenBCI Daisy 16-channel dry electrode EEG cap, Unity engine development system, OpenBCI GUI streaming, Python torch deep-learning model, HP computer, Bluetooth keyboard, Bluetooth mouse, and iPad. Task design: The experimenter introduced the interactive system to the participant and collected pre-test data. Under guidance, 5 min of tongue movement pre-training data were collected, and a model was fitted using this 5-minute data. After the participant tried interacting with the fitted model for ten minutes, they formally entered the target selection mode: selecting random highlighted targets for five time.(the false chosen will be counted in Interaction count.)

4.5 Measures

Both objective and subjective indicators were recorded to comprehensively evaluate the interaction performance, user experience, and system usability of the TongueBCI. These measures were selected based on established assessment frameworks in human-computer interaction and BCI research to ensure validity and comparability with existing literature.

Objective Indicators

Objective metrics were automatically logged by the system to quantify interaction efficiency, accuracy, and stability, minimizing subjective bias:

- One hit rate: The ratio of times a participant selects a target directly and correctly. $Accuracy = \frac{\text{single correct selection amount}}{\text{total test amount}}$.
- Interaction time: The average time for participants' interactions. $Interaction\ time = \frac{\text{total time of interactions}}{\text{total number of interactions}}$.
- Interaction count: Total number of interactions.

Subjective Indicators

Subjective metrics were collected via validated questionnaires to assess user perceptions of task burden, system usability, and comfort, complementing objective data with qualitative insights:

- Participant task perception: The NASA-TLX task scale [10] was used as a post-task questionnaire.
- Perceived usability and ease of use: The System Usability Scale (SUS) [2] was used as a post-system questionnaire.

4.6 Procedure

After the completion of the pre-test questionnaire, each experimental session was conducted in similar order:

- The experimenter instructed the participant on the interaction type corresponding to the session, utilizing the system's built-in pre-training mode to collect data for that session, which was subsequently used for model training.
- After the model had been trained, the experimenter proceeded to activate or deactivate the auxiliary design, after which the participant engaged in a trial operation lasting between five and fifteen minutes.
- The experimenter used the system to randomly assign options. The participant controlled the system to make selections, repeated five times, after which they filled out a questionnaire of NASA-TLX.
- The experimenter then switched the auxiliary design and conducted another five rounds of specified option selection, after which the participant completed another questionnaire of NASA-TLX.
- The experiment proceeded with the other type of interaction method, repeating the aforementioned experimental procedures.

Upon completion of all experimental procedures, subjects were requested to complete the SUS questionnaire.

5 Results

5.1 Comparison with Other Studies

Despite established evidence that channel reduction compromises MI classification accuracy–as shown by Mahdieh Mohseni et al. [19] where accuracy dropped from 93.7% to 70% when channels were reduced from 64 to 10–this work effectively overcomes this limitation. We implemented an interactive system using a practical 16-channel dry-electrode setup, demonstrating that high performance is achievable without high-density wet electrodes (Table 1).

Table 1. Research on Tongue-Machine Interaction

Author	Interactive Method	Signals Used	Accuracy	Applications
Chris Salem and Shumin Zhai	Joysticks	computer input	None	None
Q. Peng and T. F. Budinger	Intraoral Sensors	computer input	None	Cursors, wheelchair and so on
T. Scott Saponas et al.	Intraoral Sensors	computer input	90.00%	Tetris
Xueliang Huo et al.	Intraoral Sensors	computer input	87.00%	Computer, wheelchair and so on
Zheng Li et al.	ME	micro-radars	95.00%	Tongue-n-cheek
Qiao Zhang	ME	EMG	94.17%	None
Tan Gemicioglu	ME	IMU, PPG, EEG	90.00%	hands-free games
Yunjun Nam	ME	EEG(GKPs)	None	wheelchair
Kæseler et al.	MI	EEG(64 channel)	86–95%	None
Our	MI	EEG(16 channel)	81–94%	TongueBCI
Our	ME	EEG(16 channel)	85–92%	TongueBCI

5.2 Usability Analysis

We converted all the SUS scores obtained. For odd-numbered items, the scoring was done using the formula "original score - 1", while for even-numbered items, the scoring was "5 - original score". The converted scores of all items were then added and multiplied by 2.5, resulting in the final SUS score of 73.25. According to the relationship between words, letters, acceptable range, and SUS scores obtained by Bangor et al. [2], our system met the usability criteria and had a high user acceptance with a GOOD adjective rating.

5.3 Hypothesis Verification

Hypothesis 1. The NASA-TLX scale scores were processed by unweighted averaging in order to obtain an overall estimation of the task burden. Using an independent sample t-test, the task burden of MI is demonstrably lower than that of ME ($t = 1.865$, $p \approx 0.038 < 0.05$). Furthermore, there was a significant difference in physical demand between MI and ME ($t = 4.195$, $p \approx 0 < 0.001$). The mental demand for MI was higher than ME, with a marginally significant difference ($t = -2.582$, $p \approx 0.007 < 0.05$). In light of the necessity for accessible interaction, stability and physical demands are of greater importance to users. Consequently, MI can be considered to be of greater usability than ME.

Hypothesis 2. The results of an independent sample t-test indicated that the auxiliary design had a significant impact on one-hit accuracy ($t = -1.807$, $p = 0.039 < 0.05$) (Fig. 2).

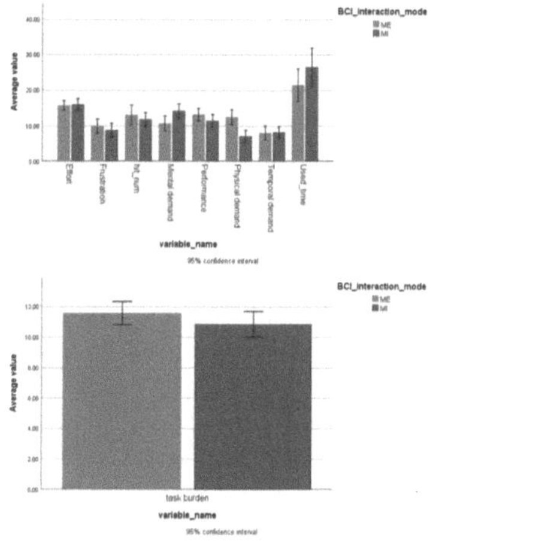

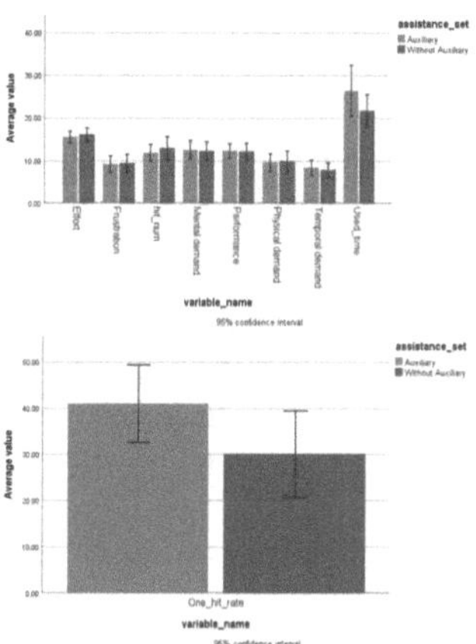

Fig. 2. Task Indicators: MI, ME and Auxiliary Design

6 Discussion and Conclusions

This study presents TongueBCI, a non-invasive BCI that utilizes EEG for interaction via tongue motor imagery (MI) and execution (ME). By integrating dataset construction, deep learning-based recognition, and real-time interaction design, it bridges key theoretical and practical gaps in tongueâĂŞmachine interfaces.

Key Contributions. This work established two EEG datasets (baseline and interaction) for three tongue movement directions and rest. An optimized EEG-GCN model achieved accuracies up to 94.1% (MI) and 88.4% (ME), validating the feasibility of pure EEG decoding for both motor execution and imagery of tongue movements, thereby eliminating the historical dependency on multimodal sensing. A practical real-time system was implemented, enabling tongue-based control of a virtual drone for daily activity selection. The design integrates anti-jitter stabilization and auxiliary scanning to mitigate user fatigue and enhance operational robustness.

Theoretical and Practical Implications. TongueBCI advances the field of tongueâĂŞmachine interaction by establishing tongue motor imagery (MI) as a standalone modality, distinct from prior systems that relied primarily on motor execution (ME) or hybrid sensing. By leveraging the neural basis of tongue movements–particularly the discriminable EEG patterns of MI (cortical origin) and ME (including non-neural artifacts such as glossokinetic potentials)–this work provides a robust decoding framework suitable for motor-impaired users.

Limitations and Future Directions. This study has limitations that inform future research. The participant cohort consisted solely of healthy adults, necessitating validation in clinical populations (e.g., ALS patients) to assess efficacy with pathological neural signatures. Model generalizability may be constrained by the relatively small dataset (N = 11); future work should expand to larger, multi-center cohorts. While the system currently supports five commands, its scalability to complex tasks (e.g., text entry) and integration of adaptive personalization algorithms present clear directions. Technically, reducing electrode count for wearability and exploring high-resolution or hybrid (e.g., EEG-fNIRS) approaches warrant further investigation.

References

1. Abiri, R., Borhani, S., Sellers, E.W., Jiang, Y., Zhao, X.: A comprehensive review of EEG-based brain–computer interface paradigms. J. Neural Eng. **16**(1), 011001 (2019). https://doi.org/10.1088/1741-2552/aaf12e

2. Bangor, A., Kortum, P., Miller, J.: Determining what individual SUS scores mean: adding an adjective rating scale. J. Usability Stud. **4**(3), 114–123 (2009)
3. Bi, T., Xia, X., Lo, D., Grundy, J., Zimmermann, T., Ford, D.: Accessibility in software practice: a practitioner's perspective. ACM Trans. Softw. Eng. Methodol. **31**(4), 1–26 (2022). https://doi.org/10.1145/3503508. https://dl.acm.org/doi/10.1145/3503508
4. Brunet, P., Feigenbaum, B.A., Harris, K., Laws, C., Schwerdtfeger, R., Weiss, L.: Accessibility requirements for systems design to accommodate users with vision impairments. IBM Syst. J. **44**(3), 445–466 (2005). https://doi.org/10.1147/sj.443.0445. http://ieeexplore.ieee.org/document/5386679/
5. Cincotti, F., et al.: Non-invasive brain-computer interface system: towards its application as assistive technology. Brain Res. Bull. **75**(6), 796–803 (2008). https://doi.org/10.1016/j.brainresbull.2008.01.007. https://linkinghub.elsevier.com/retrieve/pii/S0361923008000142
6. Gao, Y., Fu, X., Ouyang, T., Wang, Y.: EEG-GCN: spatio-temporal and self-adaptive graph convolutional networks for single and multi-view EEG-based emotion recognition. IEEE Signal Process. Lett. **29**, 1574–1578 (2022). https://doi.org/10.1109/LSP.2022.3179946. https://ieeexplore.ieee.org/document/9788054/
7. Gemicioglu, T., Winters, R.M., Wang, Y.T., Gable, T.M., Paradiso, A., Tashev, I.J.: Gaze & Tongue: a subtle, hands-free interaction for head-worn devices. In: Extended Abstracts of the 2023 CHI Conference on Human Factors in Computing Systems, pp. 1–4. ACM, Hamburg, Germany (2023). https://doi.org/10.1145/3544549.3583930. https://dl.acm.org/doi/10.1145/3544549.3583930
8. Graimann, B., Allison, B., Pfurtscheller, G.: Brain-computer interfaces: a gentle introduction. In: Graimann, B., Pfurtscheller, G., Allison, B. (eds.) Brain-Computer Interfaces. The Frontiers Collection, pp. 1–27. Springer, Heidelberg (2009). https://doi.org/10.1007/978-3-642-02091-9_1
9. Klem, G.H.: The ten-twenty electrode system of the international federation. The international federation of clinical neurophysiology. Electroencephalogr. Clin. Neurophysiol. Suppl. **52**, 3–6 (1999). https://cir.nii.ac.jp/crid/1574231874767178624
10. Hart, S.G.: Nasa-task load index (NASA-TLX); 20 years later. In: Proceedings of the Human Factors and Ergonomics Society Annual Meeting, vol. 50, no. 9, pp. 904–908 (2006). https://doi.org/10.1177/154193120605000909. http://journals.sagepub.com/doi/10.1177/154193120605000909
11. Huo, X., Wang, J., Ghovanloo, M.: A magneto-inductive sensor based wireless tongue-computer interface. IEEE Trans. Neural Syst. Rehabil. Eng. **16**(5), 497–504 (2008). https://doi.org/10.1109/TNSRE.2008.2003375. https://ieeexplore.ieee.org/document/4595652/
12. Kaeseler, R.L., Johansson, T.W., Struijk, L.N.S.A., Jochumsen, M.: Feature and classification analysis for detection and classification of tongue movements from single-trial pre-movement EEG. IEEE Trans. Neural Syst. Rehabil. Eng. **30**, 678–687 (2022). https://doi.org/10.1109/TNSRE.2022.3157959. https://ieeexplore.ieee.org/document/9734730/
13. Kawala-Sterniuk, A., et al.: Summary of over fifty years with brain-computer interfaces-a review. Brain Sci. **11**(1), 43 (2021). https://doi.org/10.3390/brainsci11010043. https://www.mdpi.com/2076-3425/11/1/43
14. Kübler, A.: The history of BCI: From a vision for the future to real support for personhood in people with locked-in syndrome. Neuroethics **13**(2), 163–180 (2020). https://doi.org/10.1007/s12152-019-09409-4. http://link.springer.com/10.1007/s12152-019-09409-4

15. Leys, D., Hénon, H., Mackowiak-Cordoliani, M.A., Pasquier, F.: Post-stroke dementia. Lancet Neurol. **4**(11), 752–759 (2005). https://doi.org/10.1016/S1474-4422(05)70221-0. https://linkinghub.elsevier.com/retrieve/pii/S1474442205702210
16. Li, Z., Robucci, R., Banerjee, N., Patel, C.: Tongue-n-cheek: non-contact tongue gesture recognition. In: Proceedings of the 14th International Conference on Information Processing in Sensor Networks, pp. 95–105. ACM, Seattle, Washington (2015). https://doi.org/10.1145/2737095.2737109. https://dl.acm.org/doi/10.1145/2737095.2737109
17. Martin, R.E., et al.: Cerebral areas processing swallowing and tongue movement are overlapping but distinct: a functional magnetic resonance imaging study. J. Neurophysiol. **92**(4), 2428–2443 (2004). https://doi.org/10.1152/jn.01144.2003. https://www.physiology.org/doi/10.1152/jn.01144.2003
18. Mohamed, N.A.R.: A deep learning-based brain-computer interaction system for speech and motor impairment. J. Eng. Appl. Sci. **70**(1), 40 (2023). https://doi.org/10.1186/s44147-023-00212-w. https://jeas.springeropen.com/articles/10.1186/s44147-023-00212-w
19. Mohseni, M., Shalchyan, V., Jochumsen, M., Niazi, I.K.: Upper limb complex movements decoding from pre-movement EEG signals using wavelet common spatial patterns. Comput. Methods Programs Biomed. **183**, 105076 (2020). https://doi.org/10.1016/j.cmpb.2019.105076. https://www.sciencedirect.com/science/article/pii/S0169260719307588
20. Nicolas-Alonso, L.F., Gomez-Gil, J.: Brain computer interfaces, a review. Sensors **12**(2), 1211–1279 (2012). https://doi.org/10.3390/s120201211. http://www.mdpi.com/1424-8220/12/2/1211
21. Pai, K., Kallimani, R., Iyer, S., Maheswari, B.U., Khanai, R., Torse, D.: A Survey on Brain-Computer Interface and Related Applications (2022). https://doi.org/10.48550/ARXIV.2203.09164, publisher: arXiv Version Number: 1
22. Peng, Q., Budinger, T.F.: ZigBee-based wireless intra-oral control system for quadriplegic patients. In: 2007 29th Annual International Conference of the IEEE Engineering in Medicine and Biology Society, pp. 1647–1650. IEEE, Lyon, France (2007). https://doi.org/10.1109/IEMBS.2007.4352623. http://ieeexplore.ieee.org/document/4352623/. iSSN 1557-170X
23. Salem, C., Zhai, S.: An isometric tongue pointing device. In: Proceedings of the ACM SIGCHI Conference on Human Factors in Computing Systems, pp. 538–539. ACM, Atlanta, Georgia USA (1997). https://doi.org/10.1145/258549.259021. https://dl.acm.org/doi/10.1145/258549.259021
24. Saponas, T.S., Kelly, D., Parviz, B.A., Tan, D.S.: Optically sensing tongue gestures for computer input. In: Proceedings of the 22nd Annual ACM Symposium on User Interface Software and Technology, pp. 177–180. ACM, Victoria, BC, Canada (2009). https://doi.org/10.1145/1622176.1622209. https://dl.acm.org/doi/10.1145/1622176.1622209
25. Sinanović, O., Mrkonjić, Z., Zukić, S., Vidović, M., Imamović, K., et al.: Post-stroke language disorders. Acta Clin. Croat. **50**(1), 79–94 (2011)
26. Zhang, Q., Gollakota, S., Taskar, B., Rao, R.P.: Non-intrusive tongue machine interface. In: Proceedings of the SIGCHI Conference on Human Factors in Computing Systems, pp. 2555–2558. ACM, Toronto, Ontario, Canada (2014). https://doi.org/10.1145/2556288.2556981. https://dl.acm.org/doi/10.1145/2556288.2556981

XR Headset-Empowered Sketch Art Education: Enhancing Learning Outcomes Through Spatial Perception and Layered Teaching

Lijia Li[1], Zeya Wang[2], Sen-Zhe Xu[3](✉), Qi Wen Gan[4], and Song-Hai Zhang[5,6]

[1] Tsinghua-Qingdao Institute of Arts and Science Innovation, Qingdao, China
llj21@tsinghua.org.cn
[2] Dalian Jiaotong University, Dalian, China
[3] University of Science and Technology Beijing, Beijing, China
senzhe@ustb.edu.cn
[4] University of Arizona, Tucson, USA
qiwengan@arizona.edu
[5] BNRist, Beijing, China
[6] Tsinghua University, Beijing, China
shz@tsinghua.edu.cn

Abstract. Sketching education, a cornerstone of visual arts, often leads to a disconnect between abstract theory and practical application when teaching spatial relationships and dynamic light or shadow principles. This study presents an XR headset application built on a novel three-layer teaching framework: basic modeling, cognitive deepening, and creative expression. Leveraging XR's immersive capabilities, the system integrates real-time sketch conversion, dynamic light source simulation, and spatial walking interaction. Small-scale user experiments confirm this paradigm, which merges real-object observation with XR enhancement, significantly improves learning outcomes, particularly in enhancing structural understanding and achieving a 75% cognitive transfer rate. The application offers a dynamic model that facilitates the leap from technical skill acquisition to creative expression, providing valuable insights for future XR-driven educational content design.

Keywords: Extended Reality (XR) · Head-Mounted Displays (HMD) · Spatial Perception · Layered Teaching · Digital Interactive Design

1 Introduction

Sketching, as the cornerstone of visual arts, holds core value in cultivating a learner's precise control over form, volume, light, and shadow, alongside their

L. Li and Z. Wang—Contributed equally to this work (Co-First Authors).

A. Hinkenjan et al. (Eds.): ICXR 2025, LNCS 16428, pp. 381–392, 2026.
https://doi.org/10.1007/978-981-95-7195-6_27

logical interpretation of spatial relationships [1]. However, traditional sketch education faces persistent limitations that impede learning efficacy: 1) **Static Light and Shadow:** Reliance on observing static still life causes learners to memorize specific shadow performances rather than grasping the underlying dynamic principles [2,3]. 2) **Abstract Structural Logic:** Teaching often remains superficial, as 2D static diagrams fail to build a cognitive path from the appearance of shadows to the essence of structure [4,5], leading to mechanical imitation. 3) **Passive Expression:** Existing methods predominantly focus on realistic imitation skills, which struggle to guide learners beyond "replicating reality" to cultivate emotional expression [6,7].

Extended Reality (XR) headset technology offers an innovative solution to these dilemmas [8]. Leveraging its advantages in immersive experience, spatial interaction, and dynamic simulation, XR can convert real-world objects into sketch-like forms in real-time and dynamically simulate multi-dimensional lighting effects [9]. This approach effectively bridges the cognitive gap between abstract theory and concrete perception that exists in traditional teaching [10].

1.1 Research Aims

This study aims to design and validate an XR headset application for sketch education. We construct a three-layer teaching framework—**basic modeling, cognitive deepening, and creative expression**—that aligns with cognitive progression from beginner to advanced. Based on this, we developed an XR system to directly address the pain points of "static light and shadow perception, abstract structural understanding, and passive creative expression".

The contributions of this study are threefold, forming a valuable addition to the fields of sketch learning, mixed reality, and spatial interaction:

1. The construction of a three-layer sketch education model that integrates XR technology to form a systematic teaching framework, providing theoretical support and a practical path for layered teaching.
2. The design of an innovative interactive teaching solution based on XR headsets, which utilizes real-time sketch conversion and multi-perspective light source simulation to offer a new pedagogical paradigm for sketch education.
3. Empirical validation through a controlled experiment and expert interviews, confirming the positive effect of the XR technology on sketch learning outcomes, particularly in enhancing structural understanding and achieving a 75% cognitive transfer rate.

2 Related Works

This study's theoretical and design framework is built on three core areas: layered theories of sketch education, the application and limitations of XR technology in art education, and the interactive design of educational XR applications.

2.1 Layered Theory of Sketch Education

Basic Modeling Layer. Existing research suggests implicit cognitive stages informing our three-layer framework. The Basic Modeling Layer is grounded in Betty Edwards' perceptual modeling theory [11], complemented by the traditional "Five-Tones" theory (light/shadow rules) [12]. The Cognitive Deepening Layer is based on Russian structural sketching [13,14], which, combined with the "deconstruction-recomposition" logic from contemporary sketching [15], validates guiding light-and-shadow through structural logic. The Creative Expression Layer is supported by "expressive sketching" theory [16,17], emphasizing sketching as a "vehicle for personal emotion and spatial understanding", centered on the active organization of visual elements [18–20].

2.2 Application and Limitations of XR Technology in Art Education

Prior work confirms XR's value but highlights limitations. Augmented Reality (AR) applications enhance form control via contour overlay but often lack support for dynamic lighting and spatial perception [21]. Virtual Reality (VR) systems aid structural understanding but the "reality-virtuality gap" impedes knowledge transfer to physical sketching [22–27]. Current prominent applications (e.g., Gesture VR, Tilt Brush, SketchAR) generally lack layered modules aligned with sketch learning traits, offering insufficient support for the "skill-to-creation" transition and weak transferability to physical media [28].

2.3 Interactive Design in Educational XR Applications

Interactive design focuses on "precise information presentation" and "natural user operation" [29–32]. Progressive guidance models from educational games effectively reduce anxiety and boost self-exploration [33]. Furthermore, spatial interaction based on physical movement enhances users' spatial presence and knowledge retention [34,35]. While our study adopts these principles, existing designs often fail to fully consider the necessary synergy between "visual observation, hand operation, cognitive processing" in art learning. Our interactive design therefore emphasizes layered support for this conversion process.

3 Design and Implementation

3.1 Overall Design Goals

This application, utilizing an XR headset as the carrier, aims to cultivate three core sketch skills: establishing a basic cognitive system of "form, volume, and light or shadow", deeply understanding object structural logic and spatial change principles, and achieving personalized creative expression. To accomplish this, the system integrates core functions such as real-time sketch conversion, dynamic multi-dimensional light source simulation, precise layered guidance, and spatial walking-based interaction. By matching these technical characteristics with cognitive principles, it constructs a complete "observation - understanding - expression" learning loop. From the perspective of technical constraints, the design mandates three key indicators to ensure the "cognitive flow is not interrupted": real-time performance (latency < 0.3 s), spatial positioning accuracy (within $pm5$ cm), and interaction naturalness (accuracy $\geq 95\%$), as excessive errors in latency or positioning, or overly complex interactions, would disrupt observation continuity and occupy cognitive resources needed for core sketching principles.

3.2 Layered Teaching Design

Basic Modeling Layer. This layer leverages **Betty Edwards's "perceptual modeling"** and traditional "five-tone" sketching principles. The XR system actively identifies the light source, using an interface to mark the **"light source direction indicator"** and **"light or shadow layer labels"** on the still life. This visually simplifies the process for beginners to establish the cognition of **"form, volume, and light or shadow".** Users can also filter secondary details, retaining only core outlines and key light/shadow boundaries to **reduce cognitive load** (see Fig. 1).

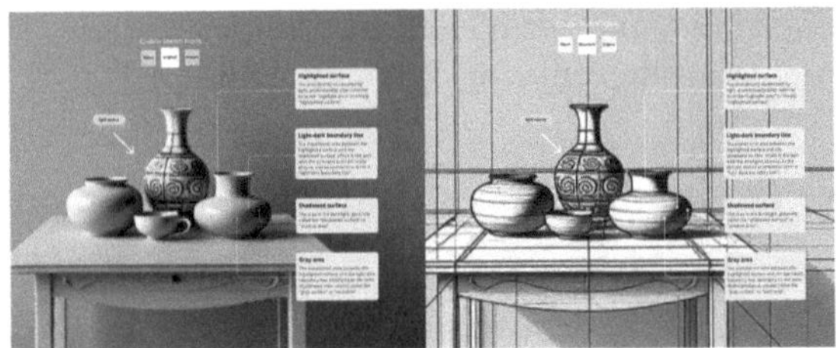

Fig. 1. Original Mode: Identifies the real space light source and labels basic form information. & **Structure Mode**: Retains core outlines and key light/shadow boundaries.

Cognitive Deepening Layer. Based on **structural sketching theory** and the **"structure-first"** methodology, the XR system uses a **"semi-structural sketch"** visual form (see Fig. 1). This transforms the abstract theory that "shadow is the external manifestation of structure" into a visible relationship. The interactive design allows learners to **walk freely** around the object, with **real-time updates** to light and shadow forms based on viewpoint changes. Users can switch between real-world, structural, and sketch-like effects. Light source simulation offers various types (e.g., point light, parallel light) to demonstrate the link between "perspective - form - light/shadow".

Creative Expression Layer. This final layer, based on **expressive sketching theory**, recommends different **perspectives and sketch styles** for users (see

Fig. 2). Learners select an observation perspective by walking, after which the system suggests relevant sketch styles while reserving the final choice for the user. Based on their selection, the system provides **example drawings** and **guidance suggestions**. These suggestions analyze the spatial environment (e.g., cool color palette in a cold environment) and suitable expressive methods, ensuring **ample space for personalized expression** without interference.

Fig. 2. Real-world still life, semi-structural still life sketch, and still life sketch interfaces from different XR perspectives.

3.3 Core Function Implementation

The system's functions are implemented using a Video-See-Through (VST) XR headset. All virtual content is rendered and superimposed onto the live video feed in real-time to ensure accurate registration with the real environment. The real-space perception function uses SLAM technology, fusing the device's LiDAR and RGB camera to build a 3D environmental map. By tracking the learner's position with IMU and visual algorithms at a 50 Hz refresh rate, the system maintains a crucial spatial positioning error of 5 cm. This precision prevents virtual structural overlays from visually detaching from the physical object.

Light source perception and simulation employ a **PBR engine**, supporting 3D adjustments for **azimuth, intensity, and color temperature**. Light/shadow calculations strictly adhere to physical laws; cast shadow length is precisely calculated using the geometric relationship:

$$\text{shadow length} = \text{object height} \times \cot(\theta)$$

This state updates in real-time as the learner moves, intuitively demonstrating the position-perspective-lighting relationship.

The real-time sketch conversion relies on a computer vision fusion algorithm. It first uses an improved Canny edge detection operator to extract contours, which are then optimized. The contour data and grayscale image are input into a lightweight style transfer network based on MobileNetV2 (parameter count reduced by 40%). The network's optimized low latency (<0.3 s) is vital for maintaining the real-time VST cycle and ensuring the observation-perception flow remains uninterrupted. Finally, the example drawing resource library contains 20 layered cases, displayed in a flexibly adjusted, semi-transparent floating window that supports dynamic recommendations based on learning progress (see Fig. 3).

Fig. 3. Dynamic Adjustment and Intelligent Recommendation of the Auxiliary Teaching Information Box.

3.4 System Environment and Hardware Configuration

The application was developed using the Unity Engine (version 2022.3) and the Mixed Reality Toolkit (MRTK). The core deployment device for the user experiment was the Pico 4 Enterprise headset (Qualcomm Snapdragon XR2). This hardware-software combination was selected to specifically meet the ±5 cm SLAM accuracy and the <0.3 s VST latency requirements demonstrated in Sect. 3.3.

4 Experiment

This study's methodological approach integrates two empirical studies—expert interviews and a small-scale user experiment—to validate the pedagogical efficacy of the proposed XR system. The research addresses three core questions regarding its contribution to broader domain concepts: **First**, how does a layered, XR-enhanced teaching framework affect students' overall learning outcomes compared to traditional methods? **Second**, what is the effect of XR spatial perception enhancement (structural overlay, dynamic light) on improving structural understanding and lowering cognitive load? **Finally**, what is the relationship between XR-mediated tools and the successful cognitive transfer of observational experience to subsequent physical artistic expression? The study was designed to sequentially gather qualitative feedback on system design and quantitative evidence on learning performance.

4.1 Experiment 1: Expert Interviews

This experiment involved **five experts with over 10 years of sketch teaching experience**, including three university art teachers and two senior art exam trainers. All participants possessed familiarity with the challenges of traditional sketch instruction and had basic experience with XR technology. The procedure consisted of three structured stages: **First**, experts were introduced to the system's design philosophy and core functions via a demonstration video. **Next**, participants used the system for 30 min, experiencing the three-layer teaching process. **Finally**, a 40-minute semi-structured interview was conducted, with all content recorded and transcribed for analysis. Interview transcripts underwent **Thematic Content Analysis**. Transcripts were open-coded and categorized under the three evaluation dimensions. Statements expressing consensus or clear trends were subsequently quantified to derive the reported percentages and synthesize qualitative insights into results.

4.2 Experiment 2: Small-Scale User Experiment

The experiment recruited **40 university students** (20 male, 20 female, aged 1822) with no prior professional sketch training, randomly assigning them to an experimental and a control group (n = 20 each). Baseline equivalence was established via a pre-test sketch of a plaster cone. **Scoring Criteria** used a comprehensive **100-point scale** across three dimensions: **Basic Modeling**(max 30), **Cognitive Deepening** (max 30), and **Creative Expression** (max 40). Scores were calculated as the average of two professional teachers' double-blind assessments. Independent samples **t-tests** confirmed baseline balance, showing **no statistically significant differences** ($p>0.05$) between groups across any dimension (see Table 1).

Table 1. Pre-test Score Comparison between Groups (Mean ± SD)

Ability Dimension (Max Score)	Experimental Group (Pre-test)	Control Group (Pre-test)	Significance of Difference (p-value)
Basic Modeling (30)	17.8 ± 2.3	18.1 ± 2.1	0.68
Cognitive Deepening (30)	15.5 ± 2.0	15.3 ± 2.2	0.73
Creative Expression (0–40)	22.3 ± 3.1	22.5 ± 2.9	0.85

The study spanned **5 days**: Day 1 for the pre-test, Days 2–4 for the intervention, and Day 5 for the post-test. Both groups completed 40 min of daily instruction (XR application vs. traditional). The XR system, built on Unity/MRTK and deployed on the Pico 4 Enterprise headset, was selected to meet the critical ±5 cm SLAM accuracy and <0.3 s VST latency requirements. Table 2 visually details the contrast between the XR and traditional intervention processes (see Table 2).

Table 2. Intervention Content Comparison: XR-Enhanced vs. Traditional Copying

Teaching Layer	XR System Presentation (Advantage)	Traditional Teaching Limitation	Clarified Learning Effect
Basic Modeling (Day 2)	Dynamic Light Simulation; Spatial Interaction	Teacher explanation; Textbook Copying	Overcomes "fixed perspective errors"; Quickly grasps volume/form
Cognitive Deepening (Day 3)	Structure/Perspective Overlay (X-ray View)	Relies on high mental abstraction	Directly visualizes structural principles; Reduces cognitive load; Enhances spatial understanding
Creative Expression (Day 4)	Real-time Style Conversion & Comparison	Lacks immediate feedback; Limited style exploration	Promotes style transfer and creative exploration; Provides instant feedback

Measurement and Result Clarification: Measurement metrics included drawing time and final quality (see Table 3). To ensure methodological rigor, we clarified the calculation of key data: The **32% increase in spatial perception scores** was calculated as the percentage difference between the Experimental and Control groups' mean post-test scores on the dedicated 'perspective and structural projection' sub-item, relative to the Control group's mean. The **75% cognitive transfer rate** was derived from the proportion of experimental group participants who answered "Yes" or "Strongly Yes" to a mandatory post-experiment self-assessment question regarding the successful application of XR observation experience to physical sketching (see Table 4).

Table 3. Comparison of Drawing Time between Experimental and Control Group

Group	Average Pre-test Time (minutes)	Average Post-test Time (minutes)	Time Reduction (minutes)
Experimental Group	38.2 ± 4.5	28.5 ± 3.2	9.7
Control Group	37.8 ± 4.3	35.2 ± 4.1	2.6
Significance of Difference	-	$p < 0.01$	-

Table 4. Dimensional Score Improvement Comparison ($\bar{X} \pm SD$)

Ability Dimension	Experimental Group (Post-test - Pre-test)	Control Group (Post-test - Pre-test)	Improvement Ratio (Experimental Group/Control Group)
Basic Modeling	9.8 ± 2.5	5.1 ± 2.0	1.9 times
Cognitive Deepening	12.6 ± 3.1	4.2 ± 1.8	3.0 times
Creative Expression	7.2 ± 2.8	3.5 ± 1.5	2.1 times
Total Score	29.6 ± 5.3	12.8 ± 4.1	2.3 times

5 Results

The experimental results integrate expert qualitative feedback, user quantitative performance, and system usability assessment. This section presents the findings sequentially and discusses them in relation to the research questions.

5.1 Expert Interview Results

Qualitative expert feedback confirmed the XR framework's effectiveness, particularly in addressing the cognitive challenge of **light and shadow dynamics** in relation to structure. Experts universally affirmed the **Cognitive Deepening Layer's** success, noting that the combination of spatial overlay and light source switching transformed abstract theory into perceivable and actionable spatial information. Expert C summarized this advantage: "The **dynamic lighting feature is crucial.** It allowed me to visually perceive the dynamic relationship between structure and light for the first time; it is far more effective than any textbook".

However, feedback also highlighted interaction limitations and necessary design modifications. While the **Spatial Walking Interaction** was praised for fostering multi-view observation, its **excessive frequency and necessity were questioned**, with Expert D noting it "can lead to fatigue". Regarding the **Creative Expression Layer**, experts endorsed the concept but suggested expanding its expressive possibilities. They felt the current functionality (style switching) made it function more like a **"renderer"** than an "active creation tool", lacking user control over elements like line or color. Expert A advised: "We need **more interactive features** to genuinely stimulate proactive artistic creation, not just offer style filters".

5.2 User Experiment Results: Learning Efficiency and Outcomes

The user experiment validated the significant advantage of the XR-enhanced intervention in both learning efficiency and final quality. Table 2, which visually details the differences between the XR and traditional interventions, provides direct context for these outcomes (see Table 2). Drawing Time Efficiency: Analysis of drawing time revealed the experimental group achieved a statistically significant reduction in task completion time, suggesting improved efficiency (see Table 3). Learning Outcome Comparison: Score analysis showed the experimental group's mean post-test score was significantly higher than the control group's (see Table 4), confirming the effectiveness of the teaching framework (supporting RQ1).

6 Conclusion

6.1 Results Discussion and Conclusion

To address abstract spatial and light/shadow challenges in sketch education, this study introduced an XR headset-based three-layer progressive framework (basic modeling, cognitive deepening, and creative expression). By integrating real-time sketch conversion, dynamic light, and spatial walking interaction, the system successfully bridged the theory-observation gap. Efficacy was strongly confirmed: the largest and most significant post-test score gain was in Cognitive Deepening ($t(38) = 4.21$, $p < 0.001$), with spatial perception increasing by **32%** (Table 4), validating that XR spatial enhancement resolves the challenging "light-to-structure" cognitive barrier. Furthermore, the Mixed Reality paradigm (real object + XR) proved highly effective for transfer, achieving a remarkable 75% cognitive transfer rate (vs. 42% for pure VR), mitigating cognitive disconnect and facilitating transfer to physical sketching. Despite positive learning outcomes, System Usability Scale (SUS) data highlighted the need for interaction optimization: feedback on spatial walking frequencysuggests finding a necessary balance between immersion and user comfort. This work provides an empirically validated, innovative model for XR art education, offering valuable practical insights for future technology-enabled content design.

6.2 Limitations and Future Work

This study's limitations guide future research in three primary areas. First, the limited scale and duration of the user experiment ($N = 40$,5 days) restrict the long-term generalizability of the findings; future work must involve larger cohorts and extended intervention periods. Second, the current scope was restricted to simple still life compositions; the system's efficacy requires further validation with complex, dynamic subjects (e.g., human figures). Finally, to enhance the objectivity of creative assessment, future research should integrate computational measures (e.g., complexity analysis) alongside the current subjective scoring methods.

Acknowledgement. This work was supported by the National Natural Science Foundation of China (62402281, 62361146854), the Fundamental Research Funds for the Central Universities (FRF-TP-25-036), and the Tsinghua-Tencent Joint Laboratory for Internet Innovation Technology.

References

1. Hillkurtz, A.: Sketching Techniques for Artists: In-Studio and Plein-Air Methods for Drawing and Painting Still Lifes, Landscapes, Architecture, Faces and Figures, and More. Rockport Publishers (2021)
2. Sorby, S.A.: Developing 3-D spatial visualization skills. Eng. Des. Graph. J. **63**(2) (1999)
3. Ivins, W.M., Jr.: Art & Geometry: A Study in Space Intuitions. Harvard University Press (1946)
4. Shan, W.: Study on sketch teaching in design specialty. In: 3rd International Conference on Culture, Education and Economic Development of Modern Society (ICCESE 2019), pp. 912–914. Atlantis Press (2019)

5. Wang, N.: The philosophy of "form" and "modeling" in sketching education. In: 2015 2nd International Conference on Education, Language, Art and Intercultural Communication (ICELAIC 2015), pp. 137–139. Atlantis Press (2015)
6. Ding, Y.: The relationship between space field and real space in art. In: The 6th International Conference on Arts, Design and Contemporary Education (ICADCE 2020), pp. 7–10. Atlantis Press (2021)
7. Edwards, B.: Understanding Architecture Through Drawing. Taylor & Francis (2008)
8. Rauschnabel, P.A., Felix, R., Hinsch, C., et al.: What is XR? Towards a framework for augmented and virtual reality. Comput. Hum. Behav. **133**, 107289 (2022)
9. Thoravi Kumaravel, B., Nguyen, C., DiVerdi, S., et al.: TutoriVR: a video-based tutorial system for design applications in virtual reality. In: Proceedings of the 2019 CHI Conference on Human Factors in Computing Systems, pp. 1–12 (2019)
10. Machuca, M.D.B., Israel, J.H., Keefe, D.F., et al.: Toward more comprehensive evaluations of 3D immersive sketching, drawing, and painting. IEEE Trans. Vis. Comput. Graph. **30**(8), 4648–4664 (2023)
11. Edwards, B.: Drawing on the Right Side of the Brain: A Course in Enhancing Creativity and Artistic Perception, 4th edn. TarcherPerigee, New York (2012)
12. Speed, H.: The Practice and Science of Drawing. Dover Publications, New York (1960)
13. Mogilevtsev, V.A.: Fundamentals of Drawing. 4art (2023)
14. Nicolaides, K.: The Natural Way to Draw: A Working Book for the Student. Houghton Mifflin Harcourt (1941)
15. Hale, R.B.: Drawing Lessons from the Great Masters. Watson-Guptill Publications (1964)
16. Pipes, A., Mittler, G.A.: Art in Focus. McGraw Hill Education (2006)
17. Drawing: A Complete Guide. Laurence King Publishing (2007)
18. Goldstein, N.: Drawing: A Contemporary Approach, 6th edn. Prentice Hall (2008)
19. Brommer, G.F., Kinne, R.M.: Art in Your World. Davis Publication (1993)
20. Berger, J.: Ways of Seeing. Penguin Books (1972)
21. An, Q.: Implementation of intelligent painting systems in art education as a way of developing student self-efficacy and involvement: post Lingnan Painting Spirit. Educ. Inf. Technol. **29**(12), 15173–15189 (2024)
22. Alnagrat, A., Ismail, R.C., Idrus, S.Z.S., et al.: A review of extended reality (XR) technologies in the future of human education: current trend and future opportunity. J. Hum. Centered Technol. **1**(2), 81–96 (2022)
23. Nurhidayat, M., Azhar, H.: The effectiveness of using augmented reality learning media in improving the ability to draw sketches. J. La Edusci. **4**(6), 450–459 (2023)
24. Asdiansyah, M., Sitompul, N.C.: Pengaruh project based learning dan Minat Belajar Terhadap Hasil Belajar Menggambar Bentuk (still life) Dalam Pelajaran visual art. Teknologi Pendidikan **5**(2), 119–128 (2020)
25. Antonietti, A., Cantoia, M.: To see a painting versus to walk in a painting: an experiment on sense-making through virtual reality. Comput. Educ. **34**(3–4), 213–223 (2000)
26. Sun, R., Wu, Y.J., Cai, Q.: The effect of a virtual reality learning environment on learners' spatial ability. Virtual Reality **23**(4), 385–398 (2019)
27. Yi, J.: A Conceptual Model of Enhancing Spatial Ability Through Immersive Learning Environment for Art Students
28. Hsu, Y.C., Tsai, M.J., Chang, Y.H.: The effects of immersive virtual reality on artistic creativity: a review of empirical studies. Educ. Technol. Soc. (2020)

29. Li, Z., Chen, X.: Sustainable development of diversified teaching mode from ecological perspective: a case study on metaverse-based landscape oil painting course. J. Multimed. Inf. Syst. **10**(3), 259–270 (2023)
30. Bäck, R., Plecher, D.A., Wenrich, R., et al.: Mixed reality in art education. In: 2019 IEEE Conference on Virtual Reality and 3D User Interfaces (VR), pp. 1583–1587. IEEE (2019)
31. Dafiotis, P., Sylaiou, S., Stylianidis, E., et al.: Evaluating uses of XR in fostering art students' learning. Multimodal Technol. Interact. **9**(4), 36 (2025)
32. Petersen, G.B., Petkakis, G., Makransky, G.: A study of how immersion and interactivity drive VR learning. Comput. Educ. **179**, 104429 (2022)
33. Williford, B.: Sketchtivity: improving creativity by learning sketching with an intelligent tutoring system. In: Proceedings of the 2017 ACM SIGCHI Conference on Creativity and Cognition, pp. 477–483. (2017)
34. Meccawy, M.: Creating an immersive XR learning experience: a roadmap for educators. Electronics **11**(21), 3547 (2022)
35. Liu, H.: Application and development of VR technology in painting. In: Journal of Physics: Conference Series, vol. 1744, no. 4, p. 042225. IOP Publishing (2021)

The Effects of Head Pitch on Translation Gain in Virtual Reality Environments

Hong-Ru Ji[1], Sen-Zhe Xu[2], Yang-Fu Ren[1,3](✉), Fang-Lue Zhang[3,4], and Song-Hai Zhang[1,3,5]

[1] Qinghai University, Xining, China
[2] University of Science and Technology Beijing, Beijing, China
senzhe@ustb.edu.cn
[3] Tsinghua University, Beijing, China
ryf21@mails.tsinghua.edu.cn, shz@tsinghua.edu.cn
[4] Victoria University of Wellington, Wellington, New Zealand
[5] BNRist, Beijing, China
fanglue.zhang@vuw.ac.nz

Abstract. Redirected Walking (RDW) in virtual reality relies on carefully calibrated translation gain to maintain a natural mapping between physical and virtual spaces. However, most existing gain strategies assume the user maintains a horizontal viewing direction, ignoring the potential effects of head pitch angle. This oversight can lead to perceptual bias and reduce redirection quality. In this paper, we investigate how the user's Point of Subjective Equality (PSE) and perceived threshold (σ) for virtual speed changes vary with head pitch. Using a psychophysical approach, we guided users through a speed discrimination task and collected speed perception judgments and subjective discomfort scores across seven pitch angles. Results showed that users tended to underestimate speed when looking upward (with significantly higher PSE), while speed was overestimated and σ decreased in downward conditions, indicating increased speed sensitivity. This trend held across scenes, though exact values varied. SSQ assessments further showed that upward views were more likely to induce motion sickness, whereas horizontal and mildly upward views were more comfortable. These findings reveal the impact of head pitch on speed perception and user experience, providing an empirical basis for adaptive gain control in VR.

Keywords: Virtual Reality · Redirected Walking · Translation Gain · Head Pitch Angle

1 Introduction

Natural walking is widely considered one of the most intuitive and immersive locomotion methods in virtual reality (VR), as it enhances spatial orientation, distance perception and user presence through real-world body movements [36]. However, practical implementation is limited by the constrained physical spaces

A. Hinkenjan et al. (Eds.): ICXR 2025, LNCS 16428, pp. 393–405, 2026.
https://doi.org/10.1007/978-981-95-7195-6_28

typical of homes, labs, or exhibitions, which rarely match the scale of the virtual environments (VEs) users are meant to explore. To address this mismatch, Redirected Walking (RDW) has been widely explored in immersive systems [17]. RDW specifically leverages the inherent perceptual inaccuracies that occur when users wear a head-mounted display, allowing subtle manipulations of translation, rotation, and curvature gains during natural walking without the user's conscious awareness. This provides continuous proprioceptive feedback and a more natural sense of movement, enhancing immersion and spatial awareness [27,31,34]. In contrast, other locomotion methods in VR, such as walking-in-place or turn-based techniques, do not exploit these perceptual limitations and cannot provide the same natural proprioceptive feedback. Consequently, RDW was selected to explore the role of head pitch in shaping locomotion perception.

In RDW systems, various forms of redirection gains have been proposed to subtly adjust the mapping between users' physical and virtual motion, thereby steering their trajectory in physical space while preserving a natural walking experience in the virtual scene [27]. Prior studies have examined them for redirection gains under standard conditions, they often assume an idealized posture in which users maintain a level gaze. However, in practical VR usage, users naturally vary their head pitch, and the potential effects of these variations on translation gain perception have not yet been systematically quantified.

Together, this body of work highlights head pitch as a critical factor in the integration of sensory cues underlying locomotion and gain perception in VR. To this end, we designed and conducted controlled user experiments to investigate the following research questions (RQ):

RQ1: How does head pitch angle affect users' point of subjective equality (PSE, μ) and perceptual sensitivity (σ) for translation gain?

RQ2: Are the effects of head pitch on gain perception (PSE and σ) consistent across different virtual environments?

RQ3: How does head pitch angle influence users' severity of motion sickness during VR locomotion?

2 Related Work

2.1 Redirected Walking: Techniques and Perceptual Thresholds

Redirected Walking (RDW) [27] subtly alters users' walking paths to expand the navigable area in virtual environments. Building on this concept, Steinicke et al. [32] classified RDW manipulations into three types of gains: translation gain, rotation gain, and curvature gain. Translation gain scales physical movement along the walking direction to alter perceived distance. Rotation gain adjusts the mapping between physical head turns and virtual scene rotation, affecting perceived angular motion. Curvature gain imperceptibly redirects users along a circular arc while maintaining the illusion of walking straight.

Subsequent work has refined RDW through adaptive gain models and investigation of gain interactions. Neth et al. [24] introduced a dynamic curvature gain approach that varies gain strength based on walking speed, enabling more aggressive redirection at lower speeds without detection. Grechkin et al. [9] showed that translation and curvature gains can be combined without significantly increasing perceptibility. Cho et al. [5] extended gain analysis to non-forward locomotion, demonstrating that curvature gain thresholds are more permissive during lateral and backward movements, while translation gain thresholds remain relatively stable across directions. Most recently, Xu et al. [38] proposed BiRD, a bidirectional rotation gain technique synchronized with natural head movement.

In recent years, several new types of redirection gains have been introduced, such as bending gain [16,29], jumping gain [21], and strafing gain [41]. The successful implementation of these novel gains has further expanded the possibilities of redirected walking, enabling users to navigate larger virtual environments through natural locomotion without the need for additional input devices [8,19,25]. Existing studies on translation gain perception typically require subjects to maintain a horizontal viewpoint in order to exclude interference from changes in viewpoint [4,20,33]. However, in real virtual reality use situations, users often walk with a non-horizontal viewpoint, which may have an impact on gain perception. Therefore, this study further investigated the effect of pitch angle on translation gain.

2.2 Algorithmic Techniques for Redirected Walking

In terms of algorithm design on RDW, researchers have explored various strategies that combine different types of redirection gains to guide user locomotion effectively. Razzaque et al. proposed three RDW strategies: Steer-to-Center (S2C), Steer-to-Orbit (S2O), and Steer-to-Multiple-Targets (S2M) [26]. Hodgson et al. proposed Steer-to-Multiple+Center [10]. These strategies aim to redirect users back toward the center or interior of the tracked space when they approach physical boundaries. Xu et al. [39] proposed a method to analyze a user's possible movement directions and positional redirection of walking through a series of standard postures, which reduces the number of resets, improving the accuracy of path planning. Li et al. [18] introduced a skeleton graph mapping approach to guide user navigation. Bachmann et al. [2] employed artificial potential fields to steer users away from physical obstacles and nearby individuals. Building on similar principles, Thomas et al. [35]developed the Push/Pull Reactive (P2R) method, which dynamically repels users from obstacles and attracts them toward designated targets.

With the advancement of virtual reality technology, the focus of redirected walking (RDW) has gradually shifted from single-user experiences to multi-user interactions. Bachmann et al. [3] and Azmandian et al. [1] proposed methods aimed at avoiding collisions between users in dual-user scenarios. To avoid user collisions, Dong et al. [7] and Jeon et al. [13] proposed methods based on dynamic user density and optimal space partitioning. These methods focus on avoiding collisions but neglect perceptual differences. This study examines how head pitch affects translation gain perception to guide redirected walking design.

2.3 Head Orientation Effects on Locomotion and Perception in VR

Head orientation, especially along the pitch axis, significantly influences motion perception and gait behavior in VR environments. Jaekl et al. [11] found that perceptual stability persists despite mismatches between visual and physical motion, with head pitch relative to gravity having minimal impact. Crane et al. [6] extended this by showing that while isolated head pitch had a limited effect, body tilt or combined head-body tilt biased translation perception, highlighting the vestibular system's reliance on integrated orientation cues. In immersive VR, adaptive changes in head pitch often emerge in response to visual uncertainty. For instance, Janeh et al. [12] reported increased downward head tilt under low translation gains, likely as a strategy to enhance optic flow.

Other studies have manipulated or controlled head pitch to investigate its role in perceived locomotion. Yamamoto et al. [40] and Meyer et al. [23] showed that visually induced pitch shifts can simulate slope walking without physical inclines. Redirection techniques [22] and gaze fixation tasks [15,28] further demonstrate that consistent head pitch aids in stabilizing motion cues, especially when peripheral feedback is limited. Shimamura et al. [30] linked subtle posture changes to perceived effort and embodiment, while Williams et al. [37] showed that high rotation gains disrupt natural head-gaze coordination, implicating vestibulo-ocular mechanisms. Despite these findings, there has been little systematic investigation into how head pitch angle affects users' sensitivity to translation gain.

3 Study of the Effect of Pitch Angle on Translation Gain

3.1 Pilot Experiment on Effect of Pitch Angle on Translation Gain

Our work aims to determine translation gain detection thresholds across pitch angles. First, we needed to verify whether pitch angle affects translation gain perception.

The pitch angles, translation gain ranges, step lengths, and virtual environment used in the pilot experiment were identical to those in the main experiment. Two participants with virtual reality experience were invited to evaluate their sensitivity to changes in translation gain under the various pitch angle conditions using a 2AFC (two-alternative forced choice) task [33]. The results showed that, despite the limited sample size, the points of subjective equality (PSEs) differed across pitch angles. Participants also reported feeling more fatigued at extreme pitch angles, both high and low. Therefore, in the main experiment, the pitch angles used were −60°, −40°, −20°, 0°, 20°, 40°, and 60°, where positive values indicate downward head tilt and negative values indicate upward tilt.

3.2 Apparatus

The main experimental equipment included an HTC Vive (basic version) headset, Unity3D, and SteamVR from the Steam platform. The computer used was equipped with an NVIDIA GeForce RTX 4060 graphics card, an Intel Core i7-7700HQ CPU, and 16GB of memory. To ensure the validity of the data and the comparability of conditions, potential confounding variables—such as the physical starting position, display settings, background illumination, and movement speed—were strictly controlled throughout the experiment. Photos from the user experiment are shown in Fig. 1.

3.3 Participants

All participants were students recruited from the university. A total of 20 subjects participated in our study, comprising 10 females and 10 males. Participants' ages ranged from 20 to 26 years, with a mean age of 24.15 and a median age of 24.00. All participants had normal or corrected-to-normal vision. Before the experiment, 2 participants had no prior VR experience, while 18 had some experience. All participants were right-handed.

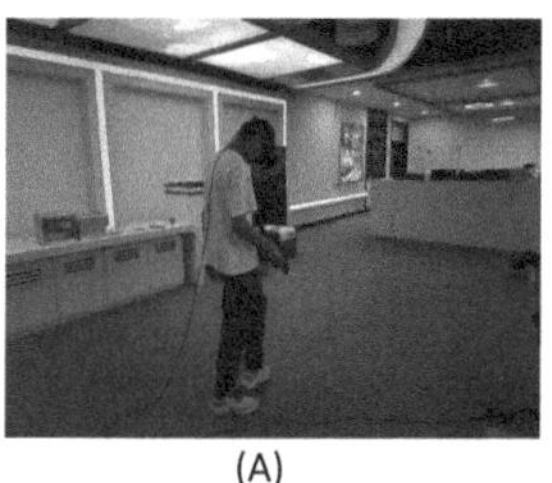
(A)
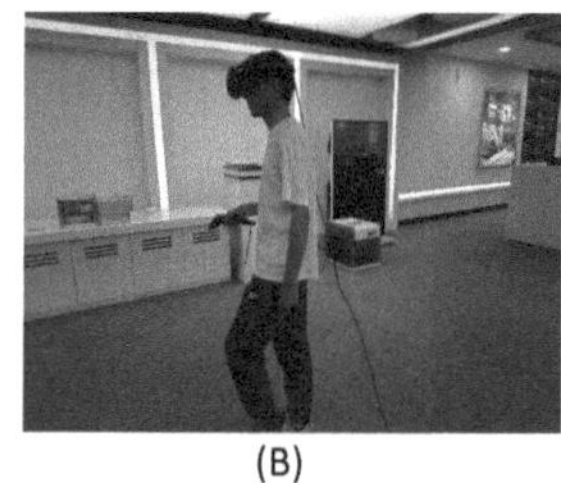
(B)
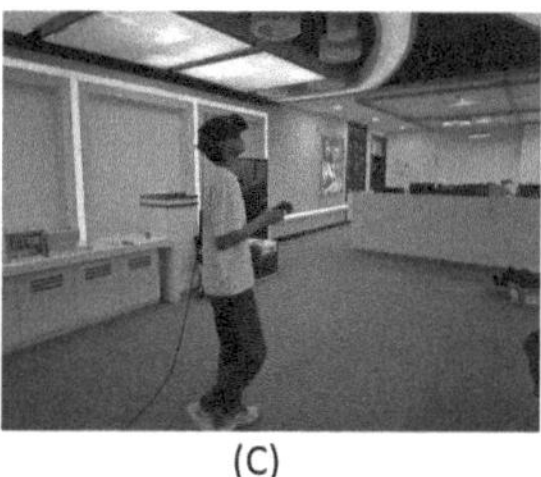
(C)

Fig. 1. Overview of the user study setup. (A) Downward view. (B) Horizontal view. (C) Upward view.

3.4 Experiment Design

To investigate the effect of pitch angle on users' perception of translation gain, we set seven pitch angle conditions in this study: –60°, –40°, –20°, 0° (level), 20°, 40°, and 60°. The seven pitch angles were determined based on pilot testing, aiming to systematically cover the full range of head orientations in VR. For each pitch angle, a tolerance range of ±10° was allowed to ensure the user's viewpoint remained approximately stable at the target angle during the experiment. A total of four types of virtual scenes (as shown in Fig. 2) and 11 translation gain values were used. The types of virtual scenes [42,43] are as follows: (1) high outdoor density, (2) low outdoor density, (3) high indoor density, and (4) low indoor density. The 11 gain values ranged from 0.5 to 1.5 in increments of 0.1.

Before the experiment began, participants were explicitly informed of potential adverse effects such as vertigo and nausea. Basic information, including age, gender, and VR experience, was collected via a questionnaire. Participants were also asked to complete the Simulator Sickness Questionnaire (SSQ) [14] before

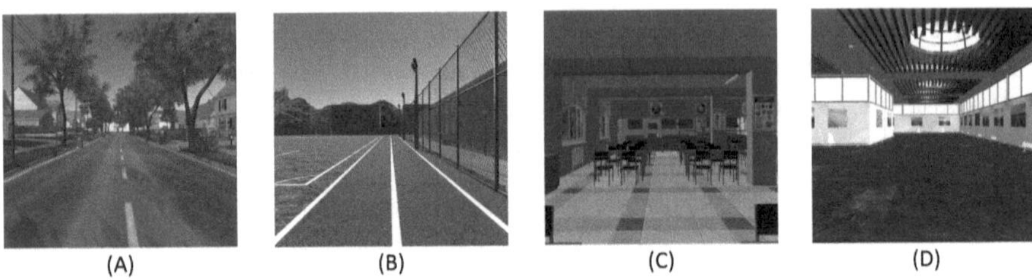

Fig. 2. The four virtual environments used in the experiment. (A) Scene A. (B) Scene B. (C) Scene C. (D) Scene D.

and after each pitch condition. We then explained the purpose and procedures of the study and assisted each participant in putting on the VR headset. Participants completed the task for each pitch condition, with a sufficient break to mitigate fatigue and VR discomfort.

During the experiment, For each pitch angle, four virtual scenes and 11 translation gains were randomly combined to form a trial set, repeated three times with randomized order to reduce learning and order effects. A visual cue (a small ball) assisted participants in maintaining the target pitch angle: the ball disappeared when the head pitch was within the target range and reappeared with size proportional to deviation. The cue vanished automatically within a $\pm10°$ tolerance to minimize visual interference while still providing necessary feedback (as shown in Fig. 3).

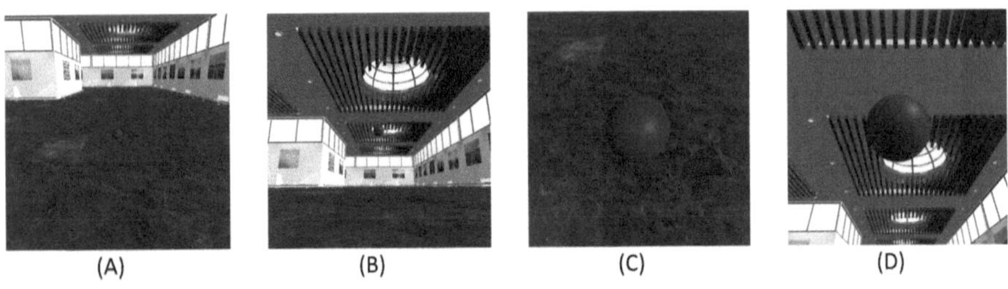

Fig. 3. Control of pitch angle deviations. (A) Downward pitch, $+5°$ from the target angle. (B) Upward pitch, $+5°$. (C) Downward pitch, $+30°$. (D) Upward pitch, $+30°$.

After adjusting the pitch angle, the user walks along the physical environment for four meters, and then a question about the feeling of virtual walking relative to physical walking appears through the 2AFC task "Was virtual walking slower or faster than physical walking?", choosing either "Slower" or "Faster". To minimize the possibility of bias and random responses, there is no "moderate" option in this setting. After the selection, a red arrow will appear in the user's current direction, and the user needs to be guided by the arrow to rotate it to coincide with the green arrow, and then the user will be redirected to the next virtual scenario for the next experiment.

4 Results

A total of 18,480 user response data points were collected in the experiment (7 pitch angles × 11 gain levels × 4 virtual scenes × 3 repetitions × 20 participants), along with 280 SSQ entries. To model the probability of a participant's perceptual response under different translation gain conditions, we applied a nonlinear least squares method to fit a cumulative Gaussian psychometric function, based on the error function (erf). The form of the fitting function is shown in formula (1).

$$P(\text{faster}) = 0.5 + 0.5 \cdot \text{erf}\left(\frac{x-\mu}{\sigma\sqrt{2}}\right) \tag{1}$$

Where x represents the translation gain, P(faster) is the probability that the subject reports "moving faster virtually". The parameter μ (Point of Subjective Equality, PSE) indicates the gain at which virtual and real speeds are perceived as equal, reflecting perceptual bias; The parameter σ (Perceptual Threshold, Just Noticeable Difference, JND) represents the smallest change in translation gain that a user can perceive, indicating sensitivity, with smaller values corresponding to higher discrimination. PSE = 1 serves as the baseline of no bias, PSE > 1 indicates underestimation, and PSE < 1 indicates overestimation of virtual speed.

In the process of data analysis, this paper is based on the Python scientific computing environment, and the `curve_fit` function in the SciPy library is used to perform nonlinear least squares fitting on the above model, so as to estimate the μ and σ parameters under each condition.

4.1 Characterization of Translation Gain Perception at Different Pitch Angles

In order to explore the characteristics of users' perception of translation gain under different pitch angles, we will analyze both the subjective point of equivalence (PSE) and the perception threshold (σ).

In this experiment, the PSE values were lower than 1 for most of the pitch angle conditions, indicating that users generally tend to overestimate the virtual velocity, i.e., they perceive the motion consistent with the real velocity at a lower gain. The perceptual threshold (σ) across different head pitch angles were below 1, indicating that participants were highly sensitive to translation gain changes under all tested conditions.

Psychometric functions were fitted to the 2AFC response data for each pitch angle to derive perceptual probability distributions (as shown in Fig. 4(A)). The results show a gradual decrease in PSE values from upward to downward viewing angles (as shown in Fig. 4(B)), and the change in perceptual threshold σ across pitch conditions was also plotted (as shown in Fig. 4(C)). The results showed that both the PSEs and perceptual thresholds (σ) were higher at upward viewing angles compared to downward viewing angles. This indicates that participants

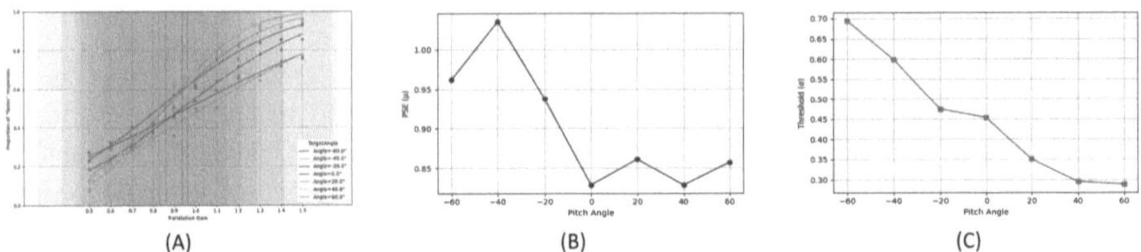

Fig. 4. Analysis of 2AFC results across seven pitch angles. (A) Psychometric curve fitting. (B) Point of Subjective Equality (PSE) variation. (C) Standard deviation (σ) variation.

were less sensitive to changes in translation gain when looking upward, requiring larger gain differences to perceive a change.

4.2 Analysis of Pitch Angle on Perceived Characteristics of Translation Gain in Different Scenes

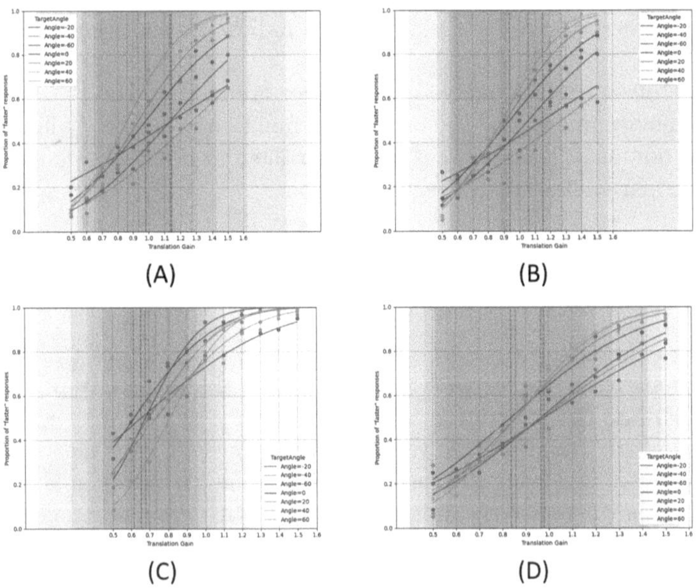

Fig. 5. Psychometric curve fitting of 2AFC data under four different virtual environments. (A)–(D) correspond to Scenes A–D, each showing the fitted curve across seven pitch angles.

In order to investigate whether the trend of the influence of the pitch angle on the translation gain perception (PSE) and perception threshold (σ) metrics is similar under different scene characteristics, this section compares and analyzes the PSE values and perception threshold (σ) metrics under different pitch angles in four different types of virtual scenes.

Figure 5 presents the probability distributions of perceived translation gain at different pitch angles across four scenario types. The corresponding PSE trends for these scenarios are shown in Fig. 6(A), revealing noticeable differences in how PSE varies with pitch angle. Figure 6(B) shows the trend of σ value with pitch angle in different virtual scenes. In different types of virtual scenes, translation gain perception exhibits scene-dependence. Specifically, in outdoor scenes, the PSE is higher than 1 under all upward-viewing conditions, indicating that users tend to underestimate their virtual movement speeds in such scenes; whereas the PSE is lower than 1 under both level-viewing and downward-viewing conditions, reflecting a certain degree of overestimation of speed. In contrast, in indoor scenes, the PSE remained below 1 in all the pitch angle conditions, suggesting that users were generally more likely to overestimate their virtual movement speed in indoor environments. Furthermore, for upward-looking conditions, σ was higher in outdoor scenes than in indoor scenes, likely due to the scarcity of nearby visual references in open environments. In contrast, σ under forward- and downward-facing conditions showed little difference between indoor and outdoor scenes, likely due to nearby visual cues dominating perceptual sensitivity.

4.3 Simulator Sickness Questionnaire

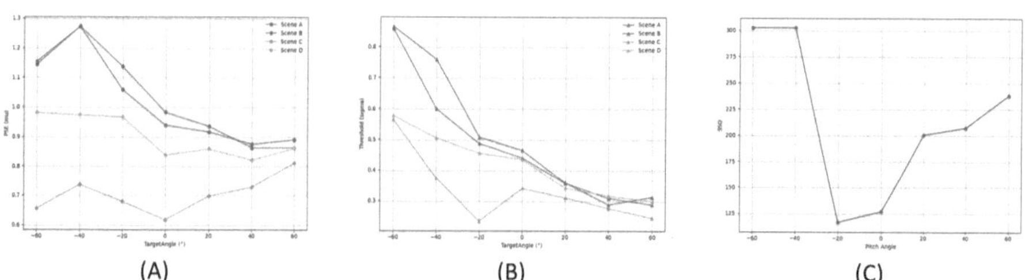

Fig. 6. Summary of variations. (A) PSE variation across four virtual environments. (B) Standard deviation (σ) variation across virtual environments. (C) Simulator Sickness Questionnaire (SSQ) variation across different pitch angles.

We analyzed participants' SSQ scores across seven gaze angles. Shapiro-Wilk tests indicated that none of the groups followed a normal distribution ($p < 0.05$), so a non-parametric method was used for overall comparison. Kruskal-Wallis test showed no significant differences among the seven angles ($\chi^2 = 1.214, p = 0.976$), indicating that participants' motion sickness scores did not differ significantly across angles. Figure 6(C) presents the total SSQ scores reported by participants under various pitch angles. The results show that users experienced the least discomfort at the horizontal viewing angle (0°) and the mildly upward angle (-20°). However, these differences were not statistically significant, indicating that participants' motion sickness responses were generally stable across the tested gaze angles.

4.4 Discussion

Head pitch and scene factors affect perception of translation gain in redirected walking, likely due to changes in visual perspective and spatial cues. Extending prior VR research on natural walking [36], these findings show that both user posture and environment influence locomotion perception, emphasizing their consideration in redirected walking to preserve naturalness and improve navigation.

5 Limitations and Future Work

Our work has some limitations. A small sample and narrow age range limit generalizability; future studies will increase sample size and age diversity. Measuring only discrete pitch angles with subjective questionnaires constrains understanding. Continuous angles and multimodal data could be used in future work. This study examined translation gain under specific head pitch conditions. It is subtle but common, and has often been overlooked in locomotion research. This study highlights its effect on translation gain perception. Future work could extend the investigation to broader VR scenarios to strengthen generalizability.

6 Conclusion

In this paper, we investigated the effects of different pitch angles and scene characteristics on the translation gain. We found that participants' sensitivity to translation gain decreased when looking upward, requiring larger gain differences to detect changes. Additionally, translation gain perception exhibited scene-dependence, with sensitivity varying according to the type of virtual environment. SSQ showed that users had the best experience under horizontal and mildly upward conditions, while extreme upward significantly exacerbated the symptoms of motion sickness.

Acknowledgments. This work was supported by the National Natural Science Foundation of China (62402281, 62361146854 and 62562052), the Fundamental Research Funds for the Central Universities (FRF-TP-25-036), and the Tsinghua-Tencent Joint Laboratory for Internet Innovation Technology.

References

1. Azmandian, M., Grechkin, T., Rosenberg, E.S.: An evaluation of strategies for two-user redirected walking in shared physical spaces. In: 2017 IEEE Virtual Reality (VR), pp. 91–98. IEEE (2017)

2. Bachmann, E.R., Hodgson, E., Hoffbauer, C., Messinger, J.: Multi-user redirected walking and resetting using artificial potential fields. IEEE Trans. Visual Comput. Graphics **25**(5), 2022–2031 (2019)
3. Bachmann, E.R., Holm, J., Zmuda, M.A., Hodgson, E.: Collision prediction and prevention in a simultaneous two-user immersive virtual environment. In: 2013 IEEE Virtual Reality (VR), pp. 89–90. IEEE (2013)
4. Bruder, G., Interrante, V., Phillips, L., Steinicke, F.: Redirecting walking and driving for natural navigation in immersive virtual environments. IEEE Trans. Visual Comput. Graphics **18**(4), 538–545 (2012)
5. Cho, Y.H., Min, D.H., Huh, J.S., Lee, S.H., Yoon, J.S., Lee, I.K.: Walking outside the box: Estimation of detection thresholds for non-forward steps. In: 2021 IEEE Virtual Reality and 3D User Interfaces (VR), pp. 448–456. IEEE (2021)
6. Crane, B.T.: The influence of head and body tilt on human fore-aft translation perception. Exp. Brain Res. **232**(12), 3897–3905 (2014). https://doi.org/10.1007/s00221-014-4060-4
7. Dong, T., Shen, Y., Gao, T., Fan, J.: Dynamic density-based redirected walking towards multi-user virtual environments. In: 2021 IEEE virtual reality and 3D user interfaces (VR), pp. 626–634. IEEE (2021)
8. Fan, L., Li, H., Shi, M.: Redirected walking for exploring immersive virtual spaces with hmd: a comprehensive review and recent advances. IEEE Trans. Visual Comput. Graph. **29**(10), 4104–4123 (2022)
9. Grechkin, T., Thomas, J., Azmandian, M., Bolas, M., Suma, E.: Revisiting detection thresholds for redirected walking: combining translation and curvature gains. In: Proceedings of the ACM Symposium on Applied Perception, pp. 113–120. ACM (2016)
10. Hodgson, E., Bachmann, E.: Comparing four approaches to generalized redirected walking: simulation and live user data. IEEE Trans. Visual Comput. Graph. **19**(4), 634–643 (2013)
11. Jaekl, P.M., et al.: Perceptual stability during head movement in virtual reality. In: Proceedings IEEE virtual reality 2002, pp. 149–155. IEEE (2002)
12. Janeh, O., Langbehn, E., Steinicke, F., Bruder, G., Gulberti, A., Poetter-Nerger, M.: Walking in virtual reality: effects of manipulated visual self-motion on walking biomechanics. ACM Trans. Appl. Percept. (TAP) **14**(2), 1–15 (2017)
13. Jeon, S.B., et al.: Dynamic optimal space partitioning for redirected walking in multi-user environment. ACM Trans. Graph. (TOG) **41**(4), 1–14 (2022)
14. Kennedy, R.S., Lane, N.E., Berbaum, K.S., Lilienthal, M.G.: Simulator sickness questionnaire: an enhanced method for quantifying simulator sickness. Int. J. Aviat. Psychol. **3**(3), 203–220 (1993)
15. Kruse, L., Langbehn, E., Steinicke, F.: I can see on my feet while walking: sensitivity to translation gains with visible feet. In: 2018 IEEE Conference on Virtual Reality and 3D User Interfaces (VR), pp. 305–312. IEEE (2018)
16. Langbehn, E., Lubos, P., Bruder, G., Steinicke, F.: Bending the curve: sensitivity to bending of curved paths and application in room-scale vr. IEEE Trans. Visual Comput. Graphics **23**(4), 1389–1398 (2017)
17. Lemic, F., Struye, J., Famaey, J.: User mobility simulator for full-immersive multiuser virtual reality with redirected walking. In: Proceedings of the 12th ACM Multimedia Systems Conference, pp. 293–299 (2021)
18. Li, H., Fan, L.: Mapping various large virtual spaces to small real spaces: a novel redirected walking method for immersive VR navigation. IEEE Access **8**, 180210–180221 (2020)

19. Li, Y.J., Steinicke, F., Wang, M.: A comprehensive review of redirected walking techniques: taxonomy, methods, and future directions. J. Comput. Sci. Technol. **37**(3), 561–583 (2022)
20. Luo, E.X., Tang, K.Y., Xu, S.Z., Tong, Q., Zhang, S.H.: Walking telescope: Exploring the zooming effect in expanding detection threshold range for translation gain. In: Zhang, FL., Sharf, A. (eds.) International Conference on Computational Visual Media, pp. 252–273. Springer, Cham (2024). https://doi.org/10.1007/978-981-97-2095-8_14
21. Matsumoto, K., Langbehn, E., Narumi, T., Steinicke, F.: Detection thresholds for vertical gains in vr and drone-based telepresence systems. In: 2020 IEEE Conference on Virtual Reality and 3D User Interfaces (VR), pp. 101–107. IEEE (2020)
22. Matsumoto, K., Narumi, T., Tanikawa, T., Hirose, M.: Walking uphill and downhill: redirected walking in the vertical direction. In: ACM SIGGRAPH 2017 Posters, pp. 1–2 (2017)
23. Meyer, M., Zank, M.: Walking of uphill slopes in immersive virtual environments. In: Proceedings of the 30th ACM Symposium on Virtual Reality Software and Technology, pp. 1–2 (2024)
24. Neth, C.T., Souman, J.L., Engel, D., Kloos, U., Bülthoff, H.H., Mohler, B.J.: Velocity-dependent dynamic curvature gain for redirected walking. IEEE Trans. Visual Comput. Graph. **18**(7), 1041–1052 (2012)
25. Nilsson, N.C., et al.: 15 years of research on redirected walking in immersive virtual environments. IEEE Comput. Graph. Appl. **38**(2), 44–56 (2018)
26. Razzaque, S.: Redirected Walking. Ph.d. thesis, University of North Carolina at Chapel Hill (2005)
27. Razzaque, S., Kohn, Z., Whitton, M.C.: Redirected walking. In: EUROGRAPHICS. The Eurographics Association (2001)
28. Reimer, D., Langbehn, E., Kaufmann, H., Scherzer, D.: The influence of full-body representation on translation and curvature gain. In: 2020 IEEE Conference on Virtual Reality and 3D User Interfaces Abstracts and Workshops (VRW), pp. 154–159. IEEE (2020)
29. Sakono, H., Matsumoto, K., Narumi, T., Kuzuoka, H.: Redirected walking using continuous curvature manipulation. IEEE Trans. Visual Comput. Graph. **27**(11), 4278–4288 (2021)
30. Shimamura, R., Kayukawa, S., Nakatsuka, T., Miyakawa, S., Morishima, S.: A study on the sense of burden and body ownership on virtual slope. In: 2019 IEEE Conference on Virtual Reality and 3D User Interfaces (VR), pp. 1154–1155. IEEE (2019)
31. Steinicke, F., Bruder, G., Hinrichs, K., Jerald, J., Frenz, H., Lappe, M.: Real walking through virtual environments by redirection techniques. J. Virtual Reality Broadcast. **6** (2009)
32. Steinicke, F., Bruder, G., Jerald, J., Frenz, H., Lappe, M.: Analyses of human sensitivity to redirected walking. In: Proceedings of ACM Symposium on Applied Perception, ACM (2008)
33. Steinicke, F., Bruder, G., Jerald, J., Frenz, H., Lappe, M.: Estimation of detection thresholds for redirected walking techniques. IEEE Trans. Visual Comput. Graph. **16**(1), 17–27 (2009)
34. Sun, Q., et al.: Towards virtual reality infinite walking: dynamic saccadic redirection. ACM Trans. Graph. (TOG) **37**(4), 1–13 (2018)
35. Thomas, J., Rosenberg, E.S.: A general reactive algorithm for redirected walking using artificial potential functions. In: 2019 IEEE Conference on Virtual Reality and 3D User Interfaces (VR), pp. 56–62. IEEE (2019)

36. Usoh, M., et al.: Walking> walking-in-place> flying, in virtual environments. In: Proceedings of the 26th Annual Conference on Computer Graphics and Interactive Techniques, pp. 359–364 (1999)
37. Williams, N.L., Stevens, L.C., Bera, A., Manocha, D.: Sensitivity to redirected walking considering gaze, posture, and luminance. IEEE Trans. Visual. Comput. Graph. (2025)
38. Xu, S.Z., Chen, F.X.Y., Gong, R., Zhang, F.L., Zhang, S.H.: Bird: using bidirectional rotation gain differences to redirect users during back-and-forth head turns in walking. IEEE Trans. Visual. Comput. Graph. (2024), to appear
39. Xu, S.Z., Lv, T., He, G., Chen, C.H., Zhang, F.L., Zhang, S.H.: Optimal pose guided redirected walking with pose score precomputation. In: 2022 IEEE Conference on Virtual Reality and 3D User Interfaces (VR), pp. 655–663. IEEE (2022)
40. Yamamoto, T., et al.: Mobius walker: pitch and roll redirected walking. In: SIGGRAPH Asia 2017 Emerging Technologies, pp. 1–2 (2017)
41. You, C., Benda, B., Rosenberg, E.S., Ragan, E., Lok, B., Thomas, J.: Strafing gain: redirecting users one diagonal step at a time. In: 2022 IEEE international Symposium on Mixed and Augmented Reality (ISMAR), pp. 603–611. IEEE (2022)
42. Zhang, S.K., Li, Y.X., He, Y., Yang, Y.L., Zhang, S.H.: Mageadd: real-time interaction simulation for scene synthesis. In: Proceedings of the 29th ACM International Conference on Multimedia, pp. 965–973 (2021)
43. Zhang, S.K., Tam, H., Li, Y., Ren, K.X., Fu, H., Zhang, S.H.: Scenedirector: interactive scene synthesis by simultaneously editing multiple objects in real-time. IEEE Trans. Visual Comput. Graph. **30**(8), 4558–4569 (2023)

DCT-SR: Single Image Super-Resolution via Deeply Coupled Transformer-Enhanced Network

Ya-Feng Du[1], Bing-Feng Seng[1,2](✉), Zheng-Jun Du[1,2], Shu-Hong Wang[2], and Xiao-Jing Liu[1,2]

[1] School of Computer Technology and Application, Qinghai University, Xining, China
sbf@qhu.edu.cn, Yafengdu@formail.com

[2] Qinghai Provincial Key Laboratory of Media Integration Technology and Communication, Xining, China

Abstract. Single image super-resolution (SISR) is a classic task in computer vision, aiming to reconstruct high-resolution (HR) images from low-resolution (LR) images. Deep neural networks (DNNs) perform exceptionally well on the SISR task by learning complex nonlinear mappings in an end-to-end manner. Transformer-based methods have made significant progress due to their ability to model global information, but the local receptive field of windowed self-attention limits their capacity to capture long-range dependencies, affecting the accuracy of detail reconstruction. To address these issues, this paper proposes a Deeply Coupled Transformer Enhancement Network (DCT-SR). DCT-SR extracts long-range image features through a deep auxiliary network, making full use of global context information; it designs an Adaptive Fusion Module (AFM) to dynamically calibrate the contribution weights of local features from each Transformer layer and the deep global features, achieving efficient local-global feature coupling; it introduces discrete wavelet convolution (DWT) to enhance shallow high-frequency feature representation, improving texture and edge detail reconstruction. Experiments show that DCT-SR significantly outperforms existing methods on multiple benchmark datasets, demonstrating its effectiveness and generalization ability.

Keywords: Single Image Super-Resolution · Transformer · Deep Auxiliary Coupled Transformer-enhanced Network · Adaptive Fusion Module

1 Introduction

Single Image Super-Resolution (SISR) aims to restore a clean High-Resolution (HR) image from a single degraded Low-Resolution (LR) image. Since mapping LR to HR images is an ill-posed problem with infinite possible HR images downsampling to the same LR image [1], the space of possible LR-to-HR mapping functions becomes huge. This makes learning a good solution in such a large space difficult, limiting learning performance. Thus, reducing the space of possible mapping functions to enhance SR model training is crucial.

A. Hinkenjan et al. (Eds.): ICXR 2025, LNCS 16428, pp. 406–417, 2026.
https://doi.org/10.1007/978-981-95-7195-6_29

Image SR techniques have evolved from early Markov random field and Dictionary Learning methods to advanced deep learning approaches. The rise of Deep Neural Network (DNN), particularly Convolutional Neural Network (CNN), has marked significant progress in this field as they effectively learn the LR-to-HR mapping function [2–6]. Recently, Transformer-based neural networks have outperformed CNN [7–9] in image SR by using self-attention mechanisms to better model long-range image structures. Despite recent advances in image SR, challenges remain. A key issue for SR Transformers is balancing satisfactory SR accuracy and computational complexity management. Due to the quadratic computational complexity of self-attention mechanisms, previous methods have restricted attention computation to local windows to manage the computational load. However, this window-based approach constrains the receptive field, impacting performance. While recent studies [7, 8] indicate that enlarging window sizes can improve the receptive field and SR performance, it exacerbates the curse of dimensionality. This highlights the need for an efficient way to model long-range dependencies without local window constraints.

Against this background, to alleviate the local window limitations in SwinIR, this paper proposes a Deeply Coupled Transformer-enhanced Network (DCT-SR). It introduces more information to mitigate the receptive field insufficiency of local windows. Specifically, the framework introduces information through improvements in shallow and deep feature extraction. In the shallow feature extraction stage, wavelet convolution modules replace traditional convolution modules. Convolution operations are performed on wavelet-decomposed features at different scales, with each convolution kernel focusing on different frequency bands of the input. This approach emphasizes low-frequency information in a larger receptive field while preserving details and acquiring more information. In the deep feature extraction stage, a deep feature auxiliary network is introduced. By inputting the LR image into this network, deep global features are obtained and dynamically fused with the features from the Transformer's feature extraction module through an Adaptive Fusion Module (AFM). This enhances the model's utilization of global context information and improves detail reconstruction accuracy. In this way, the proposed method alleviates the local window limitations of existing SwinIR and achieves better results.

Our contributions can be summarized as follows:

1. We introduce a deep auxiliary network to extract deep global features from low-resolution images. By using an Adaptive Fusion Module (AFM), we dynamically combine these deep global features with features from the Transformer's feature extraction module. This enhances the model's use of global context information and improves the accuracy of detail reconstruction.
2. We replace traditional convolution modules with wavelet convolution modules. Wavelet convolution performs multi-scale decomposition, increasing the receptive field. It also strengthens the capture of texture and edge details, and effectively preserves the key structural information of images.
3. We propose a new AFM method for fusing multi-scale features. Our network dynamically combines variable acceptance domains. This ensures that original feature information is faithfully preserved at each spatial resolution, making feature fusion more efficient and precise.

2 Related Work

In recent years, deep learning has shown great potential in image super-resolution, driving the field's rapid development [15, 16]. Since SRCNN [3] first applied CNN to image SR tasks, outperforming traditional methods, many researchers have explored architecture optimization to boost SISR performance [2, 4–6, 10–17]. VDSR [4] demonstrated the effectiveness of deep networks; DRCN[11] introduced recursive structures for enhanced feature reuse; EDSR [5] and RDN [17] improved residual block designs to fully explore CNN's potential in super-resolution.

With Vision Transformer (ViT) [18] and its variants [19–21] achieving breakthroughs in image classification, Transformer-based super-resolution methods emerged. IPT [22] first applied the Transformer architecture to general image restoration tasks. Subsequently, various innovative techniques optimized Super-Resolution Transformers: SwinIR [9] and CAT [23] used shifted window self-attention to balance computational complexity and performance; ELAN [24] grouped multi-scale self-attention improved multi-scale feature capture; ART [25] and OmniSR [26] sparse self-attention effectively expanded the receptive field. Explorations like pre-training strategies [25], ConvFFN [26] introduction, and large window designs[7] highlighted the growing adaptability and influence of Transformer architecture in image super-resolution.

As deep learning progressed, wavelet convolution [45], which combines wavelet transforms with CNN and shows excellent performance in multiple tasks, gained significant attention. By extracting multi-scale features, wavelet convolution effectively processes high and low-frequency image information, enhancing performance in image restoration, denoising, and super-resolution. Recently, combining wavelet convolution with CNN and Transformer further improved model performance. For instance, WTConv [47] expanded CNN receptive field via wavelet transforms while keeping parameter growth logarithmic. WaveletFormerNet [46] embedded wavelet transforms into Vision Transformers, reducing texture detail loss and color distortion caused by downsampling.

3 Methodology

3.1 The Overall Structure

As shown in Fig. 1, our network consists of four components: shallow feature extraction, deep feature extraction, deep auxiliary network, and image reconstruction. Specifically, given a low-resolution input $I_{LR} \in R^{H \times W \times C_{in}}$, we split it into two branches. One branch uses wavelet convolution to extract features $F_0 \in R^{H \times W \times C}$, while the other branch uses the deep auxiliary network to extract global features $F_1 \in R^{H \times W \times C}$, where C_{in} and C denote the number of input and intermediate channels, respectively. Subsequently, the features obtained from the two branches are fed into residual depth coupling blocks (RDCBs) for deep feature extraction. Finally, the resulting features are passed through a reconstruction module to generate high-

resolution output. As shown in Figure a, each RDCB contains multiple depth coupling transformer (DCT) blocks and a 3 × 3 convolution layer with residual connections. Figure b illustrates the model structure of the DCT module, which employs an AFM fusion module to integrate features from the two branches and feeds them into the next

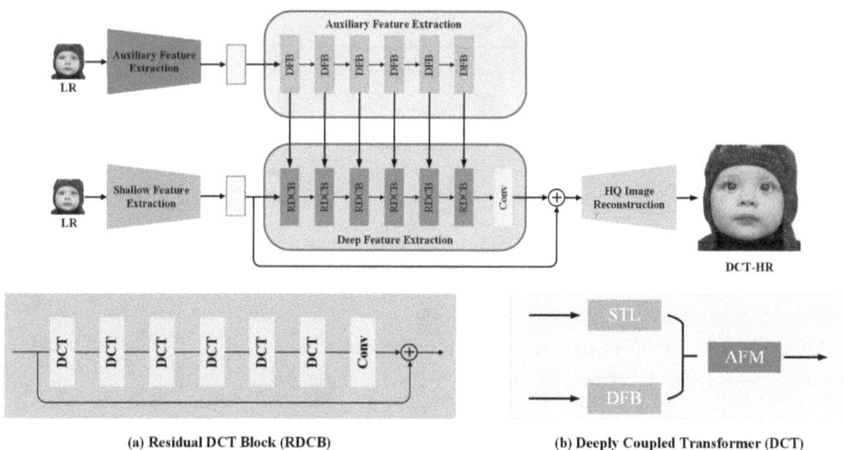

Fig. 1. The overall architecture of DCT-SR and the structure of RDCB and DCT.

DCT module. The reconstruction module utilizes pixel shuffle for upsampling of the fused features. We optimize the network parameters using a simple L_1 loss.

3.2 Haar Wavelet Convolution

In this work, we adopt the Haar Wavelet Transform due to its efficiency and simplicity[28–30]. However, our method is not confined to it as other wavelet bases can be used, albeit with increased computational cost. Given an image X, a one-level Haar Wavelet Transform (WT) in one spatial dimension (width or height) is performed via depthwise convolution with the kernels $[1,1]/\sqrt{2}$ and $[1,-1]/\sqrt{2}$, followed by a standard downsampling operator with a factor of 2. To perform 2D Haar WT, we combine operations in both dimensions using four filters, resulting in a depthwise convolution with a stride of 2:

$$f_{LL} = \frac{1}{2}\begin{bmatrix} 1 & 1 \\ 1 & 1 \end{bmatrix}, f_{LH} = \frac{1}{2}\begin{bmatrix} 1 & -1 \\ 1 & -1 \end{bmatrix}, f_{HL} = \frac{1}{2}\begin{bmatrix} 1 & 1 \\ -1 & -1 \end{bmatrix}, f_{HH} = \frac{1}{2}\begin{bmatrix} 1 & -1 \\ -1 & 1 \end{bmatrix} \quad (1)$$

Note that f_{LL} is a low-pass filter, while f_{LH}, f_{HL}, and f_{HH} are a set of high-pass filters. For each input channel, the output of the convolution:

$$[X_{LL}, X_{LH}, X_{HL}, X_{HH}] = Conv\left(\left[f_{LL}, f_{LH}, f_{HL}, f_{HH}\right], X\right) \quad (2)$$

has four channels, each with half the resolution of X in each spatial dimension. X_{LL} represents the low-frequency component of X, while X_{LH}, X_{HL}, and X_{HH} represent the

horizontal, vertical, and diagonal high-frequency components of X. Since the kernels in Eq. 1 form an orthogonal basis, the Inverse Wavelet Transform (IWT) is applied via transposed convolution:

$$X = Conv - transposed\left(\left[f_{LL}, f_{LH}, f_{HL}, f_{HH}\right], [X_{LL}, X_{LH}, X_{HL}, X_{HH}]\right) \quad (3)$$

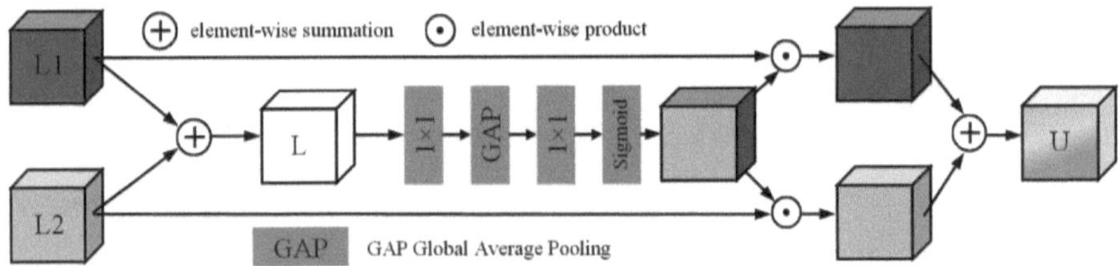

Fig. 2. Adaptive Fusion Module (AFM) schematic. It manipulates features from different resolution streams and performs aggregation based on self-concern to obtain relevant weights.

3.3 Deep Auxiliary Network for Feature Extraction

As shown in Fig. 1, we present a Deeply Coupled Transformer-enhanced Network (DCT-SR), whose deep auxiliary network leverages a pre-trained EDSR to extract long-range features from images. Given the input image x, the feature representation extracted by the EDSR network is denoted as:

$$F_{\mathrm{EDSR}}(x) = \mathrm{EDSR}(x) \tag{4}$$

where $\mathrm{EDSR}(x)$ indicates the process of feature extraction from the input image x via the pre-trained EDSR network. The resulting features $F_{\mathrm{EDSR}}(x)$ encompass rich global context information and long-range dependency features. This design of deep feature extraction lays a critical foundation for the subsequent local-global feature coupling. It enables the model to integrate global information more effectively, in turn improving the accuracy of super-resolution reconstruction.

3.4 Selective Kernel Feature Fusion

As shown in Fig. 2, we refer to HAFormer [48] feature fusion module to propose an Adaptive Fusion Module (AFM), aiming to enhance CNN feature representation by mimicking the visual cortex neurons' ability to alter receptive fields based on stimuli. The AFM module dynamically adjusts the receptive field through Fuse and Select operations to effectively integrate multi-resolution stream features.

The Fuse operator first performs an element-wise sum of input feature maps $L1$ and $L2$ from two parallel convolution streams to get the fused feature map:

$$L = L1 + L2 \tag{5}$$

Then, it applies global average pooling on L's spatial dimensions to compute channel-wise statistics:

$$s = \mathrm{GAP}(L) \tag{6}$$

The Select operator converts s into attention activations via the softmax function:

$$s' = \mathrm{softmax}(s) \tag{7}$$

It then adaptively recalibrates the original input feature maps $L1$ and $L2$ using $s\prime$. The recalibrated feature maps are summed to produce the final output feature map:

$$U = s' \cdot L1 + s' \cdot L2 \quad (8)$$

This design allows AFM to achieve more effective feature fusion with fewer parameters, thereby enhancing the network's expressiveness and performance.

4 Experiments

4.1 Experimental Setup

We use the DF2K (DIV2K [31] + Flicker2K [32]) dataset for training to avoid overfitting. We employ a pre-trained EDSR for deep auxiliary feature extraction. For the DCT structure, we maintain the same depth and width as SwinIR, with 6 RDCBs and DCTs, 180 channels, and a window size of 16. We replace traditional convolution with wavelet convolution, setting its level parameter to 1. We set the input patch size to 64 × 64 and use random rotation and horizontally flipping for data augmentation. The minibatch size is set to 32 and total training iterations are set to 500K. The learning rate is initialized as 2e-4 and reduced by half at [250K,400K,450K,475K]. We evaluate our method on five benchmark datasets: Set5 [33], Set14 [34], BSD100 [35], Urban100 [36], and Manga109 [37]. For quantitative metrics, we report PSNR and SSIM calculated on the Y channel. Following prior studies, we adopt a window size of 16 × 16 to enhance performance, especially on Urban100.

4.2 Ablation Studies

(1) **Effectiveness of WTConv and DCT.** We validate the effectiveness of the proposed WTConv and DCT through experiments. Table 1 shows the quantitative performance of × 4 super-resolution (SR) on the Urban100 dataset. Compared to the baseline results, WTConv and DCT achieve performance gains of 0.04dB and 0.06dB, respectively. Thanks to these two modules, the model's performance is further improved by 0.08dB. From the results, we can see that the model using WTConv has a larger pixel range and produces better reconstruction results. More pixels are nearly fully utilized across the image when DCT is employed.

(2) **Effects of Different Deep Auxiliary Network Designs.** We explore various deep feature auxiliary extraction network designs. Initially, using an Encode-Decode scheme resulted in a 0.15 dB performance drop compared to models without it. This suggests potential information loss and coupling issues after encoding and decoding. To address this, we retain only the feature extraction part of EDSR by fine-tuning its pre-trained model. As shown in Table 2, this approach improves performance by 0.08dB over SwinIR, confirming the effectiveness of our deep feature extraction network.

Table 1. Ablation study on the proposed WTConv and DCT.

	Baseline			
WTConv	×	√	×	√
DCT	×	×	√	√
PSNR	27.81 dB	27.85 dB	27.87 dB	27.89 dB

Table 2. Selection of depth assist modules

Structure	Encode-decode	ENSR
PNSR/SSIM	27.66 dB / 0.8284	27.89 dB / 0.8326

Table 3. The impact of feature fusion modules on the model

Structure	+ (Add)	AFM
PNSR/SSIM	27.46 dB/0.8246	27.89 dB/0.8326

(3) **Effectiveness of the AFM Module.** We compared AFM with direct feature addition in DCT. Table 3 shows that direct addition lowers performance due to inconsistent feature semantics causing mutual interference. In contrast, the AFM module, via Fuse and Select operations, dynamically adjusts the receptive field. It effectively integrates multi-resolution stream features, lessens interference in feature fusion, and uplifts the model's overall performance, confirming AFM's efficiency.

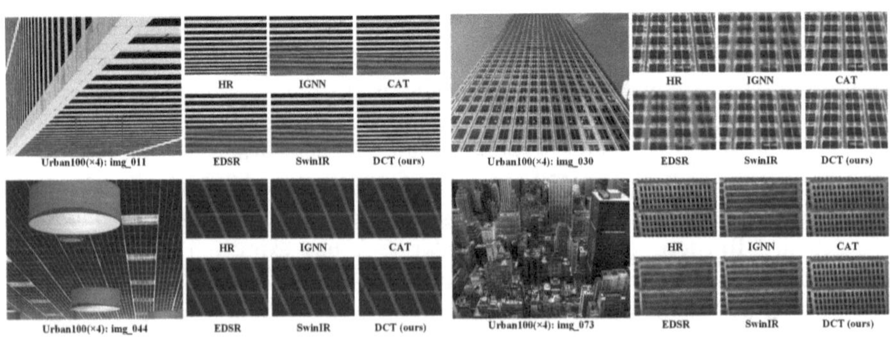

Fig. 3. Visual comparison on × 4 SR. The patches for comparison are marked with red boxes in the original images.

Table 4. Two-fold super-resolution results with existing models

Method	Scale	Training Dataset	Set5		Set14		BSD100		Urban100	
			PSNR	SSIM	PSNR	SSIM	PSNR	SSIM	PSNR	SSIM
EDSR	× 2	DIV2k	38.11	0.9602	33.92	0.9195	32.32	0.9013	32.93	0.9351
RCAN	× 2	DIV2k	38.27	0.9614	34.12	0.9216	32.41	0.9027	33.34	0.9384
SAN	× 2	DIV2k	38.31	0.9620	34.07	0.9213	32.42	0.9028	33.10	0.9370
IGNN	× 2	DIV2k	38.24	0.9613	34.07	0.9217	32.41	0.9025	33.23	0.9383
HAN	× 2	DIV2k	38.27	0.9614	34.16	0.9217	32.41	0.9027	33.35	0.9385
NLSN	× 2	DIV2k	38.34	0.9618	34.08	0.9231	32.43	0.9027	33.42	0.9394
RCAN-it	× 2	DF2k	38.37	0.9620	34.49	0.9250	32.48	0.9034	33.62	0.9410
SwinIR	× 2	DF2k	38.42	0.9623	34.46	0.9250	32.53	0.9041	33.81	0.9427
EDT	× 2	DF2k	38.45	0.9624	34.57	0.9258	32.52	0.9041	33.80	0.9425
DCT(ours)	× 2	DF2k	**38.57**	**0.9626**	**34.71**	**0.9263**	**32.57**	**0.9049**	**34.29**	**0.9453**

Table 5. Triple-fold super-resolution results with existing models

Method	Scale	Training Dataset	Set5		Set14		BSD100		Urban100	
			PSNR	SSIM	PSNR	SSIM	PSNR	SSIM	PSNR	SSIM
EDSR	× 3	DIV2k	34.65	0.9280	30.52	0.8462	29.25	0.8093	28.80	0.8653
RCAN	× 3	DIV2k	34.74	0.9299	30.65	0.8482	29.32	0.8111	29.09	0.8702
SAN	× 3	DIV2k	34.75	0.9300	30.59	0.8476	29.33	0.8112	28.93	0.8671
IGNN	× 3	DIV2k	34.72	0.9298	30.66	0.8484	29.31	0.8105	29.03	0.8696
HAN	× 3	DIV2k	34.75	0.9299	30.67	0.8483	29.32	0.8110	29.10	0.8705
NLSN	× 3	DIV2k	34.85	0.9306	30.70	0.8485	29.34	0.8117	29.25	0.8726
RCAN-it	× 3	DF2k	34.86	0.9308	30.76	0.8505	29.39	0.8125	29.38	0.8755
SwinIR	× 3	DF2k	34.97	0.9318	30.93	0.8534	29.46	0.8145	29.75	0.8826
EDT	× 3	DF2k	34.97	0.9316	30.89	0.8527	29.44	0.8142	29.72	0.8814
DCT(ours)	× 3	DF2k	**35.01**	**0.9323**	**31.03**	**0.8551**	**29.53**	**0.8158**	**30.14**	**0.8879**

Table 6. Four-fold super-resolution results with existing models

Method	Scale	Training Dataset	Set5		Set14		BSD100		Urban100	
			PSNR	SSIM	PSNR	SSIM	PSNR	SSIM	PSNR	SSIM
EDSR	× 4	DIV2k	32.46	0.8968	28.80	0.7876	27.71	0.7420	26.64	0.8033
RCAN	× 4	DIV2k	32.63	0.9002	28.87	0.7889	27.77	0.7436	26.82	0.8087
SAN	× 4	DIV2k	32.64	0.9003	28.92	0.7888	27.78	0.7436	26.79	0.8068
IGNN	× 4	DIV2k	32.57	0.8998	28.85	0.7891	27.77	0.7434	26.84	0.8090

(continued)

Table 6. *(continued)*

Method	Scale	Training Dataset	Set5		Set14		BSD100		Urban100	
			PSNR	SSIM	PSNR	SSIM	PSNR	SSIM	PSNR	SSIM
HAN	× 4	DIV2k	32.64	0.9002	28.90	0.7890	27.80	0.7442	26.85	0.8094
NLSN	× 4	DIV2k	32.59	0.9000	28.87	0.7891	27.78	0.7444	26.96	0.8109
RRDB	× 4	DF2k	32.73	0.9011	28.99	0.7917	27.85	0.7455	27.03	0.8153
RCAN-it	× 4	DF2k	32.69	0.9007	28.99	0.7922	27.87	0.7459	27.16	0.8168
SwinIR	× 4	DF2k	32.92	0.9044	29.09	0.7950	27.92	0.7489	27.45	0.8254
EDT	× 4	DF2k	32.82	0.9031	29.09	0.7939	27.91	0.7483	27.46	0.8246
DCT(ours)	× 4	DF2k	**32.92**	**0.9045**	**29.13**	**0.7958**	**27.97**	**0.7505**	**27.89**	**0.8326**

4.3 Comparison with State-of-the-Art Methods

Tables 4, 5 and 6 show the quantitative comparison of our method with state-of-the-art ones, including EDSR [5], RCAN [38], SAN [39], IGNN [40], HAN [41], NLSN [42], RCAN-it [43], and ImageNet-pretrained methods like EDT [44]. Our method outperforms others on all benchmark datasets. Specifically, DCT-SR achieves 0.39–0.48 dB higher than SwinIR on Urban100. This indicates that SwinIR has a larger performance gap compared to DCT-SR on Urban100, attributed to DCT-SR's ability to capture more structured and self-repetitive patterns. By expanding the information range, DCT-SR accesses more useful pixels for reconstruction, highlighting its effectiveness. The larger performance gap on Urban100 highlights our method's advantage in handling structured and repetitive patterns. We provide the visual comparison in Fig. 3. For the images "img 011", "img 030", "img 044" and "img 073" in Urban100, DCT successfully recovers the clear lattice content. In contrast, the other approaches all suffer from severe blurry effects. The visual results also demonstrate the superiority of our approach.

5 Limitation

While the aforementioned method delivers satisfactory performance under traditional single-degradation conditions, its effectiveness diminishes when encountering diverse or unknown degradation scenarios (e.g., DIV2K-RK, RealSR datasets), resulting in suboptimal super-resolution reconstruction outcomes in practical applications. Moreover, when dealing with highly compressed images, the method encounters performance limitations. Additionally, the inclusion of multi-layer residual networks in the selected architecture leads to longer computational inference times compared to other models, potentially compromising its performance in real-world deployment scenarios. These limitations primarily stem from the constraints of the chosen deep auxiliary network. To address these limitations, the approach can be improved by selecting alternative deep auxiliary network models and enhancing the fusion module.

6 Conclusion

This paper introduces DCT-SR, a novel single-image super-resolution framework. It combines a deep auxiliary network for global feature extraction with an Adaptive Fusion Module (AFM) to integrate local and global features effectively. Wavelet convolution replaces traditional convolution to enhance texture and edge detail capture. DCT-SR outperforms existing methods on benchmark datasets, showing significant improvements in detail reconstruction and texture preservation.

Acknowledgments. This work was supported in part by the National Natural Science Foundation of China (No. 62562052) and Qinghai University (SRT202561).

References

1. Ulyanov, D., Vedaldi, A., Lempitsky, V.: Deep image prior. In: IEEE Conference on Computer Vision and Pattern Recognition, vol. 1, pp. 9446–9454 (2018)
2. Dai, T., Cai, J., Zhang, Y., Xia, S.-T., Zhang. L.: Second-order attention network for single image super-resolution. In: 2019 IEEE/CVF Conference on Computer Vision and Pattern Recognition (CVPR) (2020)
3. Dong, C., Change Loy, C., He, K., Tang, X.: Image super-resolution using deep convolutional networks. IEEE Trans. Pattern Anal. Mach. Intell. 295–307 (2015)
4. Kim, J., Kwon Lee, J., Lee, K.M.: Accurate image super-resolution using very deep convolutional networks. In: 2016 IEEE Conference on Computer Vision and Pattern Recognition (CVPR) (2016)
5. Lim, B., Son, S., Kim, H., Nah, S., Lee, K.M.: Enhanced deep residual networks for single image super-resolution. In: 2017 IEEE Conference on Computer Vision and Pattern Recognition Workshops (CVPRW) (2017)
6. Zhang, Y., Li, K., Li, K., Wang, L., Zhong, B., Fu, Y.: Image Super-Resolution Using Very Deep Residual Channel Attention Networks, pp. 294–310 (2018)
7. Chen, X., Wang, X., Zhou, J., Qiao, Y., Dong, C.: Activating more pixels in image super-resolution transformer. In: Proceedings of the IEEE/CVF Conference on Computer Vision and Pattern Recognition (CVPR), pp. 22367–22377 (2023)
8. Li, Y., et al.: Efficient and explicit modelling of image hierarchies for image restoration. In: Proceedings ofthe IEEE Conference on Computer Vision and Pattern Recognition (2023)
9. Liang, J., Cao, J., Sun, G., Zhang, K., Gool, L.V., Swinir, R.T.: Image restoration using swin transformer (2021)
10. Gu, S., Guo, S., Zuo, W., Chen, Y., Timofte, R., Gool, L.V., Zhang, L.: Learned dynamic guidance for depth image reconstruction. IEEE Trans. Pattern Anal. Mach. Intell. **42**(10), 2437– 2452 (2019)
11. Kim, J., Lee, J.K., Lee, K.M.: Deeplyrecursive convolutional network for image super-resolution. In: Proceedings of the IEEE Conference on Computer Vision and Pattern Recognition, pp. 1637–1645 (2016)
12. Mei, Y., Fan, Y., Zhou, Y., Huang, L., Huang, T.S., Shi, H.: Image super-resolution with cross-scale non-local attention and exhaustive selfexemplars mining. In: Proceedings ofthe IEEE Conference on Computer Vision and Pattern Recognition (CVPR) (2020)
13. Mei, Y., Fan, Y., Zhou, Y.: Image superresolution with non-local sparse attention. In: 2021 IEEE/CVF Conference on Computer Vision and Pattern Recognition (CVPR), (2021)

14. Niu, B., et al.: Single Image Super-Resolution via a Holistic Attention Network, pp. 191–207 (2020)
15. Al-Mekhlafi, H., Liu, S.: Single image super-resolution: a comprehensive review and recent insight. Front. Comp. Sci. **18**(1), 181702 (2024)
16. Xiao, H., Wang, X., Wang, J., et al.: Single image super-resolution with denoising diffusion GANS. Sci. Rep. **14**(1), 4272 (2024)
17. Zhang, Y., Tian, Y., Kong, Y., Zhong, B., Fu, Y.: Residual dense network for image super-resolution (2018)
18. Dosovitskiy, A., et al.: An image is worth 16x16 words: Transformers for image recognition at scale (2020)
19. Chu, X., et al.: Twins: Revisiting the design of spatial attention in vision transformers (2021)
20. Liu, Z., et al.: Swin transformer: Hierarchical vision transformer using shifted windows (2021)
21. Wang, W., et al.: Pyramid vision transformer: a versatile backbone for dense prediction without convolutions. In: 2021 IEEE/CVF International Conference on Computer Vision (ICCV) (2022)
22. Chen, H., et al.: Pre-trained image processing transformer (20200
23. Chen, Z., Zhang, Y., Gu, J., Zhang, Y., Kong, L., Yuan, X.: Cross aggregation transformer for image restoration. In: NeurIPS (2022)
24. Zhang, X., Zeng, H., Guo, S., Zhang, L.: Efficient long-range attention network for image super-resolution. In: European Conference on Computer Vision (2022)
25. Zhang, J., Zhang, Y., Gu, J., Zhang, Y., Kong, L., Yuan, X.: Accurate image restoration with attention retractable transformer. In: ICLR (2023)
26. Wang, H., Chen, X., Ni, B., Liu, Y., Jinfan, L.: Omni aggregation networks for lightweight image super-resolution. In: Conference on Computer Vision and Pattern Recognition (2023)
27. Li, W., Lu, X., Lu, J., Zhang, X., Jia, J.: On efficient transformer and image pre-training for low-level vision. arXiv preprint arXiv:2112.10175 (2021)
28. Finder, S.E., Zohav, Y., Ashkenazi, M., Treister, E.: Wavelet feature maps compression for image-to-image cnns. In: Advances in Neural Information Processing Systems (2022)
29. Gal, R., Hochberg, D.C., Bermano, A., Cohen-Or, D.: Swagan: a style-based wavelet-driven generative model. ACM Trans. Graph. (TOG) **40**(4), 1–11 (2021)
30. Huang, H., He, R., Sun, Z., Tan, T.: Wavelet-srnet: a wavelet-based CNN for multiscale face super resolution. In: Proceedings of the IEEE International Conference on Computer Vision, pp. 1689–1697 (2017)
31. Lim, B., Son, S., Kim, H., Nah, S., Lee, K.M.: Enhanced deep residual networks for single image super-resolution. In: Proceedings of the IEEE conference on computer vision and pattern recognition workshops, pp. 136–144 (2017)
32. Timofte, R., Agustsson, E., Gool, L.V., Yang, M., Zhang, L.: Ntire 2017 challenge on single image super-resolution: Methods and results. In: Proceedings ofthe IEEE conference on computer vision and pattern recognition workshops, pp. 114–125 (2017)
33. Bevilacqua, M., Roumy, A., Guillemot, C., Alberi-Morel, M.L.: Low-complexity single-image super-resolution based on nonnegative neighbor embedding (2012)
34. Zeyde, R., Elad, M., Protter, M.: On single image scale-up using sparse-representations. In: International conference on curves and surfaces, pp. 711–730. Springer, Cham (2010)
35. Martin, D., Fowlkes, C., Tal, D., Malik, J.: A database of human segmented natural images and its application to evaluating segmentation algorithms and measuring ecological statistics. In: Proceedings Eighth IEEE International Conference on Computer Vision. ICCV 2001, vol. 2, pp. 416–423. IEEE (2001)
36. Huang, J.-B., Singh, A., Ahuja, N.: Single image super-resolution from transformed self-exemplars. In: Proceedings of the IEEE conference on computer vision and pattern recognition, pp. 5197–5206 (2015)

37. Matsui, Y., et al.: Sketch-based manga retrieval using manga109 dataset. Multimedia Tools Appl. **76**(20), 21811–21838 (2017)
38. Zhang, Y., Li, K., Li, K., Wang, L., Zhong, B., Fu, Y.: Image super-resolution using very deep residual channel attention networks. In: Proceedings of the European conference on computer vision (ECCV), pp. 286–301 (2018)
39. Dai, T., Cai, J., Zhang, Y., Xia, S.-T., Zhang, L.: Second-order attention network for single image super-resolution. In: Proceedings of the IEEE/CVF conference on computer vision and pattern recognition, pp. 11065–11074 (2019)
40. Zhou, S., Zhang, J., Zuo, W., Loy, C.C.: Cross-scale internal graph neural network for image super-resolution. Adv. Neural Inf. Process. Syst. **33**, 3499–3509 (2020)
41. Niu, B., et al.: Single image super-resolution via a holistic attention network. In: European conference on computer vision, pp. 191–207. Springer, Cham (2020)
42. Mei, Y., Fan, Y., Zhou, Y.: Image superresolution with non-local sparse attention. In: Proceedings of the IEEE/CVF Conference on Computer Vision and Pattern Recognition, pp. 3517–3526 (2021)
43. Lin, Z., et al.: Revisiting rcan: Improved training for image super-resolution (2022)
44. Li, W., Lu, X., Lu, J., Zhang, X., Jia, J.: On efficient transformer and image pre-training for lowlevel vision (2021)
45. Shahaf, F., et al.: Wavelet convolutions for large receptive fields. In: European Conference on Computer Vision. Springer, Cham (2024)
46. Zhang, S., Tao, Z., Lin, S.: WaveletFormerNet: a Transformer-based wavelet network for real-world non-homogeneous and dense fog removal. Image Vis. Comput. **146**, 105014 (2024)
47. Guanwei, J., Xu, L., Zhu, L.: WTConv-Adapter: wavelet transform convolution adapter for parameter efficient transfer learning of object detection ConvNets. In: Eighth International Conference on Video and Image Processing (ICVIP 2024). Vol. 13558. SPIE (2025)
48. Xu, Guoan, et al. "Haformer: Unleashing the power of hierarchy-aware features for lightweight semantic segmentation." IEEE Transactions on Image Processing (2024)

Personalized Visiting Route Generation for Virtual Museums Based on Large-Scale Models

Yuhan Duan and Lili Wang(✉)

State Key Laboratory of Virtual Reality Technology and Systems, School of Computer Science and Engineering, Beihang University, Beijing 100191, China
{zy2506305,wanglily}@buaa.edu.cn

Abstract. Virtual museums, as key platforms for cultural dissemination, struggle with non-personalized visiting routes and limited immersive experiences. Large-scale models, with their natural language processing and image understanding capabilities, offer solutions by enabling intelligent Q&A and image analysis. This paper presents a personalized visiting route generation system for virtual museums based on large-scale models. The system optimizes routes through three main components: (1) sampling point generation and scoring using LVLMs; (2) route generation and smoothing based on user interests; and (3) dynamic route optimization via user feedback and LLMs. It leverages the traveling salesman problem and A* algorithm for efficient route planning, and enhances user interaction through voice input and virtual reality visualization. This paper also designs user experiments to qualitatively and quantitatively demonstrate the effectiveness and convenience of the method. Results show significant improvements in user satisfaction and personalized experience.

Keywords: Large-Scale Models · Human-computer interaction · Virtual reality · Route generation

1 Introduction

With the rapid development of VR and AR technologies, virtual museums have emerged as a novel form of cultural dissemination. However, most visitors are still confined to fixed touring routes, which undermines immersion. The lack of personalization and automation in the touring experience further diminishes user engagement.

We innovatively apply large-scale models to the generation and optimization of virtual museum tour routes, focusing on developing an intelligent, dynamic, and interactive virtual museum tour route generation system. The system first analyzes the scene, then leverages the natural language processing capabilities of large language models(LLMs) to understand and process user intentions. Specifically, our contributions are threefold:

A. Hinkenjan et al. (Eds.): ICXR 2025, LNCS 16428, pp. 418–429, 2026.
https://doi.org/10.1007/978-981-95-7195-6_30

- A novel pipeline for virtual museum tour route generation based on large-scale models.
- Sampling point generation and scoring using large visual-language models(LVLMs).
- Dynamic route optimization via user feedback and large language models(LLMs).

2 Related Work

2.1 Scene Navigation

Scene navigation technology aids efficient target locating. Wang Lili et al. propose a method to automatically determine the number and location of portals and reduce back-tracing [18]. Wang Miao et al. merge isolated rooms into an integrated environment, allowing users to actively shuttle between different rooms [19]. Goal-driven visual navigation is also a core focus.Zhu Yuke et al. apply deep RL for generalizable indoor navigation, which achieves generalization capabilities for new targets and scenes [24]. Hongcheng Wang et al. propose the Demand-Driven Navigation (DDN) task, which aims to find objects without the exact names. Wang et al. propose a method to extract and align textual attribute characteristics with visual attribute features using the CLIP model to enhance scene perception during navigation [17].

2.2 Camera Path Planning

The quality of path planning algorithms is key to determining the user navigation experience. Early classic path planning algorithms include the Dijkstra algorithm [5], A* algorithm [6], and RRT algorithm [9]. With the advancement of neural networks, they have been increasingly integrated into path planning research. Chen et al. proposed a topology planning method based on the Transformer, which integrates visual and language information to generate better camera paths [4]. Some studies focus on generating camera trajectories that better align with human intentions and aesthetic standards. Li et al. proposed the Director3D framework, which uses a Transformer model to model the distribution of camera trajectories and can effectively generate camera trajectories and 3D scenes in the real world [10]. Jiang Hongda et al. addressed the problem of camera trajectory planning in virtual cinematography by using example videos to control the desired shooting methods and achieved camera trajectory prediction in new scenes [8].

2.3 Large Models

Large Language Models. From 2019 to 2023, GPT-2/3/4 demonstrated the generative and generalization power of LLMs [2,12,13]. Subsequent works—LLMR, SonifyAR, DynaVis and UFO extend the same paradigm to 3D scenes, sound, visual editing, and OS control [14–16,23]. Li's SituationAdapt further injects visual context, enabling real-time multimodal optimization of MR layouts and showcasing the potential of unified large-model reasoning in immersive environments [11].

3 Methodology

3.1 Overview

We design a personalized tour route generation system, leveraging the natural language processing and image understanding capabilities of large-scale models to analyze scenes and automatically generate tour routes for users. As shown in Fig. 1, it first analyzes the scene and selects camera poses to capture key images. LVLMs then score these images to create an initial route. After the user chooses a starting point, a personal path is instantiated. During the visit, voice feedback on needs is processed, enabling the system to dynamically adjust the route.

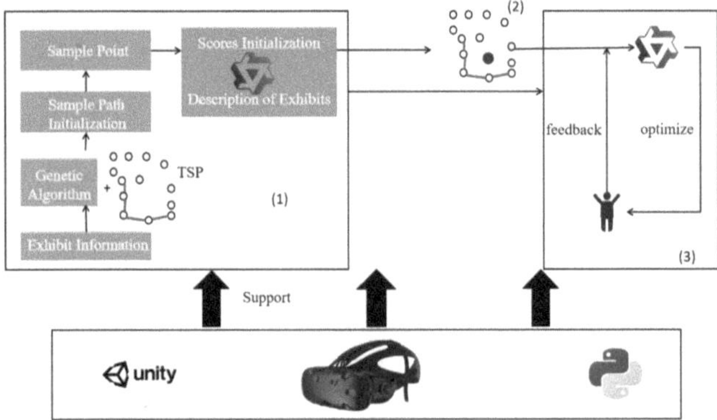

Fig. 1. System Architecture.(1) Sampling point generation and scoring using large visual-language models.(2) Route generation and smoothing based on user interests. and (3) Dynamic route optimization via user feedback and large language models

3.2 Sampling Point Generation and Scoring Using LVLMs

Sampling Path Initialization Based on Scene Analysis As shown in Fig. 2 and Fig. 3, invalid sampling points are those from which no exhibits are visible, while valid sampling points are those that clearly show exhibits. The higher the proportion of valid sampling points, the higher the degree of data effectiveness processed by the system (Fig. 4). As shown in Fig. 5, a View includes an angle(camera rotation), and a score, which represents the score of the image obtained by sampling at this point. Each sampling point includes a position, a target exhibit and three Views. Thus, scoring images becomes the problem of how to construct sampling points. The algorithm defines the R-point of an exhibit as a special sampling point. Its position is obtained by displacing the exhibit's mesh center along its forward vector:

Fig. 2. Invalid Sampling Points.

Fig. 3. Valid Sampling Points.

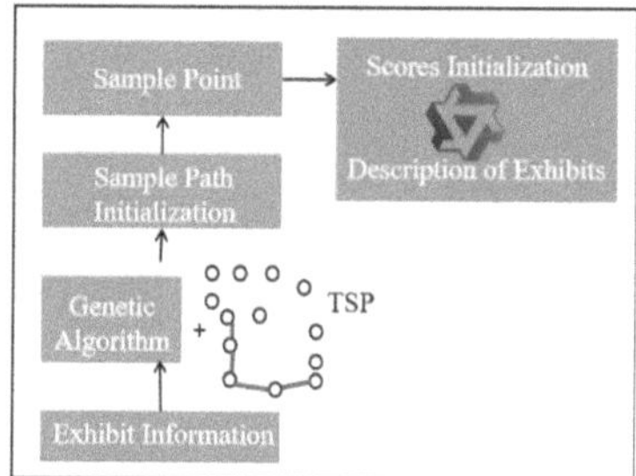

Fig. 4. Sampling Point Generation and Scoring Using LVLMs

$$Position = Target_{meshCenter} + Target_{forward} * s \tag{1}$$

$$s = 0.8 * ActualSize/0.6336 \tag{2}$$

The constants 0.8 and 0.6336 were determined by manually tuning s for each object in our sample scene and then fitting the resulting optimal distances to the objects' actual sizes.

We formulate the exhibit-visiting-order problem as a Traveling Salesman Problem and employ a heuristic genetic algorithm to solve it [22]. The entire scene is partitioned into multiple square grids(*MapGrid*). The size of each *MapGrid* is 0.3 m × 0.3 m(according to the average object size in the sample scene). These $MapGrids$ are used as nodes in the A* algorithm to generate a rough path using $orders$ [6]. The final output is a *MapGrid_path* as illustrated in Fig. 6.

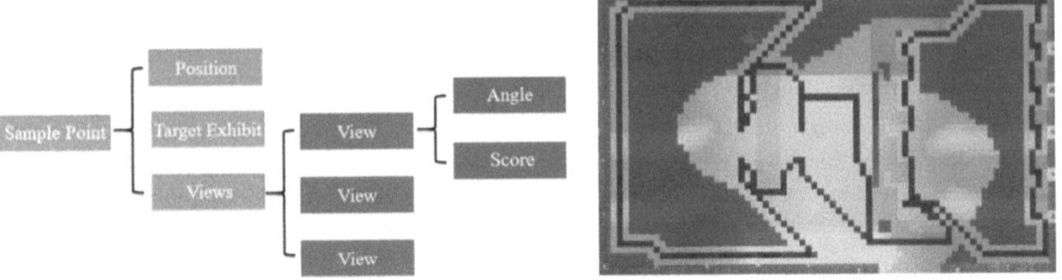

Fig. 5. Sampling Point Structure.

Fig. 6. Generated Rough Path.

Sampling Point Generation. The sampling area is defined as a collection of *MapGrid* centered on the *MapGrid* that contains the R-point, forming a square of size $(2R+1)\times(2R+1)$. This area is constructed dynamically along the coarse path produced by the A* algorithm and the set of R-points. From each area we generate k sampling points: one central point (coinciding with the R-point) and two additional points drawn uniformly at random within the area. Empirical tests show that $k = 3$ minimizes the total number of sampling points while still guaranteeing that every exhibit is captured. The central sampling point is determined by the position of the R-point, while the two random sampling points are randomly generated within the sampling area. The camera at each sampling point looks along the vector $\mathbf{v}_1$ from the point to its assigned exhibit. Through the entire algorithm, the effective rate of sampling points can reach 100% for every scene.

Scoring Initialization Based on LVLMs. During the scoring initialization phase, the LVLMs need to complete two tasks: (1) exhibit-content understanding, carried out by the Exhibit-Understanding Agent, and (2) viewpoint scoring, carried out by the Scoring Agent. The system-level prompt provided to the exhibit understanding Agent instructs the LVLMs to focus on the type, appearance, color, and content of the exhibit, and to respond in a fixed format. In the second task, Sampling points with low scores and unsuitable viewpoints can be preliminarily filtered out.

3.3 Route Generation and Smoothing Based on User Interest

After obtaining the scores, users can freely select a starting point I. The system locates the nearest sampling point P and designates its associated sampling area as the initial area A_0. Starting from A_0, the system visits all sampling areas in sequence according to *orders* $(A_1, \ldots, A_n)$, generating the tour path. First, the camera performs a smooth transition from I to P_0. Within each area A_i the point with the highest score is selected as the key sampling point P_i. The ordered sequence $\{P_i\}_{i=0}^{n}$ thus constitutes the critical way-points of the final path. Since A* plans by cost, we label colliders (walls, display cases, pillars) as occupied and others as free. The transition cost from any free cell to an occupied cell is set to

∞, thus guaranteeing obstacle avoidance. Using P_i as the starting point and P_{i+1} as the endpoint, the system successively generates a smooth path using cubic spline interpolation algorithm. The algorithm controls the overall speed based on the average score of all sampling points: the higher the average score, the slower the movement speed during the tour.

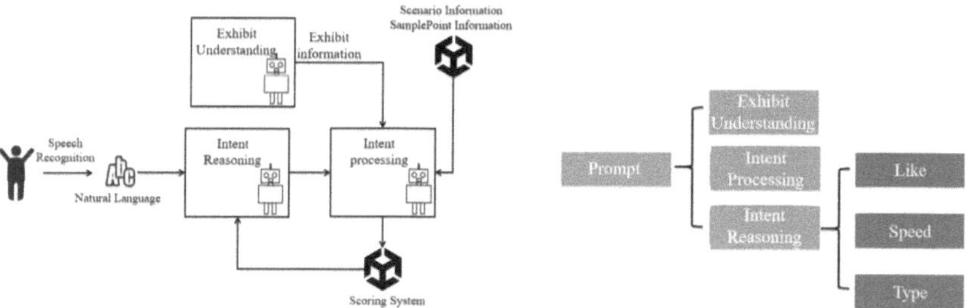

Fig. 7. Dynamic Route Optimization via User Feedback and LLMs.

Fig. 8. Prompt Structure.

3.4 Dynamic Route Optimization via User Feedback and LLMs

As shown in the workflow in Fig. 7, the Intent-Reasoning Agent(IR Agent) first identifies the user's intentions. The IR Agent categorizes user feedback into different types (preference adjustment, viewpoint adjustment, path adjustment, and touring speed). The IR Agent combines the inferred intentions with scene information and sampling point information in an appropriate format and passes them to the Intent Processing Agent(IP Agent). The IP Agent then formulates corresponding processing strategies based on the type of user feedback. As shown in Fig. 8, depending on different tasks, we design four different system-level prompts, corresponding to the Scoring Agent, Exhibit Understanding Agent(EU Agent), IR Agent and IP Agent. During the development of the system, it was found that the LLMs performs poorly with multi-step historical records; overly long historical records can cause the model to forget the initial task and produce unpredictable responses. We therefore preset core prompts for various questions, abandoning historical records each time a question is asked, and using the core prompt combined with the current question for inquiry. Taking the IR prompt as an example, every prompt we design follows two scientific principles: Clarity: instructions must be explicit, specific, and unambiguous; Structure: titles, lists and delimiters are used to organize the prompt so the model can parse complex commands more easily and return equally structured, logical outputs [20]. As shown in Fig. 9, we first apply the "persona pattern" by assigning the model an expert identity, establishing a clear framework for its subsequent reasoning [21]. Next, we explicitly enumerate all intent categories. We then specify the required input and output formats. Finally, following Brown's few-shot prompting principle, we provide a small set of concrete input-output examples to let the model learn by imitation and improve the performance [3].

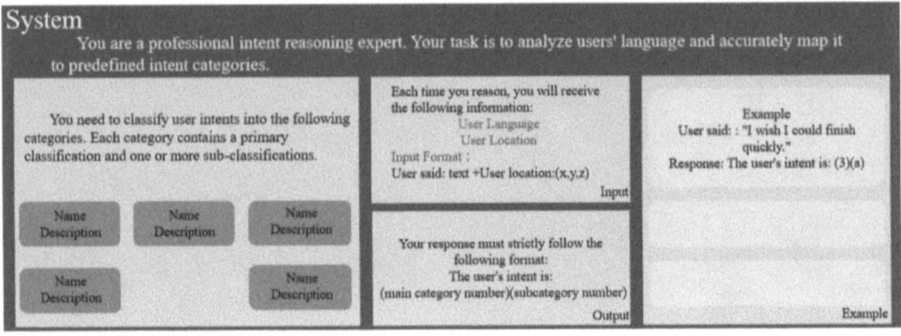

Fig. 9. Prompt Structure

4 User Experiment

4.1 Experimental Design and Content

Participants and Environment. A total of 32 volunteers aged 18 to 24 with basic computer skills were recruited; seven had prior experience with VR applications. The experimental scene was a two-storey, richly furnished virtual museum displaying ancient paintings, abstract art, photography and sculpture. The LVLM used in the experiment is Qwen-VL-Max, and the LLM is Qwen-QwQ.

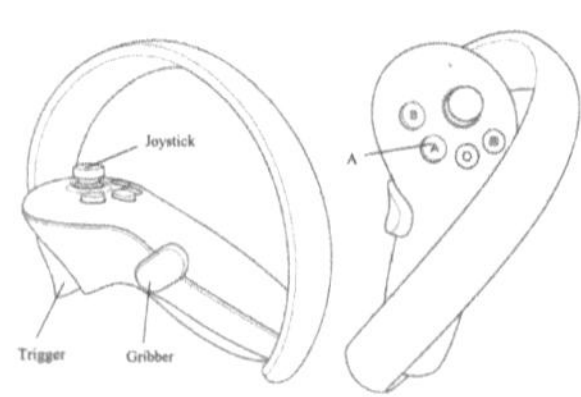

Fig. 10. Controller Button Layout.

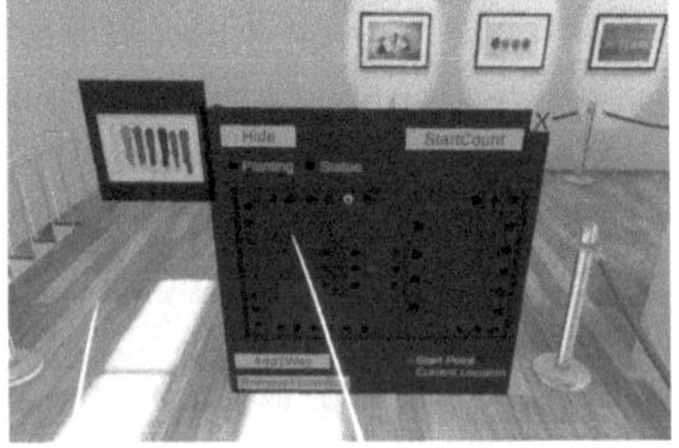

Fig. 11. Comparison Method Operation 1.

Fig. 12. Comparison Method Operation Two

Experimental Tasks and Procedures. The participants first described the exhibits they wished to view and then used two different methods to locate matching exhibits and generate routes, repeating the process for three rounds each.

The experimental methods included a comparison of the conventional ray-casting method (the comparison method) and our method. The comparison method simply lets users click on icons that represent exhibits to see the corresponding images. As shown in Figs. 11 and 12, users clicked on exhibit locations on the virtual map to view thumbnails and selected points on the route based on their descriptions, with the order of the generated route determined by the click sequence. In our method, after pressing the left trigger shown in Fig. 10, the user simply speaks the desired exhibit type; the system then generates a route. If the user doubts the route's reasonableness or coverage, they can give additional voice feedback and the system will dynamically adjust the path (Table 1).

Table 1. Evaluation Metrics.

Metric	Description
Coverage Rate	The percentage of user-required exhibits covered by the paths generated by both methods.
Error Rate	The percentage of selected exhibits that are not part of the correct answer.
Path Length Ratio	The ratio of the path length generated by the conventional ray-casting method to that generated by our method for each question.
Time	The time cost.

4.2 Result And Discussion

User Load and System Usability. The NASA Task Load Index (NASA-TLX) categorizes user workload into six dimensions [7]. The System Usability

Scale (SUS) consists of 10 statements about the system, each with a 5-point rating scale (1 – 5) corresponding to "strongly disagree," "disagree," "neutral," "agree," and "strongly agree". The higher the total score, the higher the usability of the system [1] (Table 2).

Table 2. NASA and SUS Scores.

Method	Average NASA Score↓	Average SUS Score↑
Conventional Ray Casting	54.69±5.80	64.56±8.40
Our Method	40.57±6.45	73.05±8.08
P	7.21×10^{-9}	1.20×10^{-5}

The SUS results indicate that users generally expressed higher satisfaction with this method compared to the alternative method($p = 1.20 \times 10^{-5}$). Specifically, the majority of participants found this method to be more consistent and user-friendly. This consistency and ease of use are primarily reflected in the intuitiveness and logical structure of the system's operations (Table 3).

Table 3. NASA Scores And T-Test

Method	Mental Demand↓	Physical Demand↓	Temporal Demand↓
Our Method	50.00±11.22	46.88±13.43	41.88±8.87
Conventional Ray Casting	44.06±11.10	65.16±7.13	69.84±9.63
P	0.418	1.59×10^{-8}	5.97×10^{-18}
Method	Performance Level↓	Effort↓	Frustration↓
Our Method	35.47±11.60	39.22±8.72	30.00±10.70
Conventional Ray Casting	48.3±13.83	61.25±8.70	39.53±11.53
P	1.63×10^{-4}	9.55×10^{-5}	0.002

The NASA-TLX results show the proposed method significantly outperformed conventional Ray Casting on six of seven subscales: Physical Demand and Temporal Demand dropped by over 20 points ($p = 1.59 \times 10^{-8}$ and $p = 5.97 \times 10^{-18}$), while Performance ($p = 1.63 \times 10^{-4}$), Effort ($p = 9.55 \times 10^{-5}$) and Frustration (p = 0.002) were also improved, reducing the overall score(p < 0.001). Although Mental Demand was slightly higher than the comparison method, the difference was not significant (p = 0.418), highlighting the advantage of the new method in reducing physical, temporal and affective costs.

Coverage Rate and Error Rate. As shown in Table 4, our method achieves a higher coverage rate and a lower error rate than the comparison method. Although the t-tests do not reach significance ($p = 0.061$ and $p = 0.574$), both metrics move in a consistently favorable direction; in particular, the p-value for coverage is close to the 0.05 boundary, suggesting that statistical support could be achieved with a larger sample or reduced variability. Moreover, the proposed method exhibits lower standard deviations, indicating a more stable performance among the participants (Table 4).

Table 4. Coverage Rate and Error Rate.

Method	Coverage Rate↑	Error Rate↓
Conventional Ray Casting	83.99±22.72	6.67±13.62
Our Method	91.31±12.56	4.9±13.85
P	0.061	0.574

Average Path Length Ratio. After organizing all the experimental data and excluding cases where the path length do not differ when only one or two objects are included, the average path length ratio was calculated to be 1.45. The average path length generated by our method is significantly shorter than that of the comparison method, indicating that our method is more effective in path optimization than manual selection. Compared to the user's manual and unordered selection, our method can generate shorter tour paths, improving the efficiency and reducing unnecessary tour distance.

Time. The average time required to generate a route with our method was markedly shorter than that of the comparison method ($p = 1.84 \times 10^{-17}$). The result demonstrates that our method is simple and intuitive, yielding a significant improvement in the users' operation experience. We measured the time from when users pressed the button and spoke to when they received system feedback; the average delay was approximately 18 s. Because we invoked a cloud-based API, a large portion of this latency was attributable to network delay. After deploying the Qwen-QwQ model locally, the response time per user feedback dropped sharply, demonstrating the feasibility of real-time interaction. Nevertheless, to maintain inference quality, we continued to use the cloud API during the experiment (Table 5).

Table 5. Average Time Spent.

Method	Average Time Spent (s)↓
Conventional Ray Casting	128.63±43.16
Our Method	37.50±9.23
P	1.84×10^{-17}

5 Conclusion

We present a personalized tour route generation system for virtual museums. The system analyses the scene, receives and interprets user feedback during the tour, and dynamically adapts the route to deliver a personalized and immersive experience. Through user experiments, we demonstrate the effectiveness and accuracy of our system compared to traditional methods, as well as its ability to increase user satisfaction and reduce user burden. However, our method still has shortcomings. A new initialization is required for each new scene, which objectively consumes a certain amount of time. Additionally, during the user's interaction with the system, the two-tier response process also incurs time costs. In future work, we will explore more intuitive feedback methods, improve response speed, and enhance user experience.

Acknowledgments. This work is supported by the National Natural Science Foundation of China through Project 61932003, 62372026, by Beijing Science and Technology Plan Project Z221100007722004, by National Key R&D plan 2019YFC1521102, and by the fundamental research funds for the central universities

References

1. Brooke, J.: Sus: A quick and dirty usability scale. Usability Eval. Ind. **189** (1995)
2. Brown, T.B., Mann, B.: Language models are few-shot learners. In: Proceedings of the 34th International Conference on Neural Information Processing Systems. NIPS '20, Curran Associates Inc., Red Hook, NY, USA (2020)
3. Brown, T.B., et al.: Language models are few-shot learners (2020). https://arxiv.org/abs/2005.14165
4. Chen, K., Chen, J.K., Chuang, J., Vázquez, M., Savarese, S.: Topological planning with transformers for vision-and-language navigation (2020). https://arxiv.org/abs/2012.05292
5. Dijkstra, E.W.: A note on two problems in connexion with graphs. Numer. Math. **1**(1), 269–271 (1959)
6. Hart, P.E., Nilsson, N.J., Raphael, B.: A formal basis for the heuristic determination of minimum cost paths. IEEE Trans. Syst. Sci. Cybern. **4**(2), 100–107 (1968). https://doi.org/10.1109/TSSC.1968.300136
7. Hart, S.G., Staveland, L.E.: Development of NASA-TLX (task load index): Results of empirical and theoretical research. In: Hancock, P.A., Meshkati, N. (eds.) Human Mental Workload, Advances in Psychology, vol. 52, pp. 139–183. North-Holland (1988). https://doi.org/10.1016/S0166-4115(08)62386-9. https://www.sciencedirect.com/science/article/pii/S0166411508623869
8. Jiang, H., Wang, B., Wang, X., Christie, M., Chen, B.: Example-driven virtual cinematography by learning camera behaviors. ACM Trans. Graph. **39**(4) (2020). https://doi.org/10.1145/3386569.3392427
9. Lavalle, S.M.: Rapidly-exploring random trees: A new tool for path planning. Ann. Res. Rep. (1998)
10. Li, X., et al.: Director3D: real-world camera trajectory and 3D scene generation from text (2024). https://arxiv.org/abs/2406.17601

11. Li, Z., Gebhardt, C., Inglin, Y., Steck, N., Streli, P., Holz, C.: Situationadapt: contextual UI optimization in mixed reality with situation awareness via LLM reasoning (2024). https://arxiv.org/abs/2409.12836
12. OpenAI, Achiam, J., Adler, S., Agarwal, S., Ahmad, L.: GPT-4 Technical Report (2024). https://arxiv.org/abs/2303.08774
13. Radford, A., Wu, J., Child, R., Luan, D., Amodei, D., Sutskever, I.: Language models are unsupervised multitask learners (2019). https://api.semanticscholar.org/CorpusID:160025533
14. Su, X., Froehlich, J.E., Koh, E., Xiao, C.: Sonifyar: Context-aware sound generation in augmented reality. In: Proceedings of the 37th Annual ACM Symposium on User Interface Software and Technology. UIST '24, Association for Computing Machinery, New York, NY, USA (2024). https://doi.org/10.1145/3654777.3676406
15. Torre, F.D.L., Fang, C.M., Huang, H., Banburski-Fahey, A., Fernandez, J.A., Lanier, J.: LLMR: real-time prompting of interactive worlds using large language models (2024). https://arxiv.org/abs/2309.12276
16. Vaithilingam, P., Glassman, E.L., Inala, J.P., Wang, C.: Dynavis: Dynamically synthesized UI widgets for visualization editing. In: Proceedings of the 2024 CHI Conference on Human Factors in Computing Systems. CHI '24, Association for Computing Machinery, New York, NY, USA (2024). https://doi.org/10.1145/3613904.3642639
17. Wang, H., Chen, A.G.H., Li, X., Wu, M., Dong, H.: Find what you want: learning demand-conditioned object attribute space for demand-driven navigation (2023). https://arxiv.org/abs/2309.08138
18. Wang, L., Liu, Y., Liu, X., Wu, J.: Automatic virtual portals placement for efficient VR navigation. In: 2022 IEEE Conference on Virtual Reality and 3D User Interfaces Abstracts and Workshops (VRW), pp. 628–629 (2022). https://doi.org/10.1109/VRW55335.2022.00165
19. Wang, M., Li, Y.J., Shi, J., Steinicke, F.: Scenefusion: room-scale environmental fusion for efficient traveling between separate virtual environments. IEEE Trans. Visual Comput. Graphics **30**(8), 4615–4630 (2024). https://doi.org/10.1109/TVCG.2023.3271709
20. Wei, J., et al.: Chain-of-thought prompting elicits reasoning in large language models (2023). https://arxiv.org/abs/2201.11903
21. White, J., et al.: A prompt pattern catalog to enhance prompt engineering with ChatGpt (2023). https://arxiv.org/abs/2302.11382
22. Xu, H., Ge, Y., Zhang, G.: Genetic algorithm for traveling salesman problem. In: Proceedings of the 2022 5th International Conference on Computational Intelligence and Intelligent Systems, pp. 33–40. CIIS '22, Association for Computing Machinery, New York, NY, USA (2023). https://doi.org/10.1145/3581792.3581798
23. Zhang, C., et al.: UFO: A UI-focused agent for windows OS interaction (2024). https://arxiv.org/abs/2402.07939
24. Zhu, Y., et al.: Target-driven visual navigation in indoor scenes using deep reinforcement learning (2016). https://arxiv.org/abs/1609.05143

Perceiving Safety: User Preferences and Perception of Multimodal Virtual Boundary Cues in VR

Xin Du[1], Sen-Zhe Xu[2], Yang-Fu Ren[1,3](✉), Qi-Wen Gan[4], and Song-Hai Zhang[1,3,5]

[1] Qinghai University, Xining, China
[2] University of Science and Technology Beijing, Beijing, China
senzhe@ustb.edu.cn
[3] Tsinghua University, Beijing, China
ryf21@mails.tsinghua.edu.cn, shz@tsinghua.edu.cn
[4] University of Arizona, Tucson, AZ, USA
qiwengan@arizona.edu
[5] BNRist, Beijing, China

Abstract. In immersive virtual reality (VR) environments, users often face safety risks due to limited spatial awareness, such as unintentionally approaching or crossing physical boundaries. To address this challenge, we propose a novel boundary warning risk assessment system to enhance spatial perception and operational safety. Our system continuously computes a risk score based on four key kinematic features: the user's distance to the boundary, velocity, acceleration, and the angle between movement direction and boundary orientation. Based on this score, we designed and compared four feedback strategies: a progress bar indicating risk level, a color-coded circular indicator with gradient transitions, auditory cues with varying frequencies, and a combined multimodal approach integrating visual and auditory feedback. A user study (n = 24) was conducted where participants navigated a 4×4 m virtual space with the objective of collecting as many targets as possible. We measured both objective safety metrics and subjective user experience ratings to assess the user perception of our proposed methods. Results showed that different feedback strategies led to noticeable differences in safety performance. Of the four methods tested, the Multimedia Cue was the most effective, significantly reducing boundary intrusions and receiving the highest user preference ratings.

Keywords: Virtual Reality (VR) · Spatial Awareness · Boundary Safety · Multimodal Feedback

1 Introduction

In VR environments (VEs), real walking is regarded as the most natural locomotion technique [22]. It synchronizes bodily movement with visual feedback

A. Hinkenjan et al. (Eds.): ICXR 2025, LNCS 16428, pp. 430–441, 2026.
https://doi.org/10.1007/978-981-95-7195-6_31

and enhances spatial cognition compared to controller-based navigation methods [15]. However, its application is constrained by the limited size of physical spaces, which poses safety risks when users unintentionally approach or cross real-world boundaries [19]. Ensuring safe and effective real walking within confined areas remains a key challenge in immersive VR [7].

Existing solutions include redirected walking (RDW) techniques [14] and built-in notification systems such as Chaperone and Guardian [9]. While RDW expands navigable space [23], it cannot eliminate the risk of boundary contact during highly immersive tasks. Meanwhile, threshold-based boundary warnings are often activated too late and rely heavily on visual cues, which may distract users from tasks and reduce immersion [1]. Unimodal feedback also faces inherent trade-offs: visual alerts may overload attention, while audio alerts can startle users or generate anxiety [21]. These limitations highlight the need for proactive, continuous, and multimodal boundary warning mechanisms.

To address this gap, we propose a boundary risk score assessment system. The system dynamically calculates a risk score from real-time parameters including distance to boundary, velocity, acceleration, and orientation. The score drives four boundary feedback strategies: (1) a visual progress bar directly displaying the risk score; (2) a color-coded circular indicator positioned at the top-right of the user's field of view; (3) unimodal auditory feedback using sounds of varying intensities; (4) a bimodal approach combining the visual indicator with corresponding audio cues. We design a target collection task in a $4 \times 4\,\text{m}$ space to evaluate these strategies.

Experimental results indicate that different modalities influence user responses and experiences. Bimodal feedback provides clearer guidance and higher preference while maintaining safety, whereas unimodal audio feedback triggers faster responses but increases anxiety. These findings provide empirical evidence to guide the improvement of VR boundary warning systems and offer design insights for achieving a balance between safety, immersion, and usability in multimodal human–computer interaction (HCI).

2 Related Work

2.1 Boundary Mechanisms and Dynamic Safety Zones

In VR, managing user interaction with physical boundaries is essential for safety. Existing strategies fall into two categories: static boundary warnings and dynamic boundary management. Static mechanisms are widely implemented in commercial systems such as Meta Quest's Guardian and SteamVR's Chaperone, where users predefine a safe zone and receive visual alerts when approaching the edge. While effective, these systems do not adapt to user motion states. To address this, researchers have developed dynamic approaches. Cirio et al. [3]'s Magic Barrier Tape system adjusted boundary shapes in real time using hybrid position/velocity control, creating the illusion of extended navigation. Langbehn et al. [12] combined this idea with redirected walking (RDW), subtly steering users away from boundaries without disrupting immersion. More recently, Wang et al. [20] introduced SCARF, which predicted motion trends such as step length and direction to dynamically expand or contract navigable areas. Qu et al. [13] further improved stability and adaptability for complex environments.

2.2 Multimodal Warning Mechanisms

To improve responsiveness and user experience in VEs, researchers have explored multimodal feedback. Compared to unimodal cues, multimodal designs can better capture attention, shorten reaction times, and enhance task performance [18]. For example, Khan et al. [11] found that combining visual and auditory cues stabilized gait rhythm more effectively than visual feedback alone. George et al. [5] used auditory and haptic cues to signal real-world boundaries while preserving visual immersion, showing that such allocation increased workload but improved presence and perceived safety. While multimodal cues are generally effective, excessive or poorly integrated signals may disrupt immersion. Our study therefore emphasizes balancing clear risk communication with minimal task interference. Specifically, we propose a continuous risk scoring model that drives graded peripheral visual markers and layered auditory signals, mapping risk intensity to cue strength over time. Building on George et al. [5], who combined auditory and haptic cues to represent real-world boundaries, our work advances multimodal boundary feedback in several aspects. We introduce continuous, intensity-mapped visual and auditory cues that convey graded risk levels over time, ensuring temporal continuity and minimal task interference. The system is evaluated in a room-scale target collection task with both objective safety metrics and subjective measures (SSQ, IPQ, SUS, preference). These extensions contribute a lightweight, continuous feedback approach that enhances user safety without compromising immersion.

3 Methods

3.1 Risk Assessment Algorithm

We developed a multi-feature risk evaluation model to dynamically assess users' proximity to physical boundaries in VEs. The model considers four factors: spatial distance, velocity, acceleration, and movement direction.

First, to measure spatial proximity to the physical boundary, we define a distance-based risk function:

$$f_d(d) = 1 - \frac{d}{d_{\max}} \tag{1}$$

where d denotes the Euclidean distance from the user's head position to the nearest physical boundary, and $d_{\max}$ is the normalization upper bound representing the maximum distance considered "completely safe" by the system. In this study, we set $d_{\max} = 2.0\,\mathrm{m}$.

Second, to reflect the user's approach tendency, we define a velocity-based risk function:

$$f_v(v) = \frac{\max(0, v_{\parallel})}{v_{\max}} \quad (2)$$

where $v_{\parallel} = \mathbf{v} \cdot \mathbf{n}$ is the projection of the velocity vector $\mathbf{v}$ onto the boundary's inward normal vector $\mathbf{n}$. The $\max(0, \cdot)$ operator removes negative values, ensuring that movement away from the boundary does not contribute to risk. Based on pilot testing of normal walking and high-speed approach behaviors, we set $v_{\max} = 3.0$ m/s as the normalization constant.

To account for abrupt movement, we define an acceleration-based risk function:

$$f_a(a) = \frac{\max(0, a_{\parallel})}{a_{\text{threshold}}} \quad (3)$$

where $a_{\parallel} = \mathbf{a} \cdot \mathbf{n}$ denotes the projection of the acceleration vector $\mathbf{a}$ onto the boundary's inward normal vector $\mathbf{n}$. From the same pilot study, $a_{\text{threshold}} = 4.0\ \text{m/s}^2$ was determined as the appropriate cutoff for identifying high-risk acceleration events.

In addition, directional intention is a key factor in risk estimation. We introduce a direction-based risk function as follows:

$$f_\theta(\theta) = \max(0, \cos\theta) \quad (4)$$

where θ is the angle between the user's movement direction and the inward normal vector of the nearest boundary.

To integrate all four risk components, we apply a linearly weighted risk aggregation model:

$$R = w_d \cdot f_d(d) + w_v \cdot f_v(v) + w_a \cdot f_a(a) + w_\theta \cdot f_\theta(\theta) \quad (5)$$

Here, R denotes the overall risk score, and w_d, w_v, w_a, and w_θ are the corresponding weights for the four components. To determine these weights in a principled way, we adopt the Analytic Hierarchy Process (AHP) [16]. This includes constructing pairwise comparison matrices, solving normalized eigenvectors, and performing consistency checks. Five graduate students specializing in related fields were invited to evaluate the relative importance of each factor. The final matrix satisfied the consistency condition ($CR < 0.1$), resulting in the following weight vector:

$$\mathbf{w} = [0.45,\ 0.26,\ 0.17,\ 0.12] \quad (6)$$

corresponding to distance, velocity, acceleration, and direction, respectively.

3.2 Multimodal Feedback Mechanism

To improve users' awareness of boundary proximity, we designed a risk score–based multimodal feedback system that integrates visual and auditory cues.

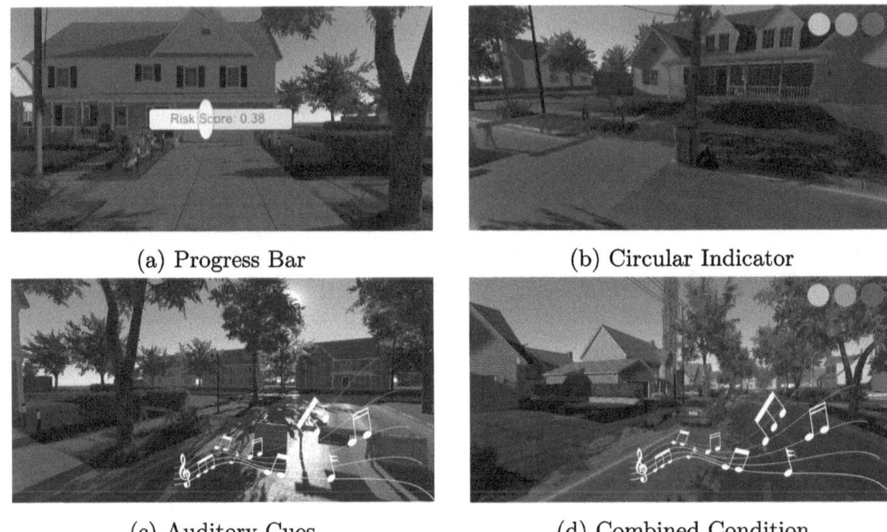

(a) Progress Bar

(b) Circular Indicator

(c) Auditory Cues

(d) Combined Condition

Fig. 1. Illustration of the four feedback strategies shown from a first-person VR viewpoint.

The visual feedback has two forms. The first is a horizontal progress bar at the center of the field of view. This design allows users to perceive quantitative risk precisely and immediately. The second is a color-coded circular indicator placed at the top-right corner of the view. This design minimizes interference with central vision while leveraging peripheral sensitivity to color changes [6]. It encodes four levels of risk: green for $R < 0.25$ (safe), yellow for $0.25 \leq R < 0.5$ (caution), orange for $0.5 \leq R < 0.75$ (moderate risk), and red for $R \geq 0.75$ (high risk), enabling rapid recognition and anticipation of increasing risk.

Auditory feedback is delivered via short "beep" sounds whose rhythm and volume correspond to R. Following auditory warning design principles [4], the beeps are slower and softer at low risk, while they become faster and louder at high risk (intervals ranging from 500 ms to 100 ms). This design conveys urgency effectively while avoiding cognitive overload.

Based on these designs, four feedback strategies were established: (1) progress bar, (2) circular indicator, (3) auditory cues, and (4) a combined condition of the circular indicator and auditory cues. All feedback types are driven by the same real-time risk scoring function. Figure 1 illustrates the geometrical forms of the four feedback cues and their placement within the field of view.

4 User Study

We conducted a user study to evaluate the effectiveness and experience of four boundary warning feedback strategies in a VR goal collection task.

4.1 User Study Design

Participants and Apparatus. Twenty-four university students (19–26 years, 12 male and 12 female) participated, all right-handed with normal or corrected vision and no major health issues; 16 had prior VR experience. The system was developed in Unity and ran on a laptop with an HTC Vive HMD and SteamVR tracking, using two base stations to cover the 4 m × 4 m area. All participants provided informed consent and received standardized training.

Task and Procedure. Participants performed a goal-collection task in a 4 m × 4 m area, freely collecting virtual targets. To encourage boundary approaches, central targets gave lower scores and boundary-near targets gave higher scores. Five conditions were tested: no feedback (baseline), visual progress bar, circular color indicator, auditory cues, and combined visual-auditory feedback, with order counterbalanced by a Latin square. Each condition lasted 3 min, followed by rest and questionnaires. Objective measures included boundary incursions, triggered warnings, and response time; subjective measures included SSQ [10], IPQ [17], SUS [2], and a custom perception questionnaire.

4.2 Results

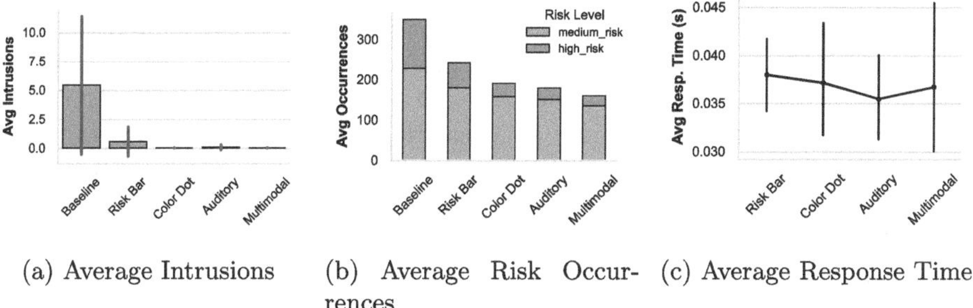

(a) Average Intrusions (b) Average Risk Occurrences (c) Average Response Time

Fig. 2. Comparison of performance metrics under different feedback conditions.

Objective Safety Index Analysis. We conducted a statistical analysis and visualized several key objective metrics, including the number of boundary intrusions, the frequency of risk-level events, and the mean response time to warnings.

The number of boundary intrusions refers to the instances when a user's physical position exceeds the predefined virtual safety boundary. Figure 2a presents a comparison of the average number of boundary intrusions across the different feedback conditions. As shown in the figure, participants under the Baseline condition exhibited significantly more boundary intrusions compared to all other conditions. A Kruskal-Wallis test confirmed significant differences in intrusion counts across the four feedback conditions ($H = 58.73, p < 0.001$).

The frequency of risk-level events captures how often users enter spatial zones that pose potential safety risks. Specifically, the system triggers a risk-level event when the user enters either the medium-risk zone (0.6–1.0 m from the boundary) or the high-risk zone (0–0.6 m from the boundary). Figure 2b presents the average number of medium-risk and high-risk events under each feedback condition. The overall trend indicates that the presence of feedback, particularly in the Multimodal Cue condition, leads to a substantial reduction in the occurrence of both medium- and high-risk behaviors. In contrast, the Baseline condition yields the highest frequency of high-risk events.

The mean response time to warnings refers to the time between the onset of a feedback cue and the user's first observable behavioral adjustment. The adjustment may involve stopping or moving away. Figure 2c shows the variation in average response time across different feedback modalities, where the Auditory Cue condition yields the shortest response times, while the Risk Bar condition produces comparatively longer reactions.

Subjective User Experience Evaluation. To evaluate whether the proposed feedback mechanisms induced cybersickness, participants completed the SSQ at the beginning of the experiment and after each feedback condition. Results showed that all values remained within a low and acceptable range, indicating minimal cybersickness symptoms across conditions.

To evaluate the impact of different feedback strategies on users' sense of presence, this study adopted the internationally recognized IPQ. Participants completed the IPQ after performing the task under each of the five feedback conditions. A non-parametric Friedman test was applied to evaluate overall differences across feedback conditions for each IPQ subscale. Whenever significant differences were observed, pairwise Wilcoxon signed-rank tests were conducted for multiple comparisons, with Bonferroni correction. The distributions of user ratings across the five conditions for each IPQ dimension are illustrated in Fig. 3, using boxplots overlaid with individual data points to visually compare differences and variances across conditions. The Friedman tests revealed no significant differences among conditions in Spatial Presence ($\chi^2(3) = 3.21$, p = 0.524, Kendall's W = 0.033, 95% CI [0.009, 0.204]) or Involvement ($\chi^2(3) = 4.66$, p = 0.324, Kendall's W = 0.049, 95% CI [0.016, 0.205]). In contrast, significant effects emerged for Realism ($\chi^2(3) = 9.57$, p = 0.048, Kendall's W = 0.100, 95% CI [0.031, 0.295]) and General Presence ($\chi^2(3) = 12.71$, p = 0.013, Kendall's W = 0.132, 95% CI [0.049, 0.351]). Post hoc Wilcoxon comparisons showed that the baseline condition (no feedback) yielded the lowest median scores in both dimensions. Specifically, in Realism, the no-feedback condition was significantly lower than the audio–visual feedback condition (p = 0.011, r = −0.61, 95% CI [−0.84, −0.24]). In General Presence, the no-feedback condition was significantly lower than the color indicator (p = 0.014, r = −0.62, 95% CI [−0.88, −0.26]), audio feedback (p = 0.013, r = −0.59, 95% CI [−0.82, −0.24]), and audio–visual feedback (p = 0.006, r = −0.82, 95% CI [−0.89, −0.59]). Taken together, these results suggest that feedback cues, and audio–visual feedback in particular, did not disrupt immersion but instead enhanced both the sense of realism and the overall presence compared to the baseline. The relatively strong effect sizes (r ranging from −0.59 to −0.82) further indicate that the differences were not only statistically significant but also of practical relevance. The lower median scores in the baseline condition can be interpreted as reflecting reduced predictability and diminished feelings of safety in the absence of boundary cues, which in turn weakened participants' sense of realism and presence.

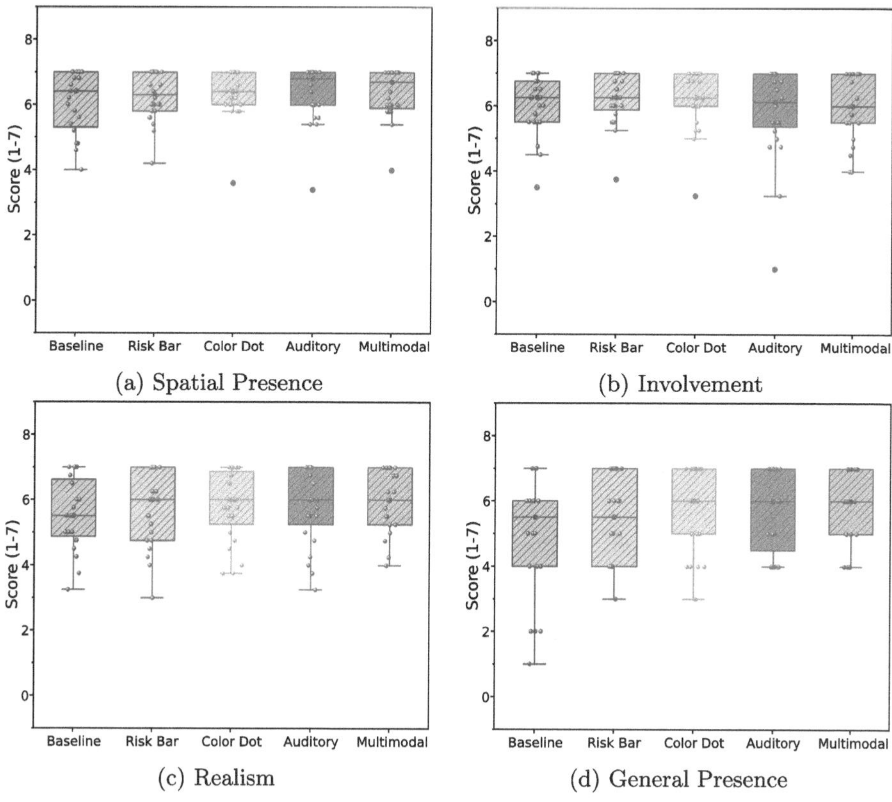

(a) Spatial Presence

(b) Involvement

(c) Realism

(d) General Presence

Fig. 3. IPQ scores across different feedback conditions.

To evaluate the usability experience of the system under different feedback conditions, this study employed the SUS. A non-parametric Friedman test was conducted to examine differences in SUS scores across the five feedback conditions, which did not reach statistical significance ($\chi^2(4) = 7.182$, $p = 0.1266$). None of the pairwise comparisons reached the corrected significance level, although the Multimodal Cue and Auditory Cue comparison ($Z = 24.000$, $p = 0.0072$) suggested a possible trend toward better usability perception with multimodal feedback.

To assess participants' subjective perception of different boundary feedback modalities, a custom-designed perception questionnaire was administered. Responses from the no-feedback condition were excluded. As illustrated in Fig. 4a, the Multimodal Cue condition notably outperformed single-modality conditions in overall perception ratings. Figure 4b presents participants' preference rankings, where the Color Dot condition was ranked first by 50% of participants, followed by Multimodal Cue, while Risk Bar and Auditory Cue received lower rankings.

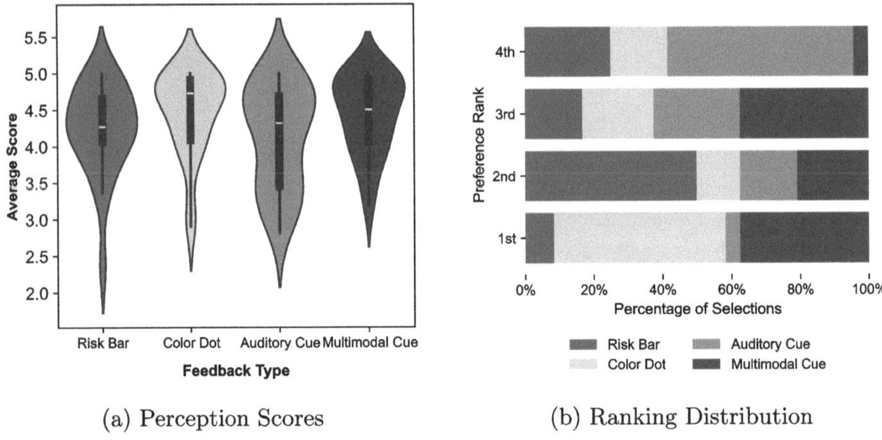

(a) Perception Scores

(b) Ranking Distribution

Fig. 4. Results of user feedback evaluation

5 Discussion

These results collectively confirm that introducing any form of boundary warning cue can substantially improve spatial boundary control in VR locomotion tasks, even when the specific feedback modality differs. As shown in Fig. 2a, all feedback conditions resulted in significantly fewer boundary intrusions compared to the Baseline condition ($H = 58.73, p < 0.001$). This finding has shown that spatial feedback, whether visual, auditory, or multimodal, can reduce unintentional boundary crossings by increasing users' spatial awareness.

The pronounced reduction in high-risk events under the Multimodal Cue condition suggests that redundancy across sensory channels enhances both perceptual stability and behavioral regulation. Figure 2b illustrates that medium- and high-risk events occurred significantly less frequently in the Multimodal Cue condition compared to all others, with the Baseline condition showing the highest frequency of high-risk events. This supports the principle of cross-modal reinforcement, whereby congruent information from different sensory streams strengthens signal salience. Such reinforcement likely leads to faster detection and more reliable user behavioral adjustments.

Response time findings further highlight modality-specific characteristics. Figure 2c shows that auditory cues triggered the fastest reactions, consistent with their ability to bypass visual attention bottlenecks and deliver immediate, high-salience alerts.

The absence of significant presence differences in Spatial Presence and Involvement suggests that safety cues, when appropriately designed, do not necessarily detract from immersion. Realism and General Presence, by contrast, showed clear benefits from feedback, with the baseline (no feedback) condition producing the lowest ratings. This pattern suggests that the lack of boundary cues may reduce participants' sense of predictability and safety, thereby undermining presence. Related work has suggested that embedding familiar objects or a 3D point cloud of the real space within the VR environment can help users perceive physical boundaries without significantly reducing immersion [8]. Inspired by this, future iterations of our system could explore integrating peripheral visual cues, such as colored dots, with familiar virtual environment elements, potentially enhancing spatial awareness and safety while further preserving immersive experience.

From a usability standpoint, SUS scores did not differ significantly among conditions ($\chi^2(4) = 7.182, p = 0.1266$), but the Multimodal Cue was generally preferred. Preference rankings depicted in Fig. 4b reveal that the Color Dot condition was favored by 50% of participants, indicating that minimal yet salient peripheral cues may provide an optimal balance between visibility and cognitive load.

6 Conclusion

This study introduced a boundary warning system for VEs that integrates users' kinematic states and spatial features to compute a real-time risk score. Based on this, we designed four feedback strategies (Risk Bar, Color Dot, Auditory Cue, and Multimodal Cue) and evaluated them through a within-subject user study. All strategies effectively reduced boundary intrusions, with the multimodal cue showing the best performance in mitigating high-risk events and minimizing response latency. Subjective measures confirmed low cybersickness and positive user preference, especially for the Color Dot and multimodal feedback. Our results demonstrate that real-time, risk-driven multimodal feedback can guide user behavior, improve safety, and preserve immersion in VEs.

Acknowledgments. This work was supported by the National Natural Science Foundation of China (62402281, 62361146854, 62562052), the Fundamental Research Funds for the Central Universities (FRF-TP-25-036), and the Tsinghua-Tencent Joint Laboratory for Internet Innovation Technology.

Disclosure of Interests. The authors declare that they have no competing interests.

References

1. Araya, R.C., Chen, Y., Rojas-Muñoz, E.: Don't walk away! Virtual safety boundaries for collaborative virtual reality learning environments. In: 2023 IEEE Frontiers in Education Conference (FIE), pp. 1–5. IEEE (2023)
2. Brooke, J., et al.: Sus-a quick and dirty usability scale. Usabil. Eval. Ind. **189**(194), 4–7 (1996)
3. Cirio, G., Marchal, M., Regia-Corte, T., Lécuyer, A.: The magic barrier tape: a novel metaphor for infinite navigation in virtual worlds with a restricted walking workspace. In: Proceedings of the 16th ACM Symposium on Virtual Reality Software and Technology, pp. 155–162 (2009)
4. Edworthy, J.: Medical audible alarms: a review. J. Am. Med. Inform. Assoc. **20**(3), 584–589 (2013)
5. George, C., Tamunjoh, P., Hussmann, H.: Invisible boundaries for VR: auditory and haptic signals as indicators for real world boundaries. IEEE Trans. Visual Comput. Graphics **26**(12), 3414–3422 (2020)
6. He, S., Cavanagh, P., Intriligator, J.: Attentional resolution and the locus of visual awareness. Nature **383**(6598), 334–337 (1996)
7. Hořejší, P., Lochmannová, A., Jezl, V., Dvořák, M.: Virtual reality locomotion methods differentially affect spatial orientation and cybersickness during maze navigation. Sci. Rep. **15**(1), 26255 (2025)
8. Kanamori, K., Sakata, N., Tominaga, T., Hijikata, Y., Harada, K., Kiyokawa, K.: Obstacle avoidance method in real space for virtual reality immersion. In: 2018 IEEE International Symposium on Mixed and Augmented Reality (ISMAR), pp. 80–89. IEEE (2018)
9. Kelly, J.W., Cherep, L.A., Siegel, Z.D.: Perceived space in the HTC vive. ACM Trans. Appl. Percept. (TAP) **15**(1), 1–16 (2017)
10. Kennedy, R.S., Lane, N.E., Berbaum, K.S., Lilienthal, M.G.: Simulator sickness questionnaire: an enhanced method for quantifying simulator sickness. Int. J. Aviat. Psychol. **3**(3), 203–220 (1993)
11. Khan, O., Ahmed, I., Cottingham, J., Rahhal, M., Arvanitis, T.N., Elliott, M.: Multisensory cues facilitate coordination of stepping movements with a virtual reality avatar. arXiv preprint arXiv:1906.09850 (2019)
12. Langbehn, E., Steinicke, F., Lappe, M., Welch, G.F., Bruder, G.: In the blink of an eye: leveraging blink-induced suppression for imperceptible position and orientation redirection in virtual reality. ACM Trans. Graphics (TOG) **37**(4), 1–11 (2018)
13. Qu, C., Che, X., Cai, Z., Li, H., Wang, S.: Safety boundary in virtual reality: an approach based on user motion analysis and prediction. In: 2022 IEEE Smartworld, Ubiquitous Intelligence & Computing, Scalable Computing & Communications, Digital Twin, Privacy Computing, Metaverse, Autonomous & Trusted Vehicles (SmartWorld/UIC/ScalCom/DigitalTwin/PriComp/Meta), pp. 1942–1947. IEEE (2022)
14. Razzaque, S.: Redirected walking. The University of North Carolina at Chapel Hill (2005)
15. Ruddle, R.A., Lessels, S.: The benefits of using a walking interface to navigate virtual environments. ACM Trans. Comput.-Hum. Interact. (TOCHI) **16**(1), 1–18 (2009)
16. Saaty, R.W.: The analytic hierarchy process—what it is and how it is used. Math. Model. **9**(3–5), 161–176 (1987)

17. Schubert, T., Friedmann, F., Regenbrecht, H.: The experience of presence: Factor analytic insights. Presence: Teleoper. Virtual Environ. **10**(3), 266–281 (2001)
18. Sigrist, R., Rauter, G., Marchal-Crespo, L., Riener, R., Wolf, P.: Sonification and haptic feedback in addition to visual feedback enhances complex motor task learning. Exp. Brain Res. **233**(3), 909–925 (2015)
19. Tseng, W.J., Kontrazis, P.D., Lecolinet, E., Huron, S., Gugenheimer, J.: Understanding interaction and breakouts of safety boundaries in virtual reality through mixed-method studies. In: 2024 IEEE Conference Virtual Reality and 3D User Interfaces (VR), pp. 482–492. IEEE (2024)
20. Wang, H., Che, X., Chang, E., Qu, C., Luo, Y., Wei, Z.: How to set safety boundary in virtual reality: a dynamic approach based on user motion prediction. Comput. Anim. Virtual Worlds **35**(1), e2210 (2024)
21. Yun, H., Yang, J.H.: Multimodal warning design for take-over request in conditionally automated driving. Eur. Transp. Res. Rev. **12**(1), 1–11 (2020). https://doi.org/10.1186/s12544-020-00427-5
22. Zhang, S.K., Li, Y.X., He, Y., Yang, Y.L., Zhang, S.H.: MageAdd: real-time interaction simulation for scene synthesis. In: Proceedings of the 29th ACM International Conference on Multimedia, pp. 965–973 (2021)
23. Zhang, S.K., Tam, H., Li, Y., Ren, K.X., Fu, H., Zhang, S.H.: SceneDirector: interactive scene synthesis by simultaneously editing multiple objects in real-time. IEEE Trans. Visual Comput. Graphics **30**(8), 4558–4569 (2023)

CPESS: Lightweight Hemiplegia Recognition Based on Video Pose Estimation and Sparse Spatiotemporal Graph Convolutional Networks

Yaoliang Wang[1], Xuesong Wang[2], Chong Chen[3], Xin He[3](✉), Baodong Wang[1], Junli Zhao[1](✉), Jianjun Sun[3](✉), Lei Peng[3], Shuzhe Yang[3], and Qiang Jian[3]

[1] College of Computer Science and Technology, Qingdao University, Qingdao 266071, Shandong, China
zjl@qdu.edu.cn
[2] School of Artificial Intelligence, Beijing Normal University, Beijing 100875, China
[3] Department of Neurosurgery, Beijing Friendship Hospital, Beijing 100050, China
hexin198383@126.com, sunjianjun@bjmu.edu.cn

Abstract. Hemiplegia recognition is crucial for early diagnosis and rehabilitation. Existing video-based methods suffer from high computational cost and parameter redundancy, hindering mobile deployment. We propose CPESS (Connect Pose Estimation Sparse-ST-GCN), a novel lightweight framework. CPESS uses AlphaPose with an SE-ResNet backbone for robust skeleton extraction, followed by a novel Sparse Spatio-Temporal Graph Convolutional Network (Sparse ST-GCN) for efficient gait analysis. This core network incorporates dynamic graph learning and explicit structural sparsification to minimize FLOPs and parameter count while maintaining accuracy. Experiments show CPESS significantly reduces redundancy compared to traditional ST-GCN, achieving 80.0% accuracy with only 0.75 G FLOPs and 3.74 M parameters. We integrate this model into an intelligent rehabilitation system based on augmented reality, demonstrating its potential for real-time clinical application.

Keywords: Sparse ST-GCN · AlphaPose · Hemiplegia Recognition · Augmented Reality

1 Introduction

Hemiplegia, a severe neurological dysfunction often caused by stroke, profoundly impairs patients' quality of life and self-sufficiency, making early and accurate intervention critical for optimizing rehabilitation outcomes [9]. Traditional hemiplegia assessments rely on clinical scales, but they are subjective and time-consuming, making continuous, objective home monitoring difficult. Therefore,

A. Hinkenjan et al. (Eds.): ICXR 2025, LNCS 16428, pp. 442–453, 2026.
https://doi.org/10.1007/978-981-95-7195-6_32

deep learning methods based on video skeletal analysis have emerged as a non-contact assessment tool.

Although deep learning offers promising assessment tools for hemiplegia recognition, its practical application faces three key hurdles: high computational cost, which prevents deployment on resource-constrained mobile devices essential for real-world monitoring [17]; scarcity of high-quality clinical data, which limits model generalization across diverse patient populations [7]; and a lack of adaptability to the dynamic changes in patients' motor function during recovery.

To achieve an objective, real-time, and deployable hemiplegia assessment, we propose the lightweight CPESS model. This solution integrates the robust AlphaPose algorithm with a novel Sparse Spatiotemporal Graph Convolutional Network (Sparse ST-GCN) to efficiently analyze human skeleton sequences from videos. Crucially, this design achieves accuracy comparable to state-of-the-art methods with significantly fewer model parameters, laying the groundwork for practical on-device deployment.

Our contributions can be summarized as follows:

- We proposed a new lightweight deep learning-based framework (CPESS), which assembles object detection, SE-ResNet-based pose estimation, and Sparse ST-GCN, forming a fully automated end-to-end pipeline for hemiplegia assessment.
- We propose an innovative Sparse Spatio-Temporal Graph Convolutional Network (Sparse ST-GCN), which significantly reduces the model's parameters and computational complexity through a customized structural sparsification strategy, enabling real-time deployment while maintaining recognition accuracy.
- We collected a set of real clinical behavior video datasets. We also integrated the CPESS model into an augmented reality (AR) rehabilitation assistance system to provide real-time, objective assessment and feedback.

2 Related Works

Hemiplegia Recognition. Research on hemiplegia focuses on developing objective assessment tools. Early studies relied on conventional biomedical signals (IMUs [18], sEMG [19]). Deep learning vision methods are promising, but the field struggles with severe data scarcity (average only 42 patient samples [4]) and the high computational cost of complex models, urgently requiring lightweighting.

Object Detection. Object detection progressed from two-stage methods (R-CNN [6], Faster R-CNN [13]) to efficient single-stage detectors like YOLO [11] and SSD [10]. Among them, the lightweight Tiny-YOLOv3 achieved high speed and multi-scale prediction capabilities.

Pose Estimation. Pose estimation is categorized into top-down (e.g., Mask R-CNN [8], AlphaPose [5], HRNet [16]) and bottom-up (e.g., OpenPose [1], CenterNet [3]) paradigms. We adopt the top-down AlphaPose (RMPE framework) for its high robustness in complex and occluded clinical scenes.

Skeleton Action Recognition. Spatio-Temporal Graph Convolutional Networks (ST-GCN) [20] are the core technology. Optimizations include dynamic graph structures (2s-AGCN [15]), directed graphs (DGNN [14]), and efficiency improvements through sparse convolution (SparseShift-GCN [21]) and shifting operations (Shift-GCN [2]). Our work enhances this field by introducing explicit structural sparsity for efficiency.

3 Method

3.1 Overview

As shown in Fig. 1, our method identifies hemiplegic gait through a three-stage automated pipeline: object detection, pose estimation, and classification via Sparse ST-GCN. This approach significantly reduces computational cost and parameter count while maintaining high recognition accuracy.

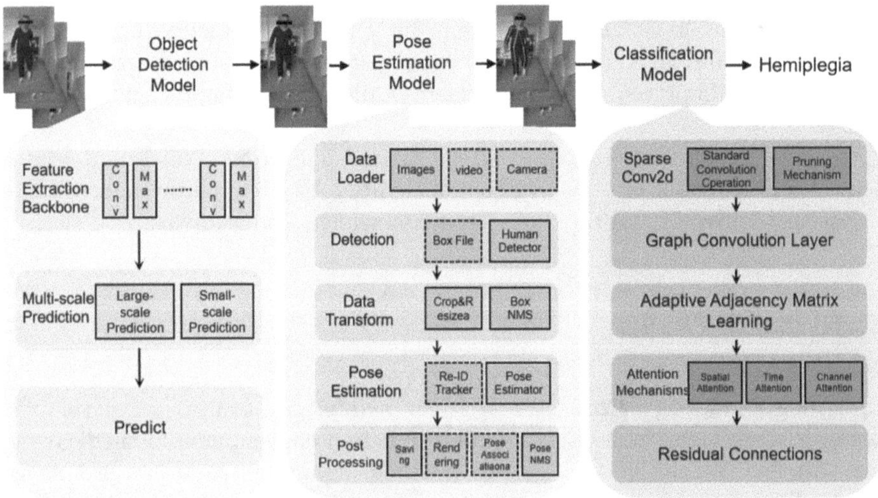

Fig. 1. The three-stage framework diagram of the hemiplegia recognition system. The system sequentially employs target detection, pose estimation, and a classification model based on sparse graph convolution to recognize the hemiplegic state of the human body from the input video.

3.2 Target Detection Model for Hemiplegic Patients Based on Tiny-YOLOv3

We employ the Tiny-YOLOv3 model [12] for its lightweight design and high speed, making it ideal for real-time processing. This model treats bounding box prediction as a regression problem, efficiently locating human targets in a single forward pass.

The total loss L_{total} is the weighted sum of Coordinate Loss (L_{coord}), Objectness Loss (L_{obj}), and Classification Loss (L_{class}):

$$L_{total} = \lambda_{coord} \cdot L_{coord} + L_{obj} + \lambda_{class} \cdot L_{class} \quad (1)$$

We chose the Tiny variant for its reduced computational requirements, crucial for our end-to-end lightweight system.

3.3 Skeleton Extraction of Hemiplegic Patients Based on AlphaPose

We adopt the robust top-down AlphaPose algorithm [5] (RMPE framework) to convert detected human figures into accurate skeletal sequences, ensuring reliability despite common issues like occlusion and complex postures.

The backbone utilizes a lightweight network based on an improved SE-ResNet architecture, integrating Batch Normalization (BN) and Squeeze-and-Excitation (SE) modules to enhance features adaptively(See Fig. 2).

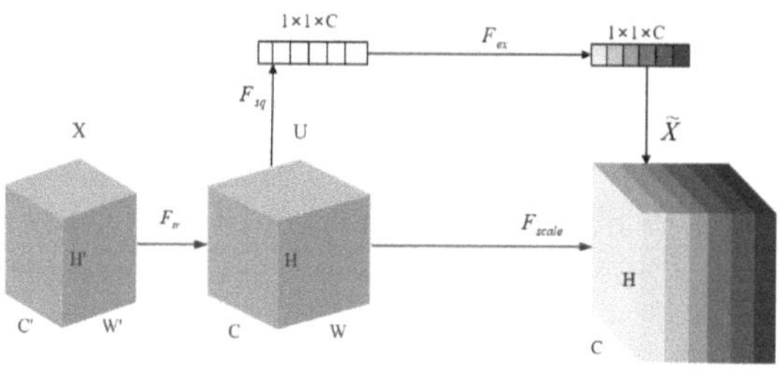

Fig. 2. Squeeze-and-Excitation (SE) module structure. This module aggregates global information through Squeeze (F_{sq}), learns channel weights through Excitation (F_{ex}), and re-weights features through Scale (F_{scale}).

The SE module explicitly models interdependencies between feature channels. This module improves the model's feature discrimination ability with minimal additional computational overhead, which is verified in our ablation studies.

3.4 Estimation of Hemiplegia Based on Sparse Spatiotemporal Graph Convolutional Networks

To address the high computational cost and parameter redundancy of Standard ST-GCN, we introduce the Sparse Spatio-Temporal Graph Convolutional Network (Sparse ST-GCN), engineered for high accuracy and efficiency.

Adaptive Graph Structure and Dynamic Adjacency Matrix. To capture dynamic joint dependencies, we use a self-attention mechanism to generate a dynamic adjacency matrix $A_{dynamic}$:

$$A_{dynamic} = Activation(Query(X) \cdot Key(X)^T) \tag{2}$$

The final adaptive adjacency matrix A_{final} combines this dynamic component with a predefined base matrix A_{base}:

$$A_{final} = A_{base} + A_{dynamic} \cdot \alpha \tag{3}$$

Explicit Sparse Graph Convolution. We enforce structural sparsity by introducing a binary sparse mask M that prunes redundant joint dependencies in A_{final}, significantly reducing computation. The sparse graph convolution operation is defined as:

$$Y_{sparse} = Conv(X \cdot (A_{final} \odot M)) \tag{4}$$

where $\odot$ is the element-wise product, and $M \in \{0,1\}^{N \times N}$ is the sparse mask.

Attention-Gated Feature Enhancement. We apply an attention-gated residual connection to enhance key features post-sparsity:

$$Y_{weight} = Y_{sparse} \cdot S + Y_{sparse} \tag{5}$$

Here, S is the attention weight. This mechanism improves feature discrimination despite structural sparsity.

3.5 Training and Optimization Settings

We implemented the CPESS framework using the PyTorch library. Experiments were conducted on a system equipped with 8 NVIDIA GeForce RTX 4090 D GPUs, as detailed in Sect. 4.1. The core hyper-parameters and optimization strategy for training the Sparse-STGCN classification network are as follows:

- Optimizer: Stochastic Gradient Descent (SGD) was used, employing a momentum of 0.9, a weight decay (ℓ_2 regularization) of 0.0005, and Nesterov acceleration.
- Initial Learning Rate: The initial learning rate was set to 0.1.
- LR Schedule: A Cosine Annealing policy was adopted to dynamically adjust the learning rate during training, with a minimum learning rate of 0.001.
- Batch Size: We utilized a per-GPU batch size of 16, resulting in an effective global batch size of 128.
- Total Epochs: The model was trained for 16 full epochs.
- Data Augmentation: The training dataset was repeated 5 times using the RepeatDataset strategy to enhance training stability and generalization.

These settings ensure stable convergence (SGD with Nesterov and high momentum) while leveraging modern LR scheduling (Cosine Annealing) for optimal performance within the constrained training budget of 16 epochs.

3.6 System Implementation and Augmented Reality Guidance

This section details the practical implementation of the hemiplegia assessment system. The prototype integrates TinyYOLOv3 and AlphaPose to analyze user motion data. The system automatically identifies the affected side and guides users through standard training movements using Augmented Reality (AR) and voice feedback.

The intelligent system generates dynamic AR visual guidance on the screen (see Fig. 3). It intuitively directs patients on 'where to move' and 'how much to move' through clear colored markers and guiding lines.

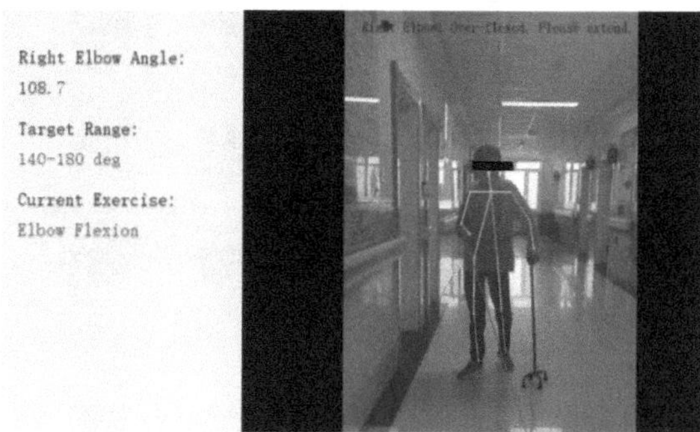

Fig. 3. Hemiplegia rehabilitation system (To protect patient privacy, the image has been obscured.)

The system achieves precise joint angle calculations (error $\pm 5^{\circ}$) for critical parameters (arm, hip, knee angles, etc.). Utilizing our lightweight CPESS pipeline, the system runs stably at 25 FPS (1080p) with a pose estimation accuracy of 81.6%, meeting real-time training needs.

4 Experiments

4.1 Dataset and Experimental Environment

The dataset was independently collected by Beijing Friendship Hospital for hemiplegic behavior recognition (patient consent obtained). It comprises 39 min of videos from 60 hemiplegic patients with a resolution of 720×1280 at 30 FPS (see Fig. 4). The data collection protocol was approved by the Ethics Committee of Beijing Friendship Hospital (Approval No. 2025-XJS-033, dated June 19, 2025). All participating patients provided written informed consent prior to the initiation of video recording. To protect patient privacy, all videos were pseudonymized, and patient faces were obscured in all figures (e.g., Fig. 3, 4, 5).

In this study, a subject-independent split was applied to the dataset. Concretely, 80% of the data samples were assigned to the training set, 10% to the validation set, and the remaining 10% to the testing set, ensuring that subjects in one set did not appear in the others. Videos are labeled as 'Hemiplegia' or 'Normal'. All experiments were conducted using an NVIDIA GeForce RTX 4090 D GPU.

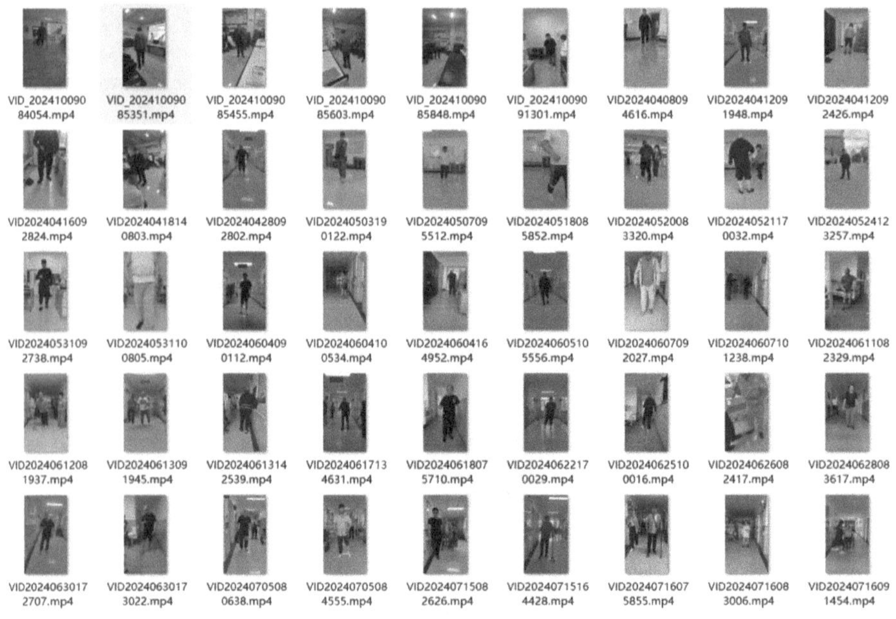

Fig. 4. Video presentation of hemiplegic patients (To protect patient privacy, the image has been obscured.).

4.2 Qualitative Analysis of Pose Estimation

We compared raw video frames with the visualized skeletal outputs (Fig. 5). This analysis focuses on the module's ability to maintain accuracy and robustness despite complex scenarios (e.g., partial self-occlusion, abnormal gait postures). The AlphaPose framework, leveraging its robust SE-ResNet backbone, accurately extracts the 13 key body points, ensuring high-quality input for the subsequent Sparse-STGCN.

4.3 Quantitative Performance Evaluation

We employed classic quantitative indicators, defining 'Normal' as the negative class and 'Hemiplegia' as the positive class. The model's performance is summarized in Table 1. Our Sparse-STGCN achieved 80.0% Accuracy and an 85.7%

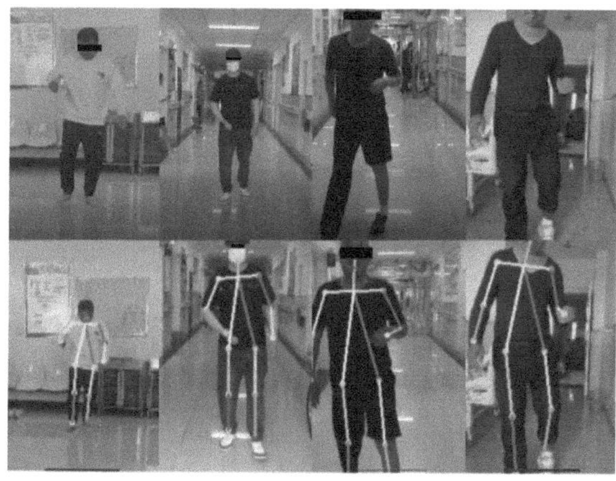

Fig. 5. Comparison between the original image (top) and the pose estimation results (bottom). The model accurately extracts the skeletal structure of 13 key points even in complex and abnormal scenarios (To protect patient privacy, the image has been obscured).

Table 1. Model Performance Metrics Comparison.

Model	Accuracy	Recall	F1-Score	Specificity
Sparse-STGCN	0.800	0.857	0.800	0.750
STGCN (Baseline)	0.753	0.782	0.760	0.720

Recall rate, which minimizes missed diagnoses. Figure 6 presents the Normalized Confusion Matrix.

The ablation study validated the contribution of key components added to the STGCN baseline (75.3% Acc., 3.80 G FLOPs). Dynamic Adjacency (DA) and the Squeeze-and-Excitation (SE) module individually improved accuracy (up to 77.1% with DA), and their synergy boosted performance to 78.5%. The final Sparse-STGCN (integrating DA, SE, and Structural Sparsity) achieved the optimal result: 80.0% accuracy (+4.7% improvement) and a substantial efficiency gain by cutting FLOPs to 0.75 G, successfully delivering a dual improvement in performance and efficiency(See Table 2).

The findings confirm the individual and synergistic contributions. Figure 7 shows that enforcing structural sparsity leads to a significant performance increase (Accuracy +6.7%, Recall +9.9%, F1-Score +6.7%) compared to a Dense GCN module, achieving the core goal of reducing FLOPs from 3.8 G to a highly efficient 0.75 G.

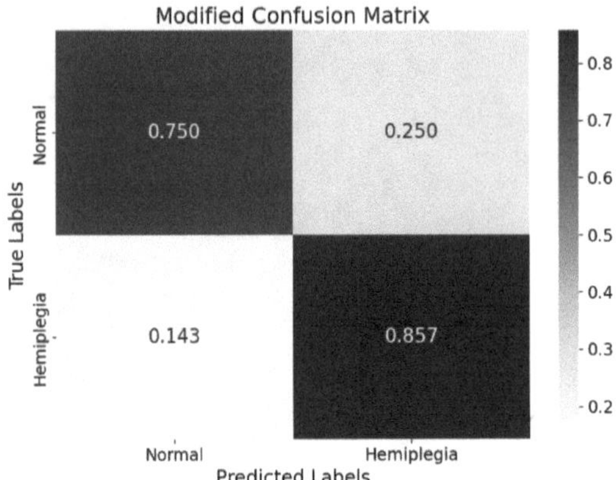

Fig. 6. Normalized Confusion Matrix for the classification of 'Normal' and 'Hemiplegia' by the Sparse-STGCN model. The values indicate the proportion of correctly and incorrectly classified samples within each true class.

Table 2. Comprehensive ablation study results on key components.

Model	DA	SE	Sp.	Acc. (%)	Δ Acc.	FLOPs (G)	Params (M)
STGCN (Baseline)				75.3	—	3.80	3.10
+ DA	✓			77.1	+1.8	3.80	3.15
+ SE		✓		76.5	+1.2	3.82	3.10
+ DA + SE	✓	✓		78.5	+3.2	3.82	3.15
Sparse-STGCN (Final)	✓	✓	✓	80.0	+4.7	0.75	3.74

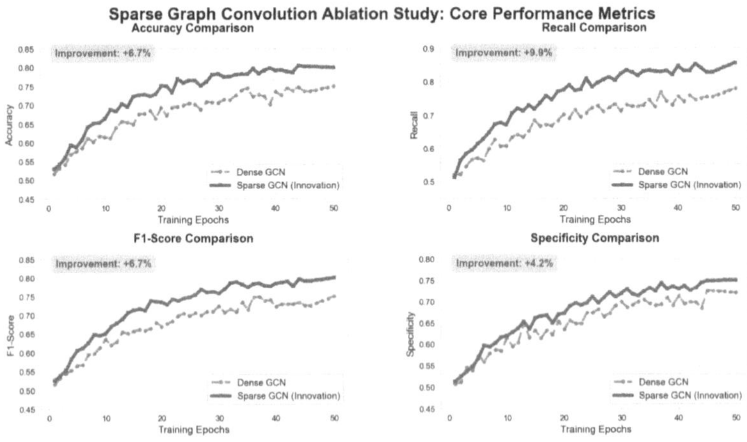

Fig. 7. Ablation study performance comparison of our proposed Sparse Graph Convolutional Networks (Sparse GCN, red solid line) versus the baseline Dense GCN (orange dashed line) across core classification metrics. (Color figure online)

4.4 Comparative Experiments and Analysis

We compared Sparse-STGCN with mainstream network architectures: the original STGCN and HRNet (Table 3).

Optimization of Model Parameters. Our Sparse-STGCN is exceptionally lightweight with only 3.74 M parameters, comparable to STGCN but significantly less than HRNet (up to 77.5 M), reducing storage and deployment costs.

Breakthrough in Computational Efficiency. The model achieves just 0.75 G FLOPs and an inference speed of 821 FPS. This represents an approximate 80% reduction in FLOPs compared to the baseline STGCN (3.8 G FLOPs), making it ideal for real-time operation on resource-limited devices.

Deployment of Adaptive Enhancement. The model size is only 4.26 MB, nearly three times smaller than the unoptimized STGCN, allowing easy integration into mobile devices or embedded systems.

In summary, Sparse-STGCN offers a superior balance of computational efficiency, model size, and inference speed, making it an ideal choice for smart rehabilitation in resource-constrained environments.

Table 3. Comparison table of different model performances.

Model	Parameter Amount (M)	FLOPs (G)	Model Size (MB)	Inference Speed (FPS)	Accuracy
Sparse-STGCN	3.74	0.75	4.26	821	80.0%
STGCN	3.1	3.8	12.4	N/A	75.3%
HRNet-W18-C-Small-v2	15.6	2.42	62.4	N/A	78.2%
HRNet-W48-C	77.5	16.1	310	N/A	81.8%

5 Conclusion

This research presents CPESS, a lightweight video-based hemiplegia recognition method utilizing AlphaPose and a novel Sparse ST-GCN. This non-contact, low-cost solution provides objective data for early screening and rehabilitation monitoring. The core Sparse ST-GCN significantly reduces computational load (80% FLOPs reduction) while maintaining high accuracy (80.0%). Future work will expand the dataset and explore multi-modal fusion for improved robustness and integration into smart rehabilitation systems.

Acknowledgments. The authors gratefully appreciate the anonymous reviewers for all of their helpful comments. This research is supported in part by the National Natural Science Foundation of China under Grant (Nos. 62172247), Natural Science Foundation of Shandong Province (No. ZR2024MF087).

References

1. Cao, Z., Hidalgo, G., Simon, T., Wei, S.E., Sheikh, Y.: Openpose: realtime multi-person 2d pose estimation using part affinity fields. IEEE Trans. Pattern Anal. Mach. Intell. **43**(1), 172–186 (2019)
2. Cheng, K., Zhang, Y., He, X., Chen, W., Cheng, J., Lu, H.: Skeleton-based action recognition with shift graph convolutional network. In: Proceedings of the IEEE/CVF Conference on Computer Vision and Pattern Recognition, pp. 183–192 (2020)
3. Duan, K., Bai, S., Xie, L., Qi, H., Huang, Q., Tian, Q.: Centernet: keypoint triplets for object detection. In: Proceedings of the IEEE/CVF International Conference on Computer Vision, pp. 6569–6578 (2019)
4. Elangovan, V.S., Devarajan, R., Khalaf, O.I., Sharif, M.S., Elmedany, W.: Analysing an imbalanced stroke prediction dataset using machine learning techniques. Karbala Int. J. Mod. Sci. **10**(2), 8 (2024)
5. Fang, H.S., Xie, S., Tai, Y.W., Lu, C.: RMPE: regional multi-person pose estimation. In: Proceedings of the IEEE International Conference on Computer Vision, pp. 2334–2343 (2017)
6. Girshick, R., Donahue, J., Darrell, T., Malik, J.: Rich feature hierarchies for accurate object detection and semantic segmentation. In: Proceedings of the IEEE Conference on Computer Vision and Pattern Recognition, pp. 580–587 (2014)
7. Guo, B., et al.: The impact of scanner domain shift on deep learning performance in medical imaging: an experimental study. arXiv preprint arXiv:2409.04368 (2024)
8. He, K., Gkioxari, G., Dollár, P., Girshick, R.: Mask R-CNN. In: Proceedings of the IEEE International Conference on Computer Vision, pp. 2961–2969 (2017)
9. Kwakkel, G., Kollen, B.J., Krebs, H.I.: Effects of robot-assisted therapy on upper limb recovery after stroke: a systematic review. Neurorehabil. Neural Repair **22**(2), 111–121 (2008)
10. Liu, W., et al.: SSD: single shot multibox detector. In: Leibe, B., Matas, J., Sebe, N., Welling, M. (eds.) ECCV 2016. LNCS, vol. 9905, pp. 21–37. Springer, Cham (2016). https://doi.org/10.1007/978-3-319-46448-0_2
11. Redmon, J., Divvala, S., Girshick, R., Farhadi, A.: You only look once: unified, real-time object detection. In: Proceedings of the IEEE Conference on Computer Vision and Pattern Recognition, pp. 779–788 (2016)
12. Redmon, J., Farhadi, A.: Yolov3: an incremental improvement. arXiv preprint arXiv:1804.02767 (2018)
13. Ren, S., He, K., Girshick, R., Sun, J.: Faster R-CNN: towards real-time object detection with region proposal networks. In: Advances in Neural Information Processing Systems, vol. 28 (2015)
14. Shi, L., Zhang, Y., Cheng, J., Lu, H.: Skeleton-based action recognition with directed graph neural networks. In: Proceedings of the IEEE/CVF Conference on Computer Vision and Pattern Recognition, pp. 7912–7921 (2019)
15. Shi, L., Zhang, Y., Cheng, J., Lu, H.: Two-stream adaptive graph convolutional networks for skeleton-based action recognition. In: Proceedings of the IEEE/CVF Conference on Computer Vision and Pattern Recognition, pp. 12026–12035 (2019)
16. Sun, K., Xiao, B., Liu, D., Wang, J.: Deep high-resolution representation learning for human pose estimation. In: Proceedings of the IEEE/CVF Conference on Computer Vision and Pattern Recognition, pp. 5693–5703 (2019)
17. Thakur, D., Biswas, S.: Attention-based deep learning framework for hemiplegic gait prediction with smartphone sensors. IEEE Sens. J. **22**(12), 11979–11988 (2022)

18. Wang, H., Wang, M., Li, D., Deng, F., Pan, Z., Song, Y.: Gait phase recognition of hip exoskeleton system based on CNN and HHO-SVM model. Electronics **14**(1), 107 (2024)
19. Wang, W., Li, K., Yue, S., Yin, C., Wei, N.: Associations between lower-limb muscle activation and knee flexion in post-stroke individuals: a study on the stance-to-swing phases of gait. PLoS ONE **12**(9), e0183865 (2017)
20. Yan, S., Xiong, Y., Lin, D.: Spatial temporal graph convolutional networks for skeleton-based action recognition. In: Proceedings of the AAAI Conference on Artificial Intelligence, vol. 32 (2018)
21. Zang, Y., Yang, D., Liu, T., Li, H., Zhao, S., Liu, Q.: SparseShift-GCN: high precision skeleton-based action recognition. Pattern Recogn. Lett. **153**, 136–143 (2022)

StepMind: Integrated Foot-Interaction System for Cognitive-Motor Executive Training

Wei Gai[1], Yu Wang[1], Chenyu Zang[1], Gaorong Lv[1](✉), Ying Yang[2], and Chenglei Yang[1]

[1] Shandong University, Jinan 250101, China
gw@sdu.edu.cn, 15953173765@163.com
[2] Shandong Mental Health Center, Jinan 250014, China

Abstract. Human daily actions rely on the coordinated cognition and movement. This paper presents StepMind, an interactive projection system integrating cognitive-motor training, which enables comprehensive executive function (EF) training through multiple moving targets. StepMind allows users to interact with virtual moving targets in real-time via foot movements, achieving training of EF subcomponents (working memory, inhibitory control and cognitive switching) through multi-target capture tasks, and dynamically adapts to meet diverse user needs. To address the challenges of low sensitivity in foot interaction and multi-target ambiguity in human-computer interaction, we innovatively combine a trivariate Gaussian footfall model with Bayesian intent inference. This framework models the spatial uncertainty of foot placements and applies probabilistic inference to improve target selection accuracy in multi-target scenarios. A 14-day user study with ten participants demonstrated overall EF improvements, while a preliminary deployment in a mental health facility highlighted the system's potential as a novel, affordable approach to cognitive rehabilitation.

Keywords: Interactive Projection · Cognitive-Motor Integration · Executive Function Training · Human–Computer Interaction

1 Introduction

Everyday activities rely on the coordination of cognition and movement. With population aging and increasing demand for cognitive rehabilitation, accessible cognitive-motor training has become increasingly important across age groups. This need is particularly evident in executive function (EF) training, which supports goal-directed behavior through three key components: working memory (maintaining task-relevant information), inhibitory control (suppressing distractions), and cognitive switching (shifting attention between tasks). EF is closely linked to real-world cognitive-motor coordination [1]. According to the brain plasticity compensation model, repeated sensorimotor engagement can enhance neural activation, particularly in aging populations, positioning integrated cognitive-motor training as a promising approach for maintaining or improving EF [2].

W. Gai and Y. Wang—These authors contributed equally to this work.

A. Hinkenjan et al. (Eds.): ICXR 2025, LNCS 16428, pp. 454–462, 2026.
https://doi.org/10.1007/978-981-95-7195-6_33

Despite increasing interest in technology-assisted EF training, existing approaches still face challenges in achieving effective cognitive-motor integration. Computerized cognitive training (CCT) platforms offer scalable interventions but isolate cognitive practice from physical engagement, relying on prolonged sedentary use and targeting limited EF subcomponents [3]. Virtual reality (VR) systems offer richer sensorimotor interaction but may cause discomfort or motion sickness due to head-mounted displays, and the use of wearable devices can hinder long-term adoption, particularly among older adults and individuals with mobility limitations [4, 5].

Building on these developments, interactive projection technology provides a natural and accessible medium for cognitive-motor training. By transforming floor spaces into responsive environments, it enables embodied interaction without wearable devices, fostering cognitive-motor synergy [6]. Previous systems have demonstrated benefits for memory and balance training in children [7], yet most rely on static or single-target tasks [20], limiting engagement and the breadth of EF training.

To advance this line of research, this study introduces StepMind, an interactive projection system designed for integrated cognitive-motor training. By projecting dynamic virtual targets onto the floor, StepMind allows users to perform real-time multi-target tasks that collectively train working memory, inhibitory control, and cognitive switching. To ensure precise foot-based interaction, the system combines a trivariate Gaussian footfall model, which captures spatial and temporal uncertainty in foot placement, with Bayesian intent inference to accurately identify target selection under complex and dynamic conditions. Building on advances in VR-based systems, StepMind focuses on natural, wearable-free interaction and supports personalized difficulty adjustment (e.g., target speed and distractor count), making it suitable for diverse age groups. Implemented with widely available hardware, including a projector and Kinect sensor, it provides a practical and adaptable platform for cognitive-motor training in both educational and clinical settings.

2 Related Work

Cognitive-motor integration has become a central approach for enhancing real-world functioning, evolving from therapist-led interventions to digital and interactive technologies. Traditional cognitive training is effective but constrained by fixed locations, high costs, and limited scalability [8–10]. Computerized Cognitive Training (CCT) platforms such as Lumosity and Peak provide accessible programs that improve working memory and reasoning [11–14], yet they largely isolate cognition from movement and promote sedentary use [15].

Virtual Reality (VR) systems embed cognitive tasks in immersive, movement-rich environments, showing gains in attention, memory, and balance [16–18]. However, VR-based EF training often targets single subcomponents and faces usability challenges-motion sickness, wearable discomfort, and limited suitability for older or mobility-impaired users [5].

Complementing the above methods, interactive projection offers a natural, wearable-free medium that integrates cognitive and physical activity through embodied interaction [6]. Prior projection systems have improved attention, balance, and memory in children and older adults [7, 19], but most employ static or single-target designs. Recent studies suggest that foot-based interaction can enhance reaction time and attentional control [20], yet comprehensive multi-target EF training remains underexplored.

Building on these foundations, this study introduces StepMind, a foot-based interactive projection system that integrates multi-target, dynamic tasks engaging all three EF subcomponents (working memory, inhibitory control, and cognitive switching) to achieve natural, embodied cognitive-motor training.

3 StepMind: Design and Implementation

3.1 System Architecture

StepMind extends a validated foot-interaction framework [20] to support dynamic multi-target tasks. Virtual targets are projected onto the floor, and users' foot trajectories are tracked in real time via Microsoft Kinect (see Fig. 1). Target size automatically scales to foot length to ensure ergonomic consistency and spatial alignment between physical and virtual spaces.

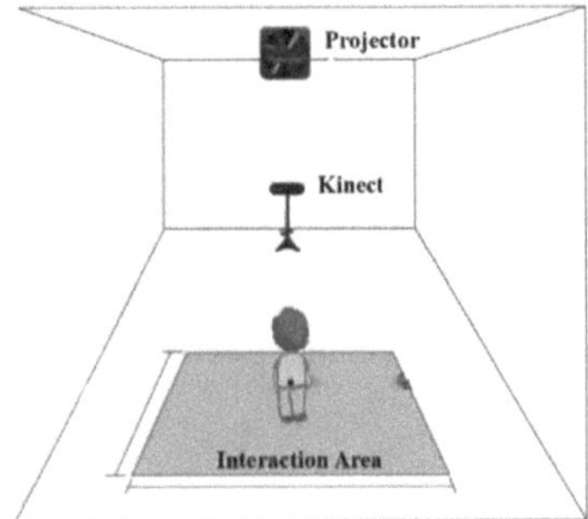

Fig. 1. System architecture.

To address selection ambiguity under dynamic conditions, StepMind integrates a trivariate Gaussian footfall model with Bayesian intent inference. The Gaussian model represents spatial-temporal uncertainty in three orthogonal dimensions: the target's motion direction, its normal direction, and the temporal deviation between footfall and target movement, thereby compensating for natural motor imprecision and improving selection accuracy over threshold-based methods [20]. The Bayesian inference module extends this framework to multi-target contexts by estimating posterior intent probabilities for all potential targets based on their motion-aligned Gaussian likelihoods. The target with the highest posterior probability is selected as the intended one, ensuring robust identification even under motion and spatial uncertainty (Fig. 2).

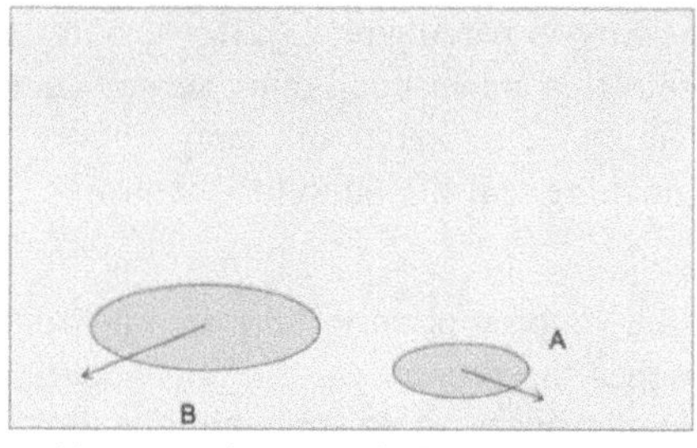

(a) Two moving targets in the interaction area

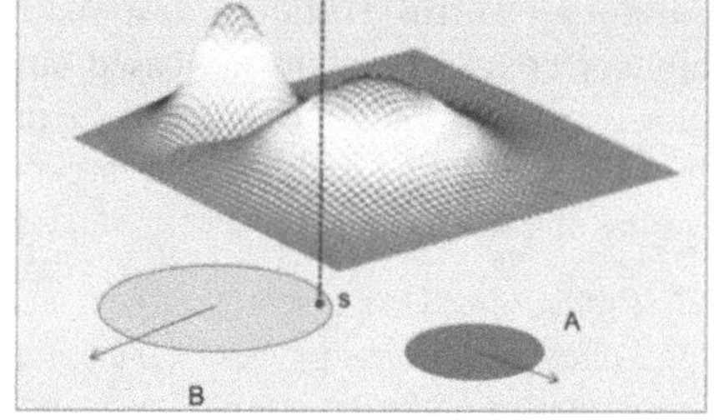

(b) Bayesian inference identifies target A as the intended selection

Fig. 2. Schematic of Bayesian Intent Inference.

3.2 Executive Function Training Task Design

StepMind incorporates three targeted tasks corresponding to the core EF subcomponents: working memory, inhibitory control, and cognitive switching. All tasks feature dynamic multi-target interactions that adjust difficulty in real time (e.g., target speed, distractor number, rule complexity) to accommodate different age groups.

Working Memory Training. Based on the numerical sequence recall paradigm [21, 22], this task strengthens working memory by combining sequence memorization with sequential target stepping. Cognitive load is scaled through sequence complexity, while motor demand increases with target dynamics, aligning with Baddeley's model of working memory.

Task Procedure. 1) Memory Phase: A numerical sequence (e.g., "2, 5, 3, 1") is presented in a prompt box. 2) Execution Phase: Users step on moving circular targets, each labeled with a number, in the same order as the memorized sequence. The interface displays the sequence prompt, countdown timer, score, and movement distance to maintain engagement (see Fig. 3).

Difficulty Progression. 1) Level 1–2: Memorize 4 single-digit numbers; targets are stationary (Level 1) or slow-moving (Level 2). 2) Level 3: Memorize 4 two-digit numbers (with identical tens digits to prevent simplified memorization); targets move at moderate speed. 3) Level 4: Memorize 4 three-digit numbers (with identical hundreds digits); targets move at increased speed.

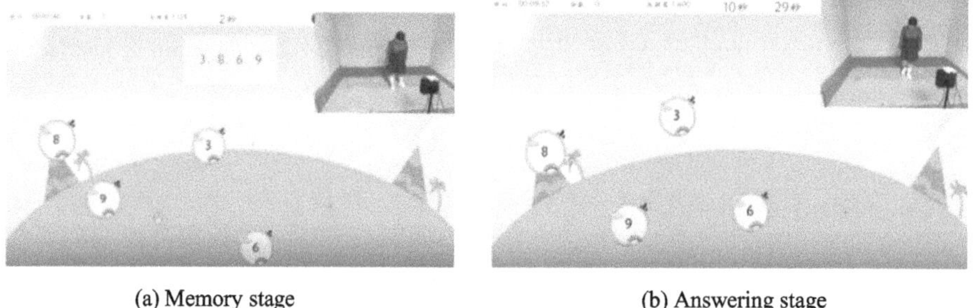

(a) Memory stage (b) Answering stage

Fig. 3. Example of the Working Memory Training Interface

Inhibitory Control Training. Inspired by the Stroop paradigm [23], this task trains inhibitory control through rule-based target selection under conflicting sensory cues (color, text, background). Users must suppress automatic responses and apply the correct rule while interacting with moving targets, mimicking real-life inhibitory control (e.g., stopping at a red light).

Task Procedure. Users select targets according to prompt-attribute matching rules (e.g., "choose the target where text color matches the prompt color"). The interface incorporates multimodal conflict cues and dynamic targets, as illustrated in Fig. 4.

Difficulty Progression. 1) Level 1–2: Two rules (e.g., text-color match vs. text-content match); two stationary (Level 1) or slow-moving (Level 2) targets. 2) Level 3: Three rules (adding background-color cues); four moving targets with conflicting text/color attributes. 3) Level 4: Nine rules (combining text, text color, and background color); four fast-moving targets with heightened sensory conflict.

Cognitive Switching Training. Adapted from the cued task-switching paradigm [24], this task enhances cognitive flexibility by requiring rapid shifts between rule conditions during dynamic foot interaction. Switching demand scales with target speed and the number of distractors, promoting multitasking and adaptive attention control.

Task Procedure. Users identify and step on the single target matching one cue's color-number combination among several moving targets before time expires. This design compels users to flexibly shift attention between cues and moving targets, enhancing cognitive switching under motor load (see Fig. 5).

Difficulty Progression. 1) Level 1–2: Four cues (three distractors); slow-moving targets. 2) Level 3: Six cues (five distractors); moderately moving targets. 3) Level 4: Eight cues (seven distractors); fast-moving targets with occasional direction changes.

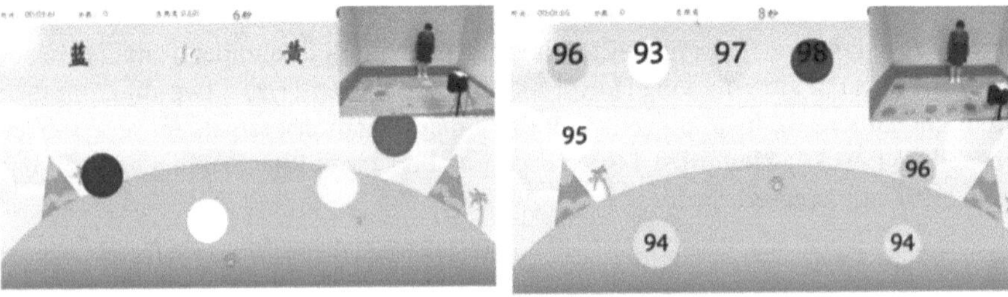

Fig. 4. Inhibitory control training interface. **Fig. 5.** Cognitive switching training interface.

4 User Study

To evaluate StepMind's effectiveness in enhancing executive function (EF) through integrated cognitive-motor training, a 14-day user study was conducted to assess improvements in working memory, inhibitory control, and cognitive switching.

4.1 Participants

Ten participants were recruited from local schools and senior centers, comprising five children (8–12 years; 2 males, 3 females) and five older adults (60–70 years; 3 males, 2 females). The mean ages were 8.2 ± 1.3 and 65.4 ± 3.7 years, respectively. All participants were cognitively healthy, physically independent, and free from conditions affecting movement. The study adhered to the Declaration of Helsinki and was approved by the university's ethics committee.

4.2 Experimental Design

All sessions took place in a quiet activity room with uniform lighting and a non-slip floor. EF performance was evaluated using StepMind's built-in assessment module, which replicated the training structure with adjusted parameters to minimize practice effects. Two metrics were collected: Accuracy, defined as the proportion of correctly selected targets; Completion Time, defined as the duration from task onset to final target selection, excluding pauses such as between encoding and execution phases.

Participants completed a 10-min familiarization session, followed by pre- and post-training assessments using standardized parameters. Training was conducted daily for 14 days, comprising three EF tasks (~15 min each) with 5-min rest intervals between tasks. Future studies may adjust rest durations by age (shorter for children, longer for older adults).

Difficulty increased progressively from Level 1 until the maximum level or time limit was reached. A trained researcher supervised all sessions to ensure calibration consistency and participant safety.

4.3 Results

Pre- and post-training performance on accuracy and completion time was analyzed using the Wilcoxon signed-rank test. In addition to significance levels, effect sizes ($r = Z/\sqrt{N}$) and 95% confidence intervals (CI) were reported to evaluate the strength and precision of the observed effects. Analyses were conducted for the overall sample ($N = 10$) and by age group (children: 8–12 years; older adults: 60–70 years).

Working Memory. Accuracy significantly improved after training ($p = .001$, $z = -2.80$, $r = .89$, 95% CI [0.053, 0.073]), corresponding to an average 5–7% gain. Similar improvements were found in both the child ($p = .031$, $r = .90$, 95% CI [0.043, 0.073]) and older adult ($p = .031$, $r = .90$, 95% CI [0.053, 0.080]) groups. Completion time did not change significantly, suggesting that training primarily enhanced accuracy rather than speed.

Inhibitory Control. Overall accuracy increased significantly ($p = .021$, $z = 2.04$, $r = .65$, 95% CI [0.014, 0.071]). Subgroup analyses indicated non-significant trends toward improvement in children ($p = .12$, $r = .54$, 95% CI [–0.002, 0.068]) and marginal effects in older adults ($p = .07$, $r = .66$, 95% CI [–0.005, 0.075]). Completion time showed no significant change, likely reflecting limited statistical power ($n = 5$ per group).

Cognitive Switching. Accuracy improved overall ($p = .016$, $z = 2.15$, $r = .68$, 95% CI [0.012, 0.062]), with a marginal reduction in completion time ($p = .049$, $z = 1.65$, $r = .52$, 95% CI [−95.2, 8.7]). By age, children showed near-significant accuracy gains ($p = .053$, $z = 1.62$, $r = .72$, 95% CI [0.013, 0.073]), while older adults exhibited faster completion times approaching significance ($p = .045$, $z = 1.70$, $r = .76$, 95% CI [−73.0, 4.4]).

Across tasks, StepMind training produced consistent accuracy improvements, while completion time effects were weaker and more variable. Exploratory subgroup trends suggested that children tended to gain more in accuracy, whereas older adults improved more in speed. Given the small sample size and multiple comparisons, these findings should be interpreted as preliminary. Nevertheless, they provide encouraging evidence for the potential of StepMind to enhance cognitive-motor integration and EF performance across age groups.

4.4 Discussion

The observed improvements in executive function (EF), particularly in accuracy, are consistent with StepMind's cognitive-motor integration design. This aligns with prior evidence that coupling physical movement with cognitive demands enhances EF-related neural pathways, particularly in the prefrontal cortex and cerebellum [2]. The relative stability of completion time, despite accuracy gains, may reflect a prioritization of precision over speed, facilitated by the system's adaptive task structure.

Although exploratory due to the small sample size, age-specific analyses revealed encouraging trends. Both children and older adults showed improvements in working memory accuracy, while cognitive switching displayed age-dependent patterns: children tended to improve in accuracy, whereas older adults exhibited shorter completion times. These findings suggest that StepMind's adaptive difficulty (e.g., adjustable target speed and task complexity) accommodates developmental and age-related differences, addressing the "one-size-fits-all" limitation of existing tools.

However, several limitations warrant caution. The small sample ($n = 10$) and short intervention (14 days) restrict generalizability and may have limited detection of speed-related changes. The absence of a control group prevents causal inference, as improvements may partly reflect practice effects. Future studies should involve larger, more diverse samples, extend the training period, and incorporate neurophysiological measures (e.g., EEG, fNIRS) to clarify the mechanisms underlying EF enhancement. A randomized design including cognitive-motor, cognitive-only, and no-training groups would further isolate the effects of integrated training and strengthen causal conclusions.

5 Conclusion and Future Work

This study presented StepMind, an interactive projection system that integrates cognitive and motor training to enhance executive function (EF). By combining a trivariate Gaussian footfall model with Bayesian intent inference, the system addresses key challenges of foot-based interaction and supports the integrated training of working memory, inhibitory control, and cognitive switching. A 14-day user study demonstrated accuracy improvements, and preliminary deployment in a mental health center indicated its potential as an accessible tool for cognitive-motor rehabilitation.

Building on the current findings, future work will explore three main directions. These include developing age- and context-specific interfaces to improve user adaptation, integrating neurophysiological measures such as EEG and fNIRS to probe the neural basis of cognitive-motor integration, and expanding scalability and ecological validity through extended studies and adaptation of StepMind's framework to VR/MR environments.

Acknowledgments. This work is supported by National Science and Technology Major Project (2022ZD0118002), the National Natural Science Foundation of China under Grant (62007021, 62277035), Shandong Provincial Natural Science Foundation (ZR2024QC304) and Shandong Province Youth Entrepreneurship Technology Support Program for Higher Education Institutions (2022KJN028).

Disclosure of Interests. The authors have no competing interests to declare that are relevant to the content of this article.

References

1. Wang, C.X., Chen, T.Y., Han, B.X.: Plasticity of the prefrontal cortex in old age and underlying mechanisms. Adv. Psychol. Sci. **26**(11), 2003–2012 (2018)
2. Park, D.C., Bischof, G.N.: The aging mind: neuroplasticity in response to cognitive training. Dialogues Clin. Neurosci. **15**(1), 109–119 (2013)
3. Hu, Y.Y.: The development of a system for cognitive ability detection and training. University of Chinese Academy of Sciences (Shenzhen Institutes of Advanced Technology, Chinese Academy of Sciences) (2020)
4. Zhu, M., Shi, J., Li, Z.: Effectiveness of computerized cognitive training for patients with cognitive dysfunction: an overview of systematic reviews. J. Nurs. **30**(21), 46–53 (2023)
5. Weech, S., Varghese, J.P., Barnett-Cowan, M.: Estimating the sensorimotor components of cybersickness. J. Neurophysiol. **120**(5), 2201–2217 (2018)
6. Van Delden, R., Moreno, A., Poppe, R., Reidsma, D., Heylen, D.: A thing of beauty: steering behavior in an interactive playground. In: Proceedings of the CHI Conference on Human Factors in Computing Systems 2017, pp. 2462–2472. ACM (2017)
7. Cornejo, R., et al.: Serious games for basic learning mechanisms: reinforcing Mexican children's gross motor skills and attention. Pers. Ubiquit. Comput. **25**(2), 375–390 (2021)
8. Kueider, A.M., Parisi, J.M., Gross, A.L., Rebok, G.W.: Computerized cognitive training with older adults: a systematic review. PLoS ONE **7**(7), e40588 (2012)
9. Wadley, V.G., Benz, R.L., Ball, K.K., Roenker, D.L., Edwards, J.D., Vance, D.E.: Development and evaluation of home-based speed-of-processing training for older adults. Arch. Phys. Med. Rehabil. **87**(6), 757–763 (2006)
10. Jak, A.J., Seelye, A.M., Jurick, S.M.: Crosswords to computers: a critical review of popular approaches to cognitive enhancement. Neuropsychol. Rev. **23**(1), 13–26 (2013)
11. Phillips, N.L., et al.: Computerized working memory training for children with moderate to severe traumatic brain injury: a double-blind, randomized, placebo-controlled trial. J. Neurotrauma **33**(23), 2097–2104 (2016)

12. Cortese, S., et al.: Cognitive training for attention-deficit/hyperactivity disorder: meta-analysis of clinical and neuropsychological outcomes from randomized controlled trials. J. Am. Acad. Child Adolescent Psychiatry **54**(3), 164–174 (2015)
13. Hardy, J.L., et al.: Enhancing cognitive abilities with comprehensive training: a large, online, randomized, active-controlled trial. PLoS ONE **10**(9), e0134467 (2015)
14. Peijnenborgh, J.C., Hurks, P.M., Aldenkamp, A.P., Vles, J.S., Hendriksen, J.G.: Efficacy of working memory training in children and adolescents with learning disabilities: a review study and meta-analysis. Neuropsychol. Rehabil. **26**(5–6), 645–672 (2016)
15. Lumsden, J., Edwards, E.A., Lawrence, N.S., Coyle, D., Munafò, M.R.: Gamification of cognitive assessment and cognitive training: a systematic review of applications and efficacy. JMIR Serious Games **4**(2), e5888 (2016)
16. Mack, D.J., Wiesmann, H., Ilg, U.J.: Video game players show higher performance but no difference in speed of attention shifts. Acta Physiol (Oxf.) **169**, 11–19 (2016)
17. Gamito, P., et al.: Cognitive stimulation of elderly individuals with instrumental virtual reality-based activities of daily life: pre-post treatment study. Cyberpsychol. Behave. Soc. Netw. **22**(1), 69–75 (2019)
18. Glueck, A.C., Han, D.Y.: Improvement potentials in balance and visuo-motor reaction time after mixed reality action game play: a pilot study. Virtual Reality **24**(2), 223–229 (2020)
19. Wang, Y., et al.: Exer-learning: a new genre combines learning, exercise and fun for children. Procedia Comput. Sci. **174**, 735–745 (2020)
20. Zang, C., et al.: Supporting foot interaction of reaction time training system. Comput. Anim. Virtual Worlds **35**(1), e2219 (2024)
21. Gevins, A.S., Cutillo, B.C.: Neuroelectric evidence for distributed processing in human working memory. Electroencephalogr. Clin. Neurophysiol. **87**(3), 128–143 (1993)
22. Cohen, J.D., et al.: Temporal dynamics of brain activation during a working memory task. Nature **386**(6625), 604–608 (1997)
23. Scarpina, F., Tagini, S.: The stroop color and word test. Front. Psychol. **8**, 557 (2017)
24. Mayr, U.: What matters in the cued task-switching paradigm: tasks or cues? Psychon. Bull. Rev. **13**(5), 794–799 (2006)

Interdisciplinary Workshop on XR and AI Interfaces for Stress Management

Ze Dong[1(✉)], Jingjing Zhang[1], Panote Siriaraya[2], Tatsunori Hirai[3], Kongmeng Liew[4], Santawat Thanyadit[5], Thanapong Intharah[6], Panida Yomaboot[7], Barrett Ens[8], Adrian Clark[1], and Thammathip Piumsomboon[1]

[1] SoPD, University of Canterbury, Christchurch, New Zealand
ze.dong@pg.canterbury.ac.nz, jzh201@uclive.ac.nz, {adrian.clark,tham.piumsomboon}@canterbury.ac.nz
[2] School of Information and Human Science, Kyoto Institute of Technology, Kyoto, Japan
[3] Global Media Studies, Komazawa University, Setagaya, Japan
thirai@komazawa.ac.jp
[4] School of Psychology, University of Canterbury, Christchurch, New Zealand
kongmeng.liew@canterbury.ac.nz
[5] Computer Science, Durham University, Durham, UK
[6] Computer Science, Khon Kaen University, Khon Kaen, Thailand
thanin@kku.ac.th
[7] Department of Psychiatry Siriraj Hospital, Mahidol University, Salaya, Thailand
Panida.yom@mahidol.ac.th
[8] Faculty of Science, The University of British Columbia, Vancouver, Canada
barrett.ens@ubc.ca

Abstract. Modern young people typically experience stress in their studies and daily lives, making management methods essential for stress reduction and psychological well-being. With the continued advancement of XR and AI, the effectiveness and functionality of these techniques in stress management are drawing increasing attention. The integration of XR and AI offers expanded possibilities for stress regulation. To explore the future potential of combinations of XR and AI in stress management, we organised an interdisciplinary workshop comprising experts in psychology, interaction design, XR and AI. This workshop generated two preliminary research concepts that served as a prelude for further research.

Keywords: Extended Reality · Artificial Intelligence · Psychology · Human Interface Design

1 Introduction

Stress is a pervasive aspect of contemporary life, frequently triggered by unforeseen events demanding rapid, informed decisions. While effectively navigating

A. Hinkenjan et al. (Eds.): ICXR 2025, LNCS 16428, pp. 463–476, 2026.
https://doi.org/10.1007/978-981-95-7195-6_34

these complexities can alleviate stress, traditional management strategies often fall short against the increasing number and variety of modern stressors [56]. Technological advancements, however, present novel opportunities to enhance stress management.

Extended Reality (XR), encompassing Virtual (VR), Augmented (AR), and Mixed Reality (MR) [28] has shown significant potential in this domain [32, 36,44]. XR technologies create immersive experiences, ranging from augmenting the real world to generating entirely virtual environments. These experiences can alter perception and facilitate collaborative decision-making [11,38,39], offering new design avenues for managing daily stress. More recently, the integration of Artificial Intelligence (AI) has begun to amplify XR's capabilities.

This paper explores the synergy between XR and AI for stress management. We conceptualise XR as a powerful front-end interface, providing immersive experiences that allow users to better understand and interact with information related to their stressors. This capacity for enhanced understanding and control aligns well with human psychological needs for agency and awareness, contributing to well-being. Conversely, AI serves as a robust back-end engine, adept at processing complex data, detecting nuanced patterns indicative of stress triggers, and identifying subtle oversight information that humans might miss. AI's analytical capabilities enable the personalisation of experiences and interventions [18].

The core motivation for the proposed workshop stems from harnessing this synergy: leveraging XR's user-facing strengths for comprehension and control, combined with AI's analytical power for detection and personalisation, to find unified design ideas for managing stress. Recognising the complexities of stress and mental health, the workshop brings together experts from psychology, interaction design, AI, and XR. Its primary objective is to investigate how integrated XR and AI systems can mitigate daily stressors, particularly focusing on those relevant to young people. Through collaborative discussion, brainstorming, and evaluation, the workshop aims to review existing technologies, identify common stress triggers, generate innovative solutions, outline initial prototype concepts, and define future research directions. Ultimately, this work aims to lay a foundational stepping stone for the development of more effective, human-centred stress management tools.

2 Background

This section reviews pertinent research on user interaction design in XR for mental health and the integration of AI and XR, providing a foundation for the workshop discussions.

2.1 XR and AI Technologies in Stress Management

Effective stress management typically involves identifying stressors, developing coping mechanisms, and addressing related emotional issues [21]. XR technologies, noted for enhancing presence and immersion [48,55], offer innovative methods for stress intervention [33,44,52]. For instance, VR allows individuals to safely confront challenging scenarios and explore coping strategies [14]. The COVID-19 pandemic further highlighted XR's value in telemedicine and remote psychological support [12,22,35]. Studies demonstrate that various VR environments [15,19] and specific elements like soundscapes [16] can alleviate negative emotions, suggesting XR's potential, including modalities like music therapy, for stress management. However, barriers such as cost, time, and energy can hinder self-managed stress interventions. Implementing technology-based solutions effectively requires interdisciplinary collaboration.

AI technologies also hold considerable promise for mental health care, including stress management, depression treatment, and diagnostics [8]. Chatbots and conversational AI offer scalable, immediate, and personalised mental health support [25]. While the rapid rise of large language models (LLMs) presents opportunities, their ethical and practical application in mental health requires careful consideration. Interdisciplinary input is crucial to navigate these complexities and ensure responsible integration.

2.2 Interaction Design and User Experience in XR for Mental Well-Being

VR and AR have been extensively explored for diagnosing and treating mental health conditions. Hardware advancements enable richer multi-sensory and multi-modal XR interactions [41]. Devices like heart rate monitors [10], breathing trainers [29], and EEGs [2] can aid in detecting psychological states and supporting relaxation techniques [44]. Yet, challenges like low sustained user interest and the need for frequent data updates can impede long-term effectiveness [41].

Personalised XR-based mental health interventions tailored to individual needs may increase user acceptance and engagement [5,17]. Encouraging open communication is also vital; research suggests that enhanced transparency and anonymity can foster user sharing and improve outcomes [1,54].

Community support and collaborative XR approaches are also important. Studies indicate XR can facilitate support networks and build empathy [24,47,53,57]. Realising XR's full potential requires considering both technology and user experience, demanding collaboration among experts from diverse fields. Effective stress management necessitates not only technological support but also active user participation, underscoring the need for interdisciplinary discussion to enhance XR's applicability.

3 Workshop Details

This online interdisciplinary workshop explored how AI and XR technologies could mitigate daily stressors for young people, bringing together experts in psychology, interaction design, AI, and XR. Given the participants' global distribution, Doodle was used for scheduling, Zoom for conducting the sessions, and Miro as the collaborative whiteboard platform. Miro allowed for personal workspaces, shared collaborative areas, and asynchronous content addition.

3.1 Participants

The workshop concept originated from discussions involving doctoral candidates and professors. A pilot workshop with specialists in relevant areas helped refine the process and inform participant invitations for the formal workshop, ensuring diverse expertise.

We recruited experts from our professional network via email. Coordinating the workshop across different global time zones presented a challenge. Consequently, participants were divided into groups, each ideally comprising experts from the four key disciplines. We successfully conducted two sessions; a third was postponed due to participant availability issues.

Session 1 involved 3 associate professors and 1 senior lecturer (4 males) with an average age of 37.5 years (SD = 3.16) and 13 years of research experience (SD = 2.71). Expertise levels in XR and AI varied as self-reported.

Session 2 included 1 associate professor, 2 lecturers, and 1 chief psychologist (3 males and 1 female) with an average age of 38.5 years (SD = 4.12) and 12.5 years of research experience (SD = 3.11). Expertise levels were self-reported. The chief psychologist possessed 13 years of clinical experience.

3.2 Research Questions

This research investigates how XR and AI can manage daily stress for young people by identifying stressors, evaluating technology effectiveness, and developing practical solutions. The central research question guiding the workshop was:

> *"How can XR technology manage the daily stress triggers of young people, and how can AI enhance this process?"*

3.3 Methodology

We applied a structured thinking technique called Edward de Bono's Six Thinking Hats [7] throughout to enhance idea generation and ensure balanced input from psychology, interaction design, AI, and XR experts. The workshop followed a four-part structure: **opening**, **warm-up**, **main session**, and **closing**. Below we outline the workshop in **seven steps** for clarity.

1. **Blue Hat (Opening & Warm-Up):** Welcome participants, provide introductions, explain the Six Thinking Hats method/goals, and set the AI/XR context.
2. **White Hat (Sharing Knowledge and Identifying Stressors):** Experts share field-specific research on stress and identify youth stressors.

3. **Yellow Hat (Evaluating Solutions and Innovations):** List advantages and developments of solutions from individual expertise areas.
4. **Black Hat (Identifying Challenges and Limitations):** Conduct interdisciplinary discussion on potential problems and negative effects.
5. **Green Hat (Generating Innovative Ideas):** Brainstorm innovative, interdisciplinary ideas.
6. **Red Hat (Emotional Considerations and Reflections):** Psychology experts lead discussion on stress control methods and summarise findings.
7. **Blue Hat (Closing):** Summarise the outcomes, collect feedback, and outline next steps for future research.

4 Results

Findings were derived from two workshop sessions involving eight experts. The Six Thinking Hats methodology structured the activities. This section summarises results from the White, Yellow, Black, Green, and Red Hat phases. Blue Hat outcomes (process management and final summary) are integrated here and further discussed in the Discussion section.

4.1 Blue Hat: Opening and Warm-Up

Both workshop sessions commenced with the *Blue Hat*. The organiser ensured that all experts understood the process and objectives. Participants were then briefed on the background story to set the stage for the following discussions.

4.2 White Hat: Sharing Knowledge and Identifying Stressors

In the *White Hat* phase, experts from both sessions identified a wide range of stressors affecting young people, including cross-cultural complexities, financial constraints, social isolation, elevated expectations, and limited opportunities for personal development. Drawing from their research in psychology, AI, and XR, participants shared relevant studies and examples to stimulate discussion. These included the use of prediction algorithms from mobile devices and wearables to detect stress and depression [9,30,46], conversational agents for stress relief [13,20,23], and VR-based therapies such as mindfulness, exposure therapy, and cognitive reappraisal [6,31,37,42,50].

Building on these insights, experts proposed multiple AI- and XR-supported approaches for stress management. Suggested methods included AI-enhanced psychotherapy, community and peer-matching systems, and VR relaxation spaces that provide culturally adaptable immersive environments [40,51]. Other ideas encompassed emotion-aware mobile or wearable devices, brainwave recognition, facial emotion detection, and chatbots offering emotional support and anonymous virtual consultation.

4.3 Yellow Hat: Evaluating Solutions and Innovations

In **Session 1**, experts evaluated previous stressors and their solutions. They synthesised and assessed these solutions across four dimensions, rating them from low to high: social, reappraisal, meditation, and avoidance. In the social dimension, the top-rated solutions were, in ascending order, the XR community support chatbot, AI-guided experience analysis, and community matching systems. For the reappraisal dimension, the preferred solutions were expectation-reality gap explanation tools and AI-enhanced digital positive psychotherapy. The meditation dimension identified VR relaxation spaces as the leading solution, while for the avoidance dimension, uncontrollable factor shields were favoured.

In **Session 2**, the second group of experts did not provide ratings but summarised solutions into three categories: alteration/stimulating environments, social-human-AI support, and detection and prevention. For altering environments, experts discussed VR mindfulness, VR relaxation, and VR music, highlighting their adaptability to different cultural contexts, non-invasiveness, support for independent task completion, and anxiety reduction through focused engagement. In terms of social-human-AI support, they suggested VR social systems, chatbots for emotional management, and anonymous consultation tools to enhance social skills, preserve anonymity, support timely emotion regulation, and reduce spatial and financial constraints of real-world interactions. For detection and prevention, they focused on AI-assisted emotional identification through images, text, sound, and brainwaves to support early stress detection, increase self-awareness, and enable empathy-based interventions using XR technologies.

4.4 Black Hat: Identifying Challenges and Limitations

In **Session 1**, in the *Black Hat* step, we assessed the potential negative impacts and disadvantages of the proposed solutions. Unlike the Yellow Hat phase, we did not ask experts to rate their answers, allowing for open-ended input without predefined criteria. Experts raised concerns about privacy and cultural isolation associated with the matching system. They also identified risks such as overdependence and privacy leakage in the use of chatbots, AI-guided experience analysis, expectation-reality gap explanation tools, and uncontrollable factor shields. The long-term effectiveness of AI-enhanced digital positive psychotherapy was questioned, with some experts suggesting it might fall short of expectations or even exacerbate existing issues. Additionally, concerns were raised about the high cost of equipment for VR relaxation spaces and the possibility of increased personal isolation and detachment.

Session 2 focused on the challenges and limitations of the identified solutions, particularly concerning data privacy, third-party access, and technological feasibility. Experts expressed concerns about the reliance on third-party support for diagnosis and treatment planning, as well as the need for substantial technological development and validation. They warned that excessive data sharing could compromise patient privacy and that third-party access to sensitive information might increase the risk of manipulation or misuse.

4.5 Green Hat: Generating Innovative Ideas

In **Session 1**, experts summarised the outcomes of prior discussions and generated innovative ideas (see Fig. 1). Through deliberation, they proposed 'XR pets' as an engaging solution. Developed using the earlier matching system, these XR pets would capture and share data while allowing users to define AI behaviours and control access to private information from the outset, addressing concerns about AI's black-box nature. Personalised XR pets could offer stress management guidance tailored to individual needs, mitigating potential drawbacks of generic interventions. As they evolve alongside users, XR pets may support emotional regulation and deliver positive psychological interventions, fostering patience and attachment through sustained familiarity.

Fig. 1. XR Pet. Social: (a) Chatbot; (b) AI-guided experience analysis; (c) community matching systems. Reappraisal: (a) expectation-reality gap explanation; (b) AI-enhanced digital psychotherapy.

Fig. 2. Stress management methods. Social-Human-AI support: (a) XR social support; (b) chatbots for stress relief and emotional management; (c) VR anonymous consultation.

Experts proposed innovative methods for stress management (see Fig. 2) in **Session 2**, such as using VR for mindfulness, relaxation, and music to create adaptable, culturally sensitive environments. They suggested that AI and XR technologies could be employed to simulate positive past experiences, including interactions with relatives, tailored through generative AI for personalised therapeutic scenarios. This concept represents a novel approach to using XR in patient treatment, providing empathy-driven interventions and enhancing emotional well-being. Additionally, the idea of AI-assisted emotional identification through images, text, and sounds, coupled with brainwave recognition, offers a creative application of technology to detect and prevent stress, potentially enabling proactive stress management strategies.

4.6 Red Hat: Emotional Considerations and Reflections

In **Session 1**, psychology experts led discussions on emotional responses to XR pets. They raised questions about the possibility of 'death' or 'illness' for these pets, how they might handle stress from unexpected events, and their potential to facilitate social interaction without replacing real-world relationships. Experts also stressed the importance of cultural sensitivity and the ability to recognise social nuances, given that XR pets would be designed using personal data. Although users can control data access, privacy remains a concern, prompting discussions about whether long-term data collection requires a regulatory framework to ensure ethical operation.

Session 2 experts, guided by participants with a background in psychology, conducted both optimistic and pessimistic evaluations of the previous discussion outputs. They acknowledged that the diagnosis and treatment plan could help therapists better understand patients' behaviour and cognitive processes. Early intervention could reduce the severity of stress problems while building patients' trust as a self-regulation mechanism.

4.7 Blue Hat: Conclusion and Future Directions

At the conclusion of **session 1**, all experts gave positive feedback on XR pets, believing they can greatly assist young people with stress management and that their effectiveness may improve as they evolve. The workshop concluded with a discussion on the role of XR pets in stress management, the necessary technology, and the dynamics of interaction between XR pets and users.

In **session 2**'s end stage, the experts summarised the strengths and weaknesses of the proposed diagnosis and treatment plan. They acknowledged its potential to improve the understanding of patient behaviour and support self-regulation but emphasised the need to address data privacy, third-party involvement, and the extensive development required to make the technology practical and ethical. Across both sessions, experts agreed that advancing XR $\times$ AI for stress management will require close interdisciplinary collaboration and the establishment of clear ethical and accessibility guidelines.

5 Discussions

This interdisciplinary workshop explored combined AI and XR approaches for stress management, yielding insights to guide future research. Our *no interruption* facilitation allowed expert discussions to evolve organically.

5.1 Impact of AI and XR on Stress Management

Previous studies have explored the impact of combining AI and XR on different populations, suggesting various directions for future research. Our study focused on stress management techniques through an interdisciplinary workshop, aiming to inspire further research in this field. After the first workshop, experts proposed that XR pets, integrating AI and XR techniques based on user preferences, could provide satisfaction and stress relief for young people as long-term virtual companions. The second workshop suggested that developing a diagnosis and treatment ecosystem with AI and XR requires a step-by-step approach, allowing for future adaptation to different populations.

5.2 Future Research Directions for Virtual Companions

Future research should focus on replicating and enhancing these interactions, including developing visualisation guidelines, smart glasses devices, empathy, multi-modal interaction design, and addressing ethical considerations. Early research [4] has shown that virtual pets can provide a certain degree of companionship compared to real pets. Lin et al. [26,27] pointed out that virtual pet games have the potential to promote user learning, cooperation, and empathy. Users expect to use virtual pets to get emotional support. They also pointed out that the progressive pet learning system allows virtual pets to be trained by users, and players can gradually understand and expect the behaviour of virtual pets, thereby deepening the relationship between the users and pets. They affirmed the value of virtual pets in providing therapy and education while pointing out the concerns about the companionship of virtual pets, the ethical issues caused by users' emotional attachment to virtual pets, and the emotional reactions of users when virtual pets are harmed.

Norouzi et al. [34] simulated the effects of virtual companion pets' effects on user behaviour and perception through AR. It found the impact of virtual pets on users' movement behaviour and spatial perception and the potential of virtual pets to enhance human interaction and emotional connection. Chahyana and Yesmaya [3] pointed out that by using emotional computing and AI, virtual pets can respond to users' emotional states and behaviours more intelligently. Based on the results of our workshop, future research can explore how different types of virtual pets interact with users, the alignment between the diversity of virtual pets and user diversity, and related social diversity issues. Additionally, research could focus on how AI can be used to train virtual pets to evolve with users' daily lives, enhancing companionship. There is also significant potential for research on using AI to enable virtual pets to provide better emotional support, such as customised stress relief, more personalised experiences, and multi-modal real-time interactions.

5.3 AI-Driven Therapeutic and Diagnostic Applications in XR

The second group of experts discussed the concept of the diagnosis and treatment plan, suggesting that creating such an ecosystem requires breaking it down into manageable parts that can be integrated as relevant technologies mature. Once trained, AI could be adapted to other populations. Some experts proposed that fully trained AI could eventually replace therapists, but they also raised ethical concerns regarding this development.

In terms of past research relevant to this context, Suzuki et al. [49] highlighted that AI-driven XR experiences can enhance user immersion and authenticity. This enhancement is achieved by real-time analysis of user behaviour and environmental contexts, which allows for natural and seamless interactions. Rueda et al. [45] emphasised the role of XR in fostering empathy and enhancing moral reasoning skills. Reed et al. [43] use generative AI to help patients create personalised background stories, demonstrating how AI can aid nursing young people in better understanding patient backgrounds and conditions, thereby highlighting the critical role of AI in education and empathy development. Based on our workshop findings, AI-driven XR can play a pivotal role in stress management by enhancing user adaptability and addressing cultural sensitivities through diverse virtual environments guided by AI.

5.4 Limitations and Future Improvements

This exploratory study presents several limitations that suggest opportunities for future research. The findings are derived from a limited sample of eight experts. While their insights are valuable, they cannot substitute for the lived experiences of the target user population. The restricted demographic diversity of our expert pool and the cancellation of a third workshop session limit the generality of our conclusions. The generated design concepts, namely the "XR Pet" and the therapeutic ecosystem, represent high-level design provocations at this stage. Critical interactional and ethical challenges have been identified, including the management of the virtual pet's lifecycle and the potential for fostering over-dependence, but these issues remain unresolved. Subsequent research should convert these concepts into more advanced prototypes and undertake thorough design investigations to tackle these intricate situations. Furthermore, the proposed AI and XR solutions may embed algorithmic bias, especially in varying cultural contexts, while the high cost of XR hardware could worsen the digital divide. Our forthcoming work will concentrate on validating and refining these initial concepts through user-centred methods, including co-design sessions with a larger and more diverse group of international students.

6 Conclusion

This paper reports on a structured, interdisciplinary inquiry into the future of mental well-being technologies. The primary contribution of this work is twofold: first, we offer a methodological case study on using a structured, expert-led approach to navigate a complex socio-technical problem space. Second, we present two generative design concepts—the "XR Pet" and a therapeutic ecosystem—that serve as tangible provocations for the HCI community, highlighting critical challenges in areas of digital companionship, data privacy, and ethical AI. The insights derived from our workshops do not offer final answers but rather provide a richer, more nuanced foundation upon which future human-centred solutions at the intersection of XR, AI, and mental health can be built.

References

1. Abraham, M., Saeghe, P., Mcgill, M., Khamis, M.: Implications of XR on privacy, security and behaviour: insights from experts. In: Nordic Human-Computer Interaction Conference, pp. 1–12 (2022)
2. Amores, J., Richer, R., Zhao, N., Maes, P., Eskofier, B.M.: Promoting relaxation using virtual reality, olfactory interfaces and wearable EEG. In: 2018 IEEE 15th International Conference on Wearable and Implantable Body Sensor Networks (BSN), pp. 98–101. IEEE (2018)
3. Chahyana, J., Yesmaya, V.: Virtual pet simulator game using augmented reality on android platform. In: Journal of Physics: Conference Series, vol. 1566, p. 012088. IOP Publishing (2020)
4. Chesney, T., Lawson, S.: The illusion of love: does a virtual pet provide the same companionship as a real one? Interact. Stud. **8**(2), 337–342 (2007)
5. Chintala, S.: Ai-driven personalised treatment plans: the future of precision medicine. Mach. Intell. Res. **17**(02), 9718–9728 (2023)
6. Cikajlo, I., Čižman-Štaba, U., Vrhovac, S., Larkin, F., Roddy, M.: Recovr: realising collaborative virtual reality for wellbeing and self-healing. In: Proceedings of the 3rd IASTED International Conference Telehealth Assistive Technology TAT, pp. 11–17 (2016)
7. De Bono, E.: Six Thinking Hats: The multi-million bestselling guide to running better meetings and making faster decisions. Penguin UK (2017)
8. Dekker, I., De Jong, E.M., Schippers, M.C., De Bruijn-Smolders, M., Alexiou, A., Giesbers, B.: Optimizing students' mental health and academic performance: AI-enhanced life crafting. Front. Psychol. **11**, 1063 (2020)
9. Diaz-Ramos, R.E., Noriega, I., Trejo, L.A., Stroulia, E., Cao, B.: Using wearable devices and speech data for personalized machine learning in early detection of mental disorders: protocol for a participatory research study. JMIR Res. Protoc. **12**(1), e48210 (2023)
10. Egan, D., Brennan, S., Barrett, J., Qiao, Y., Timmerer, C., Murray, N.: An evaluation of heart rate and electrodermal activity as an objective QoE evaluation method for immersive virtual reality environments. In: 2016 Eighth International Conference on Quality of Multimedia Experience (QoMEX), pp. 1–6. IEEE (2016)
11. Ens, B., et al.: Revisiting collaboration through mixed reality: the evolution of groupware. Int. J. Hum.-Comput. Stud. **131**, 81–98 (2019). https://www.sciencedirect.com/science/article/pii/S1071581919300606
12. Fisk, M., Livingstone, A., Pit, S.W., et al.: Telehealth in the context of covid-19: changing perspectives in Australia, the United Kingdom, and the united states. J. Med. Internet Res. **22**(6), e19264 (2020)
13. Fitzpatrick, K.K., Darcy, A., Vierhile, M.: Delivering cognitive behavior therapy to young adults with symptoms of depression and anxiety using a fully automated conversational agent (Woebot): a randomized controlled trial. JMIR Mental Health **4**(2), e7785 (2017)

14. Freeman, D., et al.: Virtual reality in the assessment, understanding, and treatment of mental health disorders. Psychol. Med. **47**(14), 2393–2400 (2017)
15. Gao, T., Zhang, T., Zhu, L., Gao, Y., Qiu, L.: Exploring psychophysiological restoration and individual preference in the different environments based on virtual reality. Int. J. Environ. Res. Public Health **16**(17), 3102 (2019)
16. Hedblom, M., Gunnarsson, B., Schaefer, M., Knez, I., Thorsson, P., Lundström, J.N.: Sounds of nature in the city: no evidence of bird song improving stress recovery. Int. J. Environ. Res. Public Health **16**(8), 1390 (2019)
17. Hickie, I.B., et al.: Right care, first time: a highly personalised and measurement-based care model to manage youth mental health. Med. J. Aust. **211**, S3–S46 (2019)
18. Hirzle, T., Müller, F., Draxler, F., Schmitz, M., Knierim, P., Hornbæk, K.: When XR and ai meet-a scoping review on extended reality and artificial intelligence. In: Proceedings of the 2023 CHI Conference on Human Factors in Computing Systems, pp. 1–45 (2023)
19. Huang, Q., Yang, M., Jane, H.A., Li, S., Bauer, N.: Trees, grass, or concrete? The effects of different types of environments on stress reduction. Landscape Urban Plann. **193**, 103654 (2020)
20. Kang, J., Wei, L.: "Give me the support i want!" the effect of matching an embodied conversational agent's social support to users' social support needs in fostering positive user-agent interaction. In: Proceedings of the 6th International Conference on Human-Agent Interaction, pp. 106–113 (2018)
21. Karyotaki, E., et al.: Sources of stress and their associations with mental disorders among college students: results of the world health organization world mental health surveys international college student initiative. Front. Psychol. **11**, 1759 (2020)
22. Kinoshita, S., et al.: Changes in telepsychiatry regulations during the covid-19 pandemic: 17 countries and regions' approaches to an evolving healthcare landscape. Psychol. Med. **52**(13), 2606–2613 (2022)
23. Kothgassner, O.D., et al.: Virtual social support buffers stress response: an experimental comparison of real-life and virtual support prior to a social stressor. J. Behav. Ther. Exp. Psychiatry **63**, 57–65 (2019)
24. Lee, Y., Yoo, B.: XR collaboration beyond virtual reality: work in the real world. J. Comput. Des. Eng. **8**(2), 756–772 (2021)
25. Li, H., Zhang, R., Lee, Y.C., Kraut, R.E., Mohr, D.C.: Systematic review and meta-analysis of AI-based conversational agents for promoting mental health and well-being. NPJ Digit. Med. **6**(1), 236 (2023)
26. Lin, C., Faas, T., Brady, E.: Exploring affection-oriented virtual pet game design strategies in VR attachment, motivations and expectations of users of pet games. In: 2017 Seventh International Conference on Affective Computing and Intelligent Interaction (ACII), pp. 362–369. IEEE (2017)
27. Lin, C., Faas, T., Dombrowski, L., Brady, E.: Beyond cute: exploring user types and design opportunities of virtual reality pet games. In: Proceedings of the 23rd ACM Symposium on Virtual Reality Software and Technology, pp. 1–10 (2017)
28. Milgram, P., Takemura, H., Utsumi, A., Kishino, F.: Augmented reality: a class of displays on the reality-virtuality continuum. In: Telemanipulator and Telepresence Technologies, vol. 2351, pp. 282–292. SPIE (1995). https://www.spiedigitallibrary.org/conference-proceedings-of-spie/2351/1/Augmented-reality--a-class-of-displays-on-the-reality/10.1117/12.197321.short

29. Miner, N., et al.: Stairway to heaven: a gamified VR journey for breath awareness. In: Proceedings of the CHI Conference on Human Factors in Computing Systems, pp. 1–19 (2024)
30. Moshe, I., et al.: Predicting symptoms of depression and anxiety using smartphone and wearable data. Front. Psych. **12**, 625247 (2021)
31. Navarro-Haro, M.V., et al.: Meditation experts try virtual reality mindfulness: a pilot study evaluation of the feasibility and acceptability of virtual reality to facilitate mindfulness practice in people attending a mindfulness conference. PLoS ONE **12**(11), e0187777 (2017)
32. Naylor, M., Ridout, B., Campbell, A.: A scoping review identifying the need for quality research on the use of virtual reality in workplace settings for stress management. Cyberpsychol. Behav. Soc. Network. **23**(8), 506–518 (2020). https://doi.org/10.1089/cyber.2019.0287. https://www.liebertpub.com/doi/10.1089/cyber.2019.0287
33. Naylor, M., Ridout, B., Campbell, A.: A scoping review identifying the need for quality research on the use of virtual reality in workplace settings for stress management. Cyberpsychol. Behav. Soc. Netw. **23**(8), 506–518 (2020)
34. Norouzi, N., et al.: Walking your virtual dog: analysis of awareness and proxemics with simulated support animals in augmented reality. In: 2019 IEEE International Symposium on Mixed and Augmented Reality (ISMAR), pp. 157–168. IEEE (2019)
35. Ohannessian, R., Duong, T.A., Odone, A., et al.: Global telemedicine implementation and integration within health systems to fight the covid-19 pandemic: a call to action. JMIR Public Health Surveill. **6**(2), e18810 (2020)
36. Pallavicini, F., Argenton, L., Toniazzi, N., Aceti, L., Mantovani, F.: Virtual reality applications for stress management training in the military. Aerosp. Med. Hum. Perform. **87**(12), 1021–1030 (2016)
37. Pallavicini, F., et al.: Is virtual reality always an effective stressors for exposure treatments? Some insights from a controlled trial. BMC Psychiatry **13**, 1–10 (2013)
38. Piumsomboon, T., Dey, A., Ens, B., Lee, G., Billinghurst, M.: The effects of sharing awareness cues in collaborative mixed reality. Front. Robot. AI **6**, 5 (2019). https://www.frontiersin.org/articles/10.3389/frobt.2019.00005/full
39. Piumsomboon, T., Lee, G.A., Irlitti, A., Ens, B., Thomas, B.H., Billinghurst, M.: On the shoulder of the giant: a multi-scale mixed reality collaboration with 360 video sharing and tangible interaction. In: Proceedings of the 2019 CHI Conference on Human Factors in Computing Systems, pp. 1–17. ACM, Glasgow, Scotland, UK (2019). https://doi.org/10.1145/3290605.3300458. https://dl.acm.org/doi/10.1145/3290605.3300458
40. Pizzoli, S.F.M., Mazzocco, K., Triberti, S., Monzani, D., Alcañiz Raya, M.L., Pravettoni, G.: User-centered virtual reality for promoting relaxation: an innovative approach. Front. Psychol. **10**, 479 (2019)
41. Pons, P., Navas-Medrano, S., Soler-Dominguez, J.L.: Extended reality for mental health: current trends and future challenges. Front. Comput. Sci. **4** (2022)
42. Pot-Kolder, R.M., et al.: Virtual-reality-based cognitive behavioural therapy versus waiting list control for paranoid ideation and social avoidance in patients with psychotic disorders: a single-blind randomised controlled trial. Lancet Psychiatry **5**(3), 217–226 (2018)
43. Reed, J.M., Dodson, T.M.: Generative ai backstories for simulation preparation. Nurse Educ. **49**(4), 184–188 (2024)

44. Riches, S., Azevedo, L., Bird, L., Pisani, S., Valmaggia, L.: Virtual reality relaxation for the general population: a systematic review. Soc. Psychiatry Psychiatric Epidemiol. **56**(10), 1707–1727 (2021). https://doi.org/10.1007/s00127-021-02110-z
45. Rueda, J., Dore-Horgan, E.: A virtual prosthesis for morality? Experiential learning through XR technologies for autonomy enhancement of psychiatric offenders. AJOB Neurosci. **13**(3), 163–165 (2022)
46. Sano, A., et al.: Identifying objective physiological markers and modifiable behaviors for self-reported stress and mental health status using wearable sensors and mobile phones: observational study. J. Med. Internet Res. **20**(6), e210 (2018)
47. Shin, D.: Empathy and embodied experience in virtual environment: to what extent can virtual reality stimulate empathy and embodied experience? Comput. Hum. Behav. **78**, 64–73 (2018)
48. Smith, V., et al.: The effectiveness of virtual reality in managing acute pain and anxiety for medical inpatients: systematic review. J. Med. Internet Res. **22**(11), e17980 (2020)
49. Suzuki, R., Gonzalez-Franco, M., Sra, M., Lindlbauer, D.: XR and AI: AI-enabled virtual, augmented, and mixed reality. In: Adjunct Proceedings of the 36th Annual ACM Symposium on User Interface Software and Technology, pp. 1–3 (2023)
50. Trappey, C.V., Trappey, A.J., Chang, C., Tsai, M., Kuo, R.R., Lin, A.P.: Virtual reality exposure therapy and physiological data analysis for treatment of stress disorders. In: Emerging Advancements for Virtual and Augmented Reality in Healthcare, pp. 143–170. IGI Global (2022)
51. Vaquero-Blasco, M.A., Perez-Valero, E., Morillas, C., Lopez-Gordo, M.A.: Virtual reality customized 360-degree experiences for stress relief. Sensors **21**(6), 2219 (2021)
52. Velana, M., Sobieraj, S., Digutsch, J., Rinkenauer, G.: The advances of immersive virtual reality interventions for the enhancement of stress management and relaxation among healthy adults: a systematic review. Appl. Sci. **12**(14), 7309 (2022)
53. Wang, X., Young, G.W., Plechatá, A., Mc Guckin, C., Makransky, G.: Utilizing virtual reality to assist social competence education and social support for children from under-represented backgrounds. Comput. Educ. **201**, 104815 (2023)
54. Wang, Y., et al.: A survey on metaverse: fundamentals, security, and privacy. IEEE Commun. Surv. Tutor. **25**(1), 319–352 (2022)
55. Wiederhold, M.D., Gao, K., Wiederhold, B.K.: Clinical use of virtual reality distraction system to reduce anxiety and pain in dental procedures. Cyberpsychol. Behav. Soc. Netw. **17**(6), 359–365 (2014)
56. Wolfers, L.N., Utz, S.: Social media use, stress, and coping. Curr. Opin. Psychol. **45**, 101305 (2022)
57. Zhang, J., et al.: Virtual triplets: a mixed modal synchronous and asynchronous collaboration with human-agent interaction in virtual reality. In: Extended Abstracts of the CHI Conference on Human Factors in Computing Systems, pp. 1–8 (2024)

Emotional Conversation: Empowering Talking Faces with Cohesive Expression, Gaze and Pose Generation

Jiadong Liang and Feng Lu(✉)

Beihang University, Beijing 10091, China
lufeng@buaa.edu.cn

Abstract. Vivid talking face generation holds immense potential applications across diverse multimedia domains, such as film and game production. While existing methods accurately synchronize lip movements with input audio, they typically ignore crucial alignments between emotion and facial cues, which include expression, gaze, and head pose. These alignments are indispensable for synthesizing realistic videos. To address these issues, we propose a two-stage audio-driven talking face generation framework that employs 3D facial landmarks as intermediate variables. This framework achieves collaborative alignment of expression, gaze, and pose with emotions through self-supervised learning. Specifically, we decompose this task into two key steps, namely speech-to-landmarks synthesis and landmarks-to-face generation. The first step focuses on simultaneously synthesizing emotionally aligned facial cues, including normalized landmarks that represent expressions, gaze, and head pose. These cues are subsequently reassembled into relocated facial landmarks. In the second step, these relocated landmarks are mapped to latent key points using self-supervised learning and then input into a pretrained model to create high-quality face images. Extensive experiments on the MEAD dataset demonstrate that our model significantly advances the state-of-the-art performance in both visual quality and emotional alignment.

Keywords: Digital Human · Talking Face Generation · AIGC

1 Introduction

The task of talking face generation involves creating a video of a talking face using a still identity image of the speaker and an audio track of their speech content. Furthermore, the generation of emotional talking face videos, featuring precise lip synchronization and vivid facial cues such as expressions, gaze, and head pose holds considerable potential for future applications. We found that these facial cue sequences exhibit consistent patterns in videos that correspond to specific emotions. For instance, in a talking face depicting contempt, individuals typically narrow their eyes, tilt their heads upward, and shift their gaze horizontally. Conversely, in videos portraying surprise, individuals generally widen their eyes while maintaining a forward-facing head pose and gaze. The alignment of these facial cues with emotions is crucial for synthesizing realistic talking

A. Hinkenjan et al. (Eds.): ICXR 2025, LNCS 16428, pp. 477–489, 2026.
https://doi.org/10.1007/978-981-95-7195-6_35

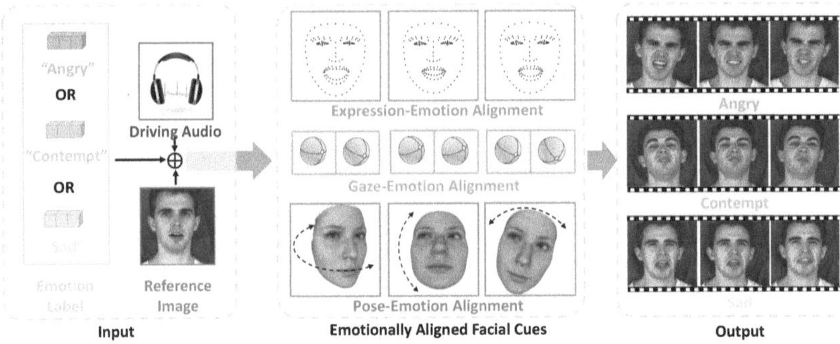

Fig. 1. We propose an advanced two-step framework for synthesizing vivid emotional talking faces with emotionally aligned facial cues. Initially, our approach utilizes the provided driving audio and an emotion label to generate three sequences of fine-grained facial cues (expression, head pose, and gaze) tailored to the specified emotion. Subsequently, these facial cues align with the specified emotion through self-supervised learning. Finally, utilizing these facial cues, we can produce vivid emotional talking face videos.

face videos. Therefore, the primary challenge of this task is to produce realistic facial videos that not only accurately reproduce lip movements in response to the driving audio but also maintain consistency between the various facial cues and corresponding emotions.

With the development of AI-Generated Content (AIGC), numerous advanced methods for generating emotional talking face have emerged. Corresponding methods can be mainly divided into audio-driven talking face generation [8,11,25] and video-driven talking face generation [12,23]. Audio-driven talking face generation synthesizes a sequence of portrait images by using both an identity image and the corresponding audio as inputs. However, most existing works focus exclusively on lip movement and often lack the ability to generate associated facial cues. The latest work, SPACE [8], is a multi-stage generative framework that achieves fine-grained control over facial expressions, emotion categories, head poses, and gaze directions of generated faces by manipulating the intermediate landmarks. Unfortunately, in SPACE, the control and generation of gaze and head pose sequences are unrelated to emotion. Although the generated faces display high visual quality, the final videos lack vividness and fail to differentiate emotions effectively. Video-driven talking face generation involves using a single identity image and multiple driving source videos as inputs. By employing a contrastive learning strategy, relevant features are extracted from various source videos to generate high-quality target talking face videos. These methods allow for the editing of facial attributes, such as head pose, facial expression, gaze, blinking, and audio, by modifying the corresponding source videos. However, these methods are not only expensive in the training stage but also incur additional costs in the inference stage due to the need for source video collection. We find that the fine-grained facial cues of the talking face video, such as expression, gaze and head pose, are closely related to emotional categories. Independently controlling these facial cues without considering emotion can lead to unrealistic results. Therefore, we require an audio-driven method that combines the low cost of audio-driven methods with the high alignment between facial cues and emotion to synthesize vivid emotional talking face videos.

In this paper, we propose an advanced audio-driven method to synthesize vivid emotional talking faces with emotionally aligned facial cue as shown in Fig. 1. We decompose the task into two sub-tasks: speech-to-landmarks synthesis and landmarks-to-face generation. Given input speech, an emotion label, and an identity image, the proposed speech-to-landmarks module can generate sequences of normalized facial landmarks (representing expressions), gaze, and head pose in an auto-regressive manner. To address the issue of substantial variations in gaze, we discretized the eye region and modeled gaze prediction as a classification task, successfully predicting gaze sequences for the first time. The alignment of emotional labels with these facial cues is achieved through self-supervised learning. These generated facial cues are synthesized into relocated 3D facial landmarks through coordinate correction and rotation. The relocated facial landmarks, driven by these cues, not only synchronize with the input audio but also enhance the alignment of expression, gaze, and pose movements with the corresponding emotion labels. We also build a collaborative emotion classifier to model the intrinsic relationships among these facial cues. Specifically, the classifier takes aggregated intermediate features from facial cues as input ensuring consistency among these facial cue sequences. The proposed landmarks-to-face module utilizes a latent keypoints space [18], capable of producing more realistic faces compared to traditional facial landmarks. Specifically, this module maps the relocated landmarks, generated by the speech-to-landmarks, to latent feature points. It then employs a pre-trained generator [27] to synthesize high-quality facial images. **To the best of our knowledge, this is the first attempt to align normalized facial landmarks, gaze, and head pose concurrently with emotional categories. Compared to existing works, these explicitly aligned facial cues significantly improve the intensity and accuracy of emotional expressions in generated talking faces.**

2 Related Work

In the following section, we provide an overview of prior research on audio-driven talking face generation and video-driven talking face generation.

Audio-Driven Talking Face Generation. The objective of Speech-driven Talking Face Generation [5,6,13,15,17,21,22,24,26,29,32] is to establish a mapping from the input speech to facial representations. MakeItTalk [34] disentangles audio content and speaker information to control lip motion and facial expressions, and effectively works with various portrait styles. Audio2Head [26] addresses challenges in achieving natural head motion by employing a motion-aware RNN for head pose prediction. With the further development of this field, there is a growing emphasis on controlling facial emotions in generated talking faces. Wang collected the MEAD [25] dataset and proposed a method that conditions talking head generation based on emotion labels. However, MEAD primarily focuses on controlling only the mouth region while leaving other parts unchanged, leading to a lack of continuity in the generated videos. Compared to MEAD, which uses a single emotion label as input to control the generation of video emotion categories, EAMM [11] achieves precise emotional control over the synthesized video by adopting features extracted from the emotion source video. However, the method still ignores the movement of the gaze direction and head pose, which results in less realistic generated videos. EMMN [20,31] employ memory networks and textual prompts, respectively, to control the emotions in the generated videos. SPACE [8] achieves fine-grained control over facial expressions, emotion categories, head poses, and gaze directions of generated faces by decomposing the generation task into multiple subtasks. While these methods are user-friendly and straightforward, they often struggle to generate emotionally aligned facial cues for generated videos.

Video-Driven Talking Face Generation. The goal of video-driven talking face generation [1,4,7,10,14,28,30] is to accurately map facial movements from a source video onto a target image. Wave2Lip [16] constructs an expert discriminator to ensure precise alignment between the lip movements and the input audio. PC-AVS [33] utilizes an implicit low-dimension pose code to separate audio-visual representations to achieve accurate lip-syncing and pose control. EVP [12] decomposes speech into two decoupled spaces to generate dynamic 2D emotional facial landmarks. PD-FGC [23] allows for the editing of facial attributes, such as head pose, facial expression, gaze, blinking, by modifying the corresponding source videos. These methods are not only costly during the training stage, but also entail additional expenses during the inference stage due to the requirement of source video collection .

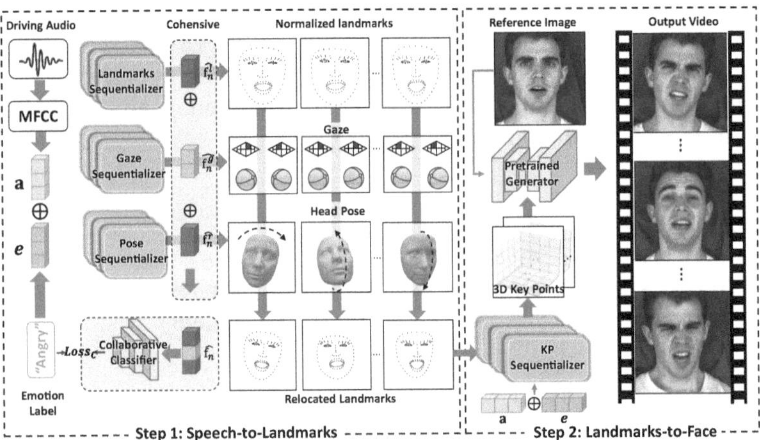

Fig. 2. Architecture of the proposed method, which performs emotional talking face generation in two steps. In Step 1, we innovatively achieved the simultaneous generation of facial cue sequences, including normalized landmarks, gaze, and head pose. These cues are then aligned with emotional labels via self-supervised learning. In Step 2, we utilize the emotionally aligned facial cues from Step 1 as inputs, employing a pre-trained model to produce vivid emotional talking face videos.

3 Two-Stage Talking Face Generation

The proposed method takes driving audio and a reference image, along with an emotion label, and produces an emotional talking face. It decomposes this task into Speech-to-Landmarks Synthesis and Landmarks-to-Face Generation. Using a pre-trained face generator, we can effectively reduce training cost while obtaining high-quality emotional talking faces. The general framework is shown in Fig. 2.

3.1 Speech-to-Landmarks Synthesis

Given an input speech, emotion label, and an identity face image, the proposed speech-to-landmarks synthesis is capable of generating sequences of normalized facial landmarks (representing expressions), gaze, and head pose in an auto-regressive manner. These facial cues are further aligned with specific emotions through self-supervised learning. Specifically, the network for speech-to-landmarks synthesis consists of three modules: Landmark Sequentializer, Gaze Sequentializer, and Pose Sequentializer, each performing auto-regressive prediction on different facial cues sequences.

Landmark Sequentializer. In talking face generation, the quality of facial landmark generation is paramount as these landmarks directly control lip movements and expressions. Given the input audio MFCC features and the normalized 3D facial landmarks of the input image. This is represented by

$$\mathbf{f}_n^l = \mathcal{S}_{\text{landmark}}(\mathbf{C}_{n-1}, \mathbf{a}_n, \mathbf{e}), \quad \mathbf{C}_n = \text{Linear}(\mathbf{f}_n^l), \tag{1}$$

where $\mathbf{f}_n^l$ and $\mathbf{a}_n$ are the facial landmarks features and audio features at time n, respectively. $\mathcal{S}_{\text{landmark}}$ represents the auto-regressive generator, and $\mathbf{C}_n \in \mathbb{R}^{147\times3}$ is the normalized 3D facial landmarks at time n. The input emotion label embedding $\mathbf{e} \in \mathbb{R}^D$ corresponds to the indexed vectorial representation in the embedding matrix $\mathbf{E} \in \mathbb{R}^{D\times K}$ for an emotion dictionary containing K emotion categories, which is learned together with the whole model. We employ a convolutional neural network (CNN) to encode the audio data, while a multi-layer perceptron (MLP) is used to encode the 3D facial landmarks. The network is trained utilizing an L1 loss function, which reduces the L1 distance between the predicted facial landmarks and the normalized ground truth landmarks. Notably, we assign a higher loss scale to the y-axis to emphasize vertical motion errors during training [8].

Pose Sequentializer. The natural movement of the head can effectively enhance the vividness of the generated video, but its motion pattern is also influenced by the emotional category. Hence, we also train an auto-regressive $\mathcal{S}_{headpose}$ that predicts the rotation and translation for the facial landmarks. The rotation is represented by three angles: yaw, pitch, and roll, and the corresponding translation is the displacement of the 3D landmarks in the x-axis, y-axis, and z-axis. The prediction is represented by

$$\mathbf{r}_n = \text{Liner}(\mathbf{f}_n^r), \quad \mathbf{r}_n = [\mathbf{m}_n, \mathbf{b}_n], \quad \mathbf{f}_n^r = \mathcal{S}_{headpose}(\mathbf{r}_{n-1}, \mathbf{a}_n, \mathbf{e}), \tag{2}$$

where $\mathbf{m}_n = [yaw, pitch, roll]$, $\mathbf{b}_n = [\Delta_x, \Delta_y, \Delta_z]$ and $\mathcal{S}_{\text{headpose}}$ represents the pose sequentializer. The poses, whether predicted or extracted from a reference video, are applied to the frontal normalized landmarks predicted by our Landmark Sequentializer. This transformation maps the normalized landmarks back to the image space after applying an appropriate scaling factor. The Pose Sequentializer is also trained utilizing an L1 loss.

Gaze Sequentializer. The eyes, as important organs for human interaction, contain abundant information in gaze direction, which can impact the emotion category of generated videos. In contrast to the prediction of facial landmarks and head pose, we transform the prediction of gaze direction from regression to classification by discretizing the eye regions as shown in Fig 5 a. It effectively enhances the accuracy of gaze direction prediction. However, in the process of predicting the sequence of gaze directions, the current gaze direction heavily relies on the previous gaze. We adopt $\mathcal{S}_{gaze}$ to model this dependency relationship. Specifically, the gaze prediction of two eyes $[\mathrm{u}_n^{left} \in [0, S-1], \mathrm{u}_n^{right} \in [1, S-1]]$ at time n can be modeled as:

$$\mathbf{f}_n^g = \mathcal{S}_{gaze}(\mathrm{v}_{n-1}, \mathbf{a}_n, \mathbf{e}).,\quad \mathrm{v}_n = \mathrm{u}_n^{left} + S \times \mathrm{u}_n^{right}, \tag{3}$$

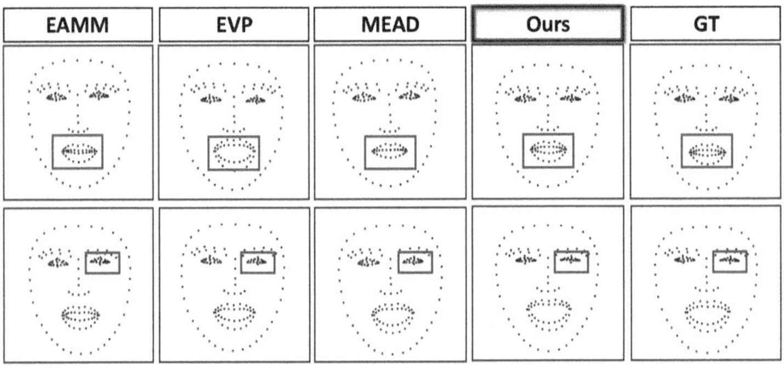

Fig. 3. Qualitative comparison of generated normalized landmarks between our method and three other methods on the MEAD dataset.

Formally, gaze decoder performs classification at n-th time step based on the hidden states $\mathbf{f}_n^g$ by

$$v_n = \underset{i \in [1, S\times S]}{\mathrm{argmax}}(\mathbf{p}_n^i),\quad \mathbf{p}_n = \mathrm{Softmax}(\mathbf{M}\mathbf{f}_n^g), \tag{4}$$

where $\mathbf{M}$ denotes a linear transformation. $\mathbf{p}_n \in \mathbb{R}^{S\times S}$ represents calculated probabilities for a total of $S \times S$ classification entries. v_n is the entry with the maximal probability, from which we can infer the corresponding gaze label $[\mathrm{u}_n^{left}, \mathrm{u}_n^{right}]$. Finally, we utilize the cross-entropy loss to optimize the gaze direction prediction model.

$$\mathrm{Loss}_{gaze} = \frac{1}{N}\sum_{n=1}^{N} \mathrm{Loss}_{\mathrm{CE}}(\mathbf{p}_n, \hat{\mathbf{p}_n}). \tag{5}$$

After obtaining these three types of facial cues, we integrate the gaze and head pose data into the normalized landmarks to obtain the relocated landmarks as shown in Fig. 2.

We also investigate the inherent relationships within these facial cues in the specific emotion. Therefore, we construct a collaborative emotion classifier to push consistency among these facial cue sequences. The classifier predicts the emotion category using the aggregated intermediate features from facial cues as input. Specifically, we can obtain the fake intermediate features $\hat{\mathbf{f}_n} = [\hat{\mathbf{f}^l_n}; \hat{\mathbf{f}^r_n}; \hat{\mathbf{f}^g_n}]$, where $[\hat{\mathbf{f}^l_n}; \hat{\mathbf{f}^r_n}; \hat{\mathbf{f}^g_n}]$ is predicted during the training stage.

$$\hat{\mathbf{l}_n} = \mathcal{F}_{classify}(\hat{\mathbf{f}_n}), \quad \text{Loss}_C = \text{L}_{\text{CE}}(\hat{\mathbf{l}_n}, \mathbf{l}_n) \tag{6}$$

where L_{CE} is cross entropy loss and $\mathbf{p}_t$ is calculated probabilities for total emotion classification entries. The total loss for the stage of speech-to-landmarks synthesis is

$$\text{Loss}_{norm} = \quad \text{Loss}_{landmarks} + \text{Loss}_{pose} + \text{Loss}_{gaze} + \text{Loss}_C. \tag{7}$$

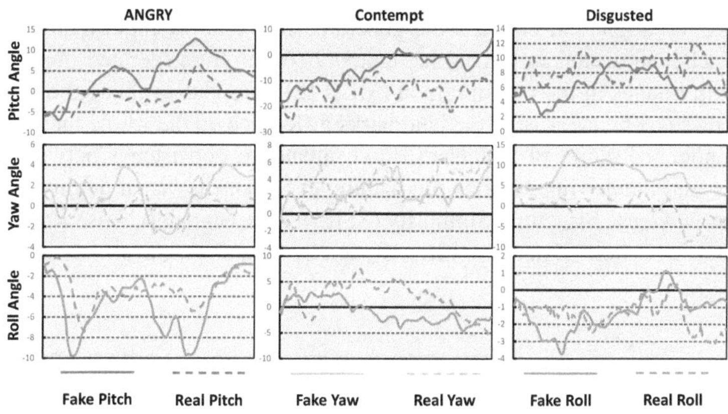

Fig. 4. Visualization of the head pose sequences in the pitch, yaw, and roll directions under different emotions.

3.2 Landmarks-to-Face Generation

The field of face generation has undergone rapid development, we find that using latent keypoints as input can generate high-quality facial images. Following SPACE [8], we utilized the pre-trained model face-vid2vid [27], a state-of-the-art framework for generating faces from latent keypoints. This approach avoids the need to learn a facial image generator from scratch, thereby reducing computational requirements and improving efficiency. Specifically, we first use the relocated landmarks in the 3D space generated in the speech-to-landmarks synthesis stage, along with the input speech and emotion labels, as input to perform autoregressive prediction of latent keypoints in a self-supervised learning manner, as shown in Fig. 2.

$$\mathbf{R}_n = \mathcal{F}_{relocate}(\mathbf{C}_n \cdot \mathbf{m}_n + \mathbf{b}_n, \mathrm{u}_n^{left}, \mathrm{u}_n^{right}), \quad \mathbf{K}_n = \mathcal{S}_{Key}(\mathbf{K}_{n-1}, \mathbf{R}_n, \mathbf{a}_n, \mathbf{e}), \tag{8}$$

where the $\mathcal{F}_{relocate}$ converts the normalized 3D facial landmarks $\mathbf{C}_n \in \mathbb{R}^{147\times 3}$ to relocated facial landmarks $\mathbf{R}_n \in \mathbb{R}^{147\times 3}$ using the gaze label $[\mathrm{u}_n^{left}, \mathrm{u}_n^{right}]$ and head pose $\mathbf{r}_n = [\mathbf{m}_n, \mathbf{b}_n]$ obtained in the stage of speech-to-landmarks. $\mathcal{S}_{Key}$ is auto-regression generator for 3D key points. Then, given the predicted latent keypoints $\mathbf{K}_n \in \mathbb{R}^{10\times 3}$ and the initial face, the pre-trained model generates high-quality facial images by using a flow-based warping field as intermediate variables. Finally, we can generate high-quality facial images with a resolution of 256, which is generally superior to previous works. By breaking down the generation of 3D facial landmarks into the collaborative production of three facial cues, we have simplified the task. Consequently, we selected a lightweight Bi-LSTM as the backbone for all auto-regressive generators ($\mathcal{S}_{lanmark}$, $\mathcal{S}_{headpose}$, $\mathcal{S}_{gaze}$, and $\mathcal{S}_{Key}$), enabling the generation of high-quality facial cues and 3D keypoints with minimal computational expense.

4 Experiment

To evaluate the alignment between the generated face and the input audio, we calculate the Euclidean distance of facial landmarks between the generated images and the ground truth images in the mouth region (MLD [2]). We also evaluate the accuracy of facial expressions by measuring the landmarks difference on the whole face (FLD). We use the confidence scores of SyncNet [3] to evaluate the consistency between the generated face and the driving audio at the feature level. For the visual quality of the synthesized face, we use Structural Similarity (SSIM), Peak Signal to Noise Ratio (PSNR), and Frechet Inception Distances (FID) [9] for quantitative analysis of the generated results.

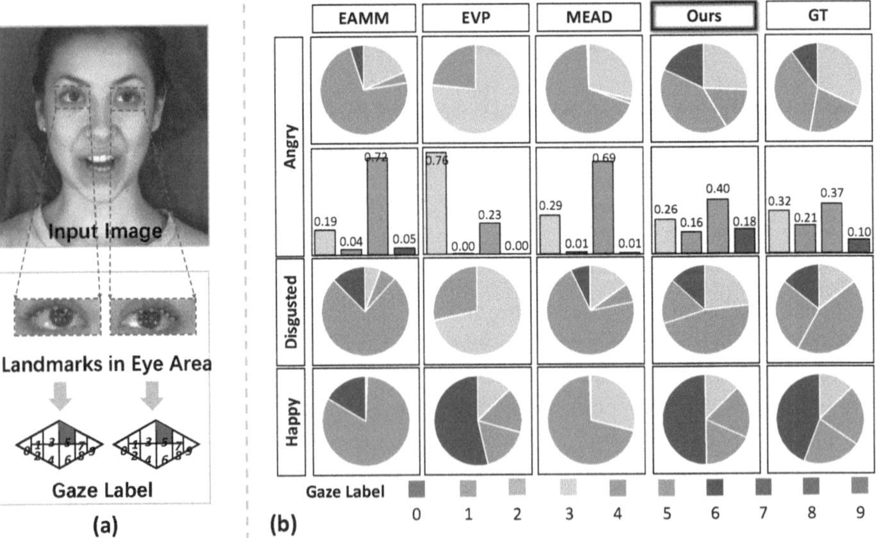

Fig. 5. (a) Pipeline of gaze direction discretization; (b) Comparison of left eye gaze distribution between our model and state-of-the-art models across different emotion categories.

4.1 Evaluation of Facial Cues

Evaluation of Normalized Landmarks. The accuracy of the generated facial landmarks critically influences the alignment of lip movements with the driving audio and the congruence between expressions and the corresponding emotion labels. The normalization of facial landmarks removes the influence of different head poses on the movement direction of facial landmarks, allowing our method to focus on predicting the vertical motions of the landmarks in the mouth and eye regions, which is crucial for prediction accuracy. We provide a qualitative comparison between the proposed Landmark Sequentializer and state-of-the-art methods for emotional talking face generation in Fig. 3. We found that only our method can effectively predict eye blinks and generate lips with better alignment (see the red boxes), which is consistent with the landmarks errors in Table 1

Evaluation of Head Pose. The generation and evaluation of head pose sequences are still challenges in this task of audio-driven talking face generation. Due to the complex relationship between driving audio and the resultant head pose sequences, which are not mapped one-to-one, quantitatively assessing head pose generation is inherently difficult. Therefore, we randomly selected generated videos across various emotional categories. Then, we plotted the pitch, yaw, and roll of the generated head pose sequences and corresponding ground truth (GT) as line charts, as shown in Fig. 4. Across different emotion categories, the generated head pose sequences exhibit similar trends to the

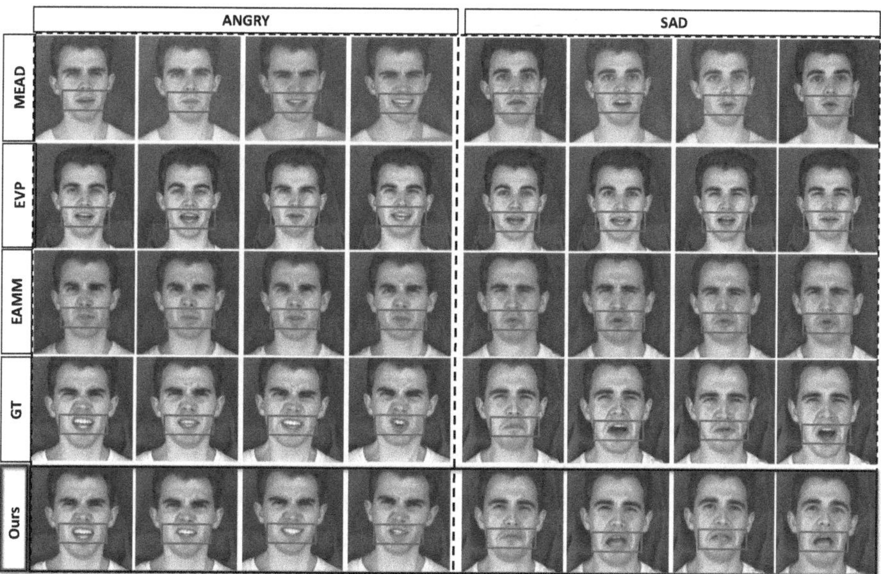

Fig. 6. Qualitative comparison of our model and other state-of-the-art models for emotional talking face generation.

ground truth (GT), demonstrating that the head poses generated by our proposed method can translate into emotionally aligned head movements.

Evaluation of Gaze. The direction of gaze is a critical facial cue in emotional talking face generation, significantly influencing the vividness of the generated video. We verify the effectiveness of the proposed Gaze Sequentializer by analyzing the spatial distribution of the pupils in the eye region. As shown in Fig. 5 b, pie charts were used to represent the gaze distribution of different methods across various emotion categories. We found that MEAD [25] and EAMM [11] exhibit identical gaze distributions across different emotion categories, with the majority of the pupils falling within the eye region "5". It implies that these two methods are incapable of generating available gaze sequences. Our method is capable of generating gaze distributions similar to the GT across all categories of emotions. These results demonstrate that the gaze sequences generated by our method effectively align with the corresponding emotional labels.

4.2 Comparison with State-of-the-Art Methods

Quantitative Evaluation. To conduct a comprehensive evaluation, we performed quantitative comparisons between our method and other approaches in both emotional and non-emotional talking face generation. Table 1 reports the quantitative experimental results. Apart from FID and SSIM, our method outperforms other approaches significantly. The improvements in MLD, FLD and SynNet shows that our approach can generate more accurate facial landmarks and achieve better lip alignment, consistent with the qualitative results shown in Fig. 3. The results of SSIM, PSNR, and FID further confirm that the proposed method can generate high-quality facial images. The results, as presented in Table 1, demonstrate that the absence of the emotion classifier, denoted as 'Ours w/o C', results in a significant decline in all quantitative metrics.

Table 1. Quantitative results of different talking face generation models on MEAD dataset.

Method	MLD ↓	FLD ↓	SynNet ↑	SSIM ↑	PSNR ↑	FID ↓
ATVG [2]	3.14	3.87	2.24	0.57	28.58	67.6
SDA [22]	3.99	4.5	1.88	0.44	28.54	-
Wave2Lip [16]	3.43	3.80	2.24	0.57	29.03	-
MakeItTalk [34]	3.80	3.92	2.20	0.56	28.92	-
PC-AVS [33]	2.97	2.74	2.10	0.60	29.02	-
Song [19]	2.54	3.49	-	0.64	29.11	36.33
MEAD [25]	2.52	3.16	-	0.68	28.61	22.52
EVP [12]	2.45	3.01	-	0.71	29.53	**7.99**
EAMM [11]	2.41	2.55	2.26	0.66	29.29	-
Xu [31]	2.31	-	3.57	**0.75**	30.10	15.89
EMMN [20]	2.78	2.87	3.57	0.66	29.38	-
Ours w/o C	2.21	2.11	4.53	0.69	30.14	9.12
Ours	**2.08**	**1.99**	**4.72**	0.74	**30.98**	8.62

Qualitative Evaluation. Figure 6 presents the qualitative comparison results of our method with other state-of-the-art emotional talking face generation methods. Due to the high alignment between facial cues and emotion categories, our method significantly outperforms other approaches in terms of normalized landmarks, gaze, and head poses.

User Study. We conducted a user study to compare our method with three SOTA models: MEAD, EVP, and EAMM. Specifically, we randomly selected five videos from each emotion category in the MEAD test set and evaluated both the overall quality and the accuracy of emotion expression in the generated videos. Human subjects were asked to vote for the video with the highest overall quality and the most accurate emotional expression. The rank-1 ratio for each method is presented in Fig. 7. Our method achieves 52% emotion accuracy and 57.88% overall quality from 20 collected human subjects, significantly outperforming other methods.

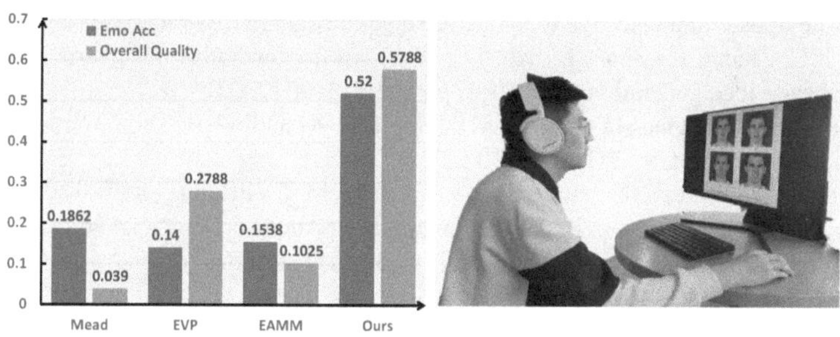

Fig. 7. User study results of talking face video generation quality and emotion accuracy.

5 Conclusion

Emotional talking face generation is a crucial part in digital human which has extensive application in virtual reality. In this paper, We proposed a two-step framework to generate vivid talking faces with emotionally aligned facial cues. In the first step, we aligned facial cues, including normalized facial landmarks, gaze, and head pose, with corresponding emotion labels in a self-supervised learning manner. In the second step, we adopted latent key points as intermediate variables and utilized a pre-trained generative model to map various facial cues into high-quality facial images. Extensive experiments on the MEAD dataset demonstrate that our model advances the state-of-the-art performance significantly.

References

1. Burkov, E., Pasechnik, I., Grigorev, A., Lempitsky, V.: Neural head reenactment with latent pose descriptors. In: CVPR, pp. 13786–13795 (2020)
2. Chen, L., Maddox, R.K., Duan, Z., Xu, C.: Hierarchical cross-modal talking face generation with dynamic pixel-wise loss. In: CVPR, pp. 7832–7841 (2019)

3. Chung, J.S., Zisserman, A.: Out of time: automated lip sync in the wild. In: Workshop on Multi-view Lip-reading, ACCV, pp. 251–263. Springer, Cham (2017). https://doi.org/10.1007/978-3-319-54427-4_19
4. Drobyshev, N., Chelishev, J., Khakhulin, T., Ivakhnenko, A., Lempitsky, V., Zakharov, E.: Megaportraits: one-shot megapixel neural head avatars. In: ACM MM, pp. 2663–2671 (2022)
5. Du, C., et al.: Dae-talker: High fidelity speech-driven talking face generation with diffusion autoencoder. In: Proceedings of the 31st ACM International Conference on Multimedia, pp. 4281–4289 (2023)
6. Fan, Y., Lin, Z., Saito, J., Wang, W., Komura, T.: Faceformer: speech-driven 3d facial animation with transformers. In: CVPR, pp. 18770–18780 (2022)
7. Gu, K., Zhou, Y., Huang, T.: Flnet: Landmark driven fetching and learning network for faithful talking facial animation synthesis. In: AAAI. vol. 34, pp. 10861–10868 (2020)
8. Gururani, S., Mallya, A., Wang, T.C., Valle, R., Liu, M.Y.: Space: speech-driven portrait animation with controllable expression. In: Proceedings of the IEEE/CVF International Conference on Computer Vision, pp. 20914–20923 (2023)
9. Heusel, M., Ramsauer, H., Unterthiner, T., Nessler, B., Hochreiter, S.: Gans trained by a two time-scale update rule converge to a local nash equilibrium. NIPS **30** (2017)
10. Hong, F.T., Zhang, L., Shen, L., Xu, D.: Depth-aware generative adversarial network for talking head video generation. In: CVPR, pp. 3397–3406 (2022)
11. Ji, X., et al.: Eamm: One-shot emotional talking face via audio-based emotion-aware motion model. In: ACM SIGGRAPH, pp. 1–10 (2022)
12. Ji, X., et al.: Audio-driven emotional video portraits. In: CVPR, pp. 14080–14089 (2021)
13. Karras, T., Aila, T., Laine, S., Herva, A., Lehtinen, J.: Audio-driven facial animation by joint end-to-end learning of pose and emotion. TOG **36**(4), 1–12 (2017)
14. Liu, J., et al.: Li-net: Large-pose identity-preserving face reenactment network. In: ICME, pp. 1–6. IEEE (2021)
15. Liu, X., Xu, Y., Wu, Q., Zhou, H., Wu, W., Zhou, B.: Semantic-aware implicit neural audio-driven video portrait generation. In: Avidan, S., Brostow, G., Cissé, M., Farinella, G.M., Hassner, T. (eds.) European Conference on Computer Vision, pp. 106–125. Springer, Cham (2022). https://doi.org/10.1007/978-3-031-19836-6_7
16. Prajwal, K., Mukhopadhyay, R., Namboodiri, V.P., Jawahar, C.: A lip sync expert is all you need for speech to lip generation in the wild. In: ACM MM, pp. 484–492 (2020)
17. Shen, S., et al.: Difftalk: Crafting diffusion models for generalized audio-driven portraits animation. In: Proceedings of the IEEE/CVF Conference on Computer Vision and Pattern Recognition, pp. 1982–1991 (2023)
18. Siarohin, A., Woodford, O.J., Ren, J., Chai, M., Tulyakov, S.: Motion representations for articulated animation. In: CVPR, pp. 13653–13662 (2021)
19. Song, L., Wu, W., Qian, C., He, R., Loy, C.C.: Everybody's talkin': let me talk as you want. IEEE Trans. Inf. Forensics Secur. **17**, 585–598 (2022)
20. Tan, S., Ji, B., Pan, Y.: Emmn: emotional motion memory network for audio-driven emotional talking face generation. In: Proceedings of the IEEE/CVF International Conference on Computer Vision, pp. 22146–22156 (2023)
21. Taylor, S., Kim, T., Yue, Y., Mahler, M., Krahe, J., Rodriguez, A.G., Hodgins, J., Matthews, I.: A deep learning approach for generalized speech animation. TOG **36**(4), 1–11 (2017)
22. Vougioukas, K., Petridis, S., Pantic, M.: End-to-end speech-driven facial animation with temporal gans. In: CVPR Workshop (2019)
23. Wang, D., Deng, Y., Yin, Z., Shum, H.Y., Wang, B.: Progressive disentangled representation learning for fine-grained controllable talking head synthesis. In: CVPR, pp. 17979–17989 (2023)

24. Wang, J., et al.: Lipformer: High-fidelity and generalizable talking face generation with a pre-learned facial codebook. In: Proceedings of the IEEE/CVF Conference on Computer Vision and Pattern Recognition, pp. 13844–13853 (2023)
25. Wang, K., Wu, Q., Song, L., Yang, Z., Wu, W., Qian, C., He, R., Qiao, Yu., Loy, C.C.: MEAD: A Large-Scale Audio-Visual Dataset for Emotional Talking-Face Generation. In: Vedaldi, A., Bischof, H., Brox, T., Frahm, J.-M. (eds.) ECCV 2020. LNCS, vol. 12366, pp. 700–717. Springer, Cham (2020). https://doi.org/10.1007/978-3-030-58589-1_42
26. Wang, S., Li, L., Ding, Y., Fan, C., Yu, X.: Audio2head: audio-driven one-shot talking-head generation with natural head motion. IJCAI (2021)
27. Wang, T.C., Mallya, A., Liu, M.Y.: One-shot free-view neural talking-head synthesis for video conferencing. In: CVPR, pp. 10039–10049 (2021)
28. Wang, Y., Yang, D., Bremond, F., Dantcheva, A.: Latent image animator: learning to animate images via latent space navigation (2022)
29. Wu, H., Zhou, S., Jia, J., Xing, J., Wen, Q., Wen, X.: Speech-driven 3d face animation with composite and regional facial movements. In: Proceedings of the 31st ACM International Conference on Multimedia, pp. 6822–6830 (2023)
30. Xiang, S., et al.: One-shot identity-preserving portrait reenactment. arXiv preprint arXiv:2004.12452 (2020)
31. Xu, C., et al.: High-fidelity generalized emotional talking face generation with multi-modal emotion space learning. In: Proceedings of the IEEE/CVF Conference on Computer Vision and Pattern Recognition, pp. 6609–6619 (2023)
32. Zhou, H., Liu, Y., Liu, Z., Luo, P., Wang, X.: Talking face generation by adversarially disentangled audio-visual representation. In: AAAI, vol. 33, pp. 9299–9306 (2019)
33. Zhou, H., Sun, Y., Wu, W., Loy, C.C., Wang, X., Liu, Z.: Pose-controllable talking face generation by implicitly modularized audio-visual representation. In: CVPR, pp. 4176–4186 (2021)
34. Zhou, Y., Han, X., Shechtman, E., Echevarria, J., Kalogerakis, E., Li, D.: Makelttalk: speaker-aware talking-head animation. TOG **39**(6), 1–15 (2020)

An AI-Enhanced VR Metaverse for Ethnic Festival Culture Protection and Inheritance

Tingyu Zhu, Jia Liu, Zhe Zhang, Yanan Liu, Qianhan Tang, Jian Gong, Hao Zhang, and Dan Xu(✉)

School of Information Science of Engineering, Yunnan University, Kunming, China
zhuty1308@stu.ynu.edu.cn, danxu@ynu.edu.cn

Abstract. In the context of globalization and digitalization, ethnic festival cultures face significant challenges in authentic inheritance and dissemination. Traditional 2D videos and live streaming often suffer from poor user interactivity and inconsistent content authenticity, with many cultural representations lacking genuine ethnic characteristics. To overcome these limitations, we developed a virtual reality (VR) metaverse centered on ethnic festivals, employing key technologies: 1) using the professional YNU-Dance motion capture dataset and skeletal animation retargeting to faithfully reproduce 11 ethnic dances with high fidelity; 2) using a multi-camera array scanning system to create personalized 3D digital avatars that enhance user immersion; 3) enabling real-time motion driving of avatars synchronized with users' actual movements through the monocular pose estimation model, without wearable devices, improving interaction naturalness and embodiment. The system is integrated in Unreal Engine 5, delivering visually compelling experiences with consistent cultural elements. Our results demonstrate the potential of VR technology to support authentic ethnic cultural preservation and interactive participation.

Keywords: Virtual Reality · Ethnic Festival · Culture Protection and Inheritance · VR Metaverse

1 Introduction

Yunnan is China's most ethnically diverse region, home to 25 indigenous minorities, 15 of which are unique to Yunnan (e.g., Bai, Hani, Dai) [1,2]. However, under modernization and globalization, ethnic minority cultural heritage faces severe challenges: the aging of heritage bearers, declining youth participation, and risks of intergenerational discontinuity [3]. For example, for the Yi people's iconic festival dance Axi Dancing Under the Moon, most inheritors are over 60 years old and lack effective succession mechanisms. Urbanization and cultural homogenization have further reduced youth willingness to engage with traditional culture [4]. As living carriers of culture, ethnic festivals integrate music, dance, costume, and ritual into a dynamic cultural ecosystem, but existing transmission models struggle to maintain their vitality.

A. Hinkenjan et al. (Eds.): ICXR 2025, LNCS 16428, pp. 490–500, 2026.
https://doi.org/10.1007/978-981-95-7195-6_36

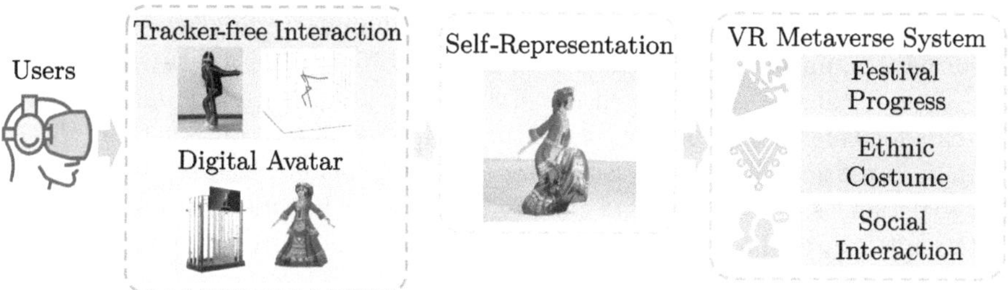

Fig. 1. The overall design of the VR metaverse.

Digital documentation efforts have increased the accessibility of intangible cultural heritage (ICH), but most rely on 2D video recording or live streaming, which suffer from low interactivity, fragmented presentation, and limited immersion [5,6]. Studies have shown that although "live streaming ICH" raises public awareness, its passive viewing format fails to trigger deep cultural participation or memory formation [7]. Similarly, many VR ICH projects employ preset characters and controller-based interactions, which cannot faithfully reproduce the spatial rhythm and embodied experience of festival dances [8]. The absence of accurate motion reproduction and personalized engagement directly weakens users' sense of presence, undermining cultural transmission efficacy [9,10].

To address these challenges, we propose an immersive VR metaverse system focused on ethnic festivals, integrating (1) multi-view motion capture data for high-fidelity NPC animation, (2) personalized 3D avatars generated through array-camera photogrammetry, and (3) wearable-free pose estimation for real-time body-driven interaction. Figure 1 presents the overall system design. Unlike traditional two-dimensional media and passive VR systems, our approach enables users to freely explore reconstructed festival villages, interact with non-player characters(NPCs) and cultural objects, and participate in narrative-guided ritual sequences using their own digital avatars. This study aims to establish a reproducible technical paradigm for dynamic cultural preservation, combining spatial authenticity, bodily presence, and cultural narrative coherence [11–13]. It further contributes to HCI knowledge by showing how embodied participation and personalized avatars can transform cultural heritage VR from a passive viewing paradigm into a participatory narrative space.

2 Related Work

2.1 Digital Preservation of Ethnic Festival Culture

Traditional digital preservation methods for ethnic culture—such as documentation, 2D videos, and image archives—offer valuable records but lack the ability to reproduce embodied elements like ritual rhythm, group participation, and interactive atmosphere [4,5]. Recent attempts to use short video and live-streaming platforms have increased exposure but still result in fragmented content and limited user engagement.

Festival culture is inherently multimodal, combining trading activities, ritual performances, music, and costumes into an integrated cultural ecosystem. However, existing digital preservation research mostly adopts a unimodal approach. Systems focusing solely on motion capture [14], costume reconstruction [15], or spatialized music [16] fail to synchronize these dimensions, leading to disjointed user experiences. This highlights the urgent need for holistic systems that integrate multi-source data and cultural semantics for immersive reconstruction.

2.2 Virtual Reality and Metaverse Applications

Virtual reality (VR) has been widely applied to education, museum curation, and cultural heritage preservation [12,13,17], providing immersive and interactive environments where users can explore historical scenes and experience traditional rituals. Some projects extend this to the metaverse concept, building virtual workshops to reproduce craft processes [18] or immersive halls to display festival decorations [19]. Digital human modeling and full-body motion capture have been introduced to simulate performer roles [20,21], yet most systems still rely on preset avatars and controller-based interactions, overlooking group dynamics and real-time body mapping.

This gap motivates the design of systems that combine multimodal motion data, personalized avatars, and natural interaction, enabling users to engage in first-person participation rather than passive viewing. The proposed VR metaverse system addresses these needs by integrating real motion capture data, avatar personalization, and wearable-free body tracking to reproduce ritual processes and enhance user embodiment.

3 Method

3.1 Overall Design of the VR Metaverse for Ethnic Festival Culture

This study constructs a VR metaverse system aimed at the preservation and dissemination of ethnic festival culture. By integrating key technologies such as immersive scene construction, intangible cultural heritage motion reproduction, digital avatar generation, and natural interaction, the system offers users an experience that is perceptible, comprehensible, and participatory. The system comprises five core functional modules: narrative guidance, digital avatar customization, ethnic costume changing, natural body interaction, and multi-user interaction. The architecture of the system is illustrated in Fig. 2.

The cultural scenes are modeled based on the spatial features and ritual processes of ethnic festivals, encompassing areas such as festive plazas, traditional villages, and performance stages. The NPC module simulates character behaviors using motion capture data to reproduce dynamic cultural activities like dances and rituals. The digital avatar module enables users to generate personalized 3D avatars via array camera scanning, enhancing a sense of identity. The natural interaction module, based on monocular camera input and pose estimation, supports real-time virtual body motion mirroring. All components are integrated and rendered using Unreal Engine 5, forming a deployable

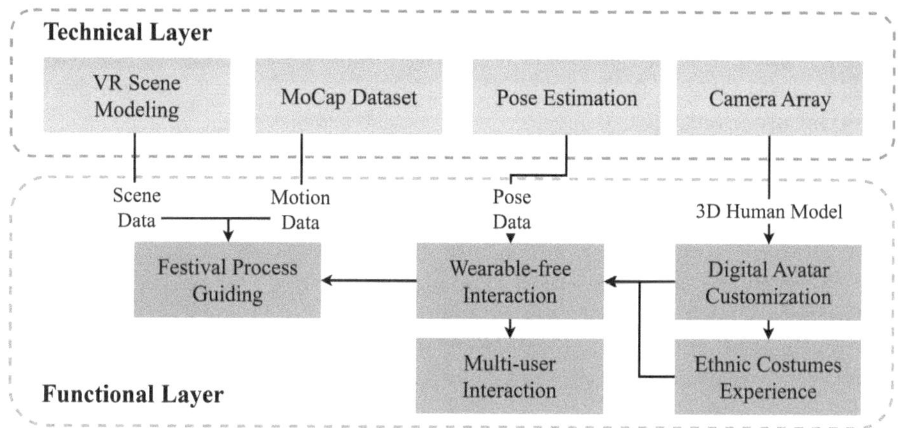

Fig. 2. The system architecture of the VR metaverse.

VR application. Cultural experts and heritage bearers reviewed elements such as architecture, movement, and clothing to ensure authenticity and cultural fidelity.

Upon logging in, users can select a specific ethnic festival scene. The system then guides them through a narrative-driven experience (Sect. 4.2.1), enabling interaction with the environment, NPCs, and other users (Sect. 4.2.5). Users may also choose to participate using their personalized digital avatar (Sect. 4.2.2) and experience ethnic costume switching (Sect. 4.2.3). Users can collect full-body images with an external camera, and this input supports pose estimation and real-time synchronization between the user's motion and their virtual representation (Sect. 4.2.4).

3.2 Enhancing Cultural Authenticity and Fidelity

Ethnic dance, as one of the most embodied and symbolic forms of expression in festival culture, serves as a key medium for immersive reproduction of intangible heritage. This study adopts the YNU-Dance dataset as the primary source for animating NPCs in festival scenes, including Dai, Yi, Bai, and Wa, etc. The dataset contains approximately five dance performances per group. Motion data were captured using three DJI OSMO Action 3 cameras and the OptiTrack passive optical MoCap system, producing high-quality skeletal animations in FBX format. The original dataset consists of 5,121 motion clips, augmented to 9,840 sequences with 543,504 RGB image frames.

To achieve natural reproduction of cultural motions in the virtual environment, the Inverse Kinematics (IK) Retargeter tool in Unreal Engine 5 is employed. It transfers skeletal animations from the source (YNU-Dance) to target NPC skeletons. The process involves bone mapping to establish structural correspondence, followed by IK optimization to maintain dynamic consistency of end effectors (e.g., hands and feet) and spatial rhythm.

This approach significantly enhances the realism and naturalness of NPC motions while preserving each ethnic group's unique bodily language and rhythmic characteristics. It also provides the technical basis for faithful reproduction of festival processes.

3.3 Enhancing User Interaction Experience

To promote user engagement and cultural immersion, the system adopts an interaction workflow that combines personalized avatar modeling with real-time motion tracking, allowing users to participate in festival scenarios through their own digital representations.

First, a high-fidelity personalized digital avatar is generated using a UStyle array camera system consisting of 140 synchronized RGB cameras (Fig. 3). Through multi-view 3D reconstruction, point cloud simplification, and AI-based modeling, users can obtain a digital avatar closely resembling their appearance by assuming a fixed pose for a single-shot capture.

Fig. 3. The array camera system we used for generating digital avatars.

Second, monocular pose estimation and inverse kinematics are used for natural motion mapping. The workflow is as follows: user motion videos are processed by HRNet [22] to extract 2D pose sequences, which are then input to a 3D pose estimation model. The resulting pose data are converted into FBX skeletal animations via IK methods and retargeted to the user's avatar. This enables full-body, device-free, real-time motion control. This low-cost and immersive interaction significantly improves users' sense of embodiment and agency in the virtual festival space.

4 Implementation and Results

4.1 System Implementation and Deployment Environment

The proposed VR system is developed using Unreal Engine 5.5. The core modules—digital avatar rendering, motion-driven logic, narrative control, and interactive feedback—are all deployed on a local computer. The design team collaborated with cultural experts through iterative workshops, including review of 3D assets, co-design of ritual sequences, and validation of costume details. This participatory process ensured cultural fidelity and reduced risks of misrepresentation. The system supports mainstream VR headsets such as Pico 4 Ultra. For digital avatar modeling, a 3D reconstruction is performed using the multi-view array camera system consisting of 140 synchronized RGB cameras. The motion-driven module leverages locally deployed pose estimation models for real-time motion tracking.

Our system has modeled substantial digital assets to construct three complete ethnic festival environments. As demonstrated in Table 1, we have implemented 857 skeletal animations covering ethnic dances and daily activities, 27 ethnic virtual avatars and 947 environmental assets including architecture, props, and natural elements.

Table 1. Modeling statistics for ethnic festival metaverse.

Scene	Asset Category	Count
Torch Festival	Skeletal Animations	386
	Ethnic Avatars	13
	Environmental Assets	420
Miao New Year	Skeletal Animations	284
	Ethnic Avatars	8
	Environmental Assets	316
Bai Village	Skeletal Animations	186
	Ethnic Avatars	6
	Environmental Assets	211

4.2 Visualization Demonstration of System Core Functions

The system implements core functional modules, including narrative guidance, avatar creation, ethnic costume switching, and natural body interaction, etc. The visualized core features of the system are as following. Figure 4 demonstrates the overall visualization effect of the ethnic festival theme.

Fig. 4. The overall visualization effect of the ethnic festival theme.

4.2.1 Narrative Guidance. The system provides UI-based and voice-assisted guidance through festival sequences, with interactive nodes such as dancing, parades, etc. NPC skeletal animations are sourced from the YNU-Dance dataset. In consultation with cultural experts, the narrative adopts a three-act structure, within which digital avatar interaction, NPC performance, and envi-

Fig. 5. The visualization effect of the digital avatar.

ronmental triggers are integrated into a coherent storyline.

4.2.2 Digital Avatar Customization. Users can either select from preset avatars or generate personalized 3D avatars using the array camera system. The standard output 3D digital avatar model has a size of 5-10M and consists of 60,000–80,000 polygons. The visualization effect is as shown in Fig. 5.

4.2.3 Ethnic Costume Switching. Users can choose from a variety of traditional ethnic costumes, each supplemented by contextual cultural descriptions to enhance immersion and understanding. Figure 6 shows the visualization of the digital avatar customization module.

4.2.4 Wearable-Free Interaction Module. Unlike traditional VR systems that require wearable sensors or multi-camera arrays, our monocular camera-based approach eliminates device constraints. Using a monocular camera, the system captures full-body images for real-time 3D pose estimation (Sect. 3.3), enabling the virtual avatar to mirror the user's movements—creating a "body-as-controller" interaction experience. The visualization effect is as shown in Fig. 7.

4.2.5 Multi-user Interaction. The system supports multiple users entering the same virtual festival scene, allowing voice communication, motion imitation, and collaborative dancing. Interactions with NPCs are also supported for enhanced engagement.

4.3 System Performance and Evaluation

System Runtime Performance. To evaluate system performance across platforms, we conducted 30 scene traversal tests on both a VR device and a PC simulation environment. For the Pico 4 Ultra, frame rates are affected by system-level VSync locking. Table 2 summarizes the average results:

The system runs stably on the Pico 4 Ultra, achieving over 72 FPS, sufficient for a smooth baseline user experience. However, it shows a 30.5% performance

A. Original digital avatar.

B. Changing costume.

C. Digital Avatar in ethnic costume.

Fig. 6. Visualization of digital avatar customization module.

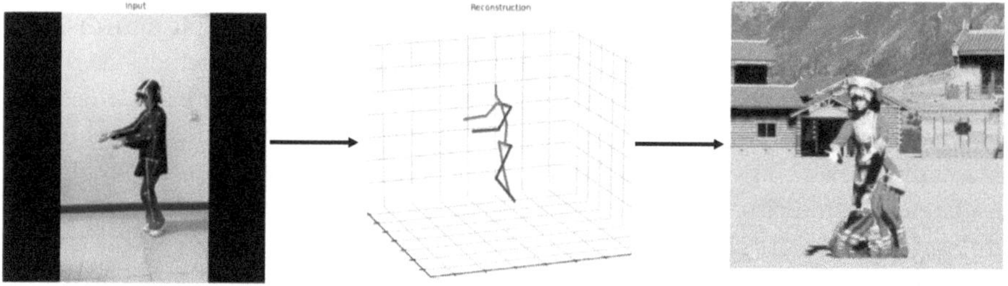

Fig. 7. The implementation of the wearable-free interaction.

gap compared to the PC simulation (104 FPS), primarily due to the computational disparity between the XR2 mobile chipset and the RTX 3070 GPU.

User Experience Evaluation. We conducted user testing with 10 ethnic cultural heritage experts and 15 general users. The evaluation involved festival participation, costume changing, motion imitation, and multi-user coordination. A 5-point Likert scale was used to assess key dimensions. Results are shown in Table 3:

The evaluation shows consistently positive feedback regarding cultural fidelity and immersive experience. Users affirmed the system's educational value and engaging interaction design.

Table 2. Runtime performance on different devices.

Device	Avg. FPS	Resolution
Pico 4 Ultra	72	1832×1920 (per eye)
PC Simulation	104	1920×2160 (per eye)

Table 3. User experience evaluation results.

Evaluation Dimension	Avg. Score (out of 5)	Description
Scene Immersion	4.7	Rich details and authentic cultural elements
Motion Fidelity	4.5	Smooth and natural, consistent with MoCap
Interaction Naturalness	4.6	Responsive and high motion freedom
Cultural Authenticity	4.8	Verified by experts, high fidelity in assets
User Engagement	4.4	Clear guidance and diverse interaction modes

5 Discussion and Conclusion

This study develops a VR metaverse system for the preservation and dissemination of ethnic festival culture, integrating ethnic dance reproduction, digital avatar generation, and natural body-driven interaction. By coordinating these core modules, users can select festival scenes, follow narrative guidance, generate personalized avatars, switch costumes, synchronize body movements in real time, and engage in multi-user interactions, forming an experience that is perceptible, intelligible, and participatory.

From a theoretical perspective, this work expands the application of VR in cultural heritage studies by embedding multimodal data—including motion capture, array-camera reconstruction, and monocular pose estimation—into a coherent system that supports both real-time rendering and embodied interaction. Compared with 2D media, the VR environment provides higher spatial fidelity and natural interaction, enabling users to cognitively and physically engage with cultural spaces and rituals.

Practically, the system demonstrates good portability and scalability for use in festival preservation, museum displays, and education. The combination of pose-driven avatar control, narrative-guided participation, and expert-verified cultural assets establishes a reproducible framework for ICH digitization and minimizes risks of cultural distortion.

Beyond the technical demonstration, the findings also prove: (1) embodied participation through body-driven control enhances cultural engagement compared with controller-based interaction; (2) personalized avatars act as identity anchors, strengthening users' connection to cultural content; (3) narrative scaffolding can balance cultural coherence with user agency. These implications extend beyond the present system and may inform future interactive heritage applications.

Future work will focus on three key areas of enhancement:

1. Expanding the range of supported festivals by incorporating more ethnic traditions and improving contextual modeling of ceremonies and processes;
2. Optimizing motion tracking algorithms under low-cost devices to lower the entry barrier for general users;

3. Integrating AI narrative engines and multi-user social systems to promote the continuous evolution and self-organizing dissemination of ethnic festival culture in virtual spaces.

References

1. Gao, W., Zhuo, X., Xiao, D.: Spatial patterns, factors, and ethnic differences: a study on ethnic minority villages in Yunnan, China. Heliyon **10**(6), e27677 (2024). https://doi.org/10.1016/j.heliyon.2024.e27677. https://www.sciencedirect.com/science/article/pii/S2405844024037083
2. Chun, L.: The inter-provincial mobility and distribution changes of the unique ethnic minorities in Yunnan: based on census data. Population Res. **49**(1), 70 (2025)
3. Li, X., Glasgow, S.N., Cheng, Z., Zhang, J.J.: Research on the problems and strategies of YI traditional dance and intangible cultural heritage "AXI dancing under the moon". Int. J. Soc. Sci. English Lit. **9**(6), 15–27 (2025)
4. Hou, Y., Kenderdine, S., Picca, D., Egloff, M., Adamou, A.: Digitizing intangible cultural heritage embodied: state of the art. J. Comput. Cult. Heritage (JOCCH) **15**(3), 1–20 (2022)
5. Liu, Q., Latiff, Z., Adnan, W.: A study on audience perception of short videos on intangible cultural heritage. Quantum J. Soc. Sci. Humanit. **5**, 474–486 (2024). https://doi.org/10.55197/qjssh.v5i6.533
6. Ponton, J.L., Keshavarz, R., Beacco, A., Pelechano, N.: Stretch your reach: Studying self-avatar and controller misalignment in virtual reality interaction. In: Proceedings of the 2024 CHI Conference on Human Factors in Computing Systems. CHI 2024. Association for Computing Machinery, New York, NY, USA (2024). https://doi.org/10.1145/3613904.3642268
7. Yun, H., Ponton, J.L., Andujar, C., Pelechano, N.: Animation fidelity in self-avatars: impact on user performance and sense of agency. In: 2023 IEEE Conference Virtual Reality and 3D User Interfaces (VR), pp. 286–296 (2023). https://doi.org/10.1109/VR55154.2023.00044
8. Wilburn, B., et al.: High performance imaging using large camera arrays. ACM Trans. Graph. **24**(3), 765–776 (2005). https://doi.org/10.1145/1073204.1073259
9. Kico, I., Grammalidis, N., Christidis, Y., Liarokapis, F.: Digitization and visualization of folk dances in cultural heritage: a review. Inventions **3**(4) (2018). https://doi.org/10.3390/inventions3040072. https://www.mdpi.com/2411-5134/3/4/72
10. Liu, G., et al.: Digital making for inheritance and enlivening intangible cultural heritage: a case of hairy monkey handicrafts. In: Proceedings of the 2023 CHI Conference on Human Factors in Computing Systems. CHI 2023. Association for Computing Machinery, New York, NY, USA (2023). https://doi.org/10.1145/3544548.3581539
11. Wang, H., Du, J., Li, Y., Zhang, L., Li, X.: Grand challenges in immersive technologies for cultural heritage. Int. J. Hum.-Comput. Interact. 1–22 (2025). https://doi.org/10.1080/10447318.2025.2475996
12. Sripan, T., Jeerapattanatorn, P.: Metaverse-based learning: a comprehensive review of current trends, challenges, and future implications. Contemp. Educ. Technol. **17**(3), ep584 (2025)

13. Gong, Q., Zou, N., Yang, W., Zheng, Q., Chen, P.: User experience model and design strategies for virtual reality-based cultural heritage exhibition. Virtual Reality **28**(2), 69 (2024)
14. Cai, W., Liu, W.: Innovative strategies of virtual reality technology in ethnic dance inheritance. Appl. Math. Nonlinear Sci. **9**(1) (2024). https://doi.org/10.2478/amns-2024-0844
15. Costello, A., Kingsland, K., Jones, B., Tanasi, D.: Virtualization and 3D visualization of historical costume replicas: accessibility, inclusivity, virtuality. In: Rousseau, J.J., Kapralos, B. (eds.) Pattern Recognition, Computer Vision, and Image Processing. ICPR 2022 International Workshops and Challenges, pp. 122–130. Springer, Cham (2023)
16. Wang, Y., Wang, S., Zhang, S., Fu, K., Lui, M., Lc, R.: From temporal to spatial: designing spatialized interactions with segmented-audios in immersive environments for active engagement with performing arts intangible cultural heritage. In: Proceedings of the 2025 ACM Designing Interactive Systems Conference, pp. 3292–3312. DIS 2025. Association for Computing Machinery, New York, NY, USA (2025). https://doi.org/10.1145/3715336.3735787
17. Zhang, J., Wan Yahaya, W.A.J., Sanmugam, M.: The impact of immersive technologies on cultural heritage: a bibliometric study of VR, AR, and MR applications. Sustainability **16**(15), 6446 (2024)
18. Nemcova, V., Thomsen, M.K., Mares, A.C., Penn, M., Ramnarain, U., Rodil, K.: Craftsmanship in virtual reality: digital development and evaluation of traditional South African beer brewing. Int. J. Intangible Heritage **18**, 128–143 (2023)
19. Chan, S.C., Cai, S.: Preserving and exhibiting intangible cultural heritage via virtual museum: a case study of the hungry ghosts festival in Hong Kong. Int. Arch. Photogramm. Remote. Sens. Spat. Inf. Sci. **48**, 405–411 (2023)
20. Ma, Y., Zhao, W., Zhang, X., Gao, Z.: Embodied cognition guides virtual-real interaction design to help yicheng flower drum intangible cultural heritage dissemination. In: 2023 Asia Conference on Cognitive Engineering and Intelligent Interaction (CEII), pp. 1–7. IEEE (2023)
21. He, W., et al.: Metadragonboat: exploring paddling techniques of virtual dragon boating in a metaverse campus. In: Proceedings of the 32nd ACM International Conference on Multimedia, pp. 6335–6344 (2024)
22. Jayaweera, S.S., Regani, S.D., Hu, Y., Wang, B., Liu, K.R.: HRNet: high-resolution neural network for human imaging using mmWave radar. IEEE Internet Things J. (2024)

MaskTalker: Audio-Driven Talking Head Generation from Masked Face Using StyleGAN

Shuai Tan, Bin Ji, Chuhang Ma, and Ye Pan(✉)

Shanghai Jiao Tong University, Shanghai, China
whitneypanye@sjtu.edu.cn

Abstract. Human mouths in the wild are often intentionally or unintentionally masked by obstacles, which hinders the lip reading for communication comprehension. To alleviate the issue, we present a novel approach called MaskTalker that generates talking head videos with lip motions, head poses, and eye blinks from the masked faces and audio. The task is innovatively formulated as seeking a trajectory navigating from the source to the target in the known latent space of StyleGAN conditioned on audio. However, two major challenges exist: the fuzzy direction forward due to coupling of current latent space, information scrambling and distortion caused by obstacles and high compression rate. To this end, we explore another LipSpace, which learns a set of directions exclusively for mouth shape transformation in a more disentangled way, clarifying the direction forward. Next, we propose a Refinement Network to compensate for the lost information. The module compares the generated coarse results with input images and employs a flow-based model to revise the distorted details, which serve as the auxiliary for fine-grained videos generation. Extensive experiments are performed to verify the effectiveness and superiority of our MaskTalker. We also present the applications of our system in real-world scenarios.

Keywords: Head avatar · Talking head generation

1 Introduction

Mouth coverings are frequently encountered in real-world scenarios, particularly due to the widespread use of masks in response to infectious diseases [6]. Consequently, lip reading, a crucial means of aiding speech comprehension, especially for individuals with hearing difficulties [10,16,36,71], is always severely impeded by the masked mouth. This has resulted in the stripping of significant information elements in messages [4,17,78], making it challenging to convey information visually in real-world scenarios such as teaching and reporting. Additionally, the masks have a negative impact on the aesthetics of public speaking.

In this study, we propose MaskTalker, a novel framework for audio-driven talking head generation with accurate lip-sync and natural head motion & eyeblinks from the masked face. Particularly, we set the most challenging

A. Hinkenjan et al. (Eds.): ICXR 2025, LNCS 16428, pp. 501–516, 2026.
https://doi.org/10.1007/978-981-95-7195-6_37

masks as a representative obstruction, which completely covers the mouth. Typically, this task can be decomposed into two sub-tasks: (1) face mask removal and (2) audio-driven talking face generation. While many previous works [2,5,12,13,15,19,21,25,32,47,82,85] have made significant progress in both sub-tasks, there has been little work to integrate them for masked face talking video generation.

Our MaskTalker breaks away from the rigid conjoining of subtasks and streamlines the process in an end-to-end fashion. As illustrated in Fig. 1, our intuition is to map the masked image into the well-known $\mathcal{W}^+$ latent space of StyleGAN [27] by GAN inversion [70] and explore a trajectory navigating from the source to the target conditioned on audio. Inspired by previous successes in single image editing for controlling head and eye movements [20,44,70], we guide the latent code to move in a certain direction by the predicted head pose & eyeblink features from audio. Hence, the generated videos can exhibit realistic head movements and blinks in a continuous and seamless manner.

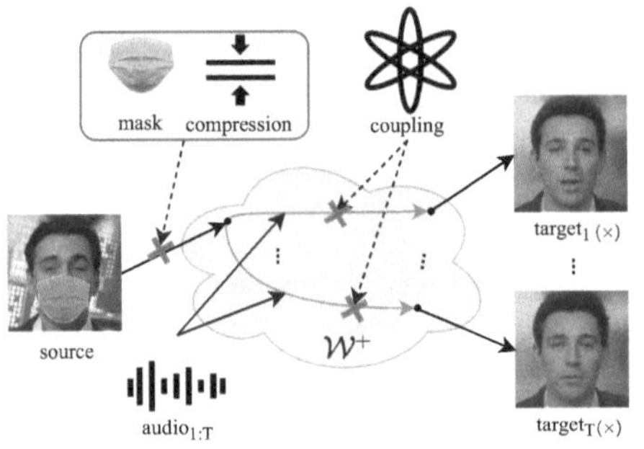

Fig. 1. The motivation of MaskTalker. Our goal is to create a trajectory in latent space that connects source latent code to target code conditioned on audio. However, masks and high compression lead to information loss, while the coupling of latent space makes it challenging to find the trajectory, resulting in inaccurate lip movements and low-quality videos.

Despite the best efforts, there are still several obstacles that impede us from finding the optimal path in Fig. 1: 1) coupling: although $\mathcal{W}^+$ space are semantically disentangled in head pose & eyeblinks, the latent code associated with some attributes may couples through the entire spacebased on DCI-based analysis [70,80], particularly for the mouth region. It can be challenging to find the correct direction to reach the target mouth shape. 2) mask and compression: wearing a mask obscures crucial facial regions, which distorts the mapping from the image to the latent space and introduces errors [45]. Moreover, $\mathcal{W}^+ \in \mathbb{R}^{18\times 512}$ is the compression and asymmetric mapping of the image [49], which entails a balance among all training data. Both issues conspire towards the lack of image-specific details in results according to Rate-Distortion theory [69,75].

To tackle these challenges, we explore LipSpace $\mathcal{L}$ designed explicitly for lip motion control. Concretely, we learn a set of directions, where each dimension independently governs a distinct visual transformation on mouth shape while maintaining other facial attributes unchanged. For this purpose, we set the found directions as orthogonal bases, which also enables us to discover new $\mathcal{L}$ latent codes through various linear combinations of the bases, to represent a wider range of lip movements. Hence, we are able to successfully find a trajectory in latent space, synthesizing talking face videos from a masked face and an audio clip via a pre-trained image generator [28].

To address low fidelity in the details, we introduce a Refinement Network that uses the difference map between the coarse results and input image as guidance to compensate for the lost image-specific details. However, the difference map cannot directly refine the results, since the obscured lower face provides erroneous reference information, and the head pose and eye regions inevitably differ from the input due to the edited latent code. To this end, we cover the lower face and only focus on the differences in unobstructed regions. Considering that the head pose & eyeblink features indicate the edited directions for latent code, we design a flow-based reviser to align the difference map conditioned on the estimated flow fields from the features. In collaboration with the detected trajectory, high-fidelity talking face videos are generated as the final results. Extensive experiments demonstrate that our method outperforms state-of-the-art (SOTA) methods, even in the presence of face masks.

The main contributions of this paper are summarized below: 1) We propose MaskTalker, which constructs a path in the latent space to generate talking face videos with lip-synchronization, head motion, and eyeblink from a masked face image and an audio clip. 2) We learn a set of orthogonal bases for lip motion control based on the explored LipSpace $\mathcal{L}$, realizing more precise lip synchronization. 3) we introduce the Refinement Network, which utilizes revised difference maps to complement missing details and achieve high-fidelity results.

2 Related Work

Latent Space Manipulation of StyleGAN. In recent times, StyleGAN [26–28] has successfully proved its power to generate impressively realistic and high-resolution images involving several latent spaces, including normally distributed $\mathcal{Z}$ latent space and semantically disentangled $\mathcal{W}^+$ space. To realize controllable image generation, GAN inversion task [1,48,70,90] is proposed to learn the mapping from images into the $\mathcal{W}^+$ latent space of the pre-trained StyleGAN via an encoder. More recently, several works have explored the manipulation of $\mathcal{W}^+$ to control specific attributes in unsupervised settings, such as head pose and eye open/close. This facilitates us to control the head pose and blinking when generating talking face videos. In contrast, Wu et al. [80] analyze another latent StyleSpace $\mathcal{S}$, which individually rigs a specific region using a single channel. Sparked by it, we further explore LipSpace $\mathcal{L}$ and learn a set of directions exclusively for mouth shape editing to achieve better lip-synchronization.

Audio-Driven Talking Face Generation. Several methods have emerged to generate talking face videos [14,23,24,33–35,37,39–41,50,55–67,79,86] from audio. On the one hand, some works [22,43,54,88] employ the encoder-decoder structure to extract and fuse features to generate talking face videos in an end-to-end manner. On the other hand, the researchers leverage explicit structure representations predicted from audio as motion guidance, such as landmark [29,72,84,89], dense motion field [51,73,74,76], and 3D models [46,53,68,83], and then synthesize result videos. Despite the previous success, they fail to generate high-resolution videos owing to the lack of corresponding training datasets. Inspired

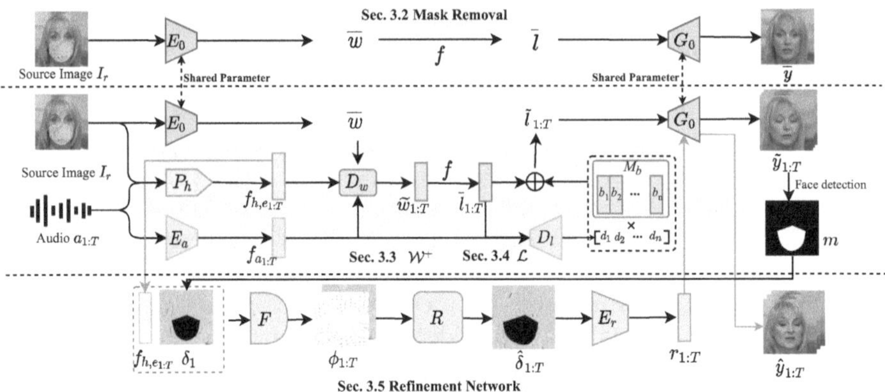

Fig. 2. The overview of MaskTalker. To generate a talking face video from a masked image and an audio clip, we first map the image into the $\overline{w} \in \mathcal{W}^+$ latent space, and predict head pose & eyeblink $f_{h,e_{1:T}}$, and audio features $f_{a_{1:T}}$ from the audio clip. Using these features, we warp the $\overline{w}$ latent code into $\widetilde{w}_{1:T}$ for realistic head pose and eyeblink (Sect. 3.2). Though applying affine transformations f to $\widetilde{w}_{1:T}$, we get $\bar{l}_{1:T} \in \mathcal{L}$, which is linearly combined with a magnitude vector $d = \{d_1, ..., d_n\}$ to perform lip-sync (Sect. 3.3). Hence, we synthesize the coarse results $\widetilde{y}_{1:T}$ and then detect the lower face mask m. Finally, we use $f_{h,e_{1:T}}$ and $\delta_1 = (\widetilde{y}_1 - I_r) \times m$ to further revise $\widetilde{y}_{1:T}$ into the high-fidelity results $\hat{y}_{1:T}$ (Sect. 3.4).

by the pre-trained StyleGAN [26–28], Yin et al. [81] modify the feature space $\mathcal{F}$ based on dense flow field to generate high-resolution talking face videos. Alghamdi et al. [3] predict the displacement of latent codes $\mathcal{W}^+$ to obtain lip motion with a fixed head pose and eyeblink. Min et al. [38] employ a VAE [31] to additionally sample the latent motion space for head motion. Nevertheless, since mouth manipulation is touch to disentangled from $\mathcal{W}^+$ as elaborated in the style mixing experiments of StyleGAN [27], both methods struggle to produce accurate lip motion. Additionally, the high-compression rate results in image-specific details loss despite fine-tuning the generator on the target image/video. On the contrary, we find an improved disentangled LipSpace $\mathcal{L}$ as complement information to enhance the lip-synchronization. Furthermore, we incorporate the difference map as a means of recovering lost details without necessitating any fine-tuning. Notably, to the best of our knowledge, our approach is the first to generate one-shot talking face from a masked face utilizing a pre-trained StyleGAN.

3 Method

Figure 2 presents the pipeline of our proposed MaskTalker, which takes a masked face and an audio clip as inputs to generate talking faces. Our MaskTalker mainly constitutes of three stages. Firstly, we project the masked face image into the latent codes of StyleGAN to remove the mask (Sect. 3.1). In the second stage, the latent codes are manipulated to adjust the head pose and eyeblink (Sect. 3.2) and generate lip motion conditioned on the audio (Sect. 3.3). Lastly, we revise the results obtained from the second stage to enhance their realistic details (Sect. 3.4).

3.1 Mask Removal

To remove the mask on the face, MaskTalker utilizes GAN Inversion methods [1, 70, 75] to extract latent representations, and StyleGAN [28] for image generation. Unlike existing methods that aim to reconstruct the input face, our approach focuses on recovering the face from an image that has been masked. Specifically, given a masked image I_r, the Image Encoder E_0 maps it into the representation $\overline{w} \in \mathcal{W}^+$, which is then transformed into $\overline{l} \in \mathcal{L}$ through affine transformations f. Subsequently, the latent code are fed into a pre-trained generator G_0 [28] to synthesize the unmasking face $\overline{y} = G_0\left(f\left(E_0\left(I_r\right)\right)\right)$.

To enable E_0 to learn the ability to generate unmasked representations, we fix G_0 and retrain E_0 using facial image pairs with and without masks. Following [70], we adopt a pre-trained ArcFace [11] network Φ and a perceptual feature extractor Ψ [52] to constrain identity preservation and perceptual performance, respectively. The process can be formulated as follows:

$$L_{\mathrm{w}} = \left\|w - \overline{w}\right\|_2, \quad L_2 = \left\|y - \overline{y}\right\|_2, \tag{1}$$

$$L_{\mathrm{ID}} = 1 - \langle \Phi(y), \Phi(\overline{y}) \rangle, \quad L_{\mathrm{LPIPS}} = \left\|\Psi(y) - \Psi(\overline{y})\right\|_2, \tag{2}$$

$$L_{\mathrm{sum}} = \lambda_{\mathrm{w}} L_{\mathrm{w}} + \lambda_2 L_2 + \lambda_{\mathrm{ID}} L_{\mathrm{ID}} + \lambda_{\mathrm{LPIPS}} L_{\mathrm{LPIPS}}, \tag{3}$$

where y and w donate ground truth unmasked face and corresponding latent code extracted by a pre-trained GAN inversion Encoder [70]. L_{sum} refers to the sum of loss functions in [70], including w loss L_{w}, reconstruction loss L_2, ID loss L_{ID} and LPIPS loss L_{LPIPS} [87]. Once E_0 is well-trained, we fix it and then use it to find the latent code w from the masked images.

3.2 Head and Eyeblink in $\mathcal{W}^+$

The first eight layers of $\overline{w}$ capture coarse and middle level facial features (e.g., pose and eyes open/closed) [27], which inspire us to warp $\overline{w}$ to perform head motion and eyeblinks. Therefore, we design a Pose Predictor P_h, consisting of a two-layer LSTM [18], to infer head pose & eyeblink features $f_{h,e_{1:T}}$ from reference image I_r and audio clip $a_{1:T}$. Since $\overline{w}$ couples multiple facial attributes such as cheeks in addition to head motion and eye blinks, we complement the attributes with audio features $f_{a_{1:T}}$ extracted from the audio signal using an Audio Encoder E_a. In this way, we construct a $\mathcal{W}^+$ space Decoder D_w to operate $\overline{w}$ conditioned on $f_{h,e_{1:T}}$ and $f_{a_{1:T}}$. Consequently, we obtain $\widetilde{w}_{1:T} = D_w\left(\overline{w}, P_h(a_{1:T}), E_a(a_{1:T})\right)$.

During the training phase, we use a mean squared error (MSE) loss L_{w} to supervise D_w. We also incorporate an inter-frame continuity loss L_{smooth} to eliminate jitters between frames, ensuring temporal coherence in the generated video. The loss functions are defined as follows:

$$L_{\mathrm{w}} = \frac{1}{T}\sum_{t=1}^{T} \|w_t - \widetilde{w}_t\|_2, \quad L_{\mathrm{smooth}} = \frac{1}{T-1}\sum_{t=1}^{T-1} \|\widetilde{w}_{t+1} - \widetilde{w}_t\|_2, \tag{4}$$

where T is the number of frames, w_t represents the latent code extracted from tth frame of ground truth video.

3.3 Lip-Sync in $\mathcal{L}$

We perform affine transformations f on $\widetilde{w}$ to obtain $\bar{l}$ in another more disentangled space, namely LipSpace $\mathcal{L}$. In the $\mathcal{L}$ space, we learn a set of bases related only to the mouth motion in a self-supervised training strategy. Specifically, we construct a lip memory $M_b = \{b_1, b_2, ..., b_n\}$ to store the learnable basis b_i and design a Lip Decoder D_l that takes in the latent code l and audio features f_a and maps them to the weight of each basis $d = \{d_1, d_2, ..., d_n\}$. Subsequently, we can calculate the overall movement direction Δ_l of the l latent code by the weight sum of bases: $\Delta_l = \sum_{i=1}^{n} d_i b_i$

In order to achieve a completely decoupled basis and prevent changes in regions other than the mouth, we enforce orthogonality between each pair of bases by setting a constraint of $\langle b_i, b_j \rangle = 0 \quad (i \neq j)$, where $\langle \cdot, \cdot \rangle$ represents the dot product operation. Hence, each basis is responsible for a unique direction of mouth shape deformation, allowing us to represent various lip movements as linear combinations of the bases while maintaining other facial attributes unchanged. In this fashion, we obtain the target latent code $\widetilde{l}_t$, and then proceed to train both the Lip Decoder D_l and lip memory M_b as follows: $\widetilde{l}_t = \bar{l}_t + \Delta_{l_t}, \quad L_{\mathrm{l}} = \frac{1}{T}\sum_{t=1}^{T} \left\| l_t - \widetilde{l}_t \right\|_2$, where l_t is ground truth l of the tth frame.

So far, we have successfully discovered a path in the latent space, enabling us to generate talking face videos with lip-sync, head motion, and eyeblink using the generator G_0. To further refine the output, we introduced a reconstruction loss L_2 and a perceptual loss L_{LPIPS}, aimed at reducing the differences between the output $\widetilde{y}$ and the ground truth y. Using the shorthand notation defined in Eq. 3, we can express the losses as: $L_2 = \frac{1}{T}\sum_{t=1}^{T} \|y_t - \widetilde{y}_t\|_2, L_{\mathrm{ID}} = \frac{1}{T}\sum_{t=1}^{T}(1 - \langle \Phi(y_t), \Phi(\widetilde{y}_t)\rangle), L_{\mathrm{LPIPS}} = \frac{1}{T}\sum_{t=1}^{T} \|\Psi(y_t) - \Psi(\widetilde{y}_t)\|_2$.

Subsequently, the total loss function L_{total} is formulated as the weighted sum of the above losses: $L_{\mathrm{total}} = \lambda_{\mathrm{w}} L_{\mathrm{w}} + \lambda_{\mathrm{smooth}} L_{\mathrm{smooth}} + \lambda_{\mathrm{l}} L_{\mathrm{l}} + \lambda_2 L_2 + \lambda_{\mathrm{ID}} L_{\mathrm{ID}} + \lambda_{\mathrm{LPIPS}} L_{\mathrm{LPIPS}}$, where λs are hyper-parameters to balance these terms.

3.4 Refinement Network

To address the low fidelity and inaccurate image-specific information in the generated videos, we introduce a Refinement Network that focuses on conveying missing details in the original image, with particular attention paid to the difference between the coarse results $\widetilde{y}$ and the input image I_r that specifies the

Table 1. Quantitative comparisons with state-of-the-art methods.

Method	LRW [7]					GRID [9]					Output		
	PSNR↑	SSIM↑	CPBD↑	LMD↓	$Sync_{conf}$ ↑	PSNR↑	SSIM↑	CPBD↑	LMD↓	$Sync_{conf}$ ↑	Resolution	Pose	Blink
MakeItTalk [89]	19.45	0.66	0.16	2.94	4.90	19.68	0.67	0.13	2.65	2.16	256^2	✓	✓
Wav2Lip [43]	19.73	**0.70**	0.21	2.61	5.22	19.96	**0.69**	0.19	2.19	**2.74**	96^2	✗	✗
Audio2Head [73]	19.63	0.66	0.17	2.83	4.96	19.71	0.65	0.15	2.42	2.32	256^2	✓	✓
PC-AVS [88]	19.80	0.67	0.18	2.63	5.04	19.82	0.68	0.17	2.34	2.48	224^2	✓	✗
MM'22 [3]	20.13	0.67	**0.25**	2.93	4.94	**20.15**	0.67	**0.26**	2.28	2.39	1024^2	✗	✗
StyleTalker [38]	19.72	0.64	0.24	2.76	5.05	19.96	0.64	**0.26**	2.25	2.37	1024^2	✓	✓
Ground Truth	-	1.00	0.26	0.00	5.30	-	1.00	0.30	0.00	2.60	256^2	-	-
Proposed with mask	20.19	0.68	0.23	2.59	5.16	20.03	0.68	0.24	2.21	2.45	1024^2	✓	✓
Proposed w/o mask	**20.25**	0.69	**0.25**	**2.53**	**5.24**	20.11	**0.69**	**0.26**	**2.16**	2.51	1024^2	✓	✓

lost information. However, I_r is occluded by a mask and $\widetilde{y}$ may differ from I_r on head pose & eyeblinks resulting from moved w. We observe that the first frame of results usually keeps the same pose as the reference image, whose difference reflects the main lost information when ignoring the mask regions. Missing information in other frames can be inferred from the first difference map based on $f_{h,e}$. Therefore, we first detect the lower face of the first frame $\widetilde{y}_1$ and represent it as a binary mask m. We further calculate the difference $\delta_1 = (I_r - \widetilde{y}_1) \times m$. Then a Flow Estimator F is designed to predict the flow field ϕ_t from δ_1 and tth $f_{h,e}$, which indicates the correction direction from δ_1 to the tth difference map $\hat{\delta}_t$. In this way, the flow field ϕ_t warps δ_1 to generate the tth corrected distortion map $\hat{\delta}_t$ by a Reviser R. Subsequently, we pass $\hat{\delta}_t$ through a Revise Encoder E_r to project it to a high-rate latent feature r_t, which refers to the lost details in $\widetilde{y}_t$. Incorporating the discovered track $\widetilde{l}_t$, G_0 competently generate high-fidelity results $\hat{y}_t = G(\widetilde{l}_t, E_r(\hat{\delta}_t)), hat\delta_t = R(F(f_{h,e_t}, \delta_1), \delta_1)$:

During training the branch, we freeze other modules and train the Refinement network using loss functions similar to Eq. 3: $L_{\mathrm{r}} = \frac{1}{T}\sum_{t=1}^{T} L_{\mathrm{sum}}(y_t, \hat{y}_t)$

4 Experiments

4.1 Experimental Setup

Datasets. We evaluate the proposed method using two widely used benchmark datasets: LRW [7] and GRID [9]. LRW comprises 1000 utterances of 500 different words, each lasting approximately one second, with various head poses captured from BBC news in the wild. GRID contains video clips of 33 speakers in a fixed head pose under experimental conditions. Thus, when testing on GRID, we fix the head pose of the results while retaining flexible blinks. Note that because there are no facial image pairs with and without masks, we train the Image Encoder for masked images in Sect. 3.1 using a synthetically generated mask dataset from LRW face images, and evaluate the model on both aforementioned datasets as well as real-world masked images.

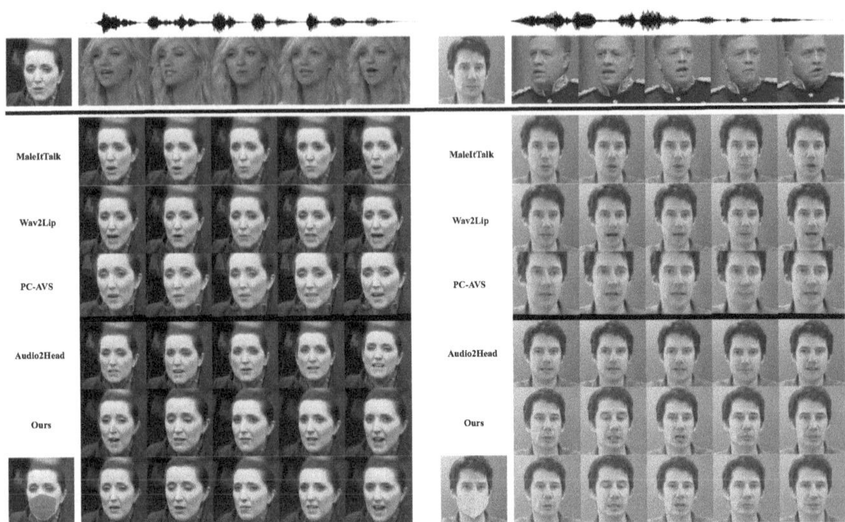

Fig. 3. Qualitative comparisons with SOTA low-resolution methods.

Fig. 4. Qualitative comparisons with state-of-the-art high-resolution audio-driven talking face generation methods.

Implementation Details. We implement our network using PyTorch and train our models on two NVIDIA GeForce GTX 3090 s with 24GB of memory. We pre-train the Image Encoder based on e4e [70] with the synthetic mask dataset and use the pre-trained image generator of StyleGAN [28]. During training, both models are kept fixed. For the other modules, we update parameters via Adam optimizer [30] with an initial learning rate of 2e-4. The bases number n in $\mathcal{L}$ space are set as 8. Moreover, we refer to previous works [70] and empirically set $\lambda_{\mathrm{w}}, \lambda_{\mathrm{smooth}}, \lambda_{1}, \lambda_{2}, \lambda_{\mathrm{ID}}$ and λ_{LPIPS} as 1, 0.001, 1, 1, 0.1, and 0.8.

Comparison Setting. We first compare our results with state-of-the-art low-resolution audio-driven talking face video generation methods: MakeItTalk [89], Wav2Lip [43], PC-AVS [88], and Audio2Head [73]. Furthermore, we compare the methods which generate high-resolution videos based on StyleGAN: MM'22 [3] and StyleTalker [38]. We assess the results using evaluation metrics including SSIM [77] and PSNR for image generation quality, cumulative probability blur detection (CPBD) for frame sharpness, the landmark distance (LMD) [5] for accuracy evaluation of lip movement. In addition, we evaluate the synchronization of lip motion with input audio by $Sync_{\mathrm{conf}}$ [8]. To ensure a fair comparison, we test all methods with the same inputs and evaluate our method under two conditions: with and without a mask.

4.2 Experimental Results

Quantitative Results. Table 1 reports the quantitative comparison to other methods on LRW and GRID datasets. Our method outperforms other methods in most evaluation metrics on both datasets. Wav2Lip achieves the highest SSIM score on LRW since it only modifies the mouth regions and maintains other parts of the reference image unchanged. Additionally, MM'22 fine-tunes the generator on each subject, which results in the highest PSNR score on GRID. Notably, despite taking a masked face as input, MaskTalker achieves comparable performance to other state-of-the-art methods.

Qualitative Results. We provide a qualitative comparison between our method and state-of-the-art low-resolution generation methods in Fig. 3. Our method benefits from the latent space representation of StyleGAN, which enables it to generate high-definition animations with natural head movements, eyeblinks, and accurate mouth shapes from both masked and unmasked face images. In contrast, other methods are unable to process faces wearing masks. For instance, MakeItTalk [89] generates talking face videos by utilizing face landmarks as an intermediate, which is the sparse representation that hardly provides accurate lip synchronization [42]. Additionally, landmark positions are difficult to detect due to the mask's concealment. Wav2Lip [43] mainly edits the mouth regions and focuses on the synchronization with the speech audio without considering head poses. While PC-AVS [88] achieves head pose control, it neglects eyeblinks for generating realistic animation. Although Audio2Head [73] can produce results with changing head pose and eye gazes, the generated faces visibly bear the deformation on the original faces. As presented in Fig. ??, we also demonstrate the practical applications of our methods in real-world scenarios, such as faces obstructed by masks and microphones.

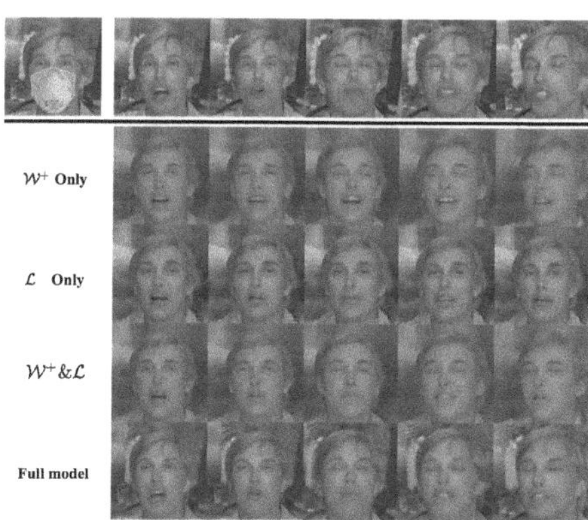

Fig. 5. Ablation study results. Top row shows the ground truth image sequence.

As illustrated in Fig. 4, we also compare our method with StyleGAN-based methods which generate the same 1024×1024 resolution videos as MaskTalker. As observed, our method produces the most precise lip motions and preserves the best fidelity, including target identity and background. Particularly, both comparison methods solely manipulate the $\mathcal{W}^+$, which couples with multiple attributes in addition to mouth shape, impairing the prediction of the lip motion. Moreover, as aforementioned, GAN Inversion tends to find the average over all training images, which results in the loss of details unique to the images. Although MM'22 retains the target identity through fine-tuning the Image Generator on a short video, the background is still distorted. Additionally, fine-tuning is a target-specific task that requires extra resources for training, and it fails to generalize to unseen images. In contrast, our method uses the difference map as a reference to capture not only identity and background differences but also characterize high generalizability. More comparison results can be found in the accompanying video.

Ablation Study. To investigate the contributions of different components in our MaskTalker, we further conduct the ablation study in a progressive way. To be specific, the experiment arrangement can be concluded as: (1) $\mathcal{W}^+$ only: We solely manipulate $\mathcal{W}^+$ to evaluate the effectiveness of the $\mathcal{W}^+$ space on performance. (2) $\mathcal{L}$ only: In order to verify that the regions affected by $\mathcal{L}$, we only edit $\mathcal{L}$ and compare the results to the reference image. (3) $\mathcal{W}^+$ & $\mathcal{L}$: We combine (1) and (3) to obtain the coarse results with head motion, eyeblinks and mouth shape. (4) Full model: Finally, we further add the Refinement Network to estimate the contribution on image quality and fidelity.

Table 2. Numerical results of ablation study on LRW.

Method/Score	PSNR ↑	SSIM ↑	CPBD ↑	LMD ↓	$Sync_{conf}$ ↑
only $\mathcal{W}^+$	19.22	0.61	0.25	3.44	4.46
only $\mathcal{L}$	18.43	0.59	**0.26**	2.68	5.07
$\mathcal{W}^+$ & $\mathcal{L}$	19.48	0.63	0.25	2.62	5.11
full model	**20.19**	**0.68**	0.23	**2.59**	**5.16**

The visual results are presented in Fig. 5. Experiment (1) imitates the correct head pose and blinks, but the mouth shapes deviate from the ground truth. Experiment (2) generates accurate lip motion while maintaining the head pose and blinks consistent with the reference image. Experiment (3) produces both dynamic head pose, eyeblinks, and mouth shape in sync with the audio, but loses details such as the background. The Refinement Network restores image-specific details. Consequently, the contribution of each module is verified. The numerical results reported in Table 2 also confirm our assumptions. We also investigate the effect of different basis numbers on the performance in the supplementary material.

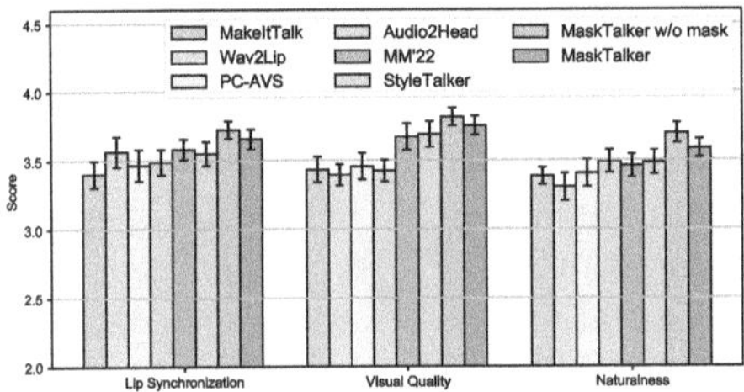

Fig. 6. User study results on three aspects. The score ranges from 1 (worst) to 5 (best), and the error bars imply deviations.

User Study. We conduct a user study to compare generation results with SOTAs. We produce 20 videos via each method, where the reference images and audios are randomly selected from LRW and GRID. Then, 20 participants (10 males, 10 females) are invited to score each video on a scale of 1 (worst) to 5 (best) in terms of lip-sync quality, visual quality and naturalness. The average scores and standard deviations are depicted in Fig. 6, demonstrating that our method outperforms other methods on all three criteria, despite masked face.

5 Conclusion

In this work, we present MaskTalker, which explores a latent space trajectory conditioned on an audio clip, artificially removes the occlusion from the masked face and drive it to talk with natural head pose & eyeblinks. Specifically, we resort to two essential latent spaces of StyleGAN: $\mathcal{W}^+$ for head pose & eyeblinks control and explored $\mathcal{L}$ for lip motion synthesis, respectively. In addition, we propose a Refinement Network to recover the image-specific details lost in the original image. Extensive evaluations illustrate that MaskTalker outperforms state-of-art algorithms on all benchmarks under both mask and unmask conditions. We postulate that our MaskTalker could pave the way for future exploration of audio-driven talking heads from faces masked by multiple obstacles.

Acknowledgements. This work is supported by National Natural Science Foundation of China (NSFC, No. 62472285 and No. 62102255), and Open Research Fund of The State Key Laboratory of Multimodal Artificial Intelligence Systems.

References

1. Abdal, R., Qin, Y., Wonka, P.: Image2stylegan: how to embed images into the stylegan latent space? In: Proceedings of the IEEE/CVF International Conference on Computer Vision, pp. 4432–4441 (2019)
2. Abdal, R., Zhu, P., Mitra, N.J., Wonka, P.: Labels4free: unsupervised segmentation using stylegan. In: Proceedings of the IEEE/CVF International Conference on Computer Vision, pp. 13970–13979 (2021)
3. Alghamdi, M.M., Wang, H., Bulpitt, A.J., Hogg, D.C.: Talking head from speech audio using a pre-trained image generator. In: Proceedings of the 30th ACM International Conference on Multimedia, pp. 5228–5236 (2022)
4. Carbon, C.C.: Wearing face masks strongly confuses counterparts in reading emotions. Front. Psychol. (2020)
5. Chen, L., Maddox, R.K., Duan, Z., Xu, C.: Hierarchical cross-modal talking face generation with dynamic pixel-wise loss. In: Proceedings of the IEEE/CVF Conference on Computer Vision and Pattern Recognition, pp. 7832–7841 (2019)
6. Chu, D.K., et al.: Physical distancing, face masks, and eye protection to prevent person-to-person transmission of sars-cov-2 and covid-19: a systematic review and meta-analysis. Lancet (2020)
7. Chung, J.S., Zisserman, A.: Lip reading in the wild. Lecture Notes in Computer Science (2016)
8. Chung, J.S., Zisserman, A.: Out of time: automated lip sync in the wild. Springer International Publishing eBooks (2016)
9. Cooke, M., Barker, J., Cunningham, S., Shao, X.: An audio-visual corpus for speech perception and automatic speech recognition. J. Acoust. Soc. Am. (2006)
10. Dell'Aringa, A.H.B., Adachi, E.S., Dell'Aringa, A.R.: Lip reading role in the hearing aid fitting process (2007)
11. Deng, J., Guo, J., Xue, N., Zafeiriou, S.: Arcface: additive angular margin loss for deep face recognition. In: Proceedings of the IEEE/CVF Conference on Computer Vision and Pattern Recognition, pp. 4690–4699 (2019)

12. Din, N.U., Javed, K., Bae, S., Yi, J.: A novel GAN-based network for unmasking of masked face. IEEE Access (2020)
13. Farahanipad, F., Rezaei, M., Nasr, M., Kamangar, F., Athitsos, V.: Gan-based face reconstruction for masked-face. In: Proceedings of the 15th International Conference on PErvasive Technologies Related to Assistive Environments, pp. 583–587 (2022)
14. Gong, B., et al.: Uknow: a unified knowledge protocol with multimodal knowledge graph datasets for reasoning and vision-language pre-training. Adv. Neural. Inf. Process. Syst. **37**, 9612–9633 (2024)
15. Guo, Y., Chen, K., Liang, S., Liu, Y.J., Bao, H., Zhang, J.: Ad-nerf: audio driven neural radiance fields for talking head synthesis. In: Proceedings of the IEEE/CVF International Conference on Computer Vision, pp. 5784–5794 (2021)
16. Haidar, L.A.: Teaching with a masked face: a challenge? Le Centre pour la Communication Scientifique Directe - HAL - memSIC (2020)
17. Han, B., Kim, G.J., Hwang, J.I.: Real-time facial animation generation on face mask. In: SIGGRAPH Asia 2022 Posters, pp. 1–2 (2022)
18. Hochreiter, S., Schmidhuber, J.: Long short-term memory. Neural Comput. (1997)
19. Hosen, M.I., Islam, M.B.: Masked face inpainting through residual attention unet (2022)
20. Hu, X., et al.: Style transformer for image inversion and editing. In: Proceedings of the IEEE/CVF Conference on Computer Vision and Pattern Recognition, pp. 11337–11346 (2022)
21. Jabbar, A., et al.: Afd-stackgan: automatic mask generation network for face de-occlusion using stackgan. Sensors (2022)
22. Jamaludin, A., Chung, J.S., Zisserman, A.: You said that?: synthesising talking faces from audio. Int. J. Comput. Vis. **127**, 1767–1779 (2019)
23. Ji, B., Pan, Y., Liu, Z., Tan, S., Jin, X., Yang, X.: Pomp: physics-consistent motion generative model through phase manifolds. In: Proceedings of the Computer Vision and Pattern Recognition Conference, pp. 22690–22701 (2025)
24. Ji, B., Pan, Y., Liu, Z., Tan, S., Yang, X.: Sport: from zero-shot prompts to real-time motion generation. IEEE Trans. Visualization Comput. Graph. (2025)
25. John, S., Danti, A.: Removal of occlusion in face images using pix2pix technique for face recognition (2022)
26. Karras, T., et al.: Alias-free generative adversarial networks. Adv. Neural. Inf. Process. Syst. **34**, 852–863 (2021)
27. Karras, T., Laine, S., Aila, T.: A style-based generator architecture for generative adversarial networks. In: Proceedings of the IEEE/CVF Conference on Computer Vision and Pattern Recognition, pp. 4401–4410 (2019)
28. Karras, T., Laine, S., Aittala, M., Hellsten, J., Lehtinen, J., Aila, T.: Analyzing and improving the image quality of stylegan. In: Proceedings of the IEEE/CVF Conference on Computer Vision and Pattern Recognition, pp. 8110–8119 (2020)
29. Kim, H., et al.: Neural style-preserving visual dubbing. ACM Trans. Graph. (TOG) **38**(6), 1–13 (2019)
30. Kingma, D.P., Ba, J.: Adam: a method for stochastic optimization. arXiv, Learning (2014)
31. Kingma, D.P., Welling, M.: Auto-encoding variational bayes. arXiv, Machine Learning (2013)
32. Li, C., Ge, S., Zhang, D., Li, J.: Look through masks: towards masked face recognition with de-occlusion distillation. In: Proceedings of the 28th ACM International Conference on Multimedia, pp. 3016–3024 (2020)

33. Ma, C., Tan, S., Pan, Y., Yang, J., Tong, X.: Esgaussianface: emotional and stylized audio-driven facial animation via 3D gaussian splatting. arXiv preprint arXiv:2601.01847 (2026)
34. Ma, C., Tan, S., Wei, J., Pan, Y.: Goes: 3D gaussian-based one-shot head animation with any emotion and any style. In: Proceedings of the 33rd ACM International Conference on Multimedia, pp. 9578–9587 (2025)
35. Ma, K., et al.: Phys-liquid: a physics-informed dataset for estimating 3d geometry and volume of transparent deformable liquids. arXiv preprint arXiv:2511.11077 (2025)
36. Mehrabian, A.: Nonverbal Communication. Routledge (2017)
37. Miao, C., et al.: Rose: remove objects with side effects in videos. arXiv preprint arXiv:2508.18633 (2025)
38. Min, D., Song, M., Hwang, S.J.: Styletalker: one-shot style-based audio-driven talking head video generation (2022)
39. Pan, Y., Liu, C., Xu, S., Tan, S., Yang, J.: Vasa-rig: audio-driven 3D facial animation with 'live' mood dynamics in virtual reality. IEEE Trans. Visualization Comput. Graph. (2025)
40. Pan, Y., Tan, S., Cheng, S., Lin, Q., Zeng, Z., Mitchell, K.: Expressive talking avatars. IEEE Trans. Visual Comput. Graph. **30**(5), 2538–2548 (2024)
41. Pan, Y., et al.: Emotional voice puppetry. IEEE Trans. Visual Comput. Graph. **29**(5), 2527–2535 (2023)
42. Park, S.J., Kim, M., Hong, J., Choi, J., Ro, Y.M.: Synctalkface: talking face generation with precise lip-syncing via audio-lip memory. In: Proceedings of the AAAI Conference on Artificial Intelligence, vol. 36, pp. 2062–2070 (2022)
43. R, P.K., Mukhopadhyay, R., Philip, J., Jha, A.K., Namboodiri, V.P., Jawahar, C.V.: Towards automatic face-to-face translation (2020)
44. Radford, A., Metz, L., Chintala, S.: Unsupervised representation learning with deep convolutional generative adversarial networks. In: International Conference on Learning Representations (2016)
45. Randhawa, Z.A., Patel, S., Adjeroh, D.A., Doretto, G.: Learning representations for masked facial recovery. In: International Symposium on Visual Computing, pp. 22–35. Springer, Cham (2022)
46. Ren, Y., Li, G., Chen, Y., Li, T.H., Liu, S.: Pirenderer: controllable portrait image generation via semantic neural rendering. In: Proceedings of the IEEE/CVF International Conference on Computer Vision, pp. 13759–13768 (2021)
47. Richard, A., Zollhöfer, M., Wen, Y., De la Torre, F., Sheikh, Y.: Meshtalk: 3D face animation from speech using cross-modality disentanglement. In: Proceedings of the IEEE/CVF International Conference on Computer Vision, pp. 1173–1182 (2021)
48. Richardson, E., et al.: Encoding in style: a stylegan encoder for image-to-image translation. In: Proceedings of the IEEE/CVF Conference on Computer Vision and Pattern Recognition, pp. 2287–2296 (2021)
49. Shannon, C.E.: Coding theorems for a discrete source with a fidelity criterion. In: IRE National Convention Record, vol. 4, pp. 142–163 (1959)
50. Shi, S., et al.: Motionstone: decoupled motion intensity modulation with diffusion transformer for image-to-video generation. In: Proceedings of the Computer Vision and Pattern Recognition Conference, pp. 22864–22874 (2025)
51. Siarohin, A., Lathuilière, S., Tulyakov, S., Ricci, E., Sebe, N.: Animating arbitrary objects via deep motion transfer. In: Proceedings of the IEEE/CVF Conference on Computer Vision and Pattern Recognition, pp. 2377–2386 (2019)

52. Simonyan, K., Zisserman, A.: Very deep convolutional networks for large-scale image recognition. In: International Conference on Learning Representations (2015)
53. Song, L., Wu, W., Qian, C., He, R., Loy, C.C.: Everybody's talkin': let me talk as you want. IEEE Trans. Inf. Forensics Secur. **17**, 585–598 (2022)
54. Song, Y., Zhu, J., Li, D., Wang, X., Qi, H.: Talking face generation by conditional recurrent adversarial network. arXiv preprint arXiv:1804.04786 (2018)
55. Tan, S., et al.: Mimir: improving video diffusion models for precise text understanding. In: Proceedings of the IEEE/CVF Conference on Computer Vision and Pattern Recognition (2025)
56. Tan, S., et al.: Animate-x++: universal character image animation with dynamic backgrounds. arXiv preprint arXiv:2508.09454 (2025)
57. Tan, S., et al.: Codance: an unbind-rebind paradigm for robust multi-subject animation. arXiv preprint arXiv:2601.11096 (2026)
58. Tan, S., et al.: Animate-x: universal character image animation with enhanced motion representation. In: International Conference on Learning Representations (2025)
59. Tan, S., et al.: Synmotion: semantic-visual adaptation for motion customized video generation. arXiv preprint arXiv:2506.23690 (2025)
60. Tan, S., Gong, B., Ji, B., Pan, Y.: Fixtalk: taming identity leakage for high-quality talking head generation in extreme cases. In: Proceedings of the IEEE/CVF International Conference on Computer Vision (2025)
61. Tan, S., Ji, B.: Edtalk++: full disentanglement for controllable talking head synthesis. arXiv preprint arXiv:2508.13442 (2025)
62. Tan, S., Ji, B., Bi, M., Pan, Y.: Edtalk: efficient disentanglement for emotional talking head synthesis. In: European Conference on Computer Vision, pp. 398–416. Springer, Cham (2025)
63. Tan, S., Ji, B., Ding, Y., Pan, Y.: Say anything with any style. In: Proceedings of the AAAI Conference on Artificial Intelligence, vol. 38, pp. 5088–5096 (2024)
64. Tan, S., Ji, B., Pan, Y.: EMMN: emotional motion memory network for audio-driven emotional talking face generation. In: Proceedings of the IEEE/CVF International Conference on Computer Vision, pp. 22146–22156 (2023)
65. Tan, S., Ji, B., Pan, Y.: Flowvqtalker: high-quality emotional talking face generation through normalizing flow and quantization. In: Proceedings of the IEEE/CVF Conference on Computer Vision and Pattern Recognition, pp. 26317–26327 (2024)
66. Tan, S., Ji, B., Pan, Y.: Style2talker: high-resolution talking head generation with emotion style and art style. In: Proceedings of the AAAI Conference on Artificial Intelligence, vol. 38, pp. 5079–5087 (2024)
67. Tan, S., et al.: Incorporating isodose lines and gradient information via multi-task learning for dose prediction in radiotherapy. In: de Bruijne, M., et al. (eds.) MICCAI 2021. LNCS, vol. 12907, pp. 753–763. Springer, Cham (2021). https://doi.org/10.1007/978-3-030-87234-2_71
68. Thies, J., Elgharib, M., Tewari, A., Theobalt, C., Nießner, M.: Neural voice puppetry: audio-driven facial reenactment. In: Vedaldi, A., Bischof, H., Brox, T., Frahm, J.-M. (eds.) ECCV 2020. LNCS, vol. 12361, pp. 716–731. Springer, Cham (2020). https://doi.org/10.1007/978-3-030-58517-4_42
69. Tishby, N., Zaslavsky, N.: Deep learning and the information bottleneck principle. In: 2015 IEEE Information Theory Workshop (ITW), pp. 1–5. IEEE (2015)
70. Tov, O., Alaluf, Y., Nitzan, Y., Patashnik, O., Cohen-Or, D.: Designing an encoder for stylegan image manipulation. ACM Trans. Graph. (TOG) **40**(4), 1–14 (2021)

71. Trecca, E.M.C., Gelardi, M., Cassano, M.: Covid-19 and hearing difficulties. Am. J. Otolaryngol. (2020)
72. Wang, K., et al.: MEAD: a large-scale audio-visual dataset for emotional talking-face generation. In: Vedaldi, A., Bischof, H., Brox, T., Frahm, J.-M. (eds.) ECCV 2020. LNCS, vol. 12366, pp. 700–717. Springer, Cham (2020). https://doi.org/10.1007/978-3-030-58589-1_42
73. Wang, S., Li, L., Ding, Y., Fan, C., Yu, X.: Audio2head: audio-driven one-shot talking-head generation with natural head motion. In: International Joint Conference on Artificial Intelligence. IJCAI (2021)
74. Wang, S., Li, L., Ding, Y., Yu, X.: One-shot talking face generation from single-speaker audio-visual correlation learning. In: Proceedings of the AAAI Conference on Artificial Intelligence, vol. 36, pp. 2531–2539 (2022)
75. Wang, T., Zhang, Y., Fan, Y., Wang, J., Chen, Q.: High-fidelity GAN inversion for image attribute editing. In: Proceedings of the IEEE/CVF Conference on Computer Vision and Pattern Recognition, pp. 11379–11388 (2022)
76. Wang, T.C., Mallya, A., Liu, M.Y.: One-shot free-view neural talking-head synthesis for video conferencing. In: Proceedings of the IEEE/CVF Conference on Computer Vision and Pattern Recognition, pp. 10039–10049 (2021)
77. Wang, Z., Bovik, A.C., Sheikh, H.R., Simoncelli, E.P.: Image quality assessment: from error visibility to structural similarity. IEEE Trans. Image Process. (2004)
78. Wegrzyn, M., Vogt, M., Kireclioglu, B., Schneider, J., Kissler, J.: Mapping the emotional face. How individual face parts contribute to successful emotion recognition. PLOS ONE (2017)
79. Wei, Y., et al.: Dreamrelation: relation-centric video customization. arXiv preprint arXiv:2503.07602 (2025)
80. Wu, Z., Lischinski, D., Shechtman, E.: Stylespace analysis: disentangled controls for stylegan image generation. In: Proceedings of the IEEE/CVF Conference on Computer Vision and Pattern Recognition, pp. 12863–12872 (2021)
81. Yin, F., et al.: Styleheat: one-shot high-resolution editable talking face generation via pre-trained stylegan. In: Computer Vision–ECCV 2022: 17th European Conference, Tel Aviv, Israel, 23–27 October 2022, Proceedings, Part XVII, pp. 85–101. Springer, Cham (2022)
82. Yin, X., Huang, D., Fu, Z., Wang, Y., Chen, L.: Segmentation-reconstruction-guided facial image de-occlusion (2023)
83. Yu, L., Yu, J., Li, M., Ling, Q.: Multimodal inputs driven talking face generation with spatial–temporal dependency. IEEE Trans. Circuits Syst. Video Technol. (2021)
84. Zakharov, E., Shysheya, A., Burkov, E., Lempitsky, V.: Few-shot adversarial learning of realistic neural talking head models. In: Proceedings of the IEEE/CVF International Conference on Computer Vision, pp. 9459–9468 (2019)
85. Zhang, C., et al.: Facial: synthesizing dynamic talking face with implicit attribute learning. In: Proceedings of the IEEE/CVF International Conference on Computer Vision, pp. 3867–3876 (2021)
86. Zhang, Q., et al.: Physrvg: physics-aware unified reinforcement learning for video generative models. arXiv preprint arXiv:2601.11087 (2026)
87. Zhang, R., Isola, P., Efros, A.A., Shechtman, E., Wang, O.: The unreasonable effectiveness of deep features as a perceptual metric. In: Proceedings of the IEEE Conference on Computer Vision and Pattern Recognition, pp. 586–595 (2018)

88. Zhou, H., Sun, Y., Wu, W., Loy, C.C., Wang, X., Liu, Z.: Pose-controllable talking face generation by implicitly modularized audio-visual representation. In: Proceedings of the IEEE/CVF Conference on Computer Vision and Pattern Recognition, pp. 4176–4186 (2021)
89. Zhou, Y., Han, X., Shechtman, E., Echevarria, J., Kalogerakis, E., Li, D.: Makelttalk: speaker-aware talking-head animation. ACM Trans. Graph. (TOG) **39**(6), 1–15 (2020)
90. Zhu, J., Shen, Y., Zhao, D., Zhou, B.: In-domain GAN inversion for real image editing. In: Vedaldi, A., Bischof, H., Brox, T., Frahm, J.-M. (eds.) ECCV 2020. LNCS, vol. 12362, pp. 592–608. Springer, Cham (2020). https://doi.org/10.1007/978-3-030-58520-4_35

A Hybrid Attention-Enhanced Network for Accurate Dental Pulp Segmentation from CBCT

Chen Wang[1], Baoyu Wu[1], Yanting Guo[1], Ruijun Liu[2](✉), and Peng Yu[3]

[1] The School of Computer and Artificial Intelligence, Beijing Technology and Business University, Beijing 100048, China
wangc@btbu.edu.cn, {2330702025,2431062175}@st.btbu.edu.cn

[2] The School of Software, Beihang University, Beijing 100191, China
liuruijun@buaa.edu.cn

[3] Department of Cariology and Endodontology, Peking University School and Hospital of Stomatology, Beijing 100081, China
yupeng@bjmu.edu.cn

Abstract. Accurate segmentation of dental pulp from cone-beam computed tomography (CBCT) is essential for digital endodontic planning, virtual surgery, and anatomical visualization. However, the intrinsic challenges of low contrast between pulp and surrounding dentin, irregular anatomical morphology, and vulnerability to imaging artifacts greatly impede robust segmentation. To address these issues, we propose PulpSegNet (PSN), a hybrid attention–enhanced segmentation framework built upon the nnUNet architecture and specifically designed for fine-grained delineation of dental pulp structures. PSN incorporates a self-calibrated convolution module SCConv and a contrast-driven feature aggregation module CDFA, strategically integrated into both deep and shallow network stages to enhance structural coherence and boundary precision simultaneously. Through hierarchical feature calibration and foreground-background contrast modeling, the network effectively mitigates the difficulties associated with small-volume targets and ambiguous tissue boundaries. Comprehensive experiments conducted on a multi-class dental pulp segmentation benchmark demonstrate that PSN consistently outperforms existing approaches and establishes a new benchmark for high-precision segmentation in digital dentistry.

Keywords: Dental pulp segmentation · CBCT images · 3D medical image analysis · Hybrid attention mechanism

1 Introduction

With the rapid advancement of Extended Reality (XR) technology, its application in medical imaging has greatly expanded, enabling intuitive visualization of

A. Hinkenjan et al. (Eds.): ICXR 2025, LNCS 16428, pp. 517–529, 2026.
https://doi.org/10.1007/978-981-95-7195-6_38

anatomical structures and surgical procedures [24]. Accurate image segmentation is fundamental for constructing realistic and interactive XR environments. In dental imaging, CBCT-based segmentation generates detailed tooth and maxillofacial models that support diagnosis, treatment planning, and evaluation [4]. Recent advances in deep learning, especially convolutional neural networks (CNNs) and Transformers, have significantly improved segmentation accuracy. CNNs capture local spatial details, while Transformers model long-range dependencies through attention mechanisms [3]. These developments provide a solid foundation for high-fidelity and anatomically precise scene reconstruction in digital dentistry.

Dental CBCT analysis has become increasingly dependent on deep learning for accurate 3D pulp segmentation, which is essential for XR-based visualization, digital restoration planning, and virtual tooth modeling [22]. Segmenting dental pulp is particularly challenging due to its small size and complex morphology, requiring models that can capture fine-grained anatomical details. Recent approaches address these challenges by incorporating attention mechanisms and geometry-aware modeling, enabling networks to focus on critical regions and differentiate pulp from surrounding tissues more effectively [15,23]. By combining anatomical priors and cross-modal strategies, these methods enhance segmentation accuracy and facilitate clinical applications such as root canal navigation, risk assessment, and patient-specific simulation in immersive XR environments.

Despite progress in dental pulp segmentation, challenges remain due to the pulp's small volume, complex morphology, and low grayscale contrast with surrounding dentin. nnUNet is a widely adopted baseline for its adaptive architecture [10], but it struggles with long-range dependencies and weak boundaries in low-contrast regions, making it susceptible to local noise. To improve segmentation accuracy and robustness, we propose a network architecture named PulpSegNet based on the nnUNet framework. The key contributions are as follows:

- PSN extends nnUNet with enhancement modules, retaining adaptive configuration and multi-scale fusion for dental pulp challenges.
- Introduce self-calibrated convolution in deep encoder to tune channels, improving fine-structure sensitivity and robustness under low contrast.
- Integrate a contrast-driven aggregation module into the decoder, enhancing foreground–background separation and boundary/detail reconstruction.

2 Related Work

Deep learning, particularly U-Net [21] and its variants, has become central to CBCT image segmentation, with CNNs and Transformers enhancing local feature discrimination and long-range dependencies through advanced architectures. These approaches improve annotation efficiency and the reliability of image-based support for digital dentistry.

2.1 CBCT-Based Medical Image Segmentation

Recent CBCT segmentation methods employ dilated convolutions and hybrid convolution-transformer architectures with sparse 3D attention, improving structural and cross-domain robustness. Noise, limited labels, and computational costs, however, still limit generalization and clinical adoption.

To address these issues, research has focused on network improvements and data handling. Representative models include nnFormer [31], a pure 3D Transformer encoder–decoder with hierarchical sparse attention, UNETR++ [25] and Swin-UMamba [17], which use lightweight attention and deformable convolutions for boundary refinement, and DPI-MoCo [8], which applies motion-compensated reconstruction for artifact reduction. Semi-supervised [9] and domain adaptation [13] approaches further exploit anatomical priors to improve structural consistency across unlabeled or cross-domain data.

2.2 CBCT-Based Dental Image Segmentation

Advances in dental CBCT segmentation emphasize feature extraction, global context, and geometric priors, though tooth crowding, metal artifacts, and grayscale inconsistencies remain challenging.

Bolelli et al. [2] proposed multi-stage cropping with a dual-branch decoder for better contour delineation. THISNet [14] integrates salient region highlighting and affinity clustering to segment teeth in dense arrangements. ToothAxis [1] reconstructs missing roots and estimates tooth axes via point cloud regression. Trans-VNet [29] combines local texture and transformer-based context modeling for improved boundaries under artifacts. Liu et al. [19] embedded ray attenuation equations in sparse-view networks to jointly optimize reconstruction and segmentation. Another work [18] uses self-supervised grayscale enhancement and Swin UNETR with FDI encoding for multi-structure segmentation and improved consistency.

2.3 CBCT-Based Pulp Structure Segmentation

Dental pulp segmentation is challenging due to small, low-contrast structures and metal artifacts. Traditional thresholding or region-growing methods are unreliable, while deep learning leverages multi-scale and geometry-aware architectures.

Tan et al. [28] introduced a dual-branch U-Net with multi-scale fusion and contextual modules for better boundary interpretation. Li et al. [12] combined multi-scale attention U-Net with level-set optimization to refine contours. Duan et al. [5] used a 3D CNN with residuals and skip connections for edge and semantic consistency. Yang et al. [30] applied a modified 3D DenseNet for multi-branch canal and cavity segmentation. Song et al. [27] presented a context-aware residual network with CBCT preprocessing for contrast enhancement. Slim et al. [26] integrated transformer-based self-attention in U-Net to improve long-range dependency modeling and boundary representation.

3 Method

3.1 Overall Architecture

In this study, CDFA [11] and SCConv [16] are integrated into nnUNet to create a layered mechanism with shallow-layer foreground enhancement and deep-layer semantic calibration. As shown in Fig. 1, by amplifying true foreground responses at high resolution and suppressing false activations in deeper layers using multi-scale context, the model achieves better recall and boundary accuracy for fine structures.

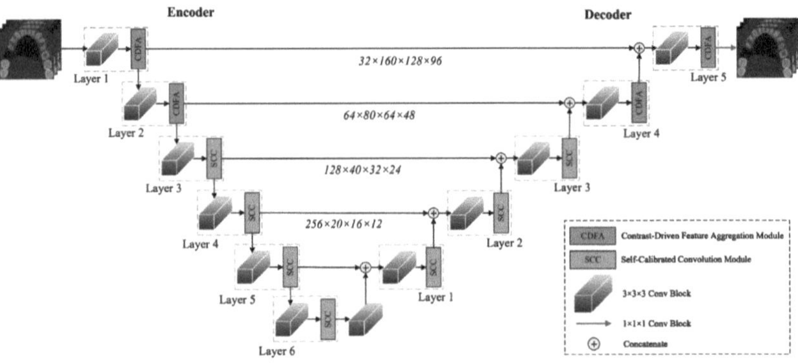

Fig. 1. Overview of the PSN architecture. It builds upon the nnUNet backbone and integrates SCConv and CDFA modules to enhance semantic calibration and boundary refinement respectively.

The encoder has six stages, with shallow layers enhancing foreground and texture, and deep layers handling semantic calibration and receptive field expansion. The decoder mirrors this with five upsampling stages. CDFA strengthens foreground signals in shallow stages, while SCConv refines semantic consistency and reduces noise in deeper layers. Skip connections transmit high-resolution, CDFA-enhanced features to preserve geometry and prevent thin structure fragmentation. Together, these modules enable early detection, semantic integrity, and precise structure reconstruction, improving representation, context modeling, and robustness.

3.2 Self-calibrated Convolution Module

For 16 class fine-grained pulp segmentation, small, sparse canals cause class imbalance and reduce sensitivity to long-range features. High-resolution CBCT requires large receptive fields to preserve slender pulp geometry, which conventional CNNs often fail to capture. As in Fig. 2, integrating SCConv into the nnUNet encoder and decoder expands plane-level receptive fields and suppresses noise in low-contrast regions.

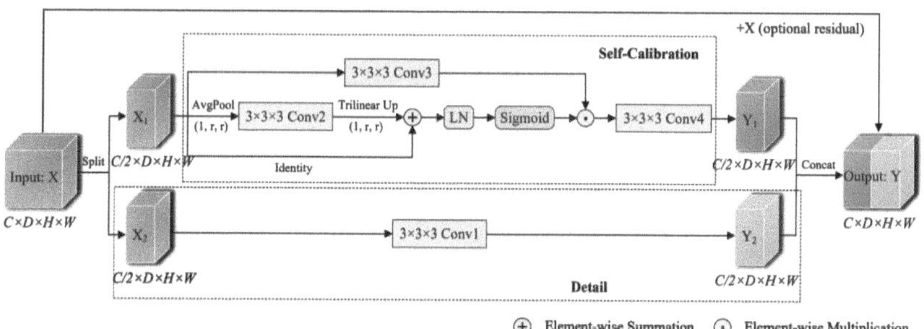

Fig. 2. Architecture of the SCConv module. SCConv introduces channel-wise feature calibration by integrating multi-scale spatial context through anisotropic pooling and selective gating.

Specifically, inspired by channel functional separation, the input feature tensor $\mathbf{X} \in \mathbb{R}^{B \times C \times D \times H \times W}$ is split along the channel dimension into calibration $\mathbf{X}_1$ and detail $\mathbf{X}_2$ branches. The former maintains structural consistency across slices, while the latter preserves local texture. Anisotropic average pooling across in-plane axes compresses $\mathbf{X}_1$, followed by 3×3 convolutions. Upsampled features are fused and passed through a sigmoid gate $\mathcal{G}$ to guide selective recalibration of channel activations:

$$\mathbf{X} = [\mathbf{X}_1, \mathbf{X}_2], \quad \mathbf{X}_1, \mathbf{X}_2 \in \mathbb{R}^{B \times \frac{C}{2} \times D \times H \times W} \tag{1}$$

$$\mathbf{T} = P_r(\mathbf{X}_1), \quad \tilde{\mathbf{T}} = F_2(\mathbf{T}), \quad \hat{\mathbf{X}}_1 = U(\tilde{\mathbf{T}}) \tag{2}$$

$$\mathbf{G} = \sigma\left(\mathrm{LN}(\hat{\mathbf{X}}_1 + \mathbf{X}_1)\right), \quad \mathbf{G} \in [0,1]^{B \times \frac{C}{2} \times D \times H \times W} \tag{3}$$

where, P_r denotes anisotropic average pooling, F_2 is $3 \times 3 \times 3$ convolution, and U is trilinear upsampling. The gating map $\mathbf{G}$ modulates $\mathbf{X}_1$, and the calibrated branch is concatenated with $\mathbf{X}_2$ and fused via $1 \times 1 \times 1$ convolution:

$$\tilde{\mathbf{Y}}_1 = F_1(\mathbf{G} \odot \hat{\mathbf{X}}_1), \quad \tilde{\mathbf{Y}}_2 = \mathbf{X}_2 \tag{4}$$

$$\mathbf{Z} = \mathrm{Cat}(\tilde{\mathbf{Y}}_1, \tilde{\mathbf{Y}}_2) \in \mathbb{R}^{B \times C \times D \times H \times W}, \quad \mathbf{Y} = F_{\mathrm{fuse}}(\mathbf{Z}) \tag{5}$$

SCConv efficiently enhances ambiguous structures via spatial-channel recalibration and context encoding, maintaining low computational overhead while improving boundary resolution and long-range geometry modeling for accurate dental pulp segmentation.

3.3 Contrast-Driven Feature Aggregation Module

To enhance feature discrimination in shallow layers with low pulp-dentin contrast, CDFA is applied at shallow encoder and decoder stages. It employs a two-stage local attention mechanism. The first branch strengthens foreground

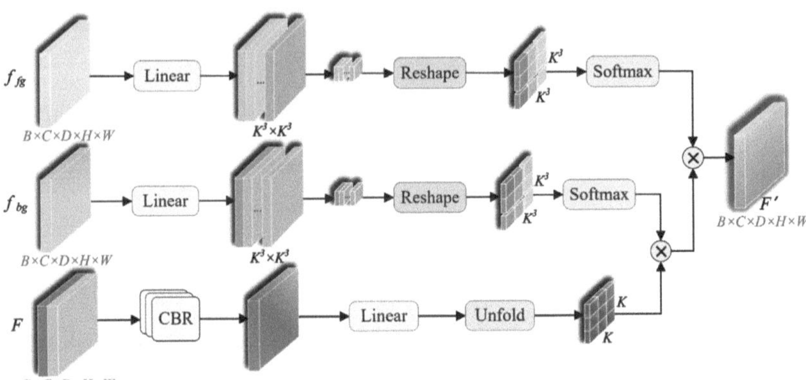

Fig. 3. Architecture of the CDFA module. CDFA enhances local contrast by leveraging intra-window attention and foreground-background reweighting to improve shallow feature discrimination.

responses, while the second suppresses irrelevant activations and reinforces boundaries, ensuring contrastive consistency.

As shown in Fig. 3, the three feature maps f_{fg}, f_{fg}, and F are derived from the same input tensor and share identical spatial dimensions. Specifically, F serves as the shared value feature, while f_{fg} and f_{fg} compute attention weights for contrastive feature refinement. Given an input feature tensor $X^{in} \in \mathbb{R}^{B\times C\times D\times H\times W}$, convolutional units first generate value representations that are reshaped into local patches for spatial correlation modeling:

$$C = h \cdot d_p \cdot w, \quad V = \text{reshape}(X)W_v \tag{6}$$

$$P_k : V_{p,h} \in \mathbb{R}^{B\times d_v \times 3^3}, \quad N = D \cdot H \cdot W \tag{7}$$

where, V represents the reshaped feature sequence, W_v is the projection matrix, C is the flattened dimension and P_k represents the $3\times 3\times 3$ local neighborhood centered at each voxel.

In the foreground enhancement stage, CDFA captures localized dependencies via an adaptive correlation matrix:

$$\alpha_{p,h}^{fg} = \text{Softmax}\left(\frac{q_{p,h}^{fg}(k_{p,h}^{fg})^T}{\sqrt{d_k}}\right) \tag{8}$$

where $q_{p,h}^{fg}$, $k_{p,h}^{fg} \in \mathbb{R}^{B\times d_k}$ are the query and key embeddings derived from V.The weighted responses within each local region are aggregated and then reconstructed into an enhanced feature map as:

$$v_{p,h}^{fg} = \sum_{l=1}^{3^3} \alpha_{p,h,l}^{fg} \cdot V_{p,h,l}, \quad X_{fg} = \mathcal{F}\left(\left\{v_{p,h}^{fg}\right\}_{p,h}\right) \tag{9}$$

where $v_{p,h}^{fg}$ represents the attention-weighted local response, and X_{fg} denotes the reconstructed foreground-enhanced feature map.

After foreground enhancement, another attention branch applies the same computation to suppress irrelevant activations and enhance boundaries. Finally, both responses are fused through a residual integration block:

$$Y = \psi(X_{fg} + X_{bg}) \tag{10}$$

where, ψ denotes a fusion block.

This two-stage local contrast modeling improves boundary continuity, enhances fine-detail recall, reduces background noise, and produces high-contrast, noise-robust shallow representations for precise 3D refinement.

4 Experiment

4.1 Dataset and Evaluation Metrics

We employed the publicly available Pulpy3D [6] dataset, which provides voxel-level annotations for 17 dental anatomical structures from high-resolution CBCT scans. For fine-grained pulp segmentation, we extracted samples containing valid labels for 16 pulp subregions. To ensure data reliability and class balance, cases with noisy annotations or limited category diversity were manually removed. After refinement, 320 samples were retained, including 288 for training and 32 for testing.

To ensure an objective and comprehensive performance assessment, four quantitative metrics were adopted, including the Dice Similarity Coefficient (DSC), Intersection over Union (IoU), Precision, and Volumetric Similarity (VS). These metrics collectively evaluate spatial overlap, volumetric consistency, and boundary accuracy, thereby providing a reliable and interpretable measure of segmentation performance for both fine-grained and binary tasks. VS specifically quantifies the degree of volumetric agreement between the predicted segmentation and the corresponding ground truth, serving as a complementary indicator to overlap-based metrics such as DSC and IoU.

4.2 Experiment Details

All experiments were conducted on a Linux workstation running Ubuntu 20.04.6, equipped with a single NVIDIA RTX 3090 GPU (24 GB memory). The software environment was configured with Python 3.9.17 and PyTorch 2.2.0. Model training was initialized with a learning rate of 0.01 and executed for 1000 epochs. To ensure fair comparison, all methods were trained using identical data preprocessing procedures and training protocols.

4.3 Experimental Result

Table 1. Qualitative 3D visualization comparison on four representative samples from the dental pulp dataset. Each row shows the segmentation results produced by different methods alongside the ground truth, allowing visual assessment of structural accuracy and completeness.

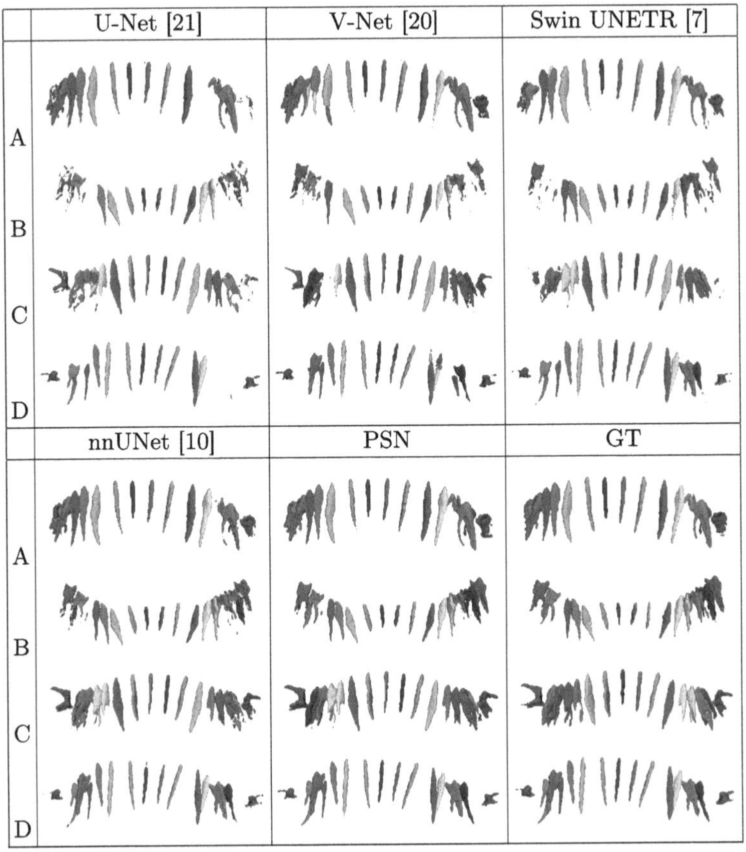

	U-Net [21]	V-Net [20]	Swin UNETR [7]
A			
B			
C			
D			
	nnUNet [10]	**PSN**	**GT**
A			
B			
C			
D			

Table 1 presents representative slice-level results across premolar, molar, and apical regions. U-Net shows discontinuities and missing regions, especially in complex posterior areas. V-Net produces disconnected segments and inconsistent anatomy. Swin UNETR exhibits fragmented pulp in the first and second molars, with non-contiguous intrapulpal components and chamber–canal discontinuities. nnUNet improves boundary alignment but retains fragmentation near terminal regions. In contrast, PSN preserves pulp connectivity, restores elongated branches, and suppresses isolated false positives. SCConv enhances feature responses in low-contrast regions, while CDFA reinforces semantic separation and local detail reconstruction, enabling more accurate 3D pulp morphology and reduced artifacts.

Table 2. Segmentation performance on the dental pulp dataset. The left section evaluates the 16 class segmentation results, while the right section computes metrics after converting all classes into a unified foreground, highlighting overall structure segmentation performance.

Method	16 class segmentation				Binary segmentation			
	DSC (%)	IoU (%)	Precision (%)	VS (%)	DSC (%)	IoU (%)	Precision (%)	VS (%)
U-Net	50.60	40.22	51.26	69.80	81.23	72.47	81.78	90.28
V-Net	51.19	41.01	52.01	69.06	82.91	71.42	81.67	90.37
Swin UNETR	57.08	47.20	63.10	76.85	86.74	77.98	87.92	95.86
nnUNet	59.12	48.99	62.25	76.12	87.31	78.60	87.25	95.53
PSN	**63.65**	**52.48**	**64.49**	**80.46**	**89.62**	**79.97**	**89.64**	**96.28**

Table 3. Comparison of GPU memory consumption and per-sample inference time among different segmentation methods.

Method	U-Net	V-Net	Swin UNETR	nnUNet	PSN
GPU Memory (GB)	16.2	16.9	18.7	8.6	9.4
Inference Time (min)	1.8	1.9	2.0	1.3	1.4

As shown in Table 2, segmentation performance was evaluated on 16 class fine-grained and binary tasks. nnUNet outperforms U-Net, V-Net [20] and Swin UNETR [7] across all metrics, while PSN achieves a DSC of 63.65 and IoU of 52.48 for 16 class segmentation, and 89.62 and 79.97 for binary classification, surpassing all baselines. These results demonstrate PSN's superior ability to capture fine structural details and delineate boundaries, largely due to the SCConv and CDFA modules.

As summarized in Table 3, relative to nnUNet our PSN exhibits higher GPU memory usage and longer per-sample inference time, this overhead is attributable to the additional modules, remains within the resource envelope of our experimental setup, and corresponds to improvements in segmentation accuracy, boundary fidelity, and pulp connectivity.

4.4 Ablation Experiment

To evaluate SCConv and CDFA in PSN, we conducted ablation experiments on the nnUNet framework under consistent training settings. Table 4 shows that both modules improve segmentation, with their combination in PSN achieving the highest scores both in 16 class and binary tasks, confirming complementary effects.

Table 4. Ablation study on the impact of SCConv and CDFA modules in both 16 class and binary segmentation settings.

Method	16 class segmentation				Binary segmentation			
	DSC (%)	IoU (%)	Precision (%)	VS (%)	DSC (%)	IoU (%)	Precision (%)	VS (%)
nnUNet [10]	59.12	48.99	62.25	76.12	87.31	78.60	87.25	95.53
+SCConv	61.23	50.75	63.71	77.54	88.42	79.13	88.10	95.80
+CDFA	61.36	50.87	63.43	78.88	88.47	78.99	88.20	95.71
PSN	**63.65**	**52.48**	**64.49**	**80.46**	**89.62**	**79.97**	**89.64**	**96.28**

SCConv, integrated into the encoder, enhances sensitivity to fine pulp structures and low-contrast regions, reducing discontinuities and improving geometric continuity through channel self-calibration. As shown in Fig. 4, it refines structural representation in challenging anatomical areas. CDFA, applied in the decoder, aggregates contrast-driven features to strengthen foreground-background distinction, refining fine anatomical details and boundaries. Combining SCConv and CDFA in PSN further improves boundary closure, regional connectivity, and overall accuracy, demonstrating their synergistic effect.

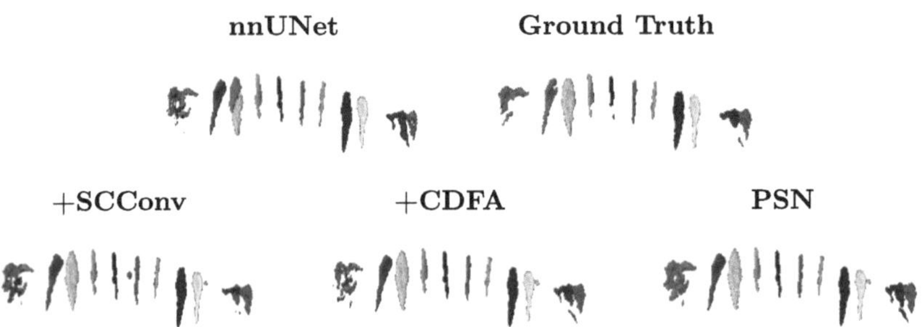

Fig. 4. Qualitative 3D visualization comparison across ablation settings on a representative sample.

5 Conclusion

This study presents PSN, a hybrid attention-enhanced network for dental pulp segmentation. Built upon nnUNet, PSN integrates SCConv and CDFA modules for complementary feature enhancement. SCConv enlarges the receptive field and suppresses false responses in low-contrast areas, while CDFA strengthens boundary cues and reduces noise through contrast-driven aggregation. Experiments show that PSN consistently surpasses U-Net, V-Net, Swin UNETR, and nnUNet on both 16 class and binary tasks, achieving superior accuracy in modeling complex pulp morphologies and maintaining structural continuity.

Overall, PSN provides an efficient solution for precise modeling of fine anatomical structures in dental CBCT, with promising potential in digital dentistry, endodontic planning, and XR-based visualization. Future work will explore multimodal extensions integrating graph neural networks and morphological priors.

Acknowledgments. This study was funded by the Beijing Natural Science Foundation and Haidian Original Innovation Joint Fund (grant number L222052), the National Natural Science Foundation of China (grant number 62201018) and the 2024 China University Industry-Research Collaboration Innovation Fund - New Generation Information Technology Innovation Project (grant number 2024IT009).

Disclosure of Interests. The authors have no competing interests to declare that are relevant to the content of this article.

References

1. Bao, N., Luo, Q., Wu, J., Cui, Z., Zhao, Y.: Toothaxis: generalizable tooth axis estimation network from CBCT or IOS models. IEEE J. Biomed. Health Inform. (2025)
2. Bolelli, F., et al.: Segmenting maxillofacial structures in CBCT volumes. In: Proceedings of the Computer Vision and Pattern Recognition Conference, pp. 5238–5248 (2025)
3. Chen, J., et al.: Transunet: transformers make strong encoders for medical image segmentation. arXiv preprint arXiv:2102.04306 (2021)
4. Cui, Z., et al.: A fully automatic AI system for tooth and alveolar bone segmentation from cone-beam CT images. Nat. Commun. **13**(1), 2096 (2022)
5. Duan, W., Chen, Y., Zhang, Q., Lin, X., Yang, X.: Refined tooth and pulp segmentation using U-Net in CBCT image. Dentomaxillofacial Radiol. **50**(6), 20200251 (2021)
6. Gamal, M., Baraka, M., Torki, M.: Automatic mandibular semantic segmentation of teeth pulp cavity and root canals, and inferior alveolar nerve on pulpy3d dataset. In: International Conference on Medical Image Computing and Computer-Assisted Intervention, pp. 14–23. Springer (2024)
7. Hatamizadeh, A., Nath, V., Tang, Y., Yang, D., Roth, H.R., Xu, D.: Swin UNETR: swin transformers for semantic segmentation of brain tumors in MRI images. In: International MICCAI Brainlesion Workshop, pp. 272–284. Springer (2021)
8. Hu, D., et al.: DPI-MoCo: deep prior image constrained motion compensation reconstruction for 4D CBCT. IEEE Trans. Med. Imaging (2024)
9. Huang, W., Zhang, L., Wang, Z., Wang, L.: Exploring inherent consistency for semi-supervised anatomical structure segmentation in medical imaging. IEEE Trans. Med. Imaging **43**(11), 3731–3741 (2024)
10. Isensee, F., Jaeger, P.F., Kohl, S.A., Petersen, J., Maier-Hein, K.H.: nnU-Net: a self-configuring method for deep learning-based biomedical image segmentation. Nat. Methods **18**(2), 203–211 (2021)

11. Lei, M., Wu, H., Lv, X., Wang, X.: Condseg: a general medical image segmentation framework via contrast-driven feature enhancement. In: Proceedings of the AAAI Conference on Artificial Intelligence, vol. 39, pp. 4571–4579 (2025)
12. Li, D., Zhu, M., Wang, S., Hu, Y., Yuan, F., Yu, J.: Accurate and automatic dental crown components segmentation with multi-scale attention based u-net and hybrid level set models. IEEE Trans. Autom. Sci. Eng. (2024)
13. Li, K., Zhu, Y., Yu, L., Heng, P.A.: A dual enrichment synergistic strategy to handle data heterogeneity for domain incremental cardiac segmentation. IEEE Trans. Med. Imaging **43**(6), 2279–2290 (2024)
14. Li, P., Gao, C., Liu, F., Meng, D., Yan, Y.: Thisnet: tooth instance segmentation on 3D dental models via highlighting tooth regions. IEEE Trans. Circuits Syst. Video Technol. **34**(7), 5229–5241 (2023)
15. Lin, X., Fu, Y., Ren, G., Yang, X., Duan, W., Chen, Y., Zhang, Q.: Micro-computed tomography-guided artificial intelligence for pulp cavity and tooth segmentation on cone-beam computed tomography. J. Endod. **47**(12), 1933–1941 (2021)
16. Liu, J.J., Hou, Q., Cheng, M.M., Wang, C., Feng, J.: Improving convolutional networks with self-calibrated convolutions. In: Proceedings of the IEEE/CVF Conference on Computer Vision and Pattern Recognition, pp. 10096–10105 (2020)
17. Liu, J., et al.: Swin-UMamba: mamba-based UNet with ImageNet-based pretraining. In: International Conference on Medical Image Computing and Computer-Assisted Intervention, pp. 615–625. Springer (2024)
18. Liu, Y., et al.: Fully automatic ai segmentation of oral surgery-related tissues based on cone beam computed tomography images. Int. J. Oral Sci. **16**(1), 34 (2024)
19. Liu, Z., et al.: Geometry-aware attenuation learning for sparse-view CBCT reconstruction. IEEE Trans. Med. Imaging (2024)
20. Milletari, F., Navab, N., Ahmadi, S.A.: V-net: fully convolutional neural networks for volumetric medical image segmentation. In: 2016 Fourth International Conference on 3D Vision (3DV), pp. 565–571. IEEE (2016)
21. Ronneberger, O., Fischer, P., Brox, T.: U-net: convolutional networks for biomedical image segmentation. In: International Conference on Medical Image Computing and Computer-Assisted Intervention, pp. 234–241. Springer (2015)
22. Santos-Junior, A.O., Fontenele, R.C., Neves, F.S., Ali, S., Jacobs, R., Tanomaru-Filho, M.: A unique AI-based tool for automated segmentation of pulp cavity structures in maxillary premolars on CBCT. Sci. Rep. **15**(1), 5509 (2025)
23. Santos-Junior, A.O., Fontenele, R.C., Neves, F.S., Tanomaru-Filho, M., Jacobs, R.: A novel artificial intelligence-powered tool for automated root canal segmentation in single-rooted teeth on cone-beam computed tomography. Int. Endod. J. **58**(4), 658–671 (2025)
24. Shaheen, E., et al.: A novel deep learning system for multi-class tooth segmentation and classification on cone beam computed tomography. A validation study. J. Dent. **115**, 103865 (2021)
25. Shaker, A., Maaz, M., Rasheed, H., Khan, S., Yang, M.H., Khan, F.S.: UNETR++: delving into efficient and accurate 3D medical image segmentation. IEEE Trans. Med. Imaging **43**(9), 3377–3390 (2024)
26. Slim, M.L., Jacobs, R., de Souza Leal, R.M., Fontenele, R.C.: AI-driven segmentation of the pulp cavity system in mandibular molars on CBCT images using convolutional neural networks. Clin. Oral Invest. **28**(12), 650 (2024)
27. Song, Y., Yang, H., Ge, Z., Du, H., Li, G.: Age estimation based on 3D pulp segmentation of first molars from CBCT images using U-Net. Dentomaxillofacial Radiol. **52**(7), 20230177 (2023)

28. Tan, M., Cui, Z., Zhong, T., Fang, Y., Zhang, Y., Shen, D.: A progressive framework for tooth and substructure segmentation from cone-beam CT images. Comput. Biol. Med. **169**, 107839 (2024)
29. Wang, C., Yang, J., Wu, B., Liu, R., Yu, P.: Trans-VNet: transformer-based tooth semantic segmentation in CBCT images. Biomed. Signal Process. Control **97**, 106666 (2024)
30. Yang, Y., et al.: Accurate and automatic tooth image segmentation model with deep convolutional neural networks and level set method. Neurocomputing **419**, 108–125 (2021)
31. Zhou, H.Y., et al.: nnFormer: volumetric medical image segmentation via a 3D transformer. IEEE Trans. Image Process. **32**, 4036–4045 (2023)

MSADM-DETR: Enhancing DETR with Multi-scale Semantic-Detail Alignment and Density-Aware Mechanisms for UAV Object Detection

Xiaopeng Liu[1], Guangyue Gao[1], Cong Liu[2], and Long Chen[3](✉)

[1] College of Computer Science and Engineering, Shandong University of Science and Technology, No. 579, Qianwangang Road, Qingdao, Shandong, China
{xiaopengliu,202383060090}@sdust.edu.cn

[2] School of Science, Nanjing University of Science and Technology, Nanjing 210094, People's Republic of China
LiuC@njust.edu.cn

[3] Department of Medical Physics and Biomedical Engineering, University College London, Charles Bell House, 43-45 Foley Street, London W1W 7TY, England, UK
chenlongcv@gmail.com

Abstract. Unmanned Aerial Vehicle Object Detection (UAV-OD) is widely used in areas such as public security, traffic management, and environmental monitoring. The DETR model removes traditional components like anchor boxes and Non-Maximum Suppression (NMS), simplifying the detection process and reducing manual design effort while enabling end-to-end object detection. However, such end-to-end models often show limited performance in complex UAV scenes with objects of different scales. To overcome these issues, this study proposes a new framework called MSADM-DETR (Multi-scale Semantic-Detail Alignment and Density-Aware Mechanisms) for UAV object detection. First, the Multi-scale Semantic-Detail Alignment (MSDA) module is designed to reduce object misalignment and detail loss during multi-scale feature fusion. Second, the Image-aware Object Density Estimation (IODE) module predicts the object density level in each image and adaptively adjusts the attention scale for different density conditions. Third, the Density-Aware Loss Weighting Mechanism (DA-Loss) dynamically adjusts the weights of classification and localization losses based on object density, improving the balance between tasks. Extensive experiments on the VisDrone2019 validation and test datasets show that MSADM-DETR achieves excellent mAP_{50} scores of 51.6% and 42.2%, respectively, outperforming existing state-of-the-art models.

Keywords: UAV object detection · DETR · small object detection · feature fusion

A. Hinkenjan et al. (Eds.): ICXR 2025, LNCS 16428, pp. 530–541, 2026.
https://doi.org/10.1007/978-981-95-7195-6_39

1 Introduction

Unmanned Aerial Vehicle (UAV) imaging has been widely applied in transportation [1], agriculture [2], ecological security [3], and search-and-rescue [4], owing to its wide coverage and flexibility. However, variations in flight altitude and viewing angles often result in dense object distributions, severe occlusions, and diverse object scales, which illustrated in Fig. 1.

Fig. 1. Representative detection challenges in UAV scenarios: (a) Occluded objects, (b) Overexposed objects, (c) Dense objects, (d) Similar backgrounds.

Existing Unmanned Aerial Vehicle Object Detection (UAV-OD) methods typically rely on complex post-processing components, such as predefined anchor boxes and Non-Maximum Suppression (NMS). These manually designed mechanisms have demonstrated strong performance in conventional object detection tasks, their effectiveness tends to diminish in UAV scenarios characterized by multi-scale objects and high-density distributions. In contrast, end-to-end detection frameworks eliminate the need for handcrafted post-processing operations, enabling a more concise and robust detection pipeline that has shown remarkable potential in UAV-based applications.

Carion et al. proposed Detection Transformer (DETR) [5], which achieves end-to-end object detection using Transformers, demonstrating strong global modeling capabilities and outstanding performance in UAV applications. Subsequent improvements [6,7] have accelerated convergence and enhanced small-object detection. However, most DETR frameworks still use a fixed attention scale, which can lead to imbalanced attention allocation and degraded detection performance in UAV scenarios with highly variable object densities.

Furthermore, UAV object detection tasks often rely on multi-scale feature fusion to address variations in object size and dense object distributions [8,9].

However, conventional multi-scale fusion may cause feature misalignment and loss of fine-grained details, leading to reduced detection accuracy. To address these issues, the main contributions of this paper are as follows:

- We propose a Multi-scale Semantic-Detail Alignment (MSDA) module that enhances fine-grained representations in low-level features and aligns spatial information between high- and low-level features, effectively reducing positional misalignment and improving localization accuracy.
- An Image-aware Object Density Estimation (IODE) module is introduced to predict object density levels and adaptively adjust the decoder's attention scale, enabling better detection performance across varying object densities.
- A Density-Aware Loss Weighting Mechanism (DA-Loss) is designed to dynamically balance classification and localization losses—emphasizing classification in dense scenes and localization in sparse ones—thereby improving detection accuracy and robustness in complex UAV scenarios.

2 Related Work

2.1 Object Detection in UAV Imagery

Early UAV object detection research focused on improving two-stage frameworks. Huang et al. [10] enhanced small-object visibility via mosaic images with higher foreground ratios, and Zhou et al. [11] improved rotated object detection using anchor refinement and a rotated IoU branch. These methods, however, suffer from high computational complexity, reliance on manual parameters, and complex pipelines. Recently, single-stage methods gained attention for balancing accuracy and efficiency. Wang et al. [12] proposed UAV-YOLOv8, optimizing feature fusion and using WIoU loss. RPLFDet [13] further improves detection via multi-scale feature fusion and refined localization. Yet, YOLO-based methods struggle in dense or occluded scenes due to NMS sensitivity, causing missed detections. Some studies introduced attention mechanisms to enhance features; Wang et al. [14] proposed Double-Head RCNN, integrating Transformer and Deformable Convolution to improve small-object detection.

2.2 End-to-End Object Detection

DETR [5] has been widely adopted in UAV object detection for its strong global modeling and end-to-end design. Liao et al. [6] introduced Pc-DETR, integrating dynamic attention and hybrid training to enhance small object detection in complex UAV scenes. Wang et al. [15] improved Deformable DETR by combining CNNs and Transformers with a non-local module for better global modeling and elongated obstacle detection. Kone et al. [7] proposed Drone-DETR, featuring a lightweight backbone and dual-path attention fusion to handle dense and complex scenes. Recent studies also integrate frequency-domain information into feature fusion [16]. However, existing DETR-based frameworks rely on a fixed number of object queries, which limits efficiency across varying object densities. To address this, our model predicts the object density level of each image to adaptively adjust attention scales.

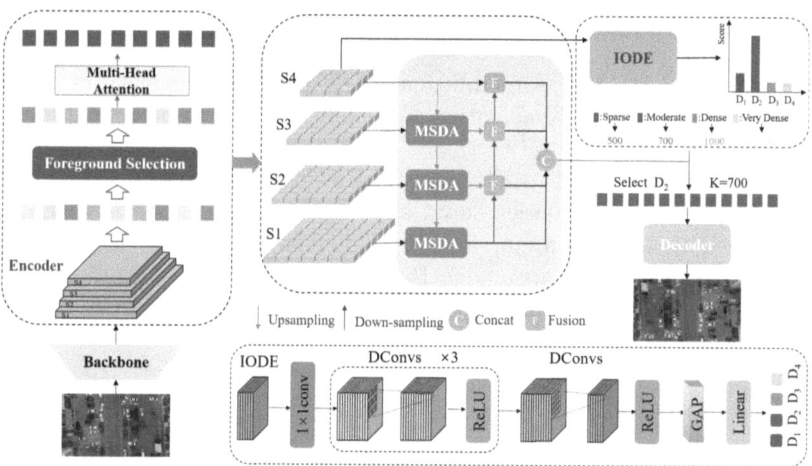

Fig. 2. Overview of MSADM-DETR. The Multi-scale Semantic-Detail Alignment (MSDA) module enables better integration of high-level semantic features with low-level spatial details; Image-aware Object Density Estimation (IODE) module predicts image-level object density to adaptively adjust attention scales.

2.3 Feature Fusion

Feature fusion can mitigate the limitations of a single feature layer and enhance a model's ability to perceive multi-scale objects. FPN [17] introduces high-level semantic information into low-level features through a top-down pathway and lateral connections, while PANet [18] extends this approach by incorporating bidirectional paths to strengthen inter-layer connections. Multi-scale fusion has been widely applied in UAV object detection. For instance, HRDNet [19] achieves balanced detection across objects of different scales, whereas CANet [9] enhances the representation of small objects through bidirectional fusion and skip connections. Overall, these methods can be seen as extensions of existing feature pyramid networks, primarily optimizing fusion pathways and connection strategies. However, in complex UAV images, the fusion of high and low-level features may still suffer from object misalignment and loss of fine-grained information, limiting detection performance. To address this, this paper introduces a linear cross-attention mechanism to achieve precise cross-scale alignment, improving the balance between multi-scale representation and detection accuracy.

3 Methodology

The overall MSADM-DETR architecture (Fig. 2) integrates three modules: the Multi-scale Semantic-Detail Alignment (MSDA) module (Sect. 3.1), the Image-aware Object Density Estimation (IODE) module (Sect. 3.2), and the Density-Aware Loss Weighting mechanism (Sect. 3.3).

3.1 Multi-scale Semantic-Detail Alignment Module

As shown in Fig. 3, the MSDA module fuses high- and low-level features via cross-scale alignment. The high-level feature $F_p \in \mathbb{R}^{B\times C\times H\times W}$ is upsampled to match the low-level feature $F_c \in \mathbb{R}^{B\times C\times h\times w}$, which is refined by the FAM module. Both features are flattened to F_p' and $F_c' \in \mathbb{R}^{B\times C\times N}$ and passed through 1×1 convolutions to produce queries, keys, and values (Q_p, K_p, V_p and Q_c, K_c, V_c). Attention weights from Q_c are applied to K_p to compute a context vector, which is then multiplied element-wise with ReLU-activated V_c for fusion. A residual connection generates the final fused output. The formulations are as follows:

$$F_c' = \text{Flatten}(\text{FAM}(F_c)), \quad F_p' = \text{Flatten}(\text{Upsample}(F_p)) \tag{1}$$

$$Q_c, K_c, V_c = \text{Conv1d}(F_c'), \quad Q_p, K_p, V_p = \text{Conv1d}(F_p') \tag{2}$$

$$F_{\text{fused}} = \&\text{Conv1d}_{\text{out}}\Big(\text{ReLU}(V_c)\cdot\Big(\sum_{i=1}^{N}\text{Softmax}(Q_c)\cdot K_p\Big)\Big) \tag{3}$$

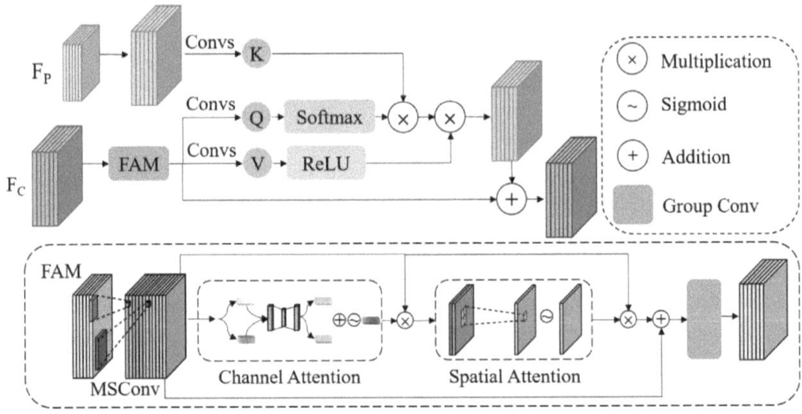

Fig. 3. Multi-scale Semantic-Detail Alignment Module.

As shown in Fig. 3, the FAM module consists of multi-scale convolutions and dual attention mechanisms. The low-level feature F_c is processed by parallel 1×1 and 3×3 convolutions, and their outputs are concatenated to generate the fused feature F_{ms}. Subsequently, a channel attention mechanism is applied to produce the channel-wise weight M_c, which enhances F_{ms} to obtain F_{ca}. This is further refined by a spatial attention mechanism, resulting in the spatially enhanced feature F_{sa}. Finally, F_{sa} is passed through a group convolution to achieve channel alignment.

3.2 Image-Aware Object Density Estimation Module

The Image-aware Object Density Estimation (IODE) module predicts the object density level of an image, enabling adaptive adjustment of the attention scale. For sparse scenes, the scale is reduced, while for dense scenes, it is increased. IODE extracts global contextual density features through multi-layer dilated convolutions with ReLU activation, followed by global average pooling and a fully connected layer that outputs the probability distribution over four density levels: sparse, moderate, dense, and extremely dense (Fig. 2). These levels are determined by the number of bounding boxes using thresholds 10, 50, 100, derived from the mean and standard deviation statistics of the VisDrone2019 dataset. The corresponding intervals are $T_d = (0, 10], (10, 50], (50, 100], (100, 500]$, and each level is assigned an attention scale $N = [500, 700, 1000, 1300]$, enabling the decoder to adaptively allocate attention according to scene density.

3.3 Density-Aware Loss Weighting Mechanism

In UAV object detection, scene density affects classification and localization difficulty. Crowded, high-density scenes make classification harder, while in sparse scenes, localization errors matter more. We propose a density-aware loss weighting mechanism that dynamically adjusts classification and regression contributions based on predicted density, improving robustness across scenarios.

The IODE module first predicts the image-level object density, which is converted into a probability vector $\mathbf{P}_d \in \mathbb{R}^4$ via a Softmax function. These probabilities are used to compute the classification and regression loss weights based on predefined density factors $\rho_{\text{cls}} = [0.8, 1.0, 1.5, 2.0]$ and $\rho_{\text{reg}} = [2.0, 1.0, 0.8, 0.5]$. To further improve adaptability, a learnable weighting module based on Gumbel-Softmax generates trainable parameters $\mathbf{g}_{\text{cls}}$ and $\mathbf{g}_{\text{reg}}$. The overall loss then incorporates these dynamic weights to balance classification and regression losses according to the predicted density level.

$$w_{\text{cls}} = \sum_{i=1}^{4} P_d^{(i)} \cdot \rho_{\text{cls}}^{(i)}, \quad w_{\text{reg}} = \sum_{i=1}^{4} P_d^{(i)} \cdot \rho_{\text{reg}}^{(i)} \tag{4}$$

$$\mathbf{g}_{\text{cls}} = \text{GumbelSoftmax}(\rho_{\text{cls}}, \tau), \quad \mathbf{g}_{\text{reg}} = \text{GumbelSoftmax}(\rho_{\text{reg}}, \tau) \tag{5}$$

$$\mathcal{L}_{\text{m}} = w_{\text{cls}} \cdot \mathbf{g}_{\text{cls}} \cdot \mathcal{L}_{\text{cls}} + w_{\text{reg}} \cdot \mathbf{g}_{\text{reg}} \cdot (\mathcal{L}_{\text{bbox}} + \mathcal{L}_{\text{giou}}) \tag{6}$$

  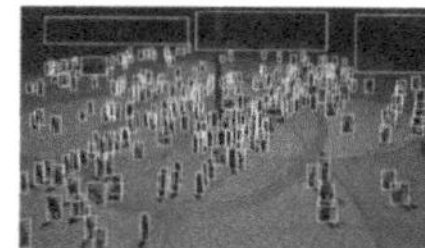 

Fig. 4. Visualization of ground-truth bounding boxes on selected images from VisDrone2019.

4 Experiments

4.1 Dataset and Experimental Setup

We use the VisDrone2019 dataset [20], containing 6,471 training, 548 validation, and 1,610 test images. Figure 4 shows the ground truth, illustrating large variations in object density. As summarized in Fig. 5: 52.9% of training images have 10âĂŞ50 objects, 10.9% have over 100, highlighting the need for density-adaptive detection; category sample sizes vary; most objects are in the lower-central region, reducing search area; and object aspect ratios are mainly in the lower-left, indicating that most objects are small. All experiments were conducted on an NVIDIA RTX 3090 GPU using PyTorch with CUDA Toolkit 11.8. The model was trained for 30 epochs with the AdamW optimizer and a batch size of 4.

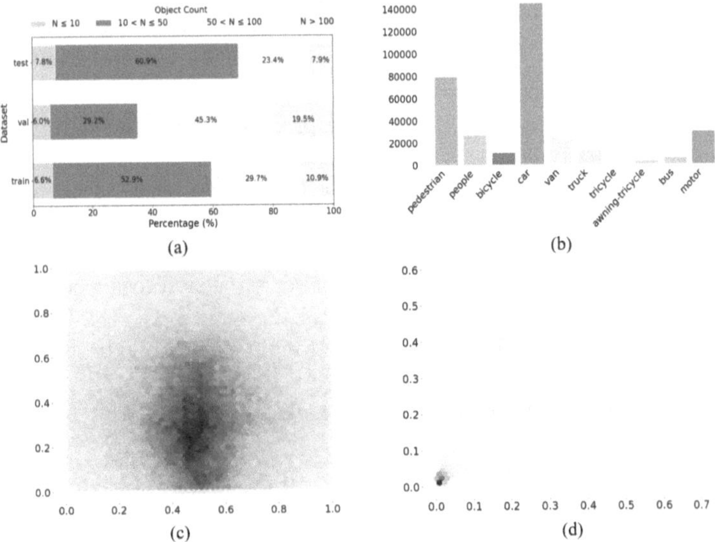

Fig. 5. VisDrone2019 dataset: (a) Object density statistics in the training, validation, and test sets; (b) Information of 10 classes; (c) Heatmap of object bounding box locations; (d) The proportion of object size.

4.2 Experimental Results

Comparison Results and Analysis of MSADM-DETR with Other SOTA Algorithms. As shown in Table 1, on the VisDrone2019 validation set, MSADM-DETR-R50 achieves mAP 31.7% and mAP_{50} 51.6%, improving over RT-DETR-R50 by 3.3% and 4.6% and slightly surpassing UAV-DETR-R50. On the test set, it attains mAP 23.8% and mAP_{50} 42.2%, outperforming

Table 1. Performance comparison of different models on VisDrone2019 val and test sets. mAP-T and mAP_{50}-T represent the results on the test set.

Method	Params	GFLOPs	mAP	mAP_{50}	mAP-T	mAP_{50}-T	FPS
Two-stage methods							
DMNet [21]	-	-	29.4	49.3	-	-	-
Faster R-CNN [22]	41.39	208	-	-	19.9	33.8	-
ARFP [23]	-	-	-	-	20.4	33.9	-
One-stage methods							
HIC-YOLOv5 [24]	-	-	25.95	44.31	20.85	36.95	-
Drone-YOLO-l [25]	76.2	-	31.9	51.3	23.8	40.7	-
YOLO-DCTI [26]	-	-	27.4	49.8	-	-	15
MHAF-YOLO [27]	15.81	67.6	28.1	45.2	22	37.2	83
RTMDet-L [28]	52.26	79.97	29.3	50.8	23.5	-	39
YOLOv10-m [29]	16.5	63.5	26.3	43.6	21.2	36.4	117
GBS-YOLOv5 [30]	-	-	-	-	20.0	35.3	-
Deformable DETR [15]	40	173	27.1	42.2	-	-	19
DAB-DETR [31]	-	-	27.8	44.9	21.9	38.6	36
RT-DETR-R50 [32]	42	136	28.4	47.0	22.4	39.3	40
UAV-DETR-R50 [16]	44.4	170	31.5	51.1	-	-	30
MSADM-DETR-R50	62	186	31.7	51.6	23.8	42.2	24

RT-DETR-R50 as well as several YOLO-based and two-stage detectors. While its inference speed is somewhat lower than that of lightweight models, MSADM-DETR demonstrates more stable and accurate detection, particularly for small, dense, and occluded objects, confirming the effectiveness of the proposed approach.

Figure 6 presents representative results on the VisDrone2019 test set. MSADM-DETR reduces false positives and missed detections in high-density scenes, outperforming RT-DETR. Faster R-CNN and YOLOv10 generate excess false positives, while DAB-DETR misses crowded objects. By using object density estimation and density-aware loss weighting, MSADM-DETR adaptively adjusts attention and balances classification and localization for more accurate detection.

Ablation Study. To evaluate the impact of each component, ablation studies were conducted on the VisDrone2019 test set (Table 2). The baseline Salience-DETR [33] achieved 22.2% mAP and 39.1% mAP_{50}. Introducing the MSDA module improved results to 22.7% mAP and 40.2% mAP_{50}, while adding the IODE module raised them to 22.9% mAP and 41.1% mAP_{50}, validating the effectiveness of multi-scale fusion and density-aware attention. Combining both modules further increased performance to 23.4% mAP and 41.5% mAP_{50}. With

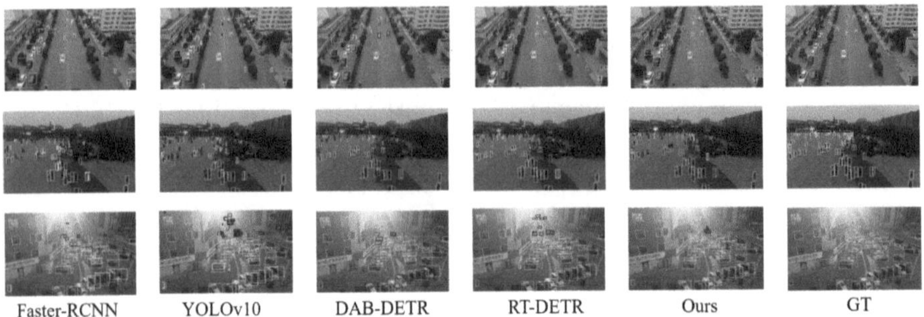

Fig. 6. The visualizations on the VisDrone2019-test set sequentially show Faster R-CNN, YOLOv10, DAB-DETR, RT-DETR, our model, and the ground truth. In the figures, blue bounding boxes indicate false positives, red bounding boxes indicate false negatives, and green bounding boxes indicate correct detections. (Color figure online)

the DA Loss mechanism, mAP_{50} reached 42.2%, demonstrating the benefit of dynamic loss weighting for UAV detection.

Table 2. Performance comparison of different models on VisDrone2019-test.

MSDA	IODE	DA Loss	mAP (%)	mAP_{50} (%)
			22.2	39.1
✓			22.7	40.2
	✓		22.9	41.1
✓	✓		23.4	41.5
✓	✓	✓	23.8	42.2

We analyzed the VisDrone2019 dataset by dividing images into four density levels based on the number of annotated objects: sparse $(0, 10]$, moderate $(10, 50]$, dense $(50, 100]$, and extremely dense $(100, 500]$ (Table 3). Model performance was evaluated under these varying densities. The baseline Salience-DETR uses a fixed attention scale of 900, while the proposed MSADM-DETR adaptively adjusts it according to object density. Experiments show that MSADM-DETR achieves higher accuracy in low-density scenes with smaller attention scales and automatically enlarges the scale beyond 1000 in high-density scenes, resulting in significantly improved performance.

The density factors are set as $\rho_{\text{cls}} = [0.8, 1.0, 1.5, 2.0]$ and $\rho_{\text{reg}} = [2.0, 1.0, 0.8, 0.5]$, where ρ_{cls} rises with density, making classification harder, while ρ_{reg} falls, reducing localization emphasis. When both factors are uniformly set to $[1.0, 1.0, 1.0, 1.0]$, the mAP_{50} on the VisDrone2019 test set is 41.5%. Applying the proposed density-dependent factors raises it to 41.9%. Using only the learnable $\mathbf{g}_{\text{cls}}$ lowers performance to 40.8%, likely due to imbalance between classification and regression. When both $\mathbf{g}_{cls}$ and $\mathbf{g}_{reg}$ are applied, mAP_{50} increases to 42.2%, showing that dual learnable weights achieve a more effective dynamic balance.

Table 3. Performance comparison (mAP (%)/mAP_{50} (%)).

Model	Density level	Attention scale	mAP (%)	mAP_{50} (%)
BASELINE	$n \leq 10$	900	29.3	48.1
	$10<n \leq 50$	900	23.8	41.2
	$50<n \leq 100$	900	22.8	41.1
	$100<n$	900	19.1	33.8
	Overall	900	22.2	39.1
MSADM-DETR (Ours)	$n \leq 10$	500	32.6	51.7
	$10<n \leq 50$	700	25	43.5
	$50<n \leq 100$	1000	23.9	43
	$100<n$	1300	21.1	38.1
	Overall	Dynamic	23.8	42.2

5 Conclusion

This paper introduces the MSADM-DETR framework, which provides a systematic solution to two major challenges in UAV object detection: spatial misalignment in multi-scale feature fusion and the imbalance of object density distributions. By incorporating Multi-scale Semantic-Detail Alignment and density-aware mechanisms, the model demonstrates improved adaptability and robustness in maintaining semantic consistency, preserving fine-grained details, and balancing task-specific losses. Experimental results on the VisDrone2019 dataset confirm significant improvements in detection accuracy, validating the effectiveness and superiority of the proposed approach in complex UAV scenarios. Overall, this work not only enriches research on Transformer-based UAV object detection but also offers new insights into addressing high-density small objects and cross-scale misalignment. Future research will focus on two directions: (1) further optimizing computational efficiency to facilitate real-time UAV deployment, and (2) integrating lightweight backbone networks to enhance the practical applicability of the model on resource-constrained platforms.

Acknowledgments. This work was supported in part by the Ministry of Education of Humanities and Social Science Project under Grant (24YJAZH092), the Fundamental Research Funds for the Central Universities (30923011022), the Natural Science Foundation of Jiangsu Province (BK20231454), the National Natural Science Foundation of China (62176183) and Jiangsu Planned Projects for Postdoctoral Research Funds.

Disclosure of Interests. The authors declare that they have no known competing financial interests or personal relationships that could have appeared to influence the work reported in this paper.

References

1. Shakhatreh, H., et al.: Unmanned aerial vehicles (UAVs): a survey on civil applications and key research challenges. IEEE Access 48572–48634 (2019)
2. Longsheng, F., Majeed, Y., Zhang, X., Karkee, M., Zhang, Q.: Faster R-CNN-based apple detection in dense-foliage fruiting-wall trees using RGB and depth features for robotic harvesting. Biosys. Eng. **197**, 245–256 (2020)
3. Lyu, X., Li, X., Dang, D., Dou, H., Wang, K., Lou, A.: Unmanned aerial vehicle (UAV) remote sensing in grassland ecosystem monitoring: a systematic review. Remote Sens. **14**(5), 1096 (2022)
4. Hao, K., Guanke Chen, L., Zhao, Z.L., Liu, Y., Wang, C.: An insulator defect detection model in aerial images based on multiscale feature pyramid network. IEEE Trans. Instrum. Meas. **71**, 1–12 (2022)
5. Carion, N., Massa, F., Synnaeve, G., Usunier, N., Kirillov, A., Zagoruyko, S.: End-to-end object detection with transformers. In: Proceedings of the European Conference on Computer Vision (ECCV), pp. 213–229. Springer (2020)
6. Liao, X., Guo, X., Rozi, A., Haizheng, Yu., Haji, A.: End-to-end polysemantic cooperative mixed task trainer for UAV target detection. Sci. Rep. **14**(1), 29775 (2024)
7. Kong, Y., Shang, X., Jia, S.: Drone-DETR: efficient small object detection for remote sensing image using enhanced RT-DETR model. Sensors **24**(17), 5496 (2024)
8. Zhu, M., Kong, E.: Multi-scale fusion uncrewed aerial vehicle detection based on RT-DETR. Electronics **13**(8), 1489 (2024)
9. Li, Y., Huang, Q., Pei, X., Chen, Y., Jiao, L., Shang, R.: Cross-layer attention network for small object detection in remote sensing imagery. IEEE J. Sel. Top. Appl. Earth Obs. Remote Sens. **14**, 2148–2161 (2020)
10. Huang, Y., Chen, J., Huang, D.: UFPMP-Det: toward accurate and efficient object detection on drone imagery. arXiv e-prints (2021)
11. Zhou, J., Feng, K., Li, W., Han, J., Pan, F.: TS4Net: two-stage sample selective strategy for rotating object detection. Neurocomputing **501**, 753–764 (2022)
12. Wang, G., Chen, Y., An, P., Hong, H., Jinghu, H., Huang, T.: UAV-YOLOv8: a small-object-detection model based on improved YOLOv8 for UAV aerial photography scenarios. Sensors **23**(16), 7190 (2023)
13. Wang, R., Lin, C., Li, Y.: RPLFDet: a lightweight small object detection network for UAV aerial images with rational preservation of low-level features. IEEE Trans. Instrum. Measur. (2025)
14. Wang, D., Lichen, H., Fang, J., Zhijie, X.: Small object detection algorithm based on improved double-head RCNN for UAV aerial images. J. Beijing Univ. Aeronaut. Astronaut. **50**(7), 2141–2149 (2023)
15. Wang, D., Li, Z., Xiaoqiang, D., Ma, Z., Liu, X.: Farmland obstacle detection from the perspective of UAVs based on non-local deformable DETR. Agriculture **12**(12), 1983 (2022)
16. Zhang, H., Zhang, H., Liu, K., Gan, Z., Zhu, G.N.: UAV-DETR: efficient end-to-end object detection for unmanned aerial vehicle imagery. arXiv preprint arXiv:2501.01855 (2025)

17. Lin, T.Y., Dollár, P., Girshick, R., He, K., Hariharan, B., Belongie, S.: Feature pyramid networks for object detection. In: Proceedings of the IEEE Conference on Computer Vision and Pattern Recognition (CVPR), pp. 2117–2125 (2017)
18. Liu, S., Qi, L., Qin, H., Shi, J., Jia, J.: Path aggregation network for instance segmentation. In: Proceedings of the IEEE Conference on Computer Vision and Pattern Recognition (CVPR), pp. 8759–8768 (2018)
19. Liu, Z., Gao, G., Sun, L., Fang, Z.: Hrdnet: high-resolution detection network for small objects. In: 2021 IEEE International Conference on Multimedia and Expo (ICME), pp. 1–6 (2021)
20. Zhu, P., et al.: Detection and tracking meet drones challenge. IEEE Trans. Pattern Anal. Mach. Intell. **44**(11), 7380–7399 (2021)
21. Li, C., Yang, T., Zhu, S., Chen, C., Guan, S.: Density map guided object detection in aerial images. In: Proceedings of the IEEE/CVF Conference on Computer Vision and Pattern Recognition Workshops (CVPRW), pp. 190–191 (2020)
22. Ren, S., He, K., Girshick, R., Sun, J.: Faster R-CNN: towards real-time object detection with region proposal networks. IEEE Trans. Pattern Anal. Mach. Intell. **39**(6), 1137–1149 (2016)
23. Wang, J., Jiong, Yu., He, Z.: ARFP: a novel adaptive recursive feature pyramid for object detection in aerial images. Appl. Intell. **52**(11), 12844–12859 (2022)
24. Tang, S., Zhang, S., Fang, Y.: HIC-YOLOv5: improved YOLOv5 for small object detection. In: 2024 IEEE International Conference on Robotics and Automation (ICRA), pp. 6614–6619. IEEE (2024)
25. Zhang, Z.: Drone-YOLO: an efficient neural network method for target detection in drone images. Drones **7**(8), 526 (2023)
26. Min, L., Fan, Z., Lv, Q., Reda, M., Shen, L., Wang, B.: YOLO-DCTI: small object detection in remote sensing based on contextual transformer enhancement. Remote Sens. **15**(16), 3970 (2023)
27. Yang, Z., et al.: MHAF-YOLO: multi-branch heterogeneous auxiliary fusion yolo for accurate object detection. arXiv preprint arXiv:2502.04656 (2025)
28. Lyu, C., et al.: RTMDet: an empirical study of designing real-time object detectors. arXiv preprint arXiv:2212.07784 (2022)
29. Wang, A., et al.: Yolov10: real-time end-to-end object detection. In: Advances in Neural Information Processing Systems (NeurIPS), vol. 37, pp. 107984–108011 (2024)
30. Liu, H., Duan, X., Lou, H., Jason, G., Chen, H., Bi, L.: Improved GBS-YOLOv5 algorithm based on YOLOv5 applied to UAV intelligent traffic. Sci. Rep. **13**(1), 9577 (2023)
31. Liu, S., et al.: DAB-DETR: dynamic anchor boxes are better queries for DETR. arXiv preprint arXiv:2201.12329 (2022)
32. Zhao, Y., et al.: DETRs beat YOLOs on real-time object detection. In: Proceedings of the IEEE/CVF Conference on Computer Vision and Pattern Recognition, pp. 16965–16974 (2024)
33. Hou, X., Liu, M., Zhang, S., Wei, P., Chen, B.: Salience DETR: enhancing detection transformer with hierarchical salience filtering refinement. In: Proceedings of the IEEE/CVF Conference on Computer Vision and Pattern Recognition, pp. 17574–17583 (2024)

Advanced Custom Gesture Recognition for Needle Manipulation in Mixed Reality Acupuncture Training

Jiayou Huang, Huayuan Zheng, and Qilei Sun(✉)

Xi'an Jiaotong–Liverpool University, Suzhou, China
{Jiayou.Huang20,Huayuan.Zheng21}@student.xjtlu.edu.cn,
qilei.sun@xjtlu.edu.cn

Abstract. Reliable gesture recognition is essential for mixed reality acupuncture training where fine motor actions must be detected in real time. We present a training-free, rule-based recognizer that operates on OpenXR-standardized hand joint streams and uses anatomy-aware, scale-normalized geometric features. The module detects four core acupuncture gestures: two-finger pinching, three-finger pinching, four-finger pinching, and tail pressing; and two action sequences: lift-thrusting and twirling. Evaluation on a remapped public dataset and a user study with twenty students shows consistently high accuracy for per-trial gestures and per-cycle sequences. On the public dataset, performance remained stable under viewpoint and distance variation. The recognizer is designed to be portable across OpenXR devices, and occlusion, field-of-view limits, and bimanual synchrony remain the primary causes of unrecognition.

Keywords: Mixed Reality · Human-centered computing · Acupuncture Training Systems · Computing methodologies · Hand Tracking · Action Recognition

1 Introduction

Acupuncture requires precise needle manipulation at prescribed acupoints. Mastery hinges on two classes of fine-motor maneuvers: needle-holding postures and manipulation actions. Canonical holding techniques are documented in clinical texts on acupuncture practice [2]. Manipulation actions such as lifting–thrusting and twirling are standard stimuli used for therapeutic effect [1]. These maneuvers demand subtle spatiotemporal coordination and are difficult to learn through observation alone, which complicates standardized instruction and objective assessment [3].

Traditional training relies on theory and demonstration and often yields variable feedback and inconsistent skill acquisition [4]. Haptic and instructional studies report a need for more consistent guidance in fine spatial control [5]. Mixed reality provides immersive practice for point localization and basic postures [6].

A. Hinkenjan et al. (Eds.): ICXR 2025, LNCS 16428, pp. 542–554, 2026.
https://doi.org/10.1007/978-981-95-7195-6_40

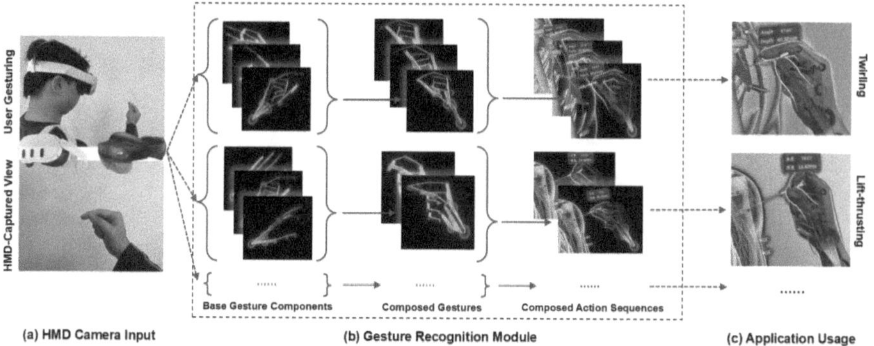

Fig. 1. Overview of the proposed gesture recognition framework. **(a)** The user performs gestures while wearing a Head-Mounted Display (HMD), capturing real-time video streams via the integrated cameras. **(b)** Base gesture components recognized from the captured hand joint data, which are then fused into composed gestures and action sequences using a hierarchical recognition pipeline. **(c)** The recognized gestures are mapped to real-time application functionalities, such as fine-grained interaction tasks like *Twirling* and *Lift-thrusting*.

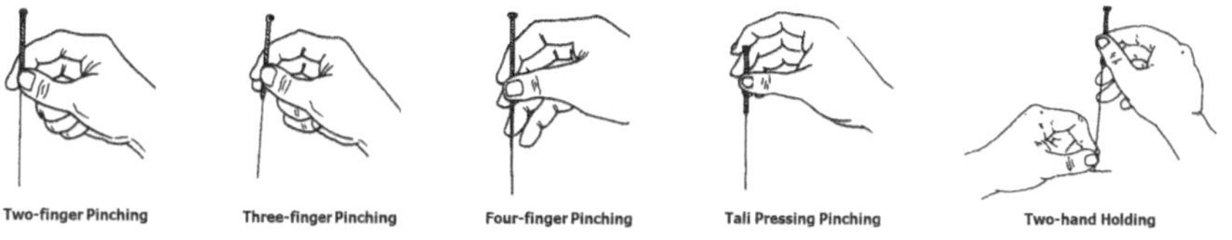

Fig. 2. Illustration of needle manipulation gestures in acupuncture, including needle-holding methods [1].

Fine-grained cross-platform monitoring of multi-style hand behavior in real time remains limited. We present a training-free, interpretable gesture-recognition module that operates on OpenXR-standardized hand-joint streams [7]. From joint positions the module constructs scale-normalized, anatomy-aware features and encodes acupuncture gestures as deterministic rules. It supports both atomic postures and temporally constrained action sequences in real time. Figure 1 overviews the pipeline. Figure 2 illustrates the needle-holding gestures adopted in this study, consistent with clinical descriptions of two-, three-, and four-finger pinching and tail pressing [2]. Figure 3 illustrates the manipulation actions adopted in this study, namely lifting–thrusting and twirling [1]. The design targets cross-platform use. Dual-hand configurations remain susceptible to occlusion and field-of-view constraints. We validate the module on a remapped public benchmark [8] and in a mixed-reality user study.

- Development of a specialized gesture-recognition module tailored for acupuncture training that reliably identifies static holding gestures and temporally constrained manipulation sequences in real time.

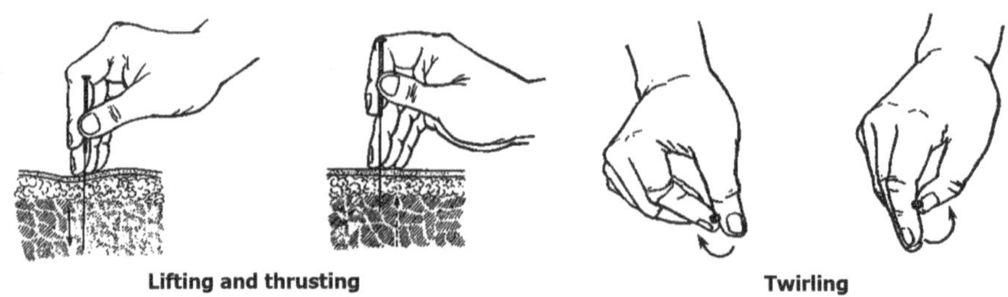

Fig. 3. Illustration of needle manipulation actions in acupuncture, including lifting–thrusting and twirling [1].

- Integration of OpenXR-standardized hand-tracking to promote platform compatibility and to provide consistent input for gesture recognition across XR systems.

2 Related Work

2.1 Needle Manipulation Simulation in Virtual Acupuncture

Early simulators reproduced haptics for single manipulation styles under fixed tissue parameters, most often lifting–thrusting [5,9,10]. Later models captured viscoelastic interactions and physiological effects of manipulation, emphasizing physical realism rather than gesture monitoring [11–14]. Prototypes with gesture cues or needle tracking appeared [4,15], yet scalability and cross-platform modularity remained limited. General frameworks enable hardware-agnostic authoring [16], but adoption in acupuncture is scarce due to subtle, domain-specific dynamics. These gaps motivate a unified, extensible module for fine-motor acupuncture gestures in mixed reality, which is the focus of this work.

2.2 Acupuncture Training Systems in Virtual Environments

XR systems have supported acupoint visualization and basic needling practice in AR and VR, and mixed-reality phantoms improved tactile engagement [17–21]. Recent systems integrate machine learning and computer vision for interaction fidelity, including human–robot manipulation, joint-trajectory recognition, and visual feedback for sensorimotor learning [22–24]. However many pipelines remain device-specific or predefined-gesture and lack cross-platform, fine-grained, multi-style monitoring in MR [15,25]. This work targets that gap with a platform-agnostic recognition module for diverse static and dynamic acupuncture gestures.

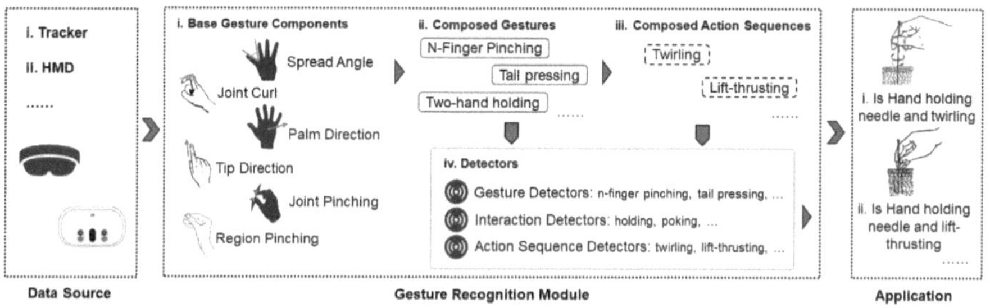

Fig. 4. Overview of the custom gesture recognition module.

2.3 Advances in Gesture Recognition for Virtual Environments

Toolkits and surveys describe customizable, hardware-agnostic composition of gestures and mixed-reality interaction design [16,26–28]. Robustness is advanced by multimodal datasets and learning across views and sequences, including HoloGesture, multi-view multi-task models, transformers, and multimodal training that improves unimodal accuracy [29–32]. Medical XR adds domain-specific procedures and safety constraints for real-time deployment [33–35]. Most prior solutions assume data-driven pipelines and do not directly address fine-motor, multi-style manipulation with cross-platform, on-device operation under occlusion and field-of-view variability. Our rule-encoded OpenXR module complements these directions by targeting acupuncture-specific postures and action sequences with interpretable, training-free, real-time behavior on device (Fig. 4).

3 Methodology

3.1 Module Overview

The module performs hierarchical, rule-based recognition on OpenXR hand-joint poses. From joint positions it derives relative, scale-normalized, anatomy-aware features, including tip and palm directions, interdigit distances, and joint curl. These features are computed from positions rather than API joint rotations to keep thresholds interpretable and behaviour consistent across devices. Because they depend on intra-hand geometry and are normalized by hand scale, they are insensitive to base-space choices and vendor-side orientation smoothing. The vocabulary comprises four acupuncture gestures (two-finger pinching, three-finger pinching, four-finger pinching, tail pressing) and two action sequences (lift-thrusting, twirling). Recognition is gesture first: a validated gesture gates a finite-state recognizer that enforces rate and extent constraints for stable sequence events. When the required joints are within the headset field of view the module emits decisions; otherwise it withholds output. These six categories cover introductory training scenarios, and all evaluations are restricted to this vocabulary. The recognizer requires no training and runs in real time on device. It is designed to be portable across OpenXR platforms, and detectors for gestures, sequences, and interactions run concurrently and dispatch confirmed events to the application layer within the same frame (Fig. 5).

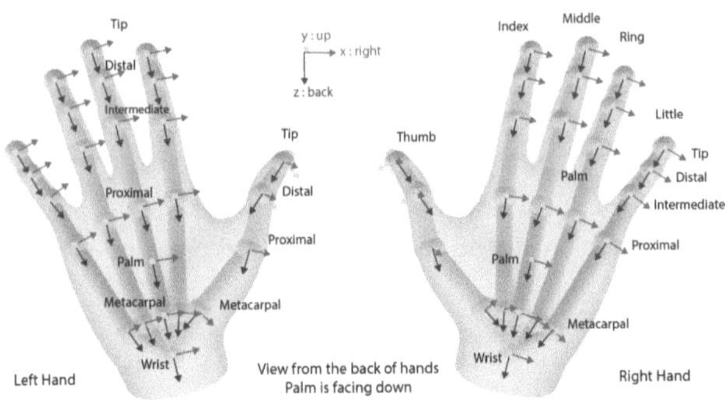

Fig. 5. OpenXR Hands tracking specification [7].

3.2 Base Hand Gesture Components

We use six primitives computed from joint positions: Joint Curl, Spread Angle, Tip Direction, Palm Direction, Joint Pinching, and Region Pinching. All distances are normalized by the target-finger length to achieve scale invariance. All decisions are conditioned on the visibility of the required joints to suppress spurious activations when key joints are out of view. Formal definitions of the primitives and their decision roles are given below:

Joint Curl. Let $\theta = \angle(\mathbf{v}_1, \mathbf{v}_2)$ between the distal–to–tip and distal–to–proximal segments. Map to $B = 1 - \theta/\theta_{\max} \in [0, 1]$ and threshold B for open versus bent.

Spread Angle. Finger separation $\phi = \angle(\mathbf{u}, \mathbf{v})$ on the skeleton; small ϕ indicates grouped fingers, large ϕ indicates splay.

Tip Direction. Finger pointing $\hat{\mathbf{D}} = \mathbf{D}/\|\mathbf{D}\|$, compared to a palm or task reference for pressing/twirling checks.

Palm Direction. Palm facing $\mathbf{N} = \mathbf{u} \times \mathbf{v}$ (palm normal); bound its deviation from the chosen reference to disambiguate similar finger layouts.

Joint Pinching. Thumb–target proximity $D_{\text{joint}} = \|\mathbf{P}_{\text{ThumbTip}} - \mathbf{P}_{\text{Joint}}\|/L_{\text{finger}}$; detect a pinch if $D_{\text{joint}} \leq \tau_p$ together with a consistent fingertip–orientation check.

Region Pinching. For a monitored segment with samples $\mathbf{P}_{\text{Monitor},k}$, use $D_k = \|\mathbf{P}_{\text{ThumbTip}} - \mathbf{P}_{\text{Monitor},k}\|/L_{\text{finger}}$ and an orientation score $R_\psi = 1 - \left|\psi/90° - 1\right|$. Fire when $\min_k D_k \leq \tau_\Omega$ and R_ψ is high with contact inside the region of interest. All thresholds are angles or normalized distances, giving translation and scale invariance; temporal debouncing and a finite–state gate apply these components over short windows.

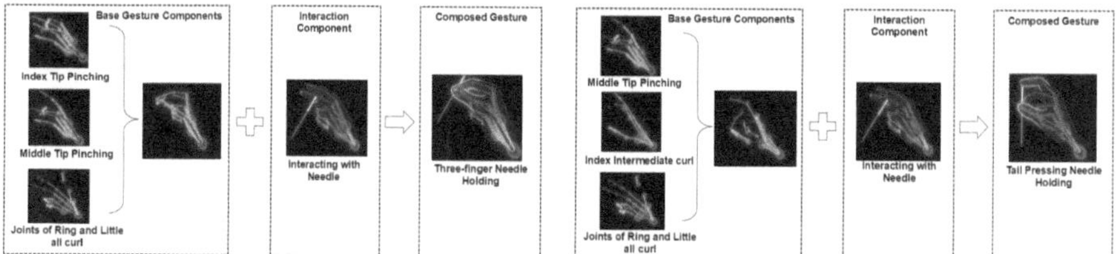

(a) Three-finger Pinching gesture (b) Tail Pressing gesture

Fig. 6. Composition of needle manipulation gestures.

3.3 Composed Gestures and Acupuncture Gestures

Composed gestures are defined as conjunctions of base hand components together with a needle interaction constraint.

N-Finger Pinching. As illustrated in Fig. 6a. Two-finger, three-finger and four-finger variants. Joint Pinching where the thumb contacts one or more target fingertips. Joint Curl for non-pinching fingers. In two-finger and three-finger grips these fingers curl for stability. In the four-finger variant the little finger may relax.

Tail Pressing. As shown in Fig. 6b. Joint Pinching where the thumb contacts the tip of the middle finger. Joint Curl for the index at the intermediate and distal joints, and for the ring and little across all joints to stabilise the grip.

Two-Hand Holding. The dominant hand uses Joint Pinching with thumb, index and middle, and curls the other fingers. The supporting hand uses Joint Pinching with thumb and index, and curls the other fingers.

Detectors apply the same visibility gate and short window temporal debouncing as the module.

3.4 Composed Action Sequences and Acupuncture Action Sequences

Composed action sequences order predefined gestures under explicit timing constraints for robust recognition. Two sequence types are supported: regular sequences reset after completion, and cyclic sequences alternate forward and reverse. Order and per-step time limits are verified; any skipped step or timeout triggers a reset.

Twirling. As illustrated in Fig. 7a. A cyclic sequence of three gestures executed forward then reversed. Step 1 uses a two-finger pinching pose with all non-pinching fingers fully curled. Step 2 employs region pinching between the thumb tip and the segment from the distal joint to the tip of the index finger. Step 3 applies joint pinching at the distal joint of the index finger. Non-pinching fingers remain curled throughout, and the order then reverses to form a continuous loop.

Lifting and Thrusting. As shown in Fig. 7b. A regular sequence of two gestures that alternate. The first gesture is a two-finger pinching pose with greater flexion at the thumb distal joint and the index intermediate joint. The second gesture keeps the pinch and overall curl with reduced flexion, producing a straighter alignment. The recognizer alternates the two gestures under the same timing limits.

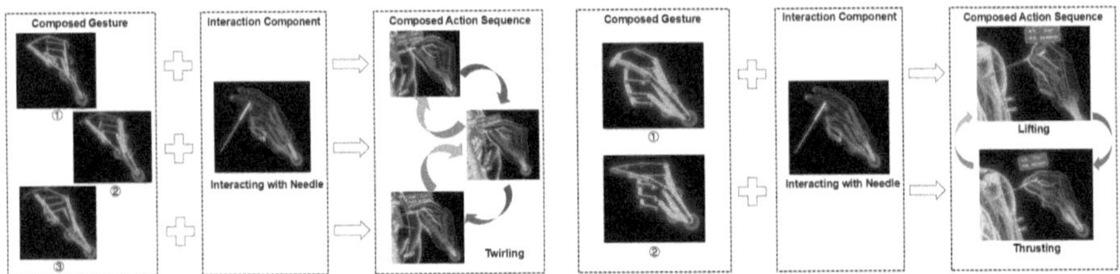

(a) Twirling Action Sequence (b) Lifting and Thrusting Sequence

Fig. 7. Composition of needle manipulation actions.

4 Module Validation

4.1 General Hand Gestures and Action Sequences

We use the Leap Motion Dynamic Hand Gesture (LMDHG) dataset [8] as a device-agnostic baseline. LMDHG provides frame-level annotations of single-hand dynamic gestures with 23 tracked joints. Joint positions are converted to the OpenXR layout so that the same rule set runs unchanged across devices. The LMDHG classes we evaluate are expressible by our rule vocabulary: pinch/open is represented by Joint or Region Pinching with finger-curl constraints; clockwise and anticlockwise rotation by cyclic changes in tip and palm orientation; and linear translation by axial motion under a stable pinch. The dataset is behaviourally related to our target tasks but is not task-equivalent to acupuncture.

LMDHG labels are remapped to our gesture names where applicable and evaluated frame by frame. To emulate view and scale variation we apply in-plane rotations up to 45° and vary depth between 30 and 100 cm. For each annotated frame we report three rates: **recognition rate**, **misclassification rate**, and **unrecognition rate**. LMDHG consists of single-hand motions and does not include bimanual occlusion or field-of-view limits.

4.2 Needle Manipulation Gestures and Actions

We evaluated the module on a Meta Quest 3 with twenty participants. All of the participants were approved by the institutional Ethical Review Panel of the university. Each participant performed five acupuncture gestures: Two-finger

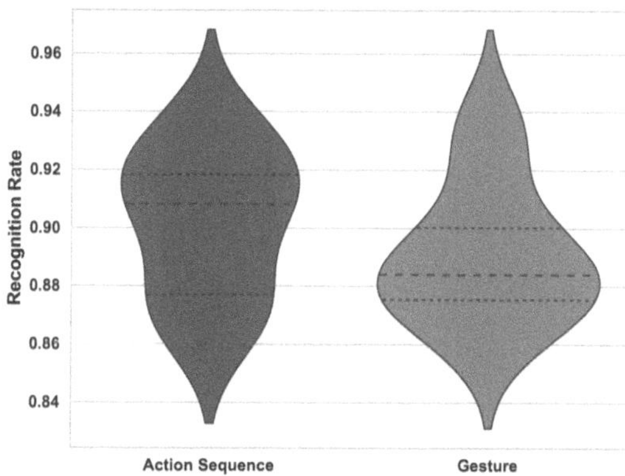

Fig. 8. LMDHG frame-level accuracy distribution.

Pinching, Three-finger Pinching, Four-finger Pinching, Tail Pressing and Two-hand Holding. They also performed two action sequences: Lift-Thrusting and Twirling. Participants were twenty students enrolled in acupuncture-related programmes and none were licensed practitioners. Natural variation in hand size, movement speed and articulation was not constrained. OpenXR hand tracking recorded joint poses in real time.

Metrics used consistent definitions. For gestures we report per-trial recognition rate, misclassification rate and unrecognition rate. For action sequences we report per-cycle recognition rate and unrecognition rate using a finite-state recogniser. Trials or cycles with no decision because the gating conditions are not met, such as outside the defined gesture vocabulary, insufficient hold duration or missing required joints, are counted as unrecognised.

4.3 Results

On LMDHG, after label remapping the frame-level recognition rate ranged from 88% to 94% across the evaluated classes, as shown in Fig. 8. Performance remained stable under in-plane rotations up to 45° and depth changes from 30 to 100 cm.

In the user study shown in Fig. 9 with 95% confidence intervals, per-trial gesture recognition rates were Two-finger Pinching 94.31%, Tail Pressing 94.28%, Four-finger Pinching 88.93%, Three-finger Pinching 88.30%, and Two-hand Holding 82.65%. Misclassification rates were 7.17% for Four-finger Pinching and 7.67% for Three-finger Pinching and were minimal for the other gestures. The unrecognition rate for Two-hand Holding was 12.14%. For action sequences evaluated per cycle, recognition rates were 89.12% for Lift–Thrusting and 91.88% for Twirling. Runtime on the training scenes was adequate for on-device interaction: the recogniser sustained 60–75 FPS (median 69 FPS), and the end-to-end detection latency was approximately 40 ms. These numbers were obtained under typical load and characterise the operating point rather than worst-case bounds.

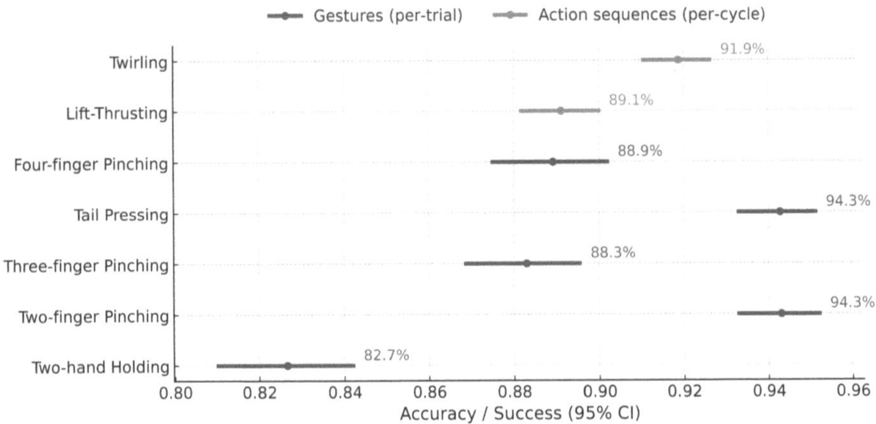

Fig. 9. User study performance per category with 95% CI. Blue: gestures (per-trial); orange: action sequences (per-cycle). (Color figure online)

5 Discussion

The module targets real-time recognition of acupuncture gestures and action sequences from OpenXR-standardised joint streams [7]. We discuss observed performance, limitations, and implications for immersive medical training.

5.1 Module Performance and Limitations

Results show stable behaviour under view and depth changes on a standardised joint stream. For action sequences the recogniser operates per cycle with a binary outcome, so failures appear as unrecognition rather than misclassification. For single-hand gestures most errors arise from ambiguity between structurally similar grips, as in Three-finger and Four-finger Pinching. Two-hand Holding attains the lowest recognition because both hands must satisfy pose and timing gates at the same moment, which increases no-decision events. Field-of-view limits and occasional overlap can further reduce the availability of required joints.

The approach depends on OpenXR joint poses, which assumes vendor conformance. We did not conduct a component-wise or threshold-sensitivity analysis. The rule set and thresholds were fixed a priori from anatomical constraints, and disabling rules or retuning thresholds would change the deployed operating point. A meaningful component study would require a dedicated protocol with broader task coverage and a larger sample and is left for future work. On LMDHG, labels were remapped to our vocabulary to approximate gesture semantics rather than to assert task equivalence, so those numbers serve as a device-agnostic baseline. The user study cohort comprised students in acupuncture-related programmes rather than licensed practitioners, which also constrains generalisability.

Future work will expand the gesture vocabulary and expert cohorts, quantify the gap between position-derived angles and API-provided joint orientations, and investigate sensor fusion or predictive tracking to mitigate joint unavailability during bimanual interaction.

5.2 Advancements Over Existing Systems and Implications

Relative to appearance-based training systems that rely on RGB or RGB-D streams [4,15], using standardised joint input reduces sensitivity to lighting and texture when joints are visible and enables direct rule-based modelling of clinically described grips and sequences. It does not resolve occlusion, and bimanual cases can still yield no-decision events. In contrast to haptic-focused simulators that prioritise force feedback with limited gesture monitoring [5,9], the present design provides active recognition for needle manipulation in mixed reality. Compared with general-purpose XR gesture toolkits that emphasise hardware-agnostic custom sets [16,26], our module is domain-specific and encodes acupuncture manipulation semantics while remaining portable across OpenXR devices.

Recognising temporally structured gestures in real time supports formative feedback and objective logging in training scenarios. Beyond acupuncture, this rule-based formulation can be used to custom task-specific gesture vocabularies and action sequences for other mixed-reality training tasks, such as laparoscopic instrument grips, ultrasound probe manipulation, and upper-limb rehabilitation reach-to-grasp patterns, provided that task semantics and validation protocols are defined.

6 Conclusion and Future Work

We presented a rule-based gesture recogniser for acupuncture training in mixed reality that operates on OpenXR-standardized joint streams. The module identifies acupuncture gestures and action sequences without training and runs on device, enabling real-time feedback within our training framework. Evaluation on a remapped LMDHG baseline and on a twenty-participant user study with Meta Quest 3 showed high per-trial and per-cycle accuracy with narrow confidence intervals under varied hand configurations and spatial viewpoints.

Future work will expand the gesture vocabulary and recruit expert practitioners in collaboration with licensed acupuncturists and clinical instructors, provide component-wise and threshold-sensitivity analyses, and add head-to-head baselines under a shared protocol. We will investigate sensor fusion and predictive tracking to mitigate joint unavailability during bimanual interaction, quantify the gap between position-derived angles and API-provided joint orientations, and conduct cross-platform runtime profiling to characterise latency and throughput.

References

1. Zhang, D.: Acupuncture: A Comprehensive Text, 2 edn. Traditional Chinese Medicine Press (2020)

2. Li, X., Wang, Y.: Chinese Acupuncture and Moxibustion, 3 edn. China Medical Science Press (2018)
3. Amori, P., Aldo, L.: Acupuncture. In: França, K., Lotti, T. (eds.) Advances in Integrative Dermatology, pp. 467–475. Wiley-Blackwell, Hoboken (2019)
4. Zhang, M., Zheng, Y., Cui, C., Meng, Z., Own, C.M.: Preliminary application of gesture recognition to virtual acupuncture. In: 2017 10th International Symposium on Computational Intelligence and Design (ISCID), pp. 1–4. IEEE (2017). https://doi.org/10.1109/ISCID.2017.201
5. Leung, K.M., Heng, P.A., Sun, H., Wong, T.T.: A haptic needle manipulation simulator for Chinese acupuncture. In: Studies in Health Technology and Informatics, vol. 119, pp. 242–244. IOS Press (2006). https://doi.org/10.3233/978-1-60750-942-4-242. https://ebooks.iospress.nl/volumearticle/20349
6. Sun, Q., Huang, J., Zhang, H., Craig, P., Yu, L., Lim, E.G.: Design and development of a mixed reality acupuncture training system. In: 2023 IEEE Conference Virtual Reality and 3D User Interfaces (VR), pp. 265–275. IEEE (2023)
7. The Khronos Group: OpenXR Specification. Khronos Group (2021). https://www.khronos.org/registry/OpenXR/specs/1.0/html/xrspec.html. Accessed 19 Sept 2024
8. Boulahia, S.Y., Anquetil, E., Multon, F., Kulpa, R.: Dynamic hand gesture recognition based on 3D pattern assembled trajectories. In: Proceedings of the 7th IEEE International Conference on Image Processing Theory, Tools and Applications (IPTA), pp. 1–6 (2017)
9. Man, L.K.: Computer simulated needle manipulation of Chinese acupuncture with realistic haptic feedback. Ph.D. thesis, The Chinese University of Hong Kong (2002)
10. Lee, I.S., et al.: Haptic simulation for acupuncture needle manipulation. J. Alternative Complement. Med. **20**(8), 654–660 (2014)
11. Yao, W., Yu, Y., Ding, G.: A hybrid method to study the mechanical information induced by needle rotating. Math. Methods Appl. Sci. **41**(15), 5939–5953 (2018). https://doi.org/10.1002/mma.5111
12. Yao, W., Shen, Z., Yu, Y., Ding, G.: Mechanical effects of acupuncture. Math. Methods Appl. Sci. **43**(10), 6268–6282 (2019). https://doi.org/10.1002/mma.5980
13. Gang, X., et al.: Effect of different twirling and rotating acupuncture manipulation techniques on the blood flow perfusion at acupoints. J. Traditional Chinese Med. **39**(5), 730–738 (2019). https://doi.org/10.1155/2019/1725936. https://onlinelibrary.wiley.com/doi/abs/10.1155/2019/1725936
14. Zhu Sun, M., Wang, X., Chen Li, Y., Yao, W., Gu, W.: Mechanical effects of needle texture on acupoint tissue. J. Integrative Med. (2023). https://doi.org/10.1016/j.joim.2023.03.005
15. Luu, T.H., Cao, H.L., Pham, D.D., Tran, L.T.C., Verstraten, T.: Development and validation of a vision-based needling training system for acupuncture on a phantom model. J. Acupuncture Res. (2022). https://doi.org/10.13045/jar.2022.00024
16. Schäfer, A., Reis, G., Stricker, D.: Anygesture: arbitrary one-handed gestures for augmented, virtual, and mixed reality applications. Appl. Sci. **12**(4), 1888 (2022)
17. Lee, V.R., Shapiro, R.B.: A broad view of wearables as learning technologies: current and emerging applications. In: Díaz, P., Ioannou, A., Bhagat, K.K., Spector, J.M. (eds.) Learning in a Digital World. SCI, pp. 113–133. Springer, Singapore (2019). https://doi.org/10.1007/978-981-13-8265-9_6
18. Zhang, M., Schulze, J.P., Zhang, D.: E-faceatlasar: extend atlas of facial acupuncture points with auricular maps in augmented reality for self-acupressure. Virtual Reality **26**, 1763–1776 (2022). https://doi.org/10.1007/s10055-022-00568-9

19. Wang, Y., Zhang, M.: Application of virtual reality and 4D imaging technology in the wisdom of interactive guidance of acupuncture and massage. In: 2022 3rd International Conference on Electronics and Sustainable Communication Systems (ICESC), pp. 1–5. IEEE (2022). https://doi.org/10.1109/ICESC54411.2022.9885547. https://ieeexplore.ieee.org/document/9885547
20. Lo, C.: An acupuncture VR game. In: Smart Science, Design and Technology, p. 4, 1st edn. CRC Press (2019). https://www.routledge.com/Smart-Science-Design--Technology/Lin-Lu-Lu-Hsieh-Huang/p/book/9780429058127
21. Ryu, C.J., Lee, S.D., Han, S.J.: Design of acupuncture controller and dummy for acupuncture training system based MR. Smart Media J. **9**(2), 86–91 (2020). https://doi.org/10.30693/SMJ.2020.9.2.8
22. Yu, H., Zhu, Z., Wang, C., Wang, J., Liu, C.: Kinematic-driven human-robot interaction system with deep learning for flexible acupuncture needling manipulations. Biomed. Signal Process. Control (2024). https://doi.org/10.1016/j.bspc.2024.106098
23. Jia, Y., Ding, R., Ren, W., Shu, J., Jin, A.: Gesture recognition of somatosensory interactive acupoint massage based on image feature deep learning model. Traitement du Signal **38**(3) (2021)
24. Jung, W.M., Lim, J., Lee, I.S., Park, H.J., Wallraven, C., Chae, Y.: Sensorimotor learning of acupuncture needle manipulation using visual feedback. PLoS ONE **10**(9), e0139340 (2015). https://doi.org/10.1371/journal.pone.0139340. https://journals.plos.org/plosone/article?id=10.1371/journal.pone.0139340
25. Zhang, M., Chen, C., Yarmand, M., Rajeshkumar, A., Weibel, N.: Acuvr: enhancing acupuncture training workflow with virtual reality. arXiv preprint arXiv:2407.02614 (2024)
26. Mo, G.B., Dudley, J.J., Kristensson, P.O.: Gesture knitter: a hand gesture design tool for head-mounted mixed reality applications. In: Proceedings of the 2021 CHI Conference on Human Factors in Computing Systems, pp. 1–13 (2021)
27. Nguyen, R., Gouin-Vallerand, C., Amiri, M.: Hand interaction designs in mixed and augmented reality head mounted display: a scoping review and classification. Front. Virtual Reality **4**, 1171230 (2023)
28. Papadopoulos, T., Evangelidis, K., Kaskalis, T.H., Evangelidis, G., Sylaiou, S.: Interactions in augmented and mixed reality: an overview. Appl. Sci. **11**(18), 8752 (2021)
29. Park, J., Hong, J.H.: Hologesture: a multimodal dataset for hand gesture recognition robust to hand textures on head-mounted mixed-reality devices. In: 2024 IEEE International Conference on Image Processing (ICIP), pp. 1–7. IEEE (2024)
30. Cunico, F., Girella, F., Avogaro, A., Emporio, M., Giachetti, A., Cristani, M.: Oo-dmvmt: a deep multi-view multi-task classification framework for real-time 3d hand gesture classification and segmentation. In: Proceedings of the IEEE/CVF Conference on Computer Vision and Pattern Recognition, pp. 2745–2754 (2023)
31. Shi, C., Zheng, Y., Fey, A.M.: Recognition and prediction of surgical gestures and trajectories using transformer models in robot-assisted surgery. In: 2022 IEEE/RSJ International Conference on Intelligent Robots and Systems (IROS), pp. 8017–8024. IEEE (2022)
32. Abavisani, M., Joze, H.R.V., Patel, V.M.: Improving the performance of unimodal dynamic hand-gesture recognition with multimodal training. In: Proceedings of the IEEE/CVF Conference on Computer Vision and Pattern Recognition, pp. 1165–1174 (2019)

33. Zhao, H., et al.: A virtual surgical prototype system based on gesture recognition for virtual surgical training in maxillofacial surgery. Int. J. Comput. Assist. Radiol. Surg. **18**(5), 909–919 (2023)
34. Rebol, M., et al.: Collaborative system design of mixed reality communication for medical training. arXiv preprint arXiv:2312.09382 (2023)
35. Uhl, J.C., Schrom-Feiertag, H., Regal, G., Gallhuber, K., Tscheligi, M.: Tangible immersive trauma simulation: is mixed reality the next level of medical skills training? In: Proceedings of the 2023 CHI Conference on Human Factors in Computing Systems, pp. 1–17 (2023)

Estimating Cluster Stability in Adaptive Resonance Theory for XR Image Understanding

Junjun Gu[1], Xiaozheng Qu[2], Zhaochuan Li[3], Zhuang Qi[1], Xiang Li[1], Haibei Huang[3], Lei Meng[1](✉), and Xiangxu Meng[1]

[1] Shandong University, Jinan 250101, Shandong, China
lmeng@sdu.edu.cn
[2] Beijing Government Service Center, Beijing 100073, China
[3] Inspur, Jinan 250101, Shandong, China

Abstract. Clustering techniques play a crucial role in scene understanding in extended reality (XR) applications such as user perspective analysis and visual localization. Fuzzy Adaptive Resonance Theory (Fuzzy ART) is a fast and convenient clustering method; however, its performance is significantly affected by the preset vigilance parameter. Although existing improvement methods incorporate mechanisms for adjusting the vigilance parameter, their complex algorithmic frameworks or processes often hinder the transparency and usability of the algorithms. To address this issue, we retain the simplicity and ease of use of Fuzzy ART and propose Stability-Based Vigilance Adjustment Fuzzy ART (SV-ART). Specifically, SV-ART integrates the Stability Assessment (SA), Vigilance Adjustment (VA), and Extinct Cluster Deletion (ED) modules into the iterative process of Fuzzy ART, uncovering implicit knowledge throughout the iterations to personalize the fine-tuning of vigilance values for each cluster, thereby optimizing the clustering structure through continuous iterations. We conducted experimental evaluations on 12 datasets and found that SV-ART improves both the optimal and overall clustering performance. This demonstrates that SV-ART improves its sensitivity to the vigilance parameter while retaining the robustness of Fuzzy ART. This makes it particularly suitable for non-expert users in scenarios where prior knowledge is scarce.

Keywords: Fuzzy Adaptive Resonance Theory · Clustering · Vigilance Adjustment · Parameter Adaptation · Stability Assessment

1 Introduction

Clustering techniques play a crucial role in scene understanding in extended reality (XR) applications such as user perspective analysis and visual localization [6,8,12,25]. Fuzzy Adaptive Resonance Theory (Fuzzy ART) [5] is a fast and convenient clustering method. The performance of Fuzzy ART is fundamentally determined by the vigilance parameter ρ, which influences the granularity of

A. Hinkenjan et al. (Eds.): ICXR 2025, LNCS 16428, pp. 555–567, 2026.
https://doi.org/10.1007/978-981-95-7195-6_41

cluster formation by controlling the range of vigilance regions (VRs). A higher ρ enforces stricter similarity constraints, promoting fine-grained clustering but potentially leading to overfitting; conversely, a lower ρ allows for broader category integration but may result in underfitting. Traditional static configurations of ρ are limited by excessive sensitivity to initial parameter selection, making the dynamic adjustment of ρ mechanisms critically important.

In recent years, various improvement schemes have emerged for the adjustment mechanisms of the vigilance parameter in Fuzzy ART. Three adjustment rules for the vigilance parameter have been proposed: activation maximization rules (AMRs) [19], confliction minimization rules [19], and hybrid integration rules [20]; the combination with particle swarm optimization and cluster validity indices [32] along with modeling it as a fuzzy membership function [13]. Although these methods have shown improvements, they still present a high barrier to understanding and use. We aim to enhance adaptive capabilities while ensuring that the algorithm remains simple and efficient, making it easier for users to comprehend and utilize.

To reduce the usability difficulty for users and improve the clustering performance of the Fuzzy ART algorithm under suboptimal initial vigilance settings, we propose Stability-Based Vigilance Adjustment Fuzzy ART (SV-ART). Building upon the iterative process of traditional Fuzzy ART, SV-ART incorporates three core phases after each execution of Fuzzy ART to form a new Iterations Module, which includes: Stability Assessment (SA), Vigilance Adjustment (VA), and Extinct Cluster Deletion (ED). These three phases do not involve reallocating samples; instead, they fine-tune the vigilance value by analyzing implicit information during the iterative process, thus laying a solid foundation for the next iteration. Specifically, in the SA phase, we design an evaluation mechanism based on changes in sample size (the number of samples within clusters) to assess the stability of all clusters and calculate their stability scores. The subsequent VA phase then fine-tunes the vigilance values of the existing clusters to varying degrees based on the stability scores from the SA phase, optimizing the cluster structure for the next iteration. Finally, the ED phase deletes all "extinct clusters" to ensure the efficiency of SV-ART. By designing the Iterations Module, SV-ART retains the operational simplicity of Fuzzy ART while enhancing its robustness against variations in ρ, enabling it to achieve satisfactory clustering results even under suboptimal vigilance settings.

We conducted experiments using a set of reasonable parameters uniformly applied across 12 datasets, validating the effectiveness and universality of our method in terms of average performance, general performance, and standard deviation. By plotting line graphs of clustering metrics as a function of ρ, we demonstrated the performance improvements of SV-ART, highlighting the algorithm's robustness to variations in ρ and its user-friendliness for individuals without specialized knowledge.

The main contributions of this paper are as follows:

- This study presents an innovative method for assessing and quantifying cluster stability, which classifies clusters and quantifies their stability by analyzing

changes in sample sizes throughout the iterative process, without requiring complex computations, thus ensuring the efficiency.
- SV-ART achieves personalized and controllable fine-tuning of the vigilance value without increasing preset parameters, enabling self-adjustment of the vigilance parameter to enhance robustness.
- Purification mechanism is introduced in the iterative process to ensure the efficient and stable operation of the algorithm.

2 Related Work

The evolution of Adaptive Resonance Theory (ART) highlights continuous theoretical advancements in pattern recognition and online learning. Initially, ART focused on stable self-organizing category recognition for analog inputs [2,24]. Key developments followed in three major variants: Fuzzy ART, designed for rapid stable learning [5,10,18], ARTMAP for supervised classification of non-stationary data [3], and ART 2-A, which accelerated category acquisition [4]. Together, these formed the foundation for modern ART systems.

Subsequent enhancements included vigilance adaptation mechanisms [19], extended to adaptive boundary scaling for social media applications [20]. Research also explored community detection using Fuzzy ART [21] and integrated deep learning with ART frameworks [21]. Innovations in vigilance testing with validity indices further refined the ART framework [30].

More recent work addresses multidimensional challenges, such as uncertainty handling through interval type-2 fuzzy methods [13], and visualization techniques to mitigate ordering effects [31]. Salience-aware mechanisms improved sparse data processing [17], while dual-vigilance architectures [26], hypersphere-based formulations [7], and topological clustering with information-theoretic learning [14] further expanded ART's capabilities. Bayesian methods with kernel techniques also enhanced ART's adaptability [15].

Current innovations continue diversifying, with distributed learning frameworks combining dual-vigilance mechanisms for arbitrary cluster retrieval [23, 27], and resonance network architectures [22]. Clustering adaptations have also shown promise in multi-label classification tasks [16]. Furthermore, incremental validation indices with adaptive reset features [28,29] and topological biclustering extensions [34] reflect emerging trends, while hierarchical clustering through parameter-free growth mechanisms [35] broadens ART's scalability.

3 Preliminary on Fuzzy ART

Fuzzy ART comprises two primary components: an input field F_1 for data reception and a category field F_2 for cluster representation. Consider a sample $\mathbf{x} = (x_1, \ldots, x_m)$ in the m-dimensional feature space, where each feature $x_i \in [0, 1]$. Before processing, $\mathbf{x}$ undergoes complement coding, producing an augmented input vector $\mathbf{I} = (\mathbf{x}, \bar{\mathbf{x}})$ in the input field F_1, where $\bar{\mathbf{x}} = \mathbf{1} - \mathbf{x}$. This expansion prevents the weight vectors of the clusters from decreasing so much that new clusters must be created, a phenomenon known as category proliferation. This architecture enables incremental clustering of normalized data while balancing plasticity and stability through parameterized vigilance constraints inherent in the Fuzzy ART framework, as illustrate below.

Cluster Prototypes: Each category C_j ($j = 1, \ldots, J$) in F_2 corresponds to a weight vector $\mathbf{w}_j$.

Parameters: The algorithm employs three critical parameters. The choice parameter $\alpha > 0$ regulates the sensitivity of cluster activation, usually set close to zero. The learning rate $\beta \in [0, 1]$ controls the speed at which prototypes adapt. The vigilance parameter $\rho \in [0, 1]$ determines the threshold that controls the threshold of a sample belonging to a cluster.

The algorithm operates through three phases:

1. **Category choice:** For input $\mathbf{I}$, the choice function T_j for each cluster C_j is computed as:
$$T_j = \frac{|\mathbf{I} \wedge \mathbf{w_j}|}{\alpha + |\mathbf{w_j}|}, \tag{1}$$
where operation $\wedge$ is defined by $(\mathbf{p} \wedge \mathbf{q})_i \equiv \min(p_i, q_i)$ and $|\cdot|$ is the L_1-norm. The winning cluster C_{j^*} satisfies $j^* = \arg\max_j T_j$.
2. **Template matching:** The match function between $\mathbf{I}$ and C_{j^*} evaluates:
$$M_{j^*} = \frac{|\mathbf{I} \wedge \mathbf{w}_{j^*}|}{|\mathbf{I}|}. \tag{2}$$
Resonance occurs if $M_{j^*} \geq \rho$, leading to the conclusion that $\mathbf{x}$ belongs to cluster C_{j^*}. Then go to step 3 and update the cluster weight. Otherwise, select a new winner cluster from the remaining clusters in F_2. If no cluster satisfies ρ, a new cluster will be generated to encode $\mathbf{I}$.
3. **Prototype learning:** Under resonance, the weight vector $\mathbf{w}_{j^*}$ updates via:
$$\mathbf{w}_{j^*}^{(\text{new})} = \beta(\mathbf{I} \wedge \mathbf{w}_{j^*}) + (1 - \beta)\mathbf{w}_{j^*}, \tag{3}$$
enabling dynamic refinement of cluster boundaries while preserving prior knowledge.

4 Stability-Based Vigilance Adjustment in Fuzzy ART

It is well-known that the iterative process of traditional Fuzzy ART refers to refining cluster weights and enhancing performance by iteratively processing all samples in the dataset. Meanwhile, the AMR [19,20] allows for adaptive increases or decreases in the vigilance value of the winning cluster to enhance the robustness of Fuzzy ART. Inspired by AMR, we introduce it into the iterative process, resulting in a new method called SV-ART. The overall framework of SV-ART is illustrated in Fig. 1, and the pseudocode is provided in Algorithm 1.

4.1 Stability Assessment Module

The SA phase is illustrated in part (A) of Fig. 1. As mentioned earlier, inputting the same data over multiple iterations can effectively improve the clustering performance of Fuzzy ART. The underlying mechanism is that, with an increasing

---

Algorithm 1. SV-ART

Input: Set of input vectors $V = \{\mathbf{I}_1, ..., \mathbf{I}_N\}$, vigilance parameter ρ_0, choice parameter $\alpha = 0.001$, expansion parameter $\tau = 0.1$, maximum number of iterations $t_{\max}$.
Output: Set of clusters K, set of weight vectors W, sample assignment A_t in Iteration t.
1: Initialize $K = \emptyset$, $W = \emptyset$.
2: Initialize current number of iterations $t = 1$ and initialize A_t.
3: Initialize $\mathbf{G}$ to store the change in sample size for each cluster.
4: Create cluster C_1 using the first sample $\mathbf{I}_1$ and ρ_0.
5: Update K and W, set $A_1[1] = 1$.
6: **for** each input vector $\mathbf{I}_n$ $(n = 2, \ldots, N)$ **do**
7:     **for** each cluster C_j in K **do**
8:         Calculate the choice function T_j.
9:     Select the winner cluster index $j^* = \arg\max_j T_j$.
10:     Calculate the match function M_{j^*}.
11:     **if** $M_{j^*} < \rho_{j^*}$ **then**
12:         Select a new winner cluster index j^* and go to step **9**.
13:     **else**
14:         Update w_{j^*} in W.
15:         Update $A_t[n] = j^*$.
16:     **if** no winner satisfies the vigilance parameter **then**
17:         Let ind = new cluster index.
18:         Create a new cluster c_{ind} using $\mathbf{I}_n$ and ρ_0.
19:         Update K, W.
20:         Update $A_t[n] = ind$.
21: **while** true **do**
22:     Set $t = t + 1$.
23:     **for** each input vector $\mathbf{I}_n$ $(n = 1, \ldots, N)$ **do**
24:         Perform Fuzzy ART, the same as steps **7** to **21**.
25:     **if** $t = t_{\max}$ or $A_t = A_{t-1}$ **then**
26:         **return** K, W and A_t.
27:     **else**
28:         Compare A_t and A_{t-1} to update $\mathbf{G}$.
29:         Initialize stable cluster set $L = \emptyset$.
30:         Initialize unstable cluster set $U = \emptyset$.
31:         Compare A_t and A_{t-1} to identify clusters with a increased sample size and add them to L.
32:         Compare A_t and A_{t-1} to identify clusters with a reduced sample size and add them to U.
33:         **for** each cluster C_j in K **do**
34:             **if** C_j is in L **then**
35:                 Compute s_j using Equation (7).
36:                 Update $\rho_j^{(\text{new})}$ using Equation (8).
37:             **if** C_j is in U **then**
38:                 Compute s_j using Equation (7).
39:                 Update $\rho_j^{(\text{new})}$ using Equation (9).
40:         **for** each cluster C_j in K **do**
41:             **if** the sample size of $C_j = 0$ **then**
42:                 Delete C_j from K and delete w_j from W.
43:                 Update A_t.

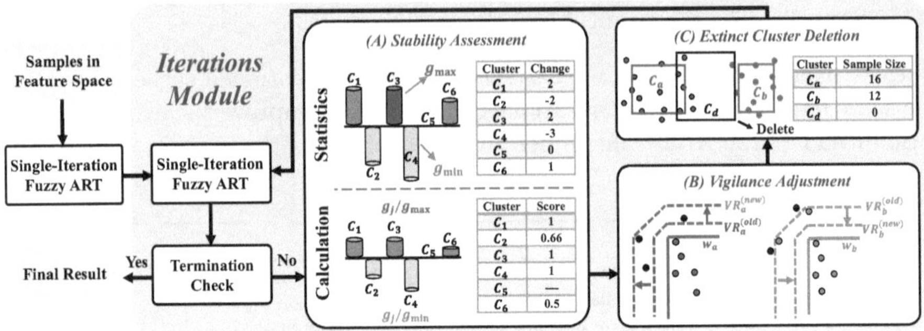

Fig. 1. The framework of SV-ART.

number of iterations, the weight vectors of each cluster are gradually adjusted and optimized, encouraging some samples to migrate to better-matching clusters. Based on this observation, we propose a cluster stability assessment mechanism based on changes in sample size (the number of samples within a cluster). Specifically, let J denote the number of existing clusters. We use $\mathbf{G} = (g_1, g_2, \ldots, g_J)$ to represent the changes in sample size for each cluster. By tracking the sample assignment A_t and A_{t-1} from adjacent iterations, we can analyze the changes in sample size across the clusters. For any C_j in F_2, if the sample size in the current iteration decreases compared to the previous one ($g_j < 0$), the cluster is deemed unstable. Conversely, clusters with an increased sample size ($g_j > 0$), including newly formed ones, are classified as stable. The theoretical basis for this assessment mechanism lies in the fact that clusters losing samples often tend to reflect the fact that their weight vector or corresponding ρ is non-optimal, which prevents them from maintaining structural robustness during the iterative process. In contrast, clusters with increased sample sizes signify a more discriminative partitioning of the feature space, thus gaining a competitive advantage. It is also clear that since the gain and loss of samples are interdependent, the following holds true in each Iteration:

$$\sum_{j=1}^{J} g_j = 0, \tag{4}$$

indicating that stable and unstable clusters either coexist or do not exist simultaneously. Let $g_{\max}$ denote the maximum increment and $g_{\min}$ denote the minimum decrement, calculated as follows:

$$g_{\max} = \max\{g_1, g_2, \ldots, g_J\}, \tag{5}$$

$$g_{\min} = \min\{g_1, g_2, \ldots, g_J\}. \tag{6}$$

When both stable and unstable clusters are present, $g_{\max} > 0$ and $g_{\min} < 0$ hold true. We aim to fully utilize this information to control the magnitude of vigilance adjustments in the next phase. We define $\mathbf{S} = (s_1, s_2, \ldots, s_J)$ to represent the stability scores of each cluster, calculated as follows:

$$s_j = \begin{cases} \frac{g_j}{g_{\max}}, & \text{if } C_j \text{ is a stable cluster,} \\ \frac{g_j}{g_{\min}}, & \text{if } C_j \text{ is an unstable cluster.} \end{cases} \tag{7}$$

It is readily observed that $s_j \in (0, 1]$. Furthermore, clusters that are not classified as stable or unstable do not have their s_j computed, as they will not be adjusted in the next phase.

4.2 Vigilance Adjustment

The VA phase is represented in section (B) of Fig. 1. In Fuzzy ART, the vigilance parameter ρ determines the degree of similarity required for a sample to be allocated to a particular cluster, and only samples that meet the threshold may occur resonance. As mentioned above, the AMR [19] selectively increases or decreases the vigilance value for different clusters, thus alleviating cases arising from improper initial vigilance values.

Inspired by AMR, we adjust the vigilance values in this phase based on the stability assessment results from the SA phase. Specifically, for all existing clusters C_j in category field F_2, if it is a stable cluster, its corresponding ρ value is adjusted using the following formula:

$$\rho_j^{(\text{new})} = (1 - \tau \cdot s_j)\rho_j^{(\text{old})}, \tag{8}$$

whereas if C_j is an unstable cluster, the adjustment formula is as follows:

$$\rho_j^{(\text{new})} = (1 + \tau \cdot s_j)\rho_j^{(\text{old})}. \tag{9}$$

For the remaining clusters, no adjustments are made. In these equations, τ is a small positive value, and s_j is the stability score calculated during the SA phase. To ensure the usability of our method, τ defaults to the commonly used setting of 0.1, which guarantees a reasonably small range of adjustments.

Through these operations, for stable clusters, we can slightly reduce the threshold without compromising their overall structure, thereby increasing the influence of high-quality clusters in subsequent iterations. At the same time, the probability of resonance emerging in the subsequent iteration for unstable clusters can be slightly diminished. Additionally, we leverage the stability scores to reasonably control the magnitude of adjustment according to the stability levels of the clusters. This ensures that more stable clusters are reinforced while less stable clusters are diminished.

4.3 Extinct Cluster Deletion

The ED phase is illustrated in section (C) of Fig. 1. It is evident that during the iterative process, a cluster that originally contained samples may lose all its points in a particular iteration, resulting in a sample size of zero. We refer to this cluster as the "extinct cluster". There are two main causes for this situation: first, unreasonable cluster weights may lead to the original samples being absorbed

Table 1. Summary of the datasets.

Dataset	Samples	Features	Clusters	Type
Aggregation	788	2	7	Artificial
Chainlink	1000	3	2	Artificial
Compound	399	2	6	Artificial
Dermatology	358	34	6	Real World
Face	320	2	4	Artificial
Flame	240	2	2	Artificial
Ionosphere	351	34	2	Real World
Jain	373	2	2	Artificial
Lsun	400	2	3	Artificial
Spiral	312	2	3	Artificial
Synthetic Control	600	60	6	Real World
Wave	287	2	2	Artificial

by other clusters; second, adjustments made during the VA phase can cause the vigilance values of certain clusters to become excessively high, preventing any samples from resonating with them.

In this phase, we delete all information related to the extinct clusters, such as cluster weights and vigilance values, and update the sample assignment A_t with new cluster indices. Ultimately, through the ED phase, we streamline the number of clusters and optimize the clustering structure across the entire space, laying a solid foundation for the next iteration. It also reduces unnecessary computations and ensures that computational efficiency is not compromised by the emergence of extinct clusters.

5 Experiments

5.1 Datasets

We adopted the selection of datasets from [27], utilizing 12 datasets with varying features. These datasets can be obtained from [1,9,11,33], and their characteristics are summarized in Table 1. Before the experiments, all datasets were preprocessed using Min-Max normalization to scale their characteristic values to the range $[0, 1]$, followed by complement coding to obtain input vectors [27].

5.2 Experimental Setup

Our experiments attempt to simulate the clustering performance obtained by users lacking expertise in the use of ART-based clustering methods. Thus, we compared SV-ART with Fuzzy ART [5], and four methods mentioned in Introduction: CM-ART [19], AM-ART [19], HI-ART [20], and SA-ART [17], as they have few preset parameters and exhibit a certain degree of adaptability to ρ.

Table 2. The clustering performance of different algorithms.

		Peak Performance						Mean Performance						Standard Deviation	
		FA	CM-ART	AM-ART	HI-ART	SA-ART	Ours	FA	CM-ART	AM-ART	HI-ART	SA-ART	Ours	SA-ART	Ours
Agg	ARI	0.566	0.345	0.600	0.399	0.776	**0.798**	0.374	0.203	0.311	0.222	0.340	**0.486**	0.232	**0.173**
	NMI	0.727	0.590	0.679	0.604	0.822	**0.866**	0.591	0.521	0.546	0.536	0.518	**0.658**	0.281	**0.127**
Chain	ARI	0.316	0.084	0.454	0.094	0.281	**0.889**	0.154	0.057	0.130	0.061	0.077	**0.351**	**0.094**	0.214
	NMI	0.389	0.309	0.397	0.325	0.438	**0.820**	0.280	0.260	0.254	0.267	0.190	**0.438**	0.187	**0.141**
Com	ARI	0.690	0.483	0.614	0.485	**0.755**	**0.755**	0.377	0.226	0.334	0.234	0.344	**0.494**	0.274	**0.200**
	NMI	0.704	0.597	0.661	0.597	0.771	**0.781**	0.541	0.469	0.527	0.477	0.451	**0.609**	0.301	**0.160**
Derm	ARI	0.326	0.089	0.179	0.097	0.580	**0.639**	0.137	0.059	0.091	0.064	0.136	**0.335**	0.206	**0.160**
	NMI	0.497	0.500	0.495	0.501	0.646	**0.714**	0.451	0.413	0.424	0.418	0.227	**0.523**	0.285	**0.114**
Face	ARI	0.510	0.402	0.574	0.397	0.261	**0.624**	0.150	0.148	0.152	0.132	0.115	**0.240**	**0.088**	0.163
	NMI	0.477	0.475	0.550	0.454	0.477	**0.605**	0.317	0.310	0.294	0.298	0.265	**0.412**	0.170	**0.092**
Flame	ARI	0.284	0.165	0.336	0.177	0.397	**0.435**	0.154	0.063	0.149	0.066	0.163	**0.231**	0.152	**0.126**
	NMI	0.404	0.327	0.372	0.331	0.507	**0.514**	0.288	0.241	0.276	0.244	0.235	**0.337**	0.190	**0.098**
Iono	ARI	0.128	**0.274**	0.133	0.241	0.149	0.247	0.048	0.098	0.041	0.104	0.055	**0.135**	**0.051**	0.058
	NMI	0.215	0.226	0.215	0.227	0.251	**0.273**	0.184	0.190	0.181	0.193	0.130	**0.196**	0.112	**0.063**
Jain	ARI	0.685	0.376	0.757	0.311	0.557	**0.773**	0.287	0.174	0.279	0.147	0.203	**0.374**	**0.190**	0.191
	NMI	0.543	0.370	0.627	0.340	0.500	**0.660**	0.384	0.282	0.362	0.270	0.284	**0.422**	0.193	**0.094**
Lsun	ARI	0.539	0.311	0.465	0.303	0.601	**0.708**	0.314	0.138	0.283	0.139	0.251	**0.386**	0.218	**0.161**
	NMI	0.624	0.523	0.572	0.523	0.736	**0.773**	0.476	0.365	0.453	0.363	0.373	**0.535**	0.276	**0.158**
Spiral	ARI	0.099	0.092	0.065	0.093	0.122	**0.127**	**0.054**	0.047	0.030	0.046	0.024	0.034	0.041	**0.036**
	NMI	0.445	0.441	0.416	0.442	**0.468**	0.447	0.169	**0.246**	0.150	**0.245**	0.085	0.114	0.147	**0.122**
Syn	ARI	0.074	0.103	0.130	0.184	**0.606**	0.487	0.035	0.051	0.070	0.077	0.180	**0.258**	0.216	**0.164**
	NMI	0.466	0.476	0.488	0.484	**0.755**	0.668	0.358	0.361	0.391	0.383	0.317	**0.435**	0.310	**0.209**
Wave	ARI	0.175	0.124	0.150	0.124	0.147	**0.191**	0.102	0.080	0.069	0.080	0.062	**0.111**	0.047	**0.046**
	NMI	0.383	0.359	0.332	0.360	0.385	**0.392**	0.209	**0.264**	0.173	0.263	0.124	0.200	0.133	**0.113**

Instead of complex tuning of each dataset, we use uniform reasonable parameter settings that do not change to ensure low dependence on a priori knowledge and to maintain fair comparisons. Specifically, the choice parameter $\alpha = 10^{-3}$, and learning rate $\beta = 0.5$ for moderate adaptation. Method-specific configurations used empirically validated values: AM-ART's restraint parameter $\sigma = 10^{-4}$, SA-ART's stability-frequency balance $\lambda = 0.5$, with $\delta = 10^{-4}$ and $\Delta = 10^{-4}$ for SA-ART and CM-ART respectively. In particular, σ and δ were chosen among $\{10^{-1}, 10^{-2}, 10^{-3}, 10^{-4}, 10^{-5}\}$ because this value would perform best on most datasets. Except for CM-ART and HI-ART, all other methods iterate multiple times with $t_{\max} = 20$, and the termination criteria are consistent with that in line 25 of the pseudocode. CM-ART and HI-ART perform only a single iteration, as experiments revealed that the number of clusters they produced increased rapidly with each iteration. We hypothesize that the significant adjustments to ρ caused by CMR [20] are not suitable for the datasets we selected. For all methods, the initial vigilance parameter ρ is scanned within the range $[0.05, 0.95]$ with a step size of 0.02, executed across five random orders of the dataset, recording the average performance for each ρ.

Cluster quality assessment used Normalized Mutual Information (NMI) and Adjusted Rand Index (ARI) [35], both generating normalized scores in the range $[0, 1]$ with higher values indicating better label alignment.

5.3 Clustering Performance Comparison

We recorded the experimental results of all methods across five random data input sequences and calculated the average NMI (aNMI) and average ARI (aARI) for each value of ρ. These two metrics represent the clustering performance of a particular method on a specific dataset at a given ρ value. Subsequently, we extracted the maximum and average values of aARI and aNMI from the ρ scanning process and presented them in Table 2 under the Peak Performance and Mean Performance sections. These sections reflect the best clustering performance and general clustering performance achieved by the algorithm during the scanning process.

Regarding Peak Performance, we observed that CM-ART, AM-ART, and HI-ART exhibited varying levels of performance across different datasets. This indicates that these methods require appropriate parameter tuning tailored to specific data conditions to achieve better results, which places high demands on prior knowledge. In high-dimensional data, SA-ART demonstrated the best performance, as seen in the Synthetic Control dataset, confirming that SA-ART is more suitable for high-dimensional datasets [17]. Conversely, SV-ART consistently showed optimal performance across most datasets. Therefore, in scenarios where prior knowledge is limited and targeted parameter adjustments are not made, both SA-ART and SV-ART often outperformed other methods, with SV-ART being the most versatile and suitable for a majority of datasets.

In reality, users lacking prior knowledge are more likely to select a suboptimal value; therefore, exploring Mean Performance is essential. The results indicate that SV-ART achieves the best general clustering performance across most datasets, although it performs poorly on a few datasets with unique cluster shapes, such as the Spiral dataset. Other methods exhibit varying strengths and weaknesses across different datasets. Additionally, to investigate the fluctuations of aNMI and aARI during the scanning process, we calculated their variances, denoted as standardized NMI (sNMI) and standardized ARI (sARI), and compared them with SA-ART, as shown in the Standard Deviation section of Table 2. The results suggest that SV-ART is less responsive to changes in ρ during the scanning process, while SA-ART shows greater sensitivity. Overall, when users randomly select ρ due to a lack of prior knowledge, SV-ART offers the best clustering expectations and the strongest robustness, often making it the preferred choice among these methods. In contrast, other algorithms are more susceptible to the detrimental effects of poor ρ choices, which can lower average performance or lead to significant fluctuations. This, to some extent, demonstrates that SV-ART successfully enhances overall performance and mitigates the sensitivity of ART-based clustering algorithms to ρ. Furthermore, SV-ART displays greater stability in its fluctuations compared to SA-ART, ensuring that actual performance does not deviate significantly from expectations.

6 Conclusion

This paper presents a heuristic improvement to the iterative process of Fuzzy ART, resulting in a new clustering algorithm called Stability-Based Vigilance Adjustment Fuzzy ART. It integrates three key phases after each execution of Fuzzy ART, extracting implicit knowledge from adjacent iterations to estimate cluster stability and stability scores. Our experimental results verified that SV-ART does not increase the number of preset parameters, while retaining the simplicity and efficiency of Fuzzy ART.

However, we observed some limitations of SV-ART during the experiments, including its inability to handle specific cluster shapes. Thus, there is considerable room for improvement in various aspects of SV-ART. Additionally, this method can serve as a general framework for heuristic approaches to cluster stability assessment and quantification, which can be integrated with other ART-based clustering algorithms in future research.

Acknowledgments. This work was supported by the Key R&D Program of Shandong Province (Founding no.: 2024TATSGC033).

References

1. Bache, K., Lichman, M.: UCI machine learning repository (2013). http://archive.ics.uci.edu/ml
2. Carpenter, G.A., Grossberg, S.: Art 2: self-organization of stable category recognition codes for analog input patterns. Appl. Opt. **26**(23), 4919–4930 (1987)
3. Carpenter, G.A., Grossberg, S., Reynolds, J.H.: Artmap: supervised real-time learning and classification of nonstationary data by a self-organizing neural network. Neural Netw. **4**(5), 565–588 (1991)
4. Carpenter, G.A., Grossberg, S., Rosen, D.B.: Art 2-a: an adaptive resonance algorithm for rapid category learning and recognition. Neural Netw. **4**(4), 493–504 (1991a)
5. Carpenter, G.A., Grossberg, S., Rosen, D.B.: Fuzzy art: fast stable learning and categorization of analog patterns by an adaptive resonance system. Neural Netw. **4**(6), 759–771 (1991b)
6. Dharmasiri, A., Kattadige, C., Zhang, V., Thilakarathna, K.: Viewport-aware dynamic 360° video segment categorization. In: Proceedings of the 31st ACM Workshop on Network and Operating Systems Support for Digital Audio and Video, pp. 114–121 (2021)
7. Elnabarawy, I., Wunsch, D.C., da Silva, L.E.B.: Dual vigilance hypersphere adaptive resonance theory. In: 2019 IEEE Symposium Series on Computational Intelligence (SSCI), pp. 2425–2532. IEEE (2019)
8. Feng, G., Jiang, Z., Tan, X., Cheng, F.: Hierarchical clustering-based image retrieval for indoor visual localization. Electronics **11**(21), 3609 (2022)
9. Fränti, P., Sieranoja, S.: K-means properties on six clustering benchmark datasets (2018). http://cs.uef.fi/sipu/datasets/
10. Guo, W., Zhang, Y., Cai, X., Meng, L., Yang, J., Yuan, X.: LD-man: layout-driven multimodal attention network for online news sentiment recognition. IEEE Trans. Multimed. **23**, 1785–1798 (2020)
11. Ilc, N., Dobnikar, A.: Gravitational clustering of the self-organizing map. In: Dobnikar, A., Lotrič, U., Šter, B. (eds.) ICANNGA 2011. LNCS, vol. 6594, pp. 11–20. Springer, Heidelberg (2011). https://doi.org/10.1007/978-3-642-20267-4_2
12. Jiang, J., Zou, Y., Chen, L., Fang, Y.: A visual and VAE based hierarchical indoor localization method. Sensors **21**(10), 3406 (2021)

13. Majeed, S., Gupta, A., Raj, D., Rhee, F.C.H.: Uncertain fuzzy self-organization based clustering: interval type-2 fuzzy approach to adaptive resonance theory. Inf. Sci. **424**, 69–90 (2018)
14. Masuyama, N., Loo, C.K., Ishibuchi, H., Kubota, N., Nojima, Y., Liu, Y.: Topological clustering via adaptive resonance theory with information theoretic learning. IEEE Access **7**, 76920–76936 (2019)
15. Masuyama, N., Loo, C.K., Wermter, S.: A kernel Bayesian adaptive resonance theory with a topological structure. Int. J. Neural Syst. **29**(05), 1850052 (2019)
16. Masuyama, N., Nojima, Y., Loo, C.K., Ishibuchi, H.: Multi-label classification via adaptive resonance theory-based clustering. IEEE Trans. Pattern Anal. Mach. Intell. **45**(7), 8696–8712 (2022)
17. Meng, L., Tan, A.H., Miao, C.: Salience-aware adaptive resonance theory for large-scale sparse data clustering. Neural Netw. **120**, 143–157 (2019)
18. Meng, L., Tan, A.H., Wunsch, D.: Adaptive Resonance Theory in Social Media Data Clustering. Springer, Cham (2019)
19. Meng, L., Tan, A.H., Wunsch, D.C.: Vigilance adaptation in adaptive resonance theory. In: The 2013 International Joint Conference on Neural Networks (IJCNN), pp. 1–7. IEEE (2013)
20. Meng, L., Tan, A.H., Wunsch, D.C.: Adaptive scaling of cluster boundaries for large-scale social media data clustering. IEEE Trans. Neural Netw. Learn. Syst. **27**(12), 2656–2669 (2015)
21. Park, G.M., Kim, J.H.: Deep adaptive resonance theory for learning biologically inspired episodic memory. In: 2016 International Joint Conference on Neural Networks (IJCNN), pp. 5174–5180. IEEE (2016)
22. Park, G.M., Kim, J.H.: Adaptive developmental resonance network. IEEE Trans. Neural Netw. Learn. Syst. **32**(10), 4347–4361 (2020)
23. Qi, Z., Wang, Y., Chen, Z., Wang, R., Meng, X., Meng, L.: Clustering-based curriculum construction for sample-balanced federated learning. In: CAAI International Conference on Artificial Intelligence, pp. 155–166. Springer, Cham (2022)
24. Qu, X., et al.: Towards initialization-agnostic clustering with iterative adaptive resonance theory (2025). https://arxiv.org/abs/2505.04440
25. Rossi, S., De Simone, F., Frossard, P., Toni, L.: Spherical clustering of users navigating 360 content. In: 2019 IEEE International Conference on Acoustics, Speech and Signal Processing (ICASSP), ICASSP 2019, pp. 4020–4024. IEEE (2019)
26. da Silva, L.E.B., Elnabarawy, I., Wunsch, D.C., II.: Dual vigilance fuzzy adaptive resonance theory. Neural Netw. **109**, 1–5 (2019)
27. da Silva, L.E.B., Elnabarawy, I., Wunsch, D.C., II.: Distributed dual vigilance fuzzy adaptive resonance theory learns online, retrieves arbitrarily-shaped clusters, and mitigates order dependence. Neural Netw. **121**, 208–228 (2020)
28. da Silva, L.E.B., Rayapati, N., Wunsch, D.C.: icvi-artmap: using incremental cluster validity indices and adaptive resonance theory reset mechanism to accelerate validation and achieve multiprototype unsupervised representations. IEEE Trans. Neural Netw. Learn. Syst. **34**(12), 9757–9770 (2022a)
29. da Silva, L.E.B., Rayapati, N., Wunsch, D.C.: Incremental cluster validity index-guided online learning for performance and robustness to presentation order. IEEE Trans. Neural Netw. Learn. Syst. **34**(10), 6686–6700 (2022b)
30. da Silva, L.E.B., Wunsch, D.C.: Validity index-based vigilance test in adaptive resonance theory neural networks. In: 2017 IEEE Symposium Series on Computational Intelligence (SSCI), pp. 1–8. IEEE (2017)

31. da Silva, L.E.B., Wunsch, D.C.: A study on exploiting vat to mitigate ordering effects in fuzzy art. In: 2018 International Joint Conference on Neural Networks (IJCNN), pp. 1–8. IEEE (2018)
32. Smith, C., Wunsch, D.: Particle swarm optimization in an adaptive resonance framework. In: 2015 International Joint Conference on Neural Networks (IJCNN), pp. 1–4. IEEE (2015)
33. Thrun, M.C., Ultsch, A.: Clustering benchmark datasets exploiting the fundamental clustering problems. Data Brief **30**, 105501 (2020)
34. Yelugam, R., da Silva, L.E.B., Wunsch, D.C., II.: Topological biclustering artmap for identifying within bicluster relationships. Neural Netw. **160**, 34–49 (2023)
35. Zhou, S., et al.: A comprehensive survey on deep clustering: taxonomy, challenges, and future directions. ACM Comput. Surv. **57**(3), 1–38 (2024)

Author Index

A. Hinkenjan et al. (Eds.): ICXR 2025, LNCS 16428, pp. 569–571, 2026.
https://doi.org/10.1007/978-981-95-7195-6

Zeitfracht Medien GmbH
Ferdinand-Jühlke-Straße 7
99095 Erfurt, Deutschland
produktsicherheit@kolibri360.de